Microeconomic Foundations of Employment and Inflation Theory

EDMUND S. PHELPS
Columbia University

ARMEN A. ALCHIAN
University of California (Los Angeles)

CHARLES C. HOLT
Urban Institute

DALE T. MORTENSEN
Northwestern University

G. C. ARCHIBALD
University of British Columbia

ROBERT E. LUCAS, JR.
Carnegie-Mellon University

LEONARD A. RAPPING
Carnegie-Mellon University

SIDNEY G. WINTER, JR.
University of Michigan

JOHN P. GOULD
University of Chicago

DONALD F. GORDON
University of Rochester

ALLAN HYNES
University of Washington

DONALD A. NICHOLS
University of Wisconsin

PAUL J. TAUBMAN
University of Pennsylvania

MAURICE WILKINSON
Columbia University

Microeconomic Foundations of

Employment and Inflation Theory

W·W·NORTON & COMPANY·INC·

New York

PRINTED IN THE UNITED STATES OF AMERICA

5 6 7 8 9 0

Designed by Art Ritter

Contents

Preface

Last year several of us were excited to learn that we were not alone. Similar life existed on other campuses. Evidence was found of nearly a dozen drafts and fragments, all on the subjects of wage, price, job, and production decisions under incomplete information. An economics of disequilibrium seemed to be forming. A meeting was suggested to see whether we spoke the same language and thought the same theorems. In the course of the arrangements, we learned that most of our papers were not yet irrevocably committed for publication. Visions of a book. It was determined that those few papers already placed were copublishable or republishable. Two additional manuscripts were stimulated to fill in gaps. The result is this volume.

In the preparation of this book the authors have received corporate assistance on top of the individual help acknowledged elsewhere. A meeting of nearly all the authors took place in Philadelphia on January 25–26, 1969. Some facilities there were made available by the University of Pennsylvania. The principal economic support of the meeting came from the National Science Foundation. We are particularly grateful to James H. Blackman in this connection for his encouragement and flexibility. The publisher lent financial assistance to the conference. Particular thanks go to Donald S. Lamm whose own decision-making under incomplete information has been fast and adaptable in coping with the special problems of a fifteen-author book. Finally, we appreciate the willingness of the editors of the *Western*

Economic Journal for their willingness to see us copublish the paper by A. A. Alchian and the willingness of the editor of the *Journal of Political Economy* to have us copublish the paper by L. A. Rapping and R. E. Lucas, Jr., and to reprint with revisions the paper by E. S. Phelps.

Philadelphia
March 24, 1969

E.S.P.

Microeconomic Foundations of Employment and Inflation Theory

Introduction:
The New
Microeconomics
in Employment
and Inflation Theory*

EDMUND S. PHELPS

The conventional neoclassical theory of the supply decisions of the household and of the firm, the theory we all teach though rarely practice, is well known to be inconsistent with Keynesian models of employment and with post-Keynesian models of inflation. It contains no road from the fall of aggregate demand[1] to the fall of output and employment airily reached by Keynes. Only the esoteric non-neutrality of the particular demand shift at hand would lead us to expect more than pure money price and money wage effects. Inflation has no tendency in the neoclassical theory to stimulate output, there being full employment with or without inflation.

Relentless application of neoclassical principles to either a competitive industry or a pure monopoly shows that output and employment in the corn industry will fall, given the technology and fixed factors, if and only if there is a rise of the product wage—the wage in terms of

*This essay is intended to elucidate the general contribution that this volume seeks to make and to indicate some of the similarities and differences of treatment in the individual papers. It does not fully summarize any of the papers, however, and does not necessarily have the concurrence of any other author in whole or in part. The author's work on the present paper was supported by the Brookings Institution.

[1]By "aggregate demand" I mean (throughout) a schedule in the price–real income (or output) plane. This schedule may be vertical or, under the "Keynes" and "Pigou" effects, negatively sloped. It shows the relation between price level and the output coordinate of intersections of Hicksian *IS–LM* curves.

corn.[2] The theory is mute as to why a fall of demand should be expected to raise product wage rates. It does not prepare us for the notion of "imperfect wage flexibility." Were neoclassical doctrine to predict such a rise of product wage rates, it would still find itself at an impasse. It is widely agreed that product wage rates do *not* rise markedly and unerringly whenever unemployment rises. While money wages are imperfectly flexible, money prices are equally so. What then is the appropriate theory of industry pricing and output?

In the same way, conventional neoclassical theory does not explain why inflation (or unexpected inflation) is said, in post-Keynesian economics, to "buy" an increase of output and employment. First of all, in the neoclassical world there are no idle resources that inflation could somehow activate. Firms might be thought, neoclassically, to require lower product wage rates to produce more while households would be unlikely to respond with a corresponding increase of labor supply if real wage rates were to fall. But if one recognizes the normal residue of frictional unemployment, there is still the question of how inflation and its concomitants operate to decrease that residue. It seems clear that macroeconomics needs a microeconomic foundation.

The Keynesians postulated money wage stickiness. After the Dunlop–Tarshis–Keynes exchanges, an equal degree of price stickiness was usually postulated too. Yet there was little microeconomic articulation of labor-market models and product-market models from which such stickiness could be derived. Several interpretations of stickiness were proposed at various times, though none can be said fully to have taken hold.

Some of Keynes' followers relied upon "money illusion." The argument was that the supply prices of workers will not fall in proportion to the price level when aggregate demand falls, so that a decline of profit-maximizing output and employment must result from a fall of the price level. But just why the money wage per se should be a matter of interest to workers was left unclear. Keynes himself argued that the worker takes pride in his *relative real wage*. A *perfect* labor market would leave relative real wages unaffected by a fall of going money wage rates; the nature of the imperfections required for a derived pride in the money wage Keynes did not elucidate.[3] Somewhat symmetrically,

---

[2]Aggregate demand can make absolutely no difference to any competitive firm's output except through the market-clearing prices and wage rates. (In the monopoly case, there is the obvious elasticity qualification.) It is true that the leftward shift of demand may eliminate the existence of a positive-price full employment equilibrium.

[3]Unions seem to work the "wrong" way. A union might succeed in imposing a money wage cut on its membership that each member, acting alone and in ignorance of others' willingness to accept cuts, would not accept because of his pride in his relative wage.

Another defense of money illusion is that the fall of the cost of living will not be perceived by workers to its full extent. (This differs a little from static illusion if the full fall of prices will eventually be perceived; in that case, we have an underemployment *dis*equilibrium in which prices and wages are falling unexpectedly.)

if the producer, because of social pressures, attaches an importance or amenity value to the price of his product per se, then a fall of aggregate demand may fail to generate price cuts or output increases in keeping with the decline of money wage rates and money marginal costs that result from the fall of demand. If the resulting fall of the real wage reduces the quantity of labor supplied, there occurs a fall of employment. Some writers have envisioned increased cartelization in depressed times while other writers have seen flatter demand curves and keener competition in hard times.

The interpretation of wage and price stickiness as money illusion is consistent with a world of price-takers operating in perfect markets. For that reason it has been a convenience in textbook expositions. However, it is usually the large sophisticated units to whom stickiness is most frequently ascribed. If one postulates a world of price-makers (e.g., oligopolists), then "frictions" are possible that can permit an underemployment disequilibrium despite the absence of any money illusion. Several writers have pointed to the "cost" of changing prices and wages. In part the reference is to the labor and printing costs of revising price lists, menus, paychecks, and the like. More important, perhaps, are the administrative costs of deciding upon prices and wages. It is unlikely that any management would find it profitable to review its prices and wage rates hourly or daily. Quarterly or annual reviews are frequently the rule. But it is not clear why, in a neoclassical world at any rate, the cost of making decisions should be significant.

There is now emerging a new kind of microeconomics of production, labor supply, wage and price decisions—a body of theory that goes beyond neoclassical intertemporal equilibrium. The theory is different from some of the previous efforts, just cited, to found a theory of aggregate supply, in that it sticks doggedly to the neoclassical postulates of lifetime expected utility maximization and net worth maximization, it makes no appeal to faulty perceptions and it does not fundamentally require that price-setters economize on their decision-making time. The present volume is devoted to the development of this new approach.

The new work illuminates, in different ways, some old problem areas in Keynesian economics and it opens up new territory of hypotheses and questions. The papers here offer new reasons why money wage rates are "sticky" in the face of price-level movements—why money wage rates (and thus prices) do not quickly respond by enough to keep employment and output at their respective equilibrium levels when aggregate demand changes.[4] They similarly explain the stickiness of prices when money production costs move; hence real wage rates are not implied necessarily to rise when employment falls despite diminish-

---

[4] It thus becomes clearer why, despite the availability of low-cost computers, workers and firms are unlikely to want to make *real* wage agreements—i.e., to avail themselves of full automatic escalation.

ing marginal productivity. Many of the models generate a momentary steady-state Phillips curve relation between the employment level and the rate of wage (or price) change. The rate of change of employment also frequently figures in the momentary general Phillips relation. Finally, the crucial role that the new theory assigns to expectations, especially expectations of wage and price change, together with the notion of adaptive expectations, have led most of the authors here to the hypothesis that the momentary Phillips curve will shift according to the point chosen on it. Today's Phillips curve may be quite stable, but tomorrow's curve will depend upon how the economy behaves today. In particular, it may be that an increase in the steady rate of inflation will have only a vanishing effect on the unemployment rate.[5]

The theoretical departure that is common to these otherwise neoclassical papers is their removal of the Walrasian postulate of complete information. In the Walrasian economy, all transactions take place under complete information on the part of each buyer and seller about his alternatives. As a consequence, the Walrasian economy satisfies the *two* conditions for economic equilibrium.

The first of these conditions is that there is no nonprice rationing. There exists no buyer who, knowing he could make both himself and some seller better off by paying a higher price in return for more of the seller's product, is yet somehow frustrated from overbidding either because the seller is ignorant of his bid or because the seller has a long-run interest in assuring his present buyers a continuing supply at the present price. Similarly, no seller is frustrated from underbidding. This condition can also be expressed by saying that prices clear markets.[6]

The other condition for equilibrium is that there be no surprise. The market-clearance condition means only that every price is market clearing among the set of people who know the price. It means that every firm knows how much output those buyers who know his price are willing to buy from him at various prices he might set, and analogously for sellers to the firm. The absence of surprise despite evolving

---

[5]This hypothesis, known variously as the "permanent unemployment thesis" or the "strong expectations hypothesis," does not shock scholarly economists. Fellner and Wallich argued it in this country more than ten years ago, and von Mises before them. Friedman and the present author have been primarily responsible for its current renaissance. The novelty of the work here in this connection is its development of the microeconomic underpinning.

[6]That prices clear markets follows from the maximization postulate that no buyer or seller would knowingly pass up an opportunity for improvement and the informational postulate that buyers and sellers can predict their purchase and sales opportunities—in the present and in the future. In the case of a monopolist firm that sets price (nondiscriminatorily), market clearance means simply that the monopolist operates "on" his demand curve; he never rations buyers and he never produces in excess of quantity demanded at the price he sets because he knows his maximum sales at every price. Similarly, the monopsonist firm setting price operates "on" his supply curve. In the competitive case, where buyer and seller act as if the price necessary to effect a purchase or a sale were independent of the quantity purchased or sold, market clearing means that supply equals demand.

conditions entails that each household and firm always know the market-clearing prices at every firm now and in the future. There is perfect knowledge of current prices in the strict sense that if a price were to change somewhere in the economy, every household would know the new price immediately.[7] Otherwise equilibrium would be limited to recurrent stationary conditions. This requires that there be no cost to learning or to advertising these prices. That future market-clearing prices are known is interpretable as costless economic forecasting.[8]

On the ice-covered terrain of the Walrasian economy, the question of a connection between aggregate demand and the employment level is a little treacherous.[9] Only one path of aggregate demand will produce the path of the price level and money wage level that people foresee. But we may ask what difference it would make if people were spontaneously to foresee inflation (of prices and money wage rates equally) rather than a stationary price and wage level, so that aggregate demand must be steadily increased to validate these expectations. Would the inflationary scenario be one of higher employment than in the stationary-price story? The answer is that there is no necessary and intrinsic connection between the rate of anticipated inflation and the level of employment. Employment, investment, and other real supplies and demands will be invariant to the difference in the anticipated price trend if all foreseen relative prices, including foreseen real rates of interest, are likewise invariant. The two tools of fiscal and monetary policy give the government enough degrees of freedom to validate and sustain a "pure" or "neutral" inflation in which real interest rates are insulated from the expectations of inflation.[10]

With the postulate of perfect information removed, the way is at last open to formal study of general disequilibrium—its manifestations

[7]It is not simply that the household thinks it knows all the prices and it happens to be right in the prevailing economic state; the weaker concept, introduced below, of non-Walrasian equilibrium involves the correctness of expectations—in the large if not in the small.

[8]The analytical construct of a comprehensive futures market to determine all future prices in advance, so that future prices are placed on a par with current prices, falls to the ground in an economy with a positive birth rate. For the present members of the economy, to achieve economic efficiency, will want to be able to trade later with the yet-unborn members of the economy who cannot as yet enter into futures contracts.

[9]If one wishes to discuss money prices and inflation in the Walrasian economy, one needs to suppose that, even in the fully informed Walrasian economy, peoples' IOUs would not be completely trusted and that the government, or a few banks under government regulation, would monopolize the manufacture of currency or other money.

[10]Three qualifications may be mentioned: The expected capital loss on real money balances may substitute for taxation of income so that if taxes are not assumed to be lump sum, there will be a substitution effect favoring employment and saving. Second, if legal or technological factors prevent money (or some components of money) from bearing interest, the opportunity costs of holding money will be greater under anticipated inflation and one could imagine that the resulting additional nuisance of managing transactions balances would shorten the workday a little or divert secondary household workers from the labor market. Third, there may be "distribution effects" on labor supply if the inflation was not anticipated as early as the signing of the oldest outstanding contract expressed in money terms.

in price changes and resource use, and its determinants, among them the behavior of aggregate demand. Three types of disequilibrium models, in both the product-market and labor-market analyses, are discernible in this volume. The present eccentric guide to the volume is organized largely according to that typology. It locates the individual papers in those terms, doing violence to many of them, for seldom does any paper fall completely into one type.

1
LABOR MARKETS,
MONEY WAGE BEHAVIOR,
AND UNEMPLOYMENT

Labor economists have long noticed that, in a large complex economy, the labor market is beset by seriously incomplete information on the part of the worker and firm concerning current wage rates elsewhere in the economy; a certain amount of "search unemployment" is therefore normal. Armen Alchian's paper points out that, on a reasonable expectational hypothesis, the quantity of search unemployment and thus the level of employment will vary with aggregate demand through its effect on sampled money wage rates. Specifically, an increase of aggregate demand will reduce search unemployment by causing some searchers to mistake a *general* rise of money wage rates for the discovery of a high *relative* money wage offer, high enough that its acceptance is preferred to search for a higher one.

I have found it instructive to picture the economy as a group of islands between which information flows are costly: To learn the wage paid on an adjacent island, the worker must spend the day traveling to that island to sample its wage instead of spending the day at work. Imagine, only for simplicity, that total labor supply—the sum of employment and (search) unemployment—is a constant for every household, independent of real wage rates, expected real interest rates, and so on. Suppose also that labor is technically homogeneous in production functions and indifferent among the many heterogeneous jobs of producing a variety of products. Producers on each island are in pure competition in the labor market as well as in the interisland product markets. Each morning, on each island, workers "shape up" for an auction that determines the market-clearing money wage and employment level. To start with, imagine a very stationary setup in which there is no taste change and no technical change, with constant population size.

Initially, wage rates are moving as has been expected, and it is believed that unsampled wage rates (on other islands) are equal to the sampled (own-island) one. The economy is thus in a kind of *non-Walrasian equilibrium* in which wage rates are correctly guessed. But they are never truly known as in the Walrasian world; a change of some island's wage would not be immediately learned. For simplicity of exposition, suppose that money wages have been expected to be stationary. The initial equilibrium is therefore one of steady wages and prices.

Now let aggregate demand fall. If the decline of derived demand for labor were understood to be general and uniform across islands, money wage rates (and with them prices) would fall so as to maintain employment and the real wage rate (provided that a new equilibrium exists). But suppose that workers on every island believe the fall of demand is at least partially island-specific, owing to their island's individual product mix. It is natural then to postulate, with Alchian, that workers' expectations of money wage rates elsewhere (on other islands) will "adapt" less than proportionally to the unforeseen fall of sampled money wage rates. To the extent that the island-specific component of the wage change is believed to be enduring enough to make a search for a better money wage rate seem worthwhile, the acceptance wage on each island will fall less than proportionally to product prices; some workers will refuse employment at the new (lower) market-clearing money wage rates, preferring to spend the time searching for a better relative money wage elsewhere.[11] *Effective* labor supply thus shifts leftward at every real wage rate; real wage rates rise, and profit-maximizing output and employment fall.

The papers by Charles Holt, Dale Mortensen, and the present author discuss the generation of a Phillips curve from labor-market models that, although more realistic, are not radically different from the island parable. Before proceeding to these models, we note that the faint shape of a Phillips curve relation between the steady unemployment rate and the rate of wage change appears even in the ultrasimple island model. If the government were to manipulate aggregate demand to keep the average money level constant at its new lower level, then the unemployed would be disappointed at finding money wage rates equally low elsewhere and would hence revise downward their expectations of the mean wage elsewhere relative to sampled wage rates; search would become less attractive and effective labor supply would shift rightward. To prevent the market-clearing employment rate from rising, therefore, the government would have to continue to reduce money wage rates by contracting aggregate demand—or by holding aggregate demand steady if the quantity of aggregate output demanded is independent of the price level. This action would be effective on the hypothesis that every unexpected decrease of sampled money wage rates produces a less-than-proportional decrease of

---

[11]I assume that workers differ in age, and hence differ in their appraisal of the lifetime gain from a specified expectation of wage rate improvement, or that workers differ in the "adaptability" of their wage expectations so that each island's effective labor-supply curve slopes upward.

expected money wage rates elsewhere. Some continuing decline of money wage rates (of the right magnitude) thus accompanies the maintenance of the specified volume of search unemployment.[12] The rate of decrease of money wage rates is clearly larger the greater is the shortfall of actual wage rates from expected wage rates. It is also true that the volume of search unemployment is larger the greater is this shortfall. Hence we deduce a Phillips-like relation between the steady level of unemployment and the algebraic rate of increase of money wage rates. In this relation, the expected long-run trend rate of money wage increase figures as a parameter. If workers look backward and see that money wage rates are steadily falling and adapt their expectations of the general wage trend accordingly, an ever-accelerating rate of decrease of wage rates will occur if the search unemployment level is maintained.

In the above story, every steady state of positive unemployment is one of disequilibrium in the sense that sampled wage rates are continually and systematically different from (less than) what they were expected to be.[13] Equilibrium, in the non-Walrasian sense, denotes a state in which wage rates and other prices on average are found—over space and over time—to be what they were expected to be. Steady-state equilibrium in this sense occurs in the simplified island model only at zero unemployment. To escape this implication, it is necessary to introduce structural change, such as "real" microeconomic product-demand shifts, relative-cost shifts, or population-shifts.[14] Then the islands where money wage rates are *above* the average money wage rates expected elsewhere will be numerous enough relative to the islands where wage rates are *below* expected wage rates elsewhere that the equilibrium steady unemployment rate will be positive. There will be enough job "vacancies"—as defined by the quantity of labor that would be demanded at expected mean wage rates elsewhere minus actual employment where wage rates are "high"—in relation to the quantity of search unemployment that equilibrium "in the large" is possible, although individual searchers and nonsearchers may be disappointed or delighted.[15] In the model so extended, "overemployment" is possible.

---

[12]A rigorous argument that the rate of wage decline is constant, at least asymptotically, would require more detailed specifications of the model.

[13]If the expected long-run trend rate of money wage change is, say, 4 percent, a small enough steady unemployment rate will be associated with rising money wage rates; but they will be rising at less than 4 percent, so that the same average overestimate of wage rates elsewhere will exist and net disappointment will occur.

[14]There is a lengthier discussion of the requirements *infra* in connection with the Archibald paper.

[15]Unlike some models, in the kind of economy I have been sketching, wage rates will be high and *falling* where vacancies are defined to be present, while in sectors where wage rates are below expected wage rates elsewhere (the current loci of the unemployment), wage rates will be low and *rising*. These rates of change, I believe, need not characterize more thoroughly non-Walrasian markets where each firm is an island.

It results when, starting from the equilibrium level of search unemployment, money wage rates are driven above average expected levels. Such unexpected wage rises induce some of the search unemployed to stop earlier, to accept employment at the sampled wage rates (and some employed to postpone search)—if, as hypothesized before, every unexpected wage increase produces a less-than-proportional increase of mean expected money wage rates elsewhere.[16]

Thus the island scenario suggests a wage-change equation in which the Phillips relation is one element. The rate of wage change is connected to the level of the unemployment rate, the rate of change of employment, and the expected trend rate of increase of wage rates— the latter entering the equation with a unitary coefficient. Such an equation is also arrived at, through models that are more realistic in some respects, by the present author, Mortensen, and (with some qualification) by Holt.

Of the three papers, Mortensen's is most like the island story in two respects: Jobs and people are fundamentally alike—only wage rates (across firms) and expectations thereof (across people) are different. Second, a firm will never turn away a worker who is willing to work for less than the firm's present workers; in this sense, there is market clearing. It will be suggested later that there is some connection between the first point, homogeneity, and the second point, the absence of job rationing.

Mortensen adapts to that type of model the approach of the present author in his paper, which is to suppose that each firm is a wage-maker rather than a wage-taker. The essential idea is that the wage is an important recruiting tool of the individual firm. In Walrasian theory, each firm can have in an instant as much labor as it likes at the going wage. In seriously uninformed labor markets, it seems more natural to treat each firm as a kind of island, an island from which information about its wage is acquired only gradually. Thus the firm may be considered to have dynamical monopsony power at each point in time: A rise of its wage offer relative to wage rates elsewhere will increase the speed with which its employment roll will increase.

Mortensen is the first to elaborate a rigorous theory of optimal wage setting on those lines. The optimal wage depends upon the dynamics of response which the firm anticipates from any particular wage. Mortensen's treatment of the "flow supply" of labor to the firm grows out of Holt's approach to unemployment as a problem in "optimal

[16]I should mention a weakness in the above search-unemployment model. A fall of aggregate demand may fail to produce the expectation of finding better relative money wage rates elsewhere and thus fail to increase search unemployment if workers observe that the cost of living has fallen in proportion to sampled money wage rates (or in greater proportion) insofar as they take those consumer prices to be some indication of general wage rates. (This suggests that price-level stickiness has a role to play in search unemployment.)

stopping." In the former's version, every worker possesses a subjective probability distribution of current wage offers—one that may be stationary over the future or, more generally, expected to change at some exponential rate (the expected rate of mean wage change). The worker can sample wage rates more intensively in the unemployed state than in the employed state, but the employed worker has some probability of exposure to an outside wage offer. From these considerations the unemployed worker settles on an acceptance wage or reservation price. Some workers, from experience, are more bearish than others, and workers form a continuum in that respect. Hence the larger the firm's wage, the greater is the proportion of unemployed workers sampling its wage the firm can expect to accept its offer: similarly, the higher the rate at which it can expect to attract workers employed elsewhere. It is also supposed that an increase of the firm's wage reduces the *rate* at which its present employees will quit—this gradualness of response being primarily an analytical convenience, its interpretation being one of a wish by the firm's employees to economize on their decision-making time in the face of constant jiggling of their wage rate.

An increase of aggregate demand creates incentives for each firm to raise its wage relative to expectations of wage rates elsewhere. If the system started out in equilibrium, with the rate of average wage increase just equal to the (average) expected rate of mean wage increase, so that the unemployment was at its normal or natural level, then the increase of wage offers will gradually draw workers out of the unemployed pool. Maintenance of a lower unemployment rate requires that wage rates stay ahead of expectations as the latter are revised upward. If a steady rate of wage inflation is engineered by the monetary and fiscal authorities in excess of the (constant) expected rate of mean wage change, then the unemployment rate falls to some (disequilibrium) steady-state value where the unemployed workers have generally higher acceptance wages. But steady wage inflation will not buy a permanent reduction of the unemployment rate if workers learn to revise upward their expected rate of mean wage increase in the direction of the actual average rate of wage increase.

Though the papers by Holt and by the present author are extensively synthesized and refined in the Mortensen paper, their differences from their offspring are significant. Both papers emphasize that quit rates are high when unemployment is low. From an unadulterated Mortensen–Alchian view this is inexplicable: The same unexpected wage increases that shorten the search of those already unemployed should also cause some employed workers, pleasantly surprised with raises they believe to be unmatched elsewhere, to decide not to quit, not to join the search for a better wage. The negative association between the quit rate and the unemployment rate involves the phenomenon of job rationing in the labor market. When aggregate demand is high, jobs are made available that some workers, perhaps as qualified as present holders, were previously unable to "bid" for. As employed workers learn of these openings, they quit to take those which are preferable to their present jobs; concomitantly, unemployment falls to a lower level as searchers for available jobs find their object.

In Holt's analysis, the rate of overall wage increase is an appropriate average of the rate of wage improvement of workers who quit directly to take another job and, of course, on-the-job wage increases, which play a somewhat passive role. Those who directly change jobs do so because they have been offered a better wage. (Those who are laid off do not generally enjoy the same wage improvement.) An increase of the quit rate increases the frequency with which such wage improvements occur and thus adds to the rate of increase of the average wage received. By postulating an inverse relation between the quit rate and the level of the unemployment, Holt deduces one component of a negative relationship between the unemployment rate and the rate of wage increase in steady states.

The other component of that relationship depends upon the average duration of unemployment. The shorter unemployment on average, Holt supposes, the larger is the average algebraic wage improvement. The argument is that the unemployed worker, despite perfect knowledge of the average wage and of the degree of job availability, tends to narrow his estimate of the variance of wage offers as he acquires more experience with the distribution. Further, as more time goes by without work, his net worth falls and so, too, may his liquidity. For these reasons one may expect that his acceptance wage will fall. Holt then postulates an inverse relation between the average duration of unemployment and the unemployment rate, appealing for support to the tendency for the total separation rate (quits into the unemployment pool plus layoffs) to be independent of the unemployment rate. Thus it is argued that the smaller the level of the unemployment rate, the larger is the algebraic rate of wage improvement of that fraction of the labor force who pass through the unemployment pool and, correspondingly, the larger is the rate of increase of the average wage.

In principle the average wage received could drift up in this way without any increase of wage rates by any firm—for awhile. Interfirm movements to higher-wage firms and "up-grading" are examples. But Holt views the raise of wage rates as another device by which the firm seeks to attract additional labor when its job vacancies increase. He suggests that the wage-setting by the firm can be viewed analogously to his view of the acceptance wage of the labor supplier.

In the present author's paper, the approach to the derivation of the momentary Phillips curve is somewhat similar. Start the economy in an equilibrium where the actual rate of mean wage change conforms to average expectations of the mean wage change. An increase of aggregate demand opens up more jobs; the unemployment rate declines as searchers find these openings and as firms succeed in their additional nonwage recruitment efforts. There is some discussion of optimal recruitment effort over time. Insofar as wage increases by themselves decrease unemployment in the aggregate, they do so, in the model, by raising contractual wage rates relative to what new wage contracts are expected to offer in the near future. However, it is shown how the Alchian–Mortensen view, which depends upon misexpectations of the current mean wage, can be incorporated into the model.

If a steady state with a below-equilibrium level of unemployment is to be maintained, the job-vacancy rate must remain higher—otherwise, with workers harder to find, recruitment would be smaller; but recruitment cannot be smaller if unemployment is to remain lower, for at the lower unemployment rate the separation rate is at least as high, indeed the quit rate is higher. There is a negative steady-state relation, therefore, between the unemployment rate and the vacancy rate.

Although the greater willingness to hire and greater use of nonwage recruiting measures, such as help-wanted advertising, are the principal means by which aggregate unemployment is reduced, the individual firm regards its money wage rates as an important recruitment tool. When vacancies rise and unemployment falls, each firm will wish to raise its wage relative to its expectation of the general wage level over the near future, for such an increase of its relative wage will assist it in its recruiting. But in the disequilibrium state under discussion, every firm raises its wage more than its expectation of the increase in the average wage elsewhere. Every firm must therefore come to be disappointed in the actual results from its *ex post* wage over the wage contract. Every firm will be disappointed in its recruiting performance because its relative wage turns out to be less than intended. Firms adjust to this surprise by a further increase of money wage rates to "catch up," to attain the recruitment performance they had intended. Likewise, workers will have been disappointed with their relative wage over the past contract period and will demand such catch-up wage increases. The result is that there exists a steady-state constant rate of money wage increase (in excess of the expected rate of increase) corresponding to a steady unemployment rate below the equilibrium level. The rate of wage increase is shown to be greater the smaller the unemployment rate. (Of course, there may be requirements upon fiscal and monetary policy if, as money wage rates go up, the incentive upon firms to maintain employment is not to fall.)

It could be, incidentally, that the relation of the rate of change of money wage rates, on the one hand, to the vacancy and unemployment rates, on the other, is of the simple "excess demand" form—where only the difference between the latter two rates matters. Thus there is no conflict between "excess demand" and the Phillips curve in theories of money wage change. The point is that vacancies jointly determine unemployment and thus excess demand and the rate of inflation—more precisely, the excess of the rate of money wage increase over the expected rate of money wage increase, all in steady states.

We have been talking about a momentary Phillips curve that corresponds to a particular expected rate of money wage increase. When the actual rate of wage increase steadily exceeds that expected rate, the steady-state unemployment rate is given by the momentary steady-state Phillips curve. When the actual rate of wage increase just equals the expected rate of wage increase, the corresponding point on the curve is, by definition, the equilibrium unemployment rate. Clearly, there can be a different equilibrium unemployment rate corresponding to every value of the expected rate of wage increase. Such an equilibrium locus will generally be steeper than the family of momentary Phillips curves; it could be negatively or positively sloped. It is argued, in the present author's paper, that, to a first approximation, the equilibrium unemployment rate is independent of the expected rate of wage increase; i.e., the equilibrium locus is vertical. The unique unemployment rate has been called the warranted rate (Phelps), the natural rate (Friedman), the normal rate (Harberger), and the full employment rate (Lerner). In that case, a fluctuationless "anticipated inflation" would be associated with the same rate of unemployment as a fluctuationless regime of steady prices in which money wage rates are rising only as fast as productivity. Essentially, the argument for this proposition is that in a given real situation in terms of unemployment and vacancy rates, every worker will demand an additional point on his percentage wage increase, and each employer will want to pay an additional 1 percent increase in wages, for every one point addition to the expected percentage rate of money wage increase elsewhere in the economy. These formalisms take on significance if we introduce a behavioral hypothesis about the expected rate of wage increase, e.g., the adaptative-expectations hypothesis. Then the engineering of a faster growth of aggregate demand and hence a higher rate of inflation cannot achieve a lasting reduction of the unemployment rate below the natural rate—though it may bring enormous happiness in the transition. Several qualifications to all this are acknowledged and underlined in the present author's paper.

Job rationing, we have said, is a significant feature of the two papers last discussed. Alchian also notes the prevalence of queueing in labor and product markets. What is the microeconomic rationale for job rationing? Although it is addressed primarily to the pricing policy of a seller facing a stochastic demand, the analysis by Donald Gordon and Allan Hynes sheds light on rationing from the buying side of the labor market. Economists have become familiar with the thought that the firm, in experiencing a variable need for labor, may pay wages to a buffer stock of idle or near-idle workers to ensure its being able to meet randomly high demands for his product when marginal recruitment costs are positive and rising. Under the same recruitment conditions, it may be advantageous to the firm to pay its workers wage rates that frequently exceed the "bids" for those jobs by unemployed (or other) workers, if the employer faces a stochastic supply of labor. When the employer is not sure, at each wage, how many workers, and which workers, will quit tomorrow and how many unemployed workers will seek and accept jobs, he may find it expected-present-value maximizing to reduce the risk of a loss of workers by paying wage rates that, most of the time, are unnecessarily high for generating the average employment level the firm would like to have. This consideration is surely most important when there is considerable technical heterogeneity among workers. Then marginal recruitment costs are higher and may be rising more steeply. We shall return to further discussion of this paper.

Let us face now a question that we have so far skirted: What keeps the natural unemployment rate positive? Why is it realistic to suppose that any unemployment equilibrium tends to stay positive? It is clear we would not be able to achieve zero unemployment this year without having inflation well in excess of expectations. Everyone knows that in order to have nonpositive excess supplies in each and every submarket, it would unquestionably be necessary to have huge excess demands in some submarkets. There exist elegant static models to illustrate this. The mismatch of resources that exists this year is customarily attributed to some unevenness in shifts of demand functions and supply functions across industrial sectors and across geographical regions. The thought, presumably, is that it will take some time for workers to conclude that, this year at any rate, Nottingham is a bad scene for employment—if it has not always been that way. But it would be unlikely to find that unemployment was perennially well above average in rural areas simply because there was below-average growth in the demand for food compared to other products, above-average growth in productivity, and above-average growth of population. Such a pattern is not new in agriculture, so one presumes that the market ably "discounts" it. The kind of unevenness that makes the natural unemployment rate positive is unsystematic, unforeseen unevenness. The paper by G. C. Archibald discusses this point, introducing the term "stochastic stability" to describe the character of supply-demand shifts that keep the equilibrium unemployment rate from decaying toward zero. This view of the matter suggests that the variance of unemployment across industrial categories and regions is crucial in explaining the mean unemployment rate. Archibald finds, however, that the variance seems to make an independent contribution to the rate of wage change, given mean unemployment. The explanation may lie in certain nonlinearities, and, from this point of view, it is interesting that, if skewness of the distribution is introduced, variance adds nothing to the statistical fit.

Yet uneven shifts, differential rates of change, are not entirely essential for positivity of equilibrium unemployment rates. In an imperfectly informed labor market, it seems likely that the typical new entrant into the labor force will want to look around for his best opportunity—or one better than that which first meets the eye. Only a few workers will be able to place themselves in jobs before becoming available for work. In that case, a positive birth rate by itself ensures that the natural unemployment rate is a positive number. And indeed we find that unemployment rates are greatest among the very young—those looking for their first job and probably those looking for a job preferable to their first one. In their models, Holt, the present author, and Mortensen all find that equilibrium unemployment rates are larger the faster the rate of growth of the labor supply. The other parameter which surely plays a role is the rate of productivity growth. It will be of some interest to touch briefly on the parameters affecting the natural unemployment rate that are easily alterable by public policy. But let us first complete the taxonomy of unemployment and corresponding models of wage dynamics.

In the models of search unemployment under discussion, the alternative to accepting a job is looking for another one. It is important to recognize another possibility: accepting leisure. The corresponding idleness might be called "wait unemployment." In any real-life situation, unemployment is likely to be an admixture of search and leisure (and some of the leisure may be spent in kinds of production, such as making one's own meals or making home repairs).

Gordon and Hynes discuss a model of the intermittent idleness of a resource subject to stochastically fluctuating demand. Their principal example is the problem of pricing apartments. Probably their analysis is most importantly applicable to product markets. But their insights carry over to labor markets as well.

Every wage contract between employer and employee, Gordon and Hynes maintain, is a contract for some finite duration of time—even if this understanding is not explicit and even if there are laws against indentured servitude. If a worker who finds his service not in demand at his standard wage should reduce his wage enough to be hired, he would be taking the risk that he would have to reject, over the duration of his new job, an offer of employment at his standard wage. The supplier who faces a stochastic demand will want to set his wage high enough that, if he has correctly estimated the probability distribution of demands, he will be intermittently unemployed. This model quite obviously illuminates the sporadic unemployment of artisans, lawyers, actors, architects, consultants, and politicians. When one considers that a record of frequent quitting may stigmatize a worker, even when there has never been a definite job to complete, it is clear that the Gordon–Hynes model is relevant to a wider part of the labor market.

The quantity of wait unemployment, like the amount of search unemployment, is not impervious to changes in aggregate demand. When an increase in aggregate demand increases the mean demand for the services of workers, most suppliers who happen to have been idle will respond to the increase in demand by accepting employment at their old standard rates. But as the unusual frequency of demands persists, suppliers will adaptively revise upward their expectations of mean demand and raise their standard wages accordingly. Hence, if employment were to be maintained at some level in excess of its equilibrium level—at the latter, the mean demand is being correctly estimated— there would be a succession of wage increases (in excess of the normal trend rate of increase that sellers believe to be appropriate to the secular growth of demand). The rate of wage increase is greater the larger the excess of employment over its equilibrium value. Thus a kind of momentary Phillips curve again emerges. But Gordon and Hynes argue that as suppliers find that steady escalation of their fees has not been enough to recover equilibrium, they will accelerate their fees. They conclude that their model, too, denies the possibility of a stable tradeoff between employment and inflation.

There is available another, potentially complementary, model of wait unemployment, one that is neoclassical except for its exclusion of perfect foresight. There is no presumption that foreseen price changes cause systematic correlative changes in the anticipated real rate of interest. But it may well be that unforeseen changes of the price-level tend, as an empirical matter, to produce systematic changes in the expected real rates of interest—in such a direction, in fact, that employment changes in the same direction. This is argued by Robert Lucas and Leonard Rapping.

Consider an unforeseen rise of the price level in a competitive economy that has expected price and wage stationarity and that has, up to the present, been right. Lucas and Rapping postulate that households "adapt" their expectations of the future price level only partially in response to the unexpected price rise. In a manner of speaking, households will speculate on the gradual return of the price level to its original level. Therefore, they argue, if households expect to spend any increment of money wages partially on *future* consumption goods, a rise of money wage rates in proportion to the current price level would make additional labor supply more attractive than before. Thus the labor-supply curve shifts rightward at every real wage rate. Real wage rates fall and employment is stimulated. The analysis assumes that, if money rates of interest fall at all with the price rise, they do not fall by so much as to prevent the expected real rate of interest from rising. It is the rise of the expected real interest rate that stimulates the increase of labor supply in their model. The authors display a simple lifetime utility-maximization model of household labor supply, involving present and future consumption and leisure, as an illustration.

Out of the Lucas–Rapping model comes not only a theory of money wage stickiness but a momentary Phillips curve relation between the rate of price change and the employment rate. If aggregate demand is manipulated by the government in such a way as to keep the price level constant at its new and higher level, workers will, on the adaptive-expectations hypothesis above, successively revise upward their expectations of future consumption-goods prices; these revisions will gradually reduce labor supply (at every real wage), thus driving money wage rates up and driving profit-maximizing output and employment back toward their steady-state equilibrium levels. But there is some rate of continuing unforeseen price increases, a rate that is able to keep the expected future price level equal to a constant fraction of the actual price level—if each unforeseen increase of the current price level induces a constant and less-than-proportional increase of the expected price level—which can thus induce households to maintain their labor supply at the given "overemployment" level. Yet the required rate of inflation is constant, rather than ever-accelerating, only if what might be called the "expected trend rate of price change"—explicitly fixed at zero in their exposition—fails to adapt to the actual trend of the price level. In the Lucas–Rapping formulation of the price-change (or wage-change) equation, the expected long-run trend rate of price enters with a unitary coefficient.

It remains to point, with some pride, to the bearing of these papers on some concerns of public policy. Unemployment and inflation are matters of social as well as intellectual interest. On the other hand, it must be emphasized that the formulation of policy recommendations is beyond the scope of this book. In the main, the authors have been content with predictions of some of the effects of this or that government action, without offering any judgment as to the welfare basis for such a move or any estimate of its score in a cost-benefit test.

One of the policy arsenals, one that can do its bit even if it cannot alone bring total victory, is stocked with the weapons of money and taxes. In framing policy toward aggregate demand, the question inevitably arises as to whether a period of unexpected inflation and temporary overemployment would bring welfare gains in the interval. Alchian emphasizes that unemployment is productive. It would be as senselessly puritanical to wipe out unemployment as it would be to raise taxes in a deep depression. Today's unemployment is an investment in a better allocation of any given quantity of employed persons tomorrow; its opportunity cost, like that of any other investment, is present consumption. Similarly, Gordon and Hynes see spare capacity and wait unemployment as important for economic efficiency. They also serve who only stand and wait. But whether the natural rate of unemployment is "just right" is difficult to say. The world of frictions, uncertainties, queues, and what-not portrayed here is bound to be fraught with externalities. Hence a small amount of overemployment, for example, might be Pareto-superior to the natural amount—neglecting the effects upon expectations of inflation and the ramifications of that for economic efficiency. The distributional consequences of a deviation from the natural rate must also be reckoned.

The other policy arsenal, still being equipped, consists of the whole range of public services and fiscal incentives that might improve the effectiveness with which the labor market allocates workers to jobs. As Holt points out in the second paper of this volume, the feedback and interaction effects in these new models are sufficiently powerful and novel that certain policy measures may not have the expected effects. He finds, for example, that measures which decrease the propensity to quit, *ceteris paribus*, would increase the average duration of unemployment in equilibrium. Mortensen, in his discussion of the determinants of the natural rate of unemployment, finds that an increase in the speed with which a worker, when unemployed, can sample wage rates will increase the reservation wage of the unemployed worker, raise the average duration of unemployment, and thus quite possibly increase the natural unemployment rate. Such paradoxes do not, of course, *ipso facto*, condemn structural measures that reduce the costs of acquiring information in the labor market. The criteria for deciding on such a policy measure should involve distribution and efficiency (present-value calculations), not whether or not the measure will increase or decrease the equilibrium quantity of unemployment. On the other hand, that more and cheaper information is better should not uncritically be taken as an axiom.

2
PRICE AND OUTPUT DYNAMICS

The above models typically postulate complete information on the part of buyers about all goods prices. If a firm were to change its product price, the full effect of this change on the quantity demanded of the firm's commodity would be felt instantaneously. In that kind of model, inducing the firm to employ more—to move down its labor demand curve expressed in wage units as it were—requires a fall of product wage rates or, more loosely, of real wage rates. No one believes that production fluctuations can be accounted for completely, if at all, by such countercyclical real wage rate movements. More sophisticated views of pricing which dispense with various Walrasian informational postulates can avert the implication that real wage rates must so behave if aggregate demand changes are to have output and employment effects. They can also rationalize a kind of excess capacity phenomenon as a normal accompaniment, like unemployment, of the non-Walrasian economy.

Sidney Winter and the present writer analyze a model in which, primarily because of sluggishness in the diffusion of information, the firm finds itself at every moment having transient monopoly power: It will not instantaneously lose all its customers if it raises its price nor will it gain the whole market instantly if it cuts its price.[17] Yet the effect of such a price variation mounts over time as information on the associated price differentials is diffused through the market. This paper restricts attention to the undifferentiated atomistic case in which the firm is asymptotically competitive. The firm knows that setting a price permanently above the expected "going price" in the economy for comparable goods would ultimately cost it its entire market share, whereas setting a price permanently below the going price would ultimately capture a huge number of customers. In such an economy one can conceive of a non-Walrasian equilibrium in which, on the product side, for every firm, the inflow of newborn customers just matches the outflow of customers; the firm believes therefore that its price is just "competitive," being equal to prices charged elsewhere; likewise, its customers believe they are being charged the going price elsewhere.

There are two obvious theorems about the "markup" in that equilibrium. The first proposition is that the firm does not fully exploit its transient monopoly position. It produces beyond the point where marginal cost equals instantaneous marginal revenue, because it estimates that a temporary rise of price, while bringing a larger cash flow for the immediate future, would cost it some valuable customers and thus some future cash flow. The second proposition is that the firm produces less than that output rate at which its marginal costs would equal the equilibrium going price. To obtain the larger cash flow that greater sales at the going price would seem to offer, the firm would have temporarily to reduce its price to attract additional customers. Provided the expected real rate of interest is positive, there is some gap between marginal cost and price which is small enough that the present sacrifice of cash flow entailed by a small temporary price cut (remember the firm is already producing too much from a myopic view) is not worth the discounted future increase of cash flow which the resulting customer gain would bring.[18]

There is a kind of excess capacity in this equilibrium state. If we think of the array of "machines," each of which can produce a unit of output but which generally differ in their labor requirements, then

[17]This is the counterpart in product markets of the Phelps–Mortensen postulate of dynamical monopsony power by the firm in labor markets.

[18]The same propositions apply to the firm in an analogous position in the labor market having at every moment some transient monopsonistic power, yet being an asymptotically competitive buyer of labor. See the Mortensen paper.

some of the more labor intensive of these machines will be idle even though, at the going product wage, some revenue would be left over as rent for these machines if their output could find a buyer without the aforementioned costs. There can also be excess capacity in another sense: It can happen that output increases are obtainable from an increase of aggregate demand without any decline of product wage rates.

To see that in principle real wage rates can move procyclically, we note that, given the parameters controlling the expected rate of response of customer flow to a change in the firm's price, the firm's optimal price is homogeneous of degree one in the customer's demand price, the money wage rate, and the expected going price elsewhere. Its optimal output is homogeneous of degree zero in these variables. Suppose an increase of aggregate demand produces a neutral upward shift of the firm's demand curve and that money wage rates happen to rise in the same proportion. If the firm's expectation of the going price at competing firms is unchanged, or is revised upward in smaller proportion to the rise of its own demand, then it is possible that the firm will want to raise its price less than proportionally to its instantaneous "demand price," meeting the additional quantity demanded with greater output and hence greater employment. To raise its price in full proportion to the rise of the demand price at the initial equilibrium output would be to neglect the decline of its competitiveness that it believes such a price increase would bring. The disequilibrium result, then, is a rise of real wage rates and an increase of output and employment.[19] In the symmetrical situation—a fall of demand and of money wage rates—producers let their markups increase, failing to realize that they must cut price more if they are to maintain their competitiveness. Thus the price level may fall by less than the money wage rate level despite the fall of output and employment.

It is easy to see, having now gotten the hang of things, that a Phillips-like relation between the output level (relative to capacity) and the rate of price increase results if each firm continuously adjusts upward its price as it learns that it is not experiencing a net loss of customers from its higher price and as money wage rates keep pace with the general price level. But the now-familiar qualification must again be made: The long-run trend rates of increase of money wage rates, of demand, and of the going price elsewhere expected by the firm figure as parameters in any such steady-state Phillips relation. As these expected trend rates adapt to perceived trends, the Phillips relation floats upward.

[19]My too-brief search of the literature for the scholarly purposes of this survey turned up few writers before Keynes (or even after) who ever asked why quantity effects should be expected to accompany the price effects of monetary and other macroeconomic disturbances. To my surprise, one of the few, D. H. Robertson, put his finger on the above behavior of markups: "The stimulus of rising prices is partly founded in illusion . . . [the business leader] is spurred on . . . by imaginary gains at the expense of his fellow business men. It is so hard to believe at first that other people will really have the effrontery or the good fortune to raise their charges as much as he has raised his own." *Money* (Cambridge University Press, New York, 1929).

Obviously the soil of non-Walrasian product markets is one where any competent ad man would flourish. John Gould, after reviewing and delinearizing earlier work in that area, discusses optimal advertising outlay over time in the setting of two "diffusion" models. In both cases he finds that the firm, confined to a fixed price, chooses an advertising budget that settles down to a constant outlay over time. In one case, the "diffusion" model, advertising starts small and builds. In another case, a "contagion" model, advertising builds to a peak and then recedes. Unless one were to interpret the speed of the word-of-mouth communication as a matter of price, both are fixed-price models. Clearly the optimal advertising models by Gould could be usefully married to the optimal pricing model of Phelps and Winter.

Still another model of economic fluctuations in output emerges from recent analyses of optimal pricing and by the supplier of a good under conditions of uncertainty about future price or demand. The uncertainty attaches to the profitability of leaving some output unsold in the present when a choice must be made between selling the output in the present or in the future.

The paper by Gordon and Hynes analyzes the monopolist who faces a stochastic demand curve. Their paper fits the problem of the owner of an apartment building who must offer one-year leases on his apartments. Simplifying somewhat, they imagine that the owner sets a rental on vacant apartments each "day." The owner does not aim to set the rental so low that there would be a high probability of no vacancies each day. A higher rental is superior for the usual buffer-stock reason.

An increase of mean demand will at first reduce the vacancy rate. Rentals on vacant apartments are sticky because the increase of mean demand is mistaken for a random deviation. As this experience with the below-equilibrium vacancy rate continues, the owner will begin to adapt his subjective estimate of the mean demand at his current rental, raising his rentals accordingly. If aggregate demand is steadily increased so as to permit the below-equilibrium vacancy rate to continue, the upward adjustments of apartment rentals continue as owners grope for the changing mean of the distribution. This is the temporary Phillips relation at work. But owners eventually learn that they must raise rentals faster than they have been doing if they are to succeed in restoring their vacancy rates. Gordon and Hynes argue that there cannot be a stable law of disequilibrium price dynamics for the same reason that, it is argued, there can be no stable law for use in predicting individual stock-price movements. When others learn the law, it is no longer descriptive. An important consideration, therefore, is the cost and return to the necessary learning in the case at hand.

In this sort of analysis it can be assumed, if one likes, that all prices are known. Then the markets under discussion are imperfect because each good is not widely known. People want to inspect and compare apartments before renting one, each apartment being a little different. Donald Nichols argues that heterogeneity is the key attribute of goods that normally experience occasional idleness. The most homogeneous assets, such as money and certain industrial shares, are very liquid, i.e., quickly exchangeable. The more heterogenous assets, such as houses and paintings, are frequently unemployed.

There has been a revival of interest in the consequences of true "user cost." That term, as used here, refers to the fact that some machinery deteriorates faster the greater the speed with which it is run and the greater the number of shifts per day (because maintenance opportunities are thereby reduced). Paul Taubman and Maurice Wilkinson have looked into the consequences of user cost for the optimal output and investment decisions of the competitive firm, generally under static expectations.

The concept of user cost together with adaptive expectations may be capable of offering an additional reason why unforeseen price movements can cause output changes despite unchanged product wage rates. Let all product prices and money wage rates rise unexpectedly and in the same proportion. Suppose that prices and wages are adaptively expected to regress gradually in the direction of their previous level. Consider, as a start, the producer who can neither sell his existing capital nor buy additional capital. It is the obvious that such a firm will want to add shifts and speed up its machinery because the marginal money quasi rent from so doing increases in proportion to current prices and wage rates, while the money shadow price of capital utilization, which reflects future expected quasi rents, increases in smaller proportion.[20] Thus the process of unforeseen inflation can produce a rightward shift of output supply and labor demand through the economics of user cost. But once again, increasing inflation is presumably necessary to maintain the disequilibrium.

3
GENERALIZATIONS

A common thread runs through all these models. The actors of each model have to cope ignorant of the future or even much of the present. Isolated and apprehensive, these Pinteresque figures construct expectations of the state of the economy—over space and over time—and maximize relative to that imagined world. The supply prices of outputs and of labor services and, similarly, the demand prices for labor, are linear homogeneous in known and expected prices (including expected mean demand prices in the stochastic case)—present

---

[20]This assumes, in Lucas–Rapping fashion, that the money rate of interest at which current quasi rents can be lent has not fallen, if at all, by as much as (or more than) the expected rate of decline of future prices and wage rate.

and future. Quantity decisions are homogeneous of degree zero in these variables.

On adaptative or other error-correcting expectations hypotheses, a change of aggregate demand alters the relations between sampled prices and expected prices. The implied alteration of expected relative prices—of expected wage rates elsewhere relative to sampled rates, of expected mean future demand prices relative to current demand prices, of expected real rates of interest, etc.—causes a change in quantity decisions, hence changes in employment and output. If by accident or design there should be maintained a disequilibrium in which expectations on average are systematically in error, error-learning will cause expectations continuously to be revised and, correspondingly, successive revisions of the supply and demand prices for labor services and the supply prices of outputs. This is the process identifiable with the Phillips curve. Whether there exists a permanent Phillips curve slanting through the layers of momentary Phillips curves is another matter. It is widely believed by the authors of this volume that equilibrium output and employment are approximately independent of expectations of wage and price increases. Hence, if these expectations adapt to actual wage and price increases, little or no permanent increase of output and employment would be obtainable through rising aggregate demand.

I

Employment
and
Wage Dynamics

Information Costs, Pricing, and Resource Unemployment*

ARMEN A. ALCHIAN

1
THEORY OF EXCHANGE, UNEMPLOYMENT, AND PRICE STABILITY

A. Introduction The economic theory of exchange often appears to imply that demand changes induce instant wage and price adjustments to maintain full resource use. But unemployment, queues, rationing, and idle resources refute any such implication. And macroeconomic theory does not explain why demand decreases cause unemployment rather than immediate wage and price adjustments in labor *and* non-human resources. Instead, administered prices, monopolies, minimum wage laws, union restrictions, and "natural" inflexibilities of wages and prices are invoked.

This paper attempts to show that economic theory is capable of being formulated—consistently with each person acting as an individual utility, or wealth, maximizer without constraints imposed by competitors, and without conventions or taboos about wages or prices—so as to imply shortages, surpluses, unemployment, queues, idle resources, and nonprice rationing with price stability. The theory im-

*Acknowledgement for substantial aid is made to the Lilly Endowment, Inc., grant to UCLA for a study in the behavioral effects of different kinds of property rights.

plies massive correlated fluctuations in employment of both labor and capital in response to aggregate demand decreases—in a context of open-market individual-utility-maximizing behavior. The theory is general in that it applies to nonhuman goods as well as to human services. Though my primary motivation to explain "unemployed" resources arose from labor-market behavior, the analysis is best exposited initially without special reference to labor markets.

The key, which, until recently, seems to have been forgotten, is that *collating information about potential exchange opportunities* is costly and can be performed in various ways.[1] Nobody knows as much as he would like (at zero cost) about everyone else's offers and demands (including the properties of goods offered or demanded), but, at a cost, more information can be acquired. Two questions guide our analysis. First, what are the means of providing information more efficiently? Second, given that information is costly, what kinds of substitute arrangements are used to economize on search costs?

In equilibrium everyone has equal marginal rates of substitution, but how is that equilibrium equality approached? It is not rational to expect a person to exchange with the first person he happens to meet with a different subjective value. It will pay to seek a higher "bid" or a lower "ask." Discovery of the variety of bids and offers and the best path or sequence of actual exchange prices toward an "equilibrium" requires costly search over the population. Institutions facilitate and economize on that search. The marketplace is an example. A large and costly portion of so-called marketing activity is information-dissemination activity. Advertisements, window displays, sales clerks, specialist agents, brokers, inventories, catalogs, correspondence, phone calls, market research agencies, employment agencies, licensing, certification, and aptitude-testing services (to name a few) facilitate the spread and acquisition of knowledge about potential demanders and suppliers and their goods and about prices they can expect to see prevail.

Marketing includes many activities: (a) "extensive" searching for all possible buyers or sellers, (b) communication of information about characteristics of the goods of each party—the "intensive" search,[2]

---

[1] A study of Stigler [G. J. Stigler, "Information in the Labor Market," *Journal of Political Economy, Supplement* (October 1962, No. 5, Part 2) pp. 94–105] will reveal this paper to be a development and application of the fundamentals of that paper. See also, for earlier interest in this problem, Rees [A. Rees, "Wage Determination and Involuntary Unemployment," *Journal of Political Economy*, 59 (April 1951) pp. 143–164; "Information Networks and Labor Markets," *American Economic Review, Supplement*, 56 (May 1966) pp. 559–566]. Arrow and Capron [K. J. Arrow and W. M. Capron, "Dynamic Shortages and Price Rises: The Engineer Scientist Case," *Quarterly Journal of Economics*, 73 (May 1959) pp. 292–308] used the difficulty of knowing the true market demand and supply as a reason for individual delays in adapting to the equilibrating price and output.

[2] This terminology is taken from Rees, "Wage Determination and Involuntary Unemployment."

(c) contract formation, (d) contract enforcement, (e) "buffer inventories" by sellers, (f) queueing of buyers, and (g) provision of price predictability. Two propositions about the costs of production or market opportunity information will be critical in the ensuing analysis.

a. *Dissemination and acquisition (i.e., the production) of information conforms to the ordinary laws of costs of production: faster dissemination, or acquisition costs more.* A simple, fruitful characterization of the search for information is sampling from a distribution of "offers" (or "bids") with some mean and dispersion. As the sample is enlarged, the observed maximum value will increase *on the average* at a *diminishing* rate. Assuming search (sampling) at a constant rate, with time thereby measuring size of sample, the expected (mathematical expectation of the) maximum observed value will rise from the median at a diminishing rate toward the upper limit of the distribution.[3] That limit will exceed the past actual price, because there is no necessity for the past sale to have been negotiated at the highest possible price (with exhaustive prior sampling, regardless of cost).

b. *Like any other production activity, specialization in information is efficient. Gathering and disseminating information about goods or about oneself is in some circumstances more efficiently done while the good or person is not employed, and thus able to specialize (i.e., while specializing) in the production of information.* If seeking information about other jobs while employed is more costly than while not employed, it can be economic to refuse a wage cut, become unemployed, and look for job information.[4] The deeper the wage cut in the old job, the cheaper the choice of unemployment in order to ferret information. Without this proposition of *differential* search costs, the theory would not be able, consistently with wealth-maximizing choices, to account for the fact that some people refuse to accept a low wage while acquiring and comparing job information.

The fact that being employed is itself a recommendation to a prospective employer does not deny that it may pay to foresake that rec-

---

[3]For example, if potential prices are normally distributed with mean, m, and with variance, σ^2, then the expected maximum observed bid $W(n)$ at the nth observation is approximately

$$W(n) = m + \sigma\sqrt{2 \log n}.$$

$W(n)$ starts at m and increases at a decreasing rate with n. If we assume one observation every λ units of time, then we can replace n by λt and obtain W as a function of time of search. Further, if we increase expenditures on search, the rate of search can be increased per unit time, whatever is the environment of search; in other words, the effective λ is a function of the environment, V, and of the expenditures on search $E(t)$: $\lambda = f[V, E(t)]$. A larger expenditure implies a larger λ, and if we let a larger V denote a more costly search environment, then a larger V implies a smaller λ. This gives :

$$W(t) = m + \sigma\sqrt{2 \log \lambda t}$$

with $\lambda = f[V, E(t)]$. We will use this later. We have postulated that $(\partial E/\partial \lambda)(\lambda/E) > 1$ in proposition (2).

[4]This proposition is added to those contained in Stigler (*op. cit.*) and is crucial to much that follows.

ommendation in view of the large wage cut required to obtain it. The value of such a recommendation would imply acceptance of greater wage cuts to keep jobs. However, the question here is why anyone would choose to foresake that lower wage and accept unemployment—not why wages are sometimes cut to hold jobs.

Our choice of words is deliberate when speaking of seeking "job information" rather than seeking "jobs." Jobs are always easily available. Timely information about the pay, working conditions, and life expectancy of all available jobs is not cheap. In a sense, *this* kind of unemployment is self-employment in information collection.

This applies to nonhuman resources as well. For example, the automobile on a used-car lot—out of "normal" service (unemployed)—facilitates cheaper information to potential buyers. Similarly, unoccupied apartments and houses (like cars and people) are cheaper to show to prospective clients.[5]

B. Graphic Interpretation   Though an illustrative mathematical formulation is in the Appendix, a graphic exposition of some characteristics of search and its costs are portrayed in Figure 1. Time is on the horizontal scale and price or wage on the vertical. For any constant rate of search over the population of potential buyers, time and scope of search can both be measured on the horizontal scale. If some good (say, a car) were sold to the first found offerer now, at t_0, the price would be P_0. The height of curve P_0P_t is the "expectation" of the maximum discerned available contract price found by time, t—assuming discerned options do not disappear or dacay with time. The line rises at a decreasing rate, rather than being horizontal at P, as it would be if information about all potential offers were costless (and if all people knew all the characteristics of the good). As the sample (information) increases, the expected maximum discerned available price increases by successively smaller increments. In terms of costs, there are increasing marginal costs of unit increments of expected maximum ascertained price.[6] The curve for an unemployed searcher will be above that for an employed searcher—if unemployment is to occur. By identifying characteristics that will affect the shape and position of the curves we can deduce unemployment patterns.

[5]We can now identify a "perfect" market—one in which all potential bids and offers are known at zero cost to every other person, and in which contract-enforcement costs are zero. Characteristics of every good need to be known perfectly at zero cost. A "perfect" market would imply a "perfect" world in which all costs of production, even of "exchanges," were zero. It is curious that while we economists never formalize our analysis on the basis of an analytical ideal of a perfect world (in the sense of costless production), we have postulated costless *information* as a formal ideal for analysis. Why?

[6]If we subtract the *cumulated* search costs over the search interval from the then-best-observed sales bid price, the *net* price line, now *net* of search costs, will hit a peak, after which it will decrease, assuming no "decay" in value of earlier perceived options.

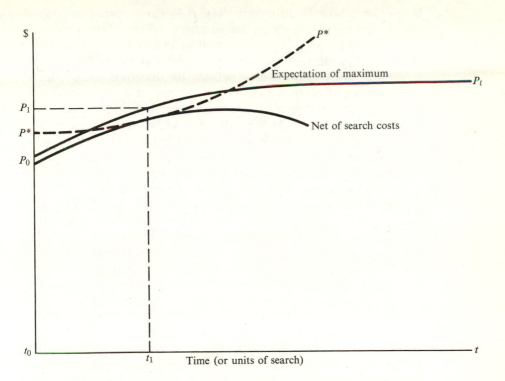

Figure 1.   Expectation of maximum discerned available bids, gross and net of search costs for specialists.

C. Liquidity   The analogy to liquidity is obvious. Liquidity concepts can be portrayed by the same diagram. The ratio of $P*$ to P is *one* dimension of the liquidity *vector*. Another, for example, is the time to t_1.

The expectation of discerned maximum offers is a function of amount of expenditures (of all types) for acquiring information up to any moment. A potential (expected maximum discerned) *gross* price will be higher, as of any time t, if more is spent on hastening the information-acquiring process. The seller nets a reward of P_1 minus *his* search costs, and the buyer pays P_1 plus his search costs. A perfectly liquid asset is one for which (a) the line starts at $P*$ rather than P (i.e., $P_1 - P* = 0$), *and also* (b) there are no costs for buyer and seller of acquiring information about the particular asset. Money is typically regarded as a resource fulfilling these criteria.[7] It enters into almost every exchange because it provides the most economical vehicle of exchange.

---

[7]For an illustration of the application of information and search costs to money and liquidity per se, see Miller [H. L. Miller, "Liquidity and Transactions Costs," *Southern Economics Journal*, 32, No. 1 (July 1965), pp. 43–48].

D. Brokers and Middlemen The P_0P_t curve reveals an opportunity for exchange with an intermediary broker. This analysis is applicable to nonhuman goods as well as to labor. It will be profitable for a "middleman" or "broker" to offer at the initial moment, t_0, a price higher than P_0, if he believes the discerned resale value of the good (net of *his* search costs) will increase at a rate greater than the interest rate and greater than that of the existing possessor of the good. The price he would offer at t_0 would be, at most, the present value of the expected maximum discerned bid price for the time his discerned price line (*net* of *his* search costs) was rising at a rate equal to the interest rate. This can be illustrated by inserting an "iso-net-present value" curve $P*P*$, the height of which *at the vertical* axis $(t = 0)$ shows that the maximum *present net* discounted value as of now, t_0, of any future net amount available (net of the *middleman's* search costs). The difference between the present-value price, $P*$, and the future selling price, P_1, is essentially the retail-wholesale price spread, or the bid-ask spread of brokers, wholesalers, or retailers. Since he is a successful specialist in search, his search costs are, by definition, lower, and hence his $P*$ is higher than for a nonmiddleman, nonspecialist.[8]

E. Price Stability: Economizing on Information and Market Adjustment Costs Aside from the obvious ways to produce information (e.g., advertising and specialist middlemen) there are less well recognized ways involving price stability, unemployed resources, and queues (in which costs are incurred to *reduce* search and other marketing costs even more). Inventories economize on costs of information. Inventories may appear to be idle, excess, or unemployed resources, but they can be interpreted as an economical use of resources.[9] Consider, as an oversimplified but suggestive example, the problem faced by a newsboy who sells an average of 100 copies of a daily paper—but not always 100 each day. The more accurately he tries to predict and the more quickly he adjusts to imperfectly predictable fluctuations in the flow of demand, the greater are the costs of his action. Potential customers may prefer that he stock an excessive number on the average with instant availability from inventories, despite higher costs caused by unsold copies. The higher cost may be manifested to customers as a smaller newspaper, fewer newsvendors, fewer editions, or a higher money price per copy sold. But this extra cost (of the unsold papers) will be less than if the newspaper sellers attempted to obtain complete information about demands at each future moment, or to make instantaneous adjustments in the number

[8]See H. Demsetz, "The Cost of Transacting," *Quarterly Journal of Economics*, 82 (February 1968), pp. 33–53.
[9]See T. L. Saaty, *Elements of Queueing Theory* (McGraw-Hill, New York, 1961).

of papers without an inventory. In brief, the costs of unsold items are incurred to reduce even more the information costs in marketing.

Another option exists. The newsvendor could change price instantly to always clear the market when demand fluctuates and thereby never have an inventory of unsold papers of a given edition awaiting purchasers.[10] Retailers would not be queued awaiting buyers. Restaurants could avoid reservations and queues by varying price instantly with the random fluctuations of appearance of customers. Why don't they? After all, that is what happens, or seems to happen, in the future markets and stock markets.[11]

Consider the consequences. Patrons appear at random intervals, though the probability density of the rate may be predictable. Would patrons prefer to see the market instantly cleared with no queues whatsoever—but only with price fluctuations to do the rationing? Not necessarily. That might *induce more search elsewhere* than under queuing. Customers may prefer more predictable prices with enhanced probability of some queues and less search. Unpredictable prices, as well as queues, impose costs on patrons; there is no reason why *only one* should be avoided regardless of the cost of the other. The restaurants must balance (a) costs of search induced by unpredictable prices and of inventories against (b) costs of queues and of waiting in queues.

For example, if gasoline were sold between 30 and 35 cents per gallon with prices fluctuating and differing among outlets for a given brand, some purchasers who paid an average of 32 cents per gallon, by prior searching for the lower price outlets, would have incurred a search cost of, let us say, 1 cent per gallon on the average. If all outlets were known to have a uniform price of 32.5 cents, search could be reduced (there would still be search for small queues) and the gross cost could fall from 33 to 32.5 cents per gallon. This is basically one of the economic defenses of manufacturer-imposed retail prices.

A seller who eliminates a nonpredictably fluctuating, transient, market-clearing price could offer his patrons a savings in costs of

[10]The expression "demand fluctuation" covers a host of mischievousness. For a more rigorous conceptualization, a "probability distribution of latent offers" is better. Reference to the mean and variance of that distribution of potentially discernable or revealed offers would provide some specification of the demand confronting a seller. Furthermore, there is not a *given* flow of *revealed* demanders. Offers could be emitted or received at a slower or faster rate. The analogy to emissions of particles from radioactive elements is apt. The emissions have a "mean" and a "range" of values (voltages) and a random time between emission, i.e., the "rate" of emission. These "randomly spaced" emissions of market offers can be characterized by a probability distribution. The *rate* at which offers are discerned by the seller can be increased or decreased by engaging in more information activity (i.e., marketing activity). This paper is not trying to specify some special underlying distribution rigorously. Some progress toward this is to be found in Stigler (*op. cit*).

[11]As a matter of fact, even on the futures markets and stock exchanges, there are specialists and "scalpers" who stabilize price by providing a buffer inventory [H. J. Working, "Test of a Theory Concerning Floor Trading on Commodity Exchanges," unpublished].

search. He could make price more predictable by carrying a larger inventory to buffer the transient demand fluctuations, and customers would reduce search costs with the assurance of a stable (i.e., predicted) price if they accepted some costs of waiting in a queue.

The queue length could vary with constant price as long as the *mean* rate of purchases is matched by the production rate. The greater the variance in the transient rate of appearance of shoppers, the greater will be the variation in the length of the queue and *also* the longer will be the average length of the line. An alternative to customer queues is "queueing" of an inventory as a buffer to eliminate customer queues while prices is constant. Among these options—transient and instant price changes, customer queues, inventories, and continued market search for better options—what determines the efficient extent of each?

Customers engage in repeat purchases; in making purchase plans, predictability of price is conducive to closer adjustment to optimal purchases. Revising purchase plans and actions is costly. If one finds a dinner price transiently high because of randomly high demand at the moment he appears in the restaurant, he will have been led to inappropriate action. He has gone to the restaurant in the expectation of a different price than that actually facing him. *Ex post* his action was not optimal. To avoid such losses, he will, thereafter, prior to concluding a purchase, engage in more search among sellers to discover unusually transiently low prices. This extra search is less costly than taking one's chances as to what price he will face in a transiently fluctuating market.

In general, smaller and more frequent random fluctuations in demand (i.e., with a fixed expectation in the probability density function), greater search costs, greater value of time, and less burdensome forms of queueing or rationing all will increase the incidence of price stability. If the demand probability density function shifted *predictably*, prices would vary—as they do for afternoon and evening restaurant and theater, for example. A lower cost of holding inventories relative to the value of the product will increase the relative size of inventories and increase price stability and shorten queues for any frequency and size of random demand fluctuations.[12]

Accordingly, we should expect to see some prices maintained relatively rigidly over time and among retail stores (with so-called fair trade laws) as *manufacturers* seek to assure the final customers of the lower *overall* costs of purchasing fair-traded items for high-quality,

---

[12]Had this paper been devoted also to the conditions that induce non-clearing-market prices, even with predictable demand, it would have included a discussion of forms of property rights in the goods being sold [A. A. Alchian and W. R. Allen, *Exchange and Production; Theory in Use* (Wadsworth Publishing Co., Belmont, Calif., 1969), Chap. 8].

but low-value, goods purchased by people whose time is relatively valuable (i.e., high-wage groups).

An obvious application of the analysis is to shop hours. Stores are open during known hours and stay open even when there are no customers in sight. A store could have lower prices if customers were to ring a bell and wait for the owner to open the store, but this would impose waiting costs on the patrons. I presume the advantage to the store operator (with lower pecuniary prices to customers) in closing his store when no customers are in sight is smaller than the convenience to shoppers.

More apartment units are built than the owner expects on the average to rent. This, of course, assumes that *revealed* demand *to him* for his apartments is neither continuous nor costlessly and perfectly predictable. Like the newsboy, it pays to build more apartments to satisfy *unpredictable* vagaries in "demand fluctuations" if such demand fluctuations cannot be accommodated by costless reallocation among demanders or "no inconvenience" from immediate rent changes. The apartment owner could always keep apartments fully rented at a lower, quickly revised rental; or at higher stable rentals he could have vacancies part of the time. A landlord, faced with an empty apartment, could cut the rent sufficiently to induce immediate rental to the first person he happened to see, if he ignored marketing (including moving) costs. But in view of costs of transactions, contract revision and displaying and arranging for new higher paying tenants of already *occupied* premises, it sometimes yields greater wealth to forego transient rent revision that would keep apartments *always* rented. In maintaining vacancies, he is responding to renters' preferences to (a) examine apartments, have rental predictability, and move more spontaneously rather than (b) to continually adjust to rental changes or (c) make plans and reservations in advance if there were price predictability *and no* inventory of vacant apartments. The "vacancies" serve as inventories; as such they do not warrant rent reductions.

If instant production were no more costly than slower production or adjustment, people could always produce whatever was wanted only at the moment it was wanted. In fact, however, producing in advance at a less hasty, less expensive rate *and* holding an "excess" for contingent demands economizes in having more services at a cost that is worth paying, taking into account the value of being able to adapt to changed demands without long, advance, "reservations-type" planning. The situation is the same for a home with enough bathrooms and dining space to accommodate more visitors than one will ordinarily have. To say there is "idle," "wasted," or "unemployed" bathroom or dining room capacity is to consider only the cost of that extra capacity while ignoring its infrequent-use value and the *greater* costs of other ways of obtaining equally high convenience or utility.

The foregoing considerations suggest that in a society with (a) costs of obtaining information about prices of all sellers, (b) costs of sellers' obtaining information about amounts of demand of customers, and (c) a tendency for unpredicted price changes to induce extra search by buyers and sellers, the "ideal" market will *not* be characterized by prices that instantly fluctuate so as always to clear the market without queues by buyers or sellers. Instead, to reduce the losses consequent to unpredictable delivery times if prices were perfectly stable, it pays (a) sellers to hold inventories, (b) buyers to accept some queueing—as a means of purchasing at predictable prices and avoiding higher search costs that would be induced if with instant price adjustments there were no queues and inventories, and (c) sometimes to continue shopping before making a contract. The stable price, accompanied by queues and inventories, will be slightly higher than if it were not stabilized by queues and inventories—but the higher pecuniary price can save on search and disappointed, incorrect price anticipations. This higher price to the buyer is lower than the sum of the average lower fluctuating price plus search and inconvenience costs to the buyer.

Before leaving the question of price stability as an information-economizing device, it is useful to try to complete the catalog of reasons for price stability in the sense that some prices are *persistently* below or above the market-clearing level. This can be done by introducing considerations of the property rights held by the allocator of the goods, of price controls, and of transaction-enforcement costs. Attenuated property rights such as prevail in nonprofit enterprises, not-for-profit institutions, or publicly owned enterprises induce prices below the market-clearing level. They do so because the higher income or wealth derivable with a higher price at a market-clearing level cannot be so easily captured by the allocator or principal to whom he may be responsible. Transactions costs also induce price inflexibility and rationing at a zero price. If the value of the item being rationed is less than the costs of collecting a fee and enforcing the contract (as in parking space or street use), the price will be chronically too low. Or if the change in price to a market-clearing level is less valuable than the costs of enforcing that changed price, the price will lag at non-market-clearing levels.[13]

2
LABOR MARKETS

Though most analyses of unemployment rely on wage conventions, and controls to retard wage adjustments above market-clearing levels,

[13]See Alchian and Allen, *op. cit.*, Chap. 8; A. A. Alchian and R. A. Kessel, "Competition, Monopoly, and the Pursuit of Pecuniary Gain," *Aspects of Labor Economics, A Conference* (*National Bureau of Economic Research*, 1962), pp. 156–83; and Arrow and Capron, *op. cit.*

Hicks and Hutt penetrated deeper.[14] Hicks suggested a solution consistent with conventional exchange theory.

> When they are not situated close together, so that knowledge of opportunities is imperfect, and transference is attended by all the difficulties of finding housing accommodation, and the uprooting and transplanting of social ties, it is not surprising that an interval of time elapses between dismissal and re-engagement, during which the workman is unemployed.[15]

He summarized:

> It has become clear that the effect of unemployment on wages can only be explained if we allow very fully for two general circumstances which do not receive much attention in equilibrium theory—the time and trouble required in making economic adjustments, and the fact of foresight . . . Their significance is immensely enchanced when we come to deal . . . with the theory of change.[16]

It is precisely this enhanced significance that this paper seeks to develop and which Hicks ignored when he immediately turned to different factors—unions and wage regulations—placing major blame on both for Britain's heavy unemployment in the 1920s and 1930s.

We digress to note that Keynes, in using a *quantity*-adjusting instead of a price-adjusting theory of exchange, merely *postulated* a "slow" reacting price, without showing that slow price responses were consistent with utility or wealth maximizing behavior in open, unconstrained markets. Keynes' analysis was altered in the subsequent income-expenditure models, where reliance was placed on "conventional" or "noncompetitive" *wage* rates. Modern "income-expenditure" theorists assumed "institutionally" or "irrationally" inflexible wages resulting from unions, money illusions, regulations, or factors allegedly idiosyncratic to labor. Keynes did not assume inflexibility only for wages. His theory rested on a more general scope of price inflexibility.[17] The present paper may in part be viewed as an attempt to "justify" Keynes' presumption about price response to disturbances in demand.

In 1939 Hutt[18] exposed many of the fallacious interpretations of idleness and unemployment. Hutt applied the analysis suggested by Hicks, but, unfortunately, he later ignored it when discussing Keynes'

---

[14]See J. R. Hicks, *The Theory of Wages* (London, 1943), pp. 42–45; W. H. Hutt, *The Theory of Idle Resources* (London, 1939).

[15]Hicks, *op. cit.*, pp. 28–29.

[16]Hicks, *op. cit.*, p. 29. And he added another type—"the unemployment of the man who gives up his job in order to look for a better."

[17]For a thorough exposition and justification of these remarks on Keynes, see Leijonhufvud [A. Leijonhufvud, *The Economics of Keynes and Keynesian Economics* (Oxford University Press, New York, 1968).

[18]Hutt, *op. cit.*

analysis of involuntary unemployment and policies to alleviate it.[19] It is unfortunate because his analysis seems to be capable of explaining and accounting for a substantial portion of that unemployment.

If we follow the lead of Hicks and Hutt and develop the implications of "frictional" unemployment for *both* human and *nonhuman* goods, we can perceive conditions that will imply *massive* "frictional" unemployment and depressions in open, unrestricted, competitive markets with rational, utility-maximizing, individual behavior. And some tests of that interpretation can be suggested.[20]

A. Unemployment   The preceding analysis shows why an employee will not necessarily accept a pay cut to *retain* a job, even though some current wage income is better than "none." An employee correctly and *sensibly* believes he can, with some search and evaluation of alternatives, get approximately his old wage at some other job; after all, that is why he was getting what he did get at his current job. If looking and "finding out" is more costly while employed, he may have reason to choose temporary unemployment as an efficient form of "producing" or investing in information.

There is reason for rejecting even a "temporary" wage cut. A subsequently restored demand will not be immediately revealed to the employee-seller at zero cost; he will continue at the lower wage than he could get elsewhere, if only he had incurred costs to "find out." Of course, employer competition would not reveal subsequent demand increases instantly; employers also have costs of getting information about alternatives. The cost of learning about all potentially available bids and offers (for employers, as well as employees, and the attributes of the goods being offered) restricts the speed of price adjustments. In sum, a refusal to cut wages enough to retain continuous present employment is neither nonoptimal behavior nor adherence to a convention as to "proper" wages.

Any firm experiencing a demand decrease could try to lower costs (to maintain output) by offering less to its inputs. But if providers of inputs know, or believe, that they have undiminished opportunities

[19]Hutt, *op. cit.*, pp. 165–169.

[20]Many labor economists have used elements of this approach in their writings. In that sense, nothing said in the preceding is new. But we are attempting to collate and assemble these elements into a general theory of pricing and exchange of goods and service in which labor is included. For examples, see the following: H. Kasper, "The Asking Price of Labor and the Duration of Unemployment," *Review of Economics and Statistics*, 49 (May 1967), pp. 165–172; R. V. Rao, "Employment Information and Manpower Utilization," *Manpower Journal*, 1 (July-September 1965), pp. 7–15; L. Reynolds, *Labor Economics and Labor Relations*, 4th ed. (Prentice-Hall, Englewood Cliffs, 1964), pp. 345–357; A. M. Roose, "Do We Have a New Industrial Feudalism?" *American Economic Review* (December 1958), pp. 903–920; H. L. Sheppard and H. A. Belitsky, *The Job Hunt: Job Seeking Behavior of Unemployed Workers in a Local Economy* (W. E. Upjohn Institute of Employment Research, 1965); V. Stoikov, "Some Determinants of the Level of Frictional Employment: A Comparative Study," *International Labor Review* (May 1966), pp. 530–549.

elsewhere, they will not accept the cut.[21] It seems exceedingly unlikely that *all* providers of inputs would know that all their alternatives
had deteriorated (if indeed, they had) so as to induce them to accept a
cut sufficient to retain their current employment. The larger the portion of the providers of inputs who do not regard their alternative discoverable opportunities as having deteriorated, the larger is the
required price cut an employer must ask the complementary inputs
to accept if he is to continue their employment in current jobs.[22]

Layoffs. There remains a phenomenon that obscures the present
interpretation. For example, we see General Motors lay off 20,000 men,
when demand for cars drops, without any negotiations about a temporary wage cut. It is tempting to blame unions or to conclude that no
wage, however low, would enable GM profitably to maintain employment, or that lower wages were impossible because of pressure from
those workers who are not laid off. But suppose there were no such
pressure and no union contracts. What would evolve as the "sensible"
response when GM's demand fell? Employers learn that wage cuts
sufficient to justify profitable maintenance of the prior rate of output
and employment would be too deep to keep employee beliefs about
alternatives. And so layoffs are announced without fruitless wage
renegotiations.

If there are job-switching costs, but a man's search costs are not
far greater when he is employed than unemployed, a *temporary* wage
cut is more likely to be acceptable. If the *temporarily* reduced wage
offer is too low to make work worthwhile, the result is a "temporary
layoff" taken without an intent of changing jobs. Insofar as onset and
duration of "temporary" conditions are *predictable*, the situation is a

[21]A seller faced with decreased demand by *one* buyer does not regard that as a reliable
indicator of similar changes in demand by all other demanders for that service. Yet such
behavior has been described as an irrational holding of "less than unity (or even zero)
elasticity of price expectation." A decrease in price available from *a* buyer does not mean
all other buyers have reduced their offer prices. To the extent *we* see only a part of the
potential "market" at any one time, it is rational to believe that a decrease in price here
does not imply all potential offers will have fallen elsewhere. Keynes, in assuming inelastic price expectations, could have been arguing that a decrease in wages from a current employer or a small set of them is not sufficient to warrant the expectation they are
lower every place as well. The contrast with securities is especially striking. Insofar as the
securities market is a cheaper market—that is, insofar as it reflects more cheaply a larger,
more complete sample of bids and offers of the population, any fall in an observed price
is more likely indicative of a decrease in other potential offers as well; the elasticity of
expectations about yet-to-be discerned available prices with search should be higher.
Thus there is nothing inconsistent in assuming different price-expectation elasticities in
different markets; in fact, there is much to be gained in detecting factors that make
them different. See Tobin [J. Tobin, "Liquidity Preference as Behavior towards Risk,"
Review of Economics Studies (1958)] and Fellner [W. Fellner, *Monetary Policies and
Full Employment* (University of California Press, Berkeley, 1946), pp. 145–151] for
examples of failures to make the distinction.

[22]The deeper the wage cut necessary to retain the old job, the greater is the incentive to
embark on a job-information search while unemployed. The greater the degree of seniority, the greater is the wage cut that could be imposed before unemployment, for
equally high seniority elsewhere cannot be obtained by a job change. The greater threatened wage cut is fought by the requirement that lower seniority men be dropped first.

recognition of normal working hours (e.g., not working at nights or on weekends) at *predictable* intervals because the worker prefers leisure to the wages available during those hours. If the onset of the decreased demand is unpredictable (building workers), but if its probability is believed known, this is again akin to weekend rest—and the wage rate is adjusted to reflect that. Building workers are an example; "casual" labor is another.[23] If the demand reduction persists longer than expected, the person will begin a job-information search.

If job-information costs depend upon whether one is employed or unemployed, then unemployment can occur (with or without moving costs). If there are moving costs also, the *length* of unemployment will be longer. But *differential* information costs are necessary for the incidence of unemployment. A *common* (i.e., *un*differentiated) search cost and/or job-switching cost would only mean a greater reduction of wealth of employees, not their unemployment as a result of unexpected demand decreases.[24]

B. Irrelevancy of Atomistic versus Monopolistic Market Types Resources sold in atomistic markets (devoid of all monopolistic or "impure" competition) experience unemployment. In any market —even in a price-taker's atomistic market, free of all price "administration" or constraints—if demand falls some sellers will be unable immediately to sell their output at the price at which others are selling, unless market (i.e., information) costs are zero. Although hazardous, it is tempting to push the analysis into the foundation of pure, perfect, and monopolistic markets; the idealized polar extreme, pure-competition market assumes zero costs of market information and product identification. If costs of either are significant, some sellers would sell less at a higher price to cater to buyers who deem it not worthwhile to look further for lower priced sellers—given the costs of canvassing the population. To attribute unemployment to monopolistic markets or to administered conventional wages and prices is to assume that market information costs the same no matter how it is produced.

C. Job Vacancies: Search by Employers Information is sought by employers also. Job vacancies, with search for best employees, are

---

[23]Hutt, *op. cit.*, Chaps. 3 and 4.

[24]Some of the preceding ideas can be summarized in terms of general economic theory by explicitly treating information as a good that is demanded and supplied. The sum of excess demands and supplies for all goods should be zero by definition. We may say that during unemployment there is an increased demand for and supply of information about market opportunities. Or we may say the market for each good is in equilibrium, but the production of market-opportunity information has increased, leaving other production at lower equilibrium rates than would have existed had resources not been diverted to production of more market-opportunity information. This method of formulating the structure of the analysis saves Say's principle that the sum of excess demands equals the sum of excess supplies—always.

the counterpart to unemployment. An employer searching (i.e., competing) for more employees will learn that a higher wage will get more employees—or that it costs more to more quickly find who will work at the same wage with the same talent. Employer search activity will increase the incidence of job changes without the employees' having experienced unemployment, because employers will seek currently employed labor and offer better wages.

Uncertainty of the employer about the quality of a potential employee induces a lower initial wage offer. The best perceived offer to a prospecting employee will reflect both the applicant's costs of canvassing all employers *and* the employer's cost of learning more about the applicant. The more homogeneous the class to which the employer believes the applicant belongs—or the less the variance of the possible marginal productivity of the applicant—the closer will the applicant's discerned offers be to the maximum. He will more quickly settle on a new job.

D. Interproduct Shift versus "Depression" Unemployment

The greater the rate of interproduct demand shifts, the larger will be unemployment. We could talk of interproduct demand shift unemployment and also of aggregate demand decrease (depression) unemployment, without any reference to *full* employment.[25] I shall occasionally use the term "full" employment to admit of unemployment in the absence of *aggregate* demand shifts. In such cases interproduct demand shifts will determine the degree of unemployment that is associated with "full" employment. That source of unemployment is usually called "frictional." But if aggregate demand changes, there is a change in the degree of unemployment, whatever it is called.

E. Output per Unit of Input

Faced with demand decreases that are regarded as transient, employers will retain employees and equipment because there is a cost of finding new employees as replacements. (Of course, any layoff probably involves loss of some employees.) Keeping "excessive" employees on the payroll is analogous to having empty apartments to allow for economic adjustment to transient unpredictable shifts in demand. Therefore, decreases in demand for an employer's products can imply a less than equivalent reduction in employment and a resultant apparent "higher cost" per output. This is more economical (efficient) than quickly adjusting the size of the work force.

F. "Depression" Unemployment

It is not necessary here to explain decreases in aggregate demand. (Our purpose is to concentrate

---

[25]Hutt, *op. cit.*, p. 35.

on the consequences of aggregate demand decreases without attention to feedback effects of unemployment on aggregate demand.) A decrease in general demand causes an increase in unemployment because more people will accept unemployment to engage in search, and each unemployed person will look longer. Wage-earning opportunities will diminish in the sense that lower wages are available elsewhere. People use time to *learn* that the failure to find other equally good job options as quickly as they thought they would reflects *diminished* alternatives in general, not unlucky search. The discerned maximum offers will be lower than if the structure of alternatives had not decreased. The lower level and slower rate of rise of best-deserved options is at first taken as an unlucky string of searches, and so unemployment is extended in the expectation of "shortly" finding that elusive best option. And with each person looking longer the total number of unemployed at any one time will be larger. (Incomes fall and feedback effects occur.) Each now has the added task of revising his whole pattern of expectations. Whereas he formerly was searching for a higher clearly formulated expected wage, now he must learn that the "best" has deteriorated.[26]

If the decrease in aggregate demand is a continuing affair (induced, we shall assume for concreteness, by a continuing fall in the quantity of money) unemployment will persist at the higher level during the continuing decrease in demand, which must be continually "discovered." The greater the rate of decrease of general demand, the greater the extent and average duration length of unemployment. Thus a *continuing* decrease in the community's stock of money is associated with a continuing decrease in general demand and with continuing unemployment of human (and nonhuman) resources. Holding general demand at its *new* level would reduce unemployment. But the costs of that mode of recovery may be greater than action designed to increase aggregate demand back to the demand beliefs that people hold.

Conversely, if the rate of increase in the quantity of money accelerates (unanticipated), the general increase in demand will increase job vacancies, increase job information dispersal activity by employers, and increase the search by employers for information about available employable resources. "Jobs are easier to get . . . ," meaning the alternatives are better than they (as well as the present job) formerly were thought to be.

Changes in aggregate demand confuse the public. Each seller notices a changed demand for his current product, but he cannot tell

[26]For an indication of the difficulties in formulating as well as solving the optimal search problem, see the following: J. MacQueen and R. G. Miller, Jr., "Optimal Persistence Policies," *Operations Research Journal*, 16 (1963), pp. 362–380; J. J. McCall, "The Economics of Information and Optimal Stopping Rules," *Journal of Business*, 38, No. 3 (July 1965), pp. 300–317; and J. J. McCall, *Economics of Information and Job Search* (Rand Corp., Santa Monica, Calif., 1968), RM–5745–OEO.

if that is a change also in aggregate demand which affects options else-where. Whether he should shift to another option, as he should not if the demand change is general, or stay where he is and change price, is the question to be answered. Should an employee switch jobs upon receipt of a superior offer or should he look over the market more fully? Given interproduct fluctuations, any person who refuses un-employment search for the best alternative option can be misled into accepting another job too soon. He will, because of increasing demand, more easily find a job with higher wages than he now gets. Yet he should have held out longer, because the upward shift means he could have done better. Unemployment will be less than "optimal"—*given* the extent of *interproduct* demand shifts and of the differential costs of knowing other job potentials. In speaking of "optimal" unemploy-ment we are not suggesting that unemployment per se is desirable. We mean that *given the fact of differential search costs and demand shifts* it pays to engage in some search more economically while not em-ployed. The opportunity to search while not employed is better than the lack of an opportunity to move to unemployment as a more effi-cient means of search. Given interproduct demand shifts, without un-employment the extent to which resources are in their most valuable uses is reduced, because the public is fooled into believing they have found the best available jobs, when in fact they have failed to invest in enough search to find "best" available jobs.

One cautionary note: Constant per capita aggregate demand is consistent with falling prices of final products. Falling consumer good prices in this case reflect lower costs of production, not reduced profit-ability of production. Resource prices will not fall. If there is an *un*anticipated inflation trend, the increased (unanticipated) aggregate demand (per capita) will reduce unemployment and maintain it at a lower level. (In this case the Phillips curve will become a pair of loops joined at the zero price-level-change rate of unemployment.) If inflation is correctly anticipated, the rate of unemployment implied for any given rate of change of aggregate demand will be lower than for un-anticipated inflation, and it will be independent of the anticipated rate.

G. Lag of What Behind What?

G. Lag of What Behind What? The analysis can be expressed more conventionally, but *not* as follows: "A reduction in demand involves a lag of wage rate decreases behind prices—which *is* a rise in real or relative wage rates. This rise implies lower employment because of diminishing marginal returns to labor inputs." That is not contained in the present analysis; wage rates and all other prices can fall at the *same* rate. But the lag that does occur is a lag of the *discernment* of the best available prices behind the new, as-yet-undiscerned, best (i.e., the new, unascertained lower *equilibrium* prices) prices which, *when* dis-covered, would restore employment to this labor. In Walrasian terms, the auctioneer does not instantaneously reveal the new equilibrium price vector. (Even in an actual auction, the time for bidders to reveal the best price is not trivial.) The "lag" is the *time for discovery*. The lag terminology tends to confuse a lag of wages behind other factor or product prices with the "lag" of discernment of the best opportunities behind the (undiscerned) equilibrating price—a price that is not freely or instantly revealed to the world. It follows that a general economy-wide demand decrease does not imply a correlation between real wage rates and depressions (and recoveries). Wage rates can fall as fast as other prices; *that* lag is not necessary for unemployment.[27]

Reduced employment of human *and nonhuman resources* when coupled with the conventional production function implies nothing about real output per employed input. Suppose that resources when faced with a demand decrease in present jobs *immediately* accepted the first available job—foregoing search for a better job. Job allocations would be "inefficient." Better allocations could be discerned with search, at a cost. The destruction of a former equilibrium is not followed by a costless immediate new equilibrium. But the faster it is sought the greater are the costs. There is some optimal rate. Insofar

---

[27]An intriguing, intellectual historical curioso may be explainable by this theory, as has been brought to my attention by Axel Leijonhufvud. Keynes' powerful, but elliptical, definition of involuntary unemployment has been left in limbo. He wrote:

> Men are involuntarily unemployed if, in the event of a small rise in the price of wage-goods relative to the money-wage, both the aggregate supply of labour willing to work for the current money wage and the aggregate demand for it at that wage would be greater than the existing volume of employment.

[J. M. Keynes, *The General Theory of Employment, Interest and Money* (The Macmillan Company, London, 1936).] To see the power and meaning of this definition (not *cause*) of unemployment, consider the following question: Why would a cut in money wages provoke a different response than *if* the price level rose relative to wages—when both would amount to the same change in relative prices, but differ only in the money price level? Almost everyone thought Keynes presumed a money wage illusion. However, an answer more respectful of Keynes is available. The price level rise conveys *different information:* Money wages everywhere have fallen relative to prices. On the other hand, a cut in one's own money wage does not imply options elsewhere have fallen. A cut only in one's present job is revealed. The money versus real wage distinction is not the relevant comparison; the wage in the present job versus the wage in all other jobs is the relevant comparison. This rationalizes Keynes' *definition* of involuntary unemployment in terms of price-level changes. If wages were cut everywhere else, and *if* employees knew it, they would not choose unemployment—but they would if they believed wages were cut just in their current job. When one employer cuts wages, this does not signify cuts elsewhere. His employees rightly think wages are not reduced elsewhere. On the other hand, with a rise in the price level, employees have less reason to think their current real wages are lower than they are elsewhere. So they do not immediately refuse a lower real wage induced by a higher price level, whereas they would refuse an equal money wage cut in their present job. It is the revelation of information about prospects elsewhere that makes the difference. And this is perfectly consistent with Keynes' definition of unemployment, and it is also consistent with his entire theory of market-adjustment processes [R. A. Kessel and A. A. Alchian, "The Meaning and Validity of the Inflation-Induced Lag of Wages behind Prices," *American Economic Review*, 50 (March 1969), pp. 43–66] because he believed wages lagged behind nonwage prices—an unproved and probably false belief (Keynes, *op. cit.*). Without that belief a general price-level rise is indeed general; it includes wages, and as such there is no reason to believe a price-level rise is equivalent in real terms to a money wage cut in a particular job [A. C. Pigou, *Lapses from Full Employment* (London, 1945), pp. 26–29.]

as resources take interim jobs, while "inefficiently" searching for better jobs or failing to search, the "total" output vector will be smaller. In other words, there is an optimal rate of unemployment *given* the rate of demand changes and *given* the differential costs of search. Very low unemployment resulting from inflationary forces can be socially inefficient, because resources mistakenly accept new jobs with too little search for better ones.

3
POTENTIAL TESTS
OF THE THEORY

Empirical tests of the theory can be sought by identifying characteristics of resources that increase the length and frequency of unemployment. Or situations in which the parameters of search conditions have changed can be compared to see if the implied changes in unemployment are observed. The class of alternative theories is open-ended, so I shall simply indicate some implications of the present theory, letting the reader conjecture whether any alternative theory contains so broad a class of phenomena.

A discriminatory test of the theory lies not in its implication of "cyclical" labor unemployment fluctuations but in its implication of unemployment, price stability, and queueing for *all* types of resources— as suggested in the preceding pages.

One aggregative unemployment feature that is implied by this analysis is a positive correlation between extent of recovery in employment from a depression with the extent of the preceding decline; a *zero* correlation is implied between the magnitude of an expansion with the subsequent decline. Absence of tendencies to restore employment would imply no correlation between either pair of movements. There is, in fact, a positive correlation of magnitude of rises with the preceding decrease, and none between contractions and preceding rises.[28]

Resources with *less differentiated* costs (while employed or unemployed) of obtaining or dispersing information will have lower incidence, as well as shorter periods, of unemployment. An employer knows more about his own employees than those of other employers, so the probability of job changes (in tasks and grades) should be greater within a firm than among firms—especially in the upward direction. But the excess probability should decrease in the higher paid tasks, because extra search is more economic the higher the marginal product of an employee's position.[29]

[28]See M. Friedman, *A Monetary History of the United States*, 1867–1960 (Princeton University Press, Princeton, N.J., 1964), pp. 493–499.
[29]See below, page 48.

Readily (i.e., cheaply) recognizable, divisible (time, place, etc.), portable (more quickly movable at a given cost), durable (more long-lived, so as to reduce contracting costs) resources should display shorter lengths of unemployment.[30] What characteristics of goods yield low costs of information? Market demands and offers of homogeneous goods ("easily and cheaply recognized") should be cheaper to survey. Tract houses built by one builder should be easier to sell or rent than custom-built houses. "Easier" to sell or buy means that for given cost of search the realized price is closer (more quickly) to the best possible price obtainable (i.e., to the price that would have resulted if every potential buyer or seller had been canvassed and if each had full information about the product). An observable magnitude correlated with search costs should be the bid-ask spread, or markup, between the buying and selling price.[31] Thus inventories should be a smaller ratio to sales for low- than for high-information-cost items. Frequent, repeated purchases by buyers should be correlated with knowledge about the item and alternative sources of purchases so that the bid-ask spread is lower. Goods sold in a formal market should have lower price spreads, reflecting the lower cost of information provided by formal markets. For example, over-the-counter stocks should have a larger bid-ask spread than stocks on more organized markets.[32] New goods, we conjecture, involve higher information dispersal costs and hence inventories relative to sales and wider price spreads.[33]

Apartments built in standard designs will have lower vacancy rates because their characteristics are more cheaply understood, being already commonly known. At one time in Southern California, homes with swimming pools were so unusual as to fall in the higher information-cost category. Brokers' fees should therefore be larger in percentage terms.

Corporation stocks and bonds can be categorized by extent of knowledge by the public about the companies. If only a few people are informed, and unless they are more easily discovered, the market will be "thin," implying longer search periods or larger bid-ask spreads. The fewness of buyers or sellers is not per se a source of thinness or high information costs. Rather it is the higher cost of finding those few potential buyers among the larger population. Thus new "unseasoned"

[30]The preceding sentence reminds us of the attributes of money, and who can doubt that money has a very low "unemployment" rate? The suggestive analogy is, in fact, precisely to the point.

[31]See Demsetz, "The Cost of Transacting."

[32]See Demsetz, "The Cost of Transacting."

[33]H. Demsetz, "Exchange and Enforcement of Property Rights," *Journal of Law Economics*, 7 (October 1964), pp. 11–26.

stocks and bonds should be markedly different in the bid-ask spread from older established stocks and bonds.[34]

Price stability with transient demand fluctuations is provided in the commodity and stock exchanges by floor traders. They trade on the "uptick and downtick" out of personal inventories, so as to reduce the variance of prices in response to what these traders regard as transient, random fluctuations in revealed market demands and supplies.[35]

The highest and the lowest priced variant of any class of goods will have a longer inventory period and larger retail-wholesale price spread than the typical or modal variant. We assume that the extremes are less familiar types; information acquisition and disbursing costs will be larger. Special-purpose machine tools should have a longer unemployment period than general-purpose widely used types of equipment. Their inventory-to-sales ratio should be larger.

Standard types of used automobiles should have a shorter inventory interval (and lower ratio of inventory to sales) than do unusual used cars because information about the standard type of car is more common among potential buyers.

The larger the dispersion of potential bid prices among buyers, the greater is the gross gain from continued search. The *absolute* (not relative) increment of discerned maximum price is larger if the dispersion is larger. Assuming that more expensive unusual items (such as paintings or works of art) are subject to a larger variance in valuation by the population, we expect a longer search period or larger markup.

The fewer the major employers in any community, the shorter will be the length and the lower will be the incidence of unemployment. Information about jobs is more readily available if there are fewer employers to search and to be told of one's talents. Wages should be more quickly adjusted in areas with only one employer. It has been suggested that the Negro in the South is faced with a fewer number of employers in the small towns than in the North and that he would therefore spend less time in job search in the South.[36]

If the highly skilled worker has a higher ratio of wages per hour to the value of self-generated income from extended job-information search, then the highly paid laborer will resort more to employment agencies to economize on his relatively valuable search time. And he will use private more than public employment agencies, because private agencies, by being able to charge higher fees for higher salaried employees, have an incentive to devote more resources to placement of such people than do public agencies. Public agencies are closer com-

---

[34]See Demsetz, "The Cost of Transacting."

[35]See Working, *op. cit.*

[36]Suggested by H. Gregg Lewis.

petitors of private agencies for lower wage job applicants. (This does not mean low-wage workers are not served by private agencies.) Looking at the employment problem from the point of view of the buyer or employer, one implication is that job vacancies for the expensive, heterogeneous executive will be longer lived than for lower productivity and standard-duty types of laborers. Some evidence of this should be revealed by employment agency fees, which, according to the present analysis, should be larger than for lower paying jobs.

Consider an employer looking for a manager and for a janitor. The value of a manager's services are higher than a janitor's, so a dollar spent for information about managers has a larger expected net marginal product. Because a better measure of the probability of the marginal product of high-marginal-product employees is worth more than a better measure of the probability of a lower marginal product employee, the employer will find it profitable to incur greater costs to get information about potential managers than for janitors. If skin color, eye shape, or sex is cheaply observable and believed to be correlated with quality of performance, the physical traits provide cheap (though incomplete) information about the quality of the person. For higher salaried jobs an extra dollar of cost for information about the potential employee is more likely to be profitable. The extra information will supplement the skin, eye, or sex indicator of quality. As a result, for higher paying jobs, the cheap information will be supplemented by other information. "Discrimination" solely according to only eye shape, sex, skin color, and ethnics is less profitable and hence less probable in higher paying jobs.[37]

If the evidence were to conform to all the foregoing implications, could this interpretation be consistent with the events of 1929–1939? There is no doubt that aggregate demand decreased rapidly from 1929 to 1932. Money stocks fell by about 15 percent per year in 1929, 1931, and 1932. That does imply decreasing aggregate demand and abnormal unemployment. But it is the prolonged high unemployment after 1932 and the slow recovery, when aggregate demand stopped decreasing, that appears inconsistent with the theory. After 1932 national income and money stocks were increasing and it is hard to believe that the rate of unemployment should not have decreased more rapidly. Even if the money stock had not increased, the convergence toward the full

[37]The example of this paragraph was developed by A. DeVany. The same principle applies to short- versus long-term employees. This test is not relevant for the *differentiated* (according to employed or unemployed) search cost, but instead is derived from presence of search costs as such. One index of discrimination is the extent to which similar types of people work in clusters. Janitors are more likely to be mostly of the same types, but managers are more likely to be of a mixed group. Discrimination by cheaply observed traits should be less frequent for managers. My impression is that, in fact, for lower paying jobs there is greater concordance or uniformity of physical types than in higher paying jobs.

equilibrium price vector should have progressed more rapidly, if one is allowed to make *ad hominem* conjectures as to the expected rate of recovery.[38]

One thing that can save the proposed interpretation despite the prolonged unemployment is the imposition of arbitrary restrictions on permissible prices. Another factor that would help to explain the prolonged unemployment without rejecting the proposed interpretation is a sequential injection of depressing policy actions.

In other words, a prolonged unemployment—without decreasing aggregate demand—would be consistent with the present interpretation of price behavior and unemployment if actual permissible (not the equilibrium) wages on prices were arbitrarily or exogenously increased. Events that support this interpretation have been chronicled by Roose and Friedman.[39] A *sequence* of measures by the government (NIRA, Guffey Coal Act, agricultural price supports, and the Labor Relations Act, minimum wages) arbitrarily and successively raised prices and wages over the period—not once and for all in 1932. In the absence of these autonomous factors pushing up permissible (though not the equilibrating) wages and prices, 1933–1937 would have shown greater employment and output. Roose attributes the low recovery to restrictive policies such as higher wages of NIRA codes, National Labor Relations Act, minimum-wage enactments, imposition of social security taxes, and unemployment and old age security taxes on employment. In the same interval other policies involving new regulatory agencies are believed to have temporarily restrained capital-goods production. Securities and exchange acts, separation of investment from commercial banking, public-utility-holding-company restrictions, the encouragement of labor strikes, and a general attack on businessmen all contributed to lower capital-goods equilibrating prices —whatever their merits. To these factors add the 1937 monetary legal reserve debacle. If all these factors had occurred once and for all in, say, 1932, the subsequent recovery rate should have been more rapid. But they, in fact, occurred in sequence over several years. If these con-

---

[38]There is one restraining factor in the unrestored quantity of money. If the quantity of money is not increased, the recovery of output and employment will imply still lower "full employment" equilibrium prices. The increased real output with constant stock of money requires still lower prices. This continuing deflationary pressure on prices would retard the return of production and employment to "full-use" levels. A sufficient increase in money stocks would have avoided the necessity of a fall in prices and wages and thereby would have speeded the rate of resource reallocation and hence the restoration of employment and output, by eliminating the cost of discerning the continuing *reduction* of potentially available prices and wages in all other opportunities. This was, of course, Keynes' advocated policy.

[39]K. D. Roose, *The Economics of Recession and Revival* (Yale University Press, New Haven, 1954), pp. 45–57; and M. Friedman, *The Monetary Studies of the National Bureau, The National Bureau Enters Its Forty-Fifth Year, Forty-Fourth Annual Report.* (Washington, 1964), pp. 14–18.

siderations are accepted, the delayed recovery until 1941 in the face of nondecreasing aggregate demand is consistent with the differential cost-of-information-about-best-available-job-opportunities theory of unemployment.

APPENDIX
MATHEMATICAL
SIMULATION:
FIXED SAMPLE SIZE

The model can be *simulated* mathematically with some arbitrary, expository functions. Formulate the problem as one of relating factors that affect the incidence and length of unemployment that maximizes the wealth of a person, given some unexpected change in demand. It is convenient to express his wealth consequent to two alternative actions: (a) he accepts the best available current employment while searching for the best job, which he accepts at some later moment, i.e., he accepts no unemployment; and (b) he terminates employment at the immediately available new wage and searches while unemployed for the best discoverable job, which he takes upon its discovery.

If his wealth with unemployment (b) is larger than for the employment (a) case, he chooses unemployment. And the length of the unemployment—the length of job-information search—is a variable of choice, rather than a parameter.

a. For the always-employed action:

$$\Omega_E = \int_0^{T_E} W_E(0)e^{-rt}\,dt + \int_{T_E}^{T_0} W_E^* e^{-rt}\,dt$$

$$- (L_E + M_E)e^{-rt}E - \int_0^{T_E} C_E(V, t)e^{-rt}\,dt,$$

where

Ω_E = wealth

$W_E(0)$ = wage now available

$W_E^*(t)$ = best wage offer found by time t with search while employed

r = interest rate

L_E = cost of leaving job while employed

M_E = cost of moving to new job while employed

$C_E(V, t)$ = rate of cost of search (depends upon the intensity of search, V, and this in turn affects W^*; C_E and T_E are chosen so as to maximize Ω_E)

T_E = date at which employment in immediately available job is terminated and new job taken

T_D = time of death or retirement from employment

b. For a person who chooses to be unemployed while searching for superior opportunities, we have

$$\Omega_U = \int_0^{T_U} U(t)e^{-rt}\,dt + \int_{T_U}^{T_D} W_U^*(t)e^{-rt}\,dt$$

$$- L_U - M_U e^{-rt_U} - \int_0^{T_U} C_U(V, t)e^{-rt}\,dt,$$

with the same variables as earlier, except that the subscript U applies to unemployment. $U(t)$ is the rate of unemployment compensation (formal, informal, value of leisure, etc.) obtained because of unemployment.

Choosing $C(V, t)$ and T_U to maximize Ω_U gives a value of Ω_U to be compared with Ω_E. If $\Omega_U > \Omega_E$, it pays to be unemployed for the length of time T_U. T_U is the *expected* date at which unemployment is terminated.

If we can now specify some of the forms of these functions and some of the parameters, we can derive some implications relating the incidence and extent of unemployment to those parameters. To this end we shall assume that the W function is monotonic, starting at the currently available best job, rising at a decreasing rate, possibly without limit or to an asymptote. We shall arbitrarily suppose the potential wage offers are distributed normally around a mean, m, the present available wage. At the nth observation, the expectation of the maximum value observed by the nth observation is approximately $W^*(n) = m + \sigma\sqrt{2\log n}$, and if we let $n = Vt$, this is a function of time, t. m and σ can also serve as variables reflecting information costs to the employer of learning more about the applicant's traits. The cheaper these costs, the less the downward bias in the employer's offers; hence the offer curve will be higher. But since the upper limit is not changed, and since we have used a normal distribution of offers function, we must reduce σ by one third the rise in m, to keep the upper value approached by the expectation of the discerned maximum wage constant (assuming the upper maximum is about 3σ above m).

To discriminate between unemployment search and employment search, we posit that C_E exceeds C_U for any given V.

The standard deviation σ can also be dependent upon employment or unemployment.

Our equations are

$$\Omega_U \equiv \int_0^{T_U} U(t)e^{-rt}\,dt + (m_0 + \sigma_U\sqrt{2\log V_U T_U}) \int_{T_U}^{T_0} e^{-rt}\,dt$$

$$- L_U - M_U e^{-rT_u} - \int_0^{T_U} C_U e^{-rt}\,dt,$$

$$\Omega_E \equiv m_0 \int_0^{T_E} e^{-rt}\,dt + (m_0 + \sigma_E\sqrt{2\log V_E T_E}) \int_{T_E}^{T_D} e^{-rt}\,dt$$

$$- (L_E + M_E)e^{-rT}E - \int_0^{T_E} C_E e^{-rt}\,dt.$$

For postulated parameter values, we solve each equation for the maximum wealth value, Ω_E and Ω_U, and determine whether unemployment or employment is chosen. Obviously, we can postulate values that will imply unemployment. However, the relevant issue is whether we can identify higher or lower values of the parameters with empirically observable kinds of resources and derive implications that are consistent with the relative unemployment rates of various resources. That remains to be seen, although in the text we presented several *nonformally* derived implications.

Instead of postulating search for a fixed sample size, we could assume that the searcher uses a sequential decision rule, in which he decides to stop whenever the accumulated evidence signals a decision. This tactic has so far defied precise formulation or solution.[40]

Still another problem is to determine not "merely" when to stop searching a fixed distribution, but when to stop searching a *shifting* distribution. Here the searcher must (a) detect the fact of a shift and (b) estimate its amount. This problem, too, has escaped formulation in terms admitting of an explicit solution.[41]

How do I justify use of the fixed-sample nonshifting-distribution model? First, it yields refutable implications. Second, the solutions it yields in terms of longer or shorter search times with known parametric changes may be in the same direction as those yielded by a more elegant model.

[40]See MacQueen and Miller, *loc. cit.*; McCall, "The Economics of Information and Optimal Stopping Rules;" and McCall, "Economics of Information and Job Search."
[41]See McCall, "The Economics of Information and Optimal Stopping Rates."

Job Search, Phillips' Wage Relation, and Union Influence: Theory and Evidence

CHARLES C. HOLT

Within the market process much more attention must be directed toward speeds of reaction. Economics has examined the allocation of resources by the pricing mechanism without much concern with timing problems. Discussion must go beyond perfect and instantaneous adjustments in markets with large costs of movement, uncertainty, limited resources of most households, and aspects of behavior ordinarily excluded from economic models.

> John T. Dunlop
> *Wage Determination under Trade Unions*, 1944

This paper derives the Phillips relation between the rate of change of money wage rates and the level of unemployment from certain be-

*This paper was written when the author was Chairman of the Social Systems Research Institute, University of Wisconsin. The research was supported by a grant from the Ford Foundation for study of dynamics of the labor market and is part of the research effort of the Institute for Research on Poverty. The author would like to acknowledge with thanks the aide of his colleagues, Martin H. David and George P. Huber, and the helpful comments by Christopher C. Archibald, Frank Brechling, Wanda Kedinger, Harry Kelejian, Ed Kuh, Richard A. Lester, Dale T. Mortensen, John G. Myers, Edmund S. Phelps, and Stanley S. Wallack.

The paper was revised when the author was on the staff of the Urban Institute with support from the Manpower Administration, U.S. Department of Labor. The views expressed are the responsibility of the author and do not represent an official position of the Department of Labor or the Urban Institute.

havioral hypotheses relating to wage changes that occur between jobs and on the job. The stress is on search processes in the labor market, but consideration also is given to the influence of unions on both relative and absolute wage levels. Relevant empirical evidence in the literature is examined briefly.

Research on the Phillips relation and on labor markets in general has tended to be heavily empirical with little attention given to the development of theory. In the interests of developing understanding and sharp hypotheses that can be subjected to rigorous tests, this paper concentrates on the development of theoretical models of the Phillips relation and on the influence of unions on wages. Because an effort is made here to find interrelations among many complex interacting processes including such subtle ones as union bargaining, this paper is necessarily exploratory. Most of the relevant literature has been covered, but an encyclopedic survey is not claimed.

Although this paper stresses the labor market interpretation of the Phillips relation, we, of course, recognize that alternative hypotheses have been developed in terms of price dynamics, expectations, monopoly power, etc. Some of these will be found in other papers in this volume. The justification for the approach presented here rests on the conviction that the labor market undoubtedly plays an important role in the inflation process. In particular, the steady drift of money wages probably arises primarily in the labor market and is transmitted recursively to prices through a markup process that determines the price level. The analytic simplicity that is obtained by assuming strictly recursive relations is clear, but, of course, this approach must stand up under empirical testing if it is to be very useful.

But whether basic labor market relations determine a stable Phillips curve or only the equilibrium level of unemployment for a floating Phillips curve, it is crucially important for policy purposes to develop a quantitative understanding of the structure of the labor market and ultimately the impacts of various manpower programs. This paper offers a start in that direction.

The general theoretical framework for this work was first presented in a paper[1] by Holt and David. It stresses the dynamic interaction between the stocks of unemployed workers and job vacancies and the relationships that govern the flows into and out of these stocks. The general approach considers the worker, both in his skills and preferences, to be complex and unique. Jobs similarly are considered to have unique and complex sets of requirements and rewards. The successful pairing of a worker and a job that leads to employment requires the mutual satisfaction of worker and employer and depends on many

---

[1]C. C. Holt and M. H. David, "The Concept of Vacancies in a Dynamic Theory of the Labor Market," *Measurement and Interpretation of Job Vacancies* (National Bureau of Economic Research, New York, 1966), pp. 73–141.

characteristics of job and worker. To obtain the large amounts of information[2] necessary for making choices, substantial resources and time are consumed by employer and employee in search, advertising, interviews, trial work periods, etc. In postulating unique rather than standardized "products" and the importance of highly specific knowledge about jobs and people, it follows that knowledge will be costly and highly imperfect, so that blind random search necessarily will play an important role.[3]

We consider here those particular stocks and flows in the labor market that lead to the Phillips relation partially because of its importance in relating two important policy variables, inflation and unemployment, and partially because it has received considerable quantitative study. However, approaching the labor markets from this point of view may not be the best way to study the underlying structural relationships. For example, there appears on theoretical and empirical grounds[4] to be a similar and more direct relationship between the stock of vacancies and the rate of change of money wages.

Stated differently, the Phillips relation reflects supply relationships most clearly. A corresponding study of the vacancy relation would show the dynamics of demand more adequately. In the Phillips relation, vacancy fluctuations are reflected only indirectly in unemployment fluctuations.

In an effort to advance beyond the stage of viewing union wage push and demand pull as an unanswerable dilemma in which interacting forces cannot be isolated, a formal model is developed of the determinants of company and union bargaining power. The approach is to analyze the strength of the bargaining threats and use these to predict negotiated settlements without getting into the detailed interactions of bargaining strategies.

[2]For theoretical and empirical work in this area see G. J. Stigler, "The Economics of Information," *Journal of Political Economics*, 69 (June 1961), pp. 213–225; "Information in the Labor Market," *Journal of Political Economics* 70, Part 2, Supplement (October 1962), pp. 94–105; and Albert Rees, "Information Networks in Labor Markets," *Papers and Proceedings of the American Economic Association* (December 1965), pp. 559–566.

[3]It might be argued that such a framework is suitable for skilled or professional jobs but not for unskilled labor. This may be true, but even where the role played in production is simple and standardized there may be many other relevant considerations that are not. The presence of an autocratic boss, company bowling league, friends, convenient transportation, compatible personality, and reliability all may significantly affect offers, acceptances, and job durations.

Standardized products, each with a unique price, and perfect knowledge have tremendous analytic appeal in terms of simplicity, but such models may miss the essence of certain economic phenomena. The dynamics of the labor market, which is undoubtedly our most important market, may well fall into this category. On this important point see C. C. Holt and G. P. Huber, "A Computer Aided Approach to Employment Service Placement and Counseling," *Management Science*, Vol. 15, No. 11, July 1969, pp. 573–94.

[4]See Holt and David, "Concept of Vacancies," and A. D. Brownlie and P. Hampton, "An Econometric Study of Wage Determination in New Zealand Manufacturing Industries," *International Economic Review*, 8, No. 3 (October 1967).

This paper is organized as follows. Section I presents an analysis of the wage dynamics in a labor market without unions. It considers the structure and functioning of the labor market and derives several versions of the Phillips relation. Section II introduces unions and analyzes bargaining power, wage drift, industrial disputes, and union influence on the Phillips relation. Section III reviews the theoretical and empirical literature dealing with labor market relationships, union phenomena, and the Phillips curve. Finally, Section IV draws conclusions and implications for further research. Because of its broad scope, this paper necessarily is exploratory in its theory development and in its use of past empirical research to test the theory.

1
BASIC WAGE DYNAMICS

A. Wage Changes and the Level of Unemployment   This section considers first the structure of the labor market and then gives an overview of the wage-change process in the absence of unions. The wage aspiration of unemployed and employed workers is analyzed. On-th-job wage changes are introduced and the Phillips relation is derived and analyzed.

The Structure of the Labor Market. A sketch of the labor market that emphasizes its structure is given in Figure 1, where the blocks contain stocks of vacancies and workers and the arrowed lines represent corresponding flows.

The continual flow of workers, particularly young and unskilled ones, through the U.S. labor market annually averages between one third and one half of the total labor force.[5] This annual flow is very large compared to the stock of unemployed workers at any one time. Quits and retirements usually force employers to engage in continual recruiting efforts, even those who maintain constant work forces. Workers flow into the market as they leave the family, graduate from schools, quit previous employment, and are laid off, and they leave the market as new hires, recalls, or they return to family or school. This high flow through the market keeps it in a constant state of flux and makes it respond quickly to changes in economic conditions.

It is more accurate to view "unemployed" as a state through which *all* workers pass periodically rather than as a description of certain kinds of people. This, of course, does not deny that some people face unemployment more often and longer than others.

---

[5]An equivalent statement is that the average duration of a job is of the order of only two or three years. Of course, some jobs last only a few weeks, while others last decades.

Robert Ozanne [*Wage Practice and Theory, A Payroll Book Study of Wage Movements*, 1860–1969, based on the McCormick and International Harvester Companies (University of Wisconsin Press, Madison, Wis., 1967)] reports a company turnover rate as high as 177 percent per year.

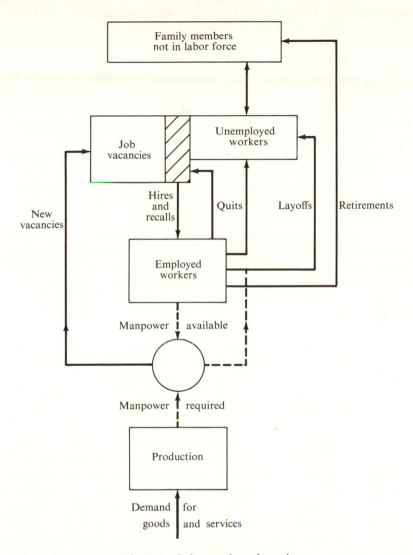

Figure 1.   Labor-market schematic.

As a result of the heterogeneity of workers and jobs and the imperfection of knowledge, the flow of new hires is best viewed as determined by a random process. Regularities can be found that explain the probabilities per period of time of finding jobs and employees, and the probability distributions of the durations of unemployment, vacancies, and jobs.

The economic choices of workers and employers are strongly influenced by the random uncertainties of the search process. Job offers typically have to be made and accepted under ignorance of what applicants or jobs may turn up tomorrow. This is not a world in which fine trade-offs can be made at the margin. Employers and workers must imperfectly search out their respective interests, economic and otherwise, presumably taking into account the costs of search.

The rapid flow in the labor market can be visualized as circular in Figure 1, in which workers flow from employment by quits and layoffs back into employment by new hires and recalls. The speed of the flow is reflected by the fact that the stock of unemployed workers is completely replaced in roughly one month.

If these *large* flows into unemployment were not very nearly equal to the flows from unemployment, the stock of unemployed workers would change drastically, and we know that unemployment changes only slowly. This near equality of the gross inflows and outflows, even during cyclical fluctuations of the economy, is the basis for considering the system always to be close to stochastic equilibrium. If the labor market were in stochastic equilibrium, the expected (mathematical expectation of) levels and composition of stocks would be constant, and the expected flows into and flows out of each stock would be equal in level and composition. Because of the high turnover rates we would expect that a disturbance to the labor market would largely die out within a quarter or half year.

To illustrate how this market operates, let us trace through the repercussions of a sudden increase in production. The desired work force now exceeds the stock of employed workers, so new vacancies are created. With the increase in the stock of vacancies the probability of worker-job matches increases with the result that new hires occur. This offsets some of the increase in vacancies and lowers the stock of unemployed workers and raises the stock of employed workers. The increase in vacancies and decrease in unemployed shorten the average duration of unemployment and lengthen the average duration of vacancies. These changes induce some employed workers to quit their present employment because of the improved opportunities in the market. These quits lower the stock of employed workers, create new vacancies, and increase the stock of the unemployed. This increase in both vacancies and unemployment increases the probability of market matches leading to new hires, thereby partially restoring the stock of employed workers. The increase in the desired work force, the lengthening duration of vacancies, and the rise in the quit rate will in the meantime lead the firms to reduce their layoffs. This increases the stock of employed workers and reduces the stock of unemployed workers. The reduction in the number of unemployed workers reduces the new hires and accentuates the lengthening of the duration of vacancies and the shortening of the duration of unemployment. These effects stimulate quits further but the improvement in employment opportunities attracts new entrants into the work force, particularly of secondary workers. This inflow offsets to some extent the decline in the stock of unemployment.

Several aspects of this market system should be noted:

a. There is a strong and fast interaction among the variables usually by several paths.

b. The system is characterized by strong negative feedback. (For example, when an increase in a stock leads to a reduction in one of the flows which determines the stock, thereby tending to restore the stock to its initial level, we have negative feedback.)

c. Two types of turnover flows show clearly in Figure 1: the quit-rehire flow and the layoff-recall flow. Both of these flows carry a worker from employment into the labor market and back to employment. The quit flow is high when the ratio of vacancies to unemployment is high, but the layoff is high when this ratio is low. Workers are laid off when they are likely to be available for recall and new workers are easy to hire. Since the total turnover flow is the sum of the quit and layoff flows, and their fluctuations are contracyclical, the total flow through the market fluctuates by relatively small percentages over the cycle.

d. Since the market is close to stochastic equilibrium, partially as the result of the negative feedbacks, the sum of new hires and recalls is nearly equal to the sum of quits and layoffs and also is nearly equal to the flow of new vacancies. For example, in the course of a year the level of unemployment might change by 1 percent (of the labor force), but the flow into and out of unemployment might be between 36 and 48 percent of the labor force. Hence it is clear that the inflow is almost equal to the outflow. Data on U.S. labor flows are plotted in Figure 2.[6]

We now turn to the examination of the wage-adjustment mechanisms that operate in the labor market.

The Wage-Change Process. In the following analysis we will consider three types of wage change: (a) that which occurs between jobs while the worker is unemployed, (b) that which occurs when there is a job change from one employer to another but without intervening unemployment, and (c) that which occurs on the job internal to the employing firm, for example by change in wage rate or by internal transfer to another job. These three types are then combined to explain changes in the general level of money wages.

Our basic hypothesis is that the Phillips relation is the result of the search processes involved in these wage changes.

In predicting the decision behavior of workers in changing from one state to another: one job to another, unemployed to working, working to unemployed, or family to labor force, we assume the following deci-

---

[6]Section II of the author's "Improving the Labor Market Tradeoff between Inflation and Unemployment," *Papers and Proceedings of the American Economic Association* (May 1969), analyzes this relation.

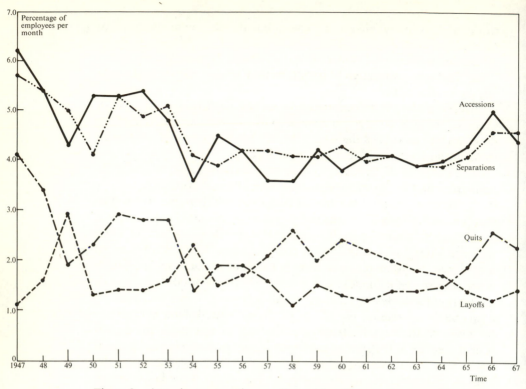

Figure 2. Accessions, separations, quits, and layoffs: annual average labor flows for U.S. manufacturing. (Source: *Employment and Earnings*, U.S. Department of Labor.)

sion process.[7] The person compares the utility of an alternative state to that of his present state. If the alternative is enough "better" to outweigh the costs of the transition, the change is made, otherwise not. The acceptance of an alternative state depends on an aspiration level. Alternatives below this level will tend to be rejected and those above accepted. For example, the present state might be "unemployed and searching" and the alternative state might be "accept the offer that has just been received." The utility of continued search, of course, involves a prediction of its risky outcome.

In the following derivation we show that a steady upward or downward drift of money wages (or more precisely, straight-time average hourly earnings plus fringe benefits) can be related to the level of unemployment. This result is based on the following premises:

a. The longer a worker is unemployed, the lower money wage or the less desirable job he is willing to accept; i.e., he has a declining aspiration level with the passage of time unemployed.

[7]This decision model is presented in *Organizations* by J. G. March and H. A. Simon (John Wiley & Sons, Inc., New York, 1958) and applied in "Computer-Aided Approach" by Holt and Huber.

b. The unemployed worker's wage aspiration level also is influenced by concurrent changes in the general wage level and by the number of job vacancies.

c. On-the-job changes in wages move in response to changes in wages between jobs.

d. The average duration of unemployment is relatively high when unemployment is high.

e. Employers usually offer higher wages to prospective employees than the bare minimum that they would accept.

f. Employed workers will tend to switch jobs, or quit to search, in response to an increase in the number of high-paying vacancies.

g. Employers make on-the-job wage increases in response to their quit losses and recruiting difficulties.

h. The general money wage level changes as the result of wage changes that unemployed workers experience between jobs, wage changes that occur when changing jobs without unemployment, and wage changes which occur on the job.

We now consider these points in greater detail.

The Wage Aspiration Level of the Unemployed Worker. The traditional static analysis of labor supply stresses the quantity of labor that will be delivered at various real wage rates. Although appropriate for some problems, it hardly seems the suitable tool for analyzing the short-term behavior of an unemployed worker who is head of a household. He does not have a *rigid* supply curve that governs whether or not he will accept a job offer.[8] Rather movements of the worker's supply curve occur with the passage of time unemployed, and we need a theory for predicting how these movements will occur.

The adaptive aspiration level that has received considerable attention by psychologists offers a suitable starting point both as a behavioral hypothesis and as a rational search strategy.

Typically job opportunities for a worker occur sequentially. An offer usually must be accepted or rejected with rather tight time constraints, so the worker must weigh his present offer against the possibility of better offers that might turn up from further search. If the present offer is good enough, wages and other things considered, he is likely to accept it and forego the costs and possible rewards of further search and waiting. This decision behavior can be analyzed in terms of an aspiration level which serves as a decision rule for distinguishing between an offer that is good enough to be accepted and the poorer offers that would be rejected.

We do not require that the aspiration level be clear and sharp, only

---

[8] We do not observe a worker holding out *permanently* for an offer that conforms to his supply curve while his children starve and his wife pleads with him. The reservation wage of economic theory traditionally has been a static concept, which hardly seems adequate for present purposes.

that it reflect some degree of regularity in probability terms. Indeed, job opportunities have so many dimensions that the decision process tends to be rather unstable as attention shifts between characteristics that are, in turn, desirable and undesirable.

In such complex choices we do not expect sophisticated optimization, but only that some degree of selection takes place that favors the better alternatives. However, MacQueen[9] has shown that, when faced with random opportunities, the use of an aspiration-level decision rule is rigorously optimal in maximizing expected outcomes, taking into account the cost of search.

A thorough understanding of the aspiration-level mechanism[10] must await further work by social psychologists, but there appears sufficient empirical support for its existence and its decline during unemployment to accept it as a working hypothesis. We will discuss some of the evidence later. Although we recognize that aspirations apply to many job dimensions, for present purposes we emphasize the wage aspiration level expressed in money terms.

The initial aspiration level is set depending on the previous experience of the worker (particularly his most recent wage), his knowledge of what other workers have achieved and his perception of what job opportunities are currently available in the market.

With the passage of time unemployed, we expect that the aspiration level would fall for several reasons:

a. Initially the aspiration level is set high to protect the worker from the risk of selling himself short by accepting the first job that comes along—unless it is a very good one. Then, as knowledge accumulates about the universe being sampled, the aspiration level is lowered.

b. When the search starts, the better job opportunities are explored first, and the aspiration level is gradually lowered as the search turns toward less attractive occupations, firms, and locations.

c. Finally, the penalties of continued searching rise with the exhaustion of financial and psychic resources and this tends to lower aspirations. With family capital reduced, income is increasingly attractive.

If, as the result of inflation or productivity changes, there is a gen-

[9]See J. MacQueen and J. J. Miller, "Optimal Persistence Policies," *Operations Research*, 8, No. 3 (May 1960) and MacQueen, "Optimal Policies for a Class of Search and Evaluation Problems," *Management Science*, 10, No. 4 (July 1964).

[10]For basic research in this area see J. Atkinson and G. Litwin, "Achievement Motive and Test Anxiety as Motive to Approach Success and Avoid Failure," *Journal of Abnormal Social Psychology*, 60 (1960), pp. 52–63; E. Burnstein, "Fear of Failure, Achievement Motivation, and Aspiring to Prestigeful Occupations," *Journal of Abnormal Social Psychology*, 67 (1963), pp. 189–193; R. R. Bush and Frederick Mosteller, *Stochastic Models of Learning* (John Wiley & Sons, Inc., New York, 1955); and K. Lewin, T. Dembo, L. Festinger, and P. Sears, "Level of Aspiration," in *Personality and the Behavior Disorders*, J. M. Hunt, ed. (Ronald, New York, 1944), Vol. I.

eral movement of all wages during the period of a worker's unemployment, we would expect his aspiration level to be gradually adjusted to compensate for this. That is, wage aspirations of the individual are set relative to the wages being received by others.

In line with the above discussion we postulate that the aspiration level of the ith unemployed worker is given by the relation

$$\mathbf{w}_{t+T}(i) = w_t(i)A_i \frac{W_{t+T}}{W_t} e^{-D_i T} r_{t+T}, \tag{1}$$

where $\mathbf{w}_{t+T}(i)$ is his wage aspiration level at the time $t + T$; t the time the worker entered the labor market; T the length of time he has been unemployed; $w_t(i)$ his wage rate at the end of his previous job; A_i a constant, usually greater than one, that sets the initial aspiration level; W_{t+T}/W_t the ratio by which general wages have changed[11] during his unemployment; D_i a constant which is the rate at which aspirations decline exponentially in response to unemployment; and r_{t+T} a random variable whose geometric mean is unity to reflect sporadic and nonwage factors that influence the wage aspiration level.

The wage from the last job, $w_t(i)$, is the initial reference for setting the acceptance level, but A_i adjusts it to take account of the worker's initial perception of his job opportunities. More on this later.

If this theory is to apply in periods of steady and possibly high rates of inflation, it is unreasonable to assume that the unemployed worker would not take this into account.

Exponential decline of the aspiration level proves to be mathematically convenient and is consistent with gradual lagged adjustments that characterize much of learning behavior. When the general wage level is constant (i.e., $W_{t+T}/W_t = 1$) and random variation is ignored, the worker's aspiration level would be that shown in Figure 3.

The Acceptance Wage. In the following derivation we assume that the employer makes a job offer and the worker either accepts or rejects it. Often an offer will exceed the worker's aspiration level, so the hiring wage will be at or above the aspiration level. We multiply the aspiration level by B, a random variable greater than one, to reflect this fact. However, presumably employers do not intentionally offer wages that are much higher than is necessary for successful recruitment:

$$w_{t+T}(i) = B\mathbf{w}_{t+T}(i), \tag{2}$$

where $w_{t+T}(i)$, the hiring wage, is the wage offered and accepted by the ith worker, *if* his unemployment were successfully terminated after

---

[11]The adjustment for changes in general wage level (W_{t+T}/W_t) probably should in a fully developed theory incorporate a lag in the perception of changes. Also, the adjustment for inflation might apply, at least partially, to the previous period of employment; see Holt, "Labor Market Tradeoff." Complete compensation for inflation proves to be a key point in challenging the uniqueness of the Phillips relation.

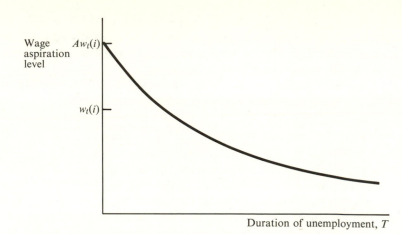

Figure 3.   Declining aspiration level during unemployment.

duration T; B reflects the offer "bonus." In subsequent derivations we suppress random variation by assuming that the probability distributions of r and B are constant and dealing with their means.

We introduce for the ith worker the proportionate rate of change of wage in the market, u_i, and the proportionate rate of change of general wages, g, defined as follows:

$$\frac{dw_t(i)}{dt}\frac{1}{w_t(i)} = u_i \quad \text{and} \quad \frac{dW_t}{dt}\frac{1}{W_t} = g. \tag{3}$$

If u_i and g are constant for the duration of unemployment T, which is of the order of a month, then integrating (3) we obtain

$$\frac{w_{t+T}(i)}{w_t} = e^{u_i T} \quad \text{and} \quad \frac{W_{t+T}}{w_t} = e^{gT}. \tag{4}$$

Combining (1), (2), and (4) yields

$$e^{u_i T} = A_i B e^{(g-D_i)T}. \tag{5}$$

Taking logarithms and simplifying yields an expression which shows that the (expected) rate of change of money wages between jobs for the ith worker depends on the rate of change of general wages and the duration of the worker's unemployment:

$$u_i = g - D_i + \frac{\ln A_i B}{T}. \tag{6}$$

The common sense of this relation can be seen from Figure 4, where we have plotted (1) suppressing the random variable and assuming that general wages are constant. The rate u is the slope (in log terms) of the line from unity to the point on the aspiration curve at the time T when a new job is found. Three alternative unemployment durations

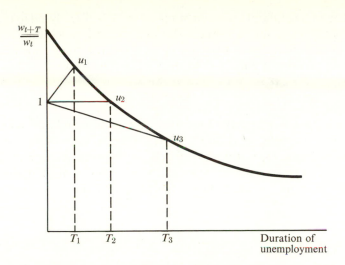

Figure 4.   Rate of change of wages between jobs.

are shown. When a job is found quickly and the aspiration level is still high, the rate of increase u_1 is high and positive. At unemployment duration T_2 the worker accepts his former wage with zero rate of wage increase, $u_2 = 0$. For a long period of unemployment T_3, the rate of change of money wages u_3 becomes negative. In this case the duration of unemployment is so great that a wage cut is accepted. If the general level of wages were not constant, then g would be added to the above rates of change of wage level.

The average rate of change of wages between jobs for all unemployed workers passing through the market is given by the aggregate relationship corresponding to (6),

$$u = g - D + \frac{\ln AB}{T},$$ (7)

where u, D, $\ln AB$, and T become averages across workers. Aggregation questions are given little consideration here, but this is not to imply that they are unimportant.

We can interpret this relation directly. The rate of change of wages for unemployed workers is the sum of three separate influences. The first is the rate of change of money wages generally, g, which enter because unemployed workers set their aspirations relative to changes in wages they see others obtaining. The second term is negative, the rate at which aspirations fall during unemployment, D. The third term is positive and reflects the effort to obtain a wage increase. To obtain a rate of wage change, the increase is divided by the time unemployed that is involved in getting it, $(\ln AB)/T$. The third term will outweigh the first if unemployment is of short duration.

The average duration of unemployment T is directly related to the number of unemployed workers through the basic stock-flow relation. The average duration of unemployment times the flow of workers into the labor market is equal to the stock of unemployed workers:

$$Tf = \mathfrak{u}, \tag{8}$$

where f is the flow largely of layoffs and quits to search, from employment into unemployment, and $\mathfrak{u}$ is the number of unemployed workers.

Substituting (8) in (7) yields a relation between the rate of change of wage rates during unemployment, the general rate of change of wage rates, the stock of unemployed workers, and the flow into unemployment:

$$u = g - D + \ln AB\frac{f}{\mathfrak{u}}. \tag{9}$$

Job Search by Employed Workers. Some workers search for new jobs while still employed. Such spare-time search will be successful in many cases, especially when vacancies are plentiful. The above analysis cannot be applied directly to this case because for zero duration of unemployment in (7) the rate of change of wages becomes infinite. However, the general notion of an aspiration level to serve as the criterion for choice in quitting one job to take another, presumably better one, still applies as does the adjustment for bonus offers in excess of aspiration level.

If workers can obtain wage increases by a factor of ABC, where C is a constant greater than unity that reflects the strong bargaining power of the employed worker, then they will quit. Otherwise they will continue on their old jobs. How much this contributes to the rate of increase of money wages depends on how many workers quit to change jobs and how often such quits are made. If T_c is the average employment duration between such quits for the employed work force, then we could write the following relations for wage changes of this type alone:

$$\frac{w_{t+T_c}}{w_t} = ABC = e^{cT_c}, \tag{10}$$

where w_t is the wage on the original job starting at t, w_{t+T} is the starting wage on the new job, and c is the average rate of change of wages from job changes alone. Thus wages increase through changing jobs at a rate that is determined by the factor of increase ABC and the time interval between such increases T_c. Using the familiar stock-flow relation, discussed above, (8), we can estimate the average duration of employment:

$$T_c = \frac{\varepsilon}{q}, \tag{11}$$

where ε is the number of employed workers in the economy and q is the rate of flow of workers changing jobs without intervening un-employment.

Substituting (11) in (10) and taking logs yields, we obtain

$$c = \ln ABC \frac{q}{\varepsilon}. \tag{12}$$

Note the strong similiarity with relation (9) for unemployed workers. Since the turnover rates, $f/\mathfrak{u}$ and q/ε, can be interpreted as the probabilities of changing states per period of time, we see that the rates of change of money wages depend on the probability per unit of time that an unemployed worker will be hired and the probability per unit of time that a worker will quit to change jobs. The higher these probabilities are, the greater upward pressure on wages.

On-the-Job Wage Changes. We now consider changes made by the employer in the wage rates of his employees. Excluding for the moment pressures from organized labor, it is clear that the opportunity for employees to quit and probably find better-paying jobs in the market will tend to induce employers to raise on-the-job wages rather than suffer serious losses of work forces. However, there are enough ties and frictions to hold most of the work forces to their current jobs in spite of the lure of better wages elsewhere unless the differential becomes too great. If employers have to make wage increases across the board, as is usually the case for morale reasons, it becomes costly to hold the mobile workers.

When workers in passing through the labor market suffer wage decreases, the employer also can cut the wages of his employees without fear of losing them, but, of course, he can expect resistance from his workers.

In recruiting new employees, the employer is again subject to pressures from the market, but here frictional attachment of workers to present jobs works against him. The probability of hiring unemployed workers or workers employed elsewhere tends to increase the higher wage offers are made. But if new recruits are brought in at higher wages or lower qualities, the morale of his present employees will suffer.

Consequently we would expect on-the-job wages to respond to the same forces and in the same direction as wage changes in the market, but adjustments are likely to be only partial.

We postulate that the rate of change of wages on the job j responds[12] to the rates of change of wages both for unemployed workers and for workers changing jobs:

$$j = k_u u + k_c c, \tag{13}$$

---

[12]In a more fully developed theory, we would expect employer behavior to be strongly influenced by his success in filling vacancies and his quit rate.

where k_u and k_c are constants a good deal less than one to reflect the partial response[13] of employers.

Even though the rate of wage increase from changing jobs u exceeds substantially the rate of wage increase on the job j, it does not follow that all will quit their jobs and look for new ones, since the high rate u is purchased by undertaking a period of unemployed job search to find the better job.

Changes in the General Wage Level. The change in the general wage level W_t depends on the wage changes of unemployed workers u and on the wage changes of the employed both on the job j and from changing jobs c. The weight given each of these changes depends on the proportion of the labor force in each category. Thus the rate of increase in the general wage level, g, is given by

$$g = Uu + (1 - U)(j + c), \tag{14}$$

where U is one of the ratio variables defined below:

$$U = \frac{u}{\mathcal{L}} \quad \text{and} \quad F = \frac{f}{\mathcal{L}}; \tag{15}$$

U is the fraction of the labor force unemployed, $\mathcal{L}$ is the size of the labor force, and the ratio $f/\mathcal{L}$ is defined as the turnover rate.

In principle, each of the relationships that has been developed is observable and amenable to direct test. However, at the present time data are lacking to distinguish clearly between the various components of wage change that make up g, the general rate of change of money wages. Since observations are available on this variable, we can combine the various linear equations to eliminate the unobserved variables and obtain an expression for g. Substituting (13) in (14) and then substituting (12) and (9) we obtain

$$g = \frac{1}{1 - k_u}\left[\left(\frac{U}{1 - U} + k_u\right)\left(-D + \ln AB\,\frac{f}{U}\right) + (1 + k_c)\left(\ln ABC\,\frac{q}{\varepsilon}\right)\right]. \tag{16}$$

Although the dependent variable is observable, accurate data probably are lacking on the flows into unemployment and flows of job-change quits. However, using approximate data the wage-adjustment relationship could be estimated in this form.

The Basic Phillips Relation. In order to get an explanatory variable closer to that of Phillips, we will use other intervening relationships. We are probably safe in assuming that quits to change jobs are a constant proportion of total quits and that the quit rate fluctuates with the

---

[13]This relation might involve a lagged response.

vacancy rate, which changes inversely with the unemployment rate.[14]

$$\frac{q}{\varepsilon} = r_q \frac{1}{U},\tag{17}$$

where r_q is a constant.

Substituting (15) and (17) into (16) yields an expression for the rate of change of money wages in terms of the unemployment rate:

$$g = \left[\frac{-D}{1 - k_u} \left(\frac{U}{1 - U} + k_u \right) \right]$$
$$+ \left[\frac{1}{1 - k_u} \right] \left[\left(\frac{U}{1 - U} + k_u \right) (\ln AB)(F) \right.$$
$$\left. + \left(\frac{1 + k_c}{1 - U} \right) (\ln ABC) r_q \right] \frac{1}{U}.\tag{18}$$

Noting that $(U/1 - U)$ is likely to be small relative to k_u and that the turnover rate F does not fluctuate much over the cycle because the fluctuations of quits and layoffs tend to cancel each other, we conclude that for small levels of unemployment the fluctuations in the $(1/U)$ term are likely to dominate the expression for g so the bracketed co-efficients of (18) may be approximated by constants, at least as a first approximation.

$$g \approx -k_1 + k_2 \frac{1}{U},\tag{19}$$

where k_1 and k_2 are approximately constant defined by reference to (18). This is the basic Phillips relation. Thus the theory predicts both the functional form and the signs that have been observed in studies of a number of countries.[15] Figure 5 shows the Phillips curve that we obtain to be a displaced rectangular hyperbola.

The rate of change of money wages is found to depend upon the behaviors of unemployed and employed workers in searching the market for their best opportunities and on employers' efforts to maintain work forces at desired levels in the face of quits and recruiting problems. These are hardly startling findings, but this formal model may increase our understanding and help in the measurement and testing of the interacting relations. In essence the model presents the theory that frictions and imperfections in knowledge in the labor market lead to time-consuming adjustment processes that are essentially stochastic and dynamic on the micro level, and they produce a continuous creeping adjustment of the wage level either upward or downward, depending on the unemployment rate.

[14]See Phillip Ross, "Labor Market Behavior and the Relationship between Unemployment and Wages," *Proceedings of the Industrial Relations Research Association* (December 1961), pp. 275–288; R. V. Eagly, "Market Power as an Intervening Mechanism in Phillips' Curve Analysis," *Economica* (February 1965), pp. 48–64; and the discussion of (20) below.

[15]See references cited in Section III.C.

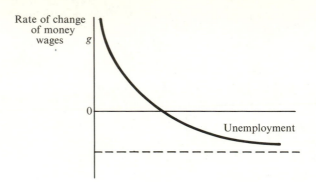

Figure 5. Basic Phillips relation.

In considering the flows into the unemployed, little stress has been put on the net flows of family members outside the labor force. This oversight might appear serious in view of the now-well-established dominance of the discouraged worker response to high unemployment in decreasing the labor force. Even though changes in employment have roughly equal impacts both on unemployment and the labor force, the *net* flow into the labor force from the family is relatively small compared to the turnover flow of quits and layoffs. In the course of a year the work force might have a net change of a few percent compared to a typical turnover flow of 24 to 36 percent. However, the steady flow of new entrants into the labor force clearly does have some influence that should be taken into account in contributing to unemployment.

The Vacancy Relation between Wage Changes and Vacancies. Even though the Phillips relation stresses unemployment and our analysis has also, we might point out in passing that the stock of vacancies is in strong stochastic interaction with the stock of unemployed workers. Empirical and theoretical works[16] suggest that as a first approximation

$$V = k_3 \frac{1}{U},\qquad(20)$$

where k_3 is a constant and V is the ratio of vacancies to labor force. Recent work[17] by the author analyzes this relation in some depth.

[16]For examples see Edward Kalacheck and James W. Knowles, *Higher Unemployment Rates, 1957–60: Structural Transformation or Inadequate Demand?* Staff Study, Joint Economic Committee, 87th Congress, 2nd Session, November 29, 1961 (U.S. Government Printing Office, Washington, 1961); J. C. R. Dow and L. A. Dicks-Mireaux, "The Excess Demand for Labor: A Study of Conditions in Great Britain, 1946–1956," *Oxford Economic Papers* (February 1958); Holt and David, "Concept of Vacancies"; and Albert Rees, "Industrial Conflict and Business Fluctuations," in *Industrial Conflict*, A. Kornhauser, R. Dubin, and A. M. Ross, eds. (McGraw-Hill, Inc., New York, 1954), pp. 213–220.

[17]See Holt, "How Can the Phillips Curve Be Moved to Reduce Both Inflation and Unemployment?", this volume.

Substituting in (19) yields a vacancy relationship that has considerable intuitive appeal, because vacancies clearly play a more active causal role in driving wage changes than does unemployment:

$$g = -k_1 + k_2 k_3 V. \tag{21}$$

This relation has found considerable empirical support using data from New Zealand and Europe. One reason for anticipating that the relationship to vacancies may be more stable than the relation to unemployment is that the latter variable is influenced directly by any changes in labor-force participation, while the former is not.

Implications of the Model. Objections may be raised that this model is too complex just to produce the result that the inflation rate depends on unemployment, and that the behavioral assumptions are gross oversimplifications. Both criticisms have validity. An effort has been made to include in the model only the most important relationships and to treat each as simply as possible.

Because the flow from employment into unemployment, f, is composed of two distinct components, it would clarify the theory above to substitute in (18),

$$f = f_l + f_q = F\mathcal{L}, \tag{22}$$

where f_l is the flow of layoffs and f_q is the flow of quits.

For policy purposes we would like to be able to lower *both* inflation and unemployment in the relevant range of the curve. To accomplish this, the above theory, (18) and (22), suggests that workers should: (a) lower their aspiration levels faster (raise D), (b) set their initial aspiration levels lower (lower A), (c) not be so prone to quit to seek a better job (lower r_q and lower f_q), and (d) require a lower compensation for changing jobs (lower C). Similarly, employers should: (e) decrease the response of on-the-job wage changes to labor market conditions and quit rates (lower k_u and k_c), (f) lower the layoff-rate contribution to labor turnover (decrease f_l), and (g) should not make bonus wage offers above the recruits' aspiration level (reduce B). Note that prescriptions (c) and (d) are partially contradictory.

Needless to say these implications require much more study, but they are interesting and appear to be reasonable. Should the present formulation receive empirical support in explaining the Phillips relation, research will be needed on ways to influence job-information flows, counseling, employment, placement, and other programs that might influence aspiration levels and employer behavior to move in the directions that would reduce inflation and unemployment.[18]

---

[18]For further analysis of this area see E. P. Kalacheck, "The Composition of Unemployment and Public Policy," in *Prosperity and Unemployment*, R. A. Gordon and M. S. Gordon, eds. (John Wiley & Sons, Inc., New York, 1966), pp. 227–262; Kalacheck and Knowles, *Structural Transformation?*; and Holt and Huber, "Computer Aided Approach."

Summary of the Wage-Creep Process. We might describe the operation of the process of wage movement as follows. When unemployment is low, workers who quit and search for better jobs usually can find them, after a time, at a higher wage than the jobs that they left. A certain fraction of other workers, by part-time search on the job, line up higher-paying jobs. When they do, they quit and go directly to the new jobs.

The employer observing this loss of employees must be recruiting constantly in order to make good his losses, but he finds that to hire new workers he usually must pay them more than they were formerly earning. He may hold his quality standards and gradually raise his wage offers, or hold his wage line and gradually lower his quality requirements. In either case his old work force is likely to become discontent and quit unless he grants them wage increases on their old jobs or upgrades them to better jobs.

This nibbling process goes on continually, and the lower the level of unemployment and the higher the number of vacancies, the higher is the probability of quits and the faster the whole process occurs. There are certain frictions in changing jobs or threatening to, in changing job assignments, and in making across-the-board wage changes, so actions are not taken until differentials gradually build up, exceed attention thresholds, and finally trigger actions.

In contrast, at high levels of unemployment workers tend to be laid off as soon as their services are not needed for the production jobs at hand. Workers find that it takes them a long time to find new jobs, and then they are likely to be at lower wages. Employers are not troubled by quits and find that they often can hire new workers at lower wages than they are currently paying or alternatively can raise their quality standards. Under these circumstances the employer can downgrade his work force to lower-paying jobs or even make across-the-board wage cuts. Knowing jobs are hard to find, the workers have little choice but to accept them. This nibbling process could make wages fall steadily, but unemployment would have to be extremely high for this to occur.

It may help to visualize the market process that we are describing by imagining a pseudophysical analogy that has similar stochastic properties. Consider a mixture of two "gases," one composed of "vacancy" molecules and one composed of "worker" molecules. Each of these individual molecules carries a price tag. When in the random flux of the gases, a vacancy and worker collide, their prices are compared and if the vacancy's price exceeds the worker's price a "placement" occurs and the molecule pair disappears from the mixture. To offset this loss from the "market" there is a continual inflow of new vacancies and workers.

Variable Initial Aspiration Levels. The foregoing theory may be elaborated readily to admit other adjustment mechanisms. For example, it is quite reasonable to suppose that parameters A, B, and C are themselves functions of the level of vacancies and/or unemployment.

For example, when the labor market is tight, workers may reasonably raise their initial aspirations resulting in an increase in A. Presumably workers can get some general information about labor-market conditions in the form of number of vacancies, the duration of unemployment that other workers have experienced, and the wages that are being offered. It seems reasonable for workers to weigh their chances in response to such information and set their aspiration levels accordingly.

When vacancies are high, employers also may tend to make higher wage offers than necessary, thereby increasing B. When jobs with other employers are plentiful, employed workers may require a higher inducement to make a job change, thereby raising C.

It may also be relevant to distinguish between the aspiration levels of unemployed workers who were laid off from those of workers who voluntarily quit. The former may only want to restore their original wage levels while the latter may have quit intending to find better jobs at higher pay. If the values of A are different for these two groups, then the *average* value of A for all unemployed workers may rise and fall with changes in the quit-layoff ratio, f_q/f_l. Since this in turn changes with the level of unemployment, we have another mechanism for changing A over the cycle.

It is possible that these changes in the aggregate aspiration level respond more strongly and directly to changes in the level of unemployment and its average duration than as the result of the decay with time unemployed of the acceptance levels of individual unemployed workers. Empirical work will be needed to determine the relative effects of various mechanisms, but there are strong reasons to anticipate that the aggregate acceptance level will decline strongly with increased average duration of unemployment.

To illustrate, Figure 6 shows in solid lines the declining acceptance wage of a typical worker under different general economic conditions as reflected by different *average* durations of unemployment T_1, T_2, and T_3 for all unemployed workers. The dashed line is drawn through the points at which the unemployment duration of worker i equals the economy average. If all workers had the same aspiration structure as worker "i", the dashed line would then be the effective aggregate acceptance curve. This might have the effect of raising both AB and D in (7).

Alternatively, variable aspiration levels might be introduced into (18) directly. For example, if

$$\ln AB = a\left(\frac{1}{U}\right)^b, \tag{23}$$

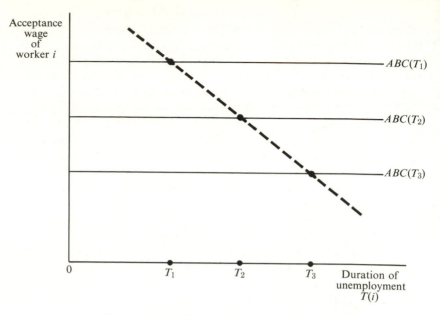

Figure 6.   Declining aggregate acceptance wage.

where a and b are positive constants, then (19) would become

$$g = -k_1 + k_3 \left(\frac{1}{U}\right)^{(1+b)}, \qquad (24)$$

where k_3 is a constant. Some empirical work seems to indicate that the exponent *is* greater than unity.[19]

B. Wage Response to Changes in Employment   Phillips and others have found some tendency for the rate of increase of money wages to be *above* the basic static relation of Figure 5 when unemployment is falling and *below* when unemployment is rising. Explanations have been advanced in terms of expectations, nonlinearities, wage norms, and other mechanisms.[20] It was a surprise to the author to discover that the theory which has already been presented automatically produces dynamic loops around the static Phillips curve.

Consider the situation in which a sudden increase in national production requires a sudden jump in the work force. The full cycle of

[19]See G. L. Perry, *Unemployment, Money Wages and Inflation* (M.I.T. Press, Cambridge, Mass., 1966).

[20]See A. W. Phillips, "The Relation between Unemployment and the Rate of Change of Money Wage Rates in the United Kingdom, 1862–1957," *Economica* (November 1958), pp. 283–299; R. G. Lipsey, "The Relation between Unemployment and the Rate of Change of Money Wage Rates in the United Kingdom, 1862–1957: A Further Analysis," *Economica* (February 1960), pp. 1–41; and E. A. Kuska, "The Simple Analytics of the Phillips' Curve," *Economica* (November 1966), pp. 462–467.

moving from one constant level of employment to a higher one can be described as follows. The unemployed workers in the market at one time have their acceptance wages scattered over a range. By cumulating the workers that would be hired if the offer level were raised, a positively sloped temporary "supply curve" could be obtained. Thus to obtain an employment increase of ΔE a certain wage increase ΔW would be required. Since changes in employment ΔE are closely correlated with changes in unemployment ΔU, we would expect to find wage changes negatively correlated with unemployment changes. Of course, both wage and unemployment changes can be expressed as time rates of change. This is the basic explanation for the change in unemployment effect on wage changes. Now we discuss the process in more detail.

Initially at constant employment, the total flow of separations is equal to the total accessions. To increase employment, the flow of new hires must be increased relative to separations. This would be done by a sudden increase in the stock of job vacancies. This would increase the probability per period of time that each unemployed worker would be hired, so the hiring rate would increase. Since the ratio of job offers to unemployed workers is increased, the workers have increased opportunities, by selecting the better offers, to increase their starting wages. The hiring gradually declines as the number of vacancies and unemployed workers in the market is reduced until a new equilibrium is established in which the hiring rate and the separation rates are equal. The hiring wage would have increased to a higher level by the process of achieving the increased employment.

A similar wage increase occurs when an employment increase stimulates the recruitment of family members outside the labor force or employees of other firms. Here if a firm is to increase its employment from these sources, it must offer more attractive vacancies than had formerly been the case in terms of higher wage offers or lower quality requirements. The larger the number of new employees it seeks to attract, the more the offers must be improved.

Stated differently, to increase new hires, offers must be made above the aspiration levels of the prospective recruits. The larger the number of recruits required, the larger is the number of aspiration levels that need to be exceeded, and the higher are the offers required to do so.

To make a downward adjustment in employment, the accession rate needs to be reduced below the separation rate. This could be done by canceling vacancies to reduce the hiring rate and/or laying off workers. The reductions in vacancies and the increase in the unemployed now gives the employers an opportunity through selective offers to hire at a higher quality level and/or lower starting wages. By the time that equilibrium is again achieved, the starting wage adjusted for quality changes will have fallen.

Actually, employment usually is increased or decreased gradually, so these processes take place over time with the result that we would expect a proportional relationship between the rates of change

$$(E_t - E_{t-1}) \quad \text{and} \quad (w_t - w_{t-1}).$$

We can incorporate this additional component of wage change into (24) to obtain a more complete Phillips relation:

$$g = -k_1 + k_3 \left(\frac{1}{U}\right)^{(1+b)} + s(U)\,\Delta E, \qquad (25)$$

where the response coefficient $s(U)$ may vary with the rate of unemployment. Phillips expressed his original relation in terms of changes in unemployment, which, of course, fluctuates closely with changes in employment.

Before leaving the free-market model of the national economy we should note that it may have application to regions as well, provided they are largely self-contained.

Also the general approach of emphasizing the implications of market search might well be applied to price behavior,[21] for example, in housing and consumer durables. Indeed, a standardized manufactured product like a Mustang may take on the character of a unique product when dealers offer significant differences in price, trade-in, and service with a consequent need for time-consuming and perhaps random search.

The foregoing analysis of free-market dynamics supplies a framework for considering the impact of union bargaining power.

C. Wage Flexibility and Differentials without Unions Before turning to the creation of wage differentials and inflexibilities by unions, we consider the cyclical fluctuations of wage differentials and wage flexibility in the absence of unions.

If a market system is to perform its allocation function efficiently, prices and wages should be subject to as little capricious variation not

---

[21]Interesting exploratory work already has been done on product pricing models, for example in Part II of this book.

The presence of uncertainty makes it economic to hold buffers of finished-goods inventory. Then short-run pricing and production decisions can be made separately, but with the fluctuations of inventory and backlog taken into account. Similarly, in the labor market firms can make wage and production decisions separately, but overtime and slack-time fluctuations need to be taken into account. What is involved in both types of markets is the development of theory that adequately takes into account both uncertainty and dynamic costs. Compared to static classical theory, these new developments offer possibilities of substantial improvement in our abilities to analyze data collected in an uncertain and dynamic world.

Alfred Kuehn (*An Analysis of the Dynamics of Consumer Behavior and Its Implications for Marketing Management*, Carnegie Mellon Graduate School of Industrial Administration, 1958, Ph.D. thesis) and others have used probability models with good results in market research on the brand loyalties of consumers. Some of these marketing models may have application in predicting occupational and regional mobility.

related to the current production and demand situation as is possible. Hence residual effects of past disturbances and adjustments should die out quickly.

Stiegler has made a notable contribution in emphasizing the contribution of search to attaining better mean prices in market transactions and in reducing the price risk attributable to random variations resulting from lack of information. These benefits are, of course, limited by the cost of search itself, and, as we have discussed above, the aspiration level can be an optimal stop-search rule.

Does the model that has been developed here have any implications for how fast relative wages will adjust and how free they are of random disequilibria? In short, does it throw light on wage flexibility?

The search in the labor market involves search initiated by both sides, firms seeking workers and workers seeking jobs, although the relative urgency of the search shifts from one side to the other over the business cycle. Can we say anything about the ransomness and friction in the labor markets at different stages of the cycle?

When unemployment is high and vacancies are low, employers have the dominant bargaining position. If an employer succeeds in finding workers who are willing to work at lower wages than he currently is paying his employees, he could fire the latter and make offers to the former, but because of employee resistance he is not likely to do so, even though it would tend to lower his wage costs. Within limits he can raise his hiring quality standards.

When vacancies are high and unemployment is low, workers have the dominant bargaining position. If a worker succeeds in finding a job vacancy at a higher wage with a willing employer, he may offer to stop searching or to change from his old job as the case may be. Granted that there are certain barriers to changing jobs, these are often *much* less binding than the corresponding constraints on the employer. Consequently, it appears much more likely that the worker will change jobs, if by doing so he can obtain higher wages or other inducements.

There also is probably less search effort when unemployment is high than when it is low. To be sure, when there are many workers unemployed they have much time for search, but they may feel that vacancies are few and success unlikely. When unemployment is low, employers greatly increase their advertising and other recruiting efforts, and an increasingly large portion of the employed work force search the vacancies on a part-time basis. Also the duration of unemployment to find a job is so short that workers can readily afford to pay this cost of finding a better job.

Thus for both reasons, search and willingness to act, we would anticipate that wages would tend to be more flexible in the sense that there would be fewer and smaller erratic wage differentials, and those that did occur would be more quickly wiped out under low unemployment than under high. If this hypothesis is correct, we would anticipate that when unemployment is low: (a) regional wage differentials resulting from the farm-to-city migration would decrease more rapidly, (b) occupational wage differentials that do not rest on skill differences would decline faster, (c) racial differentials[22] would decline faster, and (d) similarly, wage differentials between firms and industries that are not based on current conditions would decline. Stated differently, by making labor scarce through increasing aggregate demand, we may improve the efficiency of its allocation.

If these hypotheses withstand test, it will probably not be because workers have better information than business firms. Probably they do not. Rather workers are free to respond more easily to opportunities when they dominate the decisions, and search activity increases when labor is scarce and jobs are plentiful. It is important to recognize that the mere existence of a wage differential does not constitute an economic opportunity for the worker to act unless there is a vacancy that is offered to the worker.

Some increase in randomness of wage transactions may occur if the level of unemployment gets so low that the aggregate level of wages rises rapidly.

2
UNION DYNAMICS

A. The Influence of Union Bargaining Power on Relative Wages   In this section we consider the bargaining power of unions,[23] employer responses to this power, and the union wage differential. We consider only one of the consequences of the organization of unions by workers: their influence on wages. However, we do not mean to depreciate their many other roles and functions.

The organization of a union by workers, where wages are concerned, is basically an effort to substitute collective bargaining for individual bargaining in order partially to offset the concentrated power that management possesses as the result of the hierarchical organization of the firm.

In trying to determine the effects of unionization on wages, it is essential to recognize that bargaining power varies from union to

---

[22]Increasing the bargaining power and economic scarcity of unskilled workers and Negroes by maintaining a very low level of unemployment should importantly improve poverty-level incomes and job security, and it undoubtedly justifies several years of inflation to draw these people into the economic mainstream.

[23]For a good discussion of bargaining power and references to the literature, see N. W. Chamberlain and J. W. Kuhn, *Collective Bargaining* (McGraw-Hill, Inc., New York, 1965). Note particularly the analysis of costs of agreeing and disagreeing on pp. 170–187 of the second edition. Our use of the term "bargaining power" does not depend on the demands made, as theirs does.

union and over the business cycle. Without attempting to explain the process by which unions grow or the role of their leadership, etc., we can outline some of the general factors that are likely to determine their influence on wages.

We postulate that the power of a union to create a differential over individually bargained wages depends primarily on the interactions among (a) the union's ability to strike,[24] (b) the advantage of collective bargaining relative to individual bargaining, (c) the ability of the company to shift the burden of a wage increase to its customers through a price increase, and (d) the ratio of company profits to a profit norm. We discuss each in turn.

Ability to Strike. The ability of the union to strike probably depends additively on (a) the fraction of employed workers that are union members, M, and (b) the strength of worker support. The extent of membership will reflect the commitment to the union organization and will influence the size of the union treasury. The vitality of the organization and the strength of worker support would probably be reflected in the rate at which membership is growing,[25] $\Delta M = M_t - M_{t-1}$. However, when the membership already is large it becomes increasingly difficult for the union to grow further. Hence the weight put on ΔM should depend on M, which means an interaction between the variables. Specifically, we could take the probability per period of time that nonunion workers are joining the union as the measure of support $(\Delta M)/(1 - M)$. The first term plus a linearized approximation to the second gives the equation

$$\text{ability to strike} = p_1 M + p_2 (1 + p_3 M) \Delta M, \qquad (26)$$

where the p's are constants. The first term presumably represents the *amount* of organized support for the union and the second an adjustment for the *strength* of worker support, which can be positive or negative.

[24]In concentrating here on a work stoppage, we, of course, do not imply that other threats are not used. For example, the union might threaten a slowdown that would drop labor productivity enough to cause profits to go negative, but not as low as they would be if work were stopped altogether. This would hurt the company almost as much but would have very little cost to the union. The natural retaliation by the company would be to institute a lockout, which would hurt the union by depriving the workers of income but would cost the company only a small increase in its losses. Thus we would expect that once the bargaining breaks down and the threats are replaced by action, a quick escalation would result in the complete withdrawal of cooperation by both parties in the production processes. Thus the distinction between lockouts and strikes is of little analytic consequence for present purposes, as are less extreme forms of overt conflict.

[25]We adopt the rate of growth of the union as a proxy to reflect more basic variables such as strength of leadership, strength of finances, and organizing effort. If adequate data were available, probably it would be better to use the more basic relationships.

For empirical work that stresses the importance of union growth, see A. G. Hines, "Trade Unions and Inflation in the United Kingdom 1893–1961," *Review of Economic Studies* (October 1964), pp. 221–251, and Ozanne, *Wage Practice and Theory.*

The Strike Threat. Since strikes and lockouts are the ultimate threats used by unions and managements in wage bargaining, we need to examine their potential impacts on each of the parties. These are initially economic in the form of lost incomes, i.e., opportunity costs to the parties. The cost of a strike depends, of course, on its duration, but we suppress that consideration because we are not concerned with total costs but rather with the relative costs for the bargaining parties. Both parties lose by the strike, but one party is likely to lose "more" than the other in the relevant subjective sense. Bargaining power then derives from the differential cost impact. The costs and corresponding differential impacts of a strike depend sharply on the prevailing general economic conditions for which the fraction of the labor force unemployed is a relevant measure.

Since a decrease in aggregate demand both reduces company profits and raises unemployment, we would anticipate that the cost of a strike to a company would be less at higher levels of unemployment [see Figure 7(a)]. Presumably the strike interrupts production, and, after inventories are drawn down, also affects sales, revenues, and profits. The profit reduction, of course, depends on whether customer attachment to the company is sufficiently tight that their business will wait until the strike is over. In this case profits may be postponed but not lost. To be an effective threat the union needs to be prepared to strike long enough to ensure that the profit loss to the company would occur. One of the strike effects on profits comes through possible loss of work force during a protracted dispute. The tighter the labor market, the more workers are lost permanently. Even though profit losses are greatest when demand is high, the company management may feel that they can better afford strike losses then. Also the opportunities for shifting the wage increases through price increases will be better then.

A host of assumptions and qualifications could be listed, but it seems likely that the subjective cost to management of a strike rises as unemployment falls.

For the union and its members, strike costs move in the opposite direction with unemployment [see Figure 7(b)]. The basic cost is lost wages, but the tighter the labor market, the easier it is for the worker to obtain temporary and/or part-time work during the strike, and if the strike lasts so long that he quits the strike and takes a new permanent job, the less time it takes to find one.

There is an additional political cost to the union leadership of striking for higher wages when such a wage increase might increase the unemployment of its members. The higher the unemployment of union members, the more weight this consideration is given.

If at each level of unemployment we take the ratio of strike costs to the company divided by the costs to the union, we can plot in

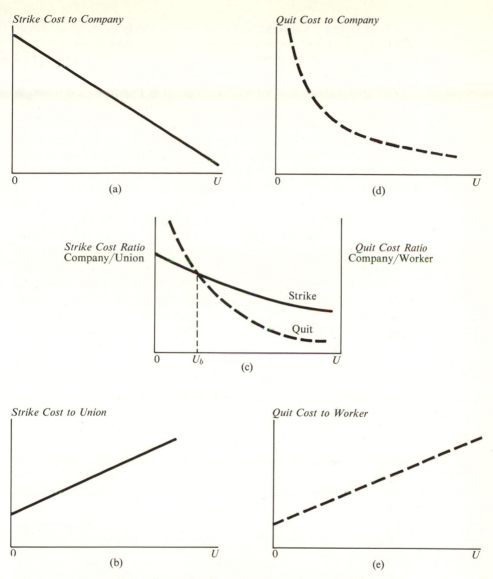

Figure 7.   Costs of strikes and quits to company, union, and worker.

Figure 7(c) the strike cost ratio which shows the relative cost to company and union. The higher this ratio, the more effective is the strike threat by the union and the greater is the union's bargaining power. Assuming linear functions, we have

$$\text{strike cost ratio} = \frac{p_4 - p_5 U}{p_6 + p_7 U} \qquad (27)$$
$$\text{(company/union)}$$

where the p's are constants and U is the unemployment rate.

Clearly when unemployment is increased, the union's strike threat falls sharply. At high levels of unemployment a strike is likely to hurt the union more than it does the company, and conversely at low unemployment levels.

The Quit Threat. The collective bargaining power of the union is always greater than that of a single worker's threat to strike, but the individual typically threatens not to strike but to *quit permanently*, which is a more drastic action. Since the union as a bargaining unit is a relatively weak democratic organization of workers all of whom have ties to the company, as does the union itself through its rights as bargaining representative with the company, it *cannot* make the strong threat of a collective *quit*. In this sense the individual workers have more bargaining power. As before, we need to determine the cost ratio to determine the bargaining power of the worker who threatens to quit.

The costs of quitting depend on general economic conditions and we will need to examine how quit costs for worker and company vary with unemployment. For the company the cost of a quit is that of recruiting a replacement, plus the opportunity cost of lost production for the duration of the vacancy, plus reduced productivity and slack-time costs that result from hoarding labor in anticipation of quits. The unexpected and short-notice character of quits and the uncertainties in the duration of vacancies account for the presence of *both* of the last two cost components; in the first case the replacement comes too late and in the second the replacement hired in anticipation comes too early, before the quit actually occurs.

The average duration of a vacancy is related to the stock of vacancies and in turn is inversely related to unemployment [see (20)], so we have the cost curve shown in Figure 7(d), which in functional form is

$$\text{cost of a quit to the company} = p_8 + p_9 \frac{1}{U}, \qquad (28)$$

where the p's are constants. When there is a large pool of unemployed workers to draw on, these recruiting costs become very low for the company.

A quit for the worker means lost income during job search, the pain and strain of job search, and some risk of a reduced wage. The duration of job search rises with unemployment [see (8)], as does the risk of a wage decrease. The linear relation of Figure 7(e) should be a reasonable approximation for present purposes.

As a consequence we can take the ratio of these costs to obtain

$$\begin{matrix}\text{quit cost ratio} \\ \text{(company/worker)}\end{matrix} = \frac{p_8 + p_9(1/U)}{p_{10} + p_{11}U}, \qquad (29)$$

where the p's are constants.

Plotting this ratio in Figure 7(c) shows that the company cost of the quit relative to the worker cost becomes very high indeed at low unemployment levels, giving the individual worker threatening to quit great bargaining power. At high unemployment levels his bargaining power is very low indeed. The effective threat when unemployment is high is that of a layoff by the company.

Comparison between the Strike and Quit Threats. If individual workers should find themselves in a tight labor market in which the quit cost ratio is greater than the strike cost ratio, they may conclude that individual bargaining based on the quit threat would advance their economic interests more effectively than collective bargaining based on the strike threat. In such a situation collective bargaining by the union would tend to lose some worker support.

Of course, the two approaches are not mutually exclusive, and workers may and do use both. However, when the individual worker feels that he can take care of himself, he will be less inclined to risk the high cost of a strike compared to the relatively low cost of a job change in a tight market.

Now comparing the strike cost ratio to the quit cost ratio in Figure 7(c) two conclusions are apparent: (a) The bargaining power of *both* union and individual workers increases with the decline in unemployment, and (b) at low levels of unemployment the bargaining power of individual workers rises much faster than the bargaining power of the union does, so that below a certain level U_b the bargaining position of the individual worker threatening to quit is relatively stronger than the union threatening to strike.

When an organization is in a bargaining situation with an opponent who can choose among various retaliatory actions, we assume that attention will focus primarily on the opponent's most serious threat. This is not to suggest that lesser threats are ignored, only that they receive much less weight. It follows that when an employer makes wage decisions at high levels of unemployment he will be much more responsive to the union's strike threat, which is relatively more serious. When unemployment is low, the employer will be much more responsive to the quit threat because the strike threat is relatively less serious.

Since we are interested in the wage differentials that unions are able to achieve relative to unorganized workers, we can obtain a relevant measure of collective bargaining advantage by determining the difference between the strike cost ratio and the quit cost ratio (see Figure 8).

Since we assume that the most serious threat to the employer is the dominant one, we see that there is a significant collective bargaining advantage relative to individual bargaining when unemployment is above U_b. At lower levels of unemployment the union threat is relatively less important than the quit threat so the union differential tends to disappear. In its simplest form the collective bargaining advantage

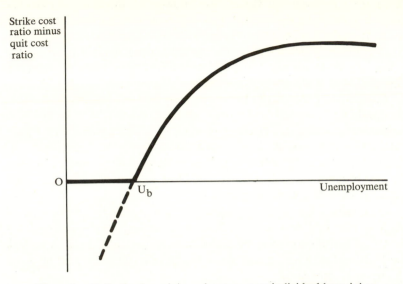

Figure 8.   Collective bargaining advantage over individual bargaining.

can be written

collective bargaining advantage
$$= \max \,[(\text{strike cost ratio} - p_{12} \cdot \text{quit cost ratio}), \, 0], \qquad (30)$$

where we have introduced the constant p_{12} to take account of the fact that the union may be more or less willing to exercise its bargaining power than is the individual worker.

Presumably union workers are never at a disadvantage because they can always use the quit threat individually. Disappearance of the collective bargaining advantage means simply that the company is even *more* responsive to the individual worker pressures in the same direction than they are to the union threat. In this sense the collective bargaining advantage can approach zero.

The full development of this analysis requires further work that will not be undertaken here.[26]

Although the above analysis is crude, it suggests a limitation on the power of unions in tight labor markets through a reduction in support by their members. Stated differently, as the quit threat takes dom-

[26]We might utilize J. R. Hicks, *Theory of Wages* (The Macmillan Company, New York, 1932); Chapter 7 of Chamberlain and Kuhn, *Collective Bargaining*; John G. Cross, "A Theory of the Bargaining Process," *American Economic Review* (March 1965), pp. 67–94; J. C. Harsanyi, "Bargaining and Conflict Situations in the Light of a New Approach to Game Theory," *Papers and Proceedings of the American Economic Association* (December 1964), pp. 447–457; or R. L. Bishop, "Game Theoretic Analyses of Bargaining," *Quarterly Journal of Economics*, 77 (November 1963), pp. 559–602.

Game theory in which the payoff matrix would change over the cycle, or, perhaps better yet, a behavioral game theory that takes into account the limited ability of the

inance over the strike threat with decreasing unemployment, the market tends to behave more and more like a free market with only individual bargaining. In the opposite direction, the higher unemployment is, the greater is the relative advantage of collective bargaining.

Shift of Wage Increases to Consumers. The resistance that the union will encounter in its push for increased wages depends on the ability of the company to raise its prices and shift the increase to customers. Presumably its ability depends on the concentration of the industry, elasticity of demand, and other product market factors. As a representative of this class of factors we propose simply the equation

$$\text{ability to shift wage increases} = CR, \tag{31}$$

where CR is the concentration ratio of the product industry, the percentage of the sales in the industry accounted for by the largest four firms.

Company Ability to Pay. The foregoing analysis has concentrated on broad national, regional, or industry variables. Some company specific factors certainly are important in determining resistance to pressure for wage increases. Company managements are judged by their abilities to keep their returns on invested capital at reasonably high levels. The management of a company that was failing to meet this norm, for whatever reason, could be expected to offer more resistance than managements with some organizational slack in the form of relatively high profits. We might measure this by the equation

$$\text{profits above norm} = \frac{1 + \pi/K}{1 + r}, \tag{32}$$

where π is the recent average of company profits, K is the invested capital in the company, and r is the normal rate of return on this type of capital taking into account its riskiness.

The Union Wage Differential. Now we have five factors that hopefully can be combined to explain the ratio between union and non-union wages. We have two kinds of variables, those that reflect the power and inclination of the union to push for wage increases (ability to strike and collective bargaining advantage) and those that reflect how successful they are likely to be if they do push (concentration and profits). If either variable in the former category were negligible, i.e.,

---

bargaining parties in solving complex probability strategies in their heads should be considered.

If instead of stressing only the dominant threat we include the sum of all threats, but with extra weight, Z, put on the dominant threat, the collective bargaining advantage would then be

collective bargaining advantage = max $Z[(\text{strike cost ratio} - \text{quit cost ratio}), 0]$.

In this case the union differential would always be greater than zero, being minimum at an intermediate unemployment level and rising at high and at low unemployment rates.

no ability to strike or no collective bargaining advantage, a union differential would not be realized no matter how great was the potential offered by the second category of factors. This suggests that the ratio of union to nonunion wages would be obtained by raising the second category to a power determined by the first. In the first category we expect that the variables would interact multiplicatively and in the second additively. Union power alone could create a differential for the whole industry, but concentration and profits add to the possibilities. Hence we obtain

$$\begin{pmatrix} \text{ratio of} \\ \text{union to} \\ \text{nonunion} \\ \text{wages} \end{pmatrix} = \begin{pmatrix} 1 + \text{concentration} + \text{profits} \end{pmatrix}^{\begin{pmatrix} \text{ability} & \text{collective} \\ \text{to} & \times \text{bargaining} \\ \text{strike} & \text{advantage} \end{pmatrix}}.$$

(33)

Introducing additional constants to reflect the strength of various effects, substituting (26), (30), (31), and (32) in (33), and taking logarithms, we obtain

$$\ln \frac{W_u}{W_{u'}} = [p_1 M + p_2(1 - p_3 M)\, \Delta M]$$

(union wage ratio)   (ability to strike)

$$\times \max\left[\left(\frac{p_4 - p_5 U}{p_6 + p_7 U} - p_{12}\frac{p_8 + p_9(1/U)}{p_{10} + p_{11}U}\right), 0\right]$$

(collective bargaining advantage)

$$\times \ln\left[p_{13} + p_{14}\,\mathrm{CR} + p_{14}\left(\frac{1 + \pi/K}{1 + r}\right)\right] = \ln(1 + d).$$

(concentration)   (profits)

(34)

where W_u is an index of union wages, $W_{u'}$ an index of corresponding nonunion wages, and d the union wage differential defined by $W_u/W_{u'} = 1 + d$. The combined multiplicative-additive form of this expression poses statistical estimation problems, but suitable approximations can be made.

Thus we conclude that the wage differential depends on the ability to strike, measured by union membership and its growth; the advantage of collective bargaining over individual bargaining, which depends on the level of unemployment in the economy; and the ability to shift wages, which depends on the industry concentration ratio and profits above norm, which depends on company profits, capital invested, and normal rate of return.

By reference to (34) and Figure 8 we can see that this theory predicts that the union differential is large at high levels of unemployment and declines as unemployment falls. This is an important conclusion.

Several qualifications should be entered here, especially since our conclusions differ from the commonly held view that union bargaining power and effect on wages are strongest in a tight market. Lacking a detailed analysis of the bargaining process, strong claims cannot be made for the functional form used in (30). Also to relate bargaining payoffs to negotiated wage differentials a more refined analysis should take into account the growing importance of institutional ties that hold the worker to a company.[27] In this, both unions and managements share responsibility. Seniority rights, the policy of hiring only at the bottom of the skill ladder, and pension rights seriously increase the costs of job changes by individual older workers, thereby reducing the effectiveness of the quit threat and individual bargaining. This makes workers increasingly dependent on collective bargaining, even in a tight labor market, and increases the burden on young workers with low seniority and low investments in pensions to respond to market adjustments. Also the possibility that union differentials rise somewhat at extremely low levels of unemployment was mentioned in footnote 13.

Such a relation as (34) must be understood as explaining at most the expected value of the union wage ratio. The subtleties of bargaining, perception of power, information, deception, and strategy will bring in many other effects that must be treated as random variables until they are better understood.

Over the business cycle, fluctuations will occur in union membership, unemployment, and profits, and hence in the union differential as well. We would anticipate that unemployment fluctuations would have the greatest effect on the union differential, and profit fluctuations would tend partially to offset the unemployment effect.

B. Wage Drift and Industrial Disputes The model developed in the preceding section has some important cyclical implications fairly directly for wage drift and the occurrence of strikes.

Wage Drift. Wage drift, the tendency in a very tight labor market for wages actually paid to exceed union contract wages, seems reasonably consistent with the above theory. In a very tight labor market companies are relatively unresponsive to collective bargaining pressure

---

[27]Although A. M. Ross ["A New Industrial Feudalism," *American Economic Review*, 48 (December 1958), pp. 903–920] found little evidence for this trend in quit-rate data, some movement in this direction seems very likely, especially in the highly unionized oligopolistic industries.

in the sense that they are being forced by the threat of quits and difficulty in recruiting to raise their wages anyway. The company managements will, of course, package these increases in terms of timing, announcements, etc.,[28] in such a way as to allay the strike threat of the union. Similarly, it is to the political interest of the union leadership to take credit for such wage increases in presenting the wage-increase package to the membership. But it is not the union's bargaining threat that is dominating the decision.

The company may seek all kinds of indirect means of raising wages through upgrading, overtime, etc., that are in excess of what they are willing to commit to the union as permanent increases. The employers undoubtedly hope that these increases are temporary. In any case the company seeks to preserve some flexibility. Consequently, we see the surprising phenomena of companies voluntarily and in their own interests paying wages in excess of the union agreements. As would be expected from the above theory, this has happened much more in Europe,[29] where unemployment has been lower than in the United States.

Industrial Disputes. Given the stress that has been placed on the strike threat it seems relevant to consider the occurrence of strikes. Because of the myriad of personality, strategy, etc., factors that enter bargaining negotiations, the most that a general analysis can hope to yield are statements about strike probabilities.

In order for the union to maintain a wage differential through the strike threat, it must act on that threat often enough to maintain its credibility. Thus there is a base "maintenance level" of the probability per period of having a strike.[30] The probability level fluctuates above and below this level presumably depending on the bargaining gap between the two parties and their willingness to accept a strike rather than back down. If the gap is small between what the union wants and what the company wants, agreement probably can be reached without the cost of a strike to bring them together. On the other hand, the probability of a strike increases as the gap gets larger.

As we have seen, the union differential tends to narrow as the labor market gets tight. The lower this differential is compared to its long-run "normal" average, the more oppressed the union is likely to feel. This happens at the time in the cycle when profits are higher than "normal." Under these circumstances the union would like to convert

[28]There is an obvious parallel here with the "packaging" of price increases by the company to coincide with union wage agreements.

[29]In Europe there also are institutional factors involved in going from national agreements on minimum wages to wage payments on the shop floor that allow much more slack for wage drift to occur than in U.S. institutions, where more of the bargaining is on the corporation level.

[30]Strikes, of course, have many other causes than wage negotiations that would contribute to this base level.

the company's "excess" profits into wage increases that would restore their differential. The management view is that the disposal of profits is its prerogative and it will resist their "dissipation" in wage increases. Thus a widening bargaining gap that can only be resolved by a strike becomes more likely as unemployment falls and hence the probability of strikes increases. The rise of free-market wages and the inability of the union to maintain its relative position and hold onto its differential even though profits are high clearly poses a serious threat to the union as an organization.

At the trough of the production cycle the union differential is higher than normal because nonunion wages have fallen so the union is less inclined to strike.

The empirical studies seem in general agreement that strikes move in phase with the business cycle. The evidence also indicates an early downturn at the peak, and a late upturn at the trough.[31]

The tendency to lead at the peaks might occur because the speed at which the union differential is decreasing and profits increasing may be a stimulus to strikes. The probability per period of time that strikes will occur, S, could be given by

$$S = s_0 - s_1(d - \bar{d}) + s_2 \, \Delta d + s_3 \left(\frac{\pi}{K} - \frac{\bar{\pi}}{K} \right),$$ (35)

where the s_i are constants, d is the fractional differential by which union wages exceed free-market wages $[d = (W_u - W_{u'})/W_{u'}]$, $\bar{d}$ is the long-term average of d, Δd is $(d_t - d_{t-1})$, π/K is the profit return on capital, and $\overline{(\pi/K)}$ is its long-term average.

Also before the peak of the cycle the union may make a strong effort to keep up with nonunion wages and, failing that, union members may find individual bargaining so effective that they are somewhat reluctant to have the union call strikes. This might account for the downturn in strikes before the peak.

Although the company's bargaining power is increased when unemployment is up, management may be constrained by its sensitivity to public relations from using that power to increase its profits by forcing union wages to follow the decline of free-market wages. Thus at the trough the union differential may be higher than union bargaining power could really support. Consequently, strikes may not start to rise until well after the trough has passed and the rise of nonunion wages has begun to reduce the union differential. This might explain the delayed troughs. Another explanation might be that the union is constrained from striking until many of its laid-off members are recalled.

[31]See F. S. O'Brien, "Industrial Conflict and Business Fluctuations, or Comment," *Journal of Political Economy*, 73 (1965), pp. 650–654, and Rees, "Industrial Conflict."

All of this is rather speculative, but it does suggest that the theory and analysis of industrial disputes may help to clarify the role that unions play in the determination of wages. The private nature of these negotiations means that there is relatively little public data until the bargaining breaks down and a strike ensues. Hence greater effort is needed to understand the significance of the data on strikes that is available. Perhaps there is an inverse relation between the number of strikes and the union differential so that the strike rate can be used as a proxy variable to detect and explain changes in the union wage differential (see Section II.A). Perhaps average strike duration has additional significance.

Paradoxically it may be true that when there are the greatest number of strikes, unions are having their smallest effect on wages—the strikes in considerable part are gestures of complaint.

C. Union Influence on the Phillips Relation We will now combine the results obtained in Sections I.A and I.B on the free-market Phillips relation with those of Section I.C on union wage differentials to show how changes in the union differential can affect the changes in money wages. Then we consider how unions may affect company responsiveness to market conditions. Finally, we consider union responses to changes.

The Effect of Changing Union Differentials. If union wages were always a constant multiple of nonunion wages, i.e., if the union differential were constant, then the existence of the differential would have little, if any, affect on the Phillips relation. Union and nonunion wages would simply move together. Since a constant union differential exists when unemployment and the other variables that affect the differential are constant,[32] the basic static Phillips relation would not be affected by the existence of unionism unless it had effects other than creating a differential. We will return to this.

However, as we have seen, the variables that determine the differential change over the cycle, so we must consider these variables in the dynamic Phillips relation.

The influence of the union differential in changing a general index of wages W depends on the number of workers paid at the union scales:

$$W = (1 - N)W_{u'} + N(1 + d)W_{u'}, \qquad (36)$$

[32]On the basis of the analysis of Section I.C we conclude that union bargaining can attain a differential over individual bargaining, but it is not within the power of the union *continually* to increase it. There are limits to squeezing company profit rates and limits to raising the relative price of the product that ultimately will set an upper limit to the union wage differential. Only a steady stream of technological innovations whose benefits the union managed to capture or a restriction on entry to union membership that was even more limiting on the supply would account for a continually increasing differential. Of course, such situations for particular unions can persist for some time.

The differential component that a restriction on entry would introduce was not considered here since it is contrary to public policy.

where N is the fraction of all employed workers paid at union rates, W_u is the index of nonunion wages, the union wage index is $W_u = (1 + d)W_{u'}$, and d is the union differential averaged across industries. We recognize that some nonunion members at organized companies and at unorganized companies are systematically paid at union rates in the latter case to forestall threatened unionization. Hence N will be greater than M, the fraction of employed workers that are union members:

$$N = mM, \qquad m > 1. \tag{37}$$

Combining (36) and (37) we have

$$W = W_{u'}(1 + mMd). \tag{38}$$

Determining the percentage rate of change we obtain

$$\frac{\partial W}{\partial t}\frac{1}{W} = \frac{\partial W_{u'}}{\partial t}\frac{1}{W_{u'}} + \frac{mM}{1 + mMd}\frac{\partial d}{\partial t}. \tag{39}$$

Note that even though the differential were large, it would not have a big effect on *changes* in the general wage level unless union membership and the followers of the union pattern constitute a substantial fraction of the work force, and the differential changed quickly.

Since the left side of (34) is approximately[33] the differential, d, we may write[34]

$$d \approx f_1(M, \Delta M) \times f_2(U) \times f_3(\pi/K), \tag{40}$$

where the $f_i(\cdot)$ are functions defined by reference to (34) and we have assumed that cyclical variations in the concentration ratios and profit norm may be neglected.

Recognizing that the influence of unions beyond unionized companies is likely to depend on whether or not unions are growing, i.e., $m = f_4(\Delta M)$, we may evaluate the right-hand term of (39), using (40), to obtain, approximately,

$$\frac{dW}{dt}\frac{1}{W} = \left[\frac{dW_{u'}}{dt}\frac{1}{W_{u'}}\right] + f_5[M, \Delta M, \Delta^2 M, U, \Delta U, \pi/K, \Delta(\pi/K)], \tag{41}$$

where f_5 is given implicitly.

The second term roughly represents the wage dynamics of a free market and corresponds to g in (25), and the third term represents the changes in the union differential occasioned by changes in union membership and influence, changes in unemployment, and changes in profit rates.

---

[33]$\ln(1 + x) \approx x$ for $|x| < 0.3$.

[34]Should strikes prove to be a useful proxy for the union differential, we might have a more direct explanation than resorting to the causal variables in (40).

Substituting (25) and using a linear approximation of $f_5(\cdot)$ we obtain from (41),

$$\frac{dW}{dt}\frac{1}{W} = -k_1 + k\left(\frac{1}{U}\right)^{1+b} + s(U)\,\Delta E + k_4 M + k_5\,\Delta M + k_6\,\Delta^2 M$$
$$+ k_7 U + k_8\,\Delta U + k_9(\pi/K) + k_{10}\,\Delta(\pi/K), \qquad (42)$$

where the k_i are positive constants. As is apparent from (40), we have neglected interactions between several cyclical variables that might be important. Such cross-product terms should come in with positive signs.

Note that the coefficients of ΔE, $\Delta\pi$, and ΔU are all positive. Since when employment and profits are rising unemployment typically is falling, the first two terms will tend to cancel the last. In a free economy with only the ΔE term, there tend to be counterclockwise loops about the basic Phillips relation. The addition of the k_8 term as the result of unionization may cancel these out or even produce clockwise loops.

The linearized version (41) does not reflect one important fact that is apparent from the original function (34) (see Figure 8). All the additional terms should decline for very small U as the collective bargaining advantage approaches zero.

The addition of volatile terms which arise from fluctuations in union differentials might conceal the basic Phillips relation in a simple graphical analysis of empirical data. A multiple regression analysis that threw these terms into the residual error would tend to find reduced correlations and possible biases in the estimate of the effect of unemployment.

Response of Bargained Wages to Market Conditions. Another way that collective bargaining might affect wages is by attenuating the responsiveness to fluctuations in market wages. According to prevailing theory, when market wages are rising, management opposes matching increases in union wages because of the anticipated difficulty later of lowering wages when free-market wages fall and the union opposes decreases. Thus the argument goes that union wages will fluctuate less in either direction—they will be inflexible.[35]

In the theory that has been developed we could say that union wages on the job respond *less* to the rates of change of wages of unemployed workers and of workers changing jobs than is the case with nonunion wages. This would correspond to replacing (13) with a response that is a weighted average of the nonunionized and unionized sectors:

$$j = (k_u u + k_c c)(1 - N) + (k_u u + k_c c)(N)K, \qquad (43)$$

where K is a constant less than one which reflects the reduced respon-

---

[35]See Milton Friedman, "Some Comments on the Significance of Labor Unions for Economic Policy," in *Impact of the Union*, D. McCord Wright, ed. (Harcourt, Brace and Company, New York, 1951).

siveness of the union sector to market conditions. This corresponds exactly to replacing k_u and k_c in the original analysis with new reduced values, $k_{u'}$ and $k_{c'}$, defined by

$$k_{u'} \equiv k_u[1 - (1 - K)N],$$
$$k_{c'} \equiv k_c[1 - (1 - K)N]. \tag{44}$$

This reduction of responsiveness reduces the rate of inflation for a given level of unemployment.

The reduced responsiveness of union wages to market conditions has been used to explain the disappearance of the union differential at the peak of the cycle and its enlargement at the trough. If on the up-swing nonunion wages rise faster than union wages, the differential will increase and conversely on the downswing.

Although (43) seems reasonable for cyclical fluctuations, it gives the unreasonable result when unemployment is constant that the union differential would be increasing or decreasing indefinitely. Consequently, it is apparent that union wages need to respond not only to wage changes associated with quits and unemployment but also to the existing differential itself. Thus (43) would need to be modified to become

$$j = [k_u u + k_c c][1 - (1 - K)N] - k_d N(d - \bar{d}), \tag{45}$$

where k_d is the feedback coefficient, which indicates that union wages tend to rise when the union differential d is lower than its long-term average $\bar{d}$. Now when nonunion wages are moving at a constant rate, union wages will move at the same rate, but the differential will be reduced somewhat when wages are rising and increased when they are falling.

Equation (13) could be replaced with (45) to obtain a union-wage-inflexibility theory which is an alternative to the bargaining theory that has been the focus of this paper. The union-wage-inflexibility theory will generate union differentials and is certainly capable of explaining some of the empirical evidence. Although such a dynamic adjustment mechanism may well play a role in the complete theory, it is not fully adequate in the absence of the bargaining theory that was presented earlier.

The insensitivity of response to nonunion wage changes is tenable only as long as a union differential exists. If a union employer is paying higher wages than corresponding nonunion wages, his quit rate is relatively low and his recruiting relatively easy. Consequently, no particular problems are raised by being unresponsive. As nonunion wages rise faster than union wages, the differential gradually disappears and the employer can no longer afford to be unresponsive to quits and recruiting problems. Thus we see that for very low unemployment the response coefficient must approach unity and the union sector behaves increasingly like the nonunion sector; i.e., K is really a function of U, $K(U)$. The union-inflexibility theory tends to break down in a tight labor market and we have to fall back on the bargaining theory.

Which theory works best or whether we need a combination of the two can only be answered by careful empirical research. The additive bargaining differential in (38) is clearly simpler than carrying the differential dynamics and inflexibilities of (45) fully through the Phillips analysis, and hence would be desirable from the analytic point of view.

Real Wage Bargaining. Real wages rather than money wages clearly are relevant in decisions to work in the market economy. They also may be relevant in the process of determining money wages particularly where unions are involved.

We write the basic profit relation:

$$\pi = PX\varepsilon - W\varepsilon, \tag{46}$$

where P is an index of finished-goods prices, $X\varepsilon$ the flow of real output, X labor productivity, and ε employment. Postulate on grounds of "fairness" that unions will seek to hold profits to no more than their existing share of gross revenue, $\pi/PX\varepsilon$. Then from (46),

$$\frac{\pi}{PX\varepsilon} = 1 - \left(\frac{W}{P}\right)\left(\frac{1}{X}\right), \tag{47}$$

we conclude that the union will try to hold $(W/P)(1/X)$ constant or make it grow.

Taking logarithms and differencing under the constancy assumption gives

$$\ln W_t - \ln W_{t-1} = (\ln P_t - \ln P_{t-1}) + (\ln X_t - \ln X_{t-1}) \tag{48}$$

or

$$j_u = p + x, \tag{49}$$

where j_u is the minimum percentage rate of change of union wages required to maintain real income share, p the percentage rate of change of finished goods prices P, and x the percentage rate of change of productivity.

Thus, at the very least, unions would like to bargain for wage increases that offset any price inflation plus an additional component that respresents their "fair share" of productivity gains. The addition of such considerations to the bargaining analysis clearly will add considerable complication through the introduction of price-markup dynamics.

From the vantage point of the individual worker it seems reasonable to assume that he maximizes his real income by maximizing his money income. He searches and sets his aspiration level accordingly, taking into account the general wage changes, g, that he perceives, but not being appreciably influenced by prices or productivities that are beyond his control and that he accepts as given.

Similarly, we would argue that the union is always bargaining for all it can get under the constraint of its bargaining power in relation to the employer. It is under continuous pressure to do so in order to justify its dues and its organizational existence. The argument that *general* price and productivity changes "justify" a wage increase will certainly be used in the rhetoric of bargaining but are probably a very secondary consideration compared to the more direct influences: union membership, its growth, and *company* prices and profits. In short, the basis for *not* building a joint wage-price theory is the conviction that wages are determined by individual and collective bargaining *in the labor market* and that demand and other variables impinging directly on that market are what determine wages. If this is true, we can study the Phillips relation as a phenomena specifically of the labor market. This is not to say that for statistical reasons we may not want to jointly estimate wage and price dynamics, but wages would be determined by the structural relations of the labor market. Again the test must be empirical.

3
REVIEW OF LITERATURE
AND EMPIRICAL EVIDENCE

A. Empirical Evidence on Labor-Market Relations   This paper has developed a rather involved set of hypothetical relationships. The virtue of such relatively complete theoretical formulations is that they (a) facilitate tests on many different levels of aggregation, (b) guide the collection of relevant data, and (c) aid the design of powerful statistical tests. It is difficult to obtain sharp tests of loosely stated relationships postulated at the macro level.

The theory development has, of course, taken into account and been influenced by empirical findings in the literature. Hence it is hardly conclusive that the theory predicts these findings correctly. However, many assumptions are introduced into the theory whose correctness is unknown and many other implications can be drawn from the theory. To stimulate the testing of these assumptions and implications is one of the important objectives of this paper.

Although rigorous statistical tests requiring new data ultimately will be needed for tests of the theory, a great deal of empirical work has been done that can be brought to bear in making preliminary tests. A complete coverage of the literature is impossible, so a selection has been made from some of the more relevant literature. These have been examined to determine inconsistencies with the above theory. Literature since early 1968 has not been included.

The Wage Aspiration Level. This key concept in the above theory has received relatively little attention by economists, especially as a dynamic adaptation process, although it is coming to play an important role in the behavioral theory of the firm.[36] Social psychologists have an extensive body of research literature on the subject. Under the label "reservation wage" the concept can be found in the economic theory literature as a static concept. However, recently data have been collected and analyzed by several researchers. Before examining these studies, we will consider briefly some of the difficulties involved in measuring the aspiration level.

When the aspiration level, *by hypothesis,* serves as a decision rule, it can be observed indirectly through the choices that people make—wage offers below the aspiration level being rejected, those above accepted. The possibility of obtaining large samples of workers should aid in its measurement.

Unfortunately a number of sticky problems must be surmounted:

a. The interview approach of asking the hypothetical question, "What is the minimum wage that you would be willing to accept today?", runs the risk of obtaining the answer to the closely related question, "What wage would you *like*?". Other difficulties arise when the question implicitly assumes that there is a static aspiration level instead of a continually changing one. In any case, such verbal responses require the subject to predict his own behavior and moreover are subject to interviewer bias. Clearly observations on decision behavior may be preferable.

b. Data on wage offers that are actually accepted encounter another difficulty. The offers are likely on the average to be somewhat above the aspiration level. Seldom would the employer's offer be just exactly the lowest that would be accepted. This brings in the probability distribution of employers' offers. The aspiration level truncates its upper tail. The observations are on the hiring wage rather than the aspiration level.

c. There is a problem of identifying the acceptance relation as distinct from the offer relation. If for a given skill class all employer offers were made at exactly the same level, no decline of hiring wage with unemployment would be *observed* even though the aspiration level were falling.

d. In any case, both verbal and decision behavior will be subject to changes in mental set and a large number of erratic influences as well as to the objective economic environment, so at best the aspiration level behavior will appear to have a large random component.

[36]For examples see William Starbuck, "The Aspiration Mechanism," *General Systems* (December 1964), pp. 191–203, and Atkinson and Litwin, "Achievement Motive."

e. In addition, there are likely to be systematic influences on aspiration levels and its rate of adjustment by dependents, financial resources, personality, age, education, social class, employment information and counseling, recent experience, reason for entering the labor market, etc. Consequently, the aspiration behavior is not apt to be a simple stable function of time unemployed. Controlling for some of these effects may be necessary to improve accuracy of measurement.

Because of these difficulties, especially as they relate to statistical problems, the following research results should be viewed critically. In the interests of brevity, qualifications are omitted.

Kasper[37] studied a 1961 recession sample of 3000 long-term unemployed workers registered with the Minnesota Employment Service. Their unemployment duration ranged from 0 to over 20 months, with an average of 7.5. They supplied information on their rates of pay from their previous employers and were asked, "What wage are you currently seeking?". His findings in brief are as follows.

Workers initially asked for wages higher than their previous wages, but after about six months of unemployment they were willing to accept less. Over the whole sample the aspiration level fell linearly by about 0.38 percent per month. A nonlinear decay function of the form $W_{t+T_u} = w_t(A/T_u^k)$, which has a falling rate of decline fitted the data better than the linear function.

Five months after the questionnaire, a check was made to see if the workers in the sample were still drawing temporary extended unemployment compensation. If not, they were assumed to be employed. Running separate regressions on the 809 who found work and those who did not, the linear rate of decline of the aspiration level was 0.76 percent per month for the former group and 0.32 percent for the latter. We infer that the members of the group with the faster-falling aspiration levels were more likely to find jobs for that reason. Kasper's very interesting work is subject to some question due to the sticky problems listed above as (a) and (c).

Sobel, Folk, and Wilcock interviewed 4000 workers registered with the employment services of six states.[38] The sampling was random with 75 percent of the sample constrained to workers over 45 years of age. The sample is probably typical of the unemployed and is heavy in unskilled blue collar workers. In their general study of the labor-market adjustments the data support the following conclusions relating to the

[37]See Hirschel Kasper, *The Relation between the Duration of Unemployment and the Change in Asking Wage*, unpublished Ph.D. dissertation, Department of Economics, University of Minnesota, 1963, and "The Asking Price of Labor and the Duration of Unemployment," *Review of Economics and Statistics* (May 1967).

[38]See Irvin Sobel and R. C. Wilcock, "Job Placement Services for Older Workers in the United States," *International Labor Review* (August 1963), pp. 1–28, and Sobel and Hugh Folk, "Labor Market Adjustments by Unemployed Older Workers," in *Employment, Policy and the Labor Market*, A. M. Ross, ed. (University of California Press, Berkeley, 1965), pp. 333–357.

duration of unemployment. As unemployment duration is considered from "less than one month" to "more than two years," the response, "work sought on a lower level," rose steadily with increasing duration from 2.4 to 15.4 percent of the respondents in the respective duration groups; "willingness to shift to a lower level" rose from 26.1 to 73.9 percent; "willingness to accept part time or seasonal work" rose from 60 to 89.9 percent. The evident willingness to seek and accept less desirable work clearly rises dramatically with increasing unemployment. This type of occupational adjustment appears to be more readily accepted by workers than a lower wage. We estimate from their data[39] that the "lowest acceptable wage" drops at the average linear rate of 0.27 percent per month for the first 4.5 months and at the rate of 0.18 percent per month for the next 14 months. Over the whole period 73 percent of the workers did not lower their aspiration wage, but 10.9 percent of the workers were willing to accept more than a 20 percent cut.

Workers' evaluations of their chances of finding jobs at acceptable wages fall with unemployment. An expectation of "good or very good chance" declines from 63 percent for those unemployed less than 1 month to 24 percent after 25 months or more of unemployment. The authors point out that many, particularly older workers, need counseling to prevent unrealistically high pay expectations from prolonging their unemployment. The author's data could support further fruitful analysis of the aspiration level using regression techniques.

Sheppard and Belitsky's study of job-seeking behavior presents a gold mine of relevant data that illustrates vividly the search process in its psychological as well as economic dimensions.[40] Their sample of 530 mostly blue collar low-income workers was drawn from the files of the Erie office of the Pennsylvania Employment Service. Workers were selected for interviewing who had been unemployed at some time during the 15 months starting in January 1963. The higher the number of companies contacted by a worker, the greater appeared the probability of his finding a job. More than half of the unemployed workers had been unemployed less than 5 weeks.

One striking finding was that about two thirds of the laid-off workers expected to be recalled to their old jobs and four fifths of these actually were recalled, but the expectation of recall adversely extended the unemployment of the others by inhibiting their job search.

To the question, "When you've been looking for a new job, do you have some hourly wage or weekly salary that you won't go below— that is, do you have in mind some *minimum* wage or salary?", 69 percent answered yes. Asked whether they had turned down job offers, 17

[39]Sobel and Wilcock, "Job Placement," Table 17.
[40]See H. L. Sheppard and A. H. Belitsky, *Job Hunt* (Johns Hopkins University Press, Baltimore, 1966).

percent answered yes. This evidence seems to support the existence of an aspiration-level phenomena in the decision process.

The aspiration level appeared to be of the order of 20 percent below the wages actually received either before or after the period of unemployment. This seems so inconsistent with findings of other researchers that this surprisingly high number must be questioned.[41]

The total number of companies contacted in the search for work ranged from zero to over 40, the average being 10.3. The number of companies contacted per month declined with the duration of unemployment, 7.2 per month for the first 2 months, 4.5 for the next 9 months, and 1.9 for longer unemployment.

The data have not been studied to determine the influence of duration of unemployment on the aspiration level. Sheppard and Belitsky found that low aspiration level was associated with low probability of finding a job, but they analyzed absolute level, not its level relative to the previous wage of the worker! Thus they were implicitly using the unwarranted assumption of homogeneous worker quality within each skill group.[42]

The United States Arms Control and Disarmament Agency had the wisdom and foresight to see the research opportunities that resulted from some sharp reductions that had occurred in space and defense spending.[43] Indeed more dramatic and painful social science "experiments" could hardly have been devised for studying labor-market adjustments. Three such studies were made.

When, in December, 1963, the Department of Defense canceled the contract to build the Dyna-Soar, a manned maneuverable space vehicle, the Boeing Company in Seattle, Washington, reduced its work force by 7700 workers in a 4-month period. Unlike the Employment Service samples of the three studies discussed above, the workers laid off by Boeing were at unusually high skill and educational levels; 50.2 percent were classed as professional, semiprofessional, technical, or skilled. Mail questionnaires were completed by 3758 workers in May 1964 and 77 percent of these filled out a second questionnaire in August. The economic shock to the Seattle community with a better than 6 percent unemployment rate was tremendous, and many of the laid-off workers were forced to sell their homes and move to other states. On the first survey 69 percent were still unemployed after an average duration of 13.8 weeks.

[41]In the reference cited above, could zero have been used for the 31 percent of the workers who did not supply a "floor wage"? (See their Chap. 4, Table 21.)

[42]Sheppard and Belitsky, *Job Hunt*; see Section IV of Chapter V.

[43]This research is presented in United States Arms Control and Disarmament Agency, *The Dyna-Soar Control Cancellation* (U.S. Government Printing Office, Washington, 1965); U.S.A.C.D.A., *Post Layoff Experiences, Republic Aviation Workers* (U.S.G.P.O., 1966); U.S.A.C.D.A., *Marten Company Employees Reemployment Experiences* (U.S.G.P.O., 1966); and Pieter de Wolff, *Wages and Labor Mobility* (Organization for Economic Cooperation and Development, Paris, 1965).

The company supplied data on the wages being paid each worker before the layoff and the worker who was still unemployed filled in the blank: "I need work that pays at least $____ per month."

The ratio of the aspiration level to the previous wage declines with duration of unemployment.[44] The average ratio for all workers with the same unemployment declines exponentially from near unity to 85.7 percent in 21 weeks. This is at the compound rate of 2.6 percent per month, a much faster rate of decline than was observed in the studies discussed above. This might be accounted for by the higher educational level and the fact that the aerospace firms were known to pay above-average wages.

Of the workers who had found jobs by May, the reduction in their median incomes was 4.6 percent for men and 18.3 percent for women, but approximately 85 percent reported that they were dissatisfied with their jobs, with low pay given as the most frequent explanation. About 73 percent indicated a willingness to undergo training.

The layoff in Denver by the Martin Company of 6800 highly skilled employees constituting 8 percent of Colorado's manufacturing employment was a similar story. When a mail questionnaire was filled out by 3000 workers it was found that more than half had found work in less than 15 weeks, but 26 percent were still unemployed. The answer to the question, "What is the minimum salary per week that you will accept?", revealed a falling aspiration level with unemployment amounting to approximately 1.4 percent per month.[45] Of those who had found work, their wages had fallen on the average approximately 10 percent.[46] The workers with more dependents were unemployed for shorter durations.

The Arms Control Agency, the Department of Defense, the various state employment services, and the companies who cooperated in the collection of this valuable data deserve high commendation. However, the analytic limitations of hundreds of 2 by 2 tables is clearly evident. In a complex situation, the examination of variables two at a time is not only clumsy but incurs serious risks of reaching invalid conclusions. These data are worthy of further analysis.

Social psychologists have evidence[47] that people who are more motivated by fear of failure than by desire to achieve tend to set unrealistically low or unrealistically high aspirations for themselves. Such people may be seriously handicapped in the effectiveness of their job-market search and might benefit from counseling attention. Sheppard and Belitsky have studied some of the psychological correlates with

---

[44] *Dyna-Soar*, Table D-49.

[45] *Dyna-Soar*, Table IV-3.

[46] *Dyna-Soar*, Table VI-2.

[47] See Atkinson and Litwin, "Achievement Motive."

market behavior.[48] For example, they found that some workers refused job offers because they felt that they were not qualified. Some people may respond so strongly to failure or fear of failure in job search that the difficult search problem posed by a low level of vacancies will seriously inhibit their search activities.

Although the fast decline of wage aspiration levels may be desirable in terms of achieving needed economic adjustments, the associated fall in income for the worker is hard to take, but perhaps of even greater importance is the attendant reduction in worker self-esteem resulting from the decline of such an obvious quantitative measure of social worth. It is quite understandable that people require time to make this adjustment and some may find it almost impossible to accept.[49] Again counseling may be helpful both to individual workers and to move the Phillips curve to the left. Much needs to be done in this area, and computers offer important possibilities to identify those who need help. The acceptance of a low-paying job on a temporary basis while continuing to look for a better one is undoubtedly a common adjustment. To deal with this case the model would have to be elaborated somewhat.

In summary, the evidence appears to support the theoretical formulation of the aspiration level given in Section I.A, but much more systematic econometric analysis of the data is needed. Although there is a great deal of variability between workers, wage aspiration levels were observed to start high and fall with unemployment but at a declining rate, and aspirations concerning the nonwage aspects of the job decline similarly. Some rich bodies of data already exist, but more are needed, particularly to distinguish between workers who quit and those who are laid off. Also, we need to examine the aspiration levels of employed workers who are searching the job market in their spare time, and we need to measure both the wage aspiration level and the acceptance wage. Finally, these empirical studies suggest that general economic conditions may affect *both* the initial aspiration level A and the rate of decline D.

Vacancies, Unemployment, and Quits. In the theory above we have argued that the stock of vacancies interacts continually with the stock of unemployed workers and that the system is always near stochastic equilibrium. Assuming that the flow through the market changes by a small percentage over the cycle, then (20) indicates that there will be systematic changes in the unemployment and vacancy stocks. When the number of vacancies increases, extra placements are made and the stock of unemployed workers declines, and conversely. Finding such

[48]Sheppard and Belitsky, *Job Hunt.*

[49]See Atkinson and Litwin, "Achievement Motive"; Burnstein, "Fear of Failure"; R. R. Bush and Frederick Mosteller, *Stochastic Models of Learning* (John Wiley & Sons, Inc., New York, 1955); and Lewin and others, "Level of Aspiration."

a stable relation between the stocks would be evidence of the existence of the stochastic equilibrium envisioned by our theory.

Dow and Dicks-Mireaux analyze the vacancy-unemployment relation corresponding to (20) on both the national and industry levels.[50] They found that for the period 1946–1950 in the United Kingdom there was a downward trend in *both* vacancy and unemployment rates, but that since then the relation has been quite stable. They fitted rectangular hyperbolas to their data (UV = constant; see Figures 1 and 2). This would give a straight line on a plot of log U versus log V with a negative slope of -1.

A linear relationship between the log of vacancies and the log of unemployment has been found for American data[51] using both the NICB Help-Wanted Index and the U.S. Employment Services Nonfarm Job Openings in Clearance. Charlotte Bochan has studied the cyclical fluctuations of vacancies.[52]

Ross and Eagley have studied a relation similar to (20), and Eagley found that for U.S. data 1931–1962 unemployment explained 69 percent of the variance of quits.[53]

Labor-Force Participation. A great deal of research has been done on the flows from the family into and out of the labor market particularly by secondary workers.[54] There is clear evidence that the labor force swells as unemployment falls, tending to offset the decline in unemployment. This important relation clearly needs to be taken into account more explicitly than we have done in our theoretical development. We have not stressed it because the net flows in to unemployment from the family resulting from changes in participation appear to be quite small relative to quit and layoff flows.

It is likely that participation is influenced both by vacancies and by unemployment, with the former variable playing the primary role. However, the close relation between vacancies and unemployment may make this difficult to determine. In any case, a nonlinear relation using the reciprocal of unemployment is apt to fit better than the linear relation which usually has been used.

[50]Dow and Dicks-Mireaux, "Excess Demand."

[51]See Kalacheck and Knowles, *Structural Transformation?*, p. 73, Chart 15.

[52]See National Bureau of Economic Research, *The Measurement and Interpretation of Job Vacancies*, Robert Ferber, ed. (Columbia University Press, New York, 1966), pp. 491–518.

[53]A. M. Ross, "Industrial Feudalism" (Chart 1), and Eagly, "Market Power."

[54]See research by G. C. Cain, "Unemployment and the Labor Force Participation of Secondary Workers," *Industrial and Labor Relations Review* (January 1967); Jacob Mincer, "Labor Force Participation of Married Women," *Aspects of Labor Economics*, National Bureau of Economic Research (Princeton University Press, Princeton, N.J., 1962), pp. 63–106; W. G. Bowen and T. A. Finegan, "Labor Force Participation and Unemployment," in *Employment Policy and the Labor Market*, A. M. Ross, ed. (University of California Press, Berkeley, 1965), pp. 115–161; John Korbel, "Labor Force Entry and Attachment of Young People," *Journal of the American Statistical Association* (March 1966).

Quits and Wage Changes. In the model above we have hypothesized that an increase in quits operates in two ways to increase wages: directly through wage increases obtained by changing jobs and indirectly by inducing on-the-job wage increases. In its stress on quits our analysis parallels that of Berman and Eagley, both of whom have seen it as a crucial "intervening" variable. In a regression analysis Berman finds that quits explain wage increases better than new hires, which she sees as reflecting only the first impact effect of an increase in vacancies. For U.S. annual data from 1946–1961 she is able to explain 90 percent of the variance of wage changes with a single variable, quit rate. Eagley in a similar analysis found that the regression fit was poor for the depression years 1931–1939. This is not surprising, because the quit mechanism is relatively inactive during periods of unemployment and in such a period at best serves as a proxy for other variables that are more directly involved.

Wage Changes on the Job and between Jobs. We are not aware of any systematic studies of the wage changes that occur as workers pass through unemployment or change jobs nor of any efforts to relate these specifically to wage changes made for workers on the job. Studies of this intermediate relationship probably will require data not formerly available.

The Relation between Wage Changes and Vacancies. The above model has not stressed vacancies because the Phillips relation is dominated by the supply side of the market, and delays in the release of vacancy data in this country have delayed the development of empirical relations. However, vacancies play the role of demand prime mover in our theory, and we derived a theoretical relation between vacancies and wage changes. Brownlie and Hampton had vacancy data for New Zealand and were able to explain 92 percent of the variance of annual wage changes, 1951–1963, with that single variable.[55] An additional variable, general wage orders which constitute statutory minimum wage rates, brought R^2 to 96 percent with the coefficients highly significant. Labor productivity, profits, and prices did not significantly improve the regression fit.

Probability Distributions of the Durations of Unemployment, Jobs, and Vacancies. If the basic premise of the model developed above is correct—that the labor-market entries, placements, quits, and layoffs of individual workers and the filling of individual vacancies act as if they were random events governed by probabilities that are determined by systematic relationships—then it follows that we should be able to observe certain stable probability distributions.

[55]See Brownlie and Hampton, "Wage Determination in New Zealand." Similar results using European data were obtained by William Fellner, Milton Gilbert, Bert Hansen, Richard Kahn, Friedrich Lutz, and Pieter de Wolff, *The Problem of Rising Prices* (Organization for European Economic Co-operation, Paris, 1961), p. 401.

In the simplest case, if the probability per period of time of leaving a particular state such as unemployment is constant, then a group of workers all unemployed at the same time would diminish in size exponentially as the workers gradually found jobs. However, some workers would be unemployed a long time just because they had a long string of bad breaks in being at the right plant gate at the wrong time. A sample of unemployed taken at one point of time would show the same exponential decay, if the percentage of workers whose unemployment already has lasted *t* or longer is plotted against *t*.

Of course, when economic conditions change, the probabilities change and different probability distributions are generated. Thus in the simplest case discussed above, there would be a whole family of exponential distributions, one for each probability level. It should be possible to estimate certain parameters from these probability distributions that should throw light on the stochastic process producing them. Some of these distributions have been explored.

Woytinski in his impressive study[56] of unemployment in the 1930s shows the cumulative distributions of the duration of unemployed men in Buffalo up to 52 weeks. His plots of the distributions for each year from 1929 through 1933 show approximately exponential distributions where the rate of decay is different for each year, depending upon the unemployment level at the time or more precisely on the current probability per week of finding a job. Since the system is not always in equilibrium, these cross-section distributions will reflect to some extent the market movements of the recent past.

In another set of data Woytinski found that Philadelphia had made an annual survey of its unemployed for the years 1931–1938. In this case the duration of unemployment was measured in *years* and some workers had been unemployed for more than four years. Here was a situation in which structural effects might well have dominated. Some recently unemployed workers might have a relatively good chance of finding a job, while the hard core of long-term unemployed might have almost no chance of finding work. The data show for the years 1934–1938 that workers whose unemployment had lasted more than three but less than four years had 42, 52, 80, 59, and 57 percent, respectively, of the probability of finding a job as did those workers unemployed less than a year. Thus years of unemployment had reduced their chances on the average by only about 40 percent of the corresponding chances of the newly unemployed.[57] There is certainly evidence here of structural factors contributing to the unemployment of certain people, but the surprising thing is that three additional years of unemployment does not affect employability even more drastically.

---

[56]W. S. Woytinsky, *Three Aspects of Labor Dynamics* (Social Science Research Council, New York, 1942), pp. 96–106.

[57]We are interpreting these data as Woytinsky did in assuming that the numbers reflect employment of the unemployed and not their withdrawal from the labor force.

When the unemployed are not equally employable, the more employable ones tend to be hired first, leaving the less employable. Thus the probability of placement gradually appears to fall with increasing duration. However, the probability of placement of each component group may actually have remained constant. It is clear that we need a better understanding of this stochastic process.

One important implication of the exponential distribution of unemployment duration is that the percentage of the unemployed above some fixed duration increases systematically with increases in the national unemployment rate. When a few years ago unemployment was still rising, concern was often expressed about the rising fraction whose unemployment exceeded 15 weeks. This was taken as an indication of increasingly serious structural effects. There may indeed have been an increase in structural problems, but the evidence cited is entirely consistent with no structural unemployment.

Berman and David and Otsuki[58] have made recent studies in which the probability of unemployment was investigated for various classifications of unemployed workers. The probability relationships show considerable stability and predictive ability. Berman finds that the exponential distribution goes far to explain the distribution of unemployment duration, but there is a clear indication that even within a year structural effects are evident.

Although his sample size is small, John Myers' data on the distribution of durations of job vacancies extending up to a year also appear to be exponential.[59]

Studies of labor turnover in Great Britain have shown that voluntary terminations range from 46 to 93 percent of all terminations. Silcock has shown[60] that the distribution of employment durations is close to being exponential, but there is a significant tendancy for the decay rate to decline with longer durations. The longer an employee has stayed, the less likely is his termination. He found that a two-parameter gamma distribution fits his data better than the exponential.

A subsequent paper by Lane and Andrew[61] concluded that the log normal distribution fits even better. It is interesting to an economist that economic fluctuations were not taken into account in these anal-

[58]Barbara Berman, "Alternative Measures of Structural Unemployment," in *Employment Policy and the Labor Market*, A. M. Ross, ed. (University of California Press, Berkeley, 1965), and Martin David and Toshio Otsuki, "Forecasting Short-Run Variation in Labor Market Activity," *Review of Economics and Statistics* (February 1968), pp. 68–77.

[59]Holt and David, "Concept of Vacancies," p. 98, and J. G. Myers, "Conceptual and Measurement Problems in Job Vacancies, A Progress Report on the NICB Study," in *Measurement and Interpretation of Job Vacancies*, R. Ferber, ed., National Bureau of Economic Research (Columbia University Press, New York, 1966), pp. 405–446.

[60]H. Silcock, "The Phenomenon of Labor Turnover," *Journal of Royal Statistical Society*, 117, Part IV, Series A (1954), pp. 429–440.

[61]K. F. Lane and J. E. Andrew, "A Method of Labor Turnover Analysis," *Journal of Royal Statistical Society*, Part III (1955), pp. 296–321.

yses, even though there are strong cyclical fluctuations of the quit rate. The high rate of early quits is explained partially by the fact that typically workers receive very little information about a job before accepting it. After this on-the-job exploration, the worker may find that the job is not to his taste, and he then quits.

The reduction of this costly turnover might be accomplished by better placement in the first place.[62]

Cyclical Fluctuations in Wage Differentials. The evidence[63] seems to show that as general unemployment rises, the unemployment rates of lower skill levels rise more than proportionally and the wages of unskilled workers fall relatively more than skilled ones.

Oi and Reder[64] have advanced closely complementary explanations. Investments by the firm in the training of skilled workers makes it reluctant to lay them off for fear of losing them. The company would prefer to downgrade skilled workers and lay off less skilled workers. Union seniority similarly may give more skilled workers priority over the unskilled ones with relatively short service. If skilled workers do lose their jobs, they can qualify for any of the jobs requiring less skill and thereby have a better chance of finding a new job than do the less skilled. When we consider that workers' energy declines with aging, and pension payments may make older workers more expensive, it is clear that the unskilled and aged may have special problems when unemployment increases.[65]

When business is on the upswing, companies often promote from within and hire at the bottom for two reasons: to promote the morale of their employees and because better information is available on their own employees.

Reder shows a remarkable relationship[66] between the unemployment rates of various skill groups: The unemployment rate of each particular skill group is a *constant* multiple or fraction of the national unemployment rate, and this important finding, if it holds up under more extensive test, may have tremendous policy implications. It may mean that the interrelations and interactions between the various skill groups are so strong that to reach effectively the unemployment problems of the unskilled, aged, and racial minority groups, we will need to reduce the unemployment levels for *all* groups. Clearly if such an important relationship is stable, we need to understand it better.

[62]Holt and David, "Concept of Vacancies."

[63]See P. W. Bell, "Cyclical Variations and Trend in Occupational Wage Differentials in American Industry since 1914," *Review of Economics and Statistics* (November 1951), pp. 329–337.

[64]W. Y. Oi, "Labor as a Quasi-fixed Factor of Production," *Journal of Political Economy* (December 1962), pp. 538–555, and M. W. Reder, "Wage Structure and Structural Unemployment," *Review of Economic Studies* (October 1964), pp. 309–322.

[65]See Sheppard and Belitsky, *Job Hunt*, and Sobel and Folk, "Labor Market Adjustments."

[66]Reder, "Wage Structure," p. 317.

One explanation that the theory in this paper suggests is that the process of stochastic interactions produces this stable relationship. For the reasons that Reder and Oi have explained, the less skilled workers have higher probabilities of being laid off and lower probabilities of being hired. The former effect decreases the length of their jobs and the latter increases the duration of their unemployment. Thus they suffer unemployment more often and longer and the combination of the two accounts for their high unemployment rates. According to classical theory, short-duration jobs would be compensated by higher wages, but the periods of unemployment may affect the unskilled workers' aspiration levels and thereby convert the additional unemployment into decreased relative wages. This may be the mechanism for widening the skill wage differentials when unemployment is high. The relationship between Reder's unemployment differentials and the corresponding wage differentials needs to be studied.

Possibly in the interests of conserving human capital that is company specific these unemployment differentials can be justified, but there is a serious policy issue here.

The theory presented in Section I.C indicated that wage flexibility increases when unemployment is low since the presence of vacancies at all skill levels offers significant opportunities for *all* workers to obtain the best job that each is capable of holding. This would suggest that the narrowed wage differentials for different skills that occur in a tight market may be socially desirable. The cure for both undesirably large differences in unemployment and undesirably large wage differentials may well be to increase aggregate demand, but this, of course, may create an inflation problem unless we can move the Phillips curve.

The basic argument here may well apply to regional, industry, and union differentials as well. To reach the socially desirable differentials assumed in static price theory, we may well need a substantial reduction in the costs of market search.

Occupational, Regional, and Industrial Mobility. The model developed in this paper is seriously deficient in not treating the various skill, occupational, industrial, and regional components of labor supply and demand. Although many of the kinds of frictional costs associated with changing jobs, moving, and searching were mentioned in passing, this analysis was not fully developed nor did we develop an adequate theory of the stochastic process.[67]

Montague and Vanderkamp have found that occupational mobility is promoted by wage incentives, lack of family responsibilities, and education.[68]

---

[67]A theoretical analysis of compartmentalization has been made by the author in "How Can?"

[68]J. T. Montague and J. Vanderkamp, *A Study in Labor Market Adjustment* (Institute of Industrial Relations, University of British Columbia, Vancouver, 1966).

The work by Parnes[69] and the more recent survey research by Lansing et al.[70] should aid in the building of the needed theory.

Albrecht[71] has shown that regional and industrial wage differentials are influenced by local unemployment, but he finds that the response is not uniform and he questions whether a national Phillips relation can have stable coefficients in the face of changes in the regional distribution of unemployment.

B. Empirical Evidence on Union Effects Here we discuss some of the empirical work on union wage differentials, bargaining power, wage drift, and strikes. Union influence on the general level of wages is considered in Section III.C.

Wage Dispersion, Union Differentials, and Unemployment. To the extent that different industries have different degrees of unionization, we would expect to find that the interindustry wage spread would tend to narrow in prosperity and widen in depression. To be sure, cyclical differences in industry demand and cyclical changes in occupational differentials also contribute to changes in the industrial wage pattern and prevent their simple interpretation in terms of union effects alone.

Lewis calculates the coefficient of variation of average annual full-time compensation across approximately 70 industries.[72] This measure of the dispersion of wages is quite stable, ranging between 24.1 and 35.1 percent from 1929 to 1958, but there is a noticeable positive correlation with the level of unemployment. He estimates that in 1958 unionism may have accounted for 2 or 3 points when the coefficient of variation was 31.5 percent.[73] The corresponding estimate for 1929, a period of lower unemployment, is "less than 1 point." These changes in both union and nonunion wage differentials are consistent with the model developed above but are considerably smaller than we had anticipated.

Rees and Hamilton also have studied the changes in the coefficient of variation as a measure of wage dispersion and have concluded that the spread of pattern bargaining across industries has contributed to the narrowing of dispersion.[74] Also the responsiveness of low-wage

[69]H. S. Parnes, *Research on Labor Mobility: An Appraisal of Research Findings in the United States* (Social Science Research Council, New York, 1954).

[70]J. B. Lansing, Eva Mueller, William Ladd, and Nancy Barth, *The Geographic Mobility of Labor: A First Report* (Survey Research Center, Institute for Social Research, Ann Arbor, Mich., 1963).

[71]W. P. Albrecht, "The Relationship between Wage Changes and Unemployment in Metropolitan Industrial Labor Markets," *Yale Economic Essays*, 6 (Fall 1966), pp. 279–341.

[72]H. G. Lewis, *Unionism and Relative Wages in the United States: An Empirical Inquiry* (University of Chicago Press, Chicago, 1963), p. 287.

[73]*Ibid.*, p. 292.

[74]Albert Rees and M. T. Hamilton, "Post War Movements of Wage Levels and Unit Labor Costs," *Journal of Law and Economics*, 6 (October 1963).

competitive industries to worsening general economic conditions and the resistance of high-wage unionized industries to these pressures has tended to increase the dispersion when unemployment increased. The narrowing of differentials that they observed in prosperity is consistent with the model presented above, which stressed the relative decline of union bargaining power over individual bargaining power and the decrease of differentials generally. Their Tables 8 and 10, when combined with unemployment data, seem to indicate a clear increase in dispersion with rising unemployment, although, of course, the war years, with wage differentials largely frozen by government order, do not follow this pattern. Also a marked time trend toward decreased dispersion seems to exist, possibly as the result of the increased industrial employment of formerly depressed agricultural populations and regions.

In observing union differentials, Eagly's cross-section study[75] of industry wage changes for years 1950–1962 is extremely interesting. He interprets a relatively low quit rate of an industry as evidence of union power in raising wages. This relation occurs for three reasons. First, in the absence of a union, workers will bargain individually and this will in some cases result in quits. Second, where a union has successfully established a wage differential over nonunion jobs, such outside jobs will be relatively unattractive and quits correspondingly low. Third, as the result of union seniority and union negotiated pensions, quits always tend to be lower in union industries.

He finds that the rankings of industries by quit rates are quite stable over time.[76] This is consistent with the stability of the pattern of unionization. He ranks the industries by the fraction of union membership and finds a significant negative correlation with ranking by quit rates— the greater the unionization, the lower the quit rate.

Next he considers[77] the cross-section relations for various years between the rate of change of money wages for 19 industries and the corresponding quit rates in the same year. A simplified version of his cross-section regression lines is shown in Figure 9. He finds in a given year that the lower the quit rate, indicating increasing unionization, the higher is the rate of change of money wages. Thus the stronger the unions, the faster industry wages rise. (He did not observe the positive slopes shown with dashed lines.) These negative slopes do not contradict the general relation that high unemployment is associated with low quits and low increases in money wages, because the whole cross-section relation shifts downward and to the left with rising unemployment. The general quit level is determined by general economic con-

[75]Eagly, "Market Power."

[76]*Ibid.*, Table 4.

[77]*Ibid.*, App. D.

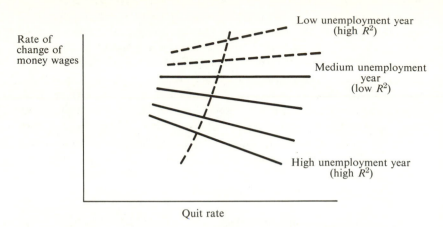

Figure 9.   Industry-cross-section regression lines for different years.

ditions in the year, but the relative quit level of individual industries is determined by degree of unionization. Thus the rate of increase of money wages in an industry depends both on its unionization and on general economic conditions.

These conclusions by Eagly are entirely consistent with the model developed above, but his analysis also allows us to test several additional implications of the model.

First, he supplies indirect evidence through the quit rate that union membership is a relevant measure of the power of unions to influence wages. Second, his correlation between quit rate and union membership fluctuates cyclically with unemployment rate. When unemployment is low, the quit rate, which serves as an inverse proxy variable for union influence on wages, correlates less well with union membership[78] indicating the decreased relative power of union bargaining (column M of his Table 4). Third, when unemployment decreases to a medium level, the slope of the wage change becomes less and less negative. This quit regression again reflects decreased differences between union and nonunion wage increases when unemployment is low. Fourth, the variance explained by the cross-section regressions of wage change on quits declines with the level of unemployment until at a medium level of unemployment the slope and R^2 are both zero. The quit rate as a measure of union power explains much more about the wage changes when unemployment is high than when it is at a medium level. Thus Eagly's analysis lends considerable support to the proposition that the influence of unions on wages is greatest when the economy is depressed. When the unemployment is at a medium level there seems to be little

[78]This analysis could be improved by using current data on the ranking of union membership, if the data can be found.

difference between union and nonunion wage changes. Unions get their increases through threatening to strike. Nonunion workers get comparable increases by threatening to quit and by quitting.

Eagly's analysis does not show cross-section regressions with positive slopes. The lowest unemployment in his sample was 2.9 percent, in 1952 which is probably not low enough for the wages of nonunion workers to rise faster than union wages and thereby decrease or eliminate the union differential. We have referred to the 3 percent neighborhood as the medium level of unemployment. If unemployment fell to lower levels, say 2 percent, we would predict that Eagly's correlation between union membership and quit rates would fall still farther, the slope of the cross-section regressions would turn positive, and the wage variance explained by quit rates would rise again. It is clear from Eagly's figure[79] that there also are some dynamic effects involved, but we have not attempted an analysis. Perhaps the rigidities and lags of union negotiations enter here.

Lewis' subtle and incisive work[80] on unionism and relative wages cannot be treated adequately in a few sentences. He reviews 18 previous studies and then goes on to make his own estimates of the percentage by which unionism raised the average wage of union labor relative to non-union labor. He concludes that the union differential was at its peak of perhaps 25 percent about 1932–1933 and close to zero—under 5 percent—during the postwar inflation of 1947–1948. In summary Lewis says, "there is substantial agreement in the evidence . . . that the impact of unionism on the union/nonunion relative wage has varied widely over time and in a systematic manner. In particular, the relative wage effect estimates appear to be negatively correlated with the rate of inflation (and, perhaps, positively correlated with the unemployment rate)."[81] His own estimates[82] show a strong correlation with the unemployment rate. He explains these changes in the differential in terms of the rigidities and lags of union wages, but his empirical estimates are equally compatible with the bargaining-power theory developed above.

Concentration, Profits, and Union Membership. Considerable effort has gone into determining the effect of these variables on union wage differentials while allowing for the possibility that their effects may be different at different stages of the business cycle. Unfortunately the variability of behavior is tremendous and clearly established empirical generalizations are hard to come by. Often the statistical techniques used have not been adequate to deal with this multicausal problem.

[79]Eagly, "Market Power," App. D.

[80]Lewis, *Unionism.*

[81]*Ibid.,* p. 191.

[82]*Ibid.,* p. 222.

Bowen, studying U.S. "two-digit" industries during 1947–1959, finds that profit, concentration ratios, and union membership all have effects on average hourly earnings in the expected directions on the average, but there appears to be substantial variability over the cycle.[83] However, when high-concentration strong-union industries were compared with low-concentration weak-union industries in recessions, wage responses to changes in employment and profit level were much stronger for the latter group.[84] "The joint effect of concentration and unionization may be greater than the algebraic sum of their individual effects. Another significant difference between these two broad sectors is that recession wage behavior in the relatively concentrated and unionized sector is much less influenced by the direct incidence of recessions on the member firms than is wage behavior in the competitive sector."[85] These findings would seem consistent with the prediction of the model presented above that the union differential depends on the triple multiplicative interaction of concentration, unionization, and unemployment.

Weiss, in a study[86] of Census population data for 1960 found that employees in concentrated industries and in unionized industries had relatively high earnings. But when allowance was made for the personal qualities that might relate to productivity, the concentration effect virtually disappeared and the union effect was reduced to perhaps 6 to 8 percent and was barely significant statistically.

Although the cross-product term between concentration and unionization seemed to show a higher significance than concentration in at least one of his basic regressions,[87] this interaction term was viewed as having second-order significance. The importance of unionization in the model developed above is supported by Weiss' results, though not strongly. The insignificance of concentration alone also is consistent with the model. How well unionization alone, the product of unionization and concentration alone, or the two terms together would correlate with the nonpersonal component of wages cannot be determined from Weiss' results. Further analysis of his data would be of great interest.

The conclusion from the present analysis is that unionized concentrated industries may pay considerably higher wages, but their labor costs may be increased only a small amount by union bargaining power. Weiss' study throws no light on the effects of changing unemployment.

Membership, Pushfulness, and Ability to Strike. In many of the

[83]W. G. Bowen, *Wage Behavior in the Post War Period—An Empirical Analysis* (Princeton University Press, Princeton, N.J., 1960), p. 64.

[84]*Ibid.*, p. 81.

[85]*Ibid.*, p. 91.

[86]L. W. Weiss, "Concentration and Labor Earnings," *American Economic Review* (March 1966), pp. 96–117.

[87]*Ibid.*, 3 on p. 106.

cross-section studies the strength of the union has been measured simply by percentage of union membership, and, as we have seen, this variable has significant explanatory power. We now consider whether or not there is empirical support for other measures of union strength that might influence the effectiveness of their strike threat and thereby influence wages. Since we have no direct way to measure union strength, we will look for its effects in wage changes.

Lewis remarks: "The annals of unionism contain a good deal of circumstantial evidence, especially during periods in which the extent of unionism in the economy *is growing*, that some non-union employers threatened with unionization raised the relative wages of their employees."[88] (Italics added.)

Ozanne on the basis of a careful study[89] of Volumes II and IV of *History of Labor* by John R. Commons, and data on strikes, numbers of workers involved in strikes, and union membership, has concluded that for the United States over the last century: "Whether unionism was growing or declining was of more actual significance to wage impact than small differences in percentages of the nonfarm work force unionized."

Hines hypothesized that the rate of change of union membership would have an effect in addition to that of the level of membership itself.[90] His tests on U.K. data for 1893–1961 supported his view. He found that the percentage rate of change in money wage rates using annual data and excluding war years was best explained by a linear relation with union membership (measured as the percentage of the labor force that was unionized) and the first difference in union membership to reflect growth or decline. This relation explained 82 percent of the variance with highly significant regression coefficients. Interestingly, the rate of change of membership alone explained 67 percent of the variance compared to only 3 percent for the level of union membership alone. This suggests that the cross-section studies that have used the latter variable may not have been using the most important measure of union strength.

Hines supports well his prime contention that union membership and change in membership have strong influences and makes tests of the lags involved to be sure that causalty does not run from wage increases to membership growth. When he ran regressions on different subperiods he found that changes in union membership had a greater effect on wages in 1949–1961 than in 1921–1938. Actually this can be predicted from his own theory,[91] which argues that a given change in

[88]Lewis, *Unionism*, p. 26.
[89]Ozanne, *Wage Practice and Theory*, Chap. 3 and Table 9.
[90]Hines, "Trade Unions."
[91]*Ibid.*, footnote, p. 229.

membership is more significant the higher is the membership level. As the level rises it becomes increasingly difficult to raise it further; 100 percent unionization is the absolute limit. It follows from his theory that wages should be influenced by an interaction (product) term between the level of membership and the change in that level. The inclusion of such a term in the regression spanning both of his subperiods should significantly improve his fit.

Dow and Dicks-Mireaux, in an effort to measure the aggressiveness of union attitudes, introduced their own subjective estimates of "pushfulness," ranging in five steps from "marked restraint" to "marked pushfulness." They found[92] this variable to have a statistically significant effect in explaining British wages 1946–1956.

Wage Drift. Under the theory developed above, we would anticipate that when the unemployment rate is very low union bargains would have little effect on money wages compared to the atomistic response to demand conditions. The phenomenon of "wage drift," in which wage incomes rise faster than contracted wage rates, seems consistent with this prediction.

The United States has had the dubious distinction of having a sufficiently high level of unemployment that the phenomena of wage drift has not been identified. Consequently, for empirical research on this topic we look to European economies in the postwar period.

There are, of course, institutional differences as well as unemployment differences that may be significant. European bargaining tends to be at the industry rather than at the firm level. Also the position of unions in labor governments forces them to take some responsibility for any inflation that could be traced to negotiated wage increases. This constrains the unions in pushing for maximum wage concessions from employers.

To answer any question about the fact of lower unemployment levels outside the United States, we show in Table 1 a spot sample for the year 1961 of unemployment rates adjusted to U.S. definitions from work by Neef.[93]

Hansen and Rehn analyzed annual data 1947–1954 for eight industries to determine the causes of wage drift, averaging about 4 percent per year, that had accounted for between one third to one half of the postwar increase in Sweden's average hourly earnings.[94] They define wage drift as the difference between the percentage increase in average hourly earnings and the corresponding increase "agreed upon at the yearly

[92]J. C. R. Dow and L. A. Dicks-Mireaux, "The Determinants of Wage Inflations: U.K. 1946–56," *Journal of the Royal Statistical Society*, 122, Series A (1959), pp. 169–170.

[93]A. F. Neef, "International Unemployment Rates, 1960–1964," *Monthly Labor Review*, 88 (March 1965), pp. 265–269.

[94]B. Hansen and G. Rehn, "On Wage Drift, A Problem in Money Wage Dynamics," in *25 Essays in Honor of Eric Lindahl* (Economisk Tidskrift, Stockholm, 1956), pp. 87–138.

Table 1

DEFINITIONALLY CONSISTENT INTERNATIONAL
UNEMPLOYMENT RATES FOR 1961

Country	Percentage
United States	6.7
Canada	7.2
France	2.4
West Germany	0.4
Great Britain	2.3
Italy	3.7
Japan	1.3
Sweden	1.5

wage negotiations between the central authorities of employers' and employees' organizations in the different industries."[95] Thus wage drift includes the effect of workers changing to better paid jobs, firms, or industries; changes in overtime; and changes in productivity under piece work. They develop a theory of wage drift in terms of (a) the adjustment mechanism by which wages respond to excess demand and approach their equilibrium, (b) profit margins, and (c) productivity changes.

Using correlation and partial correlation analyses, they conclude that the excess demand for manpower (vacancy rate minus unemployment rate for the industry) has the greatest influence on wage drift. Excess profit seems to play a minor role, and only in a few industries where piece work is important do productivity changes play a significant role. The authors qualify this result by pointing to the difficulty in estimating wage drift and the weaknesses of the data on their explanatory variables.

Marquand analyzed annual U.K. data 1948–1957 for 16 industries.[96] She defined wage drift as the difference between the change in average wage earnings once the effect of overtime working has been eliminated and the change in negotiated wage rates. Earnings drift includes overtime payments as well. She estimates that in 1955 there was a British wage drift of 7 percent with an additional 10 percent due to overtime. In explanation of this phenomena she says: "The occurrence of earnings drift (or wage drift) is frequently attributed to the difficulty employers find in recruiting sufficient labor. Thus employers will make payments above the negotiated wage rate either to attract more labor or to attempt to ensure that those who are already employed do not leave. Such payments will be related to the difficulty the employer encounters in obtaining a sufficient and suitable labor force."

[95]*Ibid.*, p. 88.

[96]Judith Marquand, "Earnings Drift in the United Kingdom, 1948–1957," *Oxford Economic Papers*, 12, No. 1 (February 1960), pp. 77–104.

Using correlation analysis and partial correlation analysis she concludes, "Overtime working, changes in productivity, and the level of advertised unfilled vacancies . . . explained 122 out of the 144 earnings-drifts."[97] Evidently piece work accounts for much of the productivity effect, and industries with many small plants seem to be more prone to drift. Profits were not found to have a significant effect.

A study for the Organization for the European Economic Co-operation by a group of independent experts considered in some detail for the period 1953–1960 the price and wage experience of Denmark, Germany, Netherlands, Sweden, the United Kingdom, and the United States with some consideration of many other European countries.[98] The problem of wage drift was analyzed for each country except the United States. The exact mechanism producing this effect is not clear, but in all cases the importance of excess demand was emphasized. For example, unfilled vacancies explained 81 percent of the variance of wage drift in Sweden.[99]

Industrial Disputes. Rees, Weintraub, and O'Brien all have made similar studies of the cyclical fluctuations of strikes over different time spans using the analytic method developed at the National Bureau of Economic Research.[100] Their findings are in general agreement that strikes move procyclically with a sizable amplitude; the troughs average about 90 percent and the peaks average about 125 percent of the long-run averages. Strikes turn down 4 to 14 months *before* the business peak and turn up *after* the business trough. The pattern of leading at the peaks and lagging at the troughs parallels that of unemployment,[101] which seems consistent with the shifts in bargaining power that our model associates with unemployment.

Before leaving the discussion of union behavior we should note that a great deal of study is summarized[102] by Rees that seems not to contradict the model developed above. Similarly, the studies discussed above seem generally consistent with the model.

C. Empirical Evidence on Phillips' Relation, including Union Wage Push

The studies of the relation between unemployment and the rate of change of money wages are so numerous and the detailed

[97]*Ibid.*, p. 98.

[98]Fellner et al., *Rising Prices.*

[99]*Ibid.*, p. 401.

[100]Rees, "Industrial Conflict"; Andrew R. Weintraub, "Prosperity versus Strikes, An Empirical Approach," *Industrial and Labor Relations Review*, 19, No. 2 (January 1966), pp. 231–238; and O'Brien, "Industrial Conflict."

[101]The President's Committee to Appraise Employment and Unemployment Statistics (R. A. Gordon, Chairman), *Measuring Employment and Unemployment* (U.S. Government Printing Office, Washington, 1962), p. 67.

[102]Albert Rees, *The Economics of Trade Unions* (University of Chicago Press, Chicago, 1962).

forms so varied that no attempt at systematic coverage will be made. Rather we will briefly examine the ability of such a macro relation to explain the historical experience of a number of different countries. Then we will consider what light our theoretical model throws on some of the more recent and thorough empirical research.

The Phillips Relation in Various Countries. The U.K. data have been studied intensively by Phillips, Dow and Dicks-Mireaux, Lipsey, Klein and Ball, and others.[103] Lipsey explained 82 percent of the variance in annual wage changes from 1862–1913 with $1/U$, $1/U^2$, and ΔU. For the years 1923–1939 and 1948–1957 the same explanatory variables plus ΔP (price change) gave an R^2 of 0.91. Using quarterly data for 1948–1957 and simultaneous estimation methods, Klein and Ball found that price changes had a much stronger effect on wages than did unemployment. These estimates put so little weight on unemployment that they raise a serious question about either the relevancy of the Phillips relation or the validity of their results. However, Ball in later theoretical work[104] does not seem inclined to minimize the importance of unemployment in influencing wages. There are so many differences between these studies that comparisons are difficult, but it seems fair to say that for considerable periods of U.K. history, unemployment and its changes had a strong influence on money wages.

In a little known paper by Phillips using quarterly data for Australia 1947–1958, he obtained quite good fits using unemployment and changes in export and import prices.[105] The government wage arbitration and prices were assumed to be endogenously determined.

Kaliski, studying Canadian data, found that $1/U$ and ΔU were significant explanatory variables for the postwar period but not for the interwar period, when prices had a strong influence on wages.[106]

Watanabe, studying quarterly data for Japan 1955–1962, found that 86 percent of the variance of four-quarter changes in wages was explained by unemployment and lagged price changes.[107] Simultaneous estimation with a price equation gave very similar results.

American data have been studied by many researchers. Bhatia for the periods 1900–1914 and 1921–1942 found that unemployment and the change in prices had a significant influence on wages, but he found

[103]Phillips, "Relation"; Dow and Dicks-Mireaux, "Determinants"; Lipsey, "A Further Analysis"; and L. R. Klein and R. J. Ball, "Some Econometrics of the Determination of Absolute Prices and Wages," *Economic Journal*, 49 (September 1959), pp. 465–482.

[104]R. J. Ball, *Inflation and the Theory of Money* (Aldine Publishing Co., Chicago, 1964).

[105]A. W. Phillips, "Wage Changes and Unemployment in Australia, 1947–58," Economic Society of Australia and New Zealand, New South Wales Branch, *Economic Monograph*, 219 (August 1959).

[106]S. F. Kaliski, "The Relation between Unemployment and the Rate of Change of Money Wages in Canada," *International Economic Review*, 5 (January 1964).

[107]Tsunekiko Watanabe, "Price Changes and the Rate of Change of Money Earnings in Japan, 1955–62," *Quarterly Journal of Economics* (February 1966), pp. 31–47.

no evidence of nonlinearity or influence by changes in unemployment.[108] In a later study he found that profits and change in profits had a significant effect. France found somewhat stronger relationships with both unemployment and change in unemployment significant.[109] Bowen and Berry found only a loose relationship between wage changes and unemployment and questioned the "existence of any long term relationship at all."[110] Bowen and Rees and Hamilton, studying the postwar period, found that both unemployment and the change in unemployment had strong effects on wage increases, but the relationship was not stable.[111]

Eckstein estimated the importance of key unions setting a national pattern taking into account the timing of negotiations.[112] He found significant evidence for such pattern setting and also found that unemployment had a significant effect. His work points up a weakness in the theoretical model that has been formulated; we have not incorporated leadership roles played by powerful unions.

Schultze and Tryon, studying six industry groupings, concluded that unemployment, profits, and consumer prices all had significant effects in explaining quarterly wage changes.[113] Perry, working with quarterly data 1947–1960, explained 87 percent of the variance of wages with significant effects from unemployment, cost of living, profits, and change of profits.[114] Kuh, using quarterly data for 1950–1960, questions unemployment and profits as explanatory variables and has somewhat better results using value productivity.[115] Differences in data and analytic treatment undoubtedly account for much of this diversity of results.

The general conclusion based on these studies of many countries is that the Phillips relation has a great deal of empirical support, but in its present formulation the estimates are rather unstable. This suggests that there is need of improving our conceptualization, data, and esti-

---

[108]R. J. Bhatia, "Profits and the Rate of Change in Money Earnings in the United States, 1935–59," *Economica* (1962), pp. 255–262, and "Unemployment and the Rate of Change of Money Earnings in the United States 1900–1958," *Economica* 28 (August 1961), pp. 286–296.

[109]R. R. France, "Wages, Unemployment and Prices in the United States 1890–1932, 1947–57," *Industrial and Labor Relations Review* (January 1962), pp. 171–190.

[110]W. G. Bowen and R. A. Berry, "Unemployment Conditions and Movements of the Money Wage Level," *Review of Economics and Statistics* (May 1963), pp. 163–172.

[111]Bowen, *Wage Behavior*, and Rees and Hamilton, "Post War Movements."

[112]Otto Eckstein, "A Theory of the Wage-Price Process in Modern Industry," *Review of Economic Studies* (October 1964), pp. 267–286.

[113]C. L. Schultze and J. L. Tryon, "Prices and Wages," in *The Brookings Quarterly Econometric Model of the United States* (Rand McNally, Chicago, 1965), pp. 281–334.

[114]Perry, *Unemployment*, p. 50.

[115]Edward Kuh, "A Productivity Theory of Wage Levels—An Alternative to the Phillips' Curve," *Review of Economic Studies* (1966), pp. 333–360.

mation of these relationships. We are beyond the point of asking whether the relation exists—it does. We need now to learn what mechanisms are responsible.

The Form and Variables of the Phillips Relation. There is evidence that the influence of unemployment is nonlinear and that consequently linear estimates will tend to be unstable as the unemployment level changes.[116] Additive linear functions in $1/U$ and $1/U^2$, etc., have all had significant effects. The model above suggests that the term should be $1/U^k$, where k is perhaps 1.5. In any case the value of k should be estimated from the data.

The model indicated that ΔU might or might not have an effect, depending upon the power of unions. This interaction may explain why the ΔU term seems to have less influence now than in earlier periods when unions were weaker.

Profits[117] and change in profits seem to have empirical support, as does union membership and change of membership.[118] Evidently effects from other terms and cross products in (41) and from ΔE have not been observed. The biggest departure from the predictions of the model is the evident importance of price changes in influencing wage changes. This result might, of course, be traceable to the influence of wages on prices.

However another possibility is that the researchers, with the exceptions of Hines and of Dow and Dicks-Mireaux, have not included direct measures of union strength. Because labor costs influence prices, their inclusion may serve as a proxy for union strength.

There are reasons from the theory for expecting an important interaction among concentration, union membership, and unemployment, and another between union membership and unemployment, but these have not been examined.

None of the aggregate work on the Phillips relation takes into account the fact that the relative influence of the unions may change for different levels of unemployment. The union effect when the labor market is so tight that there is wage drift may be quite different than in a slack market, where our model indicates that its relative effect is maximum.

The theory that is developed above is complex, and if the various effects are to be estimated to obtain a stable structure, empirical studies must be correspondingly complex.

The vacancy relation estimated for New Zealand suggests that we need to develop the demand side of the model. Perhaps only when that is done will the Phillips relation on the supply side be well defined.

---

[116]See Lipsey, "Relation," and Perry, *Unemployment*.
[117]See Perry, *Unemployment*, and Bhatia, "Profits."
[118]See Hines, "Trade Unions."

4
CONCLUSIONS
AND IMPLICATIONS
FOR FURTHER RESEARCH

In this concluding section we attempt to draw together briefly the key points that appear to have theoretical and empirical support. Then we consider some of the implications for research methodology, extensions of the theory, and implications for further research.

Summary. The existence of relationships between steady changes in money wages and the level of unemployment, and between a union wage differential and union bargaining power, has substantial support both theoretically and empirically. Also the phenomena of wage drift and industrial disputes are predicted from the theory and supported by observations. The basic behavioral mechanisms that lead to these results are the following. The wages that workers will accept fall with the duration of unemployment and increase with job vacancies. The likelihood that a worker will quit rises with job vacancies but is inhibited if the worker's present wage is relatively high. Wage offers by employers depend on their difficulty in recruiting workers to fill job vacancies, their quit rate, and the outcome of bargaining with the union. The ability of the union to establish a wage differential through bargaining increases with (a) union membership and its rate of growth, (b) the level of unemployment because of the rising relative advantage of collective bargaining compared to individual bargaining, (c) the concentration of the industry, and (d) the profitability of the firm. The likelihood of overt labor disputes rises as the conflict increases: high profits and low union differential.

Stable stochastic and dynamic relationships among various flows, stocks, wage rates, etc., appear to prevail in the labor market. These relations depend in turn on behavioral regularities expressed in probability terms that reflect the effects of uncertainty, frictional costs, etc. Such regularities and relationships have been observed on the worker, company, industry, and national levels.

Implications for Research Methodology. As the various behavioral and probability relationships are spelled out and formalized, even in the crude caricature of abstract equations, the extreme complexity of the interactions that take place in the labor-market system becomes apparent. For example, the model developed in this paper suggests that union ability to create a wage differential depends on the *multiplicative interaction* of four variables: union membership, change in membership, level of unemployment, and concentration ratio. Thus the influence of one of these variables depends on the values of all the others, and we would anticipate that they would differ over the cycle, through time and across industries. As another example the model suggests that the change in wage level depends on additive terms which are functions of quit rate, unemployment level, change in employment, and union differential.

All too often our research has asked, "What is the effect of variable X on variable Y?", and we examine the data to answer the question. We reach a conclusion and then go on to consider the effect of another variable on Y. When we are being "sophisticated" we may hold several other variables statistically constant and explore partial correlations between the two variables, or we massage the data with a multiple regression shotgun in search of high partial correlations.

Where there are many additive effects that have not been built into the analysis, there is a serious danger that the effect we are looking for will not be seen because of the variability contributed by other variables, and we may erroneously conclude that there is no *significant* effect. Where there is a multiplicative or other nonlinear relationship involving other variables, there is a serious danger that we will conclude that no *systematic* relation exists.

The moral is that we need to use statistical tools capable of detecting the simultaneous influence of multiple causes, including the effects of nonlinear interactions. But here it becomes critical to select the correct explanatory variables and functional forms. Regression methods can always find the parameters that give the best fit, but, given the complexity of the relationships and the weakness of the data, these methods cannot be relied on also to give reliable guidance for formulating the specifications of the relationships. Hence careful theoretical formulations capable of introspective and logical tests are important.

Many of the data on which we must rely are highly aggregated, so much of the information is lost or does not square with the concepts needed for analysis. Hence there is critical need for improving our data base, particularly on the micro level, and for making it more responsive to research needs.

Even though the relations are complex and the causes are many, we can as the result of fluctuations in the various causal variables statistically untangle their influences if we have adequate data and adequate theoretical understanding of the process—at least that is our hope and ultimate expectation. We are faced with severe difficulties but not unresolvable dilemmas. Provided only that union push and demand pull do not fluctuate in perfect synchronism, we should be able to measure the effects of each. Many researchers have, of course, long since appreciated these problems and successfully dealt with them. However, it is hard to escape the conclusion that if we are significantly to improve our knowledge of such a complex system as the labor market, we need increasingly to augment institutional and empirical analysis with statistical and theoretical analysis. *All* these complementary approaches are essential.

Much already has been learned, as is evident from the many relevant studies that we have used as a check on the theory that we have developed. However, some of the work was so loose methodologically that it is difficult to know how much weight should be put on its conclusions.

It is clear that the model we have developed now requires critical and systematic econometric testing using multivariate techniques. This applies both to the parts of the model that are accepted as standard doctrine and to those that contradict it.

The Demand for Labor. In the Phillips relation the demand side of the market is implicit rather than explicit; demand changes are detected by the supply response. Clearly we will obtain better understanding and estimates by considering demand relationships explicitly. We need to study how production decisions relate through a productivity relation to overtime, slack time, and the generation of vacancies.[119] We need to study how the maximum wage offer (measured in relation to the wage paid to the worker who previously occupied the job) increases with the duration of the unfilled vacancy, and similarly how the specifications on worker quality fall.

At a more modest level, estimates of the Phillips relation might be improved by including quit rate [see (16)] or by including vacancies through substituting (52).

It is clear that wages are subject to influences both from changes in vacancies and changes in unemployment. We should put both of these into our analysis and not continue to make unemployment also serve partially as a proxy for vacancies.

Further Research. Suggestions for further research and hypothesis already have been mentioned at a number of points. The hypotheses developed in this paper need critical testing at every level. The aggregation problem in particular has received no attention, even though complacency is certainly not warranted in a model in which nonlinearities play a crucial role. We consider briefly certain particular areas inviting research attention.

On the level of theory this model should be compared carefully with parallel efforts such as those of Phelps, Kuh, and Eckstein.[120]

Some of the research on mobility by region, occupation, and industry may supply a model of the disaggregated stochastic process that is a conspicuous missing link in our model when various differentials are considered; see Brechling, David, and Orcutt et al.[121]

[119]See C. C. Holt, F. Modigliani, J. F. Muth, and M. A. Simon, *Planning Production, Inventories and Work Force* (Prentice-Hall, Inc., Englewood Cliffs, N.J., 1960).

[120]E. S. Phelps, "Money Wage Dynamics and Labor Market Equilibrium," *Journal of Political Economy* (July–August 1968), Part II; Kuh, "Productivity Theory"; and Eckstein, "Wage-Price Process."

[121]Frank Brechling, "Trends and Cycles in British Regional Unemployment," *Oxford Economic Papers*, 19, No. 1 (March 1967); Martin David, "Part I: Labor Force Simula-

Cross-section and time-series studies of company responses in raising wages on the job are badly needed to put a firmer foundation under (13) and estimate its lag structure. We need to know more about the layoff and recall behavior of firms and how this relates to overtime and inventory level.

Studies are needed of workers' on-the-job market search and their aspiration levels in making decisions to quit in favor of new jobs. Exactly what moves workers to quit and search for new jobs? How long do laid-off workers wait for recall before they begin searching for new jobs?

Theoretical work is needed to relate threats and payoffs to settlements through a behavioral bargaining theory. There undoubtedly are better measures of aggressiveness of union and management leadership than change in union membership. Perhaps psychological attitudes can be measured through interview surveys.

Although the model we have developed seems quite consistent with labor-market data, high-level semipolitical bargaining among "big labor, big business, and big government" also may operate to influence patterns that affect national inflation rates, with their implications for balance-of-payments problems, etc. Progress in analyzing these effects and in evaluating the effectiveness of an income wage policy on the national level probably must await a better understanding of the dynamic operation of labor markets. One hopes that the present work will contribute to a better understanding of what lies behind Phillips' wage-adjustment relation and, even more important, will suggest measures that could be taken to move the curve so that lowered unemployment *and* rates of inflation *both* could be achieved.

tion," Household Sector Micro-Model Working Paper 6414 (mimeographed), Project MUSE, Social Systems Research Institute, University of Wisconsin, 1965; and G. H. Orcutt, A. Rivlin, M. Greenberger, and J. Korbel, *Microanalysis of Socioeconomic Systems* (Harper & Row, Publishers, New York, 1961).

Money Wage Dynamics and Labor Market Equilibrium[*]

EDMUND S. PHELPS

If the economy were always in macroeconomic equilibrium, then perhaps the full employment money-and-growth models of recent vintage would suffice to explain the time paths of the money wage and price level. But any actual economy is almost continuously out of equilibrium, so we need also to study wage and price dynamics under arbitrary conditions.

[*]This is the third version of a paper having as themes the concepts of equilibrium unemployment, excess demand, and momentary Phillips curves. The previous version was presented at the Conference of University Professors in August 1967 and published in the August 1968 *Journal of Political Economy*. An earlier version, "A Theory of Money Wage Dynamics and Its Implications for the Phillips Curve," was No. 47 in the Pennsylvania Discussion Paper Series (February 1967).

This reworking reminds me of a story about an Italian tenor singing on tour in the provinces. After noisy applause for his first aria in the opera, he repeated the aria. More insistent applause and another encore. When the audience demanded the aria a third time, the tenor addressed the audience: "*Molti grazie*, but if I sing it again I may not have enough voice left to finish the opera." Whereupon a man in the audience shouted: "You'll sing it again, and you'll keep on singing it until you get it right."

The present version resuscitates, in Appendix 2, the dynamic-programming analysis of optimal nonwage recruitment over time by the individual firm that was contained in the first version. It presents, in Appendix 1, a new mathematical treatment of a staggered wage-setting model that gives some rigorous support to the (generalized) excess-demand theory of average wage change. There are brief addenda at the ends of Sections 2 and 3 which substitute misexpectation of the current wage for misexpectation of the near-term future wage so that the compatibility of my approach with that of Alchian and Mortensen is made clear. Finally, there is an intelligible discussion (one hopes) of job-rationing and the role of heterogeneity, made possible especially by some of the ideas of Gordon and Hynes.

The Phillips curve studies of the past decade have done this with a vengeance, offering numerous independent variables in countless combinations to explain wage movements. But it is difficult to choose among these econometric models and rarely is there a clear rationale for the model used. This paper is a start toward a unified and empirically applicable theory of money wage dynamics. At the same time it tries to capture the role of expectations and thus to work into the theory the notion of labor-market equilibrium.

1
EVOLUTION OF THE
PHILLIPS CURVE AND
ITS OPPOSITION

Keynes' *General Theory*[1] and virtually all formal macroeconomic models of the postwar era postulated a minimum unemployment level— a full employment level of unemployment—which could be maintained with either stable prices or rising prices. In this happy state, additional aggregate demand would produce rising prices and wages but no reduction of unemployment. This residual unemployment was called "frictional" and "voluntary," and such unemployment was (mistakenly) assumed to be unresponsive to demand.[2] Hence there was no need to choose between low unemployment and price stability.

This doctrine depended on Keynes' notions of money wage behavior. At more than minimum unemployment, a rise (fall) of demand and employment would produce at most a once-for-all rise (fall) of the money wage, prices constant; any rise (fall) of the price level thereby induced would cause a rise (fall) of the money wage in smaller proportion. Hence, in a stationary economy at least, his theory did not predict the possibility of a secular rise of money wage rates at normal unemployment rates—let alone wage rises exceeding productivity growth— only the one-time "semi-inflation"[3] of prices and wages during the transition to minimum unemployment.

This doctrine was quickly disputed by Robinson,[4] who wrote of a conflict between moderately high employment and price stability. Dunlop[5] suggested that the *rate of change* of the money wage depends

[1]J. M. Keynes, *The General Theory of Employment, Interest and Money* (The Macmillan Company, London, 1936).

[2]A monetary economy can choose among different levels of frictional unemployment that correspond to different levels of aggregate demand and job vacancies. Some of the mechanisms that enable demand to affect frictional unemployment are discussed below, especially in Section 3.

[3]Keynes, *op. cit.*, p. 301.

[4]J. Robinson, *Essays in the Theory of Unemployment* (The Macmillan Company, New York, 1937), pp. 30–31.

[5]J. T. Dunlop, "The Movement of Real and Money Wage Rates," *Economic Journal*, 48 (September 1938), pp. 413–434.

more on the *level* of unemployment than upon the rate of change of unemployment, as Keynes had it. After the war, Singer,[6] Bronfenbrenner,[7] Haberler,[8] Brown,[9] Lerner,[10] and many others wrote that at low, albeit above-minimum, unemployment levels there occurs a process of "cost inflation," "wage-push inflation," "income inflation," "creeping inflation," "sellers' inflation," "dilemma inflation," or the "new inflation"—a phenomenon that was attributed to the discretionary power of unions or oligopolies or both to raise wages or prices or both without "excess demand."[11]

The customary attribution of cost inflation to the existence of such large economic units is unnecessary and insufficient. Like the theory of unemployment, the theory of cost inflation requires a non-Walrasian model in which there is no auctioneer continuously equilibrating commodity and labor markets. Beyond that, it is not clear to me what monopoly power contributes. An increase of monopoly power—due, say, to increased concentration—will raise prices relative to wages at any given unemployment rate and productivity level; but once, at the prevailing unemployment rate, the real wage has fallen (relative to productivity) enough to accommodate the higher markup; this process will stop and any continuation of inflation will depend on other sources.[12]

[6]H. W. Singer, "Wage Policy in Full Employment," *Economic Journal*, 62 (December 1947), pp. 438–455.

[7]M. Bronfenbrenner, "Postwar Political Economy: The President's Reports," *Journal of Political Economics*, 56 (October 1948), pp. 373–391.

[8]G. Haberler, "Causes and Cures of Inflation," *Review of Economics and Statistics*, 30 (February 1948), pp. 10–14.

[9]A. J. Brown, *The Great Inflation, 1939–51* (Oxford University Press, New York, 1955).

[10]A. P. Lerner, "Inflationary Depression and the Regulation of Administered Prices," in *The Relationship of Prices to Economic Stability and Growth*, compendium of papers submitted to panelists appearing before the Joint Economic Committee, 85th Congress, 2nd session (U.S. Government Printing Office, Washington, 1958).

[11]Quite distinct from ordinary cost inflation, though often confused with it, is the Jimmy Hoffa theory of inflation which finds the source of most inflations in the animal spirits of the largest union and corporation leaders. Wage-push theorists like S. Weintraub in his *A General Theory of the Price Level, Output, Income Distribution and Economic Growth* (Chilton Co., Philadelphia, 1959) treat inflation as almost spontaneous, virtually independent of the unemployment rate over any relevant range, and hence not induced by aggregate demand. An early paper of mine, "A Test for the Presence of Cost Inflation in the United States, 1955–57," *Yale Economic Essays*, 1 (Spring 1960), tested the hypothesis that the 1955–1957 inflation was more of this character than were the two earlier postwar inflations, making the assumption that autonomous "wage push" or "profit push" would be uneven in its sectoral incidence, so that the coefficient of correlation between sector price changes and sector output changes would (if the hypothesis were true) be algebraically smaller in the 1955–1957 period than it was earlier. It was algebraically smaller, but the statistical significance of the decline was impossible to determine. Incidentally, the paper by R. T. Selden, "Cost-Push versus Demand-Pull Inflation, 1955–57," *Journal of Political Economy*, 67 (February 1959), pp. 1–20, wrongly attributes significance to the positivity of the coefficient in 1955–1957 instead of to the magnitude of the decline.

[12]The answer of Ackley [G. Ackley, "The Contribution of Guidelines," in G. P. Shultz and R. Z. Aliber, eds., *Guidelines, Informal Controls, and the Market Place* (University of Chicago Press, Chicago, 1966)] and Lerner [A. P. Lerner, "Employment Theory and Employment Policy," *American Economic Review: Papers and Proceedings*, 57 (May

Similarly, the behavior of labor unions is not remotely sufficient to explain the cost inflation phenomenon. Whether the unions significantly exacerbate the problem—whether they increase that unemployment rate which is consistent with price stability—is, however, a difficult question. The affirmative answer frequently starts from the theory, set forth by Dunlop,[13] that a union, to maximize its utility, seeks to "trade off" the real wage rate against the unemployment of its members, raising the former (relative to productivity) until the gain from a further real wage increase is offset by the utility loss from the increase in unemployment expected to result from it. At an unemployment level below the unions' optimum, the unions then push up wage rates faster than productivity. But firms pass these higher costs on to consumers, so the real wage gains are frustrated, and as long as the government maintains the low unemployment level the rounds of inflation will continue.

I have trouble applying such a model to the American economy. Almost three quarters of the civilian labor force do not belong to unions. This fact casts doubt on the quantitative importance of the model. And perhaps the fact goes much deeper. If the union members whom the unions make unemployed have no good prospect of future union employment, they will be inclined to seek employment elsewhere. If, at the other extreme, the union unemployment is shared in the form of a short workweek, this unemployment—although real enough to the extent that members do not "moonlight"—does not add to the official unemployment rate as it is measured. Certainly the unions *participate* in the cost inflation process, and they may even increase a little the volume of unemployment consistent with price stability. But I should think that a union must offer its membership a frequency of employment opportunities that is roughly comparable to that elsewhere in order to thrive and that appreciably reduced employment opportunities require a greater wage differential between union and other employment than is commonly observed.[14]

Phillips' successful fitting of what we now call the Phillips curve[15] to a scatter diagram of historical British data deprived the discussions of some of their institutional color but neatly epitomized the new concept

---

1967), pp. 1–18] that, corresponding to every unemployment rate and productivity level, there is a natural real wage that is irreducible despite structural changes, so that money wages will keep pace with prices until unemployment is allowed to increase, seems to me to be terribly implausible. In any case, if this paper is right, cost inflation theory does not require any such "double monopoly" argument.

[13]J. T. Dunlop, *Wage Determination under Trade Unions* (A. M. Kelley, New York, 1950).

[14]It is certainly likely, however, that an *increase* of union power, even if localized, will raise the average money wage level at any constant unemployment rate. See A. G. Hines, "Trade Unions and Wage Inflation in the United Kingdom 1893–1961," *Review of Economic Studies*, 31 (October 1964), pp. 221–252.

[15]A. W. Phillips, "The Relation between Unemployment and the Rate of Change of Money Wage Rates in the United Kingdom, 1861–1957," *Economica*, 25 (November 1958), pp. 283–299.

of cost inflation—if by that term we mean (as I think most of the afore-mentioned writers intended) *that kind of inflation which can be stopped only by a reduction of the employment rate* through lower aggregate demand and which thus raises a cruel dilemma for fiscal and monetary policy.[16] The Phillips curve portrayed the rate of wage change as a continuous and decreasing function of the unemployment rate, with wage increases exceeding typical productivity growth at sufficiently low, albeit above-minimum, unemployment rates. Hence, if prices are tied to marginal or average costs, the smaller the level at which aggregate demand sets the unemployment rate, the greater is the *continuing* rate of inflation.

Strikingly, Phillips found that the nineteenth-century data pointed to a trade-off between wage increases and unemployment in the same way as contemporary data. Lipsey's sequel[17] showed a statistically significant Phillips curve relation for the subperiod 1861–1913. In fact, this early Phillips curve was *higher* (by about one percentage point) than the Phillips curve he fitted to the period 1929–1957.[18] Apparently the cost inflation tendency, if real, is not "new" in history; in Britain, anyway, it may be no worse than it used to be.

This paper will be addressed to two theoretical issues surrounding Phillips curves. The first topic is the microeconomic elaboration of the hypothesis that, *given expectations of general price and wage movements*, wage rates must *continue* to rise at a higher steady rate if a lower level of unemployment is to continue. It may be that such a theoretical contribution will swing the balance against neo-Keynesian (or more ob-scurely originating) contention that the steady-state Phillips "curve" is a flat line inasmuch as empirical investigations have not yet been widely persuasive. Though proponents of an American Phillips curve had tough sledding at first—numerous other variables were held to be impor-

---

[16]By contrast, in the pure "demand inflation" of Keynes and the classics, a reduction of the price trend could be achieved without cost to output and employment, because aggregate demand is necessarily superfluous to begin with. "Demand inflation" may be worth preserving, because a regime of "mixed inflation" is conceivable.

My earlier paper [E. S. Phelps, "A Test for the Presence of Cost Inflation in the United States 1955–57," *Yale Economic Essays*, 1 (Spring 1961), pp. 28–69] contains a fairly complete taxonomy of inflations [see also W. J. Fellner, "Demand Inflation, Cost Inflation, and Collective Bargaining," in P. D. Bradley, ed., *The Public Stake in Union Power* (University of Virginia Press, Charlottesville, Va., 1959]. Incidentally, the occasional definition of cost inflation as an autonomous upward shift of the Phillips curve is very awkward and does not imply the "policy dilemma" with which inflation analysts were concerned in the 1950s.

[17]R. G. Lipsey, "The Relation between Unemployment and the Rate of Change of Money Wage Rates in the United Kingdom, 1862–1957: A Further Analysis," *Economica*, 27 (February 1960), pp. 1–31.

[18]At a constant price level and an unemployment rate of 2 percent, Lipsey's (*op. cit.*) 1862–1913 regression (his equation [10]) predicts a 2.58 percent wage increase annually' while the 1929–1957 regression (his equation [13]) predicts a 1.65 percent annual increase. At the same 3 percent productivity growth in both periods, for example, price stability would have permitted smaller unemployment in the latter period. But Lipsey's Table 2 (p. 30) is evidence of the early Phillips curve's underestimation of the wage increases after World War II.

tant[19]—Perry's synthesis[20] of much of this early work did leave a quantitatively important role for the unemployment rate (as well as for the profit rate and the rate of change of prices) in explaining money wage movements in U.S. manufacturing. But in 1963 Bowen and Berry[21] found that the *decrease* of the unemployment rate was far more important than the level of the unemployment rate in contributing to wage increases. The more recent study of annual long-term wage data by Rees and Hamilton[22] also showed a negligible (and statistically insignificant) relation between the steady-state unemployment rate and the rate of wage increase (though wage-change effects on prices feed back strongly on wages in their equation). This evidence strongly supports the neo-Keynesian revival led by Sargan[23] and Kuh,[24] who make the level of the unemployment rate, together with productivity and the price level, determine the *level* of the money wage.[25] The underlying theory is apparently that a rise of aggregate demand creates "bottlenecks" and hence a rise of wage rates in certain areas and skills at the same time that it increases employment; once these bottlenecks have melted away and employment has reached its new and higher level there is no longer upward wage pressure. On this theory, money-wage increases go hand in hand with employment growth and not intrinsically with a high level of the employment rate.

Less frontal in a way but having equally profound policy implications is the second issue of the so-called stability of the Phillips curve. Continental economists like von Mises[26] always emphasized the role of expectations in the inflationary process. In our own day, Fellner and Wallich are most closely associated with the proposition that the maintenance of too low an unemployment rate and the resulting continued

---

[19]W. G. Bowen, *Wage Behavior in the Postwar Period* (Industrial Relations Sec., Princeton, N.J., 1960); R. J. Bhatia, "Profits and the Rate of Change of Money Earnings in the United States, 1935–1959," *Economica*, 29 (August 1962), pp. 255–262; and O. Eckstein and T. Wilson, "The Determinants of Money Wages in American Industry," *Quarterly Journal of Economics*, 70 (August 1962), pp. 379–414.

[20]G. L. Perry, "The Determinants of Wage Rate Changes and the Inflation-Unemployment Trade-off for the U.S.," *Review of Economic Studies*, 31 (October 1964), pp. 287–308.

[21]W. G. Bowen and R. A. Berry, "Unemployment Conditions and Movements of the Money Wage Level," *Review of Economics and Statistics*, 45 (May 1963), pp. 163–172.

[22]A. Rees and M. T. Hamilton, "The Wage-Price-Productivity Perplex," *Journal of Political Economics*, 75 (February 1967), pp. 63–70.

[23]J. D. Sargan, "Wages and Prices in the United Kingdom: A Study in Econometric Methodology," in P. E. Hart, G. Mills, and J. K. Whitaker, eds., *Econometric Analysis for Economic Planning: Sixteenth Symposium of the Colston Research Society* (Butterworth, London, 1964).

[24]E. Kuh, "A Productivity Theory of Wage Levels—An Alternative to the Phillips Curve," *Review of Economic Studies*, 34 (October 1967).

[25]If the *real* wage rate were made a rapidly increasing function of the employment rate, the Kuh–Sargan model could then produce (cost) inflation at low, yet above-minimum, unemployment rates.

[26]L. von Mises, *The Theory of Money and Credit* (Yale University Press, New Haven 1953).

revision of disappointed expectations will cause a runaway inflation. These ideas are reflected in the modern-day models of steady, "anticipated" inflation, begun by Lerner,[27] which imply (or assume) that high inflation confers no benefits in the form of higher employment if (or as soon as) the inflation rate is fully anticipated by firms and workers.[28] Recently, Friedman[29] and I[30] have sought to reconcile the Phillips hypothesis with the aforementioned axiom of anticipated inflation theory. I postulated that the Phillips curve, in terms of percentage price increase (or wage increase), shifts uniformly upward by one point with every one point increase of the expected percentage price increase (or expected wage increase). Then the *equilibrium* unemployment rate—the rate at which the actual and expected price increases (or wage increases) are equal— is independent of the rate of inflation. If one further postulates, as Friedman and I did, an "adaptive" or "error-correcting" theory of expectations, then the persistent underestimation of price or wage increases which would result from an unemployment level consistently below the equilibrium rate would cause expectations continually to be revised upward so that the rate of inflation would gradually increase without limit; correspondingly, an increase of the *constant* rate of inflation, while "buying" a very low unemployment rate at first, would require a gradual rise of the unemployment rate toward the equilibrium rate as expectations of that inflation developed. Therefore, society cannot trade between steady unemployment and steady inflation, on this theory; it must eventually drive (or allow) the unemployment rate toward the equilibrium level or force it to fluctuate around that equilibrium level.[31]

[27]A. P. Lerner, "The Inflationary Process—Some Theoretical Aspects," *Review of Economics and Statistics*, 31 (August 1949), pp. 193–200.

[28]Lerner ("Employment Theory and Economic Policy") now recants. My paper, "Anticipated Inflation and Economic Welfare," *Journal of Political Economy*, 73 (February 1965), pp. 1–17, contains many of the references. Two recent money-and-growth models which study the consequences of alternative anticipated price trends are those by J. Tobin, "Money and Economic Growth," *Econometrica*, 33 (October 1965), pp. 671–684, and M. Sidrauski, "Rational Choice and Patterns of Growth in a Monetary Economy," *American Economic Review: Papers and Proceedings*, 57 (May 1967), pp. 534–544.

[29]M. Friedman, "Comment," in G. P. Shultz and R. Z. Aliber, eds., *Guidelines, Informal Controls, and the Market Place* (University of Chicago Press, Chicago, 1966).

[30]E. S. Phelps, "Phillips Curves, Expectations of Inflation and Optimal Unemployment over Time," *Economica*, 34 (August 1967), pp. 254–281.

[31]On certain assumptions regarding preferences and other matters, I showed that society (or the world) would choose between an "overemployment" route *down* to the equilibrium employment rate (thus leaving a heritage of a high Phillips curve corresponding to inflationary expectations) and an "underemployment" route *up* to the equilibrium employment rate on the basis of "time preference." The role of time preference is illuminated by Friedman's characterization of "the true trade-off" (*op. cit.*, p. 59) as one between "unemployment today and unemployment at a later date"; there is such an intertemporal trade-off in the model under discussion if one holds eventual inflation rates constant, in the same way that the Fisherian trade-off between consumption today and consumption tomorrow holds subsequent wealth or capital constant. But there remains at any moment of time a statical trade-off between unemployment and inflation (with the expected inflation rate a parameter), analogous to the statical trade-off between consumption and capital formation (with initial capital stock a parameter), which lies at the roots of the intertemporal trade-off.

This paper is addressed primarily to these two issues. The next section sketches the microeconomic lines of a modified excess-demand theory of disequilibrium wage movements. This is subsequently coupled to a model of employment dynamics to show why, given expectations, both the level of unemployment *and* the rate of change of employment should be expected to be correlated with money wage movements. The last section introduces the influence of expected wage changes upon the Phillips curve.

2
TURNOVER AND "GENERALIZED EXCESS DEMAND"

For most of this section, until labor unions are fitted into the framework developed, the analysis will be confined to an "atomistic" labor market. This means that there is no collective bargaining between unions and firms. It will also be supposed that each worker is a "wage-taker."

But the labor market here is not perfectly competitive. I exclude any Walrasian auctioneer who, by collecting information on everyone's supply and demand data, might be capable of keeping the labor market in a full information, full employment equilibrium. Lacking anyone else to do so, each firm must set its own wage rates. Because suppliers of labor lack detailed information about each firm's wage rates, the individual firm has *dynamic monopsony power*: Given its other recruitment efforts, such as help-wanted advertising, the higher the wage rates it sets relative to other firms' wage rates, the faster will it attract labor. The effect of such a wage differential is "dynamic" and gradual because the diffusion of the wage information through the market takes time.[32] In a world where lives are short and information costs are high, the firm may have to pay a permanently higher wage differential the greater the employment force it wishes to sustain; but such *statical* monopsony power is not critical to the analysis that follows.[33]

The incompleteness of information arises partially from the diversity of economic experience. Even if jobs and workers were "technically" homogeneous—that is, even if every worker were to regard all firms

[32]Somewhat similarly, if the firm allows its wage rates to fall relative to what workers believe average wage rates to be, it will not expect to lose all its workers instantaneously. Some employees may engage in on-the-job search for a better paid job before quitting. The expected duration of the fall of the differential is also a factor, one not included in the formal model.

[33]At one point, in the discussion of quit rates, it is useful to appeal to incomplete information in another dimension. Some firms may ration jobs much of the time, turning away workers who would be willing to accept jobs at wage rates below those paid to its employed workers. In this event, the worker will lack complete information not only about the wage rates that each firm is paying but also about the availability of jobs at each firm.

and jobs as identical in their nonpecuniary rewards and every firm were to regard all workers as productively equivalent—the presence of ever-changing product-demand shifts, nonuniform technological progress, or uneven labor-force growth would suffice to produce some dispersion in wage rates. Workers recognize, then, that their own experience with wage offers is not to be projected to other workers and other firms. Hence workers may reject wage offers, accepting unemployment in order more easily to search for better wage offers. The expectation of dispersion of wage rates by suppliers of labor causes positive unemployment to be normal.

The existence of unemployment need not spell deflation of this world. Because the demand for labor is normally growing, owing to productivity growth and because employed workers are always retiring, quitting, or dying, firms will normally be seeking to add new employees at some positive rate. When unemployed workers are sufficiently few, the firm cannot succeed in attracting new employees unless it keeps up its wage rate relative to workers' expectations of other wage rates. Only if there were complete information, so that unemployed workers would instantaneously find the best wage and in so doing bid it down, would positive unemployment—when it fleetingly appeared— necessarily drive money wage rates to lower levels.

The time that firms require to attract new employees, even when there is some unemployment, is reflected by the presence, normally, of job "vacancies." A firm may be said to have job vacancies when the quantity of labor that it would decide to employ (at the expected average wage) *if there were complete information*—i.e., no need for capital-type information outlays in the form of temporarily higher wage rates, help-wanted advertising, and so on for the acquisition of labor—exceeds the quantity of labor it in fact has on hand under the actual informational conditions. Where vacancies are especially large, firms will pay wage rates above the expected average wage rate elsewhere. The finding of these wage rates by some of the unemployed helps to remove workers from the unemployment pool as new workers enter it; unemployed workers are not systematically and invariably disappointed and thus not led invariably to revise downward their asking wage rates. Secondly, the firm that pays a wage equal to the expected average wage elsewhere, because it is "at rest," content with attracting its "fair share" from the unemployed pool and from other firms, also has vacancies on the above definition. When the firm is "at rest," it would still gain from the free delivery of some additional employees (up to the zero vacancy point) even if each had to be paid the firm's estimate of the average wage but it does not aim to fill those vacancies because of the interest cost of the capital-type outlays it believes to be required. Positivity of vacancies, even for the representative firm in normal times, like the positivity of unemployment in normal times, signalizes the cost to both employer and worker of reaching one another under incomplete information.[34]

Yet, if jobs and workers were technically homogeneous, information costs would be less important than this paper takes them to be. Firms could cheaply announce their daily wage rates in the "wage offers" section of the local newspaper. Workers could thus sample a great many wage rates each day without giving up employment to do so. At a small subscription fee, one could read weekly newsletters from employment advisory services that would digest regional wage movements and perhaps make "go," "leave," or "stay" recommendations about various regions. Information tends to be a great deal more imperfect when there is considerable technical variety among jobs and among workers. The typical firm with heterogeneous labor requirements then has to generate more wage information to achieve the same recruitment performance. Moreover, wage information may travel more slowly if it is of only specialized interest.[35] A more important kind of heterogeneity is intra-"job." The nonpecuniary attributes of jobs in a certain category usually differ from firm to firm. In each job category, abilities and skills differ from worker to worker. As a consequence, interviewing is important and "search unemployment" is more valuable. Wage rates may be confidential, varying with the worker, so that the worker's information about alternative wage opportunities may be as seriously imperfect as his information about the nonpecuniary attributes of alternative jobs.

Analogous to the distinction between the "cost" and availability of credit is a distinction between the wage and the availability of jobs. "Job rationing" occurs when a worker is unable to find work at a firm despite his willingness to work for less than some already employed worker who is broadly like him in ability and skill. One reason, in part, why job rationing is prevalent is that workers want the promise of a degree of tenure in their jobs at the wage initially offered. They prefer this because there are frequently setup costs incurred by the individual in taking a new job, such as moving expenses; many, perhaps all, of these setup costs can be viewed as arising from the heterogeneity of jobs. By protecting workers from underbidding for the length of a

[34]One could, it is true, redefine vacancies in such a way that one nets out from marginal revenue productivity of labor the costs of holding employment at the firm constant relative to the firm's capital stock or to the total labor force so that vacancies are zero at the firm's "rest point," its steady-state target position. Similarly, one could define unemployment as the excess of unemployment above the "equilibrium" or "natural" level. For analyses of wage-marginal product relations at and away from the rest point, see the papers by Mortensen and by Phelps and Winter in this volume. See also Appendix 2.

[35]On the other hand, there may exist informational networks, formal or informal, among workers specializing in a certain job category; the sparseness of jobs in a certain category does not by itself raise the costs of sampling the corresponding wage offers to workers specializing in those categories, because the specialists may know where those offers are. But when rates are unacceptable in his otherwise preferred job category, many a worker will sometimes explore less familiar job categories where wage offers are not so easy for him to find.

"contract," the firm can normally enjoy wage savings, over the long run, compared to a policy that exposes its workers to the risk of wage fluctuations from underbidding. The second reason for job-rationing is the firm's preference for a predictable employment force (as distinct from the worker's preference for a more predictable wage). If the firm attempts to jiggle wage rates rapidly in accordance with changes in the supply of workers available to it or in its needs for workers, it will risk unexpectedly large quits in the case of wage reductions. The risk is costly because of the setup costs of hiring, rehiring, training, or retraining heterogeneous workers. The firm may find it expected-profit maximizing to delay the adjustment of its wage in response to changing supplies and demands, relying first, on refusal to hire and, second, on layoffs for "fine tuning" when buffer stocks of labor become too large.[36]

It is clear, then, that positive unemployment and positive vacancies can coexist and persist for every type of worker and job. In the more formal analysis that follows, I shall exclude serious bottlenecks in any job category in order to speak aggregatively of "the" wage rate, "the" unemployment rate, and "the" vacancy rate, as if these such statistics were pretty much uniform over the categories of workers and jobs. The focus will be on the wage decisions and employment experience of "representative" firms—that is, some average of the population of firms.

The labor supply, L, is defined as the sum of unemployed and employed workers. Letting N denote the number of persons employed, and U the number of persons unemployed, we have

$$L = N + U. \tag{1}$$

It will be supposed throughout that the size of this labor supply is a constant at each moment of time, independent of all prices, present and future, actual and expected, and independent of the availability of jobs. Because unemployed workers, by this supposition, prefer work to leisure whatever the expected average real wage, we shall identify the unemployed as consisting of those actively searching for job offers acceptable to them.

Total labor demand, N_D, is defined as the number of workers that firms would accept for employment if an indefinitely large number of workers offered to work indefinitely at the wage rates that firms believe to be the going or average wage, given expected product prices, present and future, and expected real interest rates. N_D depends upon the technology, the currently expected "product wage" (net of interest and "depreciation" on the investment outlays incurred in processing and training a new employee and calculated at the firm's planned

---

[36]In this variant of the non-Walrasian treatment of labor market, cyclical money wage increases represent to some degree the movement of workers to higher-paid (or, at any rate, preferred) job categories.

product price), and, if the firm's price is fixed so as to generate inventories and queues, directly upon aggregate demand as well. Then, with jobs filled equal to the number of persons employed (no multiple job holding or part-time jobs), job vacancies, V, are given by

$$N_D = N + V. \tag{2}$$

The concept of "excess demand" for labor, denoted X, is usually defined as

$$X = N_D - L. \tag{3}$$

Hence, using (1) and (2),

$$X = V - U. \tag{4}$$

The usual excess-demand theory of money wage dynamics states that the proportionate rate of change of the money wage is proportional to the excess demand *rate*, denoted x. The latter is excess demand per unit of labor supply, and hence equal to the excess of the vacancy rate, v, over the unemployment rate, u:

$$x = v - u, \quad x = \frac{X}{L}, \quad v = \frac{V}{L}, \quad u = \frac{U}{L}. \tag{5}$$

A widespread rationale for the simple Phillips curve relation between wage change and the unemployment rate is that, at least in sectors or economies with little or no unionization, the unemployment rate is a good proxy for the excess-demand rate and that the latter largely explains wage movements (apart from aggregation phenomena such as changes in the employment mix). Even if excess demand were the sole determinant of wage changes—this paper seeks to generalize that theory and to make it accommodate the influence of expectations—it is not obvious that the unemployment rate is a good proxy for it. What if, at times, the vacancy rate in (5) enjoys a life of its own, moving independently of the unemployment rate? (I shall later discuss the evidence on this.) Lipsey's paper brilliantly deduces from a model of employment dynamics a well-behaved relationship between the vacancy rate (hence the excess-demand rate) and the *steady* unemployment rate. I shall show, however, using a similar model, that in the non-steady-state case the unemployment rate is an inadequate indicator of the excess-demand rate and that the rate of change of employment constitutes an essential additional indicator for inferring the excess-demand rate.[37]

---

[37]These two points can perhaps be understood simply from the following exercise: Draw a nonnegatively sloped labor-supply curve and a nonpositively sloped labor-demand curve in a Marshallian plane with the expected product wage on the vertical axis and units of labor on the horizontal axis. Consider now the locus of points corresponding to a given unemployment rate; this iso-unemployment-rate curve will lie to the left of the supply curve and will also be nonnegatively sloped. It is immediately obvious that if the

The excess-demand explanation of wage movements calls for an underlying explanation. Why should it be expected that a one-unit increase of the vacancy rate always has the same wage effect as a one-unit decrease of the unemployment rate? Second, why should it be expected that most of the time, in the neighborhood of "equilibrium" (see Section 4), vacancies will equal unemployment and that a *disequilibrium* rise of wage rates requires vacancies to exceed unemployment? Why should unemployment have an effect? Why vacancies?

What follows is an attempt to rationalize a generalized excess-demand theory of money wage movements, one which is less restrictive than the simple excess-demand theory but which admits it as a special case, at least in steady states. It will be convenient to conduct the analysis in two stages: In the present section, "static" expectations of future money wage rates and product prices are postulated. By that is meant, loosely, that firms and workers expect that the average money wage prevailing in the near future will not differ from its present level or its level in the recent past, and similarly for prices. This does not mean, of course, that firms and workers do not revise over time their estimates of the past or present wage level as they observe or infer actual wage rates through time. In Section 4 the expected rate of change of the wage level will be allowed to differ from zero and to adapt to estimates of past rates of change.

We begin with the case in which each firm reviews its wage rate periodically—once a year, say. An equal number of firms, of the same average size, set wage rates each day throughout the year. This staggering of wage revisions makes the average wage move smoothly despite discrete changes in the determinants of each firm's optimal wage. The postulate that the "expected rate of wage change" is zero is most conveniently interpreted in this case as the proportionate difference between the expected average money wage one-half year hence (or over the next twelve months on average) and people's estimates of the average money wage one-half year ago (or over the past twelve months on average). The expected rate of change is thus "centered" on the current moment. In this model there is no need to suppose that events

---

demand curve is negatively sloped, or the supply curve positively sloped, then not all points on the locus represent equal algebraic excess demand; in particular, as we move down this locus from its intersection with the demand curve, vacancies and excess demand increase despite constancy of the unemployment rate. Thus the latter is not necessarily a sufficient proxy for excess demand. (This demonstration in no way contradicts the proposition that, *vacancy rate constant*, excess demand is decreasing in unemployment. The zero-vacancy, on-the-demand-curve case is a familiar example. This paper tries to get away from the supposition that we are always "on the demand curve," even the Keynesian demand curve arising from disequilibrium excess supply in commodity markets.)

As we consider situations of higher vacancies, the unemployment rate unchanged, we should expect the rate of increase of employment likewise to be higher, as employers seek to reduce vacancies through greater recruitment. The *two* pieces of information—the unemployment rate, and the rate of increase of employment—may together constitute a satisfactory proxy, or a better proxy, for excess demand.

can cause people currently to misestimate the latter, past-average money wage level; even the current *average* money wage may be correctly estimated at the current time. But the possibility, in the model, that the average wage will steadily rise or steadily fall, together with the static expectations postulate, implies that the "expected rate of wage change" can differ from the actual rate of wage change.[38] The average wage six months hence may be misforecast. (I shall subsequently discuss briefly the case in which firms review wage rates continuously. In that limiting case, misestimation of the *current* average wage level does the work of misestimation of the average wage *one-half year hence* in the model with periodic wage setting.)

Consider the ith firm at wage-setting time. It will be convenient to express its optimal wage in terms of the proportionate differential it desires to have, say Δ_i^*, between its wage and the average money wage it expects to be paid elsewhere. That is,

$$\Delta_i^* \equiv \frac{w_i^* - w^e}{w^e}, \tag{6}$$

where w_i^* is the firm's optimal wage and w^e is the average wage it expects to prevail one-half year hence. It will be supposed that workers and other firms, on average, have the same expectation of the future wage level, it being equal to their estimate of the mean wage one-half year ago.

One determinant of the desired wage differential is the firm's vacancies, V_i, calculated at the expected product wage, w^e/p, where p is the product price. An increase in the number of vacancies due either to a fall of the expected product wage or to a fall of the firm's current employment causes the firm to raise its desired differential in order to discourage quitting, to facilitate recruitment, and to encourage workers to seek employment at the firm as they learn of the higher differential.[39] A larger proportion of those who sample the firm's wage are more likely to accept employment or to stay employed at the firm the higher is this differential; and a larger number of workers are likely to learn of the firm's wage and accept employment there the higher that differential. The magnitude of the desired differential corresponding to the number of vacancies depends upon the size of the unemployment rate, u, and the size of the total labor supply, L.

The role of the unemployment rate in the determination of the desired differential is more problematical. An increase of the un-

---

[38]This is the case studied in the previous version of this paper. See, especially, pages 688 and 698.

[39]It is supposed that new and old workers receive the same wage. The two sources of an increase of vacancies need not have precisely the same effect, so that the firm's current employment, N_i, should be allowed to have some effect, positive or negative, on the desired differential even for given V_i. This effect is neglected here.

employment rate eases recruitment at every wage differential the firm might set. This is because there will then be a larger flow to the firm of unemployed workers seeking acceptable employment; employed workers are not able to sample wage and employment opportunities as intensively as the unemployed. Neglecting quit rates for the moment, we conclude that the firm can achieve the same rate of increase of employment with a smaller wage differential the larger is the un- employment rate[40]; at the other extreme, the firm can have, for the same differential, a faster increase of its employment. It will be supposed that the firm "takes out" the gain in part through a lower wage differential, though not so low that there is no increase in the current growth of the firm's employment.

When there is job rationing, the unemployment rate will influence the quit rate experienced by the firm, which, in turn, is likely to affect the firm's desired wage differential. A decrease of the unemployment rate, given the overall vacancy rate in the economy, causes employees to expect to have to spend less time in the unemployment pool if they decide to seek a job opening elsewhere and thus encourages quitting. An increase of the quit rate corresponding to any wage will increase the wage differential the firm expects to require to maintain its employment force or to add to it at any given rate. It will be supposed that the firm responds to this situation with some increase of the wage differential, though not so much as to prevent some increase of quitting. Finally, the quit rate and, thereby, the wage differential will be affected in the same way by an increase of the overall vacancy rate in the economy, because the unemployment rate and vacancy rate together affect the mean duration of unemployment expected by anyone contemplating quitting and also the probability that employees will find job openings at other firms.

The above hypotheses state that

$$\Delta_i^* = j^i(u, v, V_i, L), \qquad j_1^i < 0, \quad j_2^i > 0, \quad j_3^i > 0. \qquad (7)$$

It will be convenient to think of each firm as expanding its capital stock in proportion to the growing labor force in which case *relative* vacancies, v_i, indicates better the strength of the firm's desire for a faster (or slower) rate of growth of its employment force. If we neglect any informational economies of scale from a populous economy, we may then write

$$\Delta_i^* = k^i(u, v, v_i), \quad k_1^i < 0, \quad k_2^i > 0, \quad k_3^i > 0, \quad v_i = \frac{V_i}{L}. \qquad (8)$$

If all firms are much alike, we can express the *average* desired wage differential, denoted Δ^*, as a function of the unemployment rate and

---

[40]This is true for the indefinite future only to the extent that lifetimes are short enough that wage discrepancies can persist.

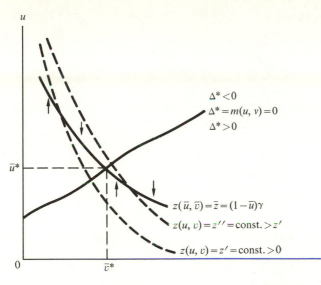

Figure 1. Relations between vacancy and unemployment rates.

of the aggregate vacancy rate, $v = \sum v_i$ [as given in (5)]:

$$\Delta^* = m(u, v), \qquad u, v > 0, \tag{9}$$

where

$$m_1 < 0, \qquad m_2 > 0 \tag{9a}$$

and, as conjectures,

$$m_{11} \gtreqless 0, \quad m_{22} \gtreqless 0, \quad m_{12} \lesseqgtr 0. \tag{9b}$$

The restrictions on the second derivatives in (9b) are inessential; they affect only the curvature of the augmented Phillips curve to be derived. The inequality $m_{11} \geqq 0$, meaning that Δ^* decreases with the unemployment rate at a nonincreasing rate, vacancy rate constant, is plausible if the quit rate is likewise convex with respect to the unemployment rate.[41] The inequality $m_{22} \geqq 0$ is suggested by the hypothesis of "rising marginal costs" to the firm of filling vacancies by means other than raising its wage differential. Finally $m_{12} \leqq 0$ makes sense if it takes a larger increase of the firm's wage differential to facilitate the filling of some fraction of a given increment in its vacancies the smaller is the unemployment pool from which workers can conveniently be drawn. The curve labeled $m(u, v) = 0$ in Figure 1 gives the combinations of u and v that makes $\Delta^* = 0$. Its slope, being $-m_2/m_1$, is necessarily positive, but the size of that slope and the curvature are indeterminate and of no qualitative consequence. To the right of this locus $\Delta^* > 0$, and to the left $\Delta^* < 0$.

[41] R. V. Eagly, "Market Power as an Intervening Mechanism in Phillips Curve Analysis," *Economica*, 32 (February 1965), pp. 48–64.

Finally, it will be argued that, approximately, the rate of change of the average wage rate, w, is proportional to Δ^*:

$$\frac{\dot{w}}{w} = \lambda\Delta^*, \quad \lambda = \text{const.} > 0, \quad \dot{w} \equiv \frac{dw}{dt}. \tag{10}$$

It is clear that, in the present model of staggered wage setting, if Δ^* has been zero for some time and w has been level for some time, then w will go on being level if Δ^* remains equal to zero. If Δ^* should rise, then, with w^e the same as it was when firms last set their wage rates, firms setting wage rates today will raise their wage rates; the average wage will therefore gradually rise as more firms reach the respective dates of the year on which they reset their wage rates. At first the instantaneous rate of change of the average wage, expressed at an annual rate, will equal Δ^* (under uniform staggering). But soon resetting will be done by firms who have noticed the average wage at the midpoint of the expiring annual contract (i.e., the average wage six months ago) to be higher than the corresponding average wage when these firms previously set their wages, and *hence higher than these firms at that time expected the midcontract average wage would be.* Consequently, these firms must add a "catch-up" wage increase to the increase they would have otherwise found sufficient to obtain the increase in their desired wage differential. The average money wage will soon tend on this account to rise faster. But there is an offsetting and stabilizing tendency: The basic wage increases will have been completed by all the firms within a "year," so only the catch-up increases remain. As the current average wage grows faster, the catch-up wage increase by firms currently raising wages makes a smaller proportionate contribution to the rise of the current average wage because this increase is based on wage observations that are centered around some past time when the average wage was lower, and because the static-expectations assumption allows no extrapolation of the prevailing wage growth. Consequently, there exists a finite, asymptotic rate of wage increase corresponding to every positive Δ^*. Further, the asymptotic $\dot{w}/w$ is well approximated by (10) over the relevant range. These propositions are demonstrated in Appendix 1. We will not go too far wrong in using (10) in and out of steady states in which u, v, and w/w^e are all constant.

One can explore the *dynamics* of the rate of wage change more conveniently if we consider a model of continuous wage setting. We retain the assumption of static expectations regarding the future trend of the average wage. Suppose, a little analogously to the staggered wage-setting model, that each firm's expectation of the current average wage level, denoted w^e, depends upon past actual values of the average wage, this time in the "adaptive" manner. Second, to maintain smoothness in wage behavior, let the ith firm adjust its wage in such a way that its expected wage differential, denoted by Δ_i^e, moves only gradually toward its "desired" differential, Δ_i^*.[42] Precisely, assume that

$$\dot{\Delta}_i^e = \mu(\Delta_i^* - \Delta_i^e), \qquad \mu > 0, \qquad \dot{\Delta}_i^e \equiv \frac{d\Delta_i^e}{dt}, \qquad (10'a)$$

where

$$\Delta_i^e \equiv \frac{w_i - w_e}{w^e}, \qquad \Delta_i^* \equiv \frac{w_i^* - w^e}{w^e}$$

and assume that [43]

$$(\dot{w}^e) = \lambda(w - w^e), \qquad \lambda > 0. \qquad (10'b)$$

Then, upon expressing the derivative $\dot{\Delta}_i^e$ in terms of $\dot{w}_i$ and $(\dot{w}^e)$ and solving for $\dot{w}_i$ we find

$$\frac{\dot{w}_i}{w_i} = \mu\left(\frac{\Delta_i^* - \Delta_i^e}{1 + \Delta_i^e}\right) + \frac{(\dot{w}^e)}{w^e},$$

where the last term is the continuous-time "catch-up" wage increase. For firms as a whole, using the adaptive-expectations relation, we then have

$$\frac{\dot{w}}{w} = \mu\left(\frac{\Delta^* - \Delta^e}{1 + \Delta^e}\right) + \lambda\Delta^e.$$

The dynamics of Δ^e, and hence of $\dot{w}/w$, is analyzed for a given Δ^* in Figure 2, where the state variable is $w/w^e = 1 + \Delta^e$. From the relation

$$\frac{(\dot{w/w^e})}{w/w^e} = \frac{\dot{w}}{w} - \frac{(\dot{w}^e)}{w^e} = \mu\left(\frac{1 + \Delta^*}{w/w^e} - 1\right)$$

it follows that w/w^e approaches $1 + \Delta^*$ monotonically. In any steady state (constant Δ^e), therefore, $\Delta^e = \Delta^*$, which means that, in steady states, all the wage increases are purely "catch up." Denoting steady-state values of variables with a bar, we have

$$\frac{\bar{\dot{w}}}{w} = \lambda\bar{\Delta}^e = \lambda\Delta^*,$$

corresponding to any steady-state $m(\bar{u}, \bar{v})$. Out of the steady state, $\lambda\Delta^*$ may still be a good approximation. If $\mu = \lambda$, $\dot{w}/w$ varies little with

---

[42]One defense of this device is that the firm may choose Δ_i^e according to estimates of the "permanent," "normal," or "near-term average," u^e, v^e, and v_i^e, and that the latter are revised adaptively in response to current u, v, and v_i.

[43]The term $(\dot{w}^e)$ means the historical time rate of change of the expected (current) wage *level*, w^e. It must be distinguished from the currently *expected rate of change* over the future of the expected wage level. The latter is zero by virtue of the assumption of static expectations.

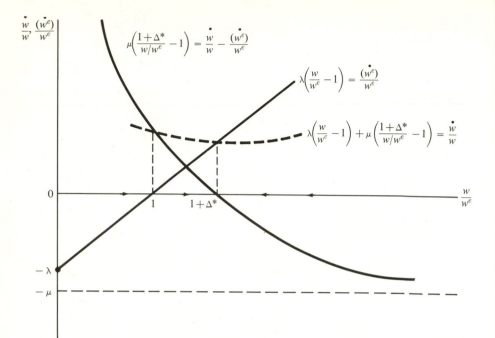

Figure 2.   Dynamics of expected wage differential and rate of wage change given Δ*.

Δ^e for small Δ^e. The direct influence of an increase of Δ^*, given Δ^e, upon the rate of wage increase wears off, but the resulting rise of Δ^e produces catch-up increases that replace that direct influence. Note, finally, that the finiteness of λ is crucial for the boundedness of $(\dot{w}/w)$. Section 4 will introduce a more general formulation of expectations.

Equations (9) and (10) constitute a generalized excess-demand theory of the rate of wage change when the expected rate of wage change is equal to zero. When $m(\cdot)$ takes the form $v - u$, we have the simple excess-demand theory: $\dot{w}/w = \lambda x$. But the theory is not closed, because u and v cannot go their own separate directions. It is desirable to add a theory of the effect of v on the path taken by u. Section 3 couples the above wage-change model with a theory of employment dynamics built upon some labor-turnover ideas of Lipsey (*loc. cit.*). The result is some implications for "momentary" relationships between unemployment and the rate of change of wage rates.

3
DERIVATION OF A MOMENTARY, AUGMENTED PHILLIPS CURVE

The absolute time rate of increase of the total number of persons employed, denoted $\dot{N} \equiv dN/dt$, consists of the number of persons hired per unit time from the unemployment pool, denoted R, less the departures (due to death and retirement) per unit time of employed persons from the labor force, denoted D, and the quitting of employees to join the unemployed in search of new jobs, denoted Q. This accounting ignores involuntary terminations and layoffs, which I shall not treat, and it assumes that entrants to the labor force first enter the unemployment pool before being hired. Of course, the accessions and separations of employed persons who transfer directly from one firm to another cancel out and do not add to $\dot{N}$. That is,

$$\dot{N} = R - D - Q. \tag{11}$$

I shall make the aggregate variables on the right-hand side of (11) depend only upon unemployment (or employment), vacancies, and the labor supply.

D will be made proportional to employment, δ being the factor of proportionality. To eliminate scale effects, I shall take new hires and quits to be homogeneous of degree one in unemployment, vacancies, and the labor supply. Hence

$$\dot{N} = R(U, V, L) - \delta N - Q(U, V, L),$$
$$R(U, V, L) = LR(u, v, 1), \qquad Q(U, V, L) = LQ(u, v, 1). \tag{12}$$

Equivalently, defining $z \equiv \dot{N}/L$,

$$z = R(u, v, 1) - \delta(1 - u) - Q(u, v, 1) = z(u, v), \qquad u, v > 0, \tag{13}$$

where I shall argue

$$z_1 > 0, \qquad z_2 > 0 \tag{13a}$$

and, more conjecturally,

$$-z_2^{-2}\left\{\left[z_{11} + z_{12}\left(\frac{-z_1}{z_2}\right)\right]z_2 - \left[z_{21} + z_{22}\left(\frac{-z_1}{z_2}\right)\right]z_1\right\} > 0. \tag{13b}$$

Thus the absolute rate of change of employment per unit labor supply is made a function of the same two variables that determine Δ^* and in so doing influence the rate of wage change.

What is the logic of the z function, in particular the role of the vacancy rate in that function? We ordinarily think of the level of labor input as determined by output, which in turn depends upon aggregate demand and productivity. There probably is a fairly tight relationship between man-hours and output (given productivity); but N is measured by the number of persons employed. In a labor market that is at least moderately tight, an increase of aggregate demand increases job vacancies. Firms respond initially to the increase of vacancies by lengthening hours worked per worker (including overtime), by more intensive use of "buffer" or "cushion" employees ("hoarded" labor), and by calls for extraordinary efforts on the part of employees. But these measures do not eliminate the job vacancies. Filling the additional vacancies requires finding additional employees, and finding new employees to fill new jobs takes time.[44] Firms will choose to take time for two reasons: because marginal recruitment costs are positive, it may pay the firm to wait for suitable persons to present themselves for employment; and because there may be "rising marginal recruitment costs,"[45] it will pay the firm to smooth its recruitment efforts over time.

Now the properties of the z function. In discussing the mechanisms by which u and v affect z, I shall rely primarily on the notion that firms, even in the aggregate, can shorten the duration of search unemployment, and thus add to employment, by intensifying nonwage recruitment efforts and by offering a larger "ration" of jobs.

It will be assumed that, the unemployment rate constant, the higher the vacancy rate, the greater is the rate at which firms will acquire unemployed workers; that is, $R_2 > 0$. A higher vacancy rate will induce more intensive recruitment, and it will increase the probability that any unemployed person contacting a firm will find a job open. This increase of accessions may itself induce more quits, as suggested in the paragraph preceding (6), so that $Q_2 > 0$ is possible. But it would be strange to find that the higher vacancy rate reduced employment growth on balance; any increase of quits will stimulate partially offsetting extra recruiting. Hence I postulate that $R_2 > Q_2 \geqq 0$, so that $z_2 = R_2 - Q_2 > 0$, for all u and v.

Clearly $R_1 > 0$ because, vacancy rate constant, the higher the unemployment rate, the greater is the flow to the firm of unemployed workers who can fill open jobs and the easier is recruitment. Since an increase of unemployment discourages quitting, $Q_1 < 0$. Hence $z_1 = R_1 + \delta - Q_1 > 0$.

Consider the dashed curves labeled $z = $ const. in Figure 1. Each depicts the locus of (u, v) combinations giving a particular value of z. The slope of such curves at any point is $-z_2/z_1 < 0$; as the unemployment rate is reduced, an increase of the vacancy rate is required to keep z constant. These z contours as drawn display strict convexity or "diminishing marginal rate of substitution," meaning that as the unemployment rate is reduced, the vacancy rate increases at an increasing rate along any contour. This convexity is the content of (13b).

The best rationale for this convexity is the presumption that $z_{21} = R_{21} - Q_{21} > 0$. This states that an increase of the vacancy rate has

[44]Some of the new employees wanted can be acquired virtually instantaneously so that the response of N to aggregate demand is not entirely the gradual or continuous response that I have postulated.

[45]That is, the additional recruitment or search costs necessary to increase by one the expected number of recruits per unit time may be greater if the firm is aiming at 500 recruits in a week than if it is aiming for only 10. This is a short-run cost curve in which we hold constant the size of the firm and its personnel office. Large firms are not implied to suffer disadvantages in recruitment.

greater effect on employment growth the greater the unemployment rate. The primary basis for that assumption is that recruitment will be more difficult the smaller is unemployment (indeed, totally unsuccessful in the aggregate at zero unemployment), so that $R_{21} > 0$. It is plausible also that an increase of the vacancy rate has less effect, if it has any, upon quits the less tight the labor market, so that $Q_{21} \leq 0$. (Since $z_{12} = z_{21}$, an equivalent view is that changes of the unemployment rate have greater impact upon z the greater the vacancy rate.) Second, we should expect that $z_{11} = R_{11} - Q_{11} \leq 0$ on the two grounds that, vacancy rates constant, an increase of the *employment* rate reduces new hires at an increasing rate and that it increases quits at an increasing rate (or at least at nondecreasing rates).[46] Third, and most controversially, it might be argued that $z_{22} = R_{22} - Q_{22} \leq 0$. $R_{22} < 0$ could result from a rising marginal recruitment cost schedule; given the unemployment rate, the new hire rate (R) might even approach an upper bound as the vacancy rate increased without limit. My guess is that $Q_{22} \geq 0$, but, in any case, (13b) shows that the suggested signs here are merely sufficient for convexity.

It is possible to supplement the mechanism by which u and v control z somewhat along the lines suggested by Alchian[47] and Mortensen.[48] Consider the staggered wage-setting model. Suppose that workers share the expectations of firms as to the average wage that will prevail one-half year hence, denoted $w^e(t)$. Then, in any steady state in which $\Delta^* > 0$, we have $w(t) > w^e(t)$; average wage offers at the current time will be regarded as higher than can be found, on the average, in months ahead; sampled wage rates will be regarded as abnormally and temporarily high, so that search unemployment will be shorter, quit rates smaller on that account, and the unemployment rate lower. Under continuous wage setting, $\Delta^* > 0$ also implies $w(t) > w^e(t)$, where the latter then means the expected *current* wage. In this case it is the underestimate by workers of the *current* average wage that lowers the unemployment rate, but in the same way. In steady states, therefore, one could write

$$Z(u, v) = R(u, v, 1, u \cdot \lambda m(u, v))$$
$$- \delta(1 - u) - Q(u, v, 1, (1 - u) \cdot \lambda m(u, v)) \qquad (13')$$

without necessarily jeopardizing (13a) and (13b). In particular, $R_4 > 0$ and $Q_4 < 0$ leaves the critical z_2 positive. I shall stick with (13) for the

---

[46]If quits *per employee* is linear in the employment rate, given the vacancy rate, then $Q(u, v, 1)$, that is, quits per unit labor supply, will be strictly convex with respect to the employment rate.

[47]"Information Costs, Pricing, and Resource Unemployment," this volume.

[48]"A Theory of Wage and Employment Dynamics," this volume.

moment and discuss subsequently the outlines of a fuller dynamic model in which neither (10) nor (13) hold except in steady states.

We can now combine (9), (10), and (13) to obtain an augmented Phillips curve in terms of the easily observed variables u and z. Since z_2 is one-signed, (13) implicitly defines v as a single-valued function of u and z, say,

$$v = \psi(u, z), \tag{14}$$

whence

$$\frac{\dot{w}}{w} = \lambda m[u, \psi(u, z)] = f(u, z), \tag{15}$$

which is our augmented Phillips curve. Since to every (u, z) pair there corresponds a unique v, there exists a derived Phillips-like relation between $\dot{w}/w$ and (u, z) pairs.

We can establish the properties of f after determining how v varies with u and z.

$$\psi_1 = \frac{-z_1[u, \psi(u, z)]}{z_2[u, \psi(u, z)]} < 0,$$

$$\psi_2 = \frac{1}{z_2[u, \psi(u, z)]} > 0,$$

$$\psi_{11} = -z_2^{-2}\left\{\left[z_{11} + z_{12}\left(\frac{-z_1}{z_2}\right)\right]z_2 - \left[z_{21} + z_{22}\left(\frac{-z_1}{z_2}\right)\right]z_1\right\} > 0, \tag{16}$$

$$\psi_{22} = -z_2^{-3}z_{22} \gtreqqless 0 \quad (?),$$

$$\psi_{21} = -z_2^{-2}\left[z_{21} + z_{22}\left(\frac{-z_1}{z_2}\right)\right] < 0 \quad (?).$$

The last two inequalities are based on the guesses discussed *in connection* with (13b), while the first three inequalities follow from (13a) and (13b).

Now we can deduce the following restrictions on the augmented Phillips curve:

$$f_1(u, z) = \lambda(m_1 + m_2\psi_1) < 0,$$

$$f_{11}(u, z) = \lambda(m_{11} + m_{12}\psi_1 + m_{22}\psi_1^2 + m_{22}\psi_{11}) > 0,$$

$$f_2(u, z) = \lambda m_2\psi_2 > 0, \tag{17}$$

$$f_{22}(u, z) = \lambda(m_{22}\psi_2^2 + m_2\psi_{22}) \gtreqqless 0 \quad (?),$$

$$f_{21}(u, z) = \lambda[(m_{21} + m_{22}\psi_1)\psi_2 + m_2\psi_{21}] < 0 \quad (?).$$

The first result states that every constant-z Phillips curve is negatively sloped: Decreased unemployment directly adds pressure on wage differentials, and this effect is reinforced by the concomitant increase of vacancies which is deducible from the constancy of z in the face of decreased unemployment. The second result states that this constant-z relation between the rate of wage change and the unemployment rate is strictly convex, as the Phillips curve is ordinarily drawn; as the unemployment rate is decreased by equal amounts the vacancy rate must increase at an increasing rate to keep z constant, by virtue of (13b), which implies $\psi_{11} > 0$, so that even in the simple excess-demand case [in which the second derivatives in (9b) are equal to zero] the rate of wage increase itself increases at an increasing rate. As for the third result, $f_2 > 0$, the higher is employment growth, the unemployment rate constant, the higher must be the vacancy rate and hence the greater the upward pressure on the money wage. Thus the association between high employment growth and high wage gains, known as the Phillips–Lipsey "loop," is consistent with the excess-demand or generalized-excess-demand theory of the Phillips curve.[49] The convexity of this relation between wage change and z is not certain because it involves the problematical ψ_{22}. Finally, there is a negative interaction between u and z, meaning $f_{21} < 0$, if my guess is right that z_{21} is strongly positive; this interaction means that a given increase of z signifies a greater increase of the vacancy rate the smaller is the unemployment rate.

The variables u and z cannot go their own way for long since a high (low) z implies a falling (rising) u. There is, therefore, some interest in the "steady-state" Phillips curve that relates the rate of wage increase to alternative, *constant* values of the unemployment rate. Let us take the proportionate rate of growth of the labor supply to be a nonnegative constant, γ. Then, corresponding to any *steady-state* unemployment rate, to be denoted $\bar{u}$, there is a steady $\bar{z}$ and a steady $\bar{v}$ which obey the relation

$$\bar{z} = z(\bar{u}, \bar{v}) = \frac{N}{L}\frac{\dot{N}}{N} = \frac{N}{L}\frac{\dot{L}}{L} = (1 - \bar{u})\gamma, \qquad \gamma \geqq 0. \qquad (18)$$

If $\gamma > 0$, then clearly $\bar{z}$ must be higher the smaller $\bar{u}$. This relation also yields a locus of steady-state $(\bar{u}, \bar{v})$ points, which is shown in Figure 1 by the solid, downward sloping curve intersecting (from below) the dashed-line iso-z contours. This locus is negatively sloped and flatter than the z contours, for as steady-state $\bar{u}$ is decreased, $\bar{v}$ must increase not only enough to keep z constant but to increase z to the required level implied by (18). Referred to the *vertical axis*, the slope is

$$\frac{d\bar{v}}{d\bar{u}} = \frac{-(z_1 + \gamma)}{z_2} < 0. \qquad (19)$$

---

[49]The lagged response of u to an increase of v produces counterclockwise loops. But the analysis of wage expectations in Section 4 implies the possibility of clockwise loops.

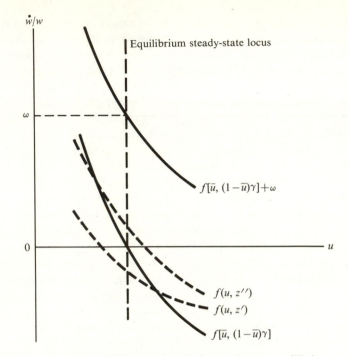

Figure 3.   Augmented Phillips curves and the steady-state equilibrium locus.

At least for sufficiently small γ, the locus will be convex like the z contours:

$$\frac{d^2\bar{v}}{d\bar{u}^2} = -z_2^{-2}\left\{\left[z_{11} + z_{12}\left(\frac{-z_1 - \gamma}{z_2}\right)\right]z_2\right.$$

$$\left. - \left[z_{21} + z_{22}\left(\frac{-z_1 - \gamma}{z_2}\right)\right](z_1 + \gamma)\right\} > 0 \quad (?). \quad (20)$$

It is not surprising, therefore, that our steady-state Phillips curve, $f[\bar{u}, (1 - \bar{u})\gamma]$, is negatively sloped and steeper than the constant-z Phillips curves:

$$\frac{\partial f[\bar{u}, (1 - \bar{u})\gamma]}{\partial \bar{u}} = f_1 - f_2\gamma < 0. \quad (21)$$

Also we find

$$\frac{\partial^2 f[\bar{u}, (1 - \bar{u})\gamma]}{\partial \bar{u}^2} = f_{11} - f_{12}\gamma - (f_{21} - f_{22}\gamma)\gamma > 0 \quad (?), \quad (22)$$

so there is some presumption of convexity (and certainly for small enough γ) in the steady-state curve as well as the constant-z curve. These results are depicted in Figure 3, which shows two constant-z Phillips curves and the steeper steady-state Phillips curve.

It might be noted that the steady-state Phillips curve is higher the greater the labor force growth rate; that is, $\partial f/\partial \gamma > 0$ for $\bar{u} < 1$. The reason is that faster growth of the labor supply requires a larger z and hence a larger vacancy rate to hold steady any given unemployment rate. This is an interesting testable implication of the theory.

Are there direct tests of the above theory of the augmented Phillips curve?[50] Quarterly British vacancy data have been prepared by Dow and Dicks-Mireaux.[51] Their study shows a scatter diagram of U and V points which, after 1950 or so, cluster around a convex, negatively sloped curve like the z contours or the steady-state locus in Figure 1. This is encouraging support for the *long-run* implications of (13) and (18). But my theory denies a strict and simple short-run relation between the unemployment rate *level* and the vacancy rate level. (Otherwise, the unemployment rate would suffice as an indicator of generalized excess demand.)

In its unadulterated form, the employment dynamics model here implies that unemployment and vacancy levels together determine the rate of change of employment and, hence, given γ, the *rate of change* of the unemployment rate. The differential equation is

$$-\dot{u} = z(u, v) - (1 - u)\gamma. \tag{23}$$

This says that if, at the prevailing u, v exceeds the corresponding $\bar{v}$ on the steady-state locus, so that $z > \bar{z} = (1 - u)\gamma$, then u will be falling (and vice versa if v is less than the corresponding $\bar{v}$). See the arrows in Figure 1.

The British data, despite being quarterly, offer a striking example that u can fall because v is high even though v is falling, which supports the emphasis on the level of v, rather than its rate of change, as a determinant of $\dot{u}$. After a sharp rise of vacancies that reduced unemployment, the latter went on falling in the second half of 1955 when vacancies had leveled off and proceeded to fall.[52] Indeed, the early postwar years in general showed a long-run trend of falling unemployment coinciding with falling vacancies. On the other hand, cyclical turning points usually occurred in the same quarter, so perhaps one should not totally neglect the rate of change of vacancies as a determinant of unemployment movements.

In the United States one has to make do with the Help-wanted Advertising Index in *Business Cycle Developments*.[53] In a recent study

---

[50]All the empirical evidence to be cited was consulted after I had arrived at an almost identical model in the first (unpublished) version of this paper, so that this evidence permits a real test of the model.

[51]J. C. R. Dow and L. A. Dicks-Mireaux, "The Excess Demand for Labor: A Study of Conditions in Great Britain, 1946–56," *Oxford Economic Papers*, 10 (February 1958), pp. 1–33.

[52]*Ibid.*, p. 3, Fig. 1B.

[53]U.S. Department of Commerce. *Business Cycle Developments* (monthly).

of this index, Cohen and Solow[54] in effect regressed the value of this index on the unemployment rate and the "new hire rate." Now (23) implies that v is a decreasing function both of u and $\dot{u}$, since points above the steady-state locus will be associated with falling u. It is of some interest, therefore, that the new hire rate, which may be a proxy for $-\dot{u}$, entered positively in that regression and the unemployment rate negatively; further, study of the residuals showed vacancies to be underestimated by this regression in cyclical phases of falling unemployment.[55]

A hasty study of the monthly data on aggregate unemployment and vacancies in Australia also appears to give some support to the present model.[56] After dividing U and V by a geometrically rising series that approximates the growth of the labor supply, I used a standard program to deseasonalize the resulting unemployment and vacancy rates. One of the best regression results was the following:

$$\log v_t = 9.76 - 0.95 \log u_t - 0.35 \log \left(\frac{u_{t+1}}{u_t}\right), \quad \bar{R}^2 = 0.925,$$
$$ (44.10) \qquad (2.40)$$
$$\text{DW} = 0.15, \tag{24}$$

where the numbers in parentheses are t-ratios and v_t and u_t denote an average of the seasonally adjusted percentage vacancy rate and unemployment rate, respectively, in month t and month $t + 1$ (multiplied by 100). Both coefficients have the predicted signs and are highly significant. The serial correlation is fearsome, but that is due partially to the monthly averaging. When only even-numbered observations were run, the Durbin–Watson statistic rose to 0.35 and the t-ratio for $\log (u_{t+1}/u_t)$ rose to 3.17, with no appreciable change in the coefficients. On the whole, these explorations offer hope of good results from a careful econometric analysis.[57]

Before we leave the analytics of the Phillips curve, let me sketch a more general analysis that (a) does not require the generalized excess-demand equation in (10) to hold out of steady states, and (b) allows w/w^e to influence z independently. The more general analysis is too complicated for any results as simple as (17), but it is more general!

[54]M. S. Cohen and R. M. Solow, "The Behavior of Help-Wanted Advertising," *Review of Economics and Statistics*, 49 (February 1967), pp. 108–110.

[55]Cohen and Solow (*op. cit.*, p. 109) wrote: "The residuals [from this regression] progressively underestimated [the help-wanted index] in the course of upswings and overestimated during downswings, the error getting worse in the course of each one-way movement." Apart from the progressivity, this constitutes additional support for the theory. As for the progressivity, the authors suggest that "formal advertising is treated as something of a last-resort method of recruitment." This means, I take it, that the help-wanted advertising index is not a totally satisfactory measure of job vacancies.

[56]I am grateful to Peter Burley for providing me with these data and to Arthur Donner and Steven Salop for carrying out these calculations.

[57]When the regression is turned around to make $\log (u_{t+1}/u_t)$ the dependent variable, the t-ratios remained significant though the R^2 was much lower.

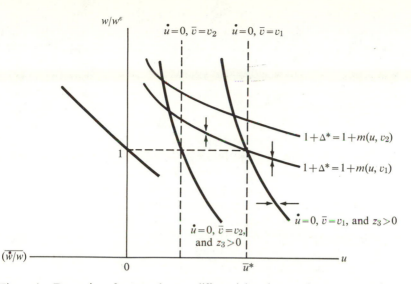

Figure 4.   Dynamics of expected wage differential and unemployment rate given the vacancy rate.

Section 2 made w/w^e a "state variable" that responds gradually to Δ^*, hence to u and v. Section 3 makes u a state variable also responding to v. Figure 4 is a phase diagram in terms of both of these state variables, with $\bar{v}$ a parameter subject to the government's fiscal and monetary control.

Consider the flatter solid curves on the right-hand side of Figure 4, each one corresponding to a different value of $\bar{v}$. Each curve indicates, for every u, that value of $w/w^e = 1 + \Delta^*$ such that w/w^e is steady. The ordinate of this curve is therefore $1 + \Delta^* = 1 + m(u, v)$, so that the curve is negatively sloped on the assumption $m_1 < 0$. Each of the steeper curves indicates, for every value of w/w^e, that value of u such that u is steady. Now if z depends only upon v, as in (11), independently of $\dot{w}/w^e$, the latter curves are vertical with intercept decreasing in $\bar{v}$. The dashed curves illustrate this case. An increase of $\bar{v}$ moves the pertinent dashed $\dot{u} = 0$ curve to the left and the pertinent $1 + \Delta^*$ upward, so that steady-state $\bar{u}$ is decreased and the steady-state w/w^e is increased. The arrow shows that u and w/w^e monotonically approach their respective steady-state values. Thus a steady-state Phillips curve emerges.

If z depends upon w/w^e as well as upon v and u, as discussed earlier, then

$$0 = -u = z(u, v, w/w^e) - (1 - u)\gamma \qquad (23')$$

gives the locus of $(\bar{u}, w/w^e)$ points for which $\dot{u} = 0$ for given v. Each such locus has the negative slope $-(z_1 + \gamma)/z_3$. If these loci are steeper than the constant (w/w^e) loci, an increase of $\bar{v}$ again produces a fall of

u and a rise of w/w^e toward their new steady-state values. So, in this case, a steady-state Phillips curve once again emerges. It can be seen that if v has no influence upon the $\dot{u} = 0$ locus except through its eventual effect upon w/w^e, a "pure" Alchian–Mortensen view, a rise of $\bar{v}$ and hence Δ^* still reduces u and increases w/w^e, despite the absence of any accompanying leftward shift of the $\dot{u} = 0$ locus.

Let me now try informally and briefly to open the model to some other factors. The "bottleneck" theory also helps to explain why wage increases should be associated with rapidly *increasing* employment. An economy adjusted to one level of aggregate demand, with its peculiar structure, cannot adapt instantaneously to a higher aggregate demand level with its new structure; certain types of labor will be in excess demand, and this will drive up the general wage index. Hansen's model[58] emphasizes that excess supplies of other types of labor, even if they sum to a figure in excess of the total of excess demands, need not hold down the wage index if wages are stickier downward than upward. In the usual bottleneck theory, however, the resulting change in wage structure will dissolve the bottlenecks, so that a low *level* of unemployment is not *ultimately* or *persistently* inflationary. It takes another slump and the passage of time if major bottlenecks are to reappear. Such a theory, therefore, seems to fit in with "ratchet inflation" of the sort analyzed by Bronfenbrenner.[59]

Lipsey attributed the influence of $\dot{u}$ in his regressions to an aggregation phenomenon.[60] To the extent that each sector of the economy has a simple and strictly convex Phillips curve of its own, the simple macro Phillips curve will shift upward with an increase in the sectoral inequality of unemployment rates. Lipsey suggested that these inequalities are worse in upturns than in downturns, so that a negative $\dot{u}$ tends to be more inflationary than a positive $\dot{u}$ at the same u. In any case, changes in the structure of vacancy and unemployment rates may be important.

What about unions? As a starting point, one might suppose the union to maximize the welfare of its members. In that case the union's wage objectives will be determined by real income opportunities outside the union. It will study and forecast the wage differential between union jobs and jobs that members could get elsewhere, weighing also the expected time required to get jobs elsewhere, hence unemployment rates and vacancy rates in the relevant areas and occupations. The average wage differential desired by unions thus depends upon our

[58]B. Hansen, "Full Employment and Wage Stability," in J. T. Dunlop, ed., *The Theory of Wage Determination* (St. Martin's Press, New York, 1957).

[59]M. Bronfenbrenner, "Some Neglected Implications of Secular Inflation," in K. K. Kurihara, ed., *Post-Keynesian Economics* (Rutgers University Press, New Brunswick, N.J., 1954).

[60]Lipsey, *op. cit.*, pp. 21–23.

pervasive u and v. At sufficiently small unemployment rates or large vacancy rates, the unions, just like individuals and firms, desire incompatibly large wage differentials, and the general index of wage rates will therefore rise.[61]

4
EXPECTATIONS AND
MACROEQUILIBRIUM

In Sections 2 and 3 it was postulated that each firm expects other firms to pay the same wage on the average over the future that was known (or believed) to have been paid in the recent past. In that case, it is natural for the firm to assume that an increase in its wage rates would attract more employees and discourage quitting, because it would expect any increase of its wage to increase its wage differential. But in the general case the firm may forecast wage changes elsewhere. How does this generalization affect the previous results?

Consider the following heuristic argument. Let each firm expect with certainty that the average wage paid elsewhere will change at a certain proportionate rate over the life of the firm's wage contract. Consider now a firm whose vacancy rate (v_i) in relation to labor-market conditions (u and v) is such that, in the absence of wage changes elsewhere, it would want to keep its present wage rate to maintain its expected wage differential at its present actual level; this firm is in equilibrium in the sense that its actual wage differential equals its desired differential. But if the firm in fact expects the average wage elsewhere to be increasing at the rate of 2 percent annually and it expects other firms to pass on the higher costs through a 2 percent rise of prices annually, then it will want to raise its wage rates by 2 percent annually; for it will calculate that it can raise its prices by 2 percent without loss of customers and thus leave unchanged its real position, that is, its real sales, its product wage and vacancy rate, and its competitiveness in the labor market. As for the disequilibrium case, if its vacancy rate and labor market conditions are such that in the absence of expectation of wage changes elsewhere it would want to raise its wage by 1 percent, say, it will, under the above expectations, want in fact to raise its wage by 3 percent for the next year. Upon averaging over firms we are then led to the proposition that we must add the expected rate of wage change, denoted $(\dot{w}/w)^e$, to the rate of wage

[61]This ties in somewhat with Keynes' (*op. cit.*, pp. 14–15) emphasis on the relative wage: "Every trade union will put up some resistance to a cut in money-wages [since such reductions 'are seldom or never of an all-round character']. But . . . no trade union would dream of striking on every occasion of a rise in the cost of living." See also J. R. Hicks, "Economic Foundations of Wage Policy," *Economic Journal*, 65 (September 1955), pp. 389–404. I should think, however, that the desired relative wage is dependent on labor-market conditions.

change that would occur under static wage expectations, to determine the actual rate of wage change per annum:

$$\frac{\dot{w}}{w} = \lambda \Delta^* + \left(\frac{\dot{w}}{w}\right)^e = f(u, z) + \left(\frac{\dot{w}}{w}\right)^e. \tag{25}$$

The result is quite natural. By "equilibrium," following Hayek, Lindahl, Harrod, and others (using varied terminology), we generally mean a path along which the relevant variables work out as people think they will. A necessary labor-market condition for what might be called a *macroequilibrium* in terms of the relevant averages and aggregates is therefore equality of the expected and actual rate of change of the average wage rate:

$$\frac{\dot{w}}{w} = \left(\frac{\dot{w}}{w}\right)^e. \tag{26}$$

Hence macroequilibrium entails

$$f(u, z) = \Delta^* = m(u, v) = 0, \tag{27}$$

meaning that generalized excess demand for labor, as measured by $m(u, v)$, be equal to zero. Any other condition would be disturbing! Note that this equilibrium admits a rising or falling average money wage. It is an egregious error to say that rising wages, or rising anything else, implies excess demand.

The fundamental result in (25) needs further interpretation and defense. First there is a matter of dating the variables. Consider again the model in which wage negotiations are annual and are evenly staggered (across firms) over the year. Consider a firm negotiating at the beginning of the calendar year. Suppose it expects average wage rates *in the future* to rise steadily at the rate of 2 percent per annum. Suppose the wage index is 100 at the beginning of the year and has been at 100 for a year. Then the firm will expect the index to stand approximately at 101 by midyear. By raising its wage by just 1 percent, the firm can expect to maintain on the average over its new contract its past average competitiveness with other employers over the old contract. We appear to get only a 1 percent wage rise resulting from a 2 percent expected rise of the index. The resolution of this puzzle, already hinted at in Section 2, consists of defining $(\dot{w}/w)^e$ as the expected rate of change of the index from six months prior to the firm's wage negotiation to six months after the wage negotiation, so that it is centered on the date of the firm's wage decision. In our example, therefore, the "expected rate of wage change" so defined is really only 1 percent. If, in the following year, the expected rate of wage change (2 percent) is unaltered and this year's expectations are borne out—so that the index will next year be expected to rise from approximately 101 (at last midyear) to approximately 103 (at the next midyear)—our firm must then raise its wage by 2 percent if it expects to stay as competitive as before with other employers. This matter is possibly of some econometric significance; the above example suggests that a perfect proxy for the expected *future* rate of wage change will tend to enter a regression equation resembling (25) with a less-than-unitary coefficient; it is only the expected rate of wage change as defined here that is predicted to enter such an equation with a unitary coefficient.[62]

There is a question of why the expected rate of wage change should enter in (25) to the exclusion of the expected price change. As I shall shortly argue, the expectation of price increases affects money wages only *through* its effects on expected vacancy rates and the expected unemployment rate. *Given the latter*, a rise of the expected rate of inflation will have little or no effect upon the wage increase that a firm grants if it expects other firms to hold the line on the money wage rates they pay; in particular, the threat of an employee expecting a rise of the cost of living to quit in search of another job will be empty if it is not expected that other firms' wages will rise with the cost of living. Whether Keynes was right that unions, too, are interested only in *relative* wages is hard to tell, but cost-of-living clauses are not very widespread in this country and have apparently never ranked very high among union objectives.

If the above result is to be really satisfactory, however, it must hold when the expected price trend is flat as well as in the case where producers can expect to pass on their wage increase in higher prices with impunity. Probably (25) *is* too simple; a full analysis requires a theory of the optimal price dynamics of the firm. Yet I am prepared to defend it as a tolerable approximation along the following lines. Continue to abstract from productivity growth and consider a firm at wage-setting time with flat price expectations. The vacancy rate of this firm, v_i, is to be calculated at a wage equal to the firm's expectation of the average money wage elsewhere at midcontract, six months hence. Imagine that *if the expected rate of wage change is zero*, the firm will find that its v_i, so calculated, would not prompt it to raise its wage. This means that its desired differential, $\Delta_i^* = k^i(u, v, v^i)$, is equal to its past wage differential at midcontract, Δ_i. As a second situation, suppose now that, *other things equal*, the firm expects a 1 percent rate of wage increase (as defined earlier, from midcontract to midcontract). Because its price expectations are flat, it does not expect to be able to

[62]The left-hand-side variable is likewise the rate of change of the actual wage index expressed at annual rates. If wage negotiations are evenly distributed over the year, the firms setting wages in January, by raising their wage rates 1 percent, will raise the index by one-twelfth of 1 percent from its December level and hence by 1 percent at an annual rate. Where annual wage negotiations are unevenly distributed over the year (producing some seasonality), one may want to work with the actual one-year rates of change of the index (for example, January to January), in which case the "expected rate of wage change" is an average of twelve figures centered (respectively) on each of the twelve months in the one-year interval.

raise its prices by an additional 1 percent without loss of customers. It will not raise its price that much. Therefore, when the firm evaluates its vacancy rate at the higher expected product wage, it will find its expected vacancy rate smaller in this second situation, so that its $\Delta_i^* = k^i(u^e, v^e, v_i^e)$ is less than its previous average wage differential, Δ_i. This means that while the firm may raise its wage it will raise it less than 1 percent in order to reduce its expected differential. To the extent that this second situation is general among firms, we will have a smaller $m(u, v)$. Firms will recruit less so that z and hence $f(u, z)$ will both be smaller. Thus a *ceteris paribus* rise of $(\dot{w}/w)^e$ in (25), to the extent that businesses do not expect to be able to shift the expected wage costs onto buyers, will be partially offset by a resulting fall of z and $f(u, z)$, so that $\dot{w}/w$ is not implied to rise by an equal amount.

Of course other things need not be equal. Like the example earlier, if the firm expects to be able to raise its price in proportion to its wage rates without loss of prospective sales—because, say, other firms are expected to raise their prices in that proportion and demand per customer is not expected on balance to fall—then neither the expected product wage, the expected wage divided by the firm's planned price, nor the firm's vacancy rate will change; thus the firm will in this case match the expected rate of wage change, adding or subtracting the wage change it would have chosen under stationary expectations. Another example of interest is the expectation by the firm of growth in the marginal and average productivity of its labor together with expected growth of its output demanded (at present prices) at a rate equal to the expected rate of wage change. Such a change in the firm's situation will leave its expected vacancy rate unchanged from its previous midcontract level, when this is evaluated at the wage expected to be necessary to keep its wage differential at its previous midcontract level. Hence the firm will raise its wage by just the amount of the expected rate of wage change if it likes its previous differential—by more (less) if that previous differential is too low (high).

In all cases, the firm is imagined notionally to increase its wage by the amount it expects is necessary to keep its past average competitiveness, to make an optimal price adjustment, and then to evaluate its expected vacancy rate at the implied product wage and expected demand for its product; if the desired differential calculated at that hypothetical vacancy rate is equal to its past average differential, it goes ahead with the "competitive" wage increase; if the desired differential is greater (less), the firm will increase its wage by more (less) than the expected or competitive amount. In mathematical terms, we can write the change in wage rate by firms currently resetting their wage rates as

$$w_t(t) - w_{t-1}(t) = (1 + \Delta_t^*)w_t^e - w_{t-1}(t)$$
$$= (1 + \Delta_t^*)(1 + \pi)w(t - \tfrac{1}{2}) - w_{t-1}(t), \quad (28)$$

where π is the expected proportionate rate of wage change. Letting Δ_t denote $w_{t-1}(t)/w(t - \frac{1}{2})$, we have

$$\frac{w_t(t) - w_{t-1}(t)}{w_{t-1}(t)} = (1 + \pi)\left(\frac{1 + \Delta_t^*}{1 + \Delta_t} - 1\right), \tag{29}$$

which may be approximated by $\pi + \Delta^* - \Delta$ for small magnitudes. In equilibrium the left-hand side must equal π, hence $\Delta_t^* = \Delta_t$. Since Δ_t must be approximately zero for firms as a whole, it follows that $\Delta^* = 0$ in equilibrium.

A rigorous argument is easier if we revert to the continuous wage-setting model together with adaptive expectations of the current wage level, as in (10'). We repeat, for the ith firm, the earlier (10'a):

$$\dot{\Delta}_i^e = \mu(\Delta_i^* - \Delta_i^e), \tag{10'a}$$

where

$$\Delta_i^e = \frac{w_i - w^e}{w^e}, \qquad \Delta_i^* = \frac{w_i^* - w^e}{w^e},$$

But we now write in place of (10'b) the generalization:

$$\dot{w}^e = \lambda(w - w^e) + \pi w^e, \tag{10'b'}$$

π being the expected rate of wage change elsewhere, that is, the rate of change of the expected current wage that would be forecast in the absence of information on a discrepancy between the actual wage level elsewhere and the currently estimated average wage level. Then

$$\frac{\dot{w}_i}{w_i} = \mu \frac{\Delta_i^* - \Delta_i^e}{1 + \Delta_i^e} + \frac{\dot{w}^e}{w^e},$$

where the second term on the right includes the "catch-up" wage increase and π as well. For firms as a whole, then,

$$\frac{\dot{w}}{w} = \mu \frac{\Delta^* - \Delta^e}{1 + \Delta^e} + \lambda \Delta^e + \pi.$$

The analysis of Figure 2 applies with slight change. In steady states we have $\Delta^e = \Delta^*$, so that

$$\frac{\dot{w}}{w} = \lambda \Delta^* + \pi,$$

which is (25). In this continuous-time model, "equilibrium" might be defined as "*ex post* $\dot{w}^e = \pi w^e$," meaning that the time change of the *estimate* (or expectation) of current w equals what was forecast for the estimate. Then, by (10'b'), $w = w^e$ is implied, whence $\Delta^e = 0$ and $\dot{w} = \dot{w}^e$. Then $\Delta^* = 0$ along any equilibrium path. If, alternatively, equilibrium were defined as *ex post* $\dot{w}/w = \pi$, so that expectations of the *level* of the current wage may be incorrect, then equilibrium implies only that $\Delta^* = 0$ when a steady state prevails. I prefer the former definition, though for steady-state analysis there is no need to choose.

The model, particularly (25) and (23), implies that there exists a unique steady-state equilibrium value of the unemployment rate, denoted by $\bar{u}^*$ and determined by the equation

$$f(\bar{u}^*, (1 - \bar{u}^*)\gamma) = 0. \tag{30}$$

This is because the steady-state $f(\bar{u}, (1 - \bar{u})\gamma)$ is strictly decreasing in $\bar{u}$ and $f(0, \gamma) > 0, f(1, 0) < 0$. At any other $\bar{u}$ there must be continuing, nonvanishing disequilibrium. Corresponding to $\bar{u}^*$ is some steady-state equilibrium vacancy rate, $\bar{v}^*$, given by the relation $m(\bar{u}^*, \bar{v}^*) = 0$.

The point about the result in (30) is that $\bar{u}^*$ is independent of π. In steady-state equilibrium the rate of wage increase is just the expected rate of wage increase, π. Hence a large $\dot{w}/w$ *in equilibrium* implies only a large π, not a small $\bar{u}$. This means that an economy that is in a steady state, and that is experiencing and expecting 10 percent money wage growth, would not have an unemployment rate different from what it would be if that economy were in a steady state and were experiencing and expecting a much smaller rate of money wage growth. Figure 3 gives the diagrammatics: A shift of the expected rate of wage change from zero to ω produces a uniform upward displacement of the steady-state Phillips curve by the same amount. As a consequence, the (dashed) *locus of steady-state equilibrium points* is a vertical line, each point having the same abscissa, $\bar{u}^*$.

Before we question whether $\bar{u}^*$ is exactly independent of monetary factors, let us consider its "real" determinants.

What if higher money wage growth in steady states is matched by higher productivity growth? It is sometimes held that an economy can maintain a steady-state equilibrium—and thus a steady state with a stationary price trend (as well as any other trend)—with a smaller steady unemployment rate the faster its productivity growth. This is obvious on the usual Phillips curve analysis where no expectational variables are introduced; and it is also valid arithmetic if the expected rate of wage change in my model is replaced by the expected rate of price change. But our theory denies that formulation if it is assumed that steady wage growth eventually generates the expectation of that growth. Then the difference in rates of wage increase consistent with price stability between rapid-productivity-growth and slow-productivity-growth situations does not permit a favorable difference in steady unemployment rates, because the difference in $\dot{w}/w$ will be matched by an equal difference in $\dot{w}^e/w$. Indeed the proposition in question could be reversed in a more general model: If rapid productivity growth and resulting obsolescence of plants strike firms unevenly and thus make greater demands for labor mobility and flexible skills, the steady-state equilibrium unemployment rate may very well be higher the faster is the growth of productivity. (But *given* productivity growth, $\bar{u}^*$ is still independent of the expected nominal wage trend.)

A rise of the rate of growth of the labor force will increase the value of z and hence the vacancy rate needed to maintain any given unemployment rate. Equilibrium $\bar{u}^*$ must then rise to accommodate a higher $\bar{v}^*$. From (30) we calculate that

$$\frac{d\bar{u}^*}{d\gamma} = \frac{-(1 - \bar{u}^*)f_2}{f_1 - f_2\gamma} > 0. \tag{31}$$

Thus rapid economic growth from any source appears to increase the equilibrium steady-state unemployment rate.

What are the implications of this theory for the consequences of policy decisions regarding $u(t)$ or, equivalently, $\dot{w}(t)/w(t)$? Nil, until we specify a theory of π. Consider two examples. Let macro policy, through v, cause $\dot{w}/w$ to be constant. Then it is natural to suppose that, at least eventually, π will approach $\dot{w}/w$. Hence $u(t)$ will eventually approach $\bar{u}^*$ independently of the selected $\dot{w}/w$. An increase of $\dot{w}/w$ above current π will "buy" a *temporary* but not a *permanent* decrease of u. As a second example, let macro policy, through v, cause $u = \bar{u} < \bar{u}^*$. Then $f[\bar{u}, (1 - \bar{u})\gamma] > 0$, so that $\dot{w}/w > \pi$ for all t. It is natural to suppose that, eventually, π tends toward $\dot{w}/w$. But each one-point increase of π makes $\dot{w}/w$ one point higher, given $u = \bar{u}$. Hence π and $\dot{w}/w$ will increase without limit. The result is hyperinflation. The latter illustration shows, by the way, that the insidious Say's law has not returned. As long as the monetary system functions, the fiscal and monetary authorities can engineer departures from the equilibrium steady-state unemployment rate. Nor do we know at what speed a hyperinflation (or inperdeflation) would develop when disequilibrium was maintained.

Suppose we are convinced that steady, nonaccelerating inflation at some moderate rate is possible in this country at a steady unemployment rate of 4 percent. In the present model this implies that $\bar{u}^*$ equals 4 percent.[63] Is it plausible that, as the above model predicts, wages and prices would spiral upward at an ever-accelerating rate if aggregate demand consistently maintained the unemployment rate at 3.5 percent? It is time to qualify the contention that $\bar{u}^*$ is independent of π. There is a lot that is hidden in the m and z functions.

One might argue that an unemployment rate as high as 4 percent is consistent with a moderate and steady rate of inflation only because some of those firms that would like to reduce substantially their wage

---

[63]Note that the unemployment rate required to keep average money wage rates in pace with productivity in the American economy at present, will exceed the American $\bar{u}^*$ because the expected rate of change of the money wage surely exceeds the rate of growth of productivity.

differentials prefer to accept below-optimal profits or even dismiss some employees rather than impose money wage cuts on their employees, and because some employees would rather quit than suffer the indignity of a money wage cut; this means that the average money wage can be rising at the expected rate of wage change even when the "true" average desired wage differential, Δ^*, is negative. But money wage cuts are occasionally appropriate for a firm that wants a lower wage differential only when the expected rate of wage change is moderately low. On this argument, therefore, a 3.5 percent unemployment rate might also be consistent with equilibrium if the expected rate of wage change were high enough that a firm could reduce its expected relative wage by the amount desired without having to impose a money wage cut.

This money-illusion variant of the model admits the possibility that a 3.5 percent unemployment rate may be a sustainable equilibrium level, too, like 4 percent, though only at a higher rate of wage increase. The steady-state equilibrium locus will be negatively sloped at least over a range, because each steady-state curve in Figure 3 will shift up by less than one point for every one-point increase of π. Nevertheless, this variant does not deny that there exists some unemployment rate such that maintenance of the unemployment rate at a level below that rate would require a disequilibrium accelerating spiral of wages and prices. Such a revision of the model appears to reinforce the earlier hypothesis that faster labor growth worsens the unemployment-inflation tradeoff if the faster labor-force growth would tend to depress the rate of growth of real wage rates. It *could* reverse the earlier hypothesis that productivity growth increases the steady-state unemployment rate necessary for price stability (or any steady-state equilibrium) if productivity growth tended to raise the rate of growth of real wage rates.

But "irrationality" is not the only ground for disclaiming any precise invariance of $\bar{u}^*$ to π. It is standard doctrine to acknowledge that an "anticipated inflation" *does* have real effects, especially through their effects upon fiscal and monetary efficiency. *If* the real rate of interest does not fall by a compensating amount, an anticipated inflation impairs the function of money as a *medium of exchange*: Nominal interest rates will be higher under anticipated inflation, and "liquidity" will thereby be reduced. This might affect $\bar{u}^*$, though it is hard to say in what way. Another effect is the impairment of money as a *unit of account*. It is harder to make intertemporal comparisons of wage offers when general wages are rising, even if rising at a known rate. It may be that, for small π, workers will neglect π in deciding to accept a job. Thus, up to a point, an increase of π may tend, comparing equilibrium steady states, to shorten the duration of search unemployment; supplies of labor may be content to use $\pi = 0$ as a convenient approximation for comparing wage offers over time even though, intellectually, they know that wage rates are trending upward. If a one-point increase of π produces a less-than-one point increase of the steady-state Phillips curve, then the equilibrium locus is negatively sloped. There may be a complementary tendency from the product side: If the real rate of interest is invariant to π, then nominal interest rates are higher. If expected inflation, like expected money wage growth, is neglected by workers for purposes of computational simplicity, then they will operate as if the real interest rate is higher when π is higher; this tendency may produce a shortening of job search, and thus a reduction of $\bar{u}^*$. Whether this alleged impairment of the money yard-stick is a Paretian improvement, in view of the many likely externalities, is beyond the scope of the present paper.

Symmetrically, the point might be made that anticipated inflation *enhances* fiscal efficiency by reducing the average tax rate necessary to induce any desired level of private consumption demand because expectations of inflation reduce the real value of the government's indebtedness. If the real rate of interest is constant, after-tax real wage rates and after-tax real interest rates will be higher, so that $\bar{u}^*$ may also change.

Enough has been said to convey the point that invariance of $\bar{u}^*$ to the rate of inflation is unlikely to be precise. But a very general theory seems to be ambiguous as to the nature of the relationship.

5
SUMMARY

A generalized excess-demand theory of the rate of change of the average money wage rate has been developed for frictional labor markets that allocate heterogeneous jobs and workers without perfect information. There are two explanatory variables: the vacancy rate and the un-employment rate. The unemployment rate and the rate of change of employment (per unit of labor supply) are shown to be joint proxies for the vacancy rate. Hence generalized excess demand can be regarded as a derived function of the unemployment rate and the rate of change of employment. This relationship is the augmented Phillips curve. Some of its properties are deduced. The steady-state Phillips curve that relates the rate of wage increase to the steady unemployment rate is also derived.

The expected rate of wage change is then added to the Phillips function—to the excess-demand term—to obtain the rate of wage increase under nonstatic expectations in a no-money-illusion world. Equilibrium entails equality between the actual and expected rates of wage change. The steady-state equilibrium locus is implied to be a vertical line at a unique steady-state equilibrium unemployment rate.

This is consistent with the usual theory of anticipated inflation. But if there are downward money-wage rigidities or important considerations of monetary and fiscal efficiency, then no precise invariance of the equilibrium steady-state unemployment rate to the equilibrium inflation rate need hold.

APPENDIX 1:
MATHEMATICS OF WAGE CHANGE UNDER STAGGERED WAGE SETTING

Let $w(t)$ denote the average wage paid at time t. Let $w_s(t)$ denote the (common) wage paid by firms whose most recent wage setting occurred at s. Resetting occurs "yearly" for each firm, so we need consider only $t - 1 \leq s \leq t$. If workers are distributed uniformly over firms and firms' wage-setting dates are distributed uniformly over the year, then

$$w(t) = \int_{t-1}^{t} w_s(t)\, ds \tag{A1}$$

with $\partial w_s(t)/\partial t = 0$ for fixed s.

The model in the text hypothesizes

$$w_t(t) = hw_t^e, \qquad h > 0, \tag{A2}$$

$$w_t^e = w(t - \tfrac{1}{2}), \tag{A3}$$

where h signifies $(1 + \Delta^*)$ in the text and is here taken to be constant over time. Then we can derive

$$w(t) = h \int_{t-\frac{3}{2}}^{t-\frac{1}{2}} w(s)\, ds \tag{A4}$$

or

$$w(t) = h \int_{\frac{1}{2}}^{\frac{3}{2}} w(t - \theta)\, d\theta. \tag{A4'}$$

For $h = 1$ it is clear that there exists just one steady-state growth rate, zero. For $h \neq 1$ we can find the steady-state growth rates, g, from

$$w'(t) = h[w(t - \tfrac{1}{2}) - w(t - \tfrac{3}{2})], \tag{A5}$$

a mixed differential-difference equation whose characteristic equation [replace $w(t)$ by e^{zt}]

$$z = h(e^{-\frac{1}{2}z} - e^{-\frac{3}{2}z}) \tag{A6}$$

every steady-state growth rate, $z \equiv w'/w$, must satisfy. It is easy to show that, outside $z = 0$, there exists just one steady-state growth rate, denoted g, with sgn $g =$ sgn$(h - 1)$, and $g < \infty$ for $h < \infty$. There are a number of approximations of (A5), good for steady states, that are of use in describing the relation between g and h. One of them is

$$gw(t) = h[gw(t - 1)], \qquad (A7)$$

whence

$$e^g = h, \quad \text{or, for small } g, g \doteq h - 1. \qquad (A8)$$

The question is now whether our equation exhibits relative stability in the sense that, as t goes to infinity, $w(t)/e^{gt}$ becomes constant; that is, does a limiting growth rate exist and equal g? [Note that $w(t)$, even so normalized, certainly does not seek any "equilibrium level" that is independent of past w.]

One approach, due to P. A. Samuelson, constructs a new variable,

$$u(t) = w(t)e^{-gt}, \qquad (A9)$$

which we desire to show tends to be constant asymptotically. Then, using (A4'),

$$u(t) = \int_{\frac{1}{2}}^{\frac{9}{2}} he^{-g\theta}u(t - \theta)\, d\theta$$

$$= \int_0^\infty f(\theta)he^{-g\theta}u(t - \theta)\, d\theta, \qquad (A10)$$

where

$$\int_0^\infty f(\theta)he^{-g\theta}\, d\theta = \int_{\frac{1}{2}}^{\frac{3}{2}} he^{-g\theta}\, d\theta = \frac{h}{g}(e^{-\frac{1}{2}g} - e^{-\frac{3}{2}g}) = 1, \quad (A11)$$

by virtue of (A6). Hence (A10) shows u at each t to be a weighted average of its own past values. It is clear, therefore, that $u(t)$ approaches a constant as t goes to infinity. The value of that constant depends only upon $u(t)$ on the initial interval, $-\frac{3}{2} \le t \le 0$. The reason for this stability is that extreme values of u are averaged out, so that any past growth of u cannot be sustained.

There exists no steady-state relation giving a finite g for every $h > 0$ when the *growth* of wages tends to be extrapolated as well as the recent level. In that case we have

$$w_t^e = w(t - \tfrac{1}{2})e^\pi, \qquad \pi = g, \qquad (A12)$$

so a steady state requires

$$gw(t) = he^g[w(t - \tfrac{1}{2}) - w(t - \tfrac{3}{2})],$$
$$g = h(e^{\frac{1}{2}g} - e^{-\frac{1}{2}g}) \doteq hg, \qquad (A13)$$

which is impossible except when $h = 1$, in which case g is indeterminate.

APPENDIX 2:
NONWAGE RECRUITMENT OVER TIME

The analysis here will be confined to a fixed-wage firm that has committed itself to invest in such a way that its capital stock, K_t^i, will grow exponentially at rate $g \geq 0$. Its cash flow (abstracting from its investment) at any time t, in real terms, is

$$\frac{p_0^i}{p_0} F(N_t^i, K_0^i e^{gt}; \mu) - \frac{w_0}{p_0} N_t^i - C(R_t^i, K_0^i e^{gt}; u) - hbK_0^i e^{gt} \qquad (A1)$$

where its money product price, p_t^i, and its money wage rate, w_t^i, are both constant relative to the consumer price index, p_t, and to other wage rates. $F(\cdot)$ is the firm's output (produced and sold), homogeneous of degree one in capital and labor with diminishing marginal productivities, and hence $p_0^i F()/p_0$ is its real value. The second term is the firm's real wage bill. $C(\cdot)$ is its real recruitment cost, also homogeneous of degree one in recruitment, denoted R, and K, with $C_R > 0$ and $C_{RR} > 0$ (rising marginal recruitment cost). The constant $h > 0$ denotes "volunteers" per unit capital whose unit processing cost is $b \geq 0$. By its homogeneity, we may write (A1) in the form (dropping unnecessary subscripts)

$$e^{gt} K_0 \left\{ \frac{p_0^i}{p_0} F(n_t, 1; \mu) - \frac{w_0}{p_0} n_t - C(r_t, 1; u) - hb \right\}, \qquad (A1')$$

where

$$r_t = \frac{R_t}{K_0 e^{gt}}, \qquad n_t = \frac{N_t}{K_0 e^{gt}}.$$

Letting R_t, H_t, D_t and Q_t denote the firm's recruits, volunteers, deaths, and quits, respectively, we have

$$\dot{N}_t = R_t + H_t - D_t - Q_t$$

$$= R_t + hK_0 e^{gt} - \delta N_t - q(u)N_t, \qquad (A2)$$

where the quit ratio, $q(u)$, is a decreasing function of the unemployment rate, u. From (A2) and differentiation of n_t we obtain

$$r_t = \dot{n}_t + \lambda(u)n_t - h, \qquad \lambda(u) \equiv g + \delta + q(u) > 0. \qquad (A2')$$

Now let us suppose that the firm maximizes, with respect to $r(t) \geq 0$, the improper integral of the discounted cash flow in (A1') subject to (A2'), where $e^{-\rho t}$ is the discount and ρ, the expected real rate of interest. I shall study only the borderline case in which $\rho = g$ and use the "overtaking principle," so that the firm maximizes the integral of the *excess* of cash flow over the exponentially rising "bliss level" of cash flow. The excess is

$$\int_0^\infty K_0 \left\{ \frac{p_0^i}{p_0} F(n, 1; \mu) - \frac{w_0}{p_0} n - C(r, 1; u) - hb \right.$$

$$\left. - \frac{p_0^i}{p_0} F(n^*, 1; \mu) + \frac{w}{p} n^* + C(\lambda n^* - h, 1; u) + hb \right\} dt, \qquad (A3)$$

where the constant (bliss-level) n^* is defined by

$$\frac{p_0^i}{p_0} F_n(n^*, 1; \mu) = \frac{w_0}{p_0} + \lambda C_R(\lambda n^* - h, 1; u) \qquad \text{(A4)}$$

and $\lambda n^* - h > 0$ by assumption.

The optimal $\dot{n}(t)$ path satisfies $\dot{n}(t) \lesseqgtr 0$ according as $n(t) \lesseqgtr n^*$. The optimal path also satisfies

$\dot{n} C_R(\dot{n} + \lambda n - h, 1; u)$

$$= \frac{p_0^i}{p_0} F(n^*, 1; \mu) - \frac{w_0}{p_0} n^* - C(\lambda n^* - h, 1; u)$$

$$- \left[\frac{p_0^i}{p_0} F(n, 1; \mu) - \frac{w_0}{p_0} n - C(\dot{n} + \lambda n - h, 1; u) \right]. \qquad \text{(A5)}$$

The level n^* is to be distinguished from the smallest "no-vacancy" level, say n^{**}, at which marginal (real) value productivity equals the real wage plus interest and "depreciation" on the sheer unit processing outlay, b:

$$\frac{p_0^i}{p_0} F_n(n^{**}, 1; \mu) = \frac{w_0}{p} + (\rho + \delta + q)b. \qquad \text{(A6)}$$

Since $\rho = g$ and $b < C_R(r, 1; u)$ for all $r \geq 0$, $n^{**} > n^*$. Hence there are positive vacancies on the bliss path. Optimal $r = 0$ at some $\bar{n}$ between n^* and n^{**} and for all $n \geq \bar{n}$. Volunteers will be accepted if only $n < n^{**}$. It is supposed throughout that $n < \bar{n}$.

Given initial n, an increase of the technological shift parameter, μ, will increase n^{**} and hence vacancies if and only if $F_{n\mu}(n^{**}, 1; \mu) > 0$. Suppose that the technical change is *not* "very labor saving" at any n; i.e., $F_{n\mu}(n, 1; \mu) > 0$ for all n. Then we calculate from (A5) that

$$\frac{d\dot{n}}{d\mu} = \frac{\dfrac{p_0^i}{p_0} [F_\mu(n^*, 1; \mu) - F_\mu(n, 1; \mu)]}{\dot{n} C_{RR}(\dot{n} + \lambda n - h, 1; u)}, \qquad \text{(A7)}$$

which is positive since $F_{n\mu} > 0$ and $(n^* - n)$ and $\dot{n}$ have the same sign. By (A2'), $dr/d\mu = d\dot{n}/d\mu$, so recruitment increases along with vacancies when labor demand increases.

Vacancies decrease with n, *ceteris paribus*. From (A5) and (A2') we find

$$\frac{dr}{dn} = \frac{-\dfrac{p_0^i}{p_0} \left[F_n(n, 1; \mu) - \dfrac{w_0}{p_0} - \lambda C_R(r, 1; u) \right]}{\dot{n} C_{RR}(r, 1; u)}. \qquad \text{(A8)}$$

The bracketed expression must have the sign of $\dot{n}$, so that $dr/dn < 0$ for all $n < \bar{n}$; hence r is monotone decreasing in n and therefore monotone increasing in vacancies. If for any n the bracketed expression were negative, then $dr/dn > 0$ for all greater n, and either the result $r = r^* \equiv \lambda n^* - h$ at $n = n^*$ or the result $r = 0$ at $n = \bar{n}$ would be contradicted.

Consider now an increase of the unemployment rate, u. This is postulated to make recruitment easier in the sense that $C_{Ru}(r, 1; u) < 0$. We calculate from (A5) that

$$\frac{d\dot{n}}{du} = \frac{[\partial C(\dot{n} + \lambda n - h, 1; u)/\partial u - \partial C(\lambda n^* - h, 1; u)/\partial u] - \dot{n}\partial C_R(\dot{n} + \lambda n - h, 1; u)/\partial u}{\dot{n}C_{RR}(r, 1; u)}, \quad (A9)$$

where it must be remembered that λ and h vary with u. If we take $\lambda'(u)$ and $h'(u)$ to be zero for the moment, the numerator can be approximated (for small $r - r^*$) by

$$C_{Ru}(r, 1; u) \cdot (r - r^*) - \dot{n}C_{Ru}(r, 1; u) = \lambda(n - n^*) \cdot C_{Ru}(r, 1; u), \quad (A10)$$

which has the sign of $\dot{n}$, so that $d\dot{n}/du > 0$ on this account. The other part of the numerator, due to the variation of λ and h with u, can be approximated by

$$[\lambda'(u)n - h'(u)]\{(r - r^*)C_{RR}(r, 1; u) - \dot{n}C_{RR}(r, 1; u)\}$$
$$+ \lambda'(u)(n - n^*)C_R(r, 1; u)$$

$$= [\lambda'(u)n - h'(u)]\lambda (n - n^*)C_{RR}(r, 1; u) + \lambda'(u)(n - n^*)C_R(r, 1; u), \quad (A11)$$

where $\lambda'(u) < 0$, $h'(u) \geq 0$. This also has the sign of $\dot{n}$, so we find that $d\dot{n}/du > 0$ unambiguously.

But recruitment need not increase with u because less recruitment is needed for given $\dot{n}$ when quits fall and volunteers increase. Using (A2'), (A10), (A11), and the relation $\lambda(n - n^*) = -\dot{n} + r - \lambda n^* + h$, we have

$$\frac{dr}{du} = \frac{\lambda(n - n^*)C_{Ru}}{\dot{n}C_{RR}} + \frac{[\lambda'(u)n - h'(u)](-\dot{n} + r - \lambda n^* + h)}{\dot{n}}$$

$$+ \frac{\lambda'(u)(n - n^*)C_R}{\dot{n}C_{RR}} + [\lambda'(u)n - h'(u)]. \quad (A12)$$

Although the troublesome last term (the reduction of quits) cancels with part of the second term, the remainder of the second term has the "wrong" sign, so dr/du *could* have the wrong sign. But $z_1 > 0$ of the text rather than $R_1 > 0$ is the interesting inequality, so it is $d\dot{n}/du > 0$ rather than $dr/du > 0$ that is important. The employment dynamics in the text can be modified considerably without loss of the end results.

A Theory of Wage and Employment Dynamics[*]

DALE T. MORTENSEN

The purpose of this paper is to provide a simple but rigorous and quantifiable theory of wage and employment dynamics. Among other things the theory purports to explain the empirical relationship known as the Phillips curve.[1] In addition, the theory suggests a sense in which there may be a trade-off between the rate of inflation and the unemployment ratio. Finally, a number of determinants of the level of "frictional unemployment" are identified in the analysis.

The essential ingredients of the theory are models of wage and job choice which together imply a non-tâtonnement wage adjustment process and a dynamic employment process, unlike static theories of wage and employment levels. The models are quite plausible as descriptions of behavior in a labor market that is essentially competitive but characterized by some degree of monopsony power on the demand side and by imperfect information on the supply side. In spite of these

*This paper developed from a research seminar on labor market problems held at Northwestern University in the spring of 1968. Many of the original ideas in the paper can be attributed to participants in that seminar. I particularly wish to acknowledge the assistance and encouragement of Professors A. Treadway, F. Brechling, and G. C. Archibald. Of course, any errors are the responsibility of the author alone. Financial support was provided partially by a National Science Foundation grant made to the author and F. Brechling.

[1]A. W. Phillips, "The Relationship between Unemployment and the Rate of Change of Money Wage Rates in the United Kingdom, 1862–1957," *Economica* (November 1958), pp. 283–299.

imperfections wages and employment respond to classical "supply and demand" factors in the model.

The idea that classical factors of supply and demand might provide a rationalization for the observations of Phillips rather than the cost-push phenomena attributed to the activities of labor unions is clearly stated by Lipsey.[2] In a more recent article Phelps defends this view with an appeal to two facts.[3] First, trade unions represent a relatively small proportion of the labor force, particularly currently in the United States. Second, Phillips and Lipsey found that the trade-off between the rate of change in the money wage and the unemployment ratio existed in the nineteenth century, when trade unionism was even weaker, as well as in contemporary data.

Two recent papers, those by Holt and Phelps, are more or less directed at the same set of problems as those considered in this research effort.[4] These papers are largely responsible for stimulating this effort and have strongly influenced the approach used in it. However, it is this author's contention that both works, for quite different reasons, fall short of the mark.

On the one hand, Holt provides us with an ingenious description of the choice and search process engaged in by an unemployed participant in the labor market when information is imperfect and search is expensive. He also gives an interpretation of the Phillips curve based on this theory. However, he does not carry his theory to its logical conclusion, which is that such conditions on the supply side imply that each firm is faced with a flow supply of labor the magnitude of which is under the control of the firm. In fact, Holt's analysis for the most part ignores demand considerations.

Phelps, on the other hand, does consider explicitly the choice problem faced by the typical firm in such a labor market. He assumes that the firm has monopsony power in a dynamic sense because of imperfect information and the cost of search. However, Phelps does not fully and rigorously analyze the implications of these assumptions for the supply conditions faced by the firm. As a result, he misses the essential dynamic nature of those conditions. Because his model lacks the structure provided by this nature, the model provides him with his principal hypothesis only with difficulty. In his own words, that hypothesis is that "the *equilibrium* unemployment rate—the rate at which the actual and expected price increases (or wage increases) are equal—is independent of the rate of inflation."[5]

---

[2]R. G. Lipsey, "The Relationship between Unemployment and the Rate of Change in the Money Wage Rates in the United Kingdom, 1862–1957: A Further Analysis," *Economica* (February 1960), pp. 1–41.

[3]See E. S. Phelps, "Money Wage Dynamics and Labor-Market Equilibrium," this volume.

[4]See C. C. Holt, "Job Search, Phillips' Wage Relation, and Union Influence: Theory and Evidence," this volume, and Phelps, *op. cit.*

[5]Phelps, *op. cit.*, p. 130.

The important postulates concerning the supply side are that particular and general information about wage offers is imperfect and that search for job opportunities and wage information is expensive and/or time consuming. It is argued that job search can be viewed usefully as a random process because of imperfect knowledge. Only a portion of the total stock of participants contact any firm in a short time interval because of the expense of search. Finally, because prospective employees possess different information about alternative opportunities, not all who contact a given firm either accept or reject the firm's offer. In other words, the net employment flow to the firm, defined as the flow of workers who are willing to accept the firm's offer from the flow of those who contact the firm less quits and attritions, is not perfectly elastic with respect to the firm's wage offer. An aggregation of the flow-supply functions for the various firms yields a relationship among the rate of change in the unemployment ratio, the unemployment ratio itself, and the difference between the actual and expected rate of wage inflation. This relationship provides an interpretation of the Phillips curve.

Since each firm is a monopsonist in the sense that it must raise its own wage relative to the average wage in the industry in order to increase the net flow of workers to it, the typical firm faces an intertemporal choice problem. The solution to this problem yields a decision rule that dictates the optimal current wage offer. If each firm attempts to maximize its present value, a relationship among the rate of wage inflation, the expected rate of product price inflation, and the ratio of the value of labor productivity to the average wage can be obtained by aggregating the decision rules. This relationship, together with the aggregate flow supply relationship, provides a model that purports to explain wage and employment dynamics in a labor market.

The model of wage and employment dynamics derived in the paper is readily quantifiable given existing data. In addition, a number of explicit empirical hypotheses are derived which can be used to test its appropriateness.

The model also provides an explanation for the observations made by Phillips and Lipsey.[6] In particular, fluctuations in the rate of product price inflation, which is taken to be exogenous, generate points that suggest a negatively sloped relationship between the proportional rate of change in the average money wage and the unemployment ratio. A cycle in the rate of product price inflation, such as might result from a cycle in general business activity, produces counterclockwise loops of points in a plane in which the rate of wage inflation is measured on the vertical and the unemployment ratio is measured on the horizontal axis.

[6]See Phillips, *op. cit.*, and Lipsey, *op. cit.*

Given the model, a trade-off between the rate of inflation and the unemployment ratio exists in the short run only. If the rate of inflation is increased by an appropriate combination of monetary and fiscal policy, it will be translated into an increase in the rate of wage inflation. To the extent that this latter increase is unanticipated, the effect is an increase in all firms' acceptance rates because unemployed workers perceive the offer of any firm to be higher relative to the average in the market than is actually the case. Thus the unemployment ratio tends to fall. However, the effect is transitory, because eventually the new higher rate of wage inflation will be anticipated. In other words, there is only one unemployment ratio consistent with equilibrium in the market and a fully anticipated rate of inflation. This unemployment ratio, dubbed the "natural rate" of unemployment recently by Friedman, is the only one consistent with the friction in the system in the long run.[7]

The model suggests a number of factors that determine the magnitude of the "natural" unemployment rate. Among these are the relative flow of new participants into the market, the cost of search, and the frequency with which current employees consider the quit decision. An interesting implication of the theory is that a decrease in the search costs incurred by unemployed participants need not necessarily reduce the natural rate of unemployment provided that search costs for employed workers do not change.

The remainder of the paper is divided into six sections. In the first a general description of the conditions envisioned in the hypothetical labor market are introduced. In addition, specific simplifying assumptions used in the analysis are stated. Section 2 deals with a theory of labor supply given imperfect information. On the basis of this theory a net employment flow equation for the typical firm is derived. The decision problem faced by each of the firms is formulated and solved in Section 3. The aggregate wage adjustment and the aggregate employment adjustment equations are derived in Section 4. Section 5 contains an analysis of the complete model. The results of this analysis, as well as other results developed elsewhere in the paper, are summarized in the final section.

1
THE NATURE OF A
LABOR MARKET

Labor markets in the United States are in a constant state of flux. As Holt has pointed out, the annual flow of those who retire or leave a

[7]Milton Friedman, "The Role of Monetary Policy," *American Economic Review* (March 1968), pp. 1–17.

particular market for some other reason is sizable relative to the stock of unemployed participants.[8] The number of employed workers who quit to find better jobs, who change jobs, or who are laid off is even larger. Thus the typical employer must continuously attract new employees just to maintain his labor force at a given size. This fact plays an important role in the model introduced in this paper.

Another important characteristic of any labor market, which will be included in the model, is that knowledge about job opportunities is imperfect. Information is imperfect because it must be obtained sequentially via a search process that takes time, because old information rapidly becomes obsolete in a dynamic setting and because extensive search is expensive. As a consequence, we view the process by which participants contact prospective employers as random, as Holt has recently suggested.[9] More important, a participant must decide on a given offer without perfect information about alternative opportunities under such circumstances. Therefore, each firm finds that its wage policy is an important recruiting tool, at least in the short run.

In this paper the labor market in question is thought to be located in space. That is, all firms in a given geographical area are assumed to face essentially the same labor market. This conceptualization need not imply that all participants in the market are equally qualified for all available jobs. Nevertheless, we make the assumption in order to simplify the analysis. The simplification might be thought to reflect the fact that interfirm mobility within a broad industry classification, such as manufacturing, is greater within a region than interregional mobility within a narrower subclassification.

From the point of view of the workers, the various jobs and firms are assumed to differ only to the extent that they offer different wages. Although this assumption violates the fact that workers have different preferences and that these different preferences are a major determinant of the wage-rate structure, the assumption allows us to concentrate more clearly on the dynamics of wage determination.

The stock-flow relationships of a typical labor market are illustrated in Figure 1. At any moment in time, t, there is a given number of participants, $L(t)$, in the market. The number of participants changes over time in accordance with the magnitude of the net flow from the population at large. For simplicity we assume that the net flow is a constant proportion of the current stock of participants. In particular,

$$\dot{L} = (\eta - \delta)L, \qquad \eta > 0, \qquad \delta > 0, \tag{1}$$

where ηL is the flow of new entrants into the market and δ is the pro-

---

[8]See Holt, *op. cit.*
[9]Holt, *op. cit.*

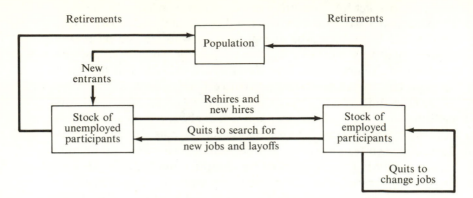

Figure 1.   The labor market.

portional rate at which current participants retire from the market.[10]
This assumption is unrealistic because the flow changes presumably
when the wages offered by firms in the market change relative to the
wage rates offered in other markets. However, our interest here is intramarket behavior, which can be analyzed without taking this fact into
account.

Participants in the market are broadly classified as employed or
unemployed. This classification does not describe a particular participant, but rather the state in which he finds himself at a given moment.
Each participant may pass through the unemployed state from time to
time, although some may do so more or less often than others.

We assume, as indicated in Figure 1, that all new participants enter
as unemployed, or equivalently that the flow into the employed state
is made up of rehires and new hires from the unemployed stock only.
This assumption is an abstraction that might be justified on the grounds
that most new entrants have only recently entered the working population. Few of these have the contacts or the information which would
enable them to become employed without some time spent searching.

The model presented in this paper purports to explain the flow of
new hires, quits to search for new jobs, and intramarket turnover of
employed participants as well as the dynamics of wage determination.
Rehires and layoffs are neglected. Although the magnitudes involved
are not small and the social importance of these flows is large, it seems
to this author that an adequate explanation of these phenomena requires an additional hypothesis to that proposed in this paper. Providing such a hypothesis is beyond the scope of the paper. Nevertheless, the author suggests that attempting to do so might prove to be a
fruitful research effort.

---

[10]A dot over a variable denotes the time derivative of the variable; e.g., $\dot{L} = dL/dt$.

2
THE FLOW SUPPLY OF
LABOR TO THE FIRM

A. New Hires from the Unemployed Stock   Because time is required to search out prospective job opportunities and because time is expensive, not all unemployed workers contact a firm in a given small time interval $(t, t + dt)$. The probability per period that an unemployed worker will make a contact, which we denote as s_0, depends on the magnitude of these costs. That is, the lower are search costs, the smaller is the expected time required to make a contact. The expected time required to make a contact is the inverse of s_0. For the purposes of this analysis, we take s_0 as given.

Presumably a large number of factors affect the ith firm's share of the unemployed participants who do make a contact. However, if information is imperfect, it may be safe to assume that the nature of the ith firm's offer does not affect it. That is, the nature of the offer is not known to the participant until after the contact is made.

Although the nature of the offer may not affect the firm's share, there are other more visible factors associated with the firm which might. For example, one would expect that the relative size of the firm is one. Participants presumably known that larger firms hire at a higher rate than smaller ones. Therefore, a proportionately larger number apply to the larger firm. For this reason we assume that the ith firm's share of contacts is equal to its share of employed workers. In other words, if U denotes the total stock of unemployed participants, N denotes total employment and N_i denotes the ith firm's labor force, then $s_0(N_i/N)U$ is the expected flow of unemployed workers who contact the ith firm in the interval $(t, t + dt)$.

Information about alternative job offers is imperfect at any point in time for two reasons: First, in a dynamic setting old information rapidly becomes obsolete. Second, the cost of obtaining up to date information is not inconsequential. In particular, time is required to search out such information. The time required for search implies that the participant must reallocate time from some other valued activity such as work or leisure. In addition to this opportunity cost, search involves "out-of-pocket" costs.

In a dynamic setting offers are usually obtained sequentially and must be responded to within a relatively short time interval. These facts, combined with the fact that obtaining more information is costly, imply that the decision to accept a given offer is often based on a comparison of the offer with the participant's rather general notions about alternatives. The extent of knowledge about alternatives that the participant does possess is obtained primarily from past offers received and previous jobs held.

Since the opportunity cost of time spent searching is higher for an employed worker than it is for an unemployed one, we assume that the probability per period of making a contact is smaller if the worker is employed than it is when the worker is not. In other words, if s_1 is the probability of making a contact, given that the worker is employed, then

$$s_0 > s_1. \tag{2}$$

Equivalently, the expected time required to make a contact is longer when the worker is employed.

Suppose that the kth unemployed participant has an offer from the ith firm at a particular moment in time. The wage offered is denoted by w_i. Although the kth participant, because of imperfect information, does not know the true average wage, $\bar{w}$, in the market, he does have an expectation concerning its level. This we denote as $\bar{w}_k^e$.

Let us assume that the participant acts as if he expects with certainty that his next offer will be $\bar{w}_k^e$. Clearly, if w_i were greater than $\bar{w}_k^e$, he would accept the job, because the wage offer is better than any he expects to receive in the future. However, if $w_i < \bar{w}_k^e$, he will continue to search whether he accepts the job or not. Of course, the probability of receiving an offer in the next period depends on his decision.

To determine whether or not the participant will accept the offer in the case of $w_i < \bar{w}_k^e$, we must take account of the different expected income streams implied by each of the alternatives. The expected income stream after a period $1/s_1$ in length will be the same whether he accepts the job or not, because after that period he expects with certainty to be earning a wage equal to $\bar{w}_k^e$. If he does accept the job, he can expect to earn an amount w_i/s_1 during the interim period. However, if he rejects it, he expects to be unemployed for a period of length $1/s_0$ and to be employed at a wage $\bar{w}_k^e$ for the remainder. Since $1/s_0$, which is the expected time unemployed if he rejects the offer, is assumed less than the $1/s_1$, his expected earnings during the interval in question are positive and equal to

$$\left(\frac{1}{s_1} - \frac{1}{s_0}\right) \bar{w}_k^e.$$

This amount represents the opportunity cost of accepting the job. Assuming that the participant accepts if and only if the expected income stream is greater by so doing, the acceptance condition is that[11]

$$cw_i \geq \bar{w}_k^e, \tag{3}$$

[11]The term $\bar{w}_k^e/c$ is analogous to what Holt, *op. cit.*, calls the acceptance wage. However, Holt assumes that the typical participant is willing to trade off time spent unemployed for a lower wage. That is, the longer a participant is unemployed, the lower is his acceptance wage. This hypothesis plays a crucial role in Holt's interpretation of the Phillips curve. Thus the interpretation given in this paper and Holt's interpretation are quite different.

where[12]

$$c = \frac{1/s_1}{(1/s_1) - (1/s_0)} = \frac{s_0}{s_0 - s_1} > 1. \tag{4}$$

Clearly, the argument above implies that some participant may accept an offer even if it is less than the expected market average. In fact, as the difference between the costs of search given unemployment and the cost of search given employment decreases, the difference between the acceptable wage and the expected market average rises. In the limiting case in which search costs are the same, all those who contact the firm will accept any positive wage; i.e., $\overline{w}_k^e/c \to 0$ as $s_1 \to s_0$. In this case the income earned while searching for a better job is simply a windfall.

The participant forms his expectation about the market average wage by combining information about wage offers that he obtained during the prior search period. If the past were identical to the present, we might think of the $\overline{w}_k^e$'s as means of samples drawn from the population of all wage offers. Should this be true, the frequency distribution of all $\overline{w}_k^e$'s would be centered around the population average, the true market average wage offer $\overline{w}$.

However, in a dynamic setting the parameters of the frequency distribution of wage offers need not be constant over time. By definition the mean of the population of wage offers is growing during a period of wage inflation. Thus, during such a period, an average of wage offers obtained in a time interval prior to an offer will underestimate the true

---

[12]In the discussion no account is taken of either expected wage inflation or time preference. These factors can be accounted for by assuming that the participant will take the alternative that yields the higher wealth. If the kth participant were to reject the offer, the present value of his future expected wage stream is given by

$$\overline{w}_k^e \int_0^\infty (1 - e^{-s_0 t}) e^{-(r - g^e)t} dt = \overline{w}_k^e \left(\frac{1}{r - g^e} - \frac{1}{s_0 + r - g^e} \right),$$

where r denotes the nominal interest rate and g^e denotes the expected rate of wage inflation. Of course, $1 - e^{-s_0 t}$ is the probability at date t in the future of having a job, because s_0 is the probability per period of receiving an offer. The present value of the kth participant's future expected wage stream is

$$\overline{w}_k^e \int_0^\infty (1 - e^{-s_1 t}) e^{-(r - g^e)t} dt + w_i \int_0^\infty e^{-(s_1 + r - g^e)t} dt$$
$$= \overline{w}_k^e \left(\frac{1}{r - g^e} - \frac{1}{s_1 + r - g^e} \right) + \frac{w_i}{s_1 + r - g^e}$$

if he were to accept the offer of the ith firm. If this term is greater than or equal to the former one, he will accept the job offered by the ith firm. In other words, he accepts if $cw_i \geq \overline{w}_k^e$, where

$$c = \frac{s_0 + r - g^e}{s_0 - s_1}.$$

The interest-rate effect on the acceptance decision as derived here is analogous to the interest-rate effect on the participation decision as derived by Lucas and Rapping, "Real Wages, Employment, and Inflation," this volume.

market average. Presumably the participant will take this fact into account by attempting to make an appropriate adjustment.

Suppose that the participant includes in his sample all information about wages obtained during a time interval $2h$ in length prior to the current date t.[13] Provided that the process by which the information is gathered is random, the sample mean, which is denoted as $\tilde{w}_k(t)$, is an unbiased estimate of the average of all offers made during the interval. If the interval is short so that the rate of wage inflation is approximately constant during it, the expectation of $\tilde{w}_k(t)$ is approximately equal to the true average of the population of wage offers at the midpoint. That is,

$$E(\tilde{w}_k(t)) = \overline{w}(t - h), \qquad (5)$$

where E denotes the expectation operator.

If participants expect wage inflation, it would be rational for them to adjust $\tilde{w}_k(t)$ for it. Suppose all participants have the same expectation about the proportional rate of wage inflation, denoted by g^e. Then, since h is small, we have

$$\overline{w}_k^e(t) = \tilde{w}_k(t)e^{hg^e}. \qquad (6)$$

Clearly, given this formulation, all unemployed participants would neither reject nor accept an offer made by the ith firm. Because of the errors made in attempting to estimate the average wage offer with limited information, the $\tilde{w}_k$'s are different for different participants. Those with generally high $\tilde{w}_k$'s will reject the offer and those whose $\tilde{w}_k$'s are relatively low will tend to accept the offer. The higher is w_i relative to the average of all $\tilde{w}_k$'s, the higher is the acceptance rate.

To make this idea more precise, we assume that the $\tilde{w}_k(t)$'s are distributed about their expectation, $\overline{w}(t - h)$. If the coefficient of variation is a constant through time and f denotes the cumulative density function, then the proportion of all participants whose $\tilde{w}_k$ is less than some value, z, is given by $f(z/\overline{w}(t - h))$. If, in addition, the distribution is symmetric and unimodal,

$$P(\tilde{w}_k \leq z) = f\left(\frac{z}{\overline{w}(t - h)}\right),$$

$$1 > f > 0, \quad f' > 0, \quad f'' \lessgtr 0 \quad \text{as} \quad z \gtrless \overline{w}(t - h). \qquad (7)$$

Since the kth unemployed participant will accept an offer from the ith firm if and only if condition (3) is satisfied, the proportion of all unemployed participants who would accept such an offer is given by

$$P(\tilde{w}_k(t) \leq cw_i(t)\overline{e}^{g^e h}) = f\left(\frac{cw_i(t)\overline{e}^{g^e h}}{\overline{w}(t - h)}\right). \qquad (8)$$

[13]The interval $(t, t - 2h)$ is the period during which information is gathered for the purpose of making decisions during the interval $(t + dt, t)$. The length of the former interval is assumed large relative to the length of the decision interval. It is also assumed that the intersection of the two intervals includes only t, the date of the offer.

Alternatively, the value of this function can be interpreted as the probability that a randomly selected participant would accept such an offer or the expected proportion of acceptances from a randomly selected sample of unemployed participants.

It proves convenient to write the first term of the argument of f in a slightly different form. Since we assume that h is a short interval of time, we know that

$$\frac{\overline{w}(t)}{\overline{w}(t-h)} \approx e^{hg},$$

where g is the rate of wage inflation during the interval. It follows, then, that

$$\frac{cw_i(t)\overline{e}^{g^e h}}{\overline{w}(t-h)} \approx c\,\frac{w_i(t)}{\overline{w}(t)}\,e^{h(g-g^e)}. \tag{9}$$

In the sequel the ratio of the ith firm's wage offer to the average offer, $w_i/\overline{w}$, is called the ith firm's own relative wage offer.

Of course, $P(\tilde{w}_k \le cw_i\overline{e}^{hg^e})$ is not the probability per period that the kth unemployed participant will be hired by the ith firm. It is instead the expected proportion of the flow of those that do receive an offer who accept the offer. To be in the former group, the kth participant must apply to the ith firm for a job and must be qualified for the job available. Since we assume all participants are qualified for all jobs, the flow of new hires from the stock of unemployed participants, H_{i0}, is given by

$$H_{i0} = s_0 f\left(c\,\frac{w_i}{\overline{w}}\,e^{h(g-g^e)}\right)\frac{N_i}{N}\,U. \tag{10}$$

B. Voluntary Quits from the Stock of Employed Participants

The problem of whether or not to quit in order to search for a better job, faced by the kth employed participant, is very similar to the acceptance decision faced by the unemployed worker. If the kth participant is employed by the ith firm, he can either continue to work for that firm at a wage w_i or quit to search for a better job. Although he can also remain employed and search for a better job, we assume that the expected time, $1/s_1$, required to find one is greater than it would be, $1/s_0$, if he were unemployed. If he acts as if he will receive his expectation concerning the market average wage, $\overline{w}_k^e$, when the job is found, he will quit if and only if the expected income stream is larger by so doing. In other words, from the argument given above, he quits if and only if

$$cw_i < \overline{w}_k^e. \tag{11}$$

The frequency with which the typical employee considers the quit decision is presumably finite. If it were not, he would have no time for any other activity. Let us assume that the probability of considering the quit decision within a small time interval $(t, t + dt)$ is positive and fixed over time. If we denote this probability as s_2, then the expected flow of the ith firm's employees who consider the decision within the interval is $s_2 N_i$.[14]

Let us assume as before that

$$\overline{w}_k^e = \tilde{w}_k e^{hg^e}, \tag{12}$$

where $\tilde{w}_k(t)$ is an average of a sample of wage information obtained by the participant during an interval $2h$ in length prior to the current date t and g^e is the expected rate of wage inflation. If the distribution of the $\tilde{w}_k$'s for employed workers is the same as that for the unemployed, and if the flow of those who are considering the quit decision can be considered a random sample in the sense that the corresponding $\tilde{w}_k$'s are a random sample from the set of all $\tilde{w}_k$'s, then the probability that one of those in the flow will quit is $P(\tilde{w}_k > cw_i \overline{e}^{hg^e})$. But, because $P(\tilde{w}_k > cw_i \overline{e}^{hg^e})$ is equal to $1 - P(\tilde{w}_k \leq cw_i \overline{e}^{hg^e})$, the expected flow of quits from the ith firm's labor force to the stock of unemployed, Q_{i0}, is given by

$$Q_{i0} = s_2 \left[1 - f\left(c \frac{w_i}{\overline{w}} e^{h(g - g^e)} \right) \right] N_i. \tag{13}$$

In other words, the proportion of those who are considering the quit decision who actually quit is equal to unity minus the proportion who would accept an offer from the ith firm if given one.

C. Intramarket Turnover   To complete a theory of the flow supply of labor to the individual firms, we turn now to a consideration of those factors which affect intramarket turnover. Since searching for a new job is expensive, no employee of the ith firm will even bother to search unless he expects that the wage to be obtained is greater than the one he currently receives. Thus, if his expectation concerning the average market wage is $\overline{w}_k^e$, then the kth employee of the ith firm will be searching for a new job at any given moment, t, if and only if

$$w_i < \overline{w}_k^e, \tag{14}$$

where again

$$\overline{w}_k^e = \tilde{w}_k e^{hg^e}. \tag{15}$$

As a consequence, the number of the ith firm's employees who are currently searching, denoted by S_i, is given by

$$S_i = P(\tilde{w}_k > w_i \overline{e}^{hg^e}) N_i \tag{16}$$

---

[14]Much of the discussion here is based implicitly on a theory of how the typical participant in the labor market allocates his time among work, search, and decision. For an excellent presentation of the economics of time allocation, see G. Becker, "A Theory of the Allocation of Time," *Economic Journal* (September 1965), pp. 493–517.

if the ith firm's labor force can be considered a random sample of all participants in the sense previously defined.

Suppose that the kth employee of the ith firm has obtained an offer from the jth firm. His decision problem is different from that of an unemployed worker with a job offer or an employed worker who is considering quitting to reenter the unemployed pool simply because the opportunity costs of rejecting the outstanding offer are different. In particular, such a worker is in the advantageous position of having two offers—one from the new prospective employer and one from his current employer.

Suppose that $\overline{w}_k^e > w_j > w_i$. In this case both the wage offered and his current wage are less than his expectation concerning the market average. Thus he will continue to search for the better job he believes exists no matter what his choice. In addition, he acts as if he expects with certainty to obtain the better job after a period of length $1/s_1$, which is the expected time required to obtain a new offer. As a consequence, if there were costs of changing jobs, such as the wages he might have to give up in order to move his household or costs he might have to incur to be adequately qualified for the new job, he would accept the offer if and only if these costs could be made up within the interim.

Suppose instead that $w_j \geq \overline{w}_k^e$. In this case he would not search further because he acts as if he believes there is no better job. Besides saving the cost of search, he can amortize any cost of changing jobs over a longer time period because he never expects to have to change jobs again. Finally, for all the reasons discussed above he would never accept if $w_j \leq w_i$.

Let us assume (a) that the costs of changing jobs are so large that they cannot be made up within a time interval of length $1/s_1$ for reasonable wage offers, but (b) that the time horizon is sufficiently long so that it always pays to change jobs if $w_j \geq \overline{w}_k^e$. Then the kth searching employee will quit the ith firm and accept the jth firm's offer if and only if

$$w_j \geq \overline{w}_k^e > w_i. \tag{17}$$

Of course, not all the ith firm's searching employees make a contact each period and not all those that do contact the jth firm. The probability that a searching employee does make a contact is s_1. If we assume as before that the jth firm's share of contacts depends on its relative size, then the expected proportion of the ith firm's searching employees who contact the jth firm is equal to $s_1 N_j/N$.

To determine the expected proportion of those who accept the offer, we must take into account the fact that each searching employee has an expected average wage that is greater than w_i. In addition, the acceptance rate is zero if $w_i \geq w_j$. Therefore, if $w_j > w_i$, then the expected acceptance rate is the probability that $w_j \geq \bar{w}_k^e$ given that $\bar{w}_k^e > w_i$. In terms of the distribution of the $\tilde{w}_k$'s, this conditional probability is equal to

$$\frac{P(\tilde{w}_k < w_j \bar{e}^{hg^e}) - P(\tilde{w}_k < w_i \bar{e}^{hg^e})}{P(\tilde{w}_k > w_i \bar{e}^{hg^e})}.$$

This fact and (16) imply that the expected flow who quit the ith firm to take a job with the jth firm, which we denote as Q_{ij}, is given by

$$Q_{ij} = \begin{cases} s_1 \dfrac{N_j}{N} [P(\tilde{w}_k < w_j \bar{e}^{hg^e}) - P(\tilde{w}_k < w_i \bar{e}^{hg^e})]N_i & \text{if } w_i \leq w_j, \\ 0 & \text{if } w_i \geq w_j. \end{cases} \tag{18}$$

But, the ith firm's losses are the jth firm's gains, i.e., $Q_{ij} = H_{ji}$, where H_{ji} denotes the jth firm's hires from the ith firm. Therefore

$$H_{ij} = \begin{cases} 0 & \text{if } w_i \leq w_j, \\ s_1 \dfrac{N_i}{N} [P(\tilde{w}_k < w_i \bar{e}^{hg^e}) - P(\tilde{w}_k < w_j \bar{e}^{hg^e})]N_j & \text{if } w_i \geq w_j. \end{cases} \tag{19}$$

Finally, since the net flow of employed workers from the jth firm to the ith firm, T_{ij}, is equal to the difference between hires and quits, it follows from (18) and (19) that

$$\begin{aligned} T_{ij} &= H_{ij} - Q_{ij} \\ &= s_1 \frac{N_i}{N} [P(\tilde{w}_k < w_i \bar{e}^{hg^e}) - P(\tilde{w}_k < w_j \bar{e}^{hg^e})]N_j, \end{aligned} \tag{20}$$

independent of the magnitudes of w_i and w_j.

By substituting for $P(\tilde{w}_k < w_i \bar{e}^{hg^e})$ and $P(\tilde{w}_k < w_j \bar{e}^{hg^e})$ from (7), we can show that (20) is equivalent to

$$T_{ij} = s_1 \frac{N_i}{N} \left[f\left(\frac{w_i}{\bar{w}} e^{h(g-g^e)} \right) - f\left(\frac{w_j}{\bar{w}} e^{h(g-g^e)} \right) \right] N_j. \tag{21}$$

Since $T_{ii} = 0$, the net expected flow of employees from all firms to the ith firm is simply $\sum_j T_{ij}$. That is,

$$T_i = \sum_j T_{ij} = \left[s_1 f\left(\frac{w_i}{\bar{w}} e^{h(g-g^e)} \right) - \alpha s_1 \right] N_i, \tag{22}$$

where

$$\alpha = \sum_j \frac{N_j}{N} f\left(\frac{w_j}{\bar{w}} e^{h(g-g^e)} \right). \tag{23}$$

D. **The Flow Supply** We can now complete the derivation of the *i*th firm's flow supply of labor. The net rate of change in the *i*th firm's labor force, $\dot{N}_i$, is equal to new hires plus net transfers from other firms less the sum of the flow who quit to reenter the unemployed pool and retirements, so

$$\dot{N}_i = H_{i0} + T_i - Q_{i0} - \delta N_i. \tag{24}$$

By substituting appropriately from (10), (13), and (22) we obtain

$$\frac{\dot{N}_i}{N_i} = \beta\left(\frac{w_i}{\bar{w}}\, e^{h(g-g^e)}, u\right)$$

$$= \left(s_0\frac{u}{1-u} + s_2\right) f\left(c\,\frac{w_i}{\bar{w}}\, e^{h(g-g^e)}\right) + s_1 f\left(\frac{w_i}{\bar{w}}\, e^{h(g-g^e)}\right)$$

$$- \alpha s_1 - s_2 - \delta. \tag{25}$$

where $u = U/L$.

The salient feature for the purpose of analyzing the optimal behavior of any firm is that the proportional rate of change in the firm's labor force is independent of the size of its labor force. It does depend on the firm's own relative wage and on the unemployment rate in the market. In particular,

$$\beta_1 = c\left(s_0\frac{u}{1-u} + s_2\right)f'\left(c\,\frac{w_i}{\bar{w}}\, e^{h(g-g^e)}\right) + s_1 f'\left(\frac{w_i}{\bar{w}}\, e^{h(g-g^e)}\right) > 0,$$

$$\beta_2 = \frac{s_0}{(1-u)^2}\, f\left(c\,\frac{w_i}{\bar{w}}\, e^{h(g-g^e)}\right) > 0. \tag{26}$$

An increase, *ceteris paribus*, in either the firm's own wage relative to the market average or in the unemployment ratio increases the net flow of labor to the firm.

The second partial derivatives follow:

$$\beta_{12} = \frac{cs_0}{(1-u)^2}\, f'\left(c\,\frac{w_i}{\bar{w}}\, e^{h(g-g^e)}\right) > 0,$$

$$\beta_{11} = c^2\left(s_0\frac{u}{1-u} + s_2\right)f''\left(c\,\frac{w_i}{\bar{w}}\, e^{h(g-g^e)}\right) + s_1 f''\left(\frac{w_i}{\bar{w}}\, e^{h(g-g^e)}\right). \tag{27}$$

Since $c > 1$ and f'' is negative (positive) when its argument is greater (less) than unity,

$$\beta_{11} = \begin{cases} <0 & \text{if } \dfrac{w_i}{\bar{w}}\, e^{h(g-g^e)} \geq 1, \\[2mm] >0 & \text{if } \dfrac{w_i}{\bar{w}}\, e^{h(g-g^e)} \leq \dfrac{1}{c}. \end{cases} \tag{28}$$

3
A THEORY OF WAGE CHOICE

The flow-supply equation, (25), has an interesting feature. Although the firm can vary the net rate of change in its employment level by appropriate choices of its own relative wage rate, there is only one such rate consistent with equilibrium in the long run. In other words, the long-run supply curve faced by the firm is perfectly elastic. The firm is a monopsonist in a dynamic sense only. In this section an optimal wage policy is derived for a firm facing this labor-supply condition.

The consequence of being a dynamic monopsonist is that the wage bill paid at any point in time depends on the rate at which the firm chooses to adjust the size of its labor force. The firm with a more rapidly growing labor force must pay a higher wage. Thus an implicit cost of adjusting the size of the labor force exists. The firm's intertemporal choice problem is a consequence of this fact.

Recently several authors have constructed theories of investment based on the concept of explicit costs of adjusting the capital stock. Included among those are Eisner and Strotz, Lucas, Gould, and Treadway.[15] The formal similarity of their models to the one developed in this paper is not coincidental.

For simplicity let us assume that the ith firm produces a single product which it sells in a perfectly competitive market at a price P_i. Labor is the only factor of production. The firm's net cash flow at date t is given by

$$R_i(t) = P_i(t)F_i(N_i(t)) - w_i(t)N_i(t), \qquad (29)$$

where $F_i(N_i)$ is the rate of production. If the firm faces a competitive capital market with a nominal interest rate, r, which is expected to prevail in the future, then the present value of the firm is defined as

$$V = \int_0^\infty R_i(t)e^{-rt}\, dt. \qquad (30)$$

The firm's optimal wage-employment policy is one for which the time path of w_i and N_i maximize V subject to (25) and the initial employment level.

A number of assumptions concerning future and current values of parameters to the firm's decision problem are necessary to obtain a solution. These follow: (a) The firm acts as if its own wage policy has

---

[15]See R. Eisner and R. H. Strotz, "Determinants of Business Investment," in Commission on Money and Credit, *Impacts of Monetary Policy* (Prentice-Hall, Inc., Englewood Cliffs, N.J., 1963), pp. 59–337; R. E. Lucas, "Optimal Investment Policy and the Flexible Accelerator," *International Economic Review* (February 1967), pp. 78–85; J. P. Gould, "Adjustment Cost in the Theory of Investment of the Firm," *Review of Economic Studies* (1968), pp. 47–55; and A. Treadway, *Rational Entrepreneurial Behavior and the Dynamics of Investment*, Ph.D. thesis, University of Chicago, 1967.

no effect on either the average market wage or the aggregate employment level; (b) the firm expects its own product price and the average market wage to inflate at the same rate, p^e, in the future; (c) the expected current level of the product price, $P_i^e(0)$, and the expected current average wage rate, $\bar{w}^e(0)$, are given; and (d) the firm expects the unemployment ratio to equal some value, u^e, in the future. How these expected values are related to the actual we leave unspecified.

Given these assumptions, (25) implies that

$$\frac{\dot{N}_i(t)}{N_i(t)} = \beta\left(\frac{w_i(t)}{\bar{w}^e(t)}, u^e\right). \tag{31}$$

Since β is monotonic, we can write

$$\frac{w_i(t)}{\bar{w}^e(t)} = \chi\left(\frac{\dot{N}_i(t)}{N_i(t)}, u^e\right). \tag{32}$$

The partial derivatives of the function χ are related to those of β in the following ways:

$$\chi_1 = \frac{1}{\beta_1} > 0, \tag{33a}$$

$$\chi_2 = -\frac{\beta_2}{\beta_1} < 0, \tag{33b}$$

$$\chi_{11} = -\frac{\beta_{11}}{\beta_1^3} \begin{cases} >0 & \text{if } \chi \geq 1, \\ <0 & \text{if } \chi \leq \frac{1}{c} < 1. \end{cases} \tag{33c}$$

The signs are implied by (26), (27), and (28). Finally, the value of the firm can be written

$$V = \bar{w}^e(0) \int_0^\infty \left[v_i F_i(N_i(t)) - \frac{w_i(t)}{\bar{w}^e(t)} N_i(t)\right] \bar{e}^{\rho t}\, dt,$$

where

$$v_i = \frac{P_i^e(0)}{\bar{w}^e(0)}, \tag{34}$$

$$\rho = r - p^e. \tag{35}$$

The parameter ρ is the real interest rate and v_i is the initial ratio of the firm's expected product price to the expected average wage rate in the labor market that the firm faces.

Formally, the firm's problem is to choose $N(t)$, $t > 0$, to

$$\max \int_0^\infty \left[v_i F_i(N_i(t)) - \chi\left(\frac{\dot{N}_i(t)}{N_i(t)}, u^e\right) N_i(t)\right] \bar{e}^{\rho t}\, dt. \tag{36}$$

This is a standard problem in the calculus of variations. A solution or extremal, denoted by $N^0(t)$, must satisfy the conditions stated below.

Define $\lambda(t)$ equal to the implicit cost of the last man added to the net employment flow at date t; i.e.,

$$\lambda(t) = \frac{\partial(\chi N_i)}{\partial \dot{N}_i} = \chi_1\left(\frac{\dot{N}_i(t)}{N_i(t)}, u^e\right). \tag{37}$$

The Euler–Lagrange condition is

$$\dot{\lambda}(t) = \left(\rho - \frac{\dot{N}_i(t)}{N_i(t)}\right)\lambda(t) + \chi\left(\frac{\dot{N}_i(t)}{N_i(t)}, u^e\right) - v_iF_i'(N_i(t)). \tag{38}$$

The Legendre condition requires that

$$\frac{\partial \lambda(t)}{\partial \dot{N}_i(t)} = \frac{\chi_{11}(\dot{N}_i/N_i(t), u^e)}{N_i(t)} \geq 0. \tag{39}$$

The transversality condition can be stated as

$$\lim_{t\to\infty} \lambda(t)\bar{e}^{\rho t} = 0. \tag{40}$$

An economic interpretation of these conditions is straightforward. Given (40), equation (38) is equivalent to

$$\lambda(t) = \int_t^\infty \left[v_iF_i'N_i(\tau) - \chi\left(\frac{\dot{N}_i(\tau)}{N_i(\tau)}, u^e\right) + \lambda(\tau)\left(\frac{\dot{N}_i(\tau)}{N_i(\tau)}\right)\right]\bar{e}^{\rho(\tau-t)}\,dt.$$

The term $v_iF_i' - \chi$ is the marginal contribution to the net cash flow at date τ of a man hired at date t. Equation (31) implies that a worker added to the labor force at date t contributes an amount equal to $\dot{N}_i(\tau)/N_i(\tau)$ at date τ. This contribution is valued by $\lambda(\tau)$, the opportunity cost of obtaining the same change through an appropriate choice of firm's own relative wage at date τ. The integral is, then, the present value of adding a man to the net employment flow at date t. Thus (38) requires that the present value of changing the level of employment must be equal to the implicit marginal cost of doing so at every date in the plan. The Legendre condition requires that the marginal cost of changing the labor force be nondecreasing. Finally, the present value at the start of the plan of changing the labor force at the end of the plan must be zero, according to the transversality condition.

Equations (37) and (38) constitute a system of autonomous differential equations in λ and N. Our task is to identify those solutions to this system which also satisfy (39) and (40). If an extremal exists, it must be an element of the set of such solutions. We can analyze the system with the aid of Figure 2.

In Figure 2(a), the relationship between the own relative wage and the rate of growth in employment is illustrated. The slope, which is the marginal cost of changing the level of employment, initially falls and

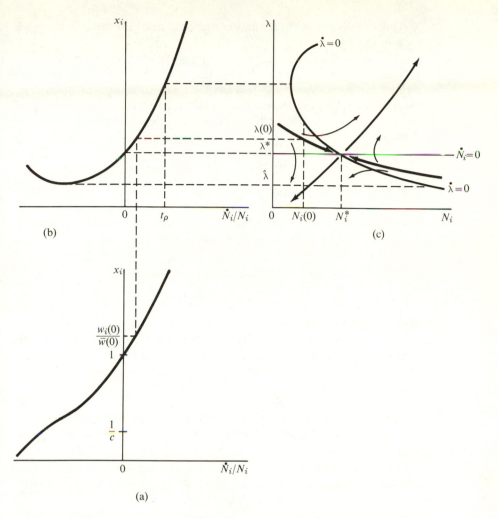

Figure 2

then rises as the rate of growth increases. The inflection point occurs in the interval $1/c < x < 1$ as implied by (33c). Although the exact position of the curve depends on a number of factors, we have drawn it through x equal to unity because the typical firm will neither gain nor lose workers when its wage equals the average in the market. The curve in Figure 2(b) relates the slope of the curve in (a) to the proportional rate of change in employment. The phase diagram, (c), illustrates the trajectories of the differential equation system.

Note that the marginal cost of changing employment is U-shaped. The Legendre condition requires that the marginal cost *not* diminish along an extremal, so the optimal choice of the rate of growth given any λ corresponds to the upward sloping portion of the curve in (b). Therefore, the extremal must be a solution to (37) and (38) such that

$\lambda(t)$ never falls below the minimum marginal cost; the latter is denoted by $\hat{\lambda}$ in the figure.

The value of λ consistent with no change in the level of employment is λ^* in the figure. Clearly employment will grow if λ is greater than λ^* and fall over time if λ is less than λ^*. The directions of motion in the various regions of the phase diagram reflect that fact.

To complete the phase diagram, we note that (38) implies

$$\left. \frac{\partial \lambda}{\partial N_i} \right|_{\dot{\lambda}=0} = \frac{v_i F_i''(N_i)}{\rho - \dot{N}_i/N_i}. \tag{41}$$

If the marginal product of labor diminishes, $F_i'' < 0$, and the real interest rate is positive, $\rho > 0$, then the slope of the $\dot{\lambda} = 0$ singular curve is positive (negative) when the rate of growth in employment is greater than (less than) the real interest rate. Equation (38) also implies that

$$\frac{\partial \dot{\lambda}}{\partial N_i} = -v_i F''(N_i). \tag{42}$$

Therefore, $\dot{\lambda}$ is positive for values of N_i sufficiently large if the marginal product diminishes.

Clearly, the singular point (λ^*, N_i^*) is a saddle. Thus there are only two trajectories, those indicated by the negatively sloped trajectories, which converge to the singular point. Since $\lambda(t) \to \lambda^*$ as $t \to \infty$ along these solutions, the transversality as well as the other necessary conditions are satisfied by them.

Provided that the integral in (36) is bounded from above and that the value of the integral is positive along either of the trajectories which converge to the origin, so that there is no incentive for the firm to go out of business, the segment of either trajectory that connects the initial employment level, $N_i(0)$, to N_i^* is the unique optimal solution to the firm's problem if the integrand of the integral in (36) is concave in the region $\lambda > \hat{\lambda}$.[16] It is a simple matter to show that the latter condition does hold given a diminishing marginal product of labor.[17] The other requirements we assume true in the sequel.

Given a particular set of parameter values, the present value of hiring an additional man is that value of λ on the optimal trajectories

---

[16]In other words, if these conditions are satisfied, any path that satisfies the necessary conditions is a unique solution to the problem specified in (36). See M. R. Hestenes, *Calculus of Variations and Optimal Control Theory* (Wiley, New York, 1966), p. 134.

[17]The integral in (36) is concave if the Hessian of the integrand is negative definite in $\dot{N}_i$ and N_i. Let H denote the Hessian; i.e.,

$$H = \begin{bmatrix} -x_{11}/N_i & \dot{N}_i x_{11}/N_i^2 \\ \dot{N}_i x_{11}/N_i^2 & v_i f'' - (\dot{N}_i/N_i)^2 x_{11}/N_i \end{bmatrix}.$$

Since $x_{11} > 0$ in the region $\lambda > \hat{\lambda}$, $-x_{11}/N_i < 0$ in that region given positive employment levels. Since $|H| = -v_i f'' x_{11}/N_i > 0$, H is negative definite in the region $\lambda > \hat{\lambda}$, $N_i > 0$.

which corresponds to the current level of employment. For example, if the current level of employment is $N_i(0)$ in the figure, then the present value of adding a man to the net employment flow is $\lambda(0)$. The optimal rate of growth is that value, $\dot{N}_i(0)/N_i(0)$, which equates the marginal cost to $\lambda(0)$. The relative wage choice implied is $w_i(0)/\overline{w}(0)$ in Figure 2(a).

Since the slope of the curve formed by the optimal trajectories is negative, the present value of adding a worker to the net employment flow falls as labor is accumulated. This result is a consequence of the assumption that the marginal product of labor diminishes or that the marginal cost of production in the static sense rises. The optimal rate of growth in the labor force declines as well as labor is accumulated. It does so because both the marginal cost of production and the marginal cost of adjusting employment rise.

A point on one of the optimal trajectories reflects the present value of adding a worker *given* the optimal future time path of employment. The values of λ along these trajectories vary because the optimal future plans differ for different initial employment levels. The optimal plans will also differ for different values of the parameters v_i, ρ, and u^e. That is,

$$\lambda^0 = \lambda^0(N_i, v_i, \rho, u^e), \tag{43}$$

where λ^0 is the imputed value at the margin of changing the net employment flow given the optimal future time path of employment. We have already proved that

$$\frac{\partial \lambda^0}{\partial N_i} = \lambda_1^0 < 0. \tag{44}$$

Below we attempt to ascertain the signs of the other partial derivatives.

Since the function χ is independent of both v_i and ρ, a change in either does not affect the position of the $\dot{N}_i = 0$ singular curve. However, it follows from (38) that

$$\left.\frac{\partial N_i}{\partial v_i}\right|_{\lambda=0} = \frac{-F_i'}{v_i F_i''} > 0,$$

$$\left.\frac{\partial N_i}{\partial \rho}\right|_{\lambda=0} = \frac{\lambda}{v_i F_i''} < 0.$$

In other words, an increase, *ceteris paribus*, in the ratio of the output price to the average wage shifts the $\lambda = 0$ singular curve everywhere to the right in Figure 2, while an increase, *ceteris paribus*, in the real interest rate shifts it leftward. The consequence is an increase in the equilibrium level of employment in the first case and a decrease in the second.

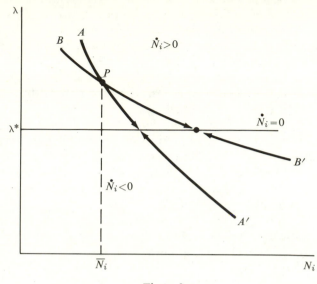

Figure 3

Although the equilibrium value of λ is unaffected in either case, the optimal trajectories shift. In particular, an increase in the price-to-average wage ratio shifts the trajectories upward. An increase in the real interest rate shifts the trajectories downward. At least such is the case near equilibrium. Below we prove that these results hold everywhere.

To prove that

$$\frac{\partial \lambda^0}{\partial v_i} = \lambda_2^0 > 0, \tag{45}$$

consider Figure 3. In the figure let the BB' curve represent the optimal trajectory that corresponds to a larger value of v_i than the value which determines the position of the trajectories represented by the AA' curve. The value of ρ is held constant.

The two curves are drawn to conform to the fact that the equilibrium employment level increases given an increase, *ceteris paribus*, in v_i. However, we assume that (45) does not hold everywhere. In particular, the two schedules intersect at some point P. The point of intersection is assumed to be in the region where $\dot{N}_i > 0$.

Clearly, if the two curves intersect at P, as assumed, then the slope of the optimal trajectory, λ_1^0, must not decrease given an increase in v_i at the point P. In other words,

$$\left.\frac{\partial \lambda_1^0}{\partial v_i}\right|_P \geq 0. \tag{46}$$

The slope of any trajectory at a point in the plane is given by

$$\frac{\partial\lambda}{\partial N_i} = \frac{\dot{\lambda}}{\dot{N}_i} = \frac{(\rho - \dot{N}_i/N_i)\lambda + \chi(\dot{N}_i/N_i, u^e) - v_i F_i'(N_i)}{\dot{N}_i}. \quad (47)$$

Since $\dot{N}_i$ does not depend directly on v_i,

$$\frac{\partial(\partial\lambda/\partial N_i)}{\partial v_i} = \frac{-F'(N_i)}{\dot{N}_i} \lessgtr 0 \qquad \text{as } \dot{N}_i \gtrless 0,$$

which contradicts (46) since $\dot{N}_i > 0$ at P. A similar argument can be used to show that no intersection occurs in the region wheren $\dot{N}_i$ is negative.

To show that

$$\frac{\partial\lambda^0}{\partial\rho} = \lambda_3^0 < 0, \quad (48)$$

simply let AA' represent the optimal trajectories for a larger value of ρ than that which determines the position of BB'. An assumed intersection at P requires

$$\left.\frac{\partial\lambda_1}{\partial\rho}\right|_P \leq 0. \quad (49)$$

However, (47) implies

$$\frac{\partial(\partial\lambda/\partial N_i)}{\partial\rho} = \frac{\lambda}{\dot{N}_i} \gtrless 0 \qquad \text{as } \dot{N}_i \gtrless 0,$$

which contradicts (49). The possibility of an intersection in the region where $\dot{N}_i$ is negative can be eliminated by a similar argument.[18]

The effect of a change in the expected unemployment rate on the optimal trajectories is ambiguous. To understand why, we first note that

$$\lambda^* = \chi_1(0, u^e). \quad (50)$$

Therefore,

$$\frac{\partial\lambda^*}{\partial u^e} = \chi_{12} < 0. \quad (51)$$

Equation (38) implies that

$$\left.\frac{\partial N_i}{\partial u^e}\right|_{\dot{\lambda}=0} = \frac{\chi_2}{v_i F''} > 0, \quad (52)$$

provided that F'' is negative. In other words, an increase in the expected unemployment rate shifts the $\dot{N}_i = 0$ singular curve down in Figure 2 while an increase causes the $\dot{\lambda} = 0$ singular curve to shift everywhere to the right. The result is an unambiguous increase in the equilibrium

---

[18]This method of proof originated with Treadway, *op. cit.*

employment level and an unambiguous decrease in the equilibrium imputed value of adding to the labor force. However, because the optimal trajectories have negative slopes, the trajectories can either shift upward, downward, or not at all. Each of the three possibilities is consistent with the change in the equilibrium.

Now that we have related the imputed values of adding a worker to the parameters faced by the firm, we can derive the qualitative properties of the relationship between the firm's optimal wage choice and these parameters. The relationship is implicit in (37). If we substitute λ^0 for λ and let χ^0 denote the optimal relative wage choice, then

$$\lambda^0 \beta_1(\chi^0, u^e) = 1, \tag{53}$$

because $\chi_1 = 1/\beta_1$. Since χ_{11} must be positive by the Legendre condition and since $\chi_{11} = -\beta_{11}/\beta_1^3$, $\beta_{11}(\chi^0, u^e)$ must be negative. Therefore,

$$\frac{\partial \chi^0}{\partial N_i} = \frac{-\lambda_1^0}{(\lambda^0)^2 \beta_{11}(\chi^0, u^e)} < 0, \tag{54a}$$

$$\frac{\partial \chi^0}{\partial v_i} = \frac{-\lambda_2^0}{(\lambda^0)^2 \beta_{11}(\chi^0, u^e)} > 0, \tag{54b}$$

$$\frac{\partial \chi^0}{\partial \rho} = \frac{-\lambda_3^0}{(\lambda^0)^2 \beta_{11}(\chi^0, u^e)} < 0, \tag{54c}$$

and

$$\frac{\partial \chi^0}{\partial u^e} = \frac{-1}{\beta_{11}(\chi^0, u^e)} \left[\frac{\lambda_4^0}{(\lambda^0)^2} + \beta_{12}(\chi^0, u^e) \right]. \tag{54d}$$

The signs of all the partials are the same as those for λ^0 except in the case of the expected unemployment rate. That is, an increase, *ceteris paribus*, in the firm's labor force induces a decrease in the optimal wage choice. Other arguments held constant, an increase in the product price-to-average wage ratio causes the firm to offer a higher wage relative to the market wage while an increase in the real interest rate has the opposite effect. These results are the consequence of the fact that the optimal wage offer and the present value of adding a worker are positively related by the marginal condition implicit in (38).

None of the results discussed above is particularly surprising. In fact, with the exception of the effect of a change in the interest rate, they are all implied by the received static short-run theory of employment. However, the ambiguity of the wage response to a change in the expected unemployment rate is of interest.

The parameter, u^e, is essentially a measure of labor-market "tightness." That is, the larger its value the larger will be the flow of prospective workers to the firm at any given wage. Phelps has argued that the typical firm will respond to a "tighter" labor market, i.e., a decrease in u^e, by raising its wage relative to its view of the average wage in the market.[19] The theory presented here does not have that implication. In fact, since β_{12} is positive from condition (27), which implies that a decrease in the expected unemployment rate increases the implicit marginal cost of adding a man, and since the same change will have little effect on the imputed value of adding a man, i.e., λ_4^0 is small in absolute value, the likely response to a decrease in u^e is a decrease, not an increase, in the offered own relative wage.

In summary let us state that

$$\frac{w_i^0}{\overline{w}^e} = \chi^0 = \psi(N_i, v_i, \rho, u^e), \qquad \psi_1 < 0, \psi_2 > 0, \psi_3 < 0, \psi_4 = ?, \quad (55)$$

where w_i^0 denotes the optimal wage choice. The optimal employment plan can now be derived, at least in principle, by substituting ψ for $w_i/\overline{w}^e$ in (31).

In the beginning of this section we noted that the firm faces a perfectly elastic labor supply curve in the long run. However, in equilibrium the value of the marginal product of labor does not equal the wage rate. In fact, the equilibrium employment level, N_i^*, is such that

$$v_i F_i'(N_i^*) - \chi(0, u^e) = \rho \chi_1(0, u^e). \quad (56)$$

Thus, in equilibrium, the value of the product of the marginal worker exceeds the wage by an amount equal to the interest charge on the implicit investment required to attract and retain that worker. The wage equals the value of the marginal product if and only if the implicit investment is zero. Therefore, the usual static competitive equilibrium condition does not hold if the firm is a dynamic monopsonist, even though the wage paid is unaffected by the degree of the firm's dynamic monopsony power. These differences provide the rationale for distinguishing the concept of a dynamic monopsonist from the concept of a static monopsonist and from the concept of a competitive employer of input services.

4
THE MARKET MODEL

The wage choices of all firms taken together determine the current value of the average market wage. If the average market wage is defined by

$$\overline{w} = \sum_i \frac{N_i}{N} w_i, \quad (57)$$

[19]Phelps, *op. cit.*

then

$$\overline{w} = \overline{w}^e \theta, \tag{58}$$

where

$$\theta = \sum_i \frac{N_i}{N} \psi(N_i, v_i, \rho, u^e) \tag{59}$$

from (55). Clearly, θ depends on the aggregate level of employment, the distribution of employment among the firms, the distribution of the v_i's, the real interest rate, and the expected unemployment ratio. If we assume that the numbers of firms, or at least the numbers of establishments, grow in proportion to the growth in participation, then under certain conditions

$$\theta = \theta(1 - u, v, \rho, u^e); \quad \theta > 0, \theta_1 < 0, \theta_2 > 0, \theta_3 < 0, \theta_4 = ?, \tag{60}$$

where $1 - u$ is the employment ratio,

$$1 - u = \frac{N}{L} \tag{61}$$

and v is the ratio of the expected average output price to the expected average wage,

$$v = \sum_i \frac{N_i}{N} v_i = \frac{1}{\overline{w}^e} \sum_i \frac{N_i}{N} P_i^e = \frac{\overline{P}^e}{\overline{w}^e}. \tag{62}$$

The signs of the partial derivatives of θ reflect those derived for ψ in Section 3. Of course, θ is positive because it is the ratio of the actual to the expected average wage.

Let us assume that the expected average wage and expected average product price each equal their respective actual values at some earlier date $t - h$, updated to account for expected inflation; i.e.,

$$\overline{w}^e(t) = \overline{w}(t - h)e^{hp^e},$$
$$\overline{P}^e(t) = \overline{P}(t - h)e^{hp^e}. \tag{63}$$

Of course, h is the length of the expectation lag.

Given these assumptions,

$$\frac{\overline{w}(t)}{\overline{w}^e(t)} = \frac{\overline{w}(t)}{\overline{w}(t - h)e^{hg^e}} \approx e^{h(g - g^e)} \tag{64}$$

if h is a small interval. Of course, g is the actual rate of inflation in the average wage rate. It follows immediately from (58), (60), and (64) that

$$g = p^e + \frac{1}{h} \ln (\theta(1 - u, v, \rho, u^e)). \tag{65}$$

The assumptions concerning expectations also imply that

$$v(t) = \frac{\overline{P}(t - h)}{\overline{w}(t - h)}. \tag{66}$$

Therefore,

$$\frac{v(t + h) - v(t)}{h} = \frac{1}{h}\left[\frac{\overline{P}(t)}{\overline{w}(t)} - \frac{\overline{P}(t - h)}{\overline{w}(t - h)}\right]$$

$$= \frac{\overline{P}(t - h)}{\overline{w}(t)} \frac{\overline{P}(t) - \overline{P}(t - h)}{h\overline{P}(t - h)}$$

$$- \frac{\overline{P}(t - h)}{w(t)} \frac{w(t) - \overline{w}(t - h)}{h\overline{w}(t - h)}.$$

If h is small, the following holds approximately:

$$\frac{\dot{v}}{v} = p - g, \tag{67}$$

where p is the actual rate of product-price inflation.

Equations (65) and (67) reflect the wage-adjustment process implicit in the theory of wage choice developed in Section III and the assumptions made about expectations. If output prices rise relative to the average wage, *ceteris paribus*, the imputed value of adding a man to the net employment flow rises for each firm. Such a change induces each firm to attempt to attract labor at a more rapid rate. This each firm does by raising its own wage offer. Since not all firms can succeed in raising their wage relative to the average, the result is an eventual increase in the average wage relative to the average product price as well as an increase in the net aggregate employment flow. As labor is accumulated by all firms, the imputed value of adding a worker tends to fall, owing to diminishing returns. The effect is a decrease in the product price-to-wage ratio. The effects of an exogenous increase in the real interest rate are the opposite of those outlined above for an increase in product prices. An increase in the expected rate of inflation for given values of the other arguments increases the rate of wage inflation by an equal amount because each firm wishes to maintain the differential between its own wage and the market average. Finally, the speed with which the price-wage ratio, v, adjusts to changes varies inversely with the length of the expectation lag.

Of course, the aggregate employment level is also endogenous. Its time rate of change is given by

$$\dot{N} = \sum_i \dot{N}_i \tag{68}$$

since the aggregate employment level is the sum of employment across all firms. Equation (68) together with (24) imply that

$$\dot{N} = \sum_i H_{i0} - \sum_i Q_{i0} - \delta N, \tag{69}$$

where H_{i0} is the flow of hires from the unemployed pool to the ith firm, Q_{i0} is the flow of quits from the ith firm to the unemployed pool, and δN is the flow of those workers who were employed who are leaving the market. From equations (10) and (13), respectively, we find that

$$\sum_i H_{i0} = s_0 \phi U, \tag{70}$$

$$\sum_i Q_{i0} = s_2(1 - \phi)N, \tag{71}$$

where

$$\phi = \sum_i \frac{N_i}{N} f\left(c \frac{w_i}{\bar{w}} e^{h(g-g^e)}\right). \tag{72}$$

Since $s_0 U$ is the number of participants in the unemployed pool per period who contact some firm, ϕ in (70) is the aggregate acceptance rate. Similarly, $(1 - \phi)$ in (71) is the proportion of employed participants who consider quitting for the purpose of searching for a new job who do quit.

It is obvious that the aggregate acceptance rate is a function of $ce^{h(g-g^e)}$ and the moments of the distribution of own relative wages across firms. Equation (57) implies that the first moment is unity, so only higher moments are of interest. The second moment about the mean of the distribution, the variance, is defined as

$$\sigma^2 = \sum_i \frac{N_i}{N} \left(\frac{w_i}{\bar{w}} - 1\right)^2. \tag{73}$$

Note that σ is the coefficient of variation of the firm's wage rates as well.

To derive the qualitative properties of the relationship between the aggregate acceptance rate and the variance of the own relative wage distribution, consider Figure 4. The value of f corresponding to a given value of $w_i/\bar{w}$ is indicated by the curve in the figure. The properties of the curve reflect the assumptions made in (7). In particular,

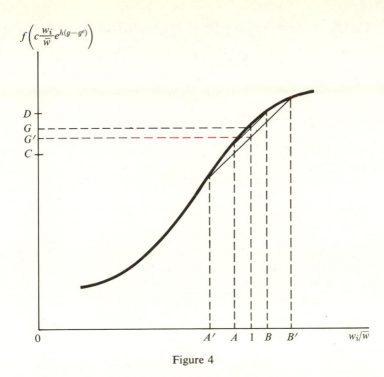

Figure 4

$f'' > 0$ when the argument is less than unity and $f'' < 0$ when the argument is greater than unity. Since $c > 1$ from (4), the mean of the relative wage distribution, unity, lies in the region when $f'' < 0$, as illustrated in the figure.

Since we proved in Section 3 that each firm will choose its wage such that $w_i/\overline{w} > 1/c$ and since $e^{h(g-g^e)} \approx 1$, the entire range of the distribution lies in the region when $f'' < 0$. Let the interval AB indicate the range of the distribution of the own relative wage offers. Clearly the acceptance rates for the various firms are values that lie along the line segment CD on the vertical axis. Suppose now that the distribution of own relative wage rates is symmetric. In this case the aggregate acceptance rate is equal to the vertical distance from the horizontal axis to the intersection of the chord drawn from E to F with the perpendicular drawn from the mean of the distribution. In other words, it is equal to the distance $0G$.

The effect of an increase in the variance on the aggregate acceptance rate can now be derived. Let the variance increase so that the new range is larger, say equal to the line segment $A'B'$. The aggregate acceptance rate is now equal to the length of the line segment $0G'$. An increase in the variance results in a decrease in the aggregate acceptance rate.

The effects of changes in $ce^{h(g-g^e)}$ can be derived directly. Note that

$$\frac{\partial \phi}{\partial ce^{h(g-g^e)}} = \sum_i \frac{N_i}{N} f'\left(c\frac{w_i}{\overline{w}} e^{h(g-g^e)}\right) \frac{w_i}{\overline{w}} > 0, \qquad (74a)$$

$$\frac{\partial^2 \phi}{(\partial ce^{h(g-g^e)})^2} = \sum_i \frac{N_i}{N} f''\left(c\frac{w_i}{\overline{w}} e^{h(g-g^e)}\right) \left(\frac{w_i}{\overline{w}}\right)^2 < 0. \qquad (74b)$$

The sign of the second partial follows from the fact that each firm chooses its wage so that $w_i/\overline{w} > 1/c$.

In summary, we have shown that

$$\phi = \phi(ce^{h(g-g^e)}, \sigma^2), \qquad 0 < \phi < 1, \phi_1 > 0, \phi_2 < 0, \phi_{11} < 0. \qquad (75)$$

Since c equals the ratio of the average market wage expected by each participant to the participant's acceptance wage, a decrease in the acceptance wage increases the aggregate rate of acceptance.[20] The acceptance wage falls if the costs of search to an employed worker decreases relative to the costs of search to an unemployed participant. An increase, *ceteris paribus*, in the difference between the actual and the expected rate of wage inflation results in an increase in the aggregate acceptance rate because the participants do not know that the higher wage offers which they receive are due only to general wage inflation. Stigler has suggested that the relative dispersion of the wage distribution is an appropriate measure of the degree of information imperfection in a labor market.[21] According to our theory, an increase in the degree of information imperfection decreases the aggregate acceptance rate. It does so because the acceptance rate of each firm increases at a decreasing rate with respect to its own relative wage rate.

To derive the adjustment equation for employment, substitute appropriately into (69) from (70) and (71). The result is

$$\dot{N} = (s_0 U + s_2 N)\phi - (s_2 + \delta)N.$$

Since total participation, L, changes over time at a proportional rate equal to $\eta - \delta$ and since the unemployment ratio equals $1 - N/L$,

$$\dot{u} = (\eta + s_2)(1 - u) - [s_0 u + s_2(1 - u)]\phi(ce^{h(g-g^e)}, \sigma^2). \qquad (76)$$

Equations (65), (67), and (76) form a complete model of wage and employment dynamics. These equations describe how the labor market envisioned in the paper adjusts to exogenous changes in the rate of product-price inflation and the real interest rate as well as to exogenous changes in certain structural parameters.

---

[20]See pp. 174–175.

[21]G. J. Stigler, "Information in the Labor Market," *Journal of Political Economy* (October 1962), Part 2, Supplement.

5
THE PHILLIPS CURVE, THE INFLATION– UNEMPLOYMENT TRADE–OFF, AND THE "NATURAL" RATE OF UNEMPLOYMENT

In this section a number of questions are asked and answered within the context of the dynamic wage-employment model developed in Section 4. (a) Can the empirical relationship known as the Phillips curve be explained? In other words, does the model suggest how the observed data were generated? (b) Is there a meaningful trade-off between inflation and unemployment? (c) Is there a "natural" rate of unemployment? If so, what are some of its determinants?

The employment equation, (76), embodies primarily supply considerations. The equation is

$$\dot{u} = (\eta + s_2)(1 - u) - [s_0 u + s_2(1 - u)]\phi(ce^{h(g-g^e)}, \sigma^2),$$

$$0 < \phi < 1, \phi_1 > 0, \phi_2 < 0, \phi_{11} < 0, \qquad (77)$$

where u denotes the unemployment ratio. All the parameters are positive and

$$c = \frac{s_0}{s_0 - s_1} > 1 \qquad (78)$$

since $s_0 > s_1$.

The parameters s_0, s_1, and s_2 are, respectively, the proportion per period of unemployed participants who make contact with a prospective employer, the proportion per period of employed participants who contact a prospective new employer, and the proportion per period of employed participants who consider quitting their current employer to reenter the unemployed pool. We argue that $s_0 > s_1$ because the frequency of contact depends inversely on the costs of search and because opportunity costs of search are presumably higher if the participant is employed. Finally, $g - g^e$ is the difference between the actual rate of wage inflation and the rate workers expect, h is an interval of time reflecting the length of the information lag, σ is the coefficient of variation of the distribution of wages, and ϕ is the aggregate acceptance rate.

As a consequence of the wage-choice decision by the various firms, the rate of wage inflation, g, is related to the unemployment rate, u, the ratio of the average product price to the average market wage, v, the rate of product price inflation expected by the firms in the market,

p^e, the unemployment ratio expected by the firms in the market, u^e, and the real interest rate ρ. In particular,

$$g = p^e + \frac{1}{h} \ln \theta(1 - u, v, \rho, u^e),$$

$$\theta > 0, \theta_1 < 0, \theta_2 > 0, \theta_3 < 0, \theta_4 = ?. \qquad (79)$$

This equation is derived as (65). Since v is the ratio of the average product price to the average market wage, where the ith firm's weight in both cases is its share of total employment,

$$\frac{\dot{v}}{v} = p - g, \qquad (80)$$

where p is the proportional rate of growth in the average product price. We assume p to be exogenous. If we substitute for g in (77) and (80) we have two differential equations in u and v. The two equations describe the wage-employment dynamics implicit in the theory.

The first question is: Can the model derived above give an interpretation to the Phillips curve? Or, more important, can the theory explain how the data observed by Phillips and others are generated? The data can be thought of as a scatter of points, each point representing a different date, in the g-u plane. There are two widely known features of these data. First, the scatter of points, given a long time span, lie generally in a downward sloping band in the g-u plane. Second, the points of sub-time-intervals describe counterclockwise loops in the plane. In other words, if one connects with a curve the point corresponding to adjacent dates, the curve so drawn for a short time interval can generally be described as a loop. As time passes during the interval, the observed point moves counterclockwise along this path.

Lipsey originally noted the existence of the loops in Phillips' data.[22] He also provides an explanation for the loops which is generally known and quite ingenious. His argument is based on two propositions: (a) The relationship between the rate of wage inflation and the unemployment ratio in each industry and/or region is convex to the origin; (b) the dispersion of unemployment ratios across industries and/or regions at a particular date spreads during the upswing of a business cycle and tightens during the downswing. Therefore, the aggregate Phillips curve, which is a convex combination of the micro curves, rises during the upswing and falls during the downswing. Since the aggregate unemployment rate falls in the upswing and rises during the down side of the business cycle, counterclockwise loops result.

[22]Lipsey, *op. cit.*

The explanation of these phenomena provided by our model depends heavily on the relationships implied by (77). Note that

$$\frac{\partial \dot{u}}{\partial u} = -[\eta + s_0 + (1 - \phi)s_2] < 0, \tag{81a}$$

$$\frac{\partial \dot{u}}{\partial g} = -[s_0 u + s_2(1 - u)]\phi_1 che^{h(g-g^e)} < 0. \tag{81b}$$

Therefore,

$$\left.\frac{\partial g}{\partial u}\right|_{\dot{u}=\text{const.}} = \frac{-[\eta + s_0 + (1 - \phi)s_2]}{[s_0 u + s_2(1 - u)]\phi_1 che^{h(g-g^e)}} < 0. \tag{82}$$

In other words, the implicit relationship between the rate of wage inflation and the unemployment ratio, given the rate of expected wage inflation and the rate of change in the unemployment ratio, is downward sloping because an increase in either the unemployment ratio or the rate of wage inflation decreases the rate of change in the unemployment ratio.

To generate the observations reported by Phillips as well as the loops observed by Lipsey, we need to make use of the demand side of the model as embodied in (79) and (80). Equation (79) implies the following results:

$$\left.\frac{\partial g}{\partial u}\right|_{v=\text{const.}} = -\frac{1}{h}\frac{\theta_1}{\theta} > 0, \tag{83a}$$

$$\frac{\partial g}{\partial v} = \frac{1}{h}\frac{\theta_2}{\theta} > 0, \tag{83b}$$

$$\frac{\partial g}{\partial p^e} = 1. \tag{83c}$$

Thus (79) implies that the rate of wage inflation increases as the unemployment ratio increases if the price/wage ratio is held constant.

It should be pointed out that (82) and (83a) are not conflicting results. The model is complete in the sense that both the rate of wage inflation and the unemployment ratio are endogenous, so time-series data on these variables are generated by the model in response to exogenous changes in its parameters. What we now wish to show is that the Phillips curve and Lipsey's loops can be generated by the business cycle. In particular, fluctuations in aggregate demand reflected in the model as fluctuations in the rate of product-price inflation produce time-series observations on g and u which lie in a negatively sloping band in the g-u plane. In addition, these observations form counterclockwise loop patterns.

To show that this is so, we use Figure 5. In the figure the curve labeled $\dot{u} = 0$ is the locus of points consistent with no change in the

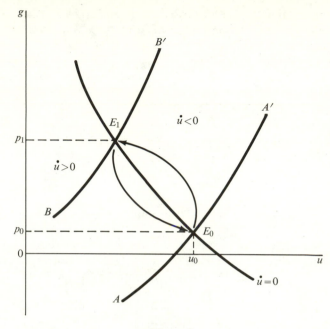

Figure 5

unemployment ratio. Since $\partial \dot{u}/\partial u < 0$, points above and to the right of the curve correspond to negative values of $\dot{u}$. In other words, if the market can be described by such a point, the unemployment ratio is falling over time. Similarly, the unemployment ratio is rising given a point to the left of the $\dot{u} = 0$ curve.

The curve AA' represents the relationship between g and u implied by (79). For the purpose of the analysis that follows we assume that the expectations variables, p^e and g^e, as well as ρ and σ^2, are held constant. Suppose that initially the rate of product price inflation is a particular value, p_0, and that the market is in equilibrium in the sense that $\dot{u} = 0$ and $\dot{v} = 0$. The assumption that $\dot{v} = 0$ and (79) and (80) imply that v is initially some particular value v_0. This value determines the position of the AA' curve. Now, since the point describing the market must lie somewhere on the AA' curve and since we are assuming $\dot{u} = 0$, the market must be at the point E_0 in the figure initially. Finally, since $\dot{v} = 0$ implies $p = g$, the rate of wage inflation is initially equal to the rate of product-price inflation, p_0.

What happens if the rate of product-price inflation increases from p_0 to a higher value p_1? Initially nothing happens, because the rate of product-price inflation is neither an argument of (77) nor (79). However, immediately after the rise $\dot{v}/v = p_1 - p_0 > 0$, because g is equal to p_0 initially. But $\partial g/\partial v > 0$. Thus the AA' schedule shifts upward as v grows in response to the positive difference between the rate of product-price inflation and the rate of wage inflation. In other words, the rate of wage inflation begins to rise. As soon as g rises above the $\dot{u} = 0$ curve, the unemployment rate begins to fall because the market is in the region where $\dot{u} < 0$. Since the $\dot{u} = 0$ curve is not affected by changes in v, the rate of wage inflation continues to rise and the unemployment rate continues to fall as described by the higher of the two arrowed paths. This process continues until a new equilibrium is reached at E_1. The new equilibrium value of the price/wage ratio determines the position of the new AA' curve denoted in the figure by BB'. By a similar argument we can show that the market follows the lower path back to E_0 if p falls back to p_0. Thus the theory does provide an explanation for counterclockwise loops based on the fact that the rate of product-price inflation fluctuates over the business cycle and the data generated by fluctuations in p are consistent with the Phillips curve.

The analysis above also implies that the rate of product-price inflation influences the unemployment ratio. Since economic policy can be used to control the rate of price inflation to a greater or lesser extent, the theory suggests that the much discussed interpretation of the Phillips curve as a social trade-off relationship may have some validity. However, we must remember that the analysis presented above is based on the assumption that the rate of wage inflation expected by participants remains constant. Although this assumption may be appropriate in the short run, it certainly is not in the long run.

To understand the consequence of relaxing the assumption of constant expectations, consider again Figure 5. Suppose that initially $p = p_0 = g = g^e$. Now suppose that policy-makers decide to maintain the rate of product price inflation forever at a higher level p_1. The initial reaction of the market is a process of adjustment along the indicated path from E_0 to E_1. However, once there, $g^e = p_0 < g = p_1$ if the expected rate of wage inflation does not change in the meanwhile.

If expectations are "adaptive" in the sense of Cagan, the inconsistency between the actual and expected rate of wage inflation will not remain forever.[23] Instead, the rate of expected wage inflation will eventually adjust until it is equal to the actual. As g^e rises, (77) implies that the $\dot{u} = 0$ curve shifts to the right. As it does so, the unemployment ratio tends to rise and, therefore, the rate of wage inflation tends to rise along the BB' schedule. But, as soon as g rises above p_1, the price/wage ratio begins to fall, which in turn shifts the BB' schedule downward. This process continues until $g^e = g$. Once the process of adjustment is complete, the unemployment ratio equals the initial value, u_0, because there is only one value consistent with $\dot{u} = 0$. and $g = g^e$ according to (77). In addition, $g = p_1$ to satisfy $\dot{v} = 0$.

[23]P. H. Cagan, "The Monetary Dynamics of Hyperinflation," in *Studies in the Quantity Theory of Money*, M. Friedman, ed. (University of Chicago Press, Chicago, 1956).

We conclude, then, that in the "long run," defined as the period of time required for the rate of expected wage inflation to adjust to the actual, our hypothetical policy-makers cannot influence the unemployment ratio by changing the rate of product-price inflation.

The results obtained seem to substantiate recent arguments by Phelps and Friedman that there is no trade-off between the rate of inflation and the unemployment ratio.[24] However, the results obtained here must be placed in their proper perspective. If the rate of wage inflation expected by participants adjusts to changes in the actual with a long lag as we have implicitly assumed, then the theory implies that control of the rate of product-price inflation with either fiscal or monetary policy can be used as a stabilization device. Surely this is a conclusion which should not shock the profession.

Moreover, if the lag in the adjustment of expectations is long, there is an intertemporal choice problem. That is, the society can "buy" a period of low unemployment now at the expense of a period of high unemployment sometime in the future. If the social rate of discount is positive, such an action may be socially optimal under appropriate circumstances. The Phillips curve provides a means of evaluating the costs and benefits of such an action. Alternatively, of course, the "price" of a permanent decrease in the rate of inflation is a period of high unemployment now.

The value of the unemployment ratio, which is consistent with no change in the unemployment ratio and the equality of the expected and actual rate of wage inflation, seems to conform to the concept of the "natural" unemployment ratio, introduced by Friedman in his recent Presidential address to the American Economic Association. According to his definition,

> The "natural rate of unemployment," in other words, is the level that would be ground out by the Walrasian system of general equilibrium equations, provided there is imbedded in them the actual structural characteristics of the labor and commodity markets, including market imperfections, stochastic variability in demands and supplies, the cost of gathering information about job vacancies and labor availabilities, the cost of mobility, and so on.[25]

Since a few of these things are "embedded" in our equations, it seems fair to make at least a partial claim that the theory developed here suggests some of the determinants of the natural rate of unemployment.

Let u^* denote the unemployment ratio consistent with $\dot{u} = 0$ and $g = g^e$. Equations (77) and (78) imply that

$$u^* = \frac{\eta + s_2(1 - \phi^*)}{\eta + s_0\phi^* + s_2(1 - \phi^*)}, \qquad (84)$$

[24]See Phelps, *op. cit.*, and Friedman, *op. cit.*
[25]Friedman, *op. cit.*, p. 8.

where

$$\phi^* = \phi\left(\frac{s_0}{s_0 - s_1}, \sigma^2\right). \tag{85}$$

Since s_0, s_1, s_2, and η are all positive, since $0 < \phi < 1$, $\phi_1 > 0$, and $\phi_2 < 0$, and since $0 < u^* < 1$, we find that

$$\frac{\partial u^*}{\partial s_0} = \frac{[s_1 s_0/(s_0 - s_1)^2](\eta + s_2)\phi_1^* - [\eta + (1 - \phi^*)s_2]\phi^*}{[\eta + s_0\phi^* + s_2(1 - \phi^*)]^2}, \tag{86a}$$

$$\frac{\partial u^*}{\partial s_1} = \frac{-[s_0^2/(s_0 - s_1)^2](\eta + s_2)\phi_1^*}{[\eta + s_0\phi^* + s_2(1 - \phi^*)]^2} < 0, \tag{86b}$$

$$\frac{\partial u^*}{\partial s_2} = \frac{s_0\phi^*(1 - \phi^*)}{[\eta + s_0\phi^* + s_2(1 - \phi^*)]^2} > 0, \tag{86c}$$

$$\frac{\partial u^*}{\partial \eta} = \frac{s_0\phi^*}{[\eta + s_0\phi^* + s_2(1 - \phi^*)]^2} > 0, \tag{86d}$$

and

$$\frac{\partial u^*}{\partial \sigma^2} = \frac{-s_0(\eta + s_2)\phi_2^*}{[\eta + s_0\phi^* + s_2(1 - \phi^*)]^2} > 0. \tag{86e}$$

To interpret these results, recall that ϕ is the aggregate acceptance rate. In other words, ϕ is the proportion of those unemployed workers considering an offer at a particular point in time who accept the offer as well as the proportion of those employed workers considering quitting who do not quit. The parameters s_0, s_1, and s_2 are, respectively, the frequency with which an unemployed worker receives offers, the frequency with which an employed worker receives offers from firms other than the one for which he works, and the frequency with which an employed worker considers quitting to search for a better job.

Further, s_0 and s_1 are assumed inversely related to the cost of search, given that the worker is unemployed and employed, respectively. η is the proportional rate at which new workers enter the market and σ is the coefficient of variation of the distribution of wages in the market. It measures the degree of wage dispersion and can be thought of as a proxy for the degree of information imperfection about alternative wage offers.

Note that the ratio $s_0/(s_0 - s_1)$ is a determinant of the aggregate acceptance rate and that $\phi_1 > 0$. That is, an increase in the cost of search given that the worker is unemployed relative to the cost of search given that he is employed, i.e., an increase in s_1/s_0, increases the acceptance rate. The reason for this implication should be clear. Such a change implies that searching for a new or better job has become relatively less expensive provided the worker is employed. Thus it tends to induce unemployed workers to take jobs. An understanding of this point is needed. Otherwise, some of the implications derived above appear to violate one's intuition.

For example, an increase in the frequency of contact by unemployed workers does not unambiguously decrease the "natural" unemployment rate. The second term on the right-hand-side of (86a) is negative because such an increase improves the chances per period that a given unemployed worker will be hired. However, an increase in s_0 reflects the fact that the cost of search has fallen for unemployed workers. Since the cost of search for employed workers is assumed unchanged, the cost of search for unemployed workers has fallen relative to that for employed workers, which, as we have noted, reduces the aggregate acceptance rate. This fact is reflected in the positive sign of the first term.

A lesson is to be learned from this result. The various schemes that have been suggested as means to reduce the cost of information about job availability may not reduce the level of frictional unemployment unless they reduce the cost to employed as well as unemployed workers. The importance of this point is underlined by (86b). This result suggests that reducing such costs for employed workers will reduce the level of frictional unemployment even though the cost of obtaining information for unemployed workers remains unchanged.

Since an increase in s_2 and an increase in η increase the relative flow of workers into the unemployment pool, it also increases the level of frictional unemployment. To the extent that the dispersion of wages in a market reflects imperfect information about alternative wage offers, an increase in the degree of imperfection decreases the acceptance rate and increases the natural unemployment ratio. Again, methods that improve the participants' knowledge about alternative wage offers may reduce this component of frictional unemployment.

In the section we provide only heuristic support for the contention that the adjustment process described by (77) to (80) is stable. In keeping with the general tone of this section, we relegate a more rigorous demonstration to an appendix.

6
SUMMARY

The principal assumptions concerning the supply side of a typical labor market are that particular and general wage information is imperfect and that searching for job opportunities and wage information is expensive. Given these assumptions, we are able to show that each firm in such a labor market faces a flow supply of labor that is not perfectly elastic with respect to the firm's own wage offer. In other words, each firm is a monopsonist in a dynamic sense. If we assume that each firm takes this fact into account and that each wishes to maximize its present value, a decision rule that dictates the firm's optimal wage offer can be derived.

By aggregating the flow-supply equations faced by the various firms, we can derive a differential equation that describes the changes in the level of employment over time. Similarly, an aggregation of the decision rules yields a wage-adjustment equation. The explicit model of wage and employment dynamics derived in this paper is summarized below:

$$\dot{u} = (\eta + s_2)(1 - u) - [s_0 u + s_2(1 - u)]\phi(ce^{h(g-g^e)}, \sigma^2),$$
$$0 < \phi < 1, \phi_1 > 0, \phi_2 < 0, \phi_{11} < 0, c = s_0/(s_0 - s_1) > 1,$$

$$\tag{87}$$

$$g = p^e + \ln \theta(1 - u, v, \rho, u^e); \quad \theta_1 < 0, \theta_2 > 0, \theta_3 < 0, \theta_4 = ?,$$

$$\tag{88}$$

$$\frac{\dot{v}}{v} = p - g. \tag{89}$$

The variables in the model are:

$u =$ unemployment ratio

$g =$ rate of money wage inflation

$v =$ ratio of the average product price to the average market wage

The parameters have the following interpretations:

$p =$ rate of product-price inflation

$g^e =$ rate of wage inflation expected by participants

$p^e =$ rate of product-price inflation expected by firms

$\rho =$ real interest rate faced by the firms

$\eta =$ rate at which new workers enter the market as a proportion of the total in the market

$s_0 =$ frequency with which unemployed workers receive job offers

$s_1 =$ frequency with which employed workers receive job offers from firms other than their employer

$s_2 =$ frequency with which employed workers consider quitting in order to reenter the unemployed pool

$h =$ length of the "information lag"

$\sigma =$ coefficient of variation of the distribution of wage offers

The value of the function ϕ is equal to the proportion of the flow of unemployed workers who have outstanding job offers who accept the offers. As well, it is the proportion of those who consider quitting to reenter the unemployment pool in each period who remain with their current employer. We refer to this proportion as the aggregate acceptance rate. Since s_0 is the average proportion per period of the stock of unemployed workers who receive an offer and s_2 is the average proportion per period of the stock of employed workers who consider quitting, (87) follows directly.

An increase in the probability of obtaining a job offer given that the participant is employed relative to the probability given that he is unemployed increases the relative attractiveness of employment. This is true because the opportunity cost of accepting a job, the income that a participant could expect to receive by continuing to search for a better job rather than accepting the opportunity before him, falls relative to the future income he can earn if he accepts his current job offer. This argument provides the rationalization for the sign of ϕ_1, since s_0 and s_1 reflect the probabilities of obtaining job offers under each of the two conditions. The argument also implies that the acceptance rate equals unity if and only if the chances are the same whether employed or not. Since it is argued that $s_0 > s_1$, ϕ is less than unity.

Given imperfect information, each participant must estimate the average market wage on the basis of wage information obtained over some period of time prior to the current date. If the relevant period is one of wage inflation or deflation, he presumably makes an adjustment for this fact. Therefore, an increase in the actual rate of wage inflation, g, relative to that expected, g^e, increases the acceptance rate because all offers appear to have increased relative to the market average. The effect can be only temporary, of course, because eventually g^e must adjust to the change in g. Nevertheless, it is important.

The signs of ϕ_2 and ϕ_{11} are not so easily explained. To understand these derivations, one must probe more deeply into the structure of the theory. It is enough to say that the derived signs of both hold if and only if a particular necessary condition for a solution to each firm's choice problem is satisfied. Therefore, they provide potential empirical tests of the appropriateness of the theory of wage choice proposed in the paper. Other additional tests are provided by (88), because that equation results from aggregating the decision rules derived from the solution to each firm's wage-choice problem.

The principal implication of the theory of wage choice is simple. Each firm attempts to attract labor at a more rapid rate the larger is its long-run target level of employment relative to its current employment level. Of course, each firm can increase the net flow of labor to it only by increasing its wage offer relative to the average market wage. An increase, *ceteris paribus*, in employment decreases algebraically the difference between the target and current level of employment. Those firms affected attempt to reduce their wages relative to the average. The result is that the market average wage falls relative to its previous level. This argument explains the sign of θ_1.

The other signs are explained by analogous arguments once one recognizes the effect of changes in the variables on the target level of employment. In particular, an increase in v reflects an improvement in the value of labor productivity relative to cost and therefore increases the target level of employment. The real interest rate enters because there are implicit costs involved in adjusting the level of employment. An increase in the real interest rate reduces the incentive to incur such costs and, therefore, reduces both the target employment level and the rate of adjustment to it. Finally, an increase in the expected rate of product-price inflation produces an equal increase in the rate of wage inflation because each firm expects the average wage to inflate at the same rate as prices in the long run.

Clearly the model does not simply relate the rate of wage inflation to the unemployment rate. In fact, both variables are endogenous to the model. How can the model, then, explain an empirical relationship between the two variables such as the Phillips curve? It can only if the relationship can be generated by the simultaneous operation of all parts of the model. In the paper we are able to show that such a relationship is generated by the model given fluctuations, owing, say, to changing demand conditions, in the rate of product-price inflation. The points in the g-u plane so generated lie in a downward sloping band. In addition, a cycle in the rate of product-price inflation generates a path of points in the g-u plane which is consistent with the counterclockwise loops observed by Lipsey.[26]

However, the possibility of a trade-off between inflation and unemployment exists in the short run only. Clearly from (87) it exists only because the rate of expected wage inflation adjusts to changes in the actual rate with a lag. The equilibrium unemployment ratio, defined as that consistent with the equality of g and g^e and no change in unemployment, is independent of the rate of inflation. It is

$$ u^* = \frac{\eta + s_2(1 - \phi(c, \sigma^2))}{\eta + s_0\phi(c, \sigma^2) + s_2(1 - \phi(c, \sigma^2))} . \qquad (90) $$

This rate seems to conform to the concept of the "natural" unemployment ratio recently introduced by Friedman.[27] It is the only value consistent with the friction in the system and rational behavior over the long run.

The direction of the changes in the equilibrium unemployment ratio induced by changes in the various parameters are all consistent with one's intuition with one exception. The sign of the effect of an increase, *ceteris paribus*, in the frequency with which unemployed participants receive job offers is ambiguous. The reason is that an increase in this frequency relative to the frequency with which employed participants receive job offers decreases the acceptance rate, for reasons already

[26]Lipsey, *op. cit.*
[27]Friedman, *op. cit.*

discussed. If the decrease in the acceptance rate is sufficient to overcome the increase in the flow of unemployed workers who receive offers, which also results from an increase in s_0, the total effect is a decrease in the flow of new hires from the unemployment pool relative to the stock of unemployed participants. If such is the case, u^* rises. If not, it falls.

The policy implications of this result are clear. Suppose that a policy were designed that would increase s_0, say by lowering the cost of search for job opportunities by unemployed workers. One cannot be sure that such a policy, if put into practice, would decrease the level of frictional unemployment unless the policy also increases the frequency with which employed workers receive job offers, s_1, by a proportionate amount.

APPENDIX:
THE STABILITY OF
THE MODEL

In the body of the paper an explicit model of the wage-employment adjustment process is derived and analyzed. Here the stability of that process is investigated.

The employment-adjustment equation is

$$\dot{u} = (\eta + s_2)(1 - u) - [s_0 u + s_2(1 - u)]$$
$$\times \phi(c[h(p^e - g^e) + \theta(1 - u, v, \rho)], \sigma^2),$$
$$0 < \phi < 1, \phi_1 > 0, \phi_2 < 0, \theta > 0, \theta_1 < 0, \theta_2 > 0, \theta_3 < 0, \qquad \text{(A1)}$$

where u is the employment ratio, v the ratio of the average product price to the average market wage, ρ the real interest rate, g^e the rate of wage inflation expected by workers, and p^e the rate of product price inflation expected by employers. All parameters are positive, including c. The wage-adjustment equation can be written

$$\frac{\dot{v}}{v} = p - p^e + \frac{1}{h}[1 - \theta(1 - u, v, \rho)]. \qquad \text{(A2)}$$

The new term, p, denotes the actual rate of product-price inflation. Both ρ and p are taken to be exogenous.[28]

A complete specification of the dynamics of the labor market requires that we describe the manner in which g^e and p^e adjust over time to g and p, respectively. However, it is useful to consider the "partial dynamics" im-

---

[28]To obtain (A1) and (A2) from (77), (79), and (80), use the following approximations:

$$e^{h(g - g^e)} \approx 1 + h(g - g^e),$$
$$e^{h(g - p^e)} \approx 1 + h(g - g^e).$$

In this section the author has chosen to ignore the expected unemployment rate, u^e, because of the ambiguity in the sign of the partial derivative of g with respect to it.

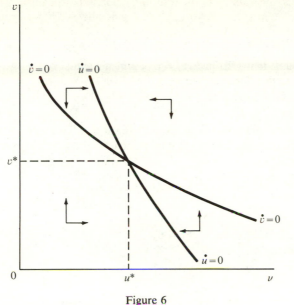

Figure 6

plicit in (A1) and (A2). In other words, is the system stable when g^e and p^e are held constant?

To answer the question, we consider Figure 6. In the figure the singular curves for both u and v are represented. The vectors indicate the direction of motion in the v-u plane. The nature of the phase plane as represented in the figure is implied by the following analytic results:

$$\left.\frac{dv}{du}\right|_{\dot{u}=0} = \frac{\theta_1}{\theta_2} - \frac{\eta + s_2(1-\phi) + s_0\phi}{[s_0u + s_2(1-u)]\phi_1c\theta_2} < \frac{\theta_1}{\theta_2} = \left.\frac{dv}{du}\right|_{\dot{v}=0} < 0, \qquad \text{(A3)}$$

$$\frac{\partial\dot{u}}{\partial u} = -[\eta + s_2(1-\phi) + s_0\phi] + [s_0u + s_2(1-u)]\phi_1c\theta_1 < 0, \qquad \text{(A4a)}$$

$$\frac{\partial\dot{v}}{\partial v} = -\frac{1}{h}\theta_2 < 0. \qquad \text{(A4b)}$$

Clearly the system is globally stable in the partial sense defined above. That is, u and v tend to their respective values at the intersection of the singular curves as time passes given any set of initial values provided that g^e and p^e remain constant. Of course, neither remains constant in reality. Nevertheless, the result does suggest that a complete system would be stable provided that the adjustment of expectations to actuality were slow enough.

Let us consider a particular version of a complete model. It is usual to assume that the expected value of a variable depends only on past actual values of that variable. Since the rate of product-price inflation is assumed exogenous to the labor market, the expected rate of product-price inflation is exogenous as well if the expectations hypothesis conforms to this rule. In other words, the stability of the resulting model is independent of the process by which p^e adjusts to p. Without losing generality, then, we can assume

$$p^e = p. \tag{A5}$$

Let us assume that g^e adjusts to changes in the actual rate of wage inflation according to the "adaptive"-expectations hypothesis introduced by Cagan[29]:

$$\dot{g}^e = \gamma(g - g^e) \qquad \gamma > 0. \tag{A6}$$

γ is a positive parameter measuring the speed of adjustment.

The complete model can now be written as the following system of differential equations[30]:

$$\dot{u} = (\eta + s_2)(1 - u) - [s_0 u + s_2(1 - u)]$$
$$\times \phi(c[h(p - g^e) + \theta(1 - u, v, \rho)], \sigma^2), \tag{A7a}$$

$$\dot{v} = \frac{v}{h}[1 - \theta(1 - u, v, \rho)], \tag{A7b}$$

$$\dot{g}^e = \gamma\left(p + \frac{1}{h}[\theta(1 - u, v, \rho) - 1] - g^e\right). \tag{A7c}$$

We consider conditions for local stability or stability in a neighborhood of equilibrium only. An equilibrium solution is said to be stable in this sense if the linear approximation to (A7) around the equilibrium solution is stable.[31] The linear approximation to (A7) about an equilibrium point (u^*, v^*, g^{*e}) is

$$\begin{bmatrix} \dot{u} \\ \dot{v} \\ \dot{g}^e \end{bmatrix} = A \begin{bmatrix} u - u^* \\ v - v^* \\ g^e - g^{*e} \end{bmatrix}, \tag{A8}$$

where

$$A = \begin{bmatrix} \delta_1 \phi_1^* c\theta_1^* - \delta_2 & -\delta_1 \phi_1^* c\theta_2^* & \delta_1 \phi_1^* ch \\ \dfrac{v^*}{h}\theta_1^* & -\dfrac{v^*}{h}\theta_2^* & 0 \\ -\dfrac{\gamma}{h}\theta_1^* & \dfrac{\gamma}{h}\theta_2^* & -\gamma \end{bmatrix} \tag{A9}$$

and where

$$\delta_1 = s_0 u^* + s_2(1 - u^*) > 0, \tag{A10}$$

$$\delta_2 = \eta + s_2(1 - \phi^*) + s_0 \phi^* > 0. \tag{A11}$$

The variables u^*, v^*, and g^{*e} denote the equilibrium values of u, v, and g^e, respectively. In other words, they satisfy the following set of equations:

[29]Cagan, *op. cit.*

[30]Equation (A7c) follows from (A6) because $g = p + 1/h\,[\theta - 1]$ when $p^e = p$.

[31]A discussion of this concept of stability and several theorems of interest can be found in Richard Bellman, *Stability Theory of Differential Equations* (McGraw-Hill, New York, 1953), pp. 78–82.

$$(\eta + s_2)(1 - u^*) - [s_0 u^* + s_2(1 - u^*)]\phi(c, \sigma^2) = 0, \quad \text{(A12a)}$$

$$1 - \theta(1 - u^*, v^*, \rho) = 0, \quad \text{(A12b)}$$

$$p - g^{*e} = 0. \quad \text{(A12c)}$$

The asterisks on the various functions in (A9), (A10), and (A11) indicate the values of the functions at the equilibrium solution.

Our next task is to show that an equilibrium solution exists and that it is unique. Clearly (A12c) implies that only one value of the expected rate of wage inflation is consistent with equilibrium. It is the rate of product-price inflation. Since $\theta_1 < 0$ and $\theta_2 > 0$, the relationship between v^* and u^* implicit in (A12b) is monotonic. Therefore, a unique equilibrium solution exists if and only if a single value of u^* satisfies (A12a). Clearly, from (A12a) only one such value does exist.

The linear system of differential equations in (A8) is stable if and only if the real parts of the characteristic roots of the matrix A are all negative. The characteristic equation is

$$|A - \lambda I| = \lambda^3 + a_1 \lambda^2 + a_2 \lambda + a_3 = 0, \quad \text{(A13)}$$

where

$$a_1 = \frac{v^*}{h} \theta_2^* + \delta_2 - \phi_1^* c \theta_1^* \delta_1 + \gamma, \quad \text{(A14a)}$$

$$a_2 = \frac{v^*}{h} \theta_2^* \delta_2 + \gamma \left(\frac{v^*}{h} \theta_2^* + \delta_2 \right), \quad \text{(A14b)}$$

$$a_3 = \gamma \frac{v^*}{h} \theta_2^* \delta_2. \quad \text{(A14c)}$$

According to Routh's theorem, the real parts of the roots of a cubic equation such as (A13) are all negative if and only if the following conditions hold[32]:

$$a_1 > 0, \ a_2 > 0, \ a_3 > 0, \quad \text{(A15a)}$$

$$a_1 a_2 > a_3. \quad \text{(A15b)}$$

Given any economically meaningful solution, i.e., $v^* > 0$, (A15a) holds because all the parameters and partial derivatives are positive except θ_1, which is negative. Since

$$a_1 a_2 = \gamma \frac{v^*}{h} \theta_2^* \delta_2 + \gamma^2 \left(\frac{v^*}{h} \theta_2^* + \delta_2 \right)$$

$$+ \left[\frac{v^*}{h} \theta_2^* + \delta_2 - \delta_1 \phi_1^* c \theta_1^* \right] \left[\frac{v^*}{h} \theta_2^* \delta_2 + \gamma \left(\frac{v^*}{h} \theta_2^* + \delta_2 \right) \right]$$

$$> \gamma \frac{v^*}{h} \theta_2^* \delta_2 = a_3, \quad \text{(A16)}$$

(A15b) holds as well. Local stability is, therefore, assured.

[32]See P. A. Samuelson, *Foundations of Economic Analysis* (Harvard University Press, Cambridge, Mass., 1961), p. 432.

The Structure of Excess Demand for Labor[*]

G. C. ARCHIBALD

The Phillips–Lipsey theory of the Phillips curve postulates a stable (but presumably nonlinear) transformation from excess demand to unemployment, and a stable[1] (but perhaps linear) reaction function mapping from excess demand to the rate of change of money wages. It will be argued here that a good deal more is required to account for an observed Phillips curve—a stable *structure* of excess demand. It will be further argued that the stability must be *stochastic*; and, finally, that some of the small amount of relevant evidence now avaliable favors this conclusion.

The argument to be developed is essentially an aggregation argument; but it will be helpful to start with a very simple point about a single (or perfectly aggregated) market. Let us postulate a linear reac-

[*]Work on which this paper is based began during my tenure of a Ford Foundation Faculty Fellowship at Northwestern University. I am greatly indebted both to the Foundation and to my hosts at Northwestern. I am alone responsible for opinions expressed here, as well as for errors.

[1]Historically stable. The argument of this paper is independent of the argument that the Phillips curve does not provide a stable frontier for the policy-maker because it would shift as expectations changed. For this argument, see E. S. Phelps, "Phillips Curves, Expectations of Inflation and Optimal Unemployment over Time," *Economica* (August 1967), and M. Friedman, "The Role of Monetary Policy," *American Economic Review* (March 1968).

tion function,[2]

$$\frac{\dot{w}}{w} = \alpha X = \alpha \left(\frac{D - S}{S} \right), \qquad \alpha > 0. \tag{1}$$

We further assume that $D = D(w, \ldots)$, $D_w < 0$. We may also assume, if we wish, that D and S are functions of time. Whether we do or not, there are only two possibilities: either (1) is stable, or it is not. Now consider the case in which D and S are invariant with respect to time, there is a unique equilibrium wage, $\bar{w}$, and the system is stable. The effects of any initial disturbance will then die away. Thus if we start with an initial nonequilibrium condition, $X_0 \neq 0$, say $X_0 > 0$, we expect a time path with $\dot{X} < 0$ and $(d/dt)(\dot{w}/w) < 0$ [because the simple form of (1) precludes oscillations].

This much is obvious and elementary. To translate to the usual Phillips curve diagram we assume a stable mapping from X to U. We note that the use of other variables, such as vacancies or U-dot, may improve the proxy measure, but this is not the point at issue here. Hence consider Figure 1. The system, if stable, will return to equilibrium at A, in the manner indicated by the dashed arrows, in response to any "one-shot" disturbance. This is not inconsistent with observation. If, of course, the value of α in (1) were such that a single market were unstable, we should have to appeal to "floors and ceilings"; but, since (1) is nonoscillatory, we should still require repeated disturbances to generate anything consistent with observation. We shall henceforth assume stability; but once we assume that more than one market exists, we shall encounter some new difficulties.

We now assume that there are two identifiable industries (labor markets) and start with a case of particular interest, in the light of postwar U.S. and U.K. experience: that in which we have simultaneously positive excess demand (unemployment less than $0A$) in one market, and negative excess demand in the other. Disaggregation into two markets merely requires that labor is not perfectly mobile between them (more mobile between firms intramarket than intermarket). The possible effects of partial mobility will be discussed below. Assume that the reaction function in market I, which will be the market to display initial excess demand, is of the form of (1). We may assume, for expositional simplicity alone, that wages are sticky downward, so that in market II, which will display initial excess supply, w_2 is a constant. Let initial conditions, X_1^0 and X_2^0, be such that weighted average un-

---

[2]The criticism that this reaction function is an *ad hoc* construct, not derived from theory, must be acknowledged and accepted. The desire to do better, to develop the micro theory of maximizing behavior under disequilibrium, and uncertainty, is the chief motivation of the present volume. The work of Holt, Phelps, and Mortensen is particularly important in this connection. The argument of this paper, however, only requires the existence of reaction functions of the type postulated: It is independent of their derivation.

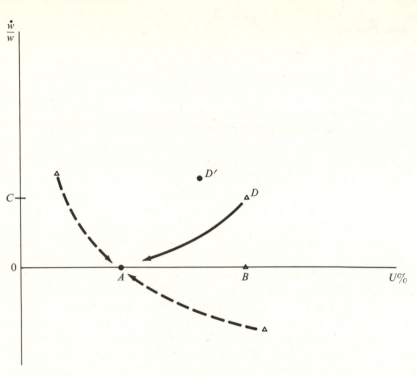

Figure 1

employment (our macro observation) is $0B > 0A$ in Figure 1. Associated with X_1^0 is an initial value, $(\dot{w}/w)_1$, which leads to a weighted-average macro observation of, say, $0C$. Our initial macro observation is thus at D, quite "off" the locus of points generated by disturbance of a single homogeneous market.

The first point to notice is the arbitrary fashion in which we have located D. Suppose that we had maintained the initial value X_2^0 but had arbitrarily doubled X_1^0. Given the nonlinear relationship between X and U (between A and 0, the range of X from zero to plus infinity maps into U from 3 or 4 percent to zero), we should not have moved B very far to the left. We should, however, have increased $0C$ by an amount equal to twice the weight of market I in the wage-rate index, generating an observation such as D'. It is abundantly obvious that initial conditions in the real, or historical, world, cannot have been arbitrary. For an observable Phillips curve to have been traced out, it must have been the case that values of X_1 and X_2 have not been independent but systematically related to one another. We shall return to this point shortly.

The second point is to notice what slope the time path from the initial observation D will have. If market I is stable, then $\dot{w}/w$ will diminish. But what of market II? And what if labor displays some mobility? Suppose that, either in response to the vacancy-unemployment differential, or the wage differential, or both, labor moves, however slowly, from market II to market I. The effect of this is to speed up the return to equilibrium in market I and to reduce unemployment in market II. Hence the time path from D will be in the direction of A, as indicated by the arrow. This is a "reverse Phillips curve."

Variation of some assumptions will not, provided that the system is stable, alter this qualitative result, although it will naturally alter the time profile of response. Thus suppose that workers in market II do not move. Unemployment will nonetheless fall over time if only workers are mortal and the proportion of new entrants who seek work in market I (where there are vacancies) rather than in market II (where there are none) is higher than the initial proportion of workers in market I. (These are sufficient conditions for structural unemployment to be a transient phenomenon.) Thus "perfect immobility" appears to be ruled out; but the extent of mobility merely alters the speed of movement from D to A, not the direction. Now let us relax our simplifying assumption that wages are pegged in market II. If wage rates are allowed to fall in market II the initial observation will be below D, but the direction of change will again be toward A. Movement from D to A involves a positive association over time between $\dot{w}/w$ and U: Both fall.

It is worth trying another experiment at this point: Can we hold U constant, and, if we do, what happens to $\dot{w}/w$? It is not, in fact, easy to hold U constant. We have already argued that structural unemployment is a transient phenomenon. This means that unemployment in market II can only be sustained by a *flow* of dismissals. Ultimately, however, this means the disappearance of industry II. This is an admissible case; but, to make any sense, we need to "invent" a new industry to replace it. In the meantime, of course, market I will have been returning to equilibrium, whether industry II vanished or not, unless we have assumed that whatever force was killing industry II was systematically maintaining excess demand in industry I. It begins to appear that we need, *inter alia*, a large stock of industries, and a "limbo" into which some may vanish and from which new ones may appear.

It is easily seen that, if the initial conditions give positive or negative excess demand in both markets, the track toward A involves a negative rather than a positive association over time between $\dot{w}/w$ and U. Thus it begins to appear that, if a macro Phillips curve is observed, it is due to the particular pattern of initial conditions (shocks) experienced by the economy. Consideration of the case of mixed excess demand and supply also suggests something about relative speeds and frequencies. If we have not observed paths like DA, it must be because the initial conditions are changed before the system has traveled far on the return path to equilibrium.

It is natural to ask how they are changed, and whether the change is exogenous. No very complete answer can be offered here, but a few suggestions can be made. If an economy has displayed a stable historical relationship between $\dot{w}/w$ and U, then the disturbances to the X's *must* have been systematic and therefore, at some level of discourse, endogenous. It is, further, easy to construct stable and consistent two-sector models in which demands are endogenous (save for exogenous components required to prevent the economy, with nonzero saving, being in neutral equilibrium on the 45-degree line) and which merely produce, in particular cases, the results argued more generally above.

The general conclusion is that we must postulate some stable relationship,

$$F(X_1, X_2) = 0 \tag{2}$$

(the extension to more sectors is obvious), to account for observations.

The next question is whether the relationship (2) could be deterministic. Simple qualitative considerations seem sufficient to rule this out. Our argument is, essentially, that there must be (must have been) a stable distribution of excess demands for labor, and one that shifted, at least cyclically, in a systematic manner. Thus the distribution of excess demands cannot have been independent of mean unemployment. It does *not* follow that whenever U has taken on a certain value, say $\bar{U}$, we have had associated values $\bar{X}_k$, $\bar{X}_j$ for given industries or markets k and j: It need only follow that there has been some associated configuration of X_i's. The deterministic case appears, indeed, to be quite impossible: It cannot have been the case that X_k and X_j have regularly stood in the same relation to one another. It is only necessary to suppose that the kth industry is bread and the jth washing machines for this to be obvious. Innovation in products, growth, and the fact that not all income elasticities of demand are unity do all that we require. There is secular change, and, with it, change in the cyclical relation of markets. Indeed, as we have argued, not only do industries vanish and new ones emerge, but it is easier to reconcile theory with observation when this is allowed for.[3]

We are thus led to interpret (2) stochastically, and write a frequency function defined over market excess demands,

$$f(X_1, \ldots, X_n). \tag{3}$$

Our argument leads to the hypothesis that there exists a stable distribution (3). At the same time, we do *not* require that the indices always attach to the same industries. To take an obvious analogy, it

---

[3]It appears, however, that regions in the United Kingdom show a good deal of what may be called "indexed stability," as opposed to merely stochastic stability. It is for this reason that there is a "regional problem." See F. P. R. Brechling, "Trends and Cycles in British Regional Unemployment," *Oxford Economic Papers* (March 1967).

is one thing to say that the heights of schoolboys in a class display a stable distribution (with appropriate parameter changes from class to class), and quite another to say that any boy called John will always be the third tallest. The second assertion is much stronger than the first and is, furthermore, unnecessary. It is also empirically preposterous while the first is not: Hence statistics!

We now wish to know if excess demands are distributed according to some recognizable law, what the law is, how the parameters may have changed, and what their economic interpretation may be. Ultimately, we wish to know how to change them, because the distribution of excess demands for labor is intimately related to some urgent social problems. At this point, however, I can only report some tentative, and apparently inconsistent, results. Lipsey argued[4] some time ago that an increase in the intermarket dispersion of unemployment would, if individual-market Phillips' curves were convex from below, lead to an increase in the macro-$\dot{w}/w$ associated with each macro value of U (mean unemployment). I have reported elsewhere[5] my test of this hypothesis. What is relevant here is the light it sheds on our distributional hypothesis. To see this, it is necessary to review briefly the earlier work.

It is not altogether clear what the "true" micro-labor markets may be; but it is clear that, whatever they are, we have no data about them. Our available data are reported for geographical or industrial units. If we assume that the geographical or industrial dispersion is at least a workable proxy for dispersion over "true" markets, then we can test Lipsey's hypothesis by computing the time series σ_t^2, where σ^2 is the cross-section variance over whatever data we have, and using σ^2 as an additional explanatory variable. The regression equation, neglecting lags, price changes, etc., then becomes

$$\left(\frac{\dot{w}}{w}\right)_t = a_0 + a_1(\overline{U})_t^b + c\sigma_t^2, \tag{4}$$

where $\dot{w}/w$ is macro and $\overline{U}$ is macro, too (the mean of the cross-section unemployment rates). b is chosen to be $+1$ or -1 as appears to fit best. σ^2 is the cross-section variance.

This model was fitted to four sets of unemployment data, two each for the United Kingdom and the United States. For the United Kingdom postwar data are available annually on a regional basis and also on an industrial (geographical) basis; for the United States it is available quarterly for states and for the 150 major labor areas. The results were broadly favorable to the hypothesis: The coefficient of σ^2 was significant

[4]R. G. Lipsey, "The Relationship between Unemployment and the Rate of Change of Money Wages in the United Kingdom, 1862–1957: A Further Analysis," *Economica* (February 1960).
[5]*American Economic Review* (May 1968, Proceedings number).

and positive, in spite of some multicollinearity. This apparently means, however, that the variance and the mean are independent, that the former can change independently of the latter, and that it exerts an independent effect on $\dot{w}/w$. This appears to be contrary to the hypothesis advanced here. In the case of the 150 major labor areas, however, the results are somewhat different. The correlation between the first *three* moments of the distribution [the third was computed so that a measure of skewness might be added to (4): the distributions are skewed, skewdness varies, and the measure proved in some cases significant] was so high as to preclude significance in multiple regression: Any moment could be made significant by exclusion of the others! This result is favorable to the hypothesis advanced here. This evidence is clearly insufficient to settle the matter; but a few more points may be made.

The theoretical prediction that σ^2 would have a positive effect, which need not be repeated here, seems quite well founded. It is also consistent with the U.K. results, and the states results. It is worth noting, however, that the U.K. regional model only offers 9 observations at each time—compared with 150! We might conjecture that, the better we are able to determine the moments, the greater is the multicollinearity, the less the "independent" effect of σ^2, and the greater the evidence for the hypothesis now under consideration. But it cannot be pretended that the data are sufficient, or sufficiently well analyzed, to permit any firm conclusion as yet. One may, however, be skeptical of attempts to explain the Phillips curve from purely deterministic constructs. Furthermore, if our distributional hypothesis were accepted, the whole debate over "structural" versus "demand-deficient" unemployment would require reconsideration, because the two would go together. We should lose interest in local explanations of particular segments of the distribution of unemployment, if we knew that the distribution were stable. Our interest would turn instead to the measurement and interpretation of the parameters and measures that might alter their values.

APPENDIX:
AN EXAMPLE OF WAGE
DYNAMICS IN A CLOSED
TWO–SECTOR MODEL

The purpose of the model to be constructed here is to explore the dynamics of wage-rate adjustment in response to initial disturbance in a case in which factor incomes feed back to commodity demands and thence to factor demands, substitution in consumption takes place, and labor can move between markets. We confine discussion to a particular disturbance: excess demand initially positive in one market and negative in the other. The model will be simplified throughout to the level required for explicit solution to be possible. This requires that all markets except the labor market clear instantaneously, and that expenditure, via factor incomes, instantaneously becomes expenditure once again. The combined effect of these assumptions is that the only dynamic behavioral equations occur in the labor market, whence stability depends solely on these equations. Our conclusions might therefore be derived directly from examination of these equations. On the other hand, this is perhaps more easily seen when the exercise is completed than before it is begun; and some other issues may be illuminated en route.

Some assumptions may be listed now. Others will be explained and motivated as we proceed.

a. Our initial conditions will be positive excess demand for labor in market 1 and negative in market 2. Hence we shall assume that output in market 1 is limited by available labor supplies, whereas in 2 it is not.

b. Wages are rigid downward in market 2: $w_2 = \bar{w}$. We could thus use $\bar{w}$ as a numeraire; but it is convenient to work in money terms throughout.

c. There is constant autonomous expenditure in the goods markets but no endogenous investment.

d. Outputs are determined by the amounts of variable labor applied under constant technology to constant capital stocks.

e. There is no monetary sector: The money supply is whatever is required to accommodate the price-quantity vectors obtained.

f. There are no intermediate products: Each sector is vertically integrated.

Some of these assumptions can, in fact, be relaxed without affecting our qualitative results. (a) is symmetrical and (b) merely a matter of convenience. Some autonomous expenditure is necessary, if households save, to yield a determinate equilibrium; but its constancy is nonessential: Exponential forcing of autonomous expenditure complicates the algebra without adding anything of substance. Endogenous investment would introduce a major complication, and has not been investigated, whence (d), but nothing of interest is added by autonomous exponential growth in productivity. (e) proves to be trivial, (f) appears essential.

The simplest way to obtain household demand functions that will "add up" to factor income, or factor income minus a constant saving ratio, is to derive them by maximizing a utility function subject to the budget constraint. Linear expenditure functions (derived from addilog utility functions) have some attractive properties but unfortunately introduce some most intractable nonlinearities. Cobb–Douglas utility functions are accordingly assumed. They sadly restrict behavior, but it will prove not to matter much. From the familiar maximizing procedure, we derive

$$q_1^d = \frac{\alpha c Y}{p_1} + \frac{Z_1}{p_1}, \tag{A1}$$

$$q_2^d = \frac{(1-\alpha)c Y}{p_2} + \frac{Z_2}{p_1}, \tag{A2}$$

and, of course,

$$Y \equiv p_1 q_1 + p_2 q_2, \tag{A3}$$

where Z_1, Z_2 are constant exogenous expenditures, fixed in money terms; $1 - c$ is the constant savings ratio; and α is the $C-D$ coefficient. Addition of (A1) and (A2) gives the familiar income-expenditure equations in money terms, i.e.,

$$Y = cY + Z_1 + Z_2,$$

whence it is seen that money income is a constant in the model, so that assumption (e) is indeed trivial.

The goods-market portion of the model is completed by adding behavior equations for firms. There is a host of interdependent possibilities: constant or diminishing returns, perfect or imperfect competition, profit maximisation or some alternative, etc. We exclude inventory[6] by assumption (a). In the interests of simplicity, we assume that in market 1, where supply is constrained by labor supply, price instantaneously clears the market, whereas in market 2 it is set by applying a constant mark-up to marginal costs. Marginal costs are given in both sectors by constant marginal productivity and the instantaneous wage rate. Thus we have

$$q_1^s = a_1 L_1^s, \tag{A4}$$

$$p_2 = \overline{w} a_2 (1 + \mu_2), \tag{A5}$$

where a_1 is the labor-productivity constant in sector 1 and a_2 the marginal cost constant (reciprocal of the productivity constant) in sector 2.

We now wish to derive the two demands for labor. In sector 1 we first need desired price and output behavior. There is, again, a host of possible behavioral assumptions. A simple, though not easily justified, assumption is that desired price is obtained by adding a constant mark-up to instantaneous marginal cost, and that desired output is the quantity that would clear the market at the administered price. These assumptions give

$$p_1^* = a_1^{-1} w_1 (1 + \mu_1), \tag{A6}$$

$$q_1^* = q_1^d(p_1^*) \tag{A7}$$

(where p_1^* and q_1^* are desired price and output, respectively), whence

$$L_1^d = a_1^{-1} q_1^*. \tag{A8}$$

In sector 2 we obviously have

$$L_2^d = a_2 q_2. \tag{A9}$$

We complete the model before starting to solve. First, we assume that the unemployed migrate from market 2 to market 1, as long as there are vacancies in market 1, according to the familiar lag form

$$-\dot{U} = \theta(U - U^*), \tag{A10}$$

where U^* is desired unemployment. We shall assume that $U^* = 0$, but it

---

[6]We exclude inventory in sector 1; in sector 2, it is unnecessary. Introduction of inventories adds realism at the expense of serious complication of the ensuing differential equations and adds little to an understanding of labor markets.

may be equal to any positive constant, if, e.g., there are some elderly unemployed unwilling to move, without altering the results. We are assuming that all the unemployed who disappear from market 2 became available in market 1, whence

$$L_1^s = L_{10}^s + \ell_1^s, \tag{A11}$$

where $\ell_1^s = \dot{U}$. Given parameter values, we may easily pick initial conditions that guard against excess demand in market 1 turning into excess supply. We could, of course, assume that migration occurs in response to wage differentials. Some results of this assumption will be noted below. Our labor-market-adjustment equations are completed by the conventional Phillips–Lipsey relation

$$\frac{\dot{w}_1}{w_1} = \frac{\delta(L_1^d - L_1^s)}{L_{10}^s}. \tag{A12}$$

The model has been designed to make solution easy. The subset of (A1) through (A5) together with the equilibrium conditions, yield two *linear* simultaneous equations in the unknowns p_1 and q_2:

$$p_1 = \frac{Z_1}{(1 - \alpha c)a_1 L_1^s} + \frac{\alpha c \overline{w} a_2 (1 + \mu_2)}{(1 - \alpha c)a_1 L_1^s} q_2, \tag{A13}$$

$$q_2 = \frac{Z_2}{\{1 - (1 - \alpha)c\}\overline{w} a_2 (1 + \mu_2)}$$
$$+ \frac{(1 - \alpha)c L_1^s}{\{1 - (1 - \alpha)c\}\overline{w} a_2 (1 + \mu_2)} p_1. \tag{A14}$$

These are solved by

$$p_1 = \frac{\{1 - (1 - \alpha)c\}Z_1 + \alpha c Z_2}{(1 - c)a_1 L_1^s}, \tag{A15}$$

$$q_2 = \frac{(1 - \alpha)c Z_1 + (1 - \alpha c)Z_2}{(1 - c)\overline{w} a_2 (1 + \mu_2)}. \tag{A16}$$

Thus p_1 is a diminishing function of available labor, L_1^s, while q_2 is a constant. Our assumptions make p_1, but not p_1^*, or L_2^d, independent of the wage rate. Thus we substitute (A15) and (A16) into the subset (A6) through (A9) to obtain

$$q_1^* = \frac{a_1}{w_1(1 + \mu_2)}\left[\frac{(1 + \alpha c)Z_1 + \alpha c Z_2}{1 - c}\right], \tag{A17}$$

$$L_1^d = \frac{(1 + \alpha c)Z_1 + \alpha c Z_2}{w_1(1 + \mu_1)(1 - c)}$$
$$= \frac{k}{w_1}, \quad \text{say,} \tag{A18}$$

$$L_2^d = \frac{(1 - \alpha)c Z_1 + (1 - \alpha c)Z_2}{\overline{w}(1 + \mu_2)(1 - c)}. \tag{A19}$$

L_2^d is a constant, of no further interest. L_1^d is negatively associated with w_1, as we should expect, and depends only indirectly on available labor supply, L_1^s (through its effect on w_1).

Now from (A10) we obtain

$$U = U_0 e^{-\theta t}. \tag{A20}$$

Substitution of (A20) into (A11) gives

$$L_1^s = L_{10}^s + U_0(1 - e^{-\theta t}). \tag{A21}$$

Substitution of (A18) and (A21) into (A12) now gives

$$\frac{\dot{w}}{w} = \frac{\delta}{L_{10}^s} \left\{ \frac{k}{w_1} - [L_{10}^s + U_0(1 - e^{-\theta t})] \right\}, \tag{A22}$$

which is solved by

$$w = \frac{k}{L_{10}^s(1 + N_0) - N_0 e^{-\theta t}} + Ce^{-[\delta t(1+N_0)+(\delta/\theta)N_0 e^{-\theta t}]}, \tag{A23}$$

where $N_0 = U_0/L_{10}^s$ and C is initial excess demand in market 1.

Some properties of (A23) are easily established. Our mobility assumptions lead to the transient terms in $e^{-\theta t}$, which go to zero, hence stability depends only on δ, as in the single-market case. Then the asymptotic solution is

$$w = \frac{K}{L_{10}^s(1 + N_0)}.$$

If initial conditions give $N_0 = 0$, we have exactly the single-market case. Differentiation of (A23) shows

$$\dot{w} \geq 0 \quad \text{and} \quad \ddot{w} \leq 0.$$

From (A22) $\dot{U} < 0$. Thus the path by which the model returns to equilibrium in the $\dot{w}/w$, U space is directed to the southwest. What pattern of disturbances would generate an observable northwest to southeast scatter can only be conjectured.

With the explicit solution of the model before us, we can easily see the price that would be paid for some alternative—and more interesting—assumptions.

Obviously matters would be seriously complicated if the subset (A1) through (A5) did not lead to linear equations. Similarly, (A6) through (A9) have been chosen to preserve linearity. Variations in (A10) through (A12) are of greater interest, and can be discussed in terms of a single market with varying supplies. Suppose first that the flow supply of new labor, $\dot{\ell}$, is proportional to vacancies (excess demand). Then we have

$$\frac{\dot{w}}{w} = \frac{\delta}{L_0} \left(\frac{K}{w} - L_0 - \ell \right), \tag{A24}$$

$$\dot{\ell} = \alpha \left(\frac{K}{w} - L_0 - \ell \right), \tag{A25}$$

which, on rearrangement, are seen to give a pair of nonlinear simultaneous differential equations. Assume alternatively that labor moves in response to wage differentials. Without troubling about lags, wages in other markets, etc., we may illustrate by writing

$$L^s = L_0 + \lambda w, \tag{A26}$$

$$\frac{\dot{w}}{w} = \frac{\delta}{L_0} \left(\frac{K}{w} - L_0 - \lambda w \right), \tag{A27}$$

which give

$$\dot{w} + \delta w + \frac{\delta \lambda}{L_0} w^2 = \frac{\delta}{L_0} K. \tag{A28}$$

It becomes very clear that economically naive assumptions readily produce the most intractable systems of equations.

How Can the Phillips Curve Be Moved to Reduce Both Inflation and Unemployment?*

CHARLES C. HOLT

In recent years national stabilization policies increasingly have confronted the conflict of attaining both inflation and full employment objectives. Although the reality of this conflict is disputed on theoretical grounds, there appears now to be overwhelming evidence[1] of its seriousness, particularly in the United States and Canada, even though empirical questions still remain about the degree of stability

*The research reported here was conducted at the Urban Institute for the Manpower Administration, U.S. Department of Labor, under the authority of the Manpower Development and Training Act.

This work is a continuation of research done by the author and his colleagues at the Social Systems Research Institute, University of Wisconsin, under a grant from the Ford Foundation for study of the dynamics of the labor market.

The author appreciates the helpful comments that were received from Frank Brechling, Martin David, Otto Eckstein, Harvey A. Garn, George P. Huber, Richard A. Lester, Joseph Lewis, Edmund S. Phelps, Paul Taubman, Donald P. Tucker, and his coauthors of the present volume.

The views presented in this paper are the responsibility of the author and do not constitute an official statement of the Urban Institute or the Department of Labor.

A complementary paper, "Improving the Labor Market Tradeoff between Inflation and Unemployment," *Papers and Proceedings of the American Economic Association* (May 1969) summarizes and extends parts of this paper.

[1]G. L. Perry, *Unemployment, Money Wage Rates, and Inflation* (M.I.T. Press, Cambridge, Mass., 1966).

R. G. Bodkin, E. P. Bond, G. L. Reuber, and T. T. Robinson, *Price Stability and High Employment: The Options for Canadian Economic Policy, An Econometric Study* (Queen's Printer, Ottawa, Canada, 1966).

of the inflation-unemployment relation, its quantitative parameters, and even its economic basis.

Observing that in different countries the Phillips curves appear to be quite different, one is led to raise the question of how the Phillips curve in the United States might be moved to the left and downward. A Canadian study[2] of the Phillips relations for various countries found the following estimates of the percentage rate of unemployment that corresponded to a 2.5 percent per year rate of increase in money wages: Canada 5.2 to 10.0 percent, United States 5.5 to 8.2, Japan 5.5, Britain 2.6 to 3.2, France 2.3, and West Germany 1.5. Ranges are shown where more than one econometric study was available. Although the studies on which these figures are based are not fully comparable, their results give strong support to the conclusion that to attain constant price levels in these countries, their unemployment rates would be substantially different. Compared to other countries, the United States appears to have substantial room for improvement.

In another international comparison, Garbarino[3] finds real growth rate correlated with inflation rate and inversely with unemployment. This is not surprising in view of the pressure for production when demand is high. Clearly it would be highly desirable to secure the low unemployment and high growth rates without inflation, if that were possible.

However, before we can consider the design of policies and programs for moving the Phillips curve, we need a conceptual understanding of its economic basis and a determination of the critical parameters that would need to be changed. An integrated and tested theory unfortunately does not yet exist, but enough work has been done on the operation of the labor market that its outline is beginning to emerge. In this paper we attempt to round out a search[4] theory of the labor market, but not its complete formal statement, and then proceed to an analysis of its policy implications. Although alternative theoretical explanations of the Phillips relation have been advanced, the labor market search theory now has enough empirical support to merit an examination of its policy implications.

Holt and David[5] presented an anatomical picture of the flows and stocks comprising the labor market and stressed the parallel roles

[2]Bodkin et al., *op. cit.*, p. 72.

[3]J. W. Garbarino, "Income Policy and Income Behavior," in *Employment Policy and the Labor Market*, A. M. Ross, ed. (University of California Press, Berkeley, 1965), pp. 56–88.

[4]Other authors are exploring the implications of search behavior and lack of knowledge, but we do not here attempt a survey of related work. Concentration on wage dynamics does not imply exclusion of price dynamics and other considerations, but it does reflect the judgment that the Phillips curve is primarily a labor-market phenomenon.

[5]C. C. Holt and M. H. David, "The Concept of Vacancies in a Dynamic Theory of the Labor Market," in *Measurement and Interpretation of Job Vacancies* (National Bureau of Economic Research, 1966), pp. 73–141.

played by stocks of workers and vacancies, probabilities of placement, and declining wage aspirations. Later Holt[6] derived several versions of the Phillips relation in a free market and then considered the effect of unions. This model was tested against empirical evidence reported in the literature.

In Section 1 of this paper, the role of vacancies in influencing wages and placements is developed and the overall operation of the market is discussed. Section 2 analyzes the basic stock, flow, and probability relationships in the market. The aggregate implications of market segmentation are analyzed in Section 3 and the Appendix. Section 4 considers briefly the argument that there can be no unique stable Phillips relation for *steady* inflation. Section 5 draws on all the above to analyze what policy measures would be effective in reducing both inflation and unemployment. Finally, Section 6 summarizes the conclusions for policy and research.

This paper attempts to go considerably beyond present knowledge in the form of rigorously complete mathematical formulations that have been fully tested empirically. Hence it must be understood that the present results are tentative. Greater certainty and especially knowledge of quantitative magnitudes must await further work.

This effort to move to policy implications may be somewhat premature, in view of our limited theoretical and empirical knowledge, but it should be helpful in pointing up those critical areas in which further basic and programmatic research is most critically needed, especially to obtain quantitative measures. However, the fact that the conclusions reached here are generally consistent with, and relevant to, existing programs designed to decrease "frictions" in the labor market lends added support to their credibility.

1
SEARCH, UNEMPLOYMENT,
VACANCIES, AND
WAGE CHANGES

In this analysis, the labor market is conceived as a dynamic stochastic system. Its anatomy is drawn crudely in Figure 1, which shows the various flows and stocks that have important influences on the labor market. This figure is discussed fully in elsewhere,[7] so we will simply note that the interaction between the two key stocks, unemployed workers and unfilled jobs (job vacancies), is critical in determining the tendency of money wages to drift upward or downward. These stocks

---

[6]C. C. Holt, "Job Search, Phillips' Wage Relation, and Union Influence: Theory and Evidence," this volume.

[7]C. C. Holt, "Improving the Labor Market Tradeoff between Inflation and Unemployment," *Papers and Proceedings of the American Economic Association* (May 1969)

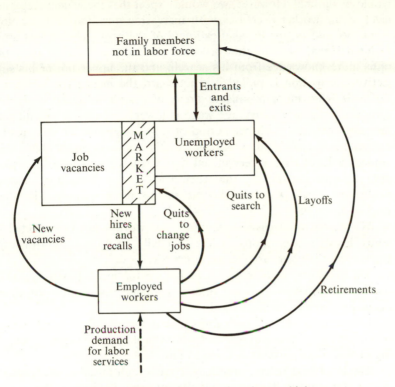

Figure 1.   Flows and stocks of workers and jobs.

in turn are determined by dynamic flows that continually replenish the stocks. We now consider the decision behaviors that determine the flows shown in the figure.

The flow of new hires results from matching up individual workers and jobs. Unemployed and employed workers, who are willing to incur the costs of doing so, search the market for job vacancies that are more attractive than continuing their present employed or unemployed states. To do as well as is feasible they set relatively high aspirations initially and gradually lower them as the search continues, until acceptable job offers are found. An optimal strategy for searching a sequence of employment opportunities that appear one at a time is to establish an acceptance level; any offers below this level are rejected and the first one above it is accepted. This search actually is concerned with many dimensions, but in the interests of simplicity in the analysis we will concentrate on money wages.

If costs of search were constant per period of time unemployed, and if a worker faced a known probability distribution of wage offers for jobs that otherwise were identical, then a constant acceptance wage, probably on the upper tail of the distribution of wage opportunities, would be optimal. However, we would expect that the wage acceptance level of the worker decreases with increasing duration of unemployment, because (a) his Baysian estimate of the probability distribution of his personal opportunities becomes gradually less diffuse as he obtains more knowledge from his search, and the upper tail of his subjective distribution is pulled down toward the mean; (b) his search proceeds from more promising areas of search to successively less promising ones whose average wage is lower; and (c) his psychic and financial costs of search per period of time increase as he depletes his financial and emotional resources and the range of his search is extended. It is, of course, recognized that a few workers may have such poor information initially that their wage expectations are unrealistically low. Such workers, who are in the minority, may raise their wage aspirations.

When general wages are changing, the worker can be expected to adjust his wage aspirations, at least partially, to take account of wage changes that workers are getting generally.

The employed worker who searches on the job behaves similarly, but his search costs are lower and he is under less pressure to adjust his wages aspirations downward.

In summary, the worker's money acceptance wage depends on his balancing the real costs of search against the gains from selective screening of the job opportunities open to him.

The employers behave similarly, setting high initial aspirations for output per wage dollar and gradually lowering them until the needed workers are hired. Of course, laid-off workers can be recalled with relatively little search.

When, in the course of recruiting, employers encounter acceptable workers, they extend offers. A worker's acceptance of an offer constitutes a placement that terminates either unemployment or employment or employment in the previous job.

The market search from the employer side involves comparing requirements of a job with the qualifications of a worker and predicting his output. The employer searches for candidates whose probable output is sufficiently high that an offer is made. The worker examines the characteristics and inducements of the jobs offered in the light of his preferences and predicts his likely satisfaction in each if he should accept. Thus, as in a marriage, both participants in the employment transaction need to be reasonably satisfied; otherwise no placement occurs. The predictions of output and satisfaction usually depend on large amounts of very specific information[8] that are not known by the parties in advance of interviews between particular worker-vacancy pairs, and hence the process of locating interesting job and worker

[8]C. C. Holt, and G. P. Huber, "A Computer Aided Approach to Employment Service Placement, and Counseling," *Management Science*, Vol. 15, No. 11, July 1969, pp. 573–94.

prospects typically involves searches on both sides of the market whose outcomes cannot be foreseen except in probability terms.

There is a great deal of variability between workers in the ratios of their aspirations to their previous employments, in the rates at which their aspirations fall, and even in the way that a single worker might respond to the same job offer on successive days. Similar kinds of variability characterize the behavior of employers but to a lesser degree. These variabilities, coupled with the random employer-worker exposures that are produced by market search, screening, and interviewing, yield a complex stochastic process that is best analyzed in probability terms.

As long as the inflows into the market of unemployed workers and vacancies continue at higher rates than the placement and recall outflows, the stocks of unemployed workers and vacancies continue to grow. An increase in the number of unemployed workers inhibits the quit flow but encourages the layoff flow into the stock of unemployed workers. An increase in the stock of vacancies discourages employers from creating new vacancies. However, the rising stocks of workers and vacancies increase the probabilities of placements and hence the outflows of workers and vacancies. For each of these stocks, the inflow decreases and the outflow increases until equality is reached and the stock level no longer changes. This process of flow equilibrium is the basic mechanism that determines the sizes of the vacancy and unemployment stocks. When inflows and outflows are equal, the stocks stabilize at constant levels.

However, the probability of placements that influences the outflows also depends on wage and other aspirations on both sides of the market. When wage offers are low and worker wage aspirations are high, the probability of an offer being both made and accepted is low, and placements are correspondingly few. Under these circumstances, the stocks of vacancies and unemployed workers grow, and as a result the durations of vacancies and unemployment increase until the gaps between worker and employer wage aspirations diminish and placement probabilities rise.

Thus the final vacancy-unemployment stock-flow equilibrium also involves an inherent wage-change equilibrium for the workers and vacancies that pass through the market.

When vacancies are filled by workers who search for better jobs while still employed, their quitting creates new vacancies (probably at lower skill requirements and wage rates) that replace the filled ones, so there is no net change in the totals of either unemployment or vacancies. However, by quitting, the workers usually obtain wage increases and lower the average wages offered by the unfilled vacancies.

To inhibit quits and to improve their chances in recruiting replacements, employers voluntarily grant on-the-job wage increases when the labor market is tight.

Through use of the strike threat in collective bargaining, union workers can raise their money wages by a certain differential relative to nonunion workers. Part of the wage increase is offset by the employer raising quality standards in hiring, and the rest comes from one or all of the following: profits, better production technology, monopoly power in the product market, or monopsony power in the purchased-goods market.

When unemployment declines, the bargaining power of the individual worker rises even more than the collective bargaining power of the union, and the union differential declines. Initially, because of the relatively high wages of the unionized firm, it enjoys relative ease in hiring and has a low quit rate. These shelter the unionized firm in a tightening labor market so that it can resist wage perssure better than the nonunion firm that must quickly raise wages in order to recruit and to hold its work force. Thus, as the market gets tighter, the nonunionized firm is more responsive and its wages rise faster than the unionized firm's. As the union differentials melt away and union leaders become aware that their wage gains have been relatively low, strikes increase when the unions try to recover their differentials.

When the labor market slackens, bargaining power of the union relative to that of the individual worker is restored. Then the unions are able to obtain higher wage increases and their differentials are regained.

It is the prime contention of the market search theory of the Phillips relation that the rate of wage inflation depends on the interaction between the size of the labor force and the level of aggregate demand, and that prices are determined primarily by adding mark-ups to costs. Monopoly power in product and labor markets can account for differentials in the levels of prices and wages relative to competitive sectors but does not affect appreciably, for any extended period, the steady-state rates of change of prices and wages.

We must concede that efforts to increase income shares by companies and unions when demand is high could speed up wage and price increases.[9] However, usually enough overage capital capacity is kept on standby basis that production can be increased substantially, if labor can be recruited. Thus demand increases tend to be transmitted quickly to the labor market, where wage changes are generated by the powerful atomistic processes discussed above.

To be sure, workers and unions are sensitive to changes in prices, but this is secondary to their responses to conditions in the labor mar-

[9] If unions and companies use their market power over wages and prices, respectively, to try to increase their shares of the real output, a wage-price spiral can indeed occur. We need to develop the theory of this phenomenon and its measurement to determine its importance. This process could occur without any reference to the unemployment rate. The empirical tie between inflation and unemployment tends to discredit this hypothesis unless the overclaim of the real output itself depends on the level of unemployment.

ket that affect the personal and collective bargaining that takes place there.

Market power on union and company sides may influence the speed with which wage and price adjustments are made, but these seem more likely to affect income distribution between groups than the basic wage-change process in the United States, where union wages account for less than a quarter of the national wage bill. These hypotheses need much more empirical testing than they have received to date.[10]

The statistical identification of causal relationships between wages and prices is complicated by the fact that there is a circular chain of causality. Wage costs affect prices, which in turn influence the conversion of money demand into real demand for goods, and through the productivity relation the real demand for labor; and this affects wages.

Wage changes experienced in passing through the market are affected by the durations of search and in turn by the sizes of the stocks of vacancies and unemployed workers. The quit rate of workers also depends on these stocks and durations. Quit turnover has little effect on the stock of vacancies or of unemployed workers, but it constitutes an important wage-increase mechanism.

Certain broad conclusions can now be drawn about this complex stochastic process which constitutes the labor market. The primary conclusion, of course, is that the wage level tends to drift upward for low levels of unemployment and even drift downward for very high levels of unemployment. A mathematical derivation of a very simple Phillips relation based on the above relationships is shown in a paper of the author's,[11] and a more complex one is derived in another paper.[12]

The inflow of new workers into the market through increased labor participation that occurs when unemployment declines tends to restore unemployment. This allows greater increases in aggregate production with less inflation response than would occur otherwise.

2
BASIC RELATIONS AMONG PROBABILITIES, STOCKS, FLOWS, AND WAGES

In order to clarify the foregoing conceptual framework, this section analyzes some of the important relations more fully.

A. Analysis of a Single Interview   In order to simplify exposition, we will consider only the wage dimension of market search and let this

[10]Holt, "Job Search, Phillips' Wage Relation and Union Influence: Theory and Evidence."
[11]Holt, "Improving the Labor Market Tradeoff between Inflation and Unemployment."
[12]Holt, "Job Search, Phillips' Wage Relation and Union Influence: Theory and Evidence."

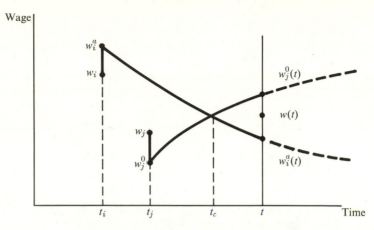

Figure 2.   Wage offer and acceptance levels.

serve as a generalized proxy for all the many complex worker and job dimensions that are involved. For example, the employer's aspiration adjustment is likely to be made by accepting less-productive workers without actually lowering the money wage offers. Clearly then, his wage offer per unit of output rises with increased vacancy duration. In the following analysis, as an analytic simplification, we hold "quality" constant and let all the adjustments take place in wages.

Consider the typical market occurrence in which market searches at time t bring together for an interview worker i and the employer who is trying to fill vacancy j (see Figure 2). Worker i quit his previous job, which paid wage w_i at time t_i, and commenced full-time search for a better job. His initial wage aspiration was w_i^a. His search has already lasted $t - t_i = T_i$, his search duration to date, and the minimum wage that he is now willing to consider is $w_i^0(t)$. The employer's position was previously filled at wage w_j, but initially he sought a higher quality replacement at the same money wage which corresponds to an initial offer level of w_j^0 for the original worker quality. Now that the vacancy duration is $T_j = t - t_j$, the employer is willing to offer as much as $w_j^0(t)$.[13]

Had this interview taken place before time t_c, there would have been a *gap* between the minimum wage that the worker would accept and the maximum offer that the employer would make. Hence the probability would have been nil of the offer being both made and accepted (see Figure 3).

However, at time t there is a wage *overlap*, i.e., the maximum offer level exceeds the minimum acceptance level, and hence there is some probability that the placement will occur at some intermediate wage

---

[13]Since we are "holding quality constant," the money wage is adjusted so that the productivity of worker i is equal to that of the earlier occupant of vacancy j.

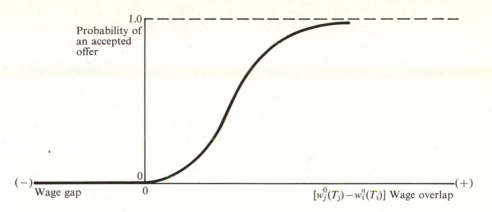

Figure 3.   Influence of wage overlap on offer–acceptance probability.

$w(t)$. Whether or not the searches of i and j continue beyond t depends, of course, on whether or not this interview ends in a placement.

The longer the vacancy and unemployment durations have been, the larger the wage overlap is likely to be and the higher the probability that an acceptable offer will be made[14] (see Figure 3). The relation between w_i and $w(t)$ shows whether the worker might succeed in raising his income. Clearly an increase is much more likely to occur when his placement occurs after a short duration of unemployment than a long one. The employer's wage change similarly would depend on the relation between $w(t)$ and w_j.

In summary, the probability $P_{0a}(ijt)$ that the ij interview would result in an offer and its acceptance, terminating search and setting a new wage agreement, depends on the initial offer and acceptance levels, their rates of adjustment, and the durations of the unemployment and the vacancy at the time t when the interview takes place.

B. Analysis of a Labor Market   Next we consider how many such possible interviews and placements would work out in a market subject to cyclical fluctuations. We assume at any period of time that the number of vacancies and workers in the market is so large that random fluctuations in placements average out in the aggregate measures.

Let T_s be the "mean search time," i.e., the time that would be required on the average for any particular worker to encounter any particular vacancy and to schedule an interview to explore the match. The implicit assumption here is that the worker is an eligible candidate for the vacancy, so that an "encounter" would be followed by an interview to determine whether an offer is made and accepted. When there is occupational and other compartmentalization, many encounters

[14]For a theoretical analysis of this probability function, see Holt and Huber, *op. cit.*

would not be followed by interviews. This case is considered later. Thus T_s is a measure of search activity and information by both workers and employers. Let P_{0a} be the average probability that an interview will result in an offer that is accepted following the above wage analysis. For brevity we might refer to P_{0a} as the offer-acceptance probability. It depends on the *averages* across unemployed workers and vacancies of the previous wages of the workers and the vacancies; the ratios of the initial offer and acceptance wages to their previous wages, respectively; the rates at which acceptance wages fall and offer wages rise with increasing durations; and the average durations of unemployment and vacancies, T_u and T_v. Because of the vagueness in what constitutes an interview, it is likely to be difficult to accurately distinguish between T_s and P_{0a}.

There is a total of $\mathcal{U}\mathcal{V}$ such potential interview encounters,[15] where $\mathcal{U}$ and $\mathcal{V}$ are the stocks of unemployed workers and vacancies, respectively. Dividing by T_s gives interviews per period of time and multiplying by P_{0a} gives the expected flow $\mathcal{F}$ of hires and recalls per period of time that are expected to result from the interviews. Thus we obtain

$$\mathcal{F} = \frac{\mathcal{U}\mathcal{V}P_{0a}}{T_s}. \tag{1}$$

If diminishing returns are introduced into equation (1), then equation (11) page 238 becomes:

$$U^x V^y = (F)(T_s)(1/P_{oa})(\mathcal{E}^{1-y}/\mathcal{L}^x)\left(1/\sum_{i=1}^{N} u_i^x v_i^y\right). \tag{11}$$

It is interesting to note that, in the special case in which $x = y = .5$, diminishing returns exactly offset the economies of scale of the large market segments. Thus in this case the degree of segmentation does not affect the aggregate levels of vacancies and unemployment under optimal allocation.

This basic relation between the flow $\mathcal{F}$ and the stocks $\mathcal{U}$ and $\mathcal{V}$ can be solved to emphasize the latter variables:

$$\mathcal{U}\mathcal{V} = \frac{\mathcal{F}T_s}{P_{0a}}. \tag{2}$$

[15]Since increases in the number of unemployed workers may to some degree interfere with the interview chances of the original unemployed workers, the number of interviews may rise less than proportionally with increases in unemployment. The same argument applies to vacancies. These diminishing return effects might be reflected by modifying (1) as follows: $\mathcal{F} = \mathcal{U}^x\mathcal{V}^y P_{0a}/T_s$, where x and y are constants, $0 < x, y < 1$.

Although the refinement will be important, especially for empirical work, it was omitted in the following theoretical analysis in the interests of simplicity. Diminishing returns may depend on the capacities of employment services and personnel offices to screen candidates, schedule interviews, etc., and this may introduce adjustment delays and other complications that are not essential for present purposes.

However, we should recognize that the omission of diminishing returns may lead to overstating the economies of scale (efficiencies of size) that are noted in large markets.

Except for trend factors, the product $\mathcal{U}\mathcal{V}$ tends to be remarkably constant over the business cycle, as Boschan[16] and Dow[17] have shown. Hence the cost of reducing unemployment is an increase in vacancies, and vice versa.

The near constancy of $\mathcal{U}\mathcal{V}$ occurs because $\mathcal{F}$, T_s, and P_{0a} all tend to have stable values except for the trend growth in $\mathcal{F}$. The quit and lay-off components, whose sum in equilibrium determines $\mathcal{F}$, fluctuates cyclically and countercyclically, respectively, so their fluctuations largely cancel out. The efficiency of search T_s seems to fluctuate little over the cycle. The probability of a placement resulting from an interview, referred to as the offer-acceptance probability P_{0a}, tends to remain constant for three reasons:

a. The average duration of vacancies moves cyclically and the average duration of unemployment moves countercyclically. These durations are given by the basic stock-flow relations,

$$T_u = \frac{\mathcal{U}}{\mathcal{F}} \quad \text{and} \quad T_v = \frac{\mathcal{V}}{\mathcal{F}}. \tag{3}$$

Thus the effects on the wage overlap tend to cancel. For example, when unemployment durations are long and workers are willing to accept relatively low wage offers, vacancy durations are short and employers are willing to make only low offers, so there is little net change in the offer-acceptance probability. The opposite canceling effects occur in a tight market.

b. The average probabilites of placing workers and filling vacancies tend to remain constant as the results of aspiration level changes with increasing durations. If workers did not lower aspirations, the workers whose acceptance wages were low relative to their productivities would have relatively high probabilities of placement and would tend to be hired first, leaving only the workers with low probabilities of placement. Thus the observed average probability of placement would fall with increases in unemployment duration. However, the workers with long unemployment durations do adjust their acceptance wages downward, thereby improving their probabilities of placement. Thus the offer-acceptance probability of workers does decline with increasing duration, but not by very much. This has been shown by empirical work by Woytinski.[18] Stated differently, workers who learn from experience that they have a low probability of receiving an offer from interviews lower their aspirations and thereby increase their chances of success.

[16]Charlotte Boschan, *Fluctuations in Job Vacancies—An Analysis of Available Measures* (National Bureau of Economic Research, forthcoming).

[17]J. C. R. Dow and L. A. Dicks-Mireaux, "The Excess Demand for Labor: A Study of Conditions in Great Britain, 1946–56," *Oxford Economic Papers* (February 1958).

[18]W. S. Woytinsky, *Three Aspects of Labor Dynamics* (Social Science Research Council, New York, 1942).

c. Employers make similar adjustments by raising wage offers and lowering job requirements when vacancies prove slow to fill, with the result that the probability of filling vacancies declines only slowly with increasing duration.[19] The most attractive vacancies tend to be filled first and the remaining ones are adjusted to increase their attractiveness.

These points are all closely related, the first stated in macro terms and the latter in micro terms. There is some evidence that frequent exposure to the labor market enables workers to have more accurate expectations of market possibilities and avoid long durations of unemployment by setting realistic aspirations initially. These adaptation mechanisms[20] tend to work in the direction of equalizing placement probabilities across workers.

The implications of these relationships will be carried further, but first we need to recognize that there is not a single labor market but many interrelated ones.

3
SEGMENTATION OF
THE LABOR MARKET

In Section 2 we implicitly assumed that every unemployed worker was a potential candidate for every vacancy. Clearly this is not true. The labor market is segmented into various submarkets: regions, occupations, sexes, races, unions, workers' ages, companies, plants, employment services, entry portals, etc. There is, of course, some interaction between these segments as the results of regional and occupational mobility by individuals, transfer of production assignments, restructuring of jobs, and even by the movement of plants.

Some of the implications of segmentation can be seen most easily by the analysis of rigid compartmentalization of the labor market into a set of noninteracting submarkets. In particular, we want to determine what effect such compartmentalization has on the total numbers of vacancies and unemployed workers and their durations.

A. Compartmentalization   Consider the situation in which the market is split into N noninteracting "compartments." The ith compartment "contains" $\mathfrak{u}_i$ unemployed workers and $\mathfrak{v}_i$ vacancies. Then using (a) we can predict that the flow of new hires from the ith com-

---

[19]See Holt and David, *op. cit.*, p. 98.

[20]Sheppard's work [H. L. Sheppard and A. H. Belitsky, *Job Hunt* (Johns Hopkins University Press, Baltimore, 1966)] on psychological variables and search effort raises the question of whether "failure" in job search may reduce search effort, thereby reducing the chances of placement. Such nonadaptive responses might lead to hard-core problem cases that would require special consideration in programs designed to improve the operation of the labor market.

partment would be

$$\mathfrak{F}_i = \frac{\mathfrak{U}_i \mathfrak{V}_i P_{0a}}{T_s} \qquad (i = 1, 2, \ldots, N). \qquad (4)$$

The aggregates for the whole economy of new hires $\mathfrak{F}$, vacancies $\mathfrak{V}$, and unemployed workers $\mathfrak{U}$ are given by

$$\mathfrak{F} = \sum_{i=1}^{N} \mathfrak{F}_i, \qquad \mathfrak{V} = \sum_{i=1}^{N} \mathfrak{V}_i, \qquad \mathfrak{U} = \sum_{i=1}^{N} \mathfrak{U}_i. \qquad (5)$$

Let lowercase letters stand for the percentage composition of each of these variables:

$$f_i = \frac{\mathfrak{F}_i}{\mathfrak{F}}, \qquad v_i = \frac{\mathfrak{V}_i}{\mathfrak{V}}, \qquad u_i = \frac{\mathfrak{U}_i}{\mathfrak{U}}. \qquad (6)$$

Substitute (6) into (4) and then into (5), to obtain

$$UV = \frac{FT_s}{P_{0a}\mathfrak{L}} \frac{1}{\sum_{i=1}^{N} v_i u_i}, \qquad (7)$$

where we define turnover rate F, vacancy rate V, and unemployment rate U as follows:

$$F = \frac{\mathfrak{F}}{\mathfrak{E}}, \qquad V = \frac{\mathfrak{V}}{\mathfrak{E}}, \qquad U = \frac{\mathfrak{U}}{\mathfrak{L}}, \qquad (8)$$

where $\mathfrak{E}$ is the number of employed workers and $\mathfrak{L}$ is the size of the labor force.

Equation (7) shows dramatically how limiting the scope of search to rigid compartments increases vacancy and unemployment rates.

For example, consider the situation in which otherwise comparable workers and vacancies are located in N identical compartments that are isolated from each other. Then u_i and v_i are $1/N$ for $(i = 1, \ldots, N)$. Substituting in (7) gives

$$UV = \frac{FT_s}{P_{0a}} N. \qquad (9)$$

Thus U and V would each tend to be increased by a factor of $\sqrt{N}$ as the result of compartmentalization compared to a unified market. An economy cut into 100 equal noninteracting compartments would tend to have ten times as many unemployed workers and vacancies. This could easily occur if each of ten isolated geographic regions had ten noncompeting occupations.

The explanation of this strong effect from compartmentalization is that the basic probability relationship in (4) that determines the placement flow incorporates a strong economy of scale. Tripling unemployment and tripling vacancies increases the new hire flow by a factor of nine!

B. Effect of Imbalances   The compartmentalization of the labor market increases vacancies and unemployment through the loss of potential economies of scale but also introduces the possibility of another type of diseconomy. Clearly the possibilities of matching workers and jobs would be reduced if most of the vacancies were in some regions and most of the unemployed workers were isolated in others. We can separate these two effects by determining what distribution of vacancies and workers would minimize aggregate unemployment and vacancies. This minimum would reflect the compartmentalization effect alone, and any additional vacancies and unemployment would be attributable to imbalance.

In the Appendix we show in equation (A5) that the minimum vacancy and unemployment rates are obtained if each region's fraction of the unemployed workers is the same as its fraction of vacancies:

$$u_i = v_i \qquad (i = 1, 2, \ldots, N). \qquad (10)$$

The regions that require the larger flow of new placements, of course, require larger stocks of vacancies and unemployed workers. These stocks rise as the square root of the flows.

The optimal allocations are designated u_1^* and v_1^*. Under this allocation the ratio of vacancies to unemployed workers is the same in all segments, and the ratio between vacancy duration and employment duration in each segment is the same as in all other segments. Thus, for minimum inflation and minimum unemployment all submarkets are equally "tight."

Substituting the results of the optimization analysis (A5) in (7), we show in (11) and (13) the desired decomposition where the various multiplicative terms that affect aggregate vacancies and unemployment are labeled in (12):

$$UV = F \quad T_s \quad \frac{1}{P_{0a}} \quad \frac{1}{\pounds} \quad \left[\frac{1}{\sum_{i=1}^{N} v_i^* u_i^*} \right] \quad \left[\frac{\sum_{i=1}^{N} v_i^* u_i^*}{\sum_{i=1}^{N} v_i u_i} \right] \qquad (11)$$

$$\begin{pmatrix} \text{product of} \\ \text{unemploy-} \\ \text{ment and} \\ \text{vacancy} \\ \text{rates} \end{pmatrix} = \begin{pmatrix} \text{turn-} \\ \text{over} \\ \text{rate} \end{pmatrix} \begin{pmatrix} \text{mean} \\ \text{search} \\ \text{time} \end{pmatrix} \begin{pmatrix} \text{offer-accept-} \\ \text{ance proba-} \\ \text{bility} \end{pmatrix} \begin{pmatrix} \text{economy} \\ \text{of} \\ \text{scale} \end{pmatrix} \begin{pmatrix} \text{compart-} \\ \text{mentali-} \\ \text{zation} \end{pmatrix} \quad \text{(imbalance)}, \qquad (12)$$

$$UV = F \quad T_s \quad \frac{1}{P_{0a}} \quad \frac{1}{\pounds} \quad \left[\left(\sum_{i=1}^{N} \sqrt{f_i} \right)^2 \right] \left[\frac{1}{\left(\sum_{i=1}^{N} \sqrt{f_i} \right)^2 \sum_{i=1}^{N} u_i v_i} \right] . \qquad (13)$$

Here we see that the product of the unemployment and vacancy rates depends on six multiplicative factors: (a) the turnover rate F;

(b) the mean time to match a worker and a vacancy for an interview within a market segment; (c) the probability that an interview will result in a placement P_{0a}; (d) the economy of scale effect reflected in the size of the work force $\mathcal{L}$; (e) the pure compartmentalization effect, which depends on the number of segments and the equality of their sizes in terms of placement flows; and (f) the imbalance effect, which depends on the allocation of vacancies and unemployment among the segments. Notice that the imbalance effect will be sensitive to cyclical fluctuations in the composition of product demand and labor supply.

Rigid compartmentalization is, of course, the extreme form of market segmentation, but it is nevertheless the relevant model for strictly noncompeting occupations and geographically isolated subeconomies. A certain degree of compartmentalization is inevitable and irreducible. However, much segmentation reflects less rigid barriers that can to some extent be crossed. To the extent that there are opportunities without prohibitive costs to migrate *between* submarkets in response to wage differentials or shorter search durations, then the compartmentalization effect declines and aggregate unemployment falls as a result. In the unlikely case of frictionless and instantaneous mobility between *all* submarkets, the compartmentalization and imbalance effects on aggregate unemployment and vacancies disappear.

How far and how fast increases in mobility among occupations, regions, and other segments of workers and employers would affect the aggregate unemployment and vacancy rates requires the development of a more complex analysis.

C. Stocks and Durations   Since vacancies and unemployment fluctuate over the business cycle, it is useful to introduce their ratio R as a cyclical variable.

$$R = \frac{V}{U}. \tag{14}$$

For ease of manipulation write (13) as

$$UV = \frac{FT_m}{P_{0a}}, \tag{15}$$

which defines T_m as a summary "market search time" that probably changes little over the cycle except for imbalances that are attributable to cyclical changes in the composition of demand. Substituting (14) in (15) and solving for unemployment and vacancy rates,

$$U = \sqrt{\frac{FT_m}{P_{0a}}} \frac{1}{\sqrt{R}} \quad \text{and} \quad V = \sqrt{\frac{FT_m}{P_{0a}}} \sqrt{R}. \tag{16}$$

Substituting these expressions in (3) and using (8) we obtain the average durations of unemployment and vacancies:

$$T_u = \sqrt{\frac{T_m}{FP_{0a}}} \frac{1}{\sqrt{R(1-U)}} \tag{17}$$

and

$$T_v = \sqrt{\frac{T_m}{FP_{0a}}} \sqrt{R}. \tag{18}$$

Thus we see that in a segmented market the unemployment and vacancy rates in (16) and unemployment and vacancy durations in (17) are determined by institutional and behavioral parameters concerned with turnover, offer-acceptance probabilities, search efficiency, compartmentalization, and imbalance, all of which tend to change slowly, and by a cyclical variable R that has inverse effects on vacancies and unemployment and their durations.

Since in Section 2 we observed that the increase or decrease of money wages experienced by workers as they flow through the labor market depends on the relation between unemployment and vacancy durations, we can see from (17) and (18) that this component in the rate of change of money wages generally depends on the ratio between job vacancies and unemployed workers R.

That wages tend to drift at a steady rate for each value of this ratio can be seen by considering an example. Suppose that 50 percent of the labor force annually flowed through the market and each time wage increases averaging 10 percent were obtained. If there were no other sources of wage change, money wages would rise at a steady rate of 5 percent per year.

Of course, other relationships are involved in wage changes that occur through job changes without unemployment and through on-the-job wage changes, but for the reasons presented in Section 1 these also would tend to respond to the vacancy-unemployment ratio. The author's analysis elsewhere[21] shows that the responsiveness to market conditions by workers in quitting and by employers in granting on-the-job wage increases influences the sensitivity of wages to the vacancy-unemployment ratio. Insufficient attention has been given to this area and hence the policy analysis later will be correspondingly limited.

Thus the rate of change of money wages, g, can be shown as a function principally of the cyclical variable R; high values of the vacancy-unemployment ratio being associated with high inflation rates,

$$g = g(R). \tag{19}$$

[21]Holt, "Improving the Labor Market Tradeoff between Inflation and Unemployment."

In view of the complex relationships involved, it would be a mistake to associate an R value of unity with the zero rate of inflation as some economists have tended to do.

Because the expression on the right of the equality in (15) tends to change slowly, we see that cyclical fluctuations in unemployment are highly correlated with those of the vacancy rate, so U can serve as a fairly good proxy for R and we can obtain a fairly stable Phillips relation that suppresses the role of vacancies. Equations (14) and (15) can be combined to eliminate V and then substituted in (19) to obtain a Phillips relation:

$$g = g\left(\frac{FT_m}{P_{0a}}\frac{1}{U^2}\right).\tag{20}$$

Since imbalances between labor market sectors may be influenced by cyclical fluctuations, the above analysis also supports the inclusion of a dynamic imbalance term in the Phillips relation as Lipsey and Archibald have urged.

4
EXISTENCE OF A
STABLE PHILLIPS
RELATION UNDER
STEADY INFLATION

Before we undertake an analysis of how the Phillips relation might be changed, we consider the argument presented by Friedman,[22] Phelps,[23] and others that *no* stable relationship exists between different rates of *steady* inflation and the level of unemployment. They concede that a dynamic relation exists, and undoubtedly would agree with Stein[24] that it is an important concern of dynamic stabilization policy.

However, their argument leads to the conclusion, which also is very important for policy purposes, that in equilibrium the level of unemployment cannot reduce unemployment *even* by paying the cost of steady inflation.

The neoclassical argument basically is that steady inflation would be predictable and people would compensate for it so that no real effects would occur. While we concede that people will *attempt* to com-

[22]M. Friedman, "Comments," in *Guidelines, Information Controls, and the Market Place*, G. P. Shultz and R. Z. Aliber, eds. (University of Chicago Press, Chicago, 1966).

[23]E. S. Phelps, "Money-Wage Dynamics and Labor-Market Equilibrium," *Journal of Political Economy* (July–August 1968), Part II.

[24]Herbert Stein, "Economic Stabilization," in *Agenda for the Nation*, Kermit Gordon, ed. (The Brookings Institution, Washington, D.C., 1968).

pensate for inflation, their decisions are made within the constraints of available information and institutions, and they may not succeed in doing so.

This neoclassical argument is presented in some detail elsewhere,[25] and a simple model of the labor market is developed which incorporates frictions at the micro level which can yield a stable Phillips curve. There it is argued that workers are partially tied to their jobs by nontransferrable skills, costs of search, etc. Employers can and, to some extent, do take advantage of this by using their bargaining power relative to the individual worker to resist responding to inflationary changes in the general wage and price level. Thus the wages of some workers will fall somewhat behind the highest wages being paid before they finally seek to catch up by searching for new jobs. It seems reasonable that the wages in the new jobs usually do not fully catch up with the inflation that accrued during the whole of their past employment because either the workers do not think it feasible or they are not able accurately to distinguish between inflation and productivity based wage changes. The lack of *complete* compensation for inflation tends to produce a stable Phillips curve rather than a floating one.

Thus the existence of a stable Phillips curve is seen to rest on the existence of frictions that cannot be ruled out simply by a priori arguments. The stability of the Phillips curve is an empirical matter, not one that can be settled by deductive arguments from premises that "obviously are true."

5
POLICIES FOR MOVING
THE PHILLIPS CURVE

On the basis of the foregoing analysis we can now identify those key parameters in the labor market that can be modified by suitable actions to lower unemployment and decrease the rate of inflation. It is convenient to consider these separately.

A. Desirable Changes in the Operation of Labor Markets
Certain changes are sufficiently symmetrical in their impacts on both the supply and the demand sides of the market that it is reasonable to assume that the wage inflation rate will not be affected.

If the offer-acceptance probability P_{0a} is increased and the market search time T_m and the turnover rate F are decreased, then the unemployment rate U and the vacancy rate V both will be decreased. These

[25]Holt, "Improving the Labor Market Tradeoff between Inflation and Unemployment."

changes would also decrease the durations of unemployment and vacancies T_u and T_v; see (16) and (17).

Decreasing the market search time would clearly reduce both durations. Increasing the offer-acceptance probability would decrease the durations, but the duration reductions would tend to lower the offer-acceptance probability, thereby tending partially to cancel out the original change.

Reducing labor turnover F surprisingly raises the durations [see (17)], but again there is a feedback effect on the offer-acceptance probability P_{0a} that tends to offset the change.

There are other interactions between changes. The increase in offer-acceptance probabilities and the decrease in market search time reduce the durations of unemployment and vacancies, which in turn would tend to increase the turnover rate, which is opposite to what is desired. However, the reduction in turnover rate increases durations, which contribute to the further reduction of the turnover rate.

The reductions of these stocks depend primarily on stock-flow dynamics. The stocks are decreased by reducing the flows into the market and increasing the probability per period of time of workers and vacancies being matched and leaving the market.

As the foregoing theory development indicates, the market search time T_m can be decreased by decreasing mean time required to search out promising interviews T_s, increasing the size of the work force to obtain economies of scale in random search, decreasing the compartmentalization of the market (number of segments and equality of their size), and decreasing the imbalances of vacancies and unemployment among submarkets.

The offer-acceptance probability P_{0a} can be raised by increasing the average wage overlap at time of interview. This would require decreasing the gap in initial wage aspirations and speeding their rates of adjustment.

We will consider specifically how these various parameter changes might be achieved, but first we examine measures that reduce inflation but do not affect unemployment.

Workers who quit are likely to have relatively high wage aspirations, because they search from the security of jobs and do not experience periods of unemployment, which tends to lower aspirations. Workers who are laid off, in contrast, are likely to have relatively low aspirations, comparable to their last job. As a consequence, decreasing the proportion of the turnover flow accounted for by quits and increasing the proportion accounted for by layoffs will lower the inflation rate.

Lowering the initial wage acceptance and offer levels of unemployed workers and vacancies entering the market lowers the inflation rate.

Increasing the rate at which workers lower their acceptance wages and decreasing the rate at which employers raise theirs will reduce the inflation rate.[26]

Lowering exaggerated expectations of the inflation rate held by workers and employers will tend to reduce the inflation rate.

Increasing productivity reduces the work force, increases unemployment, and reduces the rate of inflation. Alternatively larger output could be sold at lower prices, thereby reducing the rate of price inflation.

The above measures to reduce unemployment and inflation can be used in concert with one exception. The indicated change in employers' initial wage offer and their speeds of adjustment were in direct opposition. Hence quantitative information is needed to determine the net effect of employers' offer levels on unemployment and inflation.

The more responsive employers are to increases in the quit rate and vacancy duration in granting on-the-job wage increases, the higher the inflation rate will tend to be.

We now turn to specific measures that might be instituted by government or others for attaining the desired changes and thereby reducing both unemployment and vacancies and reducing the rate of increase of money wages.

B. Improving Economic Stability   Because of the nonlinearity of the Phillips curve, inflation is worsened for any given average level of unemployment by cyclical fluctuations that tend to increase the dispersion of regional unemployment rates. Hence there is an immediate incentive to pursue active policies and institutional changes that will promote stable growth in aggregate demand.

C. Increasing Search Efficiency   The time T_s for matching workers and vacancies for interviews would be decreased by better communications between workers and employers, i.e., by the transmission of more information that is relevant to the needs of each particular worker or employer. Only a very small fraction of the huge combinatoric number of potential matches and the attendant information would be of interest to *both* parties. To be genuinely useful, the infor-

---

[26]An example of such lowering of both worker and employer wage aspirations is the case in which both sides do not accurately adjust to an increase in the general wage level and the expectations are lower than the actual rate of change in wage level. This can readily occur from a lag in expectations and would tend to keep the inflation rate lower than it otherwise would be when there is an unanticipated increase in demand. Thus unforeseen cyclical changes in rates of inflation will tend to produce dynamic clockwise loops around the Phillips curve. These have been observed, but more often the loop movements are clockwise. This occurs because employers find it necessary to raise their offers in order to increase their hiring rates. Employers pay the worker's existing high wage aspirations because they desire to increase their current hiring in order to increase production rather than waiting for worker aspirations to decline.

mation needs to be classified, screened, selectively disseminated, and wisely used in seeking out prospective matches that are sufficiently promising mutually to justify the costs of interviews to explore in depth the prospects of placing particular workers in particular jobs. Receiving all the information on *all* the jobs or *all* the vacancies would probably be much worse than asking one's neighbors or one's employees for relevant leads.

This process involves not only information on qualifications and desires, job requirements, and inducements, but also its analysis in making decisions on the most promising directions of search and ultimately on offers and acceptances. The importance of such information and counseling services spotlights the critical role of organized employment services and their needs for powerful computerized processing.

D. Economies of Scale Although there are economies of scale in a labor market, this would hardly seem to justify any active policies to promote population growth or labor market participation. However, the consolidation of the small town populations of a region into a smaller number of urban centers should contribute to labor-market efficiencies. The same effect might be achieved more economically by extending the area of job search through better communications and increasing geographic mobility.

It is important to note that even if vacancies and workers were optimally allocated to the various submarkets so that the imbalance term contributed nothing to unemployment, the various compartments would not be equally attractive. The probabilities of matches would be larger, and durations of vacancies and unemployment would be shorter in the larger submarkets [see (A7) in the Appendix].

If the compartmentalization were geographic, there would tend to be some incentives for employers and workers to move to the larger markets with the greatest economies of scale.[27] The big city offers the potentiality of many job offers for the worker, the small town only a few. Similarly, in the larger city the employer has the pick of many workers.

However, the efficiency of the labor market is only one dimension of social welfare, so it is clear that to design population and mobility policies we need to obtain a better understanding of mobility processes and the effects of city size.

E. Decreasing the Segmentation of the Labor Market Reducing the segmentation of the labor market will increase the probability of placements. Barriers where they are irrelevant to production and job satisfaction should be questioned. Depending on circumstances, these

[27]The same mechanism may give large firms recruiting advantages over small ones.

might include race, sex, and age; excessively specialized and nonadaptive job requirements and union jurisdictions; excessive worker attachment to plant, company, occupation, region, etc.; and organization of the public employment service on a state or local basis. In short, any compartmentalization should be eliminated that is not justified on the basis of productivity, satisfaction, or transition costs (where costs are broadly interpreted).

F. Reducing Imbalances between Market Segments   To the extent that there are legitimate immobilities tending to isolate market segments, government or private actions to counter fluctuations in the regional and occupational composition of demand will help to prevent the occurrence of imbalances.

The cost and time limitations on commuting, the costs of specialized occupational training, and the costs of restructuring jobs to fit the labor supply all impose unavoidable segmentation. Although it usually is not economic for workers or jobs to jump back and forth across such segments of the market in quest of individual placements, it should be possible through job restructuring, interoccupational training, and regional labor and industry mobility programs substantially to reduce long-run imbalances among regions, occupations, etc.

In considering programs for increasing mobility, external effects are likely to be important, so the social costs of mobility may be either higher or lower than private costs. These require careful analysis in designing such programs.

By restructuring jobs, the fit between the profile of available worker skills and job requirements can be improved by employers. This can contribute to the reduction of market imbalances, particularly between skill groupings.

Such programs are essential if equality of opportunity is to have significant meaning to many American workers who are trapped in segments of the market that chronically have high unemployment and low vacancies.

In attaining the adjustment of the labor-force occupational distribution to production requirements, two kinds of situations can occur. When there are relatively more vacancies than workers at higher than at lower skill levels, training programs are needed to upgrade the work force. However, when the relative shortage of workers is at the low skill levels, the existing work force can perform the lower skill jobs without significant training, but some workers must accept the necessity of adjusting their job and income aspirations downward. The latter aspiration adjustment is likely to take less time than the training adjustment. As a consequence, relative shortages are much more likely to occur in the high-skill occupations and relative unemployment in the low-skill ones. The data seem to support this prediction.

As a consequence, when aggregate demand is cyclically low, the unemployment impact will tend to be concentrated in the low-skill occupations. Also, because advancing technology tends to open up high-skill vacancies and destroy low-skill jobs, there is a constant pressure toward unemployment among the low skilled unless training programs operate continually at all skill levels to keep work-force skills in balance with production requirements.

G. Increasing the Probability That Interviews Will Result in Placements   The offer-acceptance probability will depend on the wage overlap, i.e., the amount by which the employer's maximum wage exceeds the worker's minimum wage. Hence any reduction of the initial gaps or the hastening of their declines will help to reduce unemployment and vacancies. The gap would be reduced if workers would lower their acceptance levels for wages and job satisfactions. Employers can reduce the gap by raising wage and other inducements or by lowering their quality expectations that relate to output. The latter is less obvious to its existing work force and usually is preferred.

The following actions, aimed at inducing workers to lower their acceptance wage and firms to raise their wage to output ratios, could be taken: exhortation for the "good of the country," improved information on the distribution of opportunities available in the market, and counseling aid in using the information in making individual decisions on interviews, asking wage, offering wage, etc.

Exhortation directed at individual workers and employers, which has some conspicuous parallels to an income or guidelines policy, is unlikely to be effective if the action urged is seen as being contrary to their private interests.

In addition, the estimate of the probability distribution of market opportunities for the particular parties involved would be made less broad and diffuse by the availability of better information. The worker optimally should set his aspiration wage high enough to prevent his accepting prematurely a relatively poor opportunity before he has searched enough to get the feel of his likely options. Any reduction in his uncertainty through better information should enable him safely to set a lower initial acceptance wage.

By the same reasoning, the employer could safely offer a higher wage to output ratio, if he had better knowledge. Search of random opportunities still is required for individual jobs and vacancies, but the cutoff levels (stop rules) will be more wisely set, and the initial wage gap will be smaller. This will have the desired effect of increasing the probability of placements.

Better information and counseling may enable the worker to learn more quickly and help him to make the psychological adjustments involved in accepting lower wage aspirations that are necessitated by the economic opportunities that are available. By the same reasoning, information and consultation may help the employer learn and adjust faster to prevailing market conditions. In this case, the existing wage gaps will close more quickly, leading to a wage overlap, and the probability of placements will rise.

H. Lowering Layoff Rates   Employee assignments and reassignments within firms can be used by employers to facilitate the promotion and development of their own employees without necessitating their use of external labor markets with its attendant costly unemployment during job search. Although excessive avoidance of the external market would contribute to undesirable segmentation, the firm and the employee inherently have a great deal of information about each other that can contribute to efficiently finding good job-worker matches in the firm's internal labor market. This can reduce both the layoff rate and the quit rate for the firm and for the economy.

Business firms can smooth their work force fluctuations by (a) forecasting their sales more accurately to avoid having to make short-term responses to unanticipated sales fluctuations, (b) using inventory and back-order buffers to smooth production fluctuations, and (c) using overtime and idle time to accommodate production fluctuations rather than alternately hiring and laying off workers. A systematic strategy for making these decisions dynamically often decreases company costs.[28] The cost of training often escapes management's attention because of its "invisible" character, which frequently escapes routine accounting reports even though these costs may be quite large.[29] Because of the predictable nature of seasonal fluctuations of sales, the resulting employment fluctuations often can be reduced by better planning.

It is well known that layoff rates are higher for lower skill levels, presumably because firms have smaller training investments in these workers.[30] Public programs that induced firms to increase their investments in training should give firms stronger incentives to hold their work forces by reducing their layoffs.

[28]See, for example, C. C. Holt, F. Modigliani, J. F. Muth, and M. A. Simon, *Planning Production, Inventories and Work Force*, (Prentice-Hall, Inc., Englewood Cliffs, N.J., 1960).

[29]J. G. Myers, "Some Aspects of the Role of Job Vacancies in the Firm and the Labor Market," prepared for the Office of Manpower Policy, Evaluation, and Research (National Industrial Conference Board, 1968); J. G. Myers, "Conceptual and Measurement Problems in Job Vacancies, A Progress Report on the NICB Study," in *Measurement and Interpretation of Job Vacancies*, R. Ferber, ed., National Bureau of Economic Research (Columbia University Press, New York, 1966), pp. 405–456; and T. F. Kelly and B. P. Klotz, "A Dynamic Inventory Model of Employment" (A Progress Report), U.S. Department of Labor, Bureau of Labor Statistics (U.S. Government Printing Office, Washington, 195?).

[30]W. Y. Oi, "Labor as a Quasi-fixed Factor of Production," *Journal of Political Economy* (December 1962), pp. 538–555.

I. Lowering Quit Rates Working conditions and work organization often can be improved to make work more satisfying, and thereby decrease the frequency of quits motivated by the desire for change. Job changes internal to the firm can be used to satisfy the same need. Nonvesting pensions, seniority, etc., also reduce quits but add undesirable frictions to the labor-adjustment process.

Voluntary quits are most common among young workers. Suitable training programs might decrease their quits by developing suitable career plans and healthy attitudes toward job responsibilities and opportunities. However, it is clear that for many young workers a series of short-term jobs constitutes an extended placement process. Lacking really adequate information about career opportunities in general, or about the particular job being offered, the worker accepts it together with the company's training only to discover later that the job does not fit. Our educational system often teaches almost nothing about the world of work to help prepare young people for their important career choices ahead.

Our labor markets are often quite asymmetric in the information conveyed in the placement process. The employer characteristically collects considerable information on the worker in writing while usually the worker must be content with verbal descriptions of the job being offered that omit most of the information that is really important to him. This hardly is conducive to achieving a *mutually* satisfying job-worker match. In this situation the worker has little choice but to lightly accept the job and lightly drop it if it does not work out.

J. The Tendency toward Increased Labor Turnover The basic change needed to reduce labor turnover initiated by both employers and workers is to make better matches between jobs and workers so that a strong mutually rewarding relationship is built that will not be casually dissolved. This will become of increasing importance, if we succeed in reducing the durations of unemployment and vacancies. In a labor market with ready information on prospective jobs and new employees, the participants in existing employment relations will continually be tempted by "greener grass" elsewhere.

If the above programs were successful in increasing the probability of placements per period of time, the levels of unemployment and vacancies would decrease, and the durations of vacancies and unemployment also would decline. We can predict as an immediate consequence that an increase in the turnover rate would likely occur. The ease of finding a job from full-time search or from on-the-job search would be reflected in a shorter average duration of unemployment. This would reduce the cost of search, and we could expect that people would search more often, i.e., their employment durations between quits would decrease. The greater ease of finding new workers would be reflected in the reduced duration of vacancies, and layoff rates would tend to increase, again reducing employment durations. Not only might this increase training costs with little economic return, but the increased flow into the labor market would tend to raise the stocks of vacancies and unemployed workers and offset at least partially the reduction that was sought in unemployment and vacancies. Negative feedback makes the level of unemployment resistant to change.

The above actions will tend primarily to reduce unemployment and vacancies. We now consider actions aimed at reducing inflation.

K. Reducing the Quit-to-Layoff Ratio Little needs to be added to the foregoing discussion of methods for reducing labor turnover except to observe that voluntary quits appear to be relatively more serious than layoffs in their effects on wages. The earlier analysis[31] shows that the flow of quits through the market without intervening unemployment constitutes an important inflation mechanism directly by contributing to wage increases and indirectly through inducing employers to raise the wages of all their employees in an effort to cut their turnover rates. In the tight labor market that we hope to achieve, the quit problem could become critical.

L. Reduction of Wage Offer and Acceptance Levels Reducing workers' initial acceptance wages and speeding their decline is one objective of the information and counseling program discussed above. But now we seek ways to induce employers to *lower* their offers, which is precisely the opposite to what was needed to close the wage gap. More study is needed to determine the *net* benefit from changes in wage offers by employers.

However, information and consultation for employers could be supported for its contribution to the efficient allocation of resources. Also, greater homogeneity of vacancy duration decreases the risk of long staffing delays and hence makes employers less likely to resort to very high wage offers under panic stress.

M. Lowering Inflation Expectations Workers and employers may have a tendency to exaggerate the extent to which past and prospective wage changes are attributable to pure wage inflation. Better information and counseling may prevent such unwarranted expectations.

N. Increasing Technological Efficiency Substantial increases in labor productivity are possible on a cyclical basis as the result of slack labor.[32] However, for the long run, technological gains are slow but in the right direction in reducing real demand in the labor market and reducing pressure on prices.

[31]Holt, "Job Search, Phillips' Wage Relation and Union Influence: Theory and Evidence."
[32]Kelly and Klotz, *op. cit.*

O. Computer-Aided Counseling and Placement The proposal
to harness a computerized file of jobs and vacancies could play a very
important part in decreasing mean search time, increasing the offer-
acceptance probability, and lowering the quit and layoff rates through
higher quality placements. However, for maximum effect in aiding
counseling on training, mobility, or placement, the computer should
have enough information filed on vacancies, workers, and programs
that the machine could take over for workers and employers much
of the burden of screening the possibilities and recommending for intensive consideration by the counselor, worker, and employer *only* the
subset of information that is selected to be of greatest usefulness.[33]

However, *a warning is in order*. A computerized file of jobs and
workers could increase labor turnover and possibly even speed the inflation process, if the computer system does not also contribute significantly to improving the joint quality of job-worker matches in
terms of satisfaction and productivity. To do this most effectively, the
computer system would need to become an integral working tool for
a placement and counseling service that was keyed into a wide variety
of educational, training, counseling, mobility, and health programs in
order to serve with maximum effectiveness the individual needs of
almost all workers and employers.

P. Collective Bargaining Guidelines The government has used
"guidelines" to help regulate collective bargaining settlements where
employers and unions have significant monopoly power. However,
the theory that is presented here interprets the inflation process as
primarily the product of myriad individual decisions that occur in the
search for jobs and employees. Such a process is not likely to be significantly influenced by exhortation. Immediate interests and involve-
ments will tend to dominate concerns for the remote national welfare.
If the government cannot control these atomistic inflation processes,
it seems hardly fair, or likely to be effective, to impose controls on
collective bargains that are in a direct competitive relation with free
market wages.

This is not to say that the government cannot have some influence
on the size or timing of particular contract settlements, but rather that
it is not likely to have much long run influence on the general rate of

[33]For research on computer matching systems, see Holt and Huber, *op. cit.*; G. P. Huber
and C. H. Falker, "Computer-Based Man-Job Matching: Current Practice and Applicable Research" (Firm and Market Workshop Paper 6816, Social Systems Research
Institute, University of Wisconsin, Madison, Wis., 1968; and F. Kellogg, "Computer
Aids to the Placement Process for Internal and External Labor Markets" Proceedings
of the 20th Annual Winter meeting, Industrial Relations Research Association, Development and Use of Manpower, December 28–29, 1967; and for recommendations for the
installation of such a system, see Nixon-Agnew Campaign Committee, *Nixon on the
Issues* (New York, October 17, 1968); National Commission on Technology, Automa-
tion, and Economic Progress, *Technology and the American Economy*, 1 (February 1966);
Report to the Secretary of Labor from the Employment Service, Department of Labor,
December 23, 1965.

inflation. This area is complex and requires much more work. We need to develop methods for determining the origin of the overclaims on the real national income that constitute the driving force of the wage price spiral, *if one exists*. Should price dynamics be found to play an important role in determining the Phillips relation, a much more complex analysis will be needed.

However, in the operation of the labor market itself there may be a tendency for firms to try to outbid each other by responding vigorously to quits with on-the-job wage increases. The attempt by firms to use changes in relative wages to hold their work forces can be self-defeating for all firms collectively because the relative wage effects on quits cancel out, leaving only an increase in the money wage level. Guidelines that inhibited wage increases for all employers except those with *relatively* high quit rates might be useful in slowing the bidding process.

Q. Monopoly Power   To the extent that we are concerned about union wage differentials on equity and efficiency grounds, union jurisdictional segmentation, or overclaims on the real output by corporations and unions that would tend to cause an *autonomous* wage-price spiral, then the following policies merit consideration: (a) provision of increased job security for union and nonunion workers alike by instituting the above manpower policies in conjunction with the reduction of unemployment through a tight full employment aggregate income policy, (b) where workers elect to bargain collectively they would be represented by a union with full dues checkoff that represents *all* the firm's employees (a provision that would decrease the bargaining that reinforces occupational segmentation and decrease monopoly power in product markets[34] based on industry-wide unions), (c) enforcement of antitrust policy to decrease industry concentration and oligopoly power, and (d) reduction of tariff protection in high profit–high wage industries. The difficulty of these institutional changes should not be underestimated, but they may be more feasible in the context of an integrated manpower and full employment program.

6
CONCLUSION

Although the neoclassical argument, that no unique Phillips relation exists under constant inflation rates, has great intuitive appeal, such a stable relation can occur as the consequence of "frictions" in the job search process. Clearly the existence or nonexistence of such a relation cannot be settled by simple a priori arguments, but the conclusion on

[34]C. M. Shanks, "Should We Accept Inflation?" *Annals of the American Academy of Political and Social Science*, Philadelphia, 326 (November 1959), pp. 47–54.

this issue must rest on knowledge about the economy in question. The empirical and theoretical knowledge currently available strongly supports the view that the Phillips relation is an important characteristic of labor markets in many economies, our own included.

The operation of the labor market can be described in terms of stocks of unemployed workers and job vacancies, and a search process for mutually satisfactory matches that is best analyzed in probability terms. The various flows to and from these stocks involve many fast and powerful negative feedback effects that make disturbances die out so quickly that the market tends always to be near equilibrium. Changes in the wage level are generated by countless individual offer and acceptance decisions as workers and vacancies flow through the market, as employers grant on-the-job wage increases to inhibit this flow, and as unions push for wage increases to hold their relative positions.

The levels of unemployment and vacancies are found to depend on the turnover rates and the probability per period of time of achieving placements. This probability in turn depends on how fast the employment opportunities in the market can be searched out, how much the market is cut up unnecessarily into somewhat isolated occupations, regions, races, union jurisdictions, etc., and the extent to which an unbalanced distribution of vacancies and workers among the various segments persists. The sizes of wage changes depend on the aspirations of workers and employers and the rate at which these aspirations change with the duration of market search.

Moving the Phillips curve could be accomplished through a variety of actions taken by government, industry, unions, and individual workers, most of which would clearly be in their respective self-interests. Many of these actions are similar to familiar manpower programs designed to reduce market "frictions" and turnover and to develop the work force, but their designs differ somewhat because of their orientation toward the macroeconomic problems.

Broadly speaking, these action recommendations would (a) help workers and employers find the mutually best jobs and employees from the widest range of opportunities in a short time and with minimum upward pressure on money wages, (b) minimize the disruption of employment relationships by fluctuations in production and employment, and (c) through continuing cooperative efforts by workers and employers maintain mutually satisfying employment relationships so that quits and terminations are reduced but without resort to devices that entrap workers or employers.

Actions to accomplish these objectives complement strongly, but can be distinguished from, efforts to upgrade the productive capacities of each individual to his full potential through human resource investments that stimulate economic growth and improve the distribution of income.

A. Extended Manpower Program Proposed   The tremendously important contributions of both types of programs make urgent the consideration of a broad new manpower program that reaches the whole work force and all employers while continuing the present stress on workers with low incomes and special problems.

It has long been clear that training programs, etc., could accomplish little in reducing unemployment without stimulating the creation of new jobs with the aggregate demand policies of the New Economics. Now the inflation–unemployment dilemma threatens seriously to limit the effectiveness of the New Economics unless it is complemented by an ambitious new manpower program.

The complementarity of the two kinds of programs has long been urged by many in and out of government, but the stress usually has been on manpower programs[35] individually directed at specific poverty problems. The analysis of this paper supports the contention that attaining prosperity without inflation for the *whole* economy depends critically upon our improving the speed and efficiency with which we match the needs of individual workers and employers with suitable information, counseling, training, retraining, mobility,[36] placement, and institutional programs on a broad front. The possibilities for business and individuals to cooperate voluntarily with government in many of these programs will have great appeal to many.

The expansion of manpower programs in the United States in recent years could supply the operating experience on which some of the expanded programs could be based.[37]

Because it is critically important to obtain a fast, high-quality matching of individual workers and employers with each other and with the various manpower programs, a vastly expanded, improved, and computerized national employment service system would be essential in coupling the wide variety of individual and employer needs to the programs available.

The economic and social returns from such a coordinated effort are likely far to outweigh its costs! Inflation could be reduced and the growth in output would be sizable from several sources: reduction in unemployment, increased labor market participation, and upgrading the whole work force to achieve its full productive potential. In addi-

---

[35]A healthy start has been made with a wide variety of manpower programs, but they still reach a rather small fraction of the American work force. Space here does not permit consideration of these programs or even a listing of the relevant reports and hearings carried out by the Joint Economic Committee; the Council of Economic Advisors; the Department of Labor; the Department of Health, Education, and Welfare; the Department of Commerce; the Office of Economic Opportunity; the National Manpower Policy Task Force; etc.

[36]The need for a regional as well as a national population policy might become urgent with the easing of economic barriers to movement and the generation of adequate vacancies.

[37]G. L. Mangum, *MDTA, Foundation of Federal Manpower Policy* (Johns Hopkins University Press, Baltimore, 1968).

tion, a really tight labor market is likely to stimulate labor-saving technological innovation and reduce resistance to its introduction.

With such a coordinated aggregate demand and manpower policy, the labor market would become a much more pleasant and efficient device for coupling people to the economic needs of the country and would offer much greater security against unemployment and less risk of inflation. The Phillips curves and growth rates of other countries lead to optimism about the size of the potential improvement. The continued acceptance by the United States of a 4 percent unemployment target, which is more than double the rate of many other countries, can no longer be justified. The rationale for government intervention in the manpower area is considered further elsewhere.[38]

However, a serious limitation must be emphasized. Our knowledge in the relevant area is seriously deficient[39] as the result of inadequate manpower research in the past. Although considerable applied research has been done, and we can build on that base, much more is needed, and basic and theoretical research have been rare. For example, almost no basic research has yet been done on the critically important area of computer matching. It is important that we know what we are doing in all these areas; results do not come simply from trying. It is possible for computers to so increase the turnover rate that there will be little decrease in unemployment! Much more work will need to be done before we can determine which of the actions proposed above would be the more effective. Extensive coordinated inhouse research, grants, and contracts, both basic and applied, should certainly be undertaken by the government agencies that administer such programs. Also the possibilities are promising in this area for carefully planned systematic experimentation.

After we have successfully married a broad manpower policy with the Phillips relation, we can decide how much of the benefits we will take in real output and how much in reduction of inflation—but first we should hasten to research the still-tentative propositions on which these happy prospects are based.

APPENDIX:
OPTIMAL DISTRIBUTION OF VACANCIES AND UNEMPLOYMENT IN A SEGMENTED LABOR MARKET

We desire to determine the u_i and v_i that minimize the product of U and V given that a certain flow of the placements is needed in each of the regions. (The same answer is obtained if U is minimized given V and conversely.

[38]Holt, "Improving the Labor Market Tradeoff between Inflation and Unemployment," Section VI.

[39]For example, is Negro teenage unemployment high because of a low probability of being hired, high quit rate, high layoff rate, or all three? The action implications might be vastly different, depending on the answer.

Using (7) for the criterion and taking the constraints on u_i and v_i from (4), (5), (6), and (8), the Lagrangian expression is obtained,

$$C = \frac{FT_s}{P_{0a}\mathcal{L}}\left(\frac{1}{\sum\limits_{i=1}^{N} u_i v_i}\right) + \tau_1\left(1 - \sum_{i=1}^{N} u_i\right) + \tau_2\left(1 - \sum_{i=1}^{N} v_i\right)$$

$$+ \sum_{i=1}^{N} \tau^i\left(Ff_i - \frac{P_{0a}\mathcal{L}}{T_s} UVv_i u_i\right), \qquad \text{(A1)}$$

which is to be minimized with respect to u_i and v_i ($i = 1, 2, \ldots, N$) where τ_1, τ_2, and τ^i ($i = 1, 2, \ldots, N$) are Lagrange multipliers.

It is clear from symmetry that the optimal distribution is obtained when

$$u_i = v_i \qquad (i = 1, 2, \ldots, N). \qquad \text{(A2)}$$

Solving the last constraint for u_i and substituting (A2) gives

$$u_i = \sqrt{\frac{FT_s}{P_{0a}\mathcal{L}VU}}\sqrt{f_i} \qquad (i = 1, 2, \ldots, N). \qquad \text{(A3)}$$

Then, substituting (A3) in the first constraint,

$$1 = \sum_{i=1}^{N} u_i = \sqrt{\frac{FT_s}{P_{0a}\mathcal{L}VU}}\sum_{i=1}^{N} \sqrt{f_i}. \qquad \text{(A4)}$$

Combining (A3) and (A4) with (A2) yields the optimal distribution of unemployment and vacancies:

$$u_i^* = \frac{\sqrt{f_i}}{\sum\limits_{i=1}^{N} \sqrt{f_i}} = v_i^* \qquad (i = 1, 2, \ldots, N), \qquad \text{(A5)}$$

where u_i^* and v_i^* constitute the optimum distribution.

It is interesting to note that under optimal allocation the average duration of vacancies is not the same in all submarkets, nor are the probabilities per period of time that vacancies will be filled:

$$T_{vi} = \frac{V_i}{F_i} = \frac{Vv_i}{Ff_i}. \qquad \text{(A6)}$$

Substituting (A5),

$$T_{vi} = \frac{V}{F}\frac{1}{\sqrt{f_i}}\frac{1}{\sum\limits_{i} \sqrt{f_i}}. \qquad \text{(A7)}$$

The same kinds of differences between submarkets apply to duration of unemployment and the probabilities of being hired. In general, the larger submarkets are more attractive to both employers and workers because of the economies of scale.

Real Wages, Employment, and Inflation

ROBERT E. LUCAS, JR., and
LEONARD A. RAPPING*

The aggregate labor-supply function is a cornerstone of both neo-classical growth theory and short-run Keynesian-type employment theory. Yet no empirical estimates of the parameters of this function, comparable to estimated aggregate consumption, investment, or money demand functions, are available.[1] Despite this lack of evidence, econ-

*We wish to thank Professors T. McGuire, A. Meltzer, W. Oi, E. S. Phelps, and A. Rees, who commented on an earlier draft of this study. Their willingness to comment on our work should not be interpreted as an endorsement of our views. Indeed, at least one of the readers substantially disagreed with us, but because his disagreement aided us in clarifying our thinking, we felt obliged to acknowledge his assistance. With the exception of the material in Appendix 2, this chapter is reprinted from the *Journal of Political Economy*, v.77, no. 5 (September/October, 1969), with the permission of the University of Chicago Press.

[1]Leaving aside studies of the relative supply of labor to individual industries or firms, most of the empirical work on the supply of labor can be separated into three categories. Studies of hours of work per unit of time per member of the labor force have found a negative relationship between wage rates and hours supplied, especially for male members of the labor force. This result is reported by Finegan [T. A. Finegan, "Hours of Work in the United States," *Journal of Political Economy*, 70 (October 1962), pp. 452–470], Kosters [M. Kosters, *Income and Substitution Effects in a Family Labor Supply Model* (Rand Corp., Santa Monica, Calif., 1966), RAND P-3339], Lewis [H. G. Lewis, *Hours of Work and Hours of Leisure* (Industrial Relations Research Association, 1956), pp. 196–207], and Rosen [S. Rosen, "The Interindustry Wage and Hours Structure," *Journal of Political Economy*, 77, No. 2 (March/April 1969) pp. 249–273]. A second group of studies have examined the relationship between participation rates and wage rates. These have largely been cross-sectional studies and they have reported a positive wage-rate effect for women and a small negative effect for men. The reader will find these results in studies by Bowen and Finegan [W. G. Bowen and T. A. Finegan, "Labor Force

omists have found it necessary to proceed on the basis of certain widely accepted assumptions. In the growth literature, it is generally assumed that population growth is exogenous and that the supply of labor from any fixed population is an inelastic function of the real wage rate. In the short-run literature, on the other hand, it is commonly assumed that the labor supply is infinitely elastic at some rigid real or money wage rate. Our purpose in this paper is to construct a model of the labor market that reconciles these apparently divergent views of labor supply and to test the model on annual aggregate, U.S. time series covering the period 1929–65.

Wherever possible, we will motivate our assumptions by reference to the microeconomic labor-market literature. Yet, as with any aggregate study of a single sector of the economy, it will be necessary to gloss over much of the richness of detail provided by the many studies of particular features of labor-market behavior. We will not compensate for this loss by offering a full econometric model of the economy, but in Section I we sketch the structure of our labor-market model and its relation to the other sectors of the economy. There remains, nevertheless, an inevitable arbitrariness in our selection of two functions—the labor-supply function and a marginal productivity condition for labor—to be estimated as a simultaneous-equation system.

In addition to our primary aim of understanding the workings of the U.S. labor market, this study has as a secondary purpose the rationalization in supply and demand terms of the observed correlation between unemployment rates and the rate of inflation, or Phillips curve. Recent attempts to give a theoretical basis to the Phillips curve have been based largely on a view of the labor market as dominated by collective bargaining, where bargaining outcomes bear no explicit relation

Participation and Unemployment," in *Employment Policy and the Labor Market*, A. M. Ross, ed. (University of California Press, Berkeley, 1965)], Cain [G. Cain, *Married Women in the Labor Force: An Economic Analysis* (University of Chicago Press, Chicago, 1966)], Douglas [P. H. Douglas, *The Theory of Wages* (New York, 1934)], and Mincer [J. Mincer, "Labor Force Participation of Married Women," in *Aspects of Labor Economics*, H. G. Lewis, ed. (Princeton University Press, Princeton, N.J., 1962), pp. 63–105]. To the best of our knowledge, no attempt has been made to combine all the existing hours per head and participation rate studies in such a way as to infer an aggregate supply of labor schedule for a population fixed in terms of its demographic characteristics.

The above-mentioned studies represent attempts to isolate the long-run effect of a permanent change in real wages on labor supply. On the other hand, a third class of labor supply studies has investigated the short-run cyclical behavior of labor supply as measured by participation rates and their relationship to unemployment rates. These studies suggest a procyclical behavior in the supply of labor. See Mincer's summary of these studies [J. Mincer, "Labor Force Participation and Unemployment: A Review of Recent Evidence," in *Prosperity and Unemployment*, R. A. Gordon and M. S. Gordon, eds. (New York: Wiley, 1966)] and recent papers by Black and Russell [S. W. Black and R. R. Russell, "The Estimation of Potential Labor Force and GNP," paper presented at the Winter 1966 Econometric Society Meetings], Cain and Mincer [G. Cain and J. Mincer, "Urban Poverty and Labor Force Participation: Comment," *American Economic Review*, 59 (March 1969) pp. 185–94] and Tella [A. Tella, "Hidden Unemployment 1953–62: Comment," *American Economic Review*, 56 (December 1966), pp. 1235–1241].

to supply and demand forces.[2] Although we offer no crucial test of the two views, we shall show that a competitive market theory is rich in implications and is consistent with the U.S. experience.

The remainder of the paper is organized as follows. In Section 1 a model of the production-employment sector is discussed in general terms and related to the rest of the economy. In Section 2 an aggregate labor-supply function is developed. The demand side of the market is treated in Section 3, and the role of measured unemployment in Section 4. The model is then stated in full in Section 5, with tests reported in Section 6. Section 7 is a summary of our conclusions.

1
THE STRUCTURE OF
THE MODEL

The results reported in Section 6 are estimates of a two-equation model of the U.S. labor market, where the two equations are the labor-supply function and a marginal productivity condition for labor. The time series on which our tests were conducted are, as are all economic time series, subject to both short and long run forces. It is thus impossible, however desirable, to construct and test on these series either a "short run model" or a "long run model" of the labor market: an adequate model must contain both a short and a long run. There are, then, three features which we feel a model of the labor market (or, more broadly, the production-employment sector) should possess. First, it should incorporate the neoclassical feature that for fixed capital stock the aggregate supply schedule (relating the price of goods to real output) will become perfectly inelastic over a long period of stable aggregate demand. Second, the model should imply an elastic short run aggregate supply function, consistent with the observed fluctuations in real output and employment in the face of shifting aggregate demand.

[2]A bargaining interpretation of the Phillips relationship is given by Eckstein and Wilson [O. Eckstein and T. Wilson, "Determination of Wages in American Industry," *Quarterly Journal of Economics*, 76 (August 1962), pp. 379–444] and Perry [G. Perry, "The Determinants of Wage Rate Changes," *Review of Economic Studies*, 31 (October 1964), pp. 287–308]. Others have attempted to motivate the Phillips curve by appealing to an "out-of-equilibrium" adjustment function. This was the original motivation suggested by Phillips [A. W. Phillips, "The Relation between Unemployment and the Rate of Change of Money Wage Rates in the United Kingdom, 1861–1957," *Economica*, 25 (November 1958), pp. 283–299] and later Lipsey [R. G. Lipsey, "The Relationship between Unemployment and the Rate of Change of Money Wage Rates in the United Kingdom, 1862–1957: A Further Analysis," *Economica*, 27 (February 1960), pp. 1–31], and this view is extended in a recent paper by Phelps [E. Phelps, "Money Wage Dynamics and Labor Market Equilibrium," *Journal of Political Economy*, 76, Part 2 (August 1968), pp. 687–711]. For a discussion of the Phillips relationship and the joint influence of collective bargaining and monetary-fiscal policy see Bronfenbrenner and Holzman [M. Bronfenbrenner and F. D. Holzman, "Survey of Inflation Theory," *American Economic Review*, 53 (September 1963), pp. 593–661]. See also Bronfenbrenner's discussion of government wage-price guidelines [M. Bronfenbrenner, "A Guidepost-Mortem," *Industrial Labor Relations Review*, 20 (July 1967), pp. 637–650].

Finally, the transition from short run to long run labor-market equilibrium should be described in full.

The models tested in this paper share these three features. In implementing the models empirically, however, it is necessary to introduce a number of complications that obscure these central features. To aid in interpretating the results, we devote the remainder of this section to a simple prototype of the more complex models actually tested. In doing this, we consider the two functions actually estimated, together with the aggregate production function which was *not* estimated, as a bloc of equations determining the aggregate supply function.

Let m_t be employed persons per household in period t, k_t be capital per household, and y_t be real output per household. Let w_t be the real wage rate, and let Δp_t be the percentage rate of price increase from $t-1$ to t. We assume an aggregate production function with constant returns to scale, which can be written

$$\frac{y_t}{m_t} = f\left(\frac{k_t}{m_t}\right), \qquad f' > 0, \qquad f'' < 0. \tag{1}$$

With competitive labor markets and continuous profit maximization on the part of firms, equation (1) implies the marginal productivity condition for labor:

$$w_t = f\left(\frac{k_t}{m_t}\right) - \left(\frac{k_t}{m_t}\right)f'\left(\frac{k_t}{m_t}\right). \tag{2}$$

Equations (1) and (2) can be solved for the short run (that is, capital-fixed) output supply and labor demand functions if one wishes; their content is the same in either form. To (1) and (2) we add a labor supply function:

$$m_t = S(w_t, w_{t-1}, \Delta p_t, m_{t-1}), \tag{3}$$

where S is an increasing function of w_t, Δp_t, and m_{t-1} and a decreasing function of w_{t-1}. In Section 2 we discuss in some detail a Fisherian model motivating this labor-supply function. For the present, our interest is in the properties of the production-employment sector characterized by (1) through (3).

The supply function (3) is *not* homogeneous of degree zero in *current* prices and money wages, p_t and $w_t p_t$. Hence, in the short run, the model exhibits a form of the "money illusion" postulated in many modern, Keynesian models. If wages and prices were to remain stable over a long period, however, (3) could be solved for a long-run labor supply (relative to population), which depends only on the *real* wage rate.

Eliminating w_t, m_t, and their lagged values from (1) through (3) yields the aggregate supply function:

$$y_t = F(y_{t-1}, k_t, k_{t-1}, \Delta p_t). \tag{4}$$

The derivative of F with respect to p_t is positive, so that the short-run aggregate supply function has an upward slope—although it will not be perfectly elastic with respect to the price level. If prices are stable over a long period, and if the difference equation (4) is stable, the supply function becomes perfectly inelastic. In summary, the model (1) through (3) does possess the features discussed at the beginning of this section.

In discussing (1) through (3), we have regarded the labor market as being in *short run* equilibrium at each time t. This assumption is not inconsistent with observed fluctuations in employment, nor does it "define away" unemployment.[3] The main result of postulating a continuous short-run equilibrium is that measured unemployment, or the measured labor force, will not enter in an important way into the model. We do, however, attempt to account for movements in measured unemployment by using our model to suggest an answer to the question: What question do respondents to the employment survey think they are answering when asked if they are seeking work? This is discussed in detail in Section 4.

A second general remark is necessitated by the presence of the inflation rate Δp_t in the aggregate supply function (4). This would appear to offer the possibility that by pursuing a systematic policy of inflation, the government can raise real output arbitrarily without limit. We do *not* accept this implication. As we shall see in Section 2, if such a policy were followed, the model (1) through (3) would cease to hold.

Before turning from the general structure of the labor market to the behavior of individual suppliers and demanders of labor (Sections 2, 3, and 4), we should perhaps raise the broader question of whether a competitive supply-demand mechanism of the sort proposed above,

---

[3]Historically, much has been made of the distinction between "voluntary" and "involuntary" unemployment. When formulated carefully, however, this distinction turns out to be purely formal and serves only to obscure the important distinction between models in which labor-market equilibrium implies a particular (full employment) level of output, *independent of the level of aggregate demand*, and models in which this implication does not hold. Our model is in the latter class.

Without attempting a definitive review of the post-Keynesian literature, we wish to point out that many writers appear to treat labor markets as being in equilibrium throughout the cycle. Patinkin [D. Patinkin, *Money, Interest, and Prices* (New York, 1965), p. 341] interprets Modigliani [F. Modigliani, "Liquidity Preference and the Theory of Interest and Money," *Readings in Monetary Theory* (New York, 1951), pp. 186–239] in this way and attributes to Lange [O. Lange, *Price Flexibility and Full Employment* (The Principia Press, Bloomington, Ind., 1945)] this interpretation of Keynes. After seeking to differentiate himself from those who insist on labor suppliers being "on their supply curves" at each point in time, he himself attributes "rigidities" to the fact that "individual decisions . . . respond only 'stickily' to market changes . . ." (p. 343). Similarly, Rees [A. Rees, "Wage Determination and Involuntary Unemployment," *Journal of Political Economy*, 59 (April 1951), pp. 143–153] attributes wage rigidities to the *unwillingness* of employers to cut money wages. Of course, Patinkin is correct in asserting that it is not *necessary* to construct models in which labor markets are continuously cleared, but as his discussion of the Keynesian literature makes clear, the continuous equilibrium view is in no sense a radical departure from the views of earlier theorists, nor does it have, in itself, any obvious normative consequences.

or of *any* kind, can account for labor-market behavior. Posed in such general terms, an a priori discussion of this question is pointless, but two specific noncompetitive forces on wages and employment are sufficiently important to warrant special mention: collective bargaining and the military draft.

Clearly, the model sketched above is an inaccurate view of wage and employment determination in a single, unionized industry. In such an industry, the union imposes a higher-than-competitive wage rate, limited by the labor-demand elasticity it faces and the effectiveness of its strikes. Labor supply to the industry is irrelevant, because the excess supply that must exist is not able to bid down wages. A labor-market model for such an industry will thus consist of a demand function for labor and a "wage-setting equation." One is tempted to generalize this view of a unionized industry to the economy as a whole, and, indeed, many economists have yielded to this temptation. Over the period covered by our study, however, at most 25 percent of the labor force was employed under collective bargaining arrangements, so that this generalization makes no sense. Those who cannot find work in the unionized sector will be supplied to the nonunion sector, depressing wages there. As a result, there will be important distortions in the *relative* wage structure, but we have found neither theoretical presumption nor empirical evidence to indicate that the effect of unionism on *aggregate* wage rates is sizable (or even of predictable direction).[4]

Since the military is included in our wages and employment data, with the government treated exactly as a private employer, it is also important to consider the impact of the military draft. Ideally, one should deduct those coerced into the military (a figure that would dif-

---

[4]While the effect of collective bargaining on *relative* union/nonunion wage rates has been established (at various points in time) by Lewis [H. G. Lewis, *Unionism and Relative Wages in the United States: An Empirical Inquiry* (University of Chicago Press, Chicago, 1963)], the bargaining effect on the aggregate wage rate (weighted average of union and nonunion rates) remains uncertain and, indeed, largely unexplored. Since successful union activity will reduce employment in the unionized sector, releasing workers to the rest of the economy, there is not even a presumption that the union effect on the aggregate wage rate is positive. For example, if the demand elasticity for labor is unity in both sectors (union and nonunion) and if labor is inelastically supplied, unions will have *no* effect on either aggregate employment or the average wage rate. Even if one assumes an inelastic labor demand in the unionized sector, the union effect on wages at the peak of union power (the 1950s, when 25 percent of the work force was unionized and the relative union/nonunion wage was, according to Lewis, 1.15) is estimated at less than 4 percent.

Since the percent of the labor force covered by collective bargaining agreements has varied from 9 percent in 1929 to a high of about 25 percent in 1953, time-series analyses of the impact of bargaining on real wages have been possible. The few empirical studies we have examined suggest that collective bargaining may have a modest upward impact on aggregate real wages, but most of the observed secular and cyclical variation in this series is explained by competitive market forces. This conclusion is suggested by Rees [A. Rees, "Patterns of Wages, Price and Productivity," in *Wages, Prices, Profits and Productivity*, C. Myers, ed. (Columbia University Press, New York, 1959)] in his study of real wages in manufacturing for the period 1889–1957, and by Cagan (P. Cagan, "Theories of Mild, Continuing Inflation: A Critique and Extension," paper delivered at a symposium on inflation sponsored by New York University, Department of Economics, January 1968), who also examined the manufacturing wage data for the period 1890–1961.

fer from total draftees) from employment and from "population," deduct their pay from compensation of employees, and deduct their product from GNP—in short redo the national accounts. We have not attempted this but have instead introduced a wartime dummy variable to control for the effects of the draft during World War II—the only period in our sample where draftees form a substantial fraction of total employment. This is discussed further in Section II.

2
THE AGGREGATE SUPPLY OF LABOR

By the supply of labor we mean the quantity of man-hours supplied to the *market* economy per year.[5] There are several ways in which this quantity can vary in response to changes in the real wage rate. The wage rate may influence the size of the population through its effect on the child-bearing decision, it may affect the fraction of a given population supplied to the labor force (that is, the participation rate), or it may alter the number of hours supplied per year per labor-force member. We will examine only the last two responses—hours and participation rates—and attempt to explain changes in total labor supply for a population of fixed size and with a fixed age and sex composition.[6]

The relationship of labor supplied to the real wage, referred to in the preceding paragraph, is implied by the familiar utility analysis of the goods-leisure choice facing a single household in a competitive market. For a household facing fluctuating money wages and goods prices, this trade-off at *current* prices captures only one facet of the labor-supply decision. Equally important will be choices involving substitution between *future* goods and leisure and *current* goods and leisure. Consider, for example, the decision facing a worker who has been laid off (or who, in our terms, is confronted with a fall in the wage at which he can find work). Since accepting work at a lower wage may

---

[5] Our analysis will be restricted to the household decision problem involving the choice between market work and leisure. This is admittedly an oversimplification of a more complex decision problem involving choices among market work, leisure, home work, and school work. Our approach obviates the need for discussion of an implicit home-work wage rate and it also permits us to suppress the formal introduction of an explicit school-work wage rate. For a fuller statement of these issues see Cain (*op. cit.*), Kosters (*op. cit.*), and Mincer ("Labor Force Participation of Married Women," *loc. cit.*). It should also be stressed that since we are defining *leisure* to include *all* uses of time except remunerative labor, this term covers a variety of activities: e.g., schooling, job seeking, retirement, and housework.

[6] We are aware that in treating the population as exogenous we are failing to explain the single most important factor accounting for the secular growth in the U.S. labor force [on this point see Easterling (R. A. Easterling, Comments on paper by J. Mincer, "Labor Force Participation and Unemployment: A Review of Recent Evidence," *op. cit.*). Yet this assumption does not in any way lessen the usefulness of our model in understanding the dynamics of labor supply, and in separating short from long-run labor-supply responses to once-and-for-all real wage-rate changes.

involve, say, an investment in search or in moving to another community, the decision on current labor supply will differ depending on the wage he anticipates in the near future. If the current fall in wages is regarded as temporary, he may accept leisure now (be unemployed). If it is regarded as permanent, he may accept work elsewhere.

To examine these features of the labor-supply choice more systematically, we shall utilize an extended version of the utility analysis of a representative household, involving four commodities: current goods consumption ($\overline{C}$) and labor supply ($\overline{N}$) and "future" consumption and labor supply ($\overline{C}^*$ and $\overline{N}^*$). The household is assumed to maximize utility[7]:

$$U(\overline{C}, \overline{C}^*, \overline{N}, \overline{N}^*), \qquad U_1, \quad U_2 > 0, \quad U_3, \quad U_4 < 0, \qquad (5)$$

subject to the constraint that the present value of consumption cannot exceed the present value of income. Present values are computed using a nominal interest rate r, at which the household may lend any amount up to its current assets or borrow any amount up to that which may be secured by future income. The initial nonhuman assets, fixed in money terms, are $\overline{A}$, and present and future goods prices and money wage rates are P, P^*, W, and W^*. Thus U is maximized subject to

$$P\overline{C} + \frac{P^*}{1 + r}\,\overline{C}^* \le \overline{A} + W\overline{N} + \frac{W^*}{1 + r}\,\overline{N}^*. \qquad (6)$$

We assume that for all positive prices, a unique maximum is attained at which $\overline{C}$, $\overline{C}^*$, $\overline{N}$, $\overline{N}^* > 0$. Then the solution to the maximum problem gives each of these decision variables as a function of the four "prices" in (6) and $\overline{A}$. In particular, we have the current labor-supply function:

$$\overline{N} = F\left(W, \frac{W^*}{1 + r}, P, \frac{P^*}{1 + r}, \overline{A}\right). \qquad (7)$$

The function F is homogeneous of degree zero in its five arguments, so that if the current price level P is chosen as a deflator, (7) is equivalent to

$$\overline{N} = F\left(\frac{W}{P}, \frac{W^*}{P(1 + r)}, 1, \frac{P^*}{P(1 + r)}, \frac{\overline{A}}{P}\right). \qquad (8)$$

The theory's implications for the signs of the derivatives of F are, in general, ambiguous, as one would expect, but on the presumption that future goods and leisure are substitutes for current leisure, that

---

[7]Liviatan has shown [N. Liviatan, "Multiperiod Future Consumption as an Aggregate," *American Economic Review*, 56 (September 1966), pp. 828–840] that the common procedure of collapsing an *n*-period decision problem into a two-dimensional problem raises the usual index-number problems. These problems are neither more nor less severe than those which arise when, say, the price level is measured by an index, a procedure quite common in economics.

leisure is not inferior, and that the asset effect is small, there is a presumption that[8]

$$\partial F/\partial \left(\frac{W}{P}\right) > 0, \quad \partial F/\partial \left(\frac{W^*}{P(1+r)}\right) < 0,$$

$$\partial F/\partial \left(\frac{P^*}{P(1+r)}\right) < 0, \quad \partial F/\partial \left(\frac{\overline{A}}{P}\right) < 0. \tag{9}$$

This simple theory of a single household suggests an aggregate labor-supply function relating total manhours supplied annually, N_t, deflated by an index of the number of households, M_t, to the empirical counterparts of the arguments of F. Let W_t be an index of money wages, P_t the GNP deflator, r_t a nominal interest rate, and A_t the market value of assets held by the household sector. Let W_t^* and P_t^* be (unobservable) indexes of the anticipated prices of the composite goods "future labor" and "future consumption," based on information available at t. Then based on (8) we postulate the log-linear relationship:

$$\ln\left(\frac{N_t}{M_t}\right) = \beta_0 + \beta_1 \ln\left(\frac{W_t}{P_t}\right) - \beta_2 \ln\left[\frac{W_t^*}{P_t(1+r_t)}\right]$$

$$- \beta_3' \ln\left[\frac{P_t^*}{P_t(1+r_t)}\right] - \beta_4 \ln\left(\frac{A_t}{P_t M_t}\right), \tag{10}$$

where [see (9)] β_1, β_2, β_3', and β_4 are positive and β_0 may have either sign.[9] Letting $w_t = W_t/P_t$, $w_t^* = W_t^*/P_t^*$, $a_t = A_t/P_t$, and $\beta_3 = \beta_2 +$

[8]To obtain information on the signs of the partial derivatives of the labor-supply function F given in (7) from the hypothesis that the household maximizes (5) subject to (6), we follow the standard procedure of expressing each derivative as the sum of two terms: a Slutsky, or substitution, term and a term representing the asset (income) effect of a price change. Let $K(N, W)$ denote the substitution effect of a wage change on current labor supply, and so forth. Then

$$\frac{\partial F}{\partial W} = K(N, W) + N\frac{\partial F}{\partial A},$$

$$\partial F/\partial \left(\frac{W^*}{1+r}\right) = K\left(N, \frac{W^*}{1+r}\right) + N^*\frac{\partial F}{\partial A},$$

$$\frac{\partial F}{\partial P} = K(N, P) - C\frac{\partial F}{\partial A},$$

$$\partial F/\partial \left(\frac{P^*}{1+r}\right) = K\left(N, \frac{P^*}{1+r}\right) - C^*\frac{\partial F}{\partial A}.$$

The only implication of the utility-maximization hypothesis for the signs of the individual terms is $K(N, W) > 0$. The additional hypothesis that consumption in both periods and future leisure each are substitutes for current leisure implies that the other three substitution terms are negative. Finally, we suppose that $\partial F/\partial A$ is negative but negligible. Combining these hypotheses yields (9).

[9]The implication of our theory is that a change in the wage rate will elicit a particular labor supply response from the household. As a practical matter, of course, there is no single wage rate. Instead, wages vary according to occupation, education, sex, race, geography, and religion. When labor-supply responses vary with these characteristics, relative as well as absolute real wages will influence the aggregate supply of labor. It is assumed that over our sample period changes in the relative wage structure are such that (10) remains a good approximation of the true relation among the included variables.

$\beta_3' > 0$, and observing that $\ln (1 + r_t) \sim r_t$, (10) may be rearranged to give the more easily interpreted

$$\ln \left(\frac{N_t}{M_t} \right) = \beta_0 + \beta_1 \ln (w_t) - \beta_2 \ln (w_t^*)$$

$$+ \beta_3 \left[r_t - \ln \left(\frac{P_t^*}{P_t} \right) \right] - \beta_4 \ln \left(\frac{a_t}{M_t} \right). \qquad (11)$$

Thus labor supply is assumed to depend on current and expected real wages, on the expected real interest rate, $r_t - \ln (P_t^*/P_t)$, and on asset holdings. The presence of both current and anticipated future wage rates in this function is very much in the spirit of modern labor economics, in which the laborer is viewed as a capitalist and the decision to transfer one's supply from one market to another (which is how one typically accepts a wage cut or obtains a higher than normal increase in our economy) is recognized as an investment decision. The presence of the real interest rate [which was suggested earlier by Patinkin (*op. cit.*, p. 129)] reflects the ability to transfer consumption from one period to another.

An alternative way to view the wage response indicated by (11) is in terms of a current real wage consisting of "permanent" and "transitory" components.[10] Thus the terms involving wages on the right of (11) may be written $\beta_1 \ln (w_t/w_t^*) + (\beta_1 - \beta_2) \ln (w_t^*)$. The variable w_t^* has the natural interpretation as a permanent or normal real wage rate; the elasticity of labor supply with respect to this wage may have either sign, admitting the possibility of a backward-bending supply curve. The variable $\ln (w_t/w_t^*)$ is then the ratio of current to permanent wages. If $w_t > w_t^*$, or if current wages are abnormally high, more labor is supplied than would be implied by the long-run labor-supply function. If $w_t < w_t^*$, workers are off the long-run supply curve to the left.[11]

---

[10]The distinction between the labor-supply effect of a permanent as opposed to a transitory real wage-rate change serves as the basis of Friedman's [M. Friedman, *Price Theory: A Provisional Text* (University of Chicago Press, Chicago, 1962)] explanation of the unusually large increase in the supply of labor during World War II. To the best of our knowledge, Friedman was the first to suggest the empirical usefulness of the permanent-transitory wage rate distinction when studying the supply of labor. In studying the labor supply of married women, Mincer ("Labor Force Participation of Married Women") Cain (*op. cit.*), and Cain and Mincer (*op. cit.*) have distinguished between the effect of permanent and transitory variables on the supply of married women. But their model and objectives are different from ours. We do not address ourselves to the problems of the intrahousehold allocation of leisure and work, and it is difficult to compare directly our model with models primarily designed to explain the labor-supply behavior of the female member of the household. Nonetheless, we should stress that they have distinguished between the effect of permanent and transitory variables on the supply of female labor.

[11]Like Friedman's original permanent income hypothesis [M. Friedman, *A Theory of the Consumption Function* (Princeton University Press, Princeton, N.J., 1957)], this view of labor supply has life-cycle as well as business-cycle implications. For example, the theory "predicts" that workers will concentrate their labor supply in years of peak earnings, consuming leisure in larger than average amounts in childhood and old age. A systematic development and testing of such implications is beyond the scope of this paper.

As indicated above, there is some reason to believe that the asset effect on labor supply is minor (that β_4 is near 0), and, for this reason, this variable was originally excluded from our tests. Later we introduced some rather unsatisfactory "proxies," with generally poor results.[12] These are reported below, but for the present a_t/M_t will be dropped from the discussion. Similarly, while results with a nominal interest rate, r_t, are reported, our most satisfactory models exclude this variable, and it will be dropped from the discussion that follows.[13] Finally, it is often alleged that during World War II appeals to patriotism increased the supply of labor to both the military and nonmilitary sectors. To account for this, some of our tests introduce a zero–one dummy variable, D_t, equal to one for 1941–1945 and zero otherwise.[14]

---

[12]Our assumption that the nonhuman asset effect is small is consistent with some but not all of the available literature. Using a nonemployment income variable that includes reported income from owned assets, transfer payments, and other items, Bowen and Finegan (*loc. cit.*) obtained a negative and significant coefficient when regressing participation rates on this variable. They obtained this result for the years 1940, 1950, and 1960 and for several different age–sex groups. But another cross-sectional study by Kosters (*op. cit.*), who used the 1960 0.1 percent sample, was considerably less successful in identifying a nonemployment income effect on male hours of work. Kosters discusses the measurement problems occasioned by the use of census nonemployment income data as a proxy for income from nonhuman assets.

[13]In the model reported in Section 6, and in many of those reported in Appendix 2, either the asset variable or the nominal interest rate, or both, has been excluded from the regression equation for labor supply. In these cases the link between (9) and the version of (11) with r_t and $\ln (a_t/M_t)$ omitted needs clarification.

A household's nonhuman wealth will consist of claims to future income, partially fixed in money terms and partially in real terms. (For the representative household, A, is, of course, positive.) An increase in future prices, P^*, will then induce an increase, less than proportional, in the current market value of assets. In regressions which include an asset variable which measures market value, this capital gain or loss effect of price changes will be controlled for. Since the gain in assets is positively related to P^*, and assets are negatively related to current labor supply, the negative effect of P^* on current labor supply will be *accentuated* in regressions omitting $\ln(a_t/M_t)$. Hence β_3 is positive, whether or not an asset variable appears in (11).

When the interest rate r_t is omitted, a similar issue is raised. The nominal rate may vary with P_t^*/P_t, so that β_3 is biased toward zero in regressions with r_t excluded. There is some theoretical ground for believing this effect to be present, but there is little evidence that nominal interest rates adjust to expected inflation with sufficient speed to maintain a constant real rate. Indeed, the evidence indicates a very slow adjustment. Fisher [I. Fisher, *Theory of Interest* (New York, 1930)], who empirically investigated the relationship between interest rates and the change in prices for the United States and Great Britain, concluded: "These results suggest no direct and consistent connection of any real significance exists between P' (*the actual rate of price change*) and i (*the rate of interest*)." (The definitions in parentheses were supplied by us.) A more recent study by Sargent [T. Sargent, "Price Expectations and the Interest Rate," *Quarterly Journal of Economics*, 83 (February, 1969) pp. 127–141] corroborates Fisher's findings.

[14]We will also regard D_t as an admittedly imperfect control for the effect of the draft. Insofar as D_t indexes patriotism, it reflects a rightward shift in the supply function, resulting in increased employment and lower average wages (other things equal). As a measure of the effect of the draft, it has a positive effect on employment and an uncertain effect on the wage rate. If all the reluctant military personnel are from the nonmarket sector, the draft is simply a leftward shift in market demand, with a depressing effect on wages. On the other extreme, if all the coerced military personnel are from the nonmilitary market sector, the effect on average wages will depend on both the elasticity of labor demand in the nonmilitary sector and the difference between military pay rates and market rates. The effect of D_t will thus depend in an unknown way on patriotism and draft forces. It is our judgement that the net effect on wages will be negative; the effect on employment is positive.

Each of these variables, r_t, $\ln(a_t/M_t)$, and D_t, figures in (11) in a similar way, so the reader should have no difficulty in determining the effect on the model of adding any, or any combination, of them.

To complete the construction of an operational supply hypothesis, it is necessary to postulate a mechanism by which the real wage and price anticipations, w_t^* and P_t^*, are formed. A full analysis of this problem involves two elements: the formulation in t of forecasts for periods $t+1, t+2, \ldots$, and the construction of an index number based on these forecasts. Since we know in advance that this problem has no neat or illuminating solution, there is little incentive to conduct this analysis. Instead, we simply postulate the adaptive scheme,

$$\frac{w_t^*}{w_{t-1}^*} = \left(\frac{w_t}{w_{t-1}^*}\right)^\lambda e^{\lambda'}, \tag{12}$$

where $0 < \lambda < 1$ and where $e^{\lambda'}$ is added to permit an anticipated trend in real wages.

In logs, (12) becomes

$$\ln(w_t^*) = \lambda \ln(w_t) + (1 - \lambda)\ln(w_{t-1}^*) + \lambda'. \tag{13}$$

Similarly, we assume that price anticipations are formed adaptively, with the *same* reaction parameter λ:

$$\ln(P_t^*) = \lambda \ln(P_t) + (1 - \lambda)\ln(P_{t-1}^*) + \lambda''. \tag{14}$$

Since we will allude to the trend term λ'' at several points when interpreting our theoretical model and when evaluating our empirical results, we might mention that this term depends on major political and military events as well as the past development of prices. Its determination will not be examined in our study.

Using a Koyck transformation to eliminate w_t^* and P_t^* between (11), (13), and (14) [with r_t and a_t/M_t deleted from (11) as discussed above] we obtain

$$\ln(N_t/M_t) = [\beta_0\lambda - \lambda'\beta_2 - \lambda''\beta_3] + (\beta_1 - \lambda\beta_2)\ln(w_t)$$
$$- (1 - \lambda)\beta_1 \ln(w_{t-1}) + (1 - \lambda)\beta_3 \ln(P_t/P_{t-1})$$
$$+ (1 - \lambda)\ln(N_{t-1}/M_{t-1}). \tag{15}$$

Estimates of the parameters of (15) and its variants are reported in Section 6.[15]

Since the labor-supply equation (15) is not homogeneous in current money wages and current prices, we might say that there is "money

---

[15]One need not view (12) and (13) as exact equations. We will subsequently introduce an error term in (15) and assume that the errors are serially independent. Under this assumption, error terms in (12) and (13) are necessarily serially dependent and this dependence is broken by the Koyck transformation.

illusion" in the supply of labor. We should stress, however, that this behavior is not "irrational," nor does it stem from ignorance concerning the past course of prices. In (15), "money illusion" results not from a myopic concentration on money values but from our assumption that the suppliers of labor are adaptive on the level of prices, expecting a return to normal price levels regardless of current prices, and from the empirical fact that the nominal interest rate does not change in proportion to the actual rate of inflation. With these expectations, it is to a supplier's advantage to increase his current supply of labor and his current money savings when prices rise.[16]

Since (15) rests on the expectations hypotheses (13) and (14) fully as much as on the utility theory underlying (11), it is evident that one can expect (15) to obtain *only* in an economy where wages and prices might plausibly be forecast as (13) and (14) assume. In particular, a marked and sustained change in the trend rate of inflation (from one value of λ'' to another) will lead households using (14) to consistently over- or under-forecast prices, in which case some other forecasting scheme would presumably be adopted. We think (13) and (14) are

[16]The assumption that price expectations are formed on the (trend corrected) *level* of prices, as opposed to their rate of change, is crucial to the predictions of our model, because it accounts for the "switch" in sign on the coefficients of the inflation term in passing from (11) to (14). The appropriateness of this assumption is, of course, an empirical question, but we wish to point out that the route we have taken has a long history. To illustrate, we quote first from Hicks [J. R. Hicks, *Value and Capital* (Clarendon Press, New York, 1946), pp. 270–271]: "In order to explain the rigidity of wages, we have to assume in the parties to the wage-bargain some sense of normal prices, hardly distinguished (perhaps) from 'just' prices. The rigidity of wages extends over precisely that time—it may be quite a long time—during which the parties concerned persuade themselves that changes in related prices (whether prices of the products of labour, or of the things labour buys) are temporary changes. Once they become convinced that these changes are permanent changes, there *is* a tendency for wages to change; in situations of extreme instability, when they have lost their sense of normal prices, negotiators have recourse to automatic sliding scales and the rigidity of money wages ceases altogether."

Our treatment differs from Hicks' in its asymmetrical handling of suppliers and demanders. A still closer forerunner of our model is provided by Tobin [J. Tobin, "Money Wage Rates and Employment," in *The New Economics*, S. E. Harris, ed. (New York, 1952), p. 581]: "labor may have inelastic price expectations; a certain 'normal' price level, or range of price levels, may be expected to prevail in the future, regardless of the level of current prices. With such expectations, it is clearly to the advantage of wage earners to have, with the same current real income, the highest possible money income. For the higher their money incomes the greater will be their money savings and, therefore, their expected command over future goods."

In his celebrated study of hyperinflation, Cagan [P. Cagan, "The Monetary Dynamics of Hyperinflation," in *Studies in the Quantity Theory of Money*, M. Friedman, ed. (University of Chicago Press, Chicago, 1956)] assumed that the expected rate of price change was an exponentially weighted average of past inflation rates. Since his application involved monthly inflation rates comparable to the rate of price change per decade in our sample, there is no inconsistency between his practice and ours. Previous studies which used expectations adaptive on price *levels* include Nerlove's study of the supply of farm products [M. Nerlove, *Dynamics of Supply: Estimation of Farmers Response to Price* (Baltimore, 1958)] and Lewis's study of union/nonunion wage determination (*Unionism and Relative Wages in the United States*). More recent studies, such as Sargent (*loc. cit.*), have used hypothesis permitting both "extrapolative" (like Cagan's) and "regressive" (like ours) components in the expected inflation rate. In short, there is no empirical consensus on the formation of price expectations, nor indeed should there be, because inflation policies of governments vary over countries and over time and households are obliged to vary the way they form expectations accordingly.

plausible for the period 1929–1965 in the United States although the average inflation rate is somewhat higher in the latter part of the period than in the former. But we wish to emphasize that the theory underlying (15) shows that it is altogether illegitimate to insert an arbitrary, fixed value of P_t/P_{t-1} into (15) to obtain estimated long-run effects of inflation on labor supply.

3
THE AGGREGATE MARGINAL PRODUCTIVITY CONDITION FOR LABOR

We assume an aggregate production function of the C.E.S. form, with constant returns to scale and labor-augmenting technological change. Let y_t be the real gross national product, N_t the employment variable used in Section 2, K_t the economy's real capital stock, and Q_t an index of labor quality (in practice, a years-of-school-completed index).[17] Then

$$y_t = [a(Q_t N_t)^{-b} + c(K_t)^{-b}]^{-1/b}, \tag{16}$$

where a and c are positive and $b > -1$. Then $\sigma = 1/(1 + b)$ is the elasticity of substitution. The marginal productivity condition for labor implied by (16) and profit maximization under competition can be written in the form[18]

$$w_t = aQ_t \left(\frac{y_t}{Q_t N_t}\right)^{1+b} \tag{17}$$

Taking logs and rearranging, (17) implies

$$\ln(N_t) + \ln(Q_t) - \ln(y_t) = \sigma \ln(a) - \sigma[\ln(w_t) - \ln(Q_t)]. \tag{18}$$

Equation (17) is not a specialization of the marginal productivity condition (2); rather, it is obtained from (2) using the equality $k_t/m_t = f^{-1}(y_t/m_t)$ given by (1). The content of (16) and (17) is, of course, the same as the content of (16) and the form of (2) obtained from (16). The main virtue of (17) [or (18)] from our point of view is that it enables us to have some control over simultaneous equations problems in estimating the supply function without requiring time series on K_t.

Equation (18) is operational, and estimates of its parameters have been obtained. The use of (18), however, rests on the hypothesis that labor is a freely variable input. To the contrary, there is a good deal of

[17]While our basic model includes only labor-embodied technical change, we do not rule out other sources of technical change. In Appendix 2 we present results based on a C.E.S. production function which contains not only labor-embodied technical change but a neutral source of technical advance introduced by multiplying (16) by $e^{\lambda t}$.

[18]See Arrow et al. [K. J. Arrow, H. B. Chenery, B. S. Minhas, and R. M. Solow, "Capital-Labor Substitution and Economic Efficiency," *Review of Economics and Statistics*, 43 (August 1961), pp. 225–250].

evidence that varying labor entails adjustment costs and that this leads firms to adjust gradually to the level implied by (18), rather than attempting to maintain it continually through time.[19] We shall not pursue the analysis of the maximum problem suggested by this remark, but rather simply observe that it suggests a relation involving current *and* lagged output and employment, and the current real wage, which reduces to (18) under stationary levels of output and employment. Retaining the assumption of log linearity, this may be written

$$\ln(Q_t N_t) = c_0 - c_1 \ln\left(\frac{w_t}{Q_t}\right) + c_2 \ln(y_t)$$

$$+ c_3 \ln(y_{t-1}) + c_4 \ln(Q_{t-1} N_{t-1}), \qquad (19)$$

where $c_0, \ldots, c_4$ satisfy

$$c_0 = (1 - c_4)\sigma \ln(a), \quad c_1 = (1 - c_4)\sigma, \quad c_2 + c_3 = 1 - c_4. \qquad (20)$$

Monotonic convergence at fixed wage rates implies

$$0 < c_4 < 1, \qquad (21)$$

which implies that c_1 is positive. Using the last equality of (20) to eliminate c_3 puts (19) into the form

$$\ln\left(\frac{Q_t N_t}{y_t}\right) = c_0 - c_1 \ln\left(\frac{w_t}{Q_t}\right) + c_4 \ln\left(\frac{Q_{t-1} N_{t-1}}{y_{t-1}}\right)$$

$$+ (c_2 - 1) \ln\left(\frac{y_t}{y_{t-1}}\right). \qquad (22)$$

Estimates of the parameters of (22) are reported in Section 6.

[19]The investment in firm specific on-the-job training is perhaps the single most important factor making it costly for firms to continuously adjust their work forces. Both Becker [G. S. Becker, *Human Capital: A Theoretical and Empirical Analysis with Special Reference to Education* (New York, 1964)] and Oi [W. Oi, "Labor as a Quasi-fixed Factor of Production," *Journal of Political Economy*, 70 (December 1962), pp. 538–555] develop this argument to explain the quasi-fixity of labor inputs. Schramm (R. Schramm, *Optimal Adjustment of Factors of Production and the Study of Investment Behavior*, unpublished, Carnegie Mellon University Ph.D. dissertation, 1967) treats labor and capital inputs symmetrically as partially fixed factors and finds that in the manufacturing sector lagged values of *both* variables affect current input decisions. There is also considerable evidence to suggest that the employment/output ratio rises during downturns and falls during upturns, an observation implying labor-adjustment costs. However, there are wide differences among studies in the estimates of the short-run elasticity of labor inputs with respect to output. Using post-World War II quarterly data, estimates between 0.30 and 0.55 have been obtained by Wilson and Eckstein [T. A. Wilson and O. Eckstein, "Short-Run Productivity Behavior in U.S. Manufacturing," *Review of Economics and Statistics*, 46 (February 1964), pp. 53–64] and Kuh [E. Kuh, "Measurement of Potential Output," *American Economic Review*, 56 (September 1966), p. 762, "Cyclical and Secular Labor Productivity in United States Manufacturing," *Review of Economics and Statistics*, 47 (February 1965), pp. 11–30], but the estimated elasticity is quite sensitive to what is held constant in the regressions. McGuire (T. W. McGuire, *An Empirical Investigation of the U.S. Manufacturing Production Function in the Post-War Period*, Stanford University Ph.D. dissertation, 1968) has carefully documented this fact and has obtained estimates in the range 0.8 and 0.9 on quarterly data.

It is natural to interpret the presence of real output, y_t, in (22) as a measure of the impact of aggregate demand on the labor market. This interpretation is, however, fallacious, as should be clear from the discussion in Section 1. A fall (for example) in aggregate demand will involve a shift to the left in the *schedule* relating real output, y_t, and the price level, P_t. This event will appear to individual firms as a price decline or demand shift, and, in response, firms will vary output and labor input *simultaneously*. Our hypothesis states that as this adjustment takes place, (22) will remain valid; it does *not* state that labor demand will respond to exogenous shifts in output.

In our empirical work, however, output is treated as an exogenous variable, which gives rise to a simultaneous equations problem. This difficulty cannot be resolved by obtaining labor demand as a function of capital stock, wages, and the price level. It is true that such an equation is entitled to be called a demand function for labor, as (22) is not, but because the price level is no more exogenous than is the level of real output a simultaneity problem would persist. In short, there is, in our view, no way to set up an aggregate labor-market model in which employment and wages are affected by other variables in the economy but do not in turn affect them.

4
MEASURED
UNEMPLOYMENT

The government generates an unemployment series based on the number of persons who answer yes to the question: Are you actively seeking work?[20] There is a strong temptation to assume that respondents to this survey take the question to mean, Are you seeking work at the current wage rate?, but it is important to recognize that this assumption is simply an hypothesis, the truth of which is far from obvious. In our model it has been implicitly assumed that this interpretation is *not* correct, because the current wage is assumed to equate quantity demanded and quantity supplied exactly each period. In this section we offer an alternative hypothesis about what it is that people mean when they classify themselves as unemployed.

Our theory of the *market* behavior of suppliers of labor is developed in Section 2. We now return to this theory to see if it can also suggest

[20]The unemployment series most often used is based on a census survey. Presently unemployment is defined as follows: "Unemployed persons comprise all persons who did not work during the survey week, who made specific efforts to find a job within the past four weeks, and who were available for work during the survey week (except for temporary illness). Also included as unemployed are those who did not work at all, were available for work, and (a) were waiting to be called back to a job from which they had been laid off; or (b) were waiting to report to a new wage or salary job within 30 days" [U.S. Department of Labor, Bureau of Labor Statistics, *Employment and Earnings*, 14 (No. 7)] (January 1968)].

an hypothesis about responses to the employment survey, but before doing so, we make some general observations about wage rates and unemployment. First, an unemployed worker does not generally know what *his* current wage rate is. To find out, he must engage in a search over a variety of employment possibilities (and there are always *some*), always balancing the gains from further search against the gains from accepting a job at the best wage his search has turned up to date. As a guide in this search process, he must use some notion of his "normal" wage rate, based on wages in occupations in which he has formerly worked, wages of comparably skilled and aged workers, and so forth. The normal wage rate serves as a guide to job search. Once the searcher becomes convinced that his normal wage rate is lower than he originally thought, he may "bid" his money wage rate down by changing occupations or moving to a new location. Indeed, it is occupational or locational change which is the principal means whereby individuals can in fact cut their money wages. The search process may extend over a wide geographic area and may include search among many different potential occupations. It is not only a search for information concerning current job availabilities but concerning the future course of job development as well. Because information is limited and costly to acquire and because action on the basis of acquired information sometimes requires large resource investments in moving and retraining, the suppliers of labor will adjust slowly.[21]

In the above discussion we speak as though everyone has a reasonably firm view of his "normal" wage rate. This of course is an oversimplification. However, those unemployed persons who can speak with the least ambiguity about *their* current wage rates are those workers, primarily industrial, who have been *laid off*, as opposed to dismissed, from jobs formerly held. The term layoff has an explicit connotation of a temporary deviation from a normal or "permanent" situation.

These observations, none of which is original with us, suggest strongly that the labor force as measured by the employment survey consists of those who are employed *plus* those who are unemployed but would accept work at what they regard as their normal wage rates

---

[21]Perhaps the clearest statement of the view that unemployment is essentially employment at job search can be found in Alchian and Allen [A. Alchian and W. Allen, *University Economics* (Wadsworth Publishing Co., Belmont, Calif., 1967), pp. 494–524]. Whereas Alchian and Allen emphasize information lacunae and search costs as the source of lagged wage adjustments, a paper by Holt and David [C. Holt and M. David, "The Concept of Job Vacancies in a Dynamic Theory of the Labor Market," in *The Measurement and Interpretation of Job Vacancies* (National Bureau of Economic Research, New York, 1966)] stresses a kind of psychological resistance to wage cuts in the form of an aspiration-level model which is combined with a search process to generate unemployment. The Alchian–Allen model is closely related to an earlier paper on information by Stigler [G. Stigler, "The Economics of Information," *Journal of Political Economy*, 69 (June 1961), pp. 213–225], while the Holt–David view is very much in the spirit of Simon's work [H. A. Simon, *Models of Man* (New York, 1957)].

(or, equivalently, in their normal occupation). In Section 2, we pointed out that the index w_t^* of anticipated future wages can be interpreted as a (trend corrected) measure of normal or permanent wages. According to (13), suppliers will regard the current real wage as normal (that is, will not revise their estimates of the height of the trend line of wages) provided $w_t = w_{t-1}^*$. Similarly, a normal price level may, using (14), be defined as P_t such that $P_t = P_{t-1}^*$. Using these definitions of normal wages and prices, we may evaluate the right side of (11) at these prices to define *normal labor supply* N_t^*:

$$\ln \left(\frac{N_t^*}{M_t}\right) = \beta_0 + \beta_1 \ln (w_{t-1}^*) - \beta_2 \ln (w_t^*)$$

$$+ \beta_3 \left[r_t - \ln \left(\frac{P_t^*}{P_{t-1}^*}\right)\right] - \beta_4 \ln \left(\frac{a_t}{M_t}\right). \qquad (23)$$

Then from (11) and (23),

$$\ln \left(\frac{N_t^*}{N_t}\right) = \beta_1 \ln \left(\frac{w_{t-1}^*}{w_t}\right) + \beta_3 \ln \left(\frac{P_{t-1}^*}{P_t}\right). \qquad (24)$$

Since $\ln (N_t^*/N_t) \sim (N_t^* - N_t)/N_t^*$, the left side of (23) is a kind of unemployment rate. There are two reasons, however, why it might differ from the measured unemployment rates, U_t. First, many persons in the normal work force, N_t^*, may not report themselves as actively seeking work, especially <u>teenagers and women</u>. Second, there is a <u>frictional component of measured unemployment</u> that cannot be captured by a variable which, like our N_t^*, is defined in terms of a representative household. Since there is good reason to believe that frictional unemployment varies positively with the nonfrictional component, it will not simply appear in (24) as an additive constant.[22] To summarize these two forces, we assume that U_t and $\ln (N_t^*/N_t)$ are linearly related:

$$U_t = g_0 + g_1 \ln \left(\frac{N_t^*}{N_t}\right), \qquad g_0, \ g_1 > 0, \qquad (25)$$

Then combining (24) and (25),

$$U_t = g_0 + g_1\beta_1 \ln \left(\frac{w_{t-1}^*}{w_t}\right) + g_1\beta_3 \ln \left(\frac{P_{t-1}^*}{P_t}\right). \qquad (26)$$

Finally, using the Koyck transformation to eliminate w_{t-1}^* and P_{t-1}^*

---

[22]The argument that frictional unemployment and nonfrictional unemployment do not additively determine aggregate unemployment is developed by Gaver and Rapping (D. Gaver and L. A. Rapping, *A Stochastic Process Model of the United States Labor Market*, unpublished, Carnegie Mellon University, 1966) in terms of a stochastic job-search model with jobs being simultaneously created and destroyed.

between (26), (13), and (14), we obtain

$$U_t = [\lambda g_0 + \lambda' g_1 \beta_1 + \lambda'' g_1 \beta_3] - g_1 \beta_1 \ln \left(\frac{w_t}{w_{t-1}} \right)$$

$$- g_1 \beta_3 \ln \left(\frac{P_t}{P_{t-1}} \right) + (1 - \lambda) U_{t-1}. \tag{27}$$

Equation (27) will be added to (15) and (22) to form the three-equation system which is discussed further below. In our view it adds nothing to the theory of labor market behavior contained in (15) and (22), but it has independent interest because of its resemblance to the now-famous Phillips curve. [Indeed, defining a Phillips curve as any equality linking an inflation rate and unemployment with a negative correlation, (27) *is* a Phillips curve.] The derivation of (27) from the labor-supply theory of Section 2, together with a behavioral hypotehsis introduced in this section, leads to some strong warnings as to the empirical performance one should expect from this Phillips curve and the policy implications one should draw from it.

First, the trend rates of change in real wages and prices (λ' and λ'') appear in the constant term of (27). Hence there is no reason to expect stability of the Phillips curve across countries with different inflation rates or rates of productivity change, or in time series on a single country where these trends change sharply. Similarly, changes in the trend rate of inflation will induce a counteracting shift in the Phillips curve, so that (27) in no sense exhibits a "trade-off" offering arbitrarily low unemployment rates to a country which will tolerate sufficiently high rates of inflation. [It should be emphasized, of course, that these assertions about the way in which households perceive and adjust to changes in trend rates of inflation are not supported empirically by this study. We *test* (13) and (14), which refer to reactions to deviations from trend rates of change, and *assume* that expected trends would be revised given sufficient cause.]

If we are correct in assuming that the expected trend rate of inflation, λ'', would eventually adjust to a sustained actual rate of inflation, then there is an important sense in which there is a relevant trade-off between unemployment today and unemployment tomorrow, a proposition suggested by M. Friedman.[23] To illustrate the point consider Figure 1. Assume that there has been a *sustained* rate of inflation of 2 percent, so that the expected trend rate of inflation, λ'', equals 0.02. Let U_t^* be the steady-state value of U_t from (27). This value is g_0 when $\lambda' = \Delta \ln w_t$. Now let $\Delta \ln P_t$ rise to 0.03 and let it be maintained at this new level. From Figure 1 we see that unemployment will fall to U_1^*. But now the suppliers of labor are consistently underestimating the

[23]M. Friedman, "The Role of Monetary Theory," *American Economic Review*, 58 (March 1968) pp. 1–18.

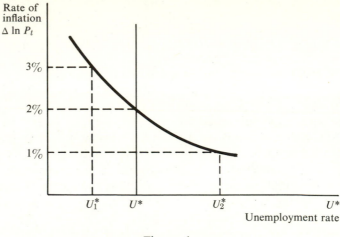

Figure 1

price level. Consequently, λ'' will eventually rise to 0.03, and then un-employment will return to U^* [see (27)]. If, on the other hand, a sus-tained 2 percent inflation is followed by a *sustained* 1 percent inflation, unemployment will *increase* to U_2^*, but eventually it will return to U^*. It appears that a policy designed to sustain an inflation can temporar-ily reduce unemployment, but unless the higher rate of increase in prices can be permanently maintained, a subsequent attempt to return to the original rate of inflation will result in an offset to the initial employment gains.[24]

5
SUMMARY STATEMENT
OF THE MODEL

In this section, the model developed in Sections 2 through 4 is re-stated in econometric form with a uniform notation. The restrictions on the regression coefficients implied by the theory are summarized, and estimation is discussed.

The marginal productivity condition for labor, corresponding to (22), is

$$\ln\left(\frac{Q_t N_t}{y_t}\right) = \beta_{10} - \beta_{11}\ln\left(\frac{w_t}{Q_t}\right) + \beta_{12}\ln\left(\frac{Q_{t-1}N_{t-1}}{y_{t-1}}\right)$$

$$+ \beta_{13}\ln\left(\frac{y_t}{y_{t-1}}\right) + u_{1t}, \tag{28}$$

[24]Our argument that there is no *long*-run unemployment-inflation trade-off is based on theoretical considerations. In another study [R. E. Lucas, Jr., and L. A. Rapping, "Price Expectations and the Phillips Curve," *American Economic Review*, 59 (June 1969) pp. 109–120] we attempt to empirically verify this position within the framework of a more general price expectations model than (14).

where

$$\beta_{11} > 0, \quad 0 < \beta_{12} < 1, \tag{29}$$

and where u_{1t} is a random error.

The labor-supply function, corresponding to (15), is

$$\ln\left(\frac{N_t}{M_t}\right) = \beta_{20} + \beta_{21} \ln(w_t) - \beta_{22} \ln(w_{t-1})$$

$$+ \beta_{23} \ln\left(\frac{P_t}{P_{t-1}}\right) + \beta_{24} \ln\left(\frac{N_{t-1}}{M_{t-1}}\right) + u_{2t}, \tag{30}$$

where[25]

$$0 < \beta_{21} < \frac{\beta_{22}}{\beta_{24}}, \quad \beta_{22} > 0, \quad \beta_{23} > 0, \quad 0 < \beta_{24} < 1, \tag{31}$$

and where u_{2t} is a random error.

The unemployment-rate function, corresponding to (27), is

$$U_t = \beta_{30} - \beta_{31} \ln\left(\frac{w_t}{w_{t-1}}\right) - \beta_{32} \ln\left(\frac{P_t}{P_{t-1}}\right) + \beta_{33} U_{t-1} + u_{3t}, \tag{32}$$

where

$$\beta_{31} > 0, \quad \beta_{32} > 0, \quad 0 < \beta_{33} < 1, \tag{33}$$

$$\beta_{31}/\beta_{32} = \beta_{21}/\beta_{23}, \quad \beta_{33} = \beta_{24}, \tag{34}$$

and where u_{3t} is a random error.

The error vectors (u_{1t}, u_{2t}, u_{3t}), $t = 1, \ldots, T$, are assumed to be independent and identically distributed, with a finite covariance matrix and a mean vector $(0, 0, 0)$. The variables Q_t, y_t, M_t, and P_t are taken to be exogenous; the endogenous variables are N_t, w_t, and U_t.[26] All three equations are overidentified.

The reduced-form equations for w_t and N_t/M_t implied by (28) and (30) are

$$\ln(w_t) \tag{35}$$

$$\ln\left(\frac{N_t}{M_t}\right) = \begin{cases} \pi_{i0} + \pi_{i1} \ln(w_{t-1}) + \pi_{i2} \ln\left(\frac{P_t}{P_{t-1}}\right) \\ + \pi_{i3} \ln\left(\frac{y_t}{M_t}\right) + \pi_{i4} \ln(Q_t) + \pi_{i5} \ln\left(\frac{Q_{t-1} N_{t-1}}{y_{t-1}}\right) \\ + \pi_{i6} \ln\left(\frac{y_t}{y_{t-1}}\right) + \pi_{i7} \ln\left(\frac{N_{t-1}}{M_{t-1}}\right) + \epsilon_{it}, \end{cases} \tag{36}$$

[25]The prediction that $\beta_{21} > 0$ follows from considerations raised in Section 1 rather than in Section 2: Since β_{21} is the short-run labor-supply elasticity, it must be positive for the aggregate supply function of goods to have the upward slope assumed in Section 1. The inequality $\beta_{21} < \beta_{22}/\beta_{24}$ follows from $\beta_2 > 0$, which is implied by the argument of Section 2. Also note that since $\beta_{22} > 0$ follows from other predictions in (31), (31) contains five (not six) independent restrictions.

[26]We have already discussed the assumption that y_t and P_t are exogenous. On the other hand, we think of M_t and Q_t as predetermined variables. The current population and its quality are the result of past decisions, which, of course, depend in part on past real wage rates.

where $i = 1$ for (35) and $i = 2$ for (36). The restrictions on $\pi_{i0}, \ldots, \pi_{i7}$, $\pi_{20}, \ldots, \pi_{27}$ implied by (29) and (31) are

$$\pi_{11} > 0, \quad \pi_{12} < 0, \quad \pi_{13} > 0, \quad \pi_{15} > 0, \quad \pi_{17} < 0, \tag{37}$$

$$\pi_{21} < 0, \quad \pi_{22} > 0, \quad \pi_{23} > 0, \quad \pi_{25} > 0, \quad \pi_{27} > 0. \tag{38}$$

In addition, the hypothesis that the difference equations (35) and (36) are stable, which was first introduced in the discussion of Section I, requires that the real parts of the roots of

$$x^2 - (\pi_{11} + \pi_{27})x + (\pi_{11}\pi_{27} - \pi_{17}\pi_{21}) = 0 \tag{39}$$

be less than one in absolute value. (If all the information in the structure were imposed on the reduced form, this quadratic would have one zero root and one nonzero real root.)

The estimated reduced-form coefficients will, under our assumptions, be consistent estimators of the true coefficients and asymptotically normally distributed when estimated by ordinary least squares. We have estimated the coefficients of (28), (30), and (32) using two-stage least squares, which involved using only (35) of the reduced form. The estimated structural coefficients will also be asymptotically normal. In addition to the coefficients and their standard errors, we report the multiple correlation coefficient and the Durbin–Watson statistic. The latter is included as a rough measure of serial correlation, although nothing is known about its distribution in models such as ours.

6
RESULTS

In this section we report estimates of the parameters of (28,) (30), (32), (35), and (36), and tests of the hypotheses (29), (31), (33), (34), (37), and (38).[27] These estimates were obtained from aggregate, U.S. time series covering the years 1930–65.

Employment is man-hours engaged in production per year in the civilian and government sectors. The money wage rate is compensation per man-hour, a measure that includes wages and salaries and public and private fringes. The price level is the GNP implicit price deflator. Real output is GNP in constant dollars. Labor quality is an

---

[27]Formally, we regard (28), (30), and (32), together with the assumptions on the error vectors, as a maintained hypothesis, and we wish to test the hypothesis that the parameters β_{11}, β_{12}, β_{21}, β_{22}, β_{23}, β_{24}, β_{31}, β_{32}, and β_{33} lie in that subset of nine-dimensional space satisfying (29), (31), (33), and (34). (The matter is further complicated if we test, rather than assume, the serial independence of the errors.) In lieu of a generally accepted test of hypotheses of this sort, we shall summarize and evaluate our results from several points of view, using the customary "t-statistics" as measures of precision. Hence our conclusion that our model is "consistent with the 1929–1965 data . . . and with several related empirical studies" should be regarded as a careful but informal conclusion on our part, *not* as a consequence of any single, formal statistical test.

index of years of school completed. Population is an index of the number of households, corrected for changes in age–sex composition.[28]

The estimated reduced-form coefficients [equations (35) and (36)] appear in lines 4 and 5 of Table 1. The five hypotheses (37) on the coefficients of the equation for ln (w_t), (35), are *all* confirmed at the 0.005 level using the relevant one-tail test of significance. Of the five hypotheses (38) on the coefficients of the equation for ln (N_t/M_t), (36), only one is confirmed at the 0.05 level: $\hat{\pi}_{17} > 0$, as predicted. The other four are neither confirmed nor contradicted, the estimated coefficients being insignificantly different from zero. Good fits were obtained on both equations; serial correlation appears to be absent. The two roots of the quadratic (39) are complex conjugates, with real parts equal to 0.68, confirming (but with no statistical significance) the predicted stability of these difference equations. In summary, of the ten sign implications placed by the theory on the reduced form, six are confirmed at the 0.05 level; four are neither confirmed nor contradicted. Equation (35) strikingly outperforms (36).

The estimated structural coefficients [equations (28) and (30)] appear on lines 1 and 2 of Table 1. Tests on these coefficients are not, of course, independent of the reduced-form tests just discussed, because the predictions on the structure imply those on the reduced form. But the converse of this statement is *not* true, so a comparison of the estimates with (29) and (31) does provide additional information as to the validity of the model.

[28]The data used in this study are contained in Appendix 1. The series on measured unemployment is from Lebergott [S. Lebergott, *Manpower in Economic Growth: The American Record since 1800* (New York, 1964)] and the 1967 Manpower Report [U.S. Department of Labor, *Manpower Report of the President* (U.S. Government Printing Office, Washington, 1967), p. 201. The Moody's Aaa rate (used later) is from the 1967 President's Economic Report [Council of Economic Advisers, *Economic Report of the President, January 1967* (U.S. Government Printing Office, Washington, 1967), p. 272]. Gross national product, the implicit GNP deflator, compensation per full-time equivalent employee, and persons engaged were all taken from Survey of Current Business sources [U.S. Department of Commerce, Office of Business Economics, *The National Income and Product Accounts of the United States, 1929–1965: Statistical Tables; A Supplement to the Survey of Current Business* (U.S. Government Printing Office, Washington, n.d.), pp. 2, 90, 102, 110, 158].

The man-hour series is the product of the number of persons engaged in production reported by the Department of Commerce times annual hours worked per year by full-time employees for the whole economy as reported by Denison [E. F. Denison, *The Sources of Economic Growth in the United States and the Alternatives Before Us* (C.E.D., 1962), Supplementary Paper 13]. Denison's series was extended beyond 1958 by regressing his series on the Bureau of Labor Statistics (BLS) weekly manufacturing hours series [U.S. Bureau of Labor Statistics, *Employment and Earnings Statistics for the United States, 1909–1966* (U.S. Government Printing Office, Washington, 1966), Bulletin 1312–4] for the years 1929–1958. Then this regression equation was used in conjunction with known BLS manufacturing hours data to predict hours for the whole economy for 1959–1965.

Compensation per man-hour was obtained by dividing annual compensation per full-time equivalent employee by annual man-hours worked by full-time employees.

The index of labor quality is taken from Denison (*op cit.*, p. 85). His data were available from 1929–1958 and were extended by a simple linear extrapolation.

The aggregate supply of labor, N_t, was deflated by a variable that accounts for changes in the total supply of labor due solely to changes in the total number of households *as well* as the joint age–sex distribution of the population. The nominal nonhuman asset

Table 1

LABOR–MARKET MODEL (1) REDUCED–FORM, SUPPLY, DEMAND, AND UNEMPLOYMENT–RATE ESTIMATES USING TWO–STAGE LEAST–SQUARES PROCEDURES

TIME SERIES 1930–1965

Equation and Dependent Variable	INDEPENDENT					
	Constant	$\ln \hat{w}_t$	$\ln w_{t-1}$	$\Delta \ln P_t$	$\ln (N/M)_{t-1}$	$\ln (\hat{w}_t/Q_t)$
Supply: $\ln (N/M)_t$	3.81 (0.93)[b]	1.40 (0.51)[b]	−1.39 (0.51)[b]	0.74 (0.17)[b]	0.64 (0.09)[b]	
First-order condition on labor: $\ln (NQ/y)_t$	−2.21 (0.70)[b]					−0.46 (0.12)[b]
Unemployment-rate function: U_t	0.042 (0.010)[b]			−0.59 (0.08)[b]		
Reduced-form wage: $\ln w_t$	−15.65 (3.50)[b]		0.44 (0.17)[b]	−0.22 (0.07)[b]	−1.15 (0.45)[b]	
Reduced-form employment: $\ln (N/M)_t$	11.60 (3.50)[b]		0.08 (0.17)	0.06 (0.07)	0.91 (0.45)[c]	

[a] All R^2 are adjusted for degrees of freedom.

[b] One-tail significance at 0.005 test level (except for intercepts, $\Delta \ln y_t$, and $\ln Q_t$, which are two-tail tests).

[c] One-tail significance at 0.05 test level (except for intercepts, $\Delta \ln y_t$, and $\ln Q_t$, which are two-tail tests).

---

variable, A_t (used later), should be deflated by an index of the number of households only. However, because our age–sex corrected population series was roughly proportional to the population over 14 years of age, we deflated both N_t and A_t by the same index, M_t.

In constructing M_t, let L_{0i} = the labor force in the zero period of the ith age–sex group and let P_{0i} = the population of the ith group again in the zero period. Then we define our population index as

$$M_t = \sum_{i=1}^{n} \frac{L_{0i}}{L_0} \frac{P_{1i}}{P_{0i}},$$

where $L_0 = \sum_{i=1}^{n} L_{0i}$. This index has two simple and equivalent interpretations. First, it is a weighted average of the percentage increase in the population of each age-sex cohort, the weights being the percent of the base-year labor force who are members of the particular age-sex group. Second, writing the index as

$$M_t = \frac{1}{L_0} \sum_{i=1}^{n} \left(\frac{L_{0i}}{P_{0i}}\right) P_{1i},$$

we interpret it as the relative increase in the labor force that would have occurred because of the change in population if the base-period participation rates had remained unchanged.

The index i covers six age–sex groups—males and females separately for age groups 14 to 20, 20 to 65, and 65 and over. We used the 1947–1949 arithmetic average of reported participation rates taken from *Manpower Report of the President (op. cit.,* p. 202). The figures include the armed forces and institutional population. The population data are taken from current population reports [U.S. Department of Commerce, Bureau of the Census, *Current Population Reports,* C.3, Nos. 186, and P. 25, Nos. 98, 114, 310, 311, and 321 (U.S. Government Printing Office, Washington)], and these data include estimates of overseas military personnel. Prior to 1940 it was assumed that there were 150,000 overseas personnel; subsequent to that date the above sources included overseas personnel.

VARIABLES						R^{2a} and d
$\ln (NQ/y)_{t-1}$	$\ln (\hat{w}_t/w_{t-1})$	$\Delta \ln y_t$	U_{t-1}	$\ln Q_t$	$\ln (y/M)_t$	
						0.798 1.56
0.58 (0.11)[b]		−0.21 (0.04)[b]				0.993 1.84
	−0.41 (0.24)[e]		0.80 (0.05)[b]			0.925 1.50
1.24 (0.44)[b]		−1.22 (0.45)[b]		0.27 (0.55)	1.25 (0.44)[b]	0.997 2.26
−0.39 (0.44)		0.80 (0.45)		−1.02 (0.55)[e]	0.02 (0.44)	0.970 1.73

N = man-hours per year
M = population over 14 years of age with constant age–sex distribution
Q = index of labor quality as measured by years of school completed
U = fraction of the labor force unemployed
w = real compensation per man-hour
P = implicit GNP deflator
y = real GNP

The three predictions (29) on the marginal productivity condition (28) are confirmed at the 0.005 level. The fit on this equation is good, and there appears to be no evidence of serial correlation. The coefficient on $\Delta \ln y_t$ is also different from zero, indicating that one cannot add an additional [to (20)] restriction on the coefficients in this equation without a significant loss in explanatory power.

The five predictions (31) on the labor-supply function (30) are also all confirmed at the 0.005 level. The fit on this equation is reasonably good. There is some slight indication of positive serial correlation.

Estimates of the employment-rate function (32) are reported on line 3 of Table 1. Three of the four predictions (33), which are independent of any implications tested elsewhere, are confirmed at the 0.005 level; the fourth is confirmed at the 0.05 level. The estimated ratios $\hat{\beta}_{31}/\hat{\beta}_{32}$ and $\hat{\beta}_{21}/\hat{\beta}_{23}$, which are predicted to be equal in (34), are, respectively, 0.70 and 1.89. To get a rough idea of the significance of this difference, one may use the approximation

$$SE\left(\frac{\hat{\beta}_{31}}{\hat{\beta}_{32}}\right) \sim \frac{SE(\hat{\beta}_{31})}{\hat{\beta}_{32}},$$

where SE(·) denotes standard error, which is valid for large samples, and similarly for the standard error of $\hat{\beta}_{21}/\hat{\beta}_{23}$. This gives standard-error estimates of 0.41 and 0.69, respectively. Hence it seems unlikely that the observed difference is significant at the 0.05 level. Finally, $\hat{\beta}_{33}$ and $\hat{\beta}_{24}$, whose equality is also predicted in (34), are 0.80 and 0.64, respectively, with standard errors of 0.05 and 0.09, respectively. In summary, (32) is a satisfactory Phillips curve, and further, the predicted link between (32) and the rest of the model appears to be consistent with the data.

In reviewing these results, the reader should be aware, as we are, that the absence of small sample tests and the arbitrary nature of the choice of significance levels makes the test results less easy to interpret than our rather formal summary might suggest. Further, as discussed below, many variants of the basic model were also tested. Finally, many predictions of "our" theory are also predictions of virtually any plausible theory (for example, the prediction that unemployment rates are positively correlated with their own lagged values). But we wish to emphasize that the configuration of signs predicted by (29), (31), and (33) only is one of $(2)^6(3)^3 = 1728$ possible outcomes. The theory has thus provided us with an extremely sharp prediction on the way the variables examined are related, and these predicted relationships have been confirmed by the 1930–1965 data.

As as second, informal, way of evaluating our results as well as an aid in interpreting them, it will be useful to compare them with results of previous studies with which ours overlaps. First, from the estimated supply-function parameters, one may compute long- and short-run elasticities with respect to the real (or money) wage rate. The estimated long run elasticity is $(1 - \hat{\beta}_{24})^{-1}(\hat{\beta}_{21} - \hat{\beta}_{22}) = (1.40 - 1.39)/0.36 = 0.03$, or essentially zero. This finding indicates that the neoclassical growth-model assumption of a zero labor-supply elasticity is approximately correct. Further, the Keynesian-type assumption of a relatively elastic short run supply schedule is also confirmed, using the estimate $\hat{\beta}_{21} = 1.40$.

From the marginal productivity condition for labor, the statistic $(1 - \hat{\beta}_{12})^{-1}\hat{\beta}_{11} = 0.46/0.42 = 1.09$ is an estimate of the aggregate elasticity of substitution. This estimate is broadly consistent with the variety of cross-sectional estimates that are available, and generally higher than other time-series estimates.[29] Aggregation introduces increased possibilities for substitution in consumption between goods of

---

[29]Both the time-series and cross-section C.E.S. production function studies are summarized and discussed by Nerlove [M. Nerlove, "Notes on Recent Empirical Studies of the C.E.S. and Related Production Functions," Institute for Mathematical Studies in the Social Sciences, Stanford University, Stanford, Calif. (July 1965), *Tech. Rept. 13*]. Additional C.E.S. time-series production function estimates can be found in a study by Lucas (E. Lucas, Jr., *Substitution between Labor and Capital in U.S. Manufacturing, 1929–1958*, unpublished, University of Chicago Ph.D. dissertation, 1964).

different factor intensities, as well as substitution in production of each good, so this latter result is perhaps not surprising. The long run elasticity of employment with respect to output has been constrained in (28) to be unity. The short run elasticity has been left free to vary, however, and is estimated to be $1 - \hat{\beta}_{13} = 0.79$. In the sense that labor inputs appear to be quasi-fixed with respect to short run output changes, this finding is consistent with those of Kuh (*loc. cit.*), McGuire (*op. cit.*), and Wilson and Eckstein (*loc. cit.*) although since different variables are controlled for in each case, this fact provides little information.

The estimated reduced-form equation for the real wage rate provides a third point of contact with earlier studies.[30] The effect of inflation on real wages has been a subject of concern to economists for some time. This concern has been motivated by interest in the wage-lag doctrine, according to which real wages fall during inflationary periods. Hamilton, Hansen, and Mitchell, each studying a different historical period, all argued for the wage-lag hypothesis, and all these writers suggest that the wage-lag results from some form of "money illusion" or contract fixity.

Mitchell and later Lerner[31] both argued that the decline in real wages during the Civil War was a result of monetary inflation. Later Kessel and Alchian[32] reinterpreted the northern Civil War experience, arguing that real, not monetary, factors account for the decline in real wages between 1860 and 1865 (without, however, controlling simultaneously for real and monetary variables). Examining a different historical period, these writers[33] were again unable to uncover any evidence in support of the wage-lag hypothesis. For the post-World War II inflation, they examined profit rates in high-labor-cost industries relative to profit rates in low-labor-cost industries and they could not find a systematic difference in the behavior of profits in the two groups of industries.

[30]One should be cautious in interpreting this equation. In particular, although the coefficient of ln Q_t is apparently near zero, this should *not* be interpreted to mean that changes in labor quality do not affect real wages, because our real income variable already includes the secular wage effect of improvements in labor quality as well as other sources of technical change. For this reason, there is an important sense in which our model does not "explain" the secular growth in real wages. Similarly, note that the population variable, like the income variable, also affects real wage movements but is left unexplained in our model.

[31]E. M. Lerner, "Inflation in the Confederacy, 1961–65," in *Studies in the Quantity Theory of Money*, M. Friedman, ed. (University of Chicago Press, Chicago, 1956); E. J. Hamilton, "Prices and Progress," *Journal of Economic History*, 12 (Fall 1952) pp. 325–349; A. Hansen, "Factors Affecting the Trend in Real Wages," *American Economic Review*, 15 (March 1925) pp. 27–42; W. C. Mitchell, *A History of the Greenbacks* (Chicago, University of Chicago Press, 1903).

[32]R. A. Kessel and A. A. Alchian, "Real Wages in the North During the Civil War: Mitchell's Data Reconsidered," *Journal of Law and Economics*, 2 (October 1959), pp, 95–114.

[33]R. A. Kessel and A. A. Alchian, "The Meaning and Validity of the Inflation-Induced Lag of Wages Behind Prices," *American Economic Review*, 50 (March 1960), pp. 43–66.

Our empirical results are not consistent with these findings. For the period 1930–65, we find that the partial effect of inflation on real wages is negative and quantitatively significant. A 10 percent increase in prices will result in a 2.2 percent decline in real wages, and this result is based on a model that controls for real factors in the form of the variable, output per capita, (y_t/M_t).[34]

To this point, we have been concerned exclusively with a single model, which has been found to be consistent with the 1929–1965 data we used and, in a general way, consistent with several previous related empirical studies. As remarked at several points above, this model is but one variant of the class of models suggested by our theory. Other variants are obtained by adding different combinations of asset variables, nominal interest rates, and a dummy variable to control for wartime phenomena. In addition, models based on a different price-and-wage-expectations hypothesis were tested. These results are tabulated and discussed briefly in Appendix 2.

There are three important reasons for including these additional results. First, since our discussion of the tests in this section emphasizes the small probability that our predictions could have been confirmed "by chance," we are anxious to make clear that the predicted configuration of coefficient signs is confirmed in all the variants estimated. Second, our selection of the model reported in this section as the "best" of those estimated was made on informal and tenuous grounds. Finally, many coefficient estimates vary rather widely depending on which other variables are included, so that the standard errors reported in Table 1 overstate considerably the accuracy of these estimates.

7
SUMMARY
AND CONCLUSIONS

The aim of this study has been to construct and test an aggregative model of the U.S. labor market. On the demand side of this market, we employed a variant of the widely used marginal productivity condition based on a C.E.S. production function. The aggregate supply function tested was suggested by a Fisherian two-period model of a representative household. This theory views suppliers of labor as reacting primarily to three variables: an anticipated "normal" or "permanent" real wage rate, which corresponds to the wage rate in the usual one-period analysis of the labor-leisure choice and has a negligible effect

[34]Kessel and Alchian [R. A. Kessel and A. A. Alchian, "Effects of Inflation," *Journal of Political Economy*, 70 (December 1962), pp. 521–537] have argued that even when inflation is fully anticipated, real wages may still decline, *ceteris paribus*, because firms will shift to more capital-intensive processes, which reduces the demand for labor.

on labor supply; the deviation of the current real wage from this normal rate, which has a strong, positive effect on labor supply; and the deviation of the price level from its perceived "normal" trend, which also has a strong positive effect on labor supply.

This labor-supply theory has been shown to resolve two apparent contradictions in the economic theory of labor markets. First, as stesssed in the introduction and in Section 1, it is consistent both with the observed wage inelasticity of labor supply in the long run and with short run fluctuations in employment, which require an elastic labor supply. Second, by regarding the labor-supply choice as depending on a multiperiod decision problem, "money illusion," in the sense of a supply function that is *not* homogeneous of zero degree in *current* money wages and prices, is reconciled with rational behavior on the part of households.

As a corollary to the supply theory utilized in this paper, the survey-measured labor force (as used to compute unemployment rates) is viewed *not* as an effective market supply, part of which cannot find employment, but rather as the supply of labor that *would be forthcoming* at perceived normal wages and prices. Measured unemployment (more exactly, its nonfrictional component) is then viewed as consisting of persons who regard the wage rates at which they could currently be employed as temporarily low, and who therefore choose to wait or search for improved conditions rather than to invest in moving or occupational change. The view that nonfrictional unemployment is, in this sense, "voluntary" does not, of course, imply that high measured unemployment rates are socially costless. Rather, it implies that economic fluctuations are costly not simply because they induce idleness, but because they lead workers as well as capitalists to make investments (in moving, training, and so forth) on the basis of perceived rates of return that cannot in fact be sustained.

We conclude with a brief mention of two problems that we regard as central to an understanding of labor markets and which our study *cannot* be used to answer. One is tempted to use our estimated structural equations to study the dynamics of the labor-market response to changes in prices and output. As we have stressed at several points above, however, this question is illegitimate: Movements over time in labor market variables will be determined simultaneously with changes in other sectors. Thus, although we know that our model is consistent with a gradual approach to full employment equilibrium, we cannot say whether or not the speed of approach is consistent with the observed business cycle. Second, our model emphasizes the crucial role of expectations formation, while testing only the very crudest expectations model. We have used an adaptive scheme that will clearly hold only under reasonably stable rates of price increase. To define what is meant by reasonable stability, and to discover how expectations are revised when such stability ceases to obtain, seems to us to be a crucial, unresolved problem.

APPENDIX 1:
VARIABLES USED
IN REGRESSIONS[a]

	w	P	N	M	Q	y	U	r
1929	100.0	100.0	100.0	100.0	100.0	100.0	3.2	4.73
1930	102.0	97.4	93.5	102.0	100.7	90.1	8.9	4.55
1931	106.7	88.5	85.5	103.0	101.5	83.2	16.3	4.58
1932	108.4	79.4	75.6	104.0	102.4	70.8	24.1	5.01
1933	104.7	77.5	76.1	105.0	103.3	69.5	25.2	4.49
1934	109.1	83.4	76.8	106.0	104.1	75.8	22.0	4.00
1935	110.5	84.2	81.1	108.0	105.0	83.3	20.3	3.60
1936	112.3	84.4	89.3	109.0	105.9	94.8	17.0	3.24
1937	114.2	87.9	93.3	111.0	106.8	99.8	14.3	3.26
1938	117.8	86.8	86.7	111.0	107.7	94.7	19.1	3.19
1939	121.1	85.4	90.7	113.0	108.6	102.8	17.2	3.01
1940	122.2	86.8	94.5	114.0	109.6	111.6	14.6	2.84
1941	124.6	93.3	104.6	115.0	110.7	129.5	9.9	2.77
1942	128.4	104.7	116.2	117.0	111.8	146.3	4.7	2.83
1943	132.7	112.3	131.2	118.0	112.1	165.6	1.9	2.73
1944	139.4	115.0	134.1	119.0	114.0	177.5	1.2	2.72
1945	148.2	118.0	125.7	120.0	115.1	174.5	1.9	2.62
1946	149.7	131.8	109.7	121.0	116.3	153.5	3.9	2.53
1947	148.5	147.4	108.6	122.0	117.4	152.2	3.9	2.61
1948	150.6	157.3	109.5	123.0	118.6	159.0	3.8	2.82
1949	157.2	156.3	105.8	125.0	119.8	159.2	5.8	2.66
1950	172.7	158.5	107.8	124.0	121.0	174.5	5.3	2.62
1951	168.5	169.2	114.1	125.0	122.2	188.3	3.3	2.86
1952	174.4	172.9	116.1	126.0	123.4	194.1	3.1	2.96
1953	183.3	174.5	116.6	127.0	124.6	202.8	2.9	3.20
1954	187.5	177.1	112.1	128.0	125.8	199.9	5.6	2.90
1955	192.7	179.6	115.3	129.0	127.1	215.1	4.4	3.06
1956	197.7	185.8	117.0	131.0	128.3	219.1	4.2	3.36
1957	202.8	192.7	115.5	132.0	129.6	222.2	4.3	3.89
1958	205.2	197.6	112.3	133.0	130.8	219.7	6.8	3.79
1959	207.5	200.8	117.7	135.0	132.1	233.7	5.5	4.38
1960	212.5	204.2	118.8	138.0	133.4	239.5	5.6	4.41
1961	218.2	206.3	117.7	139.0	134.7	244.2	6.7	4.35
1962	221.9	209.1	121.6	142.0	135.9	260.2	5.6	4.33
1963	227.3	211.9	122.9	144.0	137.2	270.6	5.7	4.26
1964	234.4	215.2	125.5	146.0	138.4	284.9	5.2	4.40
1965	238.3	219.2	129.7	149.0	139.6	301.8	4.5	4.49

Key

w = real hourly compensation; annual compensation per full-time equivalent employee

APPENDIX 2:
ADDITIONAL RESULTS

As indicated in Section 6, several versions of the basic model have been tested. We refer to the model reported in Section 6 as model 1; models 2 through 9 are described below.

Our basic model omits interest rates, real nonhuman assets per family, and the wartime zero–one dummy variable from the supply equation. Given our expectations assumption, each variable must be introduced by using both the current and one-period lagged value. In models (2) through (4), each variable is introduced separately.

We have also experimented with an alternative expectations hypothesis. Models (5) through (8) are the same as models (1) through (4) except that anticipated real wages and prices are formed in the following simple ways:

$$\ln w_t^* = \lambda \ln w_t + (1 - \lambda) \ln w_{t-1} + \lambda', \tag{A1}$$

$$\ln P_t^* = \mu \ln P_t + (1 - \mu) \ln P_{t-1} + \mu', \tag{A2}$$

where $0 \leq \lambda \leq 1$ and $0 \leq \mu \leq 1$ and λ' and μ' are the expected trend rates of growth. Substituting (A1) and (A2) into the labor supply equation (11) we obtain a different equation from (15). In particular, except for w_{t-1} and P_{t-1}, there are no other lagged independent variables nor does the lagged dependent variable appear. With this formulation there remains considerable statistical evidence of serial correlation in the residuals as measured by the d statistic.

Model (9) is the same as model (1) except that a time variable is added to the first-order condition and both reduced forms. We interpret this variable as an index of technical change.

Space limitations prevent us from discussing each estimated model in as complete detail as we have done for model (1). However, tables similar to Table 1 of the text appear at the end of this appendix and each reader is free to tabulate or summarize those aspects of our results which he thinks are most relevant. We have chosen to summarize our statistical results by stressing the estimated short and long run elasticity of labor supply and the effect of inflation on the supply of labor. The relevant supply elasticities for all the models—(1) through (9)—are summarized in Table 2. We will also summarize the overall "goodness of fit" of our models by tabulating the number (and proportion) of statistically significant reduced-form estimates

---

divided by implicit GNP deflator and annual hours worked by full-time employees; index
P = implicit GNP deflator; index
N = employment; persons engaged times annual hours worked by full-time employees; index
M = population with fixed age–sex distribution; index
Q = labor quality; index
y = real GNP; index
U = percent of the labor force unemployed
r = Moody's Aaa bond rate

[a]All regression results reported in this paper are based on data series to more significant digits than those reported in this table. The data were rounded to make the table more readable.

as well as a separate tabulation for the structural estimates. This is done in Table 3.

When the Moody's Aaa interest rate and its lagged value are added to the supply equation [model (2)], the short and long run supply elasticity is practically unchanged as compared to that obtained in model (1). And since the estimated effect of inflation is also unchanged, it would appear that omitting the interest-rate variable does not seriously bias the remaining coefficient estimates. However, we do not attach special importance to this result because we have serious reservations concerning the meaning of the Aaa rate as an index of the rate relevant to households.

When the current and lagged interest rate variables are replaced by the current and lagged World War II dummy variable [model (3)], the results are broadly consistent with our supply theory. But there is an important difference between model (3) and model (1) in that the estimated short run real wage elasticity and the inflation elasticity estimates are smaller in model (3) than in model (1). While the point estimates are significantly different in an economic sense, they are not significantly different from each other at the 5 percent t-test level. The point estimates on the dummy coefficient indicate a quantitatively important wartime effect—the supply of labor rose by 12 percent because of the war. This may reflect a patriotism effect.

We have made no attempt to construct our own nonhuman household wealth series. Instead we have used three different, readily available series on nominal, nonhuman wealth and deflated these series by the implicit GNP deflator and by our population index to obtain (a_t/M_t) in (11). Model (4) is based on the Meltzer wealth series,[35] obtained directly from Professor Meltzer.[36] This series is for reproduceable wealth less government-reproduceable wealth plus government debt. This series covers the period 1930–1958, and therefore models (4) and (8) are based on only 29 observations. In model (4), the addition of nonhuman wealth per capita increases the estimated long run supply elasticity. However, this finding is based on a model in which the estimated asset coefficients are insignificantly different from zero in both the structural equations and the reduced forms.

Estimates of the real wage and inflation coefficients for models (5) through (8) are summarized in Table 2. On the whole, the assumption that only the present and recent past influence the formation of expectations generates larger estimates of short-run supply elasticities than were previously obtained.

Model (9) yields supply elasticities similar to model (1). An examination of the estimated first-order condition indicates that all the production-function conclusions are practically unchanged when a time variable is added.

In Table 3 we show the ratio of the number of significant reduced-form and structural coefficients to the total number estimated. In this summary we omit all the coefficients for which our theory does not predict the signs.

[35]Similar results were obtained with the Ando–Brown [A. Ando and E. C. Brown, "Lags in Fiscal Policy," in *Stabilization Policies* (Englewood Cliffs, N.J.: Prentice-Hall, 1964), p. 20] and Chow [G. C. Chow, "On the Long-Run and Short-Run Demand for Money," *Journal of Political Economy*, 74 (April 1966), pp. 111–132] series. Upon request, results using these series are available.

[36]A. H. Meltzer, "The Demand for Money: The Evidence from the Time Series," *Journal of Political Economy*, 71 (June 1963), pp. 219–247.

This includes the estimated coefficients for the intercept, the change in income variable, the labor-quality variable, and the time variable. The summary results in Table 3 suggest to us that among a broad class of models using the same general body of time-series data, "significant" results are almost always obtained. And, broadly speaking, conclusions concerning the effect of transitory and permanent wage changes as well as inflation on the supply of labor remain intact regardless of which model we use.

Table 2

SOME HIGHLIGHTS OF ESTIMATES FOR MODELS (1) THROUGH (9)

Model	Short-Run Labor-Supply Elasticity	Long-Run Labor-Supply Elasticity	Effect of Inflation on Labor-Supply	Variables Held Constant
1	1.40^b	0.03	0.74^b	$(N/M)_{t-1}$
2	1.35^b	0.03	0.70^b	$(N/M)_{t-1}, r_t, r_{t-1}$
3	0.78^b	0.12	0.49^b	$(N/M)_{t-1}, D_t, D_{t-1}$
4	1.12^c	1.58	0.68^b	$(N/M)_{t-1}, a_t/M_t, a_{t-1}/M_{t-1}$
5	3.93^b	0.03	1.14^b	
6	3.59^b	0.04	1.03^b	r_t
7	2.11^b	0.10	0.55^c	D_t
8	2.93^b	−0.07	1.04^b	a_t/M_t
9	1.13^c	0.01	0.72^b	$(N/M)_{t-1}$

[b]One-tail significance at 0.005 level.
[c]One-tail significance at 0.05 level.

Table 3

SUMMARY OF ESTIMATES FOR MODELS (1) THROUGH (9)

Model	Number of Significant Reduced-Form Estimates Compared to Total	Number of Significant Structural Estimates Compared to Total
1	6/10	9/9
2	5/14	9/11
3	5/14	10/11
4	1/14	8/11
5	5/8	7/7
6	7/10	7/8
7	6/10	8/8
8	3/10	7/8
9	6/10	9/9

Table 4

LABOR–MARKET MODEL (2) NOMINAL INTEREST RATE ADDED: REDUCED–FORM, SUPPLY, DEMAND, AND UNEMPLOYMENT–RATE ESTIMATES USING TWO–STAGE LEAST–SQUARES PROCEDURES

TIME SERIES 1930–1965

Equation and Dependent Variable	Constant	$\ln \hat{w}_t$	$\ln w_{t-1}$	$\Delta \ln P_t$	INDEPENDENT $\ln (N/M)_{t-1}$	$\ln (\hat{w}_t/Q_t)$
Supply: $\ln (N/M)_t$	4.06 $(1.01)^b$	1.35 $(0.57)^c$	−1.34 $(0.58)^c$	0.70 $(0.25)^b$	0.62 $(0.09)^b$	
First-order condition on labor: $\ln (NQ/y)_t$	−2.22 $(0.70)^b$					−0.46 $(0.12)^b$
Unemployment-rate function: U_t	0.042 $(0.01)^b$			−0.59 $(0.08)^b$		
Reduced-form wage: $\ln w_t$	−15.79 $(3.96)^b$		0.44 $(0.18)^c$	−0.22 $(0.08)^b$	−1.15 $(0.50)^c$	
Reduced-form employment: $\ln (N/M)_t$	9.29 $(3.79)^c$		0.06 (0.17)	0.11 (0.08)	0.65 (0.48)	

[a]All R^2 are adjusted for degrees of freedom.

[b]One-tail significance at 0.005 test level (except for intercepts, $\Delta \ln y_t$, time, and $\ln Q_t$, which are two-tailed tests).

[c]One-tail significance at 0.05 test level (except for intercepts, $\Delta \ln y_t$, time, and $\ln Q_t$, which are two-tailed tests).

VARIABLES								R^{2a} and d
$\ln\left(\dfrac{NQ}{y}\right)_{t-1}$	$\ln\left(\dfrac{\hat{w}_t}{w_{t-1}}\right)$	$\Delta \ln y_t$	U_{t-1}	$\ln Q_t$	r_t	$\ln\left(\dfrac{y}{M}\right)_t$	r_{t-1}	
					1.89 (4.06)		--2.55 (3.79)	0.79 1.52
0.58 (0.11)[b]		−0.21 (0.04)[b]						0.993 1.83
	−0.42 (0.24)[c]		0.80 (0.05)[b]					0.925 1.49
1.24 (0.50)[c]		−1.21 (0.51)[c]		0.29 (0.61)	0.22 (1.48)	1.25 (0.51)[c]	−0.22 (1.41)	0.997 2.24
−0.09 (0.48)		0.55 (0.48)		−1.21 (0.58)[c]	1.50 (1.42)	0.30 (0.48)	−0.69 (1.35)	0.976 2.05

Key

N = man-hours per year
M = population over 14 years of age with constant age–sex distribution
Q = index of labor quality as measured by years of school completed
U = fraction of the labor force unemployed
w = real compensation per man-hour (includes wages and fringes)
P = implicit GNP deflator
y = real GNP
r = nominal rate of interest as measured by Moody's Aaa rate

Table 5

LABOR–MARKET MODEL (3) WARTIME DUMMY ADDED: REDUCED–
FORM, SUPPLY, DEMAND, AND UNEMPLOYMENT–RATE ESTIMATES
USING TWO–STAGE LEAST–SQUARES PROCEDURES

TIME SERIES 1930–1965

Equation and Dependent Variable	Constant	$\ln \hat{w}_t$	$\ln w_{t-1}$	$\Delta \ln P_t$	$\ln (N/M)_{t-1}$	$\ln (\hat{w}_t/Q_t)$
					INDEPENDENT	
Supply: $\ln (N/M)_t$	4.62 (1.02)[b]	0.78 (0.42)[c]	−0.73 (0.42)[c]	0.49 (0.16)[b]	0.58 (0.09)[c]	
First-order condition on labor: $\ln (NQ/y)_t$	−2.15 (0.68)[b]					−0.47 (0.12)[b]
Unemployment-rate function: U_t	0.04 (0.01)[b]			−0.59 (0.08)[b]		
Reduced-form wage: $\ln w_t$	−15.97 (3.71)[b]		0.41 (0.18)[c]	−0.23 (0.07)[b]	−1.14 (0.47)[b]	
Reduced-form employment: $\ln (N/M)_t$	13.81 (3.47)[b]		0.06 (0.17)	0.04 (0.07)	0.68 (0.44)	

[a] All R^2 are adjusted for degrees of freedom.

[b] One-tail significance at 0.005 test level. See notes in Table 4.

[c] One-tail significance at 0.05 test level. See notes in Table 4.

VARIABLES $\ln\left(\frac{NQ}{y}\right)_{t-1}$	$\ln\left(\frac{\hat{w}_t}{w_{t-1}}\right)$	$\Delta \ln y_t$	U_{t-1}	$\ln Q_t$	D_t	$\ln\left(\frac{y}{M}\right)_t$	D_{t-1}	R^{2a} and d
					0.12 (0.03)[b]		−0.04 (0.04)	0.869 1.82
0.57 (0.11)[b]		−0.21 (0.04)[b]						0.993 1.86
	−0.43 (0.23)[c]	0.80 (0.05)[b]						0.926 1.49
1.23 (0.45)[c]		−1.18 (0.46)[c]		0.31 (0.57)	−0.02 (0.02)	1.26 (0.45)[b]	0.01 (0.02)	0.997 2.29
−0.36 (0.42)		0.61 (0.43)		−1.21 (0.53)[c]	0.02 (0.01)	0.14 (0.42)	0.01 (0.02)	0.979 1.90

Key

N = man-hours per year
M = population over 14 years of age with constant age–sex distribution
Q = index of labor quality as measured by years of school completed
U = fraction of the labor force unemployed
w = real compensation per man-hours, (includes wages and fringes)
P = implicit GNP deflator
y = real GNP
D = zero–one wartime dummy

Table 6

LABOR–MARKET MODEL (4): REAL NONHUMAN WEALTH ADDED:
REDUCED–FORM, SUPPLY, DEMAND, AND UNEMPLOYMENT–RATE
ESTIMATES USING TWO–STAGE LEAST–SQUARES PROCEDURES

TIME SERIES 1930–1958

Equation and Dependent Variable	Constant	$\ln \hat{w}_t$	$\ln w_{t-1}$	$\Delta \ln P_t$	$\ln (N/M)_{t-1}$	$\ln (\hat{w}_t/Q_t)$
						INDEPENDENT
Supply: $\ln (N/M)_t$	5.05 (1.28)	1.12 (0.56)[c]	−0.71 (0.57)	0.68 (0.19)[b]	0.74 (0.10)[b]	
First-order condition on labor: $\ln (NQ/y)_t$	−2.19 (0.73)[b]					−0.50 (0.13)[b]
Unemployment-rate function: U_t	0.05 (0.01)[b]			−0.62 (0.09)[b]		
Reduced-form wage: $\ln w_t$	−17.58 (4.94)[b]	0.31 (0.23)	−0.26 (0.09)[b]	−0.98 (0.68)		
Reduced-form employment: $\ln (N/M)_t$	13.53 (4.79)[b]	0.21 (0.22)	0.12 (0.08)	0.59 (0.66)		

[a]All R^2 are adjusted for degrees of freedom.

[b]One-tail significance at 0.005 test level. See notes in Table 4.

[c]One-tail significance at 0.05 test level. See notes in Table 4.

$\ln\left(\dfrac{NQ}{y}\right)_{t-1}$	$\ln\left(\dfrac{\hat{w}_t}{w_{t-1}}\right)$	$\Delta \ln y_t$	U_{t-1}	$\ln Q_t$	$\left(\dfrac{a}{M}\right)_t$	$\ln\left(\dfrac{y}{M}\right)_t$	$\left(\dfrac{a}{M}\right)_{t-1}$	R^{2a} and d
					−0.12 (0.32)		−0.31 (0.24)	0.815 1.51
0.56 (0.12)[b]		−0.21 (0.04)[b]						0.989 1.94
	−0.55 (0.24)[c]		0.76 (0.06)[b]					0.935 1.57
1.12 (0.72)		−1.01 (0.69)		0.73 (0.88)	0.02 (0.14)	1.07 (0.69)	0.07 (0.11)	0.994 2.26
−0.16 (0.70)		0.46 (0.66)		−1.65 (0.85)	−0.01 (0.13)	0.34 (0.67)	−0.09 (0.11)	0.977 1.77

Key

N = man-hours per year
M = population over 14 years of age with constant age–sex distribution
Q = index of labor quality as measured by years of school completed
U = fraction of the labor force unemployed
w = real compensation per man-hour (includes wages and fringes)
P = implicit GNP deflator
y = real GNP
a/M = real nonhuman wealth per household (Meltzer's series)

Table 7

LABOR–MARKET MODEL (5): ALTERNATIVE ANTICIPATIONS ASSUMPTION: REDUCED–FORM, SUPPLY, DEMAND, AND UNEMPLOYMENT–RATE ESTIMATES USING TWO–STAGE LEAST–SQUARES PROCEDURES

TIME SERIES 1930–1965

Equation and Dependent Variable	Constant	$\ln \hat{w}_t$	$\ln w_{t-1}$	$\Delta \ln P_t$	$\ln (N/M)_{t-1}$	$\ln (\hat{w}_t/Q_t)$
						INDEPENDENT
Supply: $\ln (N/M)_t$	10.59 (0.14)[b]	3.93 (0.72)[b]	−3.90 (0.72)[b]	1.14 (0.25)[b]		
First-order condition on labor: $\ln (NQ/y)_t$	−2.38 (0.76)[b]					−0.42 (0.13)[b]
Unemployment-rate function: U_t	0.17 (0.02)[b]			−0.98 (0.23)[b]		
Reduced-form wage: $\ln w_t$	−10.84 (3.23)[b]		0.54 (0.19)[b]	−0.22 (0.08)[b]		
Reduced-form employment: $\ln (N/M)_t$	7.83 (3.11)[c]		0.00 (0.18)	0.06 (0.07)		

[a]All R^2 are adjusted for degrees of freedom.

[b]One-tail significance at 0.005 test level.

[c]One-tail significance at 0.05 test level.

VARIABLES $\ln\left(\dfrac{NQ}{y}\right)_{t-1}$	$\ln(\hat{w}_t/w_{t-1})$	$\Delta \ln y_t$	$\ln Q_t$	$\ln (y/M)_t$	R^{2a} and d
					0.550 0.85
0.61 (0.13)[b]		−0.21 (0.04)[b]			0.992 1.87
	−2.21 (0.67)[b]				0.399 0.273
0.18 (0.18)		−0.07 (0.06)	1.26 (0.43)[b]	0.12 (0.04)[b]	0.996 2.22
0.43 (0.17)[e]		−0.09 (0.05)	−1.79 (0.42)[b]	0.91 (0.04)[b]	0.974 1.68

Key

N = man-hours per year
M = population over 14 years of age with constant age–sex distribution
Q = index of labor quality as measured by years of school completed
U = fraction of the labor force unemployed
w = real compensation per man-hours (includes wages and fringes)
P = implicit GNP deflator
y = real GNP

Table 8

LABOR–MARKET MODEL (6): NOMINAL INTEREST RATE ADDED: REDUCED–FORM, SUPPLY, DEMAND, AND UNEMPLOYMENT–RATE ESTIMATES USING TWO–STAGE LEAST–SQUARES PROCEDURES

TIME SERIES 1930–1965

						INDEPENDENT
Equation and Dependent Variable	*Constant*	$\ln \hat{w}_t$	$\ln w_{t-1}$	$\Delta \ln P_t$	$\ln (N/M)_{t-1}$	$\ln (\hat{w}_t/Q_t)$
Supply: $\ln (N/M)_t$	10.66 (0.22)[b]	3.59 (0.88)[b]	−3.55 (0.90)[b]	1.03 (0.38)[b]		
First-order condition on labor: $\ln (NQ/y)_t$	−2.25 (0.74)[b]					−0.45 (0.13)[b]
Unemployment-rate function: U_t	0.17 (0.02)[b]			−0.98 (0.23)[b]		
Reduced-form wage: $\ln w_t$	−10.34 (3.28)[b]		0.54 (0.19)[b]	−0.25 (0.08)[b]		
Reduced-form employment: $\ln (N/M)_t$	6.76 (2.98)[c]		0.002 (0.17)[c]	0.13 (0.08)		

[a]All R^2 are adjusted for degrees of freedom.

[b]One-tail significance at 0.005 test level.

[c]One-tail significance at 0.05 test level.

VARIABLES $\ln\left(\dfrac{NQ}{y}\right)_{t-1}$	$\ln\left(\dfrac{\hat{w}_t}{w_{t-1}}\right)$	$\Delta \ln y_t$	$\ln Q_t$	$\ln\left(\dfrac{y}{M}\right)_t$	r_t	R^{2a} and d
					−0.90 (2.47)	0.517 0.79
0.59 (0.12)[b]		−0.21 (0.04)[b]				0.992 1.96
	−2.21 (0.65)[b]					0.405 0.27
0.16 (0.18)		−0.07 (0.06)	1.27 (0.43)[e]	0.11 (0.05)[e]	−0.52 (0.58)	0.996 2.36
0.50 (0.16)[b]		−0.09 (0.05)	−1.82 (0.39)[b]	0.95 (0.04)[b]	1.12 (0.53)[b]	0.970 2.08

Key

N = man-hours per year
M = population over 14 years of age with constant age–sex distribution
Q = index of labor quality as measured by years of school completed
U = fraction of the labor force unemployed
w = real compensation per man-hour (includes wages and fringes)
P = implicit GNP deflator
y = real GNP
r = market rate of interest as measured by Moody's Aaa rate

Table 9

LABOR–MARKET MODEL (7): WARTIME DUMMY VARIABLE ADDED:
REDUCED–FORM, SUPPLY, DEMAND, AND UNEMPLOYMENT–RATE
ESTIMATES USING TWO–STAGE LEAST–SQUARES PROCEDURES

TIME SERIES 1930–1965

Equation and Dependent Variable	Constant	$\ln \hat{w}_t$	$\ln w_{t-1}$	$\Delta \ln P_t$	INDEPENDENT $\ln (N/M)_{t-1}$	$\ln (\hat{w}_t/Q_t)$
Supply: $\ln (N/M)_t$	10.84 (0.12)[b]	2.11 (0.66)[b]	−2.01 (0.67)[b]	0.55 (0.24)[c]		
First-order condition on labor: $\ln (NQ/y)_t$	−2.20 (0.73)[b]					−0.46 (0.13)[c]
Unemployment-rate function: U_t	0.17 (0.02)[b]				−0.98 (0.22)[b]	
Reduced-form wage: $\ln w_t$	−12.34 (3.38)[b]			0.52 (0.18)[b]	−0.22 (0.07)[b]	
Reduced-form employment: $\ln (N/M)_t$	10.24 (3.07)[b]			0.03 (0.17)	0.07 (0.07)	

[a]All R^2 are adjusted for degrees of freedom.
[b]One-tail significance at 0.005 test level.
[c]One-tail significance at 0.05 test level.

VARIABLES $\ln\left(\frac{NQ}{y}\right)_{t-1}$	$\ln\left(\frac{\hat{w}_t}{w_{t-1}}\right)$	$\Delta \ln y_t$	$\ln Q_t$	$\ln\left(\frac{y}{M}\right)_t$	D_t	R^{2a} and d
					0.16 (0.03)[b]	0.704 0.88
0.58 (0.12)[b]		−0.21 (0.04)[b]				0.993 1.92
	−2.23 (0.64)[b]					0.414 0.308
0.26 (0.18)		−0.07 (0.05)	1.27 (0.43)[b]	0.17 (0.06)[b]	−0.02 (0.01)	0.996 2.28
0.31 (0.17)[c]		−0.10 (0.05)[c]	−1.81 (0.39)[b]	0.82 (0.05)[b]	0.03 (0.01)[c]	0.977 1.91

Key

N = man-hours per year
M = population over 14 years of age with constant age–sex distribution
Q = index of labor quality as measured by years of school completed
U = fraction of the labor force unemployed
w = real compensation per man-hour (includes wages and fringes)
P = implicit GNP deflator
y = real GNP
D = zero–one wartime dummy

Table 10

LABOR–MARKET MODEL (8): REAL NONHUMAN ASSETS ADDED: REDUCED–FORM, SUPPLY, DEMAND, AND UNEMPLOYMENT–RATE ESTIMATES USING TWO–STAGE LEAST–SQUARES PROCEDURES

TIME SERIES 1930–1958

Equation and Dependent Variable	Constant	$\ln \hat{w}_t$	$\ln w_{t-1}$	$\Delta \ln P_t$	$\ln (\hat{w}_t/Q_t)$
					INDEPENDENT
Supply: $\ln (N/M)_t$	9.98 (1.95)[b]	2.93 (0.90)[b]	−3.00 (0.87)[b]	1.04 (0.33)[b]	
First-order condition on labor: $\ln (NQ/y)_t$	−2.22 (0.75)[b]				−0.49 (0.13)[b]
Unemployment-rate function: U_t	0.18 (0.02)[b]			−1.02 (0.23)[b]	
Reduced-form wage: $\ln w_t$	−13.17 (3.55)[b]		0.28 (0.22)	−0.26 (0.08)[b]	
Reduced-form employment: $\ln (N/M)_t$	10.14 (3.36)[b]		0.25 (0.21)	0.10 (0.08)	

[a]All R^2 are adjusted for degrees of freedom.

[b]One-tail significance at 0.005 test level.

[c]One-tail significance at 0.05 test level.

VARIABLES $\ln\left(\dfrac{NQ}{y}\right)_{t-1}$	$\ln\left(\dfrac{\hat{w}_t}{w_{t-1}}\right)$	$\Delta \ln y_t$	$\ln Q_t$	$\left(\dfrac{a}{M}\right)_t$	$\ln\left(\dfrac{y}{M}\right)_t$	R^2 and d
				0.13 (0.35)		0.422 0.79
0.56 (0.12)[b]		−0.21 (0.04)[b]				0.989 2.08
	−2.24 (0.61)[b]					0.487 0.52
0.13 (0.19)		−0.03 (0.06)	1.75 (0.51)[b]	0.12 (0.08)	0.08 (0.05)	0.994 2.37
0.49 (0.18)[c]		−0.13 (0.06)[c]	−2.28 (0.49)[b]	−0.11 (0.07)	0.95 (0.05)[b]	0.978 2.01

Key

N = man-hours per year
M = population over 14 years of age with constant age–sex distribution
Q = index of labor quality as measured by years of school completed
U = fraction of the labor force unemployed
w = real compensation per man-hour (includes wages and fringes)
P = implicit GNP deflator
y = real GNP
a/M = real nonhuman wealth per household (Meltzer's series)

Table 11

LABOR–MARKET MODEL (9): TIME ADDED: REDUCED FORM, SUPPLY, DEMAND, AND UNEMPLOYMENT–RATE ESTIMATES USING TWO-STAGE LEAST–SQUARES PROCEDURES

TIME SERIES 1930–1965

Equation and Dependent Variable	*Constant*	$\ln \hat{w}_t$	$\ln w_{t-1}$	$\Delta \ln P_t$	$\ln (N/M)_{t-1}$	$\ln (\hat{w}_t/Q_t)$
Supply: $\ln (N/M)_t$	3.58 (0.95)[b]	1.13 (0.49)[c]	−1.12 (0.49)[c]	0.72 (0.18)[b]	0.66 (0.09)[b]	
First-order condition on labor: $\ln (NQ/y)_t$	−1.52 (1.56)					−0.43 (0.18)[c]
Unemployment-rate function: U_t	0.04 (0.01)[b]			−0.38 (0.22)[c]		
Reduced-form wage: $\ln w_t$	−33.46 (8.54)[b]		0.36 (0.17)[c]	−0.16 (0.07)[c]	−1.41 (0.44)[b]	
Reduced-form employment: $\ln (N/M)_t$	27.27 (8.72)[b]		0.15 (0.17)	0.01 (0.07)	1.13 (0.44)[c]	

[a] All R^2 are adjusted for degrees of freedom.
[b] One-tail significance at 0.005 test level.
[c] One-tail significance at 0.05 test level.

VARIABLES							R^{2a} and d
$\ln\left(\dfrac{NQ}{y}\right)_{t-1}$	$\ln\left(\dfrac{\hat{w}_t}{w_{t-1}}\right)$	$\Delta \ln y_t$	U_{t-1}	$\ln Q_t$	$\ln\left(\dfrac{y}{M}\right)_t$	t	
							0.785 1.50
0.55 (0.11)[b]		−0.20 (0.05)[b]				0.00 (0.00)	0.993 1.69
	−0.81 (0.05)[b]		0.58 (0.08)[b]				0.924 1.47
1.57 (0.44)[b]		−1.46 (0.43)[b]		3.29 (1.43)[e]	1.55 (0.43)[b]	−0.03 (0.01)[e]	0.997 2.39
−0.68 (0.44)		1.02 (0.44)[e]		−3.67 (1.46)[e]	−0.24 (0.44)	0.03 (0.01)[e]	0.978 1.64

Key

N = man-hours per year
M = population over 14 years of age with constant age–sex distribution
Q = index of labor quality as measured by years of school completed
U = fraction of the labor force unemployed
w = real compensation per man-hour (includes wages and fringes)
P = implicit GNP deflator
y = real GNP
t = time

II

Output and Price Dynamics

Optimal Price Policy
under Atomistic Competition

EDMUND S. PHELPS and
SIDNEY G. WINTER, JR.*

The world of perfect markets is at least as far removed from economic reality as the world of frictionless planes, pulleys, and pendulums is from physical reality. For neither body of theory does "unrealism" imply "irrelevance." Drastically simplifying assumptions permit a clear theoretical understanding of some of the significant aspects of all real situations and virtually all the significant aspects of a few real situations. But many of the gross features of everyday economic reality are simply not explicable, even approximately, by theories that exclude friction. The existence of spare capacity, "good will" and "pure profit," advertising, and markup behavior are a few examples. A key friction, one that helps to account for these real features, is this: In the frictionless world, a small price decrease by a firm will immediately call forth an arbitrarily large increase of quantity demanded—though the usual means of transportation will not get the customers to the store. In the world as it is, a price decrease of a penny will not instantly attract a large crowd of buyers even if shoe leather and rubber tires reliably perform their functions.

Economists have until recently done little systematic theorizing about the causes and consequences of friction. The present paper is a

*Our thanks to H. Uzawa, who, anticipating our own intention to analyze the constant-cost case of Section 2.E, actually carried out and supplied some of the necessary calculations.

contribution to the expanding theoretical literature that seeks to remedy this situation.[1] Our focus is on the problem of optimal price-making behavior for a firm which enjoys, at each instant of time, monopoly power with respect to its current customers, yet which could not indefinitely maintain a price above the going market price without losing all its customers. This feature of noninstantaneous customer response to price changes is the sole element of economic friction that we admit into the theory. Among the many phenomena not treated here, but calling for inclusion in a fully general analysis, is the input market analog of our assumption of noninstantaneous demand response.[2] Clearly, the path to a general analysis is long and difficult, especially so if it proceeds by explicit attention to the various costs of information acquisition, decision-making, and transacting that presumably are the ultimate sources of economic frictions.

Little more than a suggestion is provided as to the rationale for the particular pattern of noninstantaneous customer response investigated here. From one standpoint, this is a limitation; one would prefer to relate the firm's view of how customers behave to a fully elaborated theory of customer behavior. But it may also be argued that quite different causal mechanisms could give rise to patterns of behavior that were indistinguishable from the firm's point of view. Furthermore, a complex and analytically intractable combination of such considerations as information imperfections, habits, past investment decisions, etc., might produce results adequately approximated by relatively simple patterns.

Although our departure from the familiar Walrasian ground of perfect markets would appear to be minor, the theoretical terrain we discover is surprisingly exotic. For example, we encounter the possibility of price-making behavior that would result in the firm's choosing to pay a higher real wage in terms of its product, and at the same time increasing its output—a result that offers a possible resolution of a longstanding paradox in the microeconomic foundations of Keynesian theory. For another example, we find that even in stationary-state equilibrium there will not generally be equality between marginal cost and price; nor does the static monopoly analysis apply.

In Section 1 a model of gradual customer response to price differentials among firms is sketched out and related to the view of the situation

---

[1] By "economic friction" we mean the various considerations that make instantaneous adjustment either impossible or prohibitively costly. The literature we have in mind includes, for example, J. P. Gould, "Adjustment Cost in the Theory of Investment of the Firm," *Review of Economic Studies*, 35 (1968), pp. 47–55; R. E. Lucas, Jr., "Adjustment Costs and the Theory of Supply," *Journal of Political Economy*, 75 (1967), pp. 321–334, and most of the papers in the present volume.

[2] Mortensen's paper in the present volume analyzes a wage-determination problem closely corresponding to our price-determination problem. An analysis of the combination of the two problems remains to be done.

imputed to individual firms. In Section 2 the optimal price policy is developed, and subjected to local comparative static analysis. Section 3 offers a tentative analysis of the equilibration process for the industry as a whole, and Section 4 some concluding comments.

1
"CUSTOMER FLOW" DYNAMICS

Consider an industry consisting of a large number, m, of firms, serving a much larger number of identical customers. Let the proportion of the total number of customers buying from firm j be x_j, and assume that the number of customers is large enough so that it is a valid approximation to treat x_j as a continuous variable. Suppose further that if each firm in the industry posted price p, the quantity demanded from the industry as a whole would be $\eta(p; y)$, where y is a shift parameter that will be suppressed in the notation when it is not directly relevant. Customers buying from a particular firm are assumed to choose their purchase quantities according to the price quoted by that firm; thus, when firm j posts price p_j, it sells the quantity $x_j\eta(p_j)$.

Over time, customers gradually shift from the firms charging higher prices to those charging lower prices. The formulation of this dynamic process offered here is suggested by the thought that the process by which information about prices is transmitted is essentially one of "comparing notes" in the course of random encounters among customers.[3] Assuming that a shift of patronage occurs (at least with some probability) when a customer discovers that he is not getting the lowest possible price, one expects that the rate of customer flow between any two firms will be proportional to the product of their market shares (which determines the probability with which a particular comparison is made), and will be in favor of the firm with the lower price. Then z_{ij}, the time rate of net customer flow from firm j to firm i, is given by

$$z_{ij} = a_{ij}x_ix_j, \qquad a_{ij} \text{ independent of } x_i, x_j,$$

where

$$\text{sgn}(a_{ij}) = \text{sgn}(p_j - p_i).$$

Of course, $a_{ji} = -a_{ij}$ $(i, j = 1, \ldots, m)$, as is implied by the use of the term "net flow." Then the rate of change of firm i's proportion of the customers is given by

$$\dot{x}_i = \sum_j z_{ij} = x_i \sum_j a_{ij}x_j.$$

[3]However, as noted in the introductory remarks, this is not the only possible rationale for the model.

Suppose that k distinct prices are posted, $k \leq m$. Assume for the moment that firm numbers (i) are assigned in a way corresponding to the ordering of the prices: $i \leq i'$ implies $p_i \leq p_{i'}$ for ($i, i' = 1, \ldots, m$). Let the firms with the lowest prices be numbered from 1 to n_1, those with the next lowest from $n_1 + 1$ to $n_1 + n_2$, etc. To verify that if prices are held constant, the first n_1 firms eventually get all the customers, note that

$$\frac{d}{dt}(x_1 + \cdots + x_{n_1}) = \sum_{i \leq n_1} \sum_{j > n_1} (a_{ij} x_i x_j).$$

Let $c = \underset{\substack{(i \leq n_1) \\ (j > n_1)}}{\text{Min}} [a_{ij}]$, which is positive. Then

$$\frac{d}{dt}(x_1 + \cdots + x_{n_1}) \geq c \left(\sum_{i \leq n_1} x_i \right) \left(\sum_{j > n_1} x_j \right)$$

or

$$\frac{d}{dt} \left(\sum_{i \leq n_1} x_i \right) \geq c \left(\sum_{i \leq n_1} x_i \right) \left(1 - \left[\sum_{i \leq n_1} x_i \right] \right).$$

This says that, at any point in time, the proportion of the customers served by the firms with the lowest prices is going to one at least as fast as in a corresponding logistic process with parameter c.

In general, the coefficients a_{ij} may depend not only on the prices p_i and p_j but also directly on the indices i and j. Consistent with the spirit of the "random encounters among customers" rationale, it is possible to think of many reasons why firms in an industry might be "dynamically differentiated," i.e., why customer flow rates produced by given price discrepancies might depend on permanent characteristics of the firms. Location considerations are the most obvious. Within a broader view of the processes of transmission of price information and adjustment of buying patterns, even more reasons for such dynamic differentiation can be found, for example, advertising policies. However, problems of dynamic oligopolistic interdependence would enter the picture on the heels of the problems of dynamic differentiation. Our present analytical objectives are, necessarily, more limited.

Confining our attention to situations in which the discipline of the market is "impersonal" at every point of time, we now assume that

$$a_{ij} = \delta(p_i, p_j),$$

where $\delta(p, p') = -\delta(p', p)$, $\text{sgn} (\delta(p, p')) = \text{sgn} (p' - p)$, $\delta_1 < 0$, $\delta_2 > 0$. The equation for the change in firm i's proportion of the total customers may now be written

$$\dot{x}_i = x_i \sum_{j \neq i} \delta(p_i, p_j) x_j.$$

For each $j \neq i$, expand δ in Taylor's series with respect to its second argument, around the value $\bar{p}_i$. Neglecting terms of third and higher degree, we get

$$\dot{x}_i \cong x_i \sum [\delta(p_i, \bar{p}_i) + \delta_2(p_i, \bar{p}_i)(p_j - \bar{p}_i)$$
$$+ \tfrac{1}{2}\delta_{22}(p_i, \bar{p}_i)(p_j - \bar{p}_i)^2]x_j.$$

Since the summation extends over all $j \neq i$, we have $\sum x_j = 1 - x_i$. Define $\bar{p}_i$ as the customer-weighted mean of other firms' prices and σ_i^2 as the corresponding variance; i.e.,

$$\bar{p}_i = (1 - x_i)^{-1} \sum_{j \neq i} p_j x_j,$$

$$\sigma_i^2 = (1 - x_i)^{-1} \sum_{j \neq i} (p_j - \bar{p}_i)^2 x_j.$$

Then the approximation for $\dot{x}_i$ reads

$$\dot{x}_i \cong x_i(1 - x_i)[\delta(p_i, \bar{p}_i) + \tfrac{1}{2}\delta_{22}(p_i, \bar{p}_i)\sigma_i^2].$$

Thus the exclusion of dynamic differentiation yields a model in which the change in any given firm's proportion of the customers may be viewed as depending, at any particular point of time, on moments of the (customer-weighted) distribution of other firms' prices. Depending on the number of moments considered, the approximation involved could obviously be made as close as desired.[4]

Treating the equation above as an approximation to a supposed "objective" law by which customer flows are governed, we now assume that the individual firm chooses its price policy according to a subjectively perceived customer flow relationship that is still simpler. First, the firm attends only to its estimate of the (customer-weighted) mean price charged by other firms, disregarding variance. This neglect of variance will not involve a serious information loss if the variance is typically small or if the function δ is approximately linear. Second, we assume that competition is atomistic, in the sense that the individual firm views the industry demand as infinitely larger than its own demand. This implies that the product $x_i(1 - x_i)$ is treated simply as x_i.[5] From firm i's point of view, then,

$$\dot{x}_i = \delta(p_i, \bar{p}_i)x_i.$$

As the firm sees it, maintaining its price below the estimated industry mean price by a constant amount would result in a continuing exponential increase in its proportion of the customers. This cannot be true, given finite firms in a finite market. Similarly, in static competitive

---

[4] Assuming, of course, that δ possesses continuous derivatives of appropriately high order.
[5] It also implies that $\bar{p}_i$ is indistinguishable from $\bar{p}$, the mean price for the entire industry.

theory, it cannot be true that the demand curve facing an individual firm is horizontal. Under cost conditions consistent with competition, the invalidity of these subjective appraisals will never be clearly revealed.

2
OPTIMAL DYNAMIC
PRICE POLICY

A. The Present Value Maximization Problem   A firm that supposes itself to be operating under the regime just described must weigh short- and long-run considerations in determining its price policy. At one extreme, it could act like a monopolist toward its present customers—but in time they would drift away, and a sustained period of pricing below market would be required to build the business up again. At the other extreme, it might seek to move as quickly as possible to the competitive solution, i.e., to the output that would equate its marginal cost to the estimated prevailing industry price $\bar{p}$. This would require, of course, a short period of low or high prices to adjust its proportion of the total customers to the desired level. Neither of these policies, of course, is likely to be optimal.

By "optimal" we shall mean "present-value maximizing" under a constant instantaneous interest rate, $r > 0$. Let the firm's total variable cost function be $\phi(v; w)$, where v is output and w represents input price (or prices).[6] Quoting price p when its proportion of the total customers is x, the firm will receive revenue at the rate $px\eta(p)$ and incur costs at the rate $\phi(x\eta(p))$. The case explored here is that in which the firm displays static expectations of $\bar{p}$; i.e., its estimated industry mean price $\bar{p}$ is not expected to change over the future. Hence the present value maximization problem faced by the firm as of time zero is: Maximize

$$V = \int_0^\infty e^{-rt}[px\eta(p) - \phi(x\eta(p))]\, dt \tag{1a}$$

subject to

$$\dot{x} = \delta(p; \bar{p})x \tag{1b}$$

and

$$x(0) = x_0, \tag{1c}$$

where x_0 is the firm's initial proportion of the total customers. The object of choice is, of course, the price to be quoted at each point of time. Attention will be confined to piecewise continuous price policies $p(t)$.

The following stipulations are made concerning the various functions involved. The demand function $\eta(p)$ is defined (finite) for every

---

[6]The parameter w plays no role in this subsection and will be suppressed in the notation.

positive p, downward sloping, with downward-sloping marginal revenue (in terms of quantity), and convex to the origin. Also, as price becomes arbitrarily large, quantity demanded approaches zero. Mathematically, these assumptions are

$$\eta'(p) < 0, \quad 0 \le \eta''(p) \le \frac{2\eta'^2}{\eta}, \quad \operatorname*{Inf}_{p} \eta(p) = 0. \qquad (2a)$$

As for the cost function, marginal cost is positive (except possibly at zero output) and increasing. (We disregard fixed costs, assuming that the firm has no way whatsoever of escaping them.)

$$\phi(0) = 0, \quad \phi'(v) > 0 \text{ for } v > 0, \quad \phi''(v) > 0. \qquad (2b)$$

The properties of the function δ have already been described, except for the following: Marginal returns to price concessions are nonincreasing, in the sense that successive price reductions of equal amount yield a nonincreasing sequence of increments to the exponential growth rate of the number of customers. Consistent with this assumption, a price of zero would always produce only a finite positive growth rate, but there could be a finite price high enough to drive all the customers away instantaneously, i.e., a price $p^* > \bar{p}$ such that

$$\lim_{p \to p^{*-}} \delta(p; \bar{p}) = -\infty.$$

Since $\bar{p}$ is a constant parameter for the purposes of the dynamic optimization, its appearance in function δ will be suppressed in this subsection. The assumptions made imply the following conditions on the function $\delta(p)$:

$$\delta(\bar{p}) = 0, \quad \delta'(p) < 0, \quad \delta''(p) \le 0. \qquad (2c)$$

The combination of regularity assumptions (2) is stronger than is ever needed in the sequel. For expositional purposes it seems desirable to make the stronger assumptions rather than complicate the argument to achieve a small increase in generality.

B. Necessary Conditions Problem (1) is amenable to treatment by the methods of the theory of optimal control of dynamic systems.[7] The firm's price, p, is the *control variable*, its proportion x of the total customers is the *state variable*, and the maximand V in (1a) is a functional depending on $p(t)$, the time path of p from 0 to infinity. Each choice of a

[7]The standard reference is L. S. Pontryagin et al., *The Mathematical Theory of Optimal Processes* (Wiley-Interscience, New York, 1962). The formulation of the theory that is invoked here is lucidly expounded by K. J. Arrow in "Applications of Control Theory to Economic Growth," in *Mathematics of the Decision Sciences*, Part II (American Mathematical Society, Providence, R. I., 1969).

function $p(t)$ produces, via differential equation (1b) with initial condition (1c), a time path $x(t)$; to the pair $p(t)$, $x(t)$, the integral in (1a) assigns a present value. The problem is to assure the existence of, and characterize, a $p(t)$ that gives the maximum present value.

Necessary conditions for an optimum, as formulated in control theory, involve an auxiliary function of time here designated as $q(t)$. In the present context, this variable is essentially a nonnegative shadow price for customers as of time t. More precisely, with $x(t)$ denoting the firm's proportion of the total customers at time t, $q(t)x(t)$ represents the imputed value of that patronage—a value whose economic rationale is that the patronage costs something to acquire (through temporary price concessions) and can be reconverted to cash (through price increases).

It is notationally convenient to define the following functions:

$$F(x, p) = px\eta(p) - \phi(x\eta(p)),$$
$$G(x, p) = \delta(p)x,$$
$$H(x, p, q) = F(x, p) + qG(x, p).$$

Then the problem posed may be rewritten: Maximize

$$V = \int_0^\infty e^{-rt}F(x, p)\, dt \tag{1a$'$}$$

subject to

$$\dot{x} = G(x, p) \tag{1b$'$}$$

and

$$x(0) = x_0. \tag{1c$'$}$$

Pontryagin-type necessary conditions are[8]: If $\hat{p}(t)$ is an optimal time path of the firm's price, then there exists a function of time, $\hat{q}(t)$, defined for $t \geq 0$, such that for each $t \geq 0$,

$$\hat{p}(t) \text{ maximizes } H(\hat{x}(t), p, \hat{q}(t)) \text{ with respect to } p, \tag{3a}$$

$\hat{q}(t)$ satisfies the differential equation

$$\dot{\hat{q}} = r\hat{q} - \frac{\partial}{\partial x}[H(\hat{x}(t), \hat{p}(t), \hat{q}(t)]. \tag{3b}$$

Here, of course, the function $\hat{x}(t)$ satisfies the differential equation

$$\dot{\hat{x}} = G(\hat{x}(t), \hat{p}(t)) \tag{3c}$$

with initial condition $x(0) = x_0$.

[8]See Arrow, *op. cit.*, Proposition 6.

If the maximum in (3a) occurs at a $p > 0$, we must have

$$H_p(\hat{x}(t), \hat{p}(t), \hat{q}(t)) = 0,$$

identically in t. Translating this condition, (3b), and (1b') back into the original notation, we have the following equations that must be satisfied by an optimal triple $x(t)$, $p(t)$, $q(t)$:

$$\eta'x\left[p + \frac{\eta}{\eta'} - \phi'\right] + q\,\delta'x = 0, \tag{4a}$$

$$\dot{q} = rq - [\eta(p - \phi') + q\delta], \tag{4b}$$

$$\dot{x} = \delta x. \tag{4c}$$

Equation (4a) may be regarded as implicitly determining p as a function of q and x. The expression in brackets is marginal revenue minus marginal cost for the monopoly problem with x treated as constant. If $q = 0$, the equation calls for the monopoly solution, just as the interpretation of q as the shadow price of patronage leads us to expect. If $q > 0$, a p that solves (4a) implies marginal revenue less than marginal cost:

$$p + \frac{\eta}{\eta'} - \phi' = -q\frac{\delta'}{\eta'} < 0 \qquad \text{for } q > 0.$$

The firm sacrifices some current monopoly gain by offering a low price in the interest of keeping its customers.

It is henceforth assumed that industry marginal revenue at a sufficiently high price exceeds $\phi'(0)$, so that the monopoly solution always exists. Given the conditions (2), the monopoly price is an upper bound on the price that would ever be charged under an optimal policy, assuming $q \geqq 0$. For under the conditions imposed on η and ϕ,

$$\frac{d}{dp}\left[p + \frac{\eta}{\eta'} - \phi'\right] = 2 - \frac{\eta\eta''}{\eta'^2} - x\eta'\phi'',$$

which is positive under assumption (2). Thus the excess of marginal revenue over marginal cost is monotone increasing in p. Since $\eta(p)$ is defined for all positive p, there clearly is a p sufficiently small that marginal revenue is less than marginal cost, and it has just been assumed that there is a p sufficiently large that marginal revenue exceeds marginal cost. Hence there is a unique p, the monopoly price, at which the two are equal. Only a smaller value of p results in marginal revenue less than marginal cost.

Now consider an arbitrary piecewise continuous policy $p(t)$, disregard (4b), and treat (4a) as defining $q(t)$. If at any time the implied $q(t)$ is negative, then $p(t)$ exceeds the monopoly price; by the piecewise continuity assumption, this is true over a finite time interval. A policy $p^*(t)$ superior to $p(t)$ may then be developed as follows: Starting at a time t^* internal to the interval in which $p(t)$ exceeds the monopoly price, let $p^*(t)$ be the monopoly price, i.e., the solution to

$$p^* + \frac{\eta(p^*)}{\eta'(p^*)} - \phi'(x^*\eta(p^*)) = 0,$$

where $x^*(t)$ satisfies (4c) under policy $p^*(t)$. Since the monopoly price is by definition profit maximizing at each given x, and $x^*(t)$ departs only gradually from $x(t)$, it is clear that the revised policy yields a larger value of the integrand in (1a'), at least over a short interval t^* to $t^* + \Delta$. At time $t^* + \Delta$, $x^*(t) > x(t)$. Beginning at $t^* + \Delta$, choose $p^*(t)$ to maintain the quantity sold equal to $x(t)\eta(p(t))$:

$$x^*(t)\eta(p^*(t)) = x(t)\eta(p(t)),$$

[where $x^*(t)$ continues to be governed by differential equation (4c)]. This is always possible, by virtue of assumptions (2a), and it is clear that $p^*(t) > p(t)$ as long as $x^*(t) > x(t)$. If at a subsequent time $t^* + \Delta + \Delta'$, $x^*(t) = x(t)$, then choose $p^*(t) = p(t)$ from that time on. Over a period of length Δ', the quantity sold under the revised policy is the same as under the original policy, but the price is higher. Hence the integrand for the revised policy is the same as under the original policy before t^* and after $t^* + \Delta + \Delta'$, and it is larger in between. This shows, "constructively," that a policy $p(t)$ implying a negative $q(t)$ cannot be optimal. Hence, invoking the conclusion of the previous paragraph, optimal price $\hat{p}(t)$ is never higher than the monopoly price that would be myopically optimal given $\hat{x}(t)$.

Since time does not enter explicitly in the functions $F(x, p)$ and $G(x, p)$, an optimal policy $\hat{p}(t)$ for problem (1') actually depends on time only through $\hat{x}(t)$. That is, assuming there exists a unique $\hat{p}(t)$ solving (1'), there is some function $\psi(x)$ such that

$$\hat{p}(t) = \psi(\hat{x}(t))$$

characterizes not only the solution to the problem (1'), but also the solutions to all variants of (1') that are obtained by (a) changing the starting time from 0 to an arbitrary t_0, or (b) changing the initial condition on x.

Given that this is true of $\hat{p}(t)$, it is clear from (4a) that it is also true of $\hat{q}(t)$. There is a function $\pi(x)$ such that

$$\hat{q}(t) = \pi(\hat{x}(t)).$$

Hence $\dot{\hat{q}} = \pi'(x)\dot{\hat{x}}$, and, when $\dot{x} \neq 0$, $\pi'(x) = \dot{\hat{q}}/\dot{x}$. Dividing equation

(4b) by (4c), we obtain a differential equation satisfied by the unknown function $\pi(x)$; wherever $\dot{x} \neq 0$,

$$\pi'(x) = \frac{dq}{dx} = \frac{rq - \eta(p - \phi') - q\delta}{\delta x}. \tag{5}$$

With (4a) employed to determine the p associated with any (x, q) pair, the right-hand side of (5) is a determined function of (x, q) everywhere except where the (x, q) pair implies a price of $\bar{p}$.

The argument establishing the existence of an optimal policy $\psi(x)$ may now be outlined. Differential equation (5) is shown to have a particular solution that passes through the rest point for the system (4), i.e., the point (x, q) at which $\dot{x} = \dot{q} = 0$. This determines $\psi(x)$ by way of (4a). A solution to the dynamic system (4) is thus determined, in which $x(t)$, $q(t)$ tends to the rest point $(\bar{x}, \bar{q})$, and $p(t)$ tends to $\bar{p}$. A theorem of Arrow, involving an appropriate concavity condition on $H(x, p, q)$, is invoked to show that such a solution is, in fact, optimal.

C. **Phase Diagram Analysis**   Figure 1 illustrates the behavior of the system (4) and the related differential equation (5). The curve $\dot{x} = 0$ is the locus of (x, q) points for which the value of p implied by (4a) is $\bar{p}$, i.e., the locus defined by

$$H_p(x, \bar{p}, q) = 0. \tag{6}$$

Determining the slope of the locus by differentiating (6), we find

$$\left. \frac{dq}{dx} \right|_{p=\bar{p}} = -\frac{H_{px}}{H_{pq}}, \tag{7}$$

where

$$H_{px} = F_{px} + qG_{px} = \eta'\left[p + \frac{\eta}{\eta'} - \phi' - x\eta\phi'' \right] + q\delta'$$

$$= \frac{H_p}{x} - \eta'x\eta\phi'' = -\eta'x\eta\phi'', \tag{8}$$

$$H_{pq} = \delta'x. \tag{8a}$$

Thus

$$\left. \frac{dq}{dx} \right|_{p=\bar{p}} = \frac{\eta'}{\delta'}\, \eta\phi'' > 0, \tag{7'}$$

where, of course, the right-hand side is evaluated at $p = \bar{p}$. The intercept of the $\dot{x} = 0$ curve with the q axis is given by

$$\left. q \right|_{\substack{p=\bar{p} \\ x=0}} = -\frac{\eta'}{\delta'}\left[\bar{p} + \frac{\eta}{\eta'} - \phi'(0) \right]. \tag{9}$$

This intercept is positive or negative, according as industry marginal revenue at price $\bar{p}$ is less or greater than $\phi'(0)$—which means, according as the monopoly price corresponding to $\phi'(0)$ is greater or less than $\bar{p}$. A negative intercept for the $\dot{x} = 0$ curve simply indicates that $\bar{p}$ is definitely too high a price when $x = 0$. The monopoly price is lower and thus presents both short-run and long-run advantages over $\bar{p}$.

The region in which $\dot{x}$ is positive lies above the curve, as another differentiation of $H_p = 0$ demonstrates.

$$\left. \frac{\partial p}{\partial q} \right|_{x=\text{const.}} = - \frac{H_{pq}}{H_{pp}}. \tag{10}$$

The denominator may be written as follows:

$$H_{pp} = F_{pp} + qG_{pp}$$

$$= \eta'x\left[2 - \frac{\eta\eta''}{\eta'^2} - \eta'x\phi''\right] + \eta''x\left[p + \frac{\eta}{\eta'} - \phi'\right] + q\,\delta''x. \tag{11}$$

This implies $H_{pp} < 0$; for $\eta' < 0$, the factor in brackets in the first term is positive, η'' has been assumed positive in (2a), and the next factor is negative where $H_p = 0$ and $q > 0$, and $\delta'' < 0$. Thus a higher q, at given x, implies a lower p, and higher $\delta(p)$.

The $\dot{q} = 0$ curve in Figure 1 may be obtained by setting $\dot{q} = 0$ in (3b) or (4b), with p still determined by $H_p = 0$. Differentiation of the equation

$$rq - H_x = 0$$

yields

$$r\frac{dq}{dx} - \left[H_{xx} + H_{xp}\left(\frac{\partial p}{\partial x} + \frac{\partial p}{\partial q}\frac{dq}{dx}\right) + H_{xq}\frac{dq}{dx}\right] = 0. \tag{12}$$

Substituting for $\partial p/\partial q$ from (10), and for $\partial p/\partial x$ the analogous expression $-H_{pq}/H_{pp}$, and solving for dq/dx yields

$$\frac{dq}{dx} = \frac{H_{xx} - [(H_{xp})^2/H_{pp}]}{r + (H_{xp}H_{pq}/H_{pp}) - H_{xq}}. \tag{13}$$

Partially replacing the canonical notation and invoking (8), the denominator is

$$r - \delta - \frac{\delta'\eta'x^2\eta\phi''}{H_{pp}}. \tag{14}$$

This is positive, except perhaps for values of q large enough to imply p values satisfying $\delta(p) > r$.[9] The numerator of (13) is $1/H_{pp}$ times the

---

[9]Perhaps a closer analysis would show that it is necessarily positive. For the subsequent argument, it suffices that it is positive close to the $\dot{x} = 0$ curve.

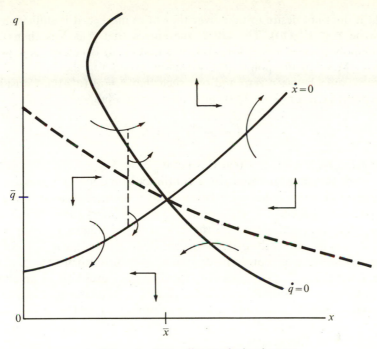

Figure 1.   Phase diagram in (x, q) space.

value of the determinant

$$\begin{vmatrix} H_{xx} & H_{xp} \\ H_{px} & H_{pp} \end{vmatrix}.$$

Noting that

$$H_{xx} = -\eta^2 \phi'',$$

and employing (8), the determinant may be evaluated as follows:

$$\begin{vmatrix} H_{xx} & H_{xp} \\ H_{px} & H_{pp} \end{vmatrix} = -\eta^2 \phi'' [H_{pp} + \eta'^2 x^2 \phi'']. \tag{15}$$

Reference to (11) now establishes that the expression in brackets is negative. Thus the determinant is positive, and the $\dot{q} = 0$ curve is negatively sloped—except possibly for values of q high enough to imply prices well below $\bar{p}$. To determine which region is the $\dot{q} > 0$ region, it suffices to note that if $q = 0$, (4a) yields the monopoly price, and (4b) then gives $\dot{q} < 0$. This shows, also, that the $\dot{q} = 0$ curve does not intersect the x axis.

The one significant feature of Figure 1 remaining to be established is that there is a point $(\bar{x}, \bar{q})$ where the $\dot{q} = 0$ curve intersects the $\dot{x} = 0$ curve, and $\bar{q} > 0, 0 < \bar{x} < 1$. If the firm is not to want to disappear, it is necessary first of all to assume that $\phi'(0) < \bar{p}$. To assure that it does not desire to take over the entire market, it is sufficient to assume $\bar{p} < \phi'(\eta(\bar{p}))$. The latter guarantees that $\bar{p}$ is less than the monopoly price when $x = 1$, and thus that $(1, 0)$ is below the $\dot{x} = 0$ curve. More to the point, the two assumptions together assure that there is an $\tilde{x}$ between zero and one such that $\bar{p} = \phi'(\eta(\bar{p})\tilde{x})$. Consider the point $(\tilde{x}, \tilde{q})$ on the $\dot{x} = 0$ curve at $\tilde{x}$. From (4a),

$$\tilde{q} = -\frac{\eta(\bar{p})}{\delta'(\bar{p})} > 0,$$

and from (4b), $\dot{q} = r\tilde{q} > 0$ at this point.

Since (4a) and (4b) give $\dot{q}$ as a continuous function of x and q, the existence of a rest point with the required properties is assured if $\dot{q}$ is negative at the point where the $\dot{x} = 0$ curve enters the nonnegative quadrant. This will always be the case if, as in Figure 1, the $\dot{q} = 0$ curve does not touch the q axis. Further, it will hold if the $\dot{x} = 0$ curve has a negative intercept with the q axis, and thus crosses the x axis, along which $\dot{q} < 0$. One possibility remains to be excluded by an additional explicit assumption, the case where $\dot{q} = 0$ intercepts the q axis *below* the $\dot{x} = 0$ curve. In (4b), let q be given by (9), and set $p = \bar{p}$. We require that the implied $\dot{q}$ be negative at this point, the intercept of the $\dot{x} = 0$ curve. This occurs if

$$-\frac{r\eta'}{\delta'}\left[\bar{p} + \frac{\eta}{\eta'} - \phi'(0)\right] - \eta[\bar{p} - \phi'(0)] < 0. \tag{16}$$

Manipulation converts this to

$$\bar{p} - \phi'(0) > \frac{-r\eta'/\delta'}{\eta + (r\eta'/\delta')}, \tag{16'}$$

where, of course, all functions on the right are evaluated at $\bar{p}$. Dividing both sides by $\bar{p}$, manipulating further, and then inverting both sides finally yields

$$\frac{\bar{p}}{\phi'(0)} > \frac{(-\eta'\bar{p}/\eta) - (\delta'\bar{p}/r)}{(-\eta'\bar{p}/\eta) - (\delta'\bar{p}/r) - 1}, \tag{16''}$$

provided that the denominator is positive. If the denominator is negative, $\dot{q}$ is necessarily positive at the point in question.

Before interpreting this condition, it may be noted that a very similar condition characterizes the rest point $(\bar{x}, \bar{q})$. Putting $p = \bar{p}$ in (4a), and $\dot{q} = 0$ in (4b), and substituting for q from (4a) in (4b) results in (16) except that $\phi'(0)$ is replaced by $\phi'(\eta(\bar{p})\bar{x})$, and the inequality is replaced by an equality. Then (16'') follows, *mutatis mutandis*. Noting that $-\eta'\bar{p}/\eta = \bar{\epsilon}$, the elasticity of industry demand at $\bar{p}$, the value $\bar{x}$ satisfies

$$\frac{\bar{p}}{\phi'(\eta(\bar{p})\bar{x})} = \frac{\bar{\epsilon} - (\delta'\bar{p}/r)}{\bar{\epsilon} - (\delta'\bar{p}/r) - 1}. \tag{17}$$

The positive term $-\delta'\bar{p}/r$ may be interpreted as the noninstantaneous component of the long-run elasticity of demand at $\bar{p}$. For small values of this quantity—resulting from sluggish customer response to price changes or from a high discount rate—the ratio between price and marginal cost at the rest point is close to that arising in static monopoly theory, $\bar{\epsilon}/(\bar{\epsilon} - 1)$. On the other hand, if small price changes around $\bar{p}$ produce very large rates of customer flow, or if the discount rate is close to zero, the ratio of price to marginal cost at the rest point will be approximately unity—the competitive result. Thus the noninstantaneous demand elasticity at $\bar{p}$ locates the rest-point solution to the dynamic problem in a continuum ranging from the static monopoly solution to the static competitive solution.

Exploiting the analogy with static monopoly theory, we obtain first an interpretation of the necessary condition

$$\bar{\epsilon} - \frac{\delta'\bar{p}}{r} > 1. \tag{18}$$

If this condition is *not* satisfied, a small temporary increase in price above $\bar{p}$ always yields an increase in the present value of revenue. Since it is also decreases the present value of cost, it is plain that a maximizing firm would never maintain price constant at $\bar{p}$. Instead, it would charge a higher price and accept the consequences in loss of patronage —the "fly-by-night" solution. But, if the sum of the instantaneous and noninstantaneous elasticities exceeds unity, price increases above $\bar{p}$ imply a loss in present value of revenue. This loss must be more than compensated by a decrease in the present value of cost if the price increase is to be worthwhile. This will be true if marginal cost is high at the point in question, but not if it is low. Equation (17) characterizes the marginal cost such that, at the margin, changes in the present value of revenue and cost just balance.

Condition (16″) simply says that, at output levels close to zero, marginal cost is low enough so that price increases above $\bar{p}$ would result in a loss in present value of revenue exceeding the cost saving. If this condition is not satisfied, a price higher than $\bar{p}$ is optimal for a firm with sufficiently small x. Since marginal cost has been assumed to be increasing throughout, optimal price is always higher than $\bar{p}$, regardless of x. Whatever its initial market proportion, the firm tends to disappear.[10]

Thus, with (16″) and (18) added to our list of assumptions, the existence of a positive $\bar{x}$ is assured. The condition $\phi'(\eta(\bar{p})) > \bar{p}$ implies $\bar{x} < 1$, but the plausibility of the behavioral assumptions made depends, of course, on $\bar{x}$ being "very small."

---

[10]If there were an initial range of decreasing marginal cost, or if the firm could at any time choose to go out of business and thereby escape some fixed costs, there would undoubtedly be solutions in which "fly by night" was optimal for x sufficiently small, but not for large x.

With the relevant features of Figure 1 logically established, we turn to the question of the existence of a function $\pi(x)$ satisfying differential equation (5) and passing through $(\bar{x}, \bar{q})$. The general existence theorem for differential equations would imply this conclusion, were it not for the fact that the denominator of (5) vanishes at $(\bar{x}, \bar{q})$. To avoid the difficulty, we back off from $\bar{x}$ to the x value corresponding to the vertical dashed-line segment in Figure 1. Solutions to the system (4), which satisfy (5) wherever it is defined, exist for all points on this segment. Those with initial q values close to the upper end point cross the $\dot{q} = 0$ curve above $\bar{q}$, while those starting close to the lower end point cross the $\dot{x} = 0$ below $\bar{q}$. By the continuity of the solutions as a function of the initial conditions, the sets of initial q values that give rise to solutions of these two types are both open. Consequently, there is a greatest lower bound to the initial q values in the first set, and this value does not lie in the second set. A solution to (4) satisfying this initial condition stays above the $\dot{x} = 0$ curve and below the $\dot{q} = 0$ curve indefinitely, and proceeds southeast at a finite rate as long as (x, q) is not close to $(\bar{x}, \bar{q})$. This can only mean that such a solution does approach $(\bar{x}, \bar{q})$ as time goes to infinity. The (x, q) path traced out is, of course, a solution to (5). No difficulty arises in extending this solution northwest from its initial point on the vertical segment.

The same construction assures the existence of the solution $\pi(x)$ to the right of $(\bar{x}, \bar{q})$, and the solution as a whole is represented by the downward-sloping dashed line of Figure 1.[11]

Given the function $\pi(x)$, the pricing rule $\psi(x)$ is defined by

$$H_p(x, \psi(x), \pi(x)) \equiv 0. \tag{19}$$

Thus we have

$$\psi'(x) = -\frac{H_{px} + H_{pq}\pi'(x)}{H_{pp}} > 0 \tag{20}$$

and, of course, $\psi(\bar{x}) = \bar{p}$.

The optimality of the solutions determined by these functions may be established by appealing to a theorem due to Arrow. According to this theorem, if $x(t)$, $p(t)$, $q(t)$ are functions satisfying conditions (3), if (x, q) converges to a limit $(\bar{x}, \bar{q})$, and if the function

$$H^0(x, q) = \max_p H(x, p, q)$$

is concave in x for every q, then these functions define an optimal path.[12] The first point to be verified is that the value of p that solves

---

[11]The argument thus far does not establish the *uniqueness* of $\pi(x)$. Presumably, however, the strict concavity subsequently displayed for the function H^0 [see (21) and subsequent discussion] assures uniqueness.

[12]Proposition 9 in Arrow, *op cit.*, stated without proof. The concavity demonstration given here is confined to nonnegative q; this presumably is sufficient—recall the earlier constructive proof that a policy implying a negative q is inferior to one in which q remains nonnegative. The fact that the function $G(x, p)$ is not concave makes the sufficiency theorem of Mangasarian [*SIAM Journal on Control*, 4 (1966), pp. 139–152] inapplicable here.

$H_p = 0$, for given nonnegative x and q, actually maximizes H as required by (3a). This is true because, as (11) shows, $H_{pp} < 0$ for all prices up to the monopoly price; at higher prices (4a) shows that H_p remains negative. The required concavity of H^0 then obtains if

$$H^0_{xx} = H_{xx} + H_{xp}\frac{dp}{dx} \leqq 0 \qquad (21)$$

holds for arbitrary nonnegative x and q, and p satisfying $H_p = 0$. In fact, $H_{xx} < 0$; the expression in question is the numerator of the right-hand side of (13). We conclude that the path determined by

$$\begin{aligned} p(t) &= \psi(x(t)), \\ \dot{x} &= \delta(p(t))x(t), \\ x(0) &= x_0, \end{aligned} \qquad (22)$$

with auxiliary variable

$$q(t) = \pi(x(t)) \qquad (23)$$

is optimal.

D. Comparative Statics in the Neighborhood of $\bar{x}$ The previous section established conditions for the existence of an optimal pricing policy that is expected to bring the firm to "rest" with some positive number of customers $\bar{x}$. In terms of the (x, p) plane, these conditions imply Figure 2, where $p = \psi(x; w, y, \bar{p})$ denotes the policy function giving optimal price as a function of the firm's x. The rest point $(\bar{x}, \bar{p})$ is now viewed as determined by the intersection of the $\dot{p} = 0$ and $\dot{x} = 0$ curves. The former is derived from the system (4) and the relation $\dot{p} = (\partial p/\partial q)\dot{q} + (\partial p/\partial x)\dot{x}$, with $H_p = 0$ now used to eliminate q:

$$\begin{aligned} 0 &= K(x, p; w, y, \bar{p}) \\ &= \left[(r - G_x)F_p + F_xG_p - G\left(F_{px} - \frac{F_p}{G_p}G_{px}\right)\right]\left[F_{pp} - \frac{F_p}{G_p}G_{pp}\right]^{-1} \\ &= [rF_p + F_xG_p - GF_{px}]\left[F_{pp} - \frac{F_p}{G_p}G_{pp}\right]^{-1}, \end{aligned} \qquad (24)$$

and the latter curve, of course, is the locus of points where

$$0 = G(x, p; \bar{p}). \qquad (25)$$

The policy function, $\psi(x; w, y, \bar{p})$, passes through the rest point and is positively sloped, as shown in (20).

We are interested in the effects of three parameters upon the policy function ψ. The first parameter is w, here identified as the competitive money wage rate. We assume that labor is the only variable input, hence that ϕ and ϕ' are proportional to w: $\phi(v; w) = w\phi(v; 1)$, and we often suppress the writing of the "1." The second is y, a shift parameter in the customer's demand function, $\eta(p; y)$; y could be interpreted as the customer's money income or, more generally, as an index of the customer's demand price. The third parameter is $\bar{p}$, the price which the firm expects other firms are charging (and will continue to charge). The analysis will be confined to the effect on price in the neighborhood of $\bar{x}$.

Since G is independent of w, a small increase of w shifts up the $\psi(x)$ function if and only if it raises the $K(x, p) = 0$ curve. The symbol on the left of (26) denotes the derivative with respect to w of the ordinate of that curve at the initial $\bar{x}$:

$$\left.\frac{dp}{dw}\right|_{\substack{K=0 \\ RP}} = \frac{rF_{pw} + G_pF_{xw}}{-(rF_{pp} + F_xG_{pp})} = \frac{-(r\eta' + \delta'\eta)\phi'x}{-(rF_{pp} + F_xG_{pp})} > 0, \quad (26)$$

where the denominator is positive by virtue of

$$H_{pp} = F_{pp} - \frac{F_p}{G_p}G_{pp} < 0,$$

and the rest-point equality $rF_p = -G_pF_x$. Accordingly, the rest point $\bar{x}$ falls with the increase of w. This can be confirmed by differentiation of (17), our implicit formula for $\eta(\bar{p})\bar{x}$,

$$\frac{w\phi'(\eta(\bar{p})\bar{x}; 1)}{\bar{p}} = 1 - \left[\frac{1}{\bar{\epsilon} - (\delta'\bar{p}/r)}\right], \quad (27)$$

where $\bar{\epsilon}$ is the instantaneous price elasticity of customer demand at $\bar{p}$. Since $\bar{\epsilon}$ is constant, we obtain

$$\frac{d\bar{x}}{dw} = \frac{-\phi'}{w\phi''\eta} < 0. \quad (28)$$

It does not follow from this local analysis that the price function shifts up at every x, only for x close to $\bar{x}$. A successful global analysis appears to be difficult.

An increase of y also affects the $\dot{p} = 0$ curve and not the $\dot{x} = 0$ line. We have

$$\left.\frac{dp}{dy}\right|_{\substack{K=0 \\ RP}} = \frac{rF_{py} + G_pF_{xy}}{-(rF_{pp} + F_xG_{pp})}$$

$$= \frac{r[\eta_y x\eta w\phi''x(p - w\phi')^{-1} - \epsilon_y p^{-1}\eta x(p - w\phi')]}{-(rF_{pp} + F_xG_{pp})}, \quad (29)$$

$$\frac{d\bar{x}}{dy} = \left(\frac{w}{\bar{p}}\phi''\eta\right)^{-1}\left[-\frac{w}{\bar{p}}\phi''x\eta_y + \epsilon_y\bigg/\left(\bar{\epsilon} - \frac{\delta'\bar{p}}{r}\right)^2\right], \quad (30)$$

where ϵ_y denotes the derivative $\partial\bar{\epsilon}/\partial y$ and η_y denotes $(\partial/\partial y)\eta(p; y)$. If $\epsilon_y = 0$ at $\bar{p}$, so that the shift of demand leaves the elasticity un-

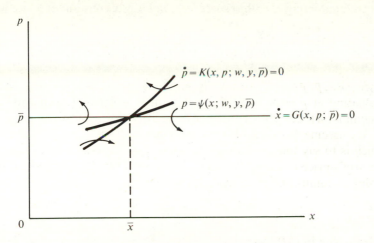

Figure 2.   Optimal pricing solution in (x, p) space.

changed at $\bar{p}$, then (dp/dy) in (29) is positive unambiguously and, correspondingly, $(d\bar{x}/dy)$ in (30) is unambiguously negative for a genuine outward shift of the customer demand curve ($\eta_y > 0$). The firm will plan on driving away customers because (27) indicates that rest-point output is independent of demand per customer; if each customer requires more output at price $\bar{p}$, proportionally fewer customers will be accommodated. The case $\epsilon_y = 0$ is "neutral," shall we say *Walras neutral*, with respect to the ratio between marginal revenue and price at $\bar{p}$.[13] If $\epsilon_y > 0$, so that the demand curve "flattens" *more* than it "shifts," reducing the ratio, the price increase is smaller than it is if ϵ_y is zero; price could decrease. The increase of ϵ at $\bar{p}$ also increases rest-point output; hence $\bar{x}$ falls less in this case than if ϵ_y is zero; it could increase. Of course, (dx/dy) and (dp/dy) are oppositely signed, the former being $K_x/K_p < 0$ times the latter.

A change of $\bar{p}$ shifts both the $K = 0$ and $G = 0$ loci in Figure 2. Since the latter is defined by $p = \bar{p}$, it is obvious that

$$\left. \frac{dp}{d\bar{p}} \right|_{G=0} \equiv 1. \tag{31}$$

If, at the initial $\bar{x}$, the $K = 0$ curve shifts down, or shifts up by a smaller amount, then the new value of $\bar{x}$ will be larger, and conversely: If $dp/d\bar{p}|_{K=0}$ exceeded one, on the other hand, $\bar{x}$ would decrease. It will be shown that, under plausible assumptions on G, the $K = 0$ curve may shift down and if it shifts up will do so by a smaller amount than G.

---

[13]When the shift is *everywhere* Walras neutral, the parameter appears in the function as $\eta(p/y; \ldots)$, i.e., as a "price-diminishing" shift.

Differentiating K with respect to $\bar{p}$, holding x constant at $\bar{x}$, we find

$$\left.\frac{dp}{d\bar{p}}\right|_{\substack{K=0 \\ RP}} = \frac{-G_{\bar{p}}F_{px} + G_{p\bar{p}}F_x}{-[rF_{pp} + F_xG_{pp}]}. \tag{32}$$

Since $G(x, \bar{p}; \bar{p}) = 0$, identically in $\bar{p}$, we have $-G_{\bar{p}} = G_p$, when evaluating at $p = \bar{p}$. Thus the first term is negative (taken with the denominator), but the second, it will be argued, is positive.

We assume now that G is homogenous of degree zero in p and $\bar{p}$—which is to say that the rate of customer flow depends on the *ratio* of the firm's price to the mean industry price.[14] Then G_p is homogeneous of degree minus one, and, by Euler's theorem,

$$G_{pp}p + G_{p\bar{p}}\bar{p} \equiv 0, \qquad G_{p\bar{p}}\bar{p} + G_{pp}p = -G_p. \tag{33}$$

Substituting in (32), we get

$$\left.\frac{dp}{d\bar{p}}\right|_{\substack{K=0 \\ RP}} = \frac{-G_{pp}F_x + G_p[F_{px} - (F_x/\bar{p})]}{-[rF_{pp} + F_xG_{pp}]}. \tag{34}$$

The first term now is nonnegative, but need not be positive. To establish that the expression as a whole is nonnegative, it would be necessary to show $F_{px} - (F_x/\bar{p})$ is negative. This seems impossible, given that F_{px} includes the term $-x\eta'\eta\phi''$, which could conceivably be large at the particular point. We conclude that the $K = 0$ curve may shift in either direction.

Equation (27) affords the simplest route to showing that $d\bar{x}/d\bar{p} > 0$, and $dp/d\bar{p}|_{\substack{K=0 \\ RP}} < 1$. Differentiating with respect to $\bar{p}$, we find

$$\frac{d\bar{x}}{d\bar{p}} = \frac{-\dfrac{w}{\bar{p}}\phi''\eta'x + \dfrac{w\phi'}{\bar{p}^2} + \left(\bar{\epsilon} - \dfrac{\delta'\bar{p}}{r}\right)^{-2} \cdot \left[\dfrac{\partial\bar{\epsilon}}{\partial\bar{p}} - \dfrac{\partial}{\partial p}\left(\dfrac{\delta'\bar{p}}{r}\right)\right]}{(w/\bar{p})\phi''\eta}. \tag{35}$$

The homogeneity assumption made on G implies that G_pp, and hence $\delta_p(p; \bar{p})p$, is homogeneous of degree zero in p and $\bar{p}$. Evaluating at $p = \bar{p}$, $\delta_p(\bar{p}; \bar{p})\bar{p}$ is therefore a constant, and the second term inside the brackets in (35) is zero. This leaves the elasticity change $\partial\bar{\epsilon}/\partial\bar{p}$ as the only potential source of sign ambiguity in (35); it appears that a sufficiently large negative value for this derivative would make $d\bar{x}/d\bar{p} < 0$. But the condition that marginal revenue be downward sloping, included in (2a), is easily shown to imply the following con-

---

[14]A generalization of this assumption is to make the rate of customer flow depend on the real value of the price discrepancy in the sense that G would be expressed as a zero-degree homogeneous function of $p - \bar{p}$ and some or all other prices. Differentiations with respect to $\bar{p}$ in the present treatment are surrogates for the effects of equiproportionate changes in $\bar{p}$ and all other prices.

dition on elasticity changes along η:

$$\frac{\partial \epsilon}{\partial p} \gtreqqless \frac{\epsilon(1 - \epsilon)}{p}. \tag{36}$$

If the elasticity increases with p, then (35) assures $d\bar{x}/d\bar{p}$ is positive. Suppose $\epsilon > 1$ and that the elasticity does decrease. Then

$$\left(\bar{\epsilon} - \frac{\delta'\bar{p}}{r}\right)^{-2} \frac{\partial \bar{\epsilon}}{\partial \bar{p}} \gtreqqless \bar{\epsilon}^{-2} \frac{\partial \bar{\epsilon}}{\partial \bar{p}} \gtreqqless \frac{\bar{\epsilon}^{-1} - 1}{\bar{p}}. \tag{37}$$

This relation may now be combined with the term $(1/\bar{p})(w\phi'/\bar{p})$ from (35), using (27) to replace $w\phi'/\bar{p}$. The final result is

$$\frac{d\bar{x}}{d\bar{p}} \gtreqqless \frac{-\eta'\bar{x}}{\eta} - \frac{\delta'\bar{p}}{rw\phi''\bar{\epsilon}[\bar{\epsilon} - (\delta'\bar{p}/r)]} > 0. \tag{38}$$

And, as a corollary, $dp/d\bar{p}\big|_{\substack{K=0 \\ RP}} - 1 < 0$. An alternative form for this

last expression, not so transparently negative, is obtained by manipulation of (34):

$$\frac{dp}{d\bar{p}}\bigg|_{\substack{K=0 \\ RP}} - 1 = \frac{rF_{pp} + G_p[F_{px} - (F_x/p)]}{-(rF_{pp} + F_x G_{pp})}. \tag{39}$$

The actual price change that occurs at the initial $\bar{x}$ when $\bar{p}$ changes, i.e., the shift in the policy function, may be obtained by differentiation of the identity $\psi(\bar{x}; w, y, \bar{p}) \equiv \bar{p}$. This gives

$$\psi_{\bar{p}} = 1 - \psi_x \frac{d\bar{x}}{d\bar{p}}. \tag{40}$$

An explicit solution for ψ_x, the slope of the policy function at the rest point, may be obtained from the following consideration: We know that setting $p = \psi(x)$ results in a solution to the dynamic system

$$\begin{aligned} \dot{p} &= K, \\ \dot{x} &= G, \\ x(0) &= x_0 \end{aligned} \tag{41}$$

that approaches the rest point. Linearizing (41) around the rest point, we obtain

$$\begin{aligned} \dot{p} &= K_p(p - \bar{p}) + K_x(x - \bar{x}), \\ \dot{x} &= G_p(p - \bar{p}) + 0(x - \bar{x}). \end{aligned} \tag{42}$$

Since $-K_x G_p < 0$, the characteristic roots of the matrix

$$\begin{bmatrix} K_p & K_x \\ G_p & 0 \end{bmatrix}$$

are real and opposite in sign. Then the slope of $\psi(x)$ at the rest point must be z_p/z_x, where (z_p, z_x) is the characteristic vector corresponding to the negative root. Any other slope would yield, locally, a solution to (41) that did not approach the rest point. Because $G_x = 0$, it is easily seen that

$$\psi_x(\bar{x}) = \frac{z_p}{z_x} = \frac{\lambda_-}{G_p}, \tag{43}$$

where λ_- is the negative root. Noting that $K_p = r$, we find

$$\lambda_- = \frac{r - \sqrt{r^2 + 4K_x G_p}}{2}, \tag{44}$$

$$\psi_x(\bar{x}) = \frac{r}{2G_p} + \sqrt{\left(\frac{r}{2G_p}\right)^2 + \frac{K_x}{G_p}}. \tag{45}$$

Differentiation of $K = 0$ yields

$$\frac{d\bar{x}}{d\bar{p}} = -\frac{K_p + K_{\bar{p}}}{K_x} = -\frac{r + K_{\bar{p}}}{K_x} \tag{46}$$

as an expression for $d\bar{x}/d\bar{p}$. Finally, substituting into (40) yields

$$\psi_{\bar{p}}(\bar{x}; w, y, \bar{p}) = 1 + \frac{r + K_{\bar{p}}}{G_p K_x} \left[\frac{r}{2} - \sqrt{\frac{r^2}{4} + G_p K_x}\right], \tag{40'}$$

where, it may be noted,

$$K_x = \frac{r\bar{x}^2 \eta^2 \phi''[\bar{\epsilon} - (\delta'\bar{p}/r)]}{F_{pp} - (F_p/G_p)G_{pp}}. \tag{47}$$

Examining (45), one sees that the policy function tends to be very flat near $\bar{x}$ if G_p is large absolutely or r is small. Under these same conditions, (40') indicates that the response to a perceived increase in the price charged by other firms is a price increase of nearly equal amount. Here, as in the case of the formula for $\bar{x}$, fast customer response and a low discount rate imply results that (in a sense) are close to the competitive extreme. But this identification obviously hinges on the firm's perceptions of $\bar{p}$ being not too far wrong. Instead of "taking" the going price as quoted on a perfect impersonal market, the firm "makes" a price that, *it believes*, is not much out of line with the industry average.

It is not apparent from (40') whether $\psi_{\bar{p}}$ is always nonnegative, but this is obviously so for cases close to the competitive extreme. A positive value of $\psi_{\bar{p}}$ is of special interest: It can be shown that under this condition the parameters $(w, y, \bar{p})$ may change in such a way that the firm increases its output while raising its price proportionately less than the rise of both the money wage and the demand price. Hence the model can generate a "procyclical" rise of the product wage, w/p, with a rise of output.

For simplicity, suppose that y shifts are everywhere Walras neutral, so that η may be written as homogeneous of degree zero in p and y:

$$\eta_p p + \eta_y y = 0. \tag{48}$$

Then an equiproportionate increase of w, y, and $\bar{p}$ leaves $\bar{x}$ unchanged and hence raises $\psi(x)$ in the same proportion. For, adding (48) to our list of assumptions leaves us with all three of the given functions in problem (1) homogeneous of degree zero in all the money prices, p, w, y, $\bar{p}$. Then raising p, at every x, in the same proportion as w, y, and $\bar{p}$ results in no change in the time path of x, and an increase in the maximand V in the same proportion as the parameters have increased. Clearly no larger increase in V can be obtained. The pertinent elasticities therefore add up to one:

$$\frac{\partial p}{\partial \bar{p}}\frac{\bar{p}}{p} + \frac{\partial p}{\partial w}\frac{w}{p} + \frac{\partial p}{\partial y}\frac{y}{p} = 1. \tag{49}$$

With the first of these elasticities positive, the sum of the two remaining elasticities must be less than one. It follows that if, say, w and y should rise in the same proportion while the firm feels no change of $\bar{p}$— or if at any rate $\bar{p}$ rises in smaller proportion—then the firm will raise its price in smaller proportion. Now, $dp/p < dy/y$ together with the Walrasian neutrality implies that price is increased less than the demand price at the initial output. Hence the firm moves down the demand curve, *increasing* its output. It does this while its product wage is actually higher because $dw/w > dp/p$. (The firm will expect its output later to fall for it will expect to lose customers in consequence of $p > \bar{p}$.) The exercise just conducted is equivalent to a *ceteris paribus* fall of $\bar{p}$. The firm, on our presumption, cuts its price (at least a little), restoring some of its competitiveness thereby, though with a smaller markup. At the lower price, more is demanded by its customers and output is increased.

If this parable of output increases "through" real wage increases is to make much sense macroeconomically, it seems necessary to suppose that the negative price elasticity of demand comes from the Pigou effect *or*, more plausibly, that when business cuts its markups, the owners of business do not reduce their real consumption by as much as workers increase theirs. Then we still write $\eta(p/y; \ldots)$, noting that y might be interpretable as after-tax money wage income. Second, in the present model with its perfect labor market, an economy-wide increase of output (coupled with higher real wage) would require a positively sloped supply-of-labor curve in the absence of fancy dynamic theories of labor supply.

It should be noted that this parable depends upon the perfectness of the labor market. There is an offsetting tendency in non-Walrasian *labor* markets for the firm, in responding to an increase in the demand price of his customers, to think that the wage paid by other firms, say $\bar{w}$, is unchanged, just as $\bar{p}$ is unchanged. Then the firm underraises its w just as it underraises its price. In a more general model, therefore, one should not expect these results to be the norm.

E. The End Case of Constant Costs: Optimal Expansion Rate

Recent studies by Gould,[15] Lucas,[16] and others have emphasized that while the firm may face a competitive demand curve, its unit costs are greater the faster is its rate of growth, because there are "adjustment costs" in absorbing more capital facilities; on certain conditions there results a determinate rate of growth of the firm's capacity. Turning those assumptions around produces a variant of the present model: While the firm can replicate and multiply familiar capital facilities at constant cost, independent of the rate of multiplication, the firm must pay an "adjustment cost" to capture more customers; the faster the rate at which it multiplies its customers, the smaller is the unit profit per customer. There results a determinate rate of expansion in the number of customers in the firm. The analysis suggests an additional basis for the Keynesian, so-called "investment-demand" function. [Think of δ as $\dot{K}/K = \rho$ (r, pure profit rate).]

Let c denote unit costs, wages plus competitive capital rents per unit of output. Then (pure) profit per customer is $(p - c)\eta(p)$. Then the firm is to maximize, with respect to $p(t)$,

$$\int_0^\infty (p - c)\eta(p)x(t)e^{-rt}\, dt \tag{50a}$$

subject to

$$\frac{\dot{x}(t)}{x(t)} = \delta(p; \bar{p}), \qquad x(0) = x_0. \tag{50b}$$

It is clear that optimal p is independent of x_0, so that $\dot{x}(t)/x(t)$ is, optimally, a constant, $\delta(p, \bar{p})$, and p is likewise constant. The optimal p therefore maximizes

$$\int_0^\infty (p - c)\eta(p)x_0 e^{[\delta(p,\bar{p})-r]t}\, dt = \frac{(p - c)\eta(p)}{r - \delta(p, \bar{p})}x_0. \tag{50a'}$$

Instead of optimizing with respect to p, let $\gamma =$ the growth rate, $p = \delta^{-1}(\gamma)$, and maximize $f(\gamma)/(r - \gamma)$, where f is defined by

$$f(\gamma) = (\delta^{-1}(\gamma) - c)\eta(\delta^{-1}(\gamma)). \tag{51}$$

The first-order condition is

$$-f'(\gamma)(r - \gamma) = f(\gamma), \tag{52}$$

[15]Gould, *op. cit.*
[16]Lucas, *op. cit.*

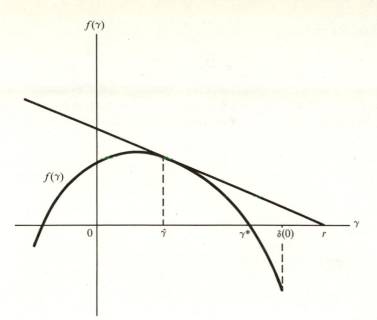

Figure 3.   Drop straight line from point $(r, 0)$ to obtain tangency with $f(\gamma)$ at optimal γ.

where $f(\gamma) > 0$ is required for a maximum at positive output. This is assured, for γ sufficiently small, if $\eta(c) > 0$.

Suppose that $r > \gamma^*$, where γ^* is the largest γ for which $f(\gamma) = 0$. Then there exists a maximum $\hat{\gamma}$ in Figure 3. It gives $\hat{\gamma} > 0$ if $-f'(0)r < f(0)$ [for $f(0) > 0$].

We need to show now that $f(\gamma)$ is, in fact, concave, as depicted in Figure 3, at least for the region in which $f'(\gamma) \leqq 0$. We have

$$f'(\gamma) = \delta_{\gamma}^{-1}[\eta + \eta'(\delta^{-1} - c)], \tag{53}$$

$$f''(\gamma) = \delta_{\gamma\gamma}^{-1}[\eta + \eta'(\delta^{-1} - c)] + (\delta_{\gamma}^{-1})^2[2\eta' + \eta'' \delta^{-1} - c\eta'']. \tag{54}$$

Like the function $\delta(p)$, the inverse function $\delta^{-1}(\gamma)$ is downward sloping and concave. Thus, comparing the first bracketed expression in (54) with (53), we see that the first term on the right-hand side of (54) is negative as required when $f'(\gamma)$ is negative. The second term is also negative, as may be shown by substituting in for η'' from downward-sloping marginal revenue assumption in (2a):

$$\eta'' \leqq \frac{2\eta'^2}{\eta}. \tag{55}$$

For comparative analysis of the solution, it is convenient to define the function

$$J(\gamma, c, \bar{p}, r) = f'(\gamma) + \frac{f(\gamma)}{r - \gamma} \equiv 0. \tag{56}$$

Then, for example,

$$\frac{d\gamma}{dc} = -\frac{J_c}{J_\gamma} = \frac{\delta_\gamma^{-1}\eta' + [\eta/(r-\gamma)]}{f''(\gamma)} < 0. \tag{57}$$

An increase in costs reduces the optimal growth rate, implying a higher optimal price. The effect of an increase in the discount rate r is in the same direction:

$$\frac{d\gamma}{dr} = -\frac{J_r}{J_\gamma} = \frac{f(\gamma)}{(r-\gamma)^2 f''(\gamma)} < 0. \tag{58}$$

3
"INDUSTRY" EQUILIBRIUM,
ITS EXISTENCE
AND STABILITY

By equilibrium is generally meant a state in which events, or at least perceptions of them, are working out as transactors have expected they would. Such changes as are occurring have already been dis-counted, as stock-traders say. Loosely, therefore, industry equilibrium requires that the average p set by firms equals the average expected p.

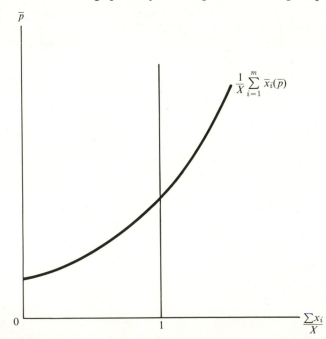

Figure 4. An equilibrium p equates the total "demand" for customers, in a state of rest, $\sum \bar{x}_i$, to the total supply of customers, X.

When average p differs from average $\bar{p}$, $\bar{p}$ is revised in an unanticipated way[17]—the system is then operating in disequilibrium. For simplicity and precision, let all firms be alike, and, in particular, share customers *equally* in the initial state. Also, let firms be alike in expectations. Then $p = \bar{p}$ is the condition for equilibrium.

We can also characterize equilibria by equality between the summed rest point $\bar{x}$'s and the number of customers to be divided in the market as in Figure 4. The rest-point "demand" for customers is positively sloped throughout by virtue of the result in (38). Hence there can exist at most one equilibrium. One could also consider the cousin to the aforementioned curve giving *rest-point output* as a function of $\bar{p}$. When ϵ is a constant, this rest-point *supply curve* is just the frictionless competitive supply curve *marked up* according to the rule in (27). By the result in (38) it is generally true that our rest-point supply curve for the industry with frictions is a marked-up version of the supply curve in the frictionless competitive case, with the size of the markup possibly varying as larger rest-point outputs are considered. Hence, our supply curve is upward sloping. An industry equilibrium will exist, therefore, if, at zero output, the demand price exceeds the corresponding marked-up marginal cost.

Consider now the stability of equilibrium. When $p < \bar{p}$, averaging over firms, firms on average will be surprised at their failure to gain

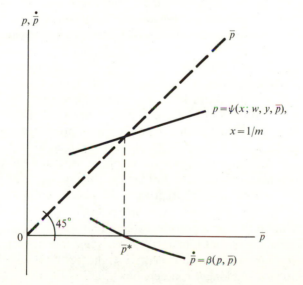

Figure 5. When $p > \bar{p}^*$, $p < \bar{p}$ and hence estimated $\bar{p}$ falls toward $\bar{p}^*$ at rate $\beta(p, \bar{p})$ where $\beta_1 > 0$, $\beta_2 < 0$.

[17]For simplicity, we assume that $\bar{p}(\tau, t)$ is independent of τ, $\tau \geq t$, meaning static expectations over future time. An obvious normalization is available for dealing with expectations of regular, steady inflation.

customers at the expense of other firms. *If* they believe they have previously estimated all *other* parameters correctly, they will revise downward their estimate of $\bar{p}$—and revise *only* that parameter estimate. The fall of (expected) $\bar{p}$ is likely to cause p to be revised downward for each firm; but this is inessential. What is essential is that each firm's optimal p is "inelastic" with respect to $\bar{p}$, $(\partial p/\partial \bar{p})(\bar{p}/p) < 1$, as was shown to hold in Section 2.D. Then, with x_i equally spread among firms, we find that $\bar{p}$ falls when $\bar{p} > \bar{p}^*$ and $\bar{p}$ rises when $\bar{p} < \bar{p}^*$ in stable fashion (see Figure 5).

4
CONCLUDING COMMENTS

We have explored some of the implications of what is at bottom a very simple assumption: The individual firm believes that maintaining a constant discrepancy between its price and the prevailing industry price will result in a constant geometric growth or decline in its share of the customers. The results, once derived and comprehended, are plausible. The firm sets its price both with an eye to the price it believes other firms are charging and to the number of customers it is serving; when it has less business than it wants, it shades its price relative to the rest of the industry. It is content to charge the prevailing price when its output level represents an appropriate balancing of the gains from more business and the costs of acquiring it through temporary price concessions. The pricing rule responds in reasonable ways to parameter changes.

Plausible and "realistic" as these results are, it is noteworthy that none of the standard analyses of firm behavior under various market structures can produce them. Perfect competitors, as every sophomore is supposed to know, do not have pricing policies at all, much less the sort of pricing policies that might be closely approximated by some fairly simple markup pricing rule, or the sort that lead to larger output levels being associated with higher values of the ratio of input prices to output prices. Monopolists need not concern themselves with alternatives open to their customers (other than those reflected in a static demand curve), while oligopolists are concerned with getting along with each other. In spirit, monopolistic competition in the large group is closest to our analysis. But our firm's "dd" is just a certain fraction of industry "DD" and has the same elasticity; the key difference between the instantaneous and longer run demand situation lies in the customer responses, not the behavior of other firms.

The agenda of unfinished business is enormous. There is first the extensive margin. The theory of the firm operating in markets with noninstantaneous quantity responses could be elaborated in many directions—simultaneous analysis of markets for inputs and outputs, integration with inventory and investment theory, advertising policy, "forced saving," dynamic differentiation, entry, and so forth. The intensive margin is equally important: the use and further development of this analysis of firm behavior as a building block for a more powerful theory of short- and intermediate-run price dynamics in "competitive" industries. The analysis of disequilibrium and equilibration is especially rich in possibilities. Unquestionably a game-theoretic approach is one of these. But enough agenda. A landing on the non-Walrasian continent has been made. Whatever further exploration may reveal, it has been a mind-expanding trip: We need never go back to $\dot{p} = \alpha(D - S)$ and $q = \min(D, S)$.

Diffusion Processes and Optimal Advertising Policy[*]

JOHN P. GOULD

The belief that the effect of an advertising expenditure persists for some period of time after the expenditure occurs has led a number of economists to treat advertising in a manner analogous to investment in durable goods.[1] One of the most noteworthy analyses along these lines is due to Nerlove and Arrow.[2] In their model, Nerlove and Arrow assume that there is a stock of goodwill, $A(t)$, which summarizes the effects of current and past advertising outlays on demand. Goodwill is measured in units having a price of $1 so that a dollar of advertising expenditure increases the stock of goodwill by a like amount. It is assumed that goodwill, like capital stock, depreciates over time and in particular that the depreciation occurs at a constant proportional

[*]I am indebted to a great number of people for their comments on an earlier draft of this paper. I would like to give special thanks to David Cass, George Haines, David Rubin, George Stigler, and Lester Telser for their helpful suggestions. I also extend my apologies to these readers for my failure to deal in a more satisfactory way with the problems they pointed out.

[1]George Haines has argued in private correspondence that there is no substantial evidence that the effect of advertising lasts for any appreciable length of time (e.g., six months to 1 year). This does not present a serious problem in this paper, however, because only continuous-time models are analyzed, and all that will be needed is the assumption that the major advertising effect lasts for some short (but finite) interval of time. Obviously, the caveat becomes quite important in the analysis of discrete-time models.

[2]Marc Nerlove and K. J. Arrow, "Optimal Advertising Policy under Dynamic Conditions," *Economica* (May 1962), pp. 124–142.

rate, δ, so that

$$\dot{A}(t) + \delta A(t) = a(t), \tag{1}$$

where $a(t)$ is the advertising expenditure at time t.[3] In terms of the capital-stock analogy, (1) states that net investment in goodwill is the difference between gross investment, $a(t)$, and depreciation.

Given these definitions and assumptions, the rate at which sales are made at time t, $q(t)$, is written as a function of the stock of goodwill, $A(t)$, and the price, $p(t)$, at time t,[4]

$$q(t) = f(p(t), A(t)).$$

Let $g(t) = C(q(t))$ be the total manufacturing cost of producing $q(t)$, so that at time t the cash flow (net of manufacturing expenses only) is

$$R(p(t), A(t)) = p(t)q(t) - g(t). \tag{2}$$

The cash flow net of advertising expenditure at time t is, therefore, $R(p(t), A(t)) - a(t)$ and the optimal time paths of advertising and price are those paths which maximize the present value of all future net cash flows. Formally, the problem is

$$\max_{a, p} \int_0^\infty e^{-rt}[R(p(t), A(t)) - a(t)]\, dt \tag{3}$$

subject to $a(t) \geq 0, p(t) \geq 0$,

$$A(0) = A_0 \text{ (i.e., initial level of goodwill is given)}$$

and

$$\dot{A} + \delta A = A(t),$$

where r is the fixed rate of interest.

The derivative $\dot{p}(t)$ is unrestricted, so that the optimal price policy is to choose $p(t)$ to maximize the integrand of (3) at each point in time for given $A(t)$ and $a(t)$.[5] Differentiating $R(p, A)$ with respect to p and setting the result equal to zero establishes a first-order condition for the optimal price, p^*,[6]

$$\left. \frac{\partial R(p, A)}{\partial p} \right|_{p=p^*} = q + p\frac{\partial f}{\partial p} - \frac{dg}{dq}\frac{\partial f}{\partial p} = 0. \tag{4}$$

[3]Throughout this paper, a dot over a variable denotes its derivative with respect to time.

[4]In the Nerlove–Arrow model, other variables, which are not controlled by the firm, such as population, consumer incomes, and prices of other goods are also included in the demand function. The reason for not introducing these exogenous variables at this point will be discussed below.

[5]It is important to note that we could not separate the price and advertising policies in this way if the demand function depended on both p and $\dot{p}$.

[6]The assumption that price is continuously adjusted, as indicated by this equation, is not an essential ingredient in any of the models discussed here. Indeed, one can easily

Define $p^*(A(t))$ to be that p for which (4) holds when goodwill is $A(t)$ and let

$$\pi(A(t)) = R(p^*, A). \tag{5}$$

Substituting (5) into (3), the problem becomes

$$\max_{a \geq 0} \int_0^\infty e^{-rt}[\pi(A(t)) - a(t)]\, dt \tag{3a}$$

subject to

$$A(0) = A_0,$$
$$\dot{A} + \delta A = a.$$

Nerlove and Arrow show, under certain regularity assumptions, that the optimal policy is to jump instantaneously from A_0 to A^* (assuming $A^* > A_0$), where

$$A^* = \frac{\beta pq}{\eta(r + \delta)}$$

and where β and η are the elasticities of demand with respect to goodwill and price, respectively. For $t > 0$, the optimal policy is $a^* = \delta A^*$. If $A^* < A_0$, the optimal policy is to set $a^* = 0$ until the stock of goodwill depreciates to the level A^* and then set $a^* = \delta A^*$ from that point on.[7]

This is clearly an interesting and imaginative model of the firm's advertising policy, but the authors point out that it has some significant shortcomings. They describe one such difficulty as follows:

> The assumption that the cost of adding to goodwill is always one, no matter at what level current advertising expenditures are carried on is actually very unrealistic. At very high levels of current advertising expenditure, resort must be had to inferior media so that the costs of adding a dollar's worth to goodwill must surely rise with the level of expenditure. One possible way of dealing with this problem is to set a finite upper bound to current advertising expenditure, below which we assume

---

construct persuasive arguments for alternative assumptions and specifications. For example, the very concept of advertising carries with it the notion of incomplete information on the part of consumers, and price itself is clearly one of the relevant pieces of information. Consequently, when the price is changed it is plausible that the firm will have to inform all customers (including previously informed customers) of this change. One way to allow for this possibility is to make δ an increasing function of price. An easier approach would be to assume that price (and thus δ) remains constant for the period of analysis. The reader may, if he wishes, make this latter assumption because it does not significantly affect the main analytical results of this paper, even though it clearly has important effects on the economic implications of these results. Our reason for using (4) at this point is to maintain consistency with the Nerlove–Arrow specification.

[7]An interesting problem arises when A^* changes over time because of changes in exogenous variables. In this case, the best policy may be to keep A below the instantaneous optimal level for some finite period of time because of anticipated future decreases in A^*.

a proportional cost of adding to goodwill . . . Alternatively and more generally, one might introduce a nonlinear cost function for additions to goodwill . . . lack of one or the other of these assumptions leads to policies which may have a jump (in $A(t)$) at $t = 0$. Since we are primarily interested in the characteristics of the optimal policy after $t = 0$, however, we shall restrict ourselves to the simpler, but more unrealistic case.[8]

The situation is somewhat worse than might be implied by the concluding sentence of this quotation. In particular, the model indicates that when the optimal level of goodwill is expected to remain constant for some time the firm should jump to this level immediately and remain there until the optimal level changes.[9] Thus the "characteristics of the optimal policy" after time $t = 0$ tend to be static rather than dynamic in nature. In contrast, a model that introduces a nonlinear cost function for additions to goodwill has an optimum path which has characteristics that differ from those of a static model for times after $t = 0$, even when the ultimate equilibrium is stationary. Since the assumption that the costs of adding to goodwill are linear is unrealistic, this difference in the characteristics of the alternative models for times after $t = 0$ is important on both theoretical and empirical grounds.

Another problem with the Nerlove–Arrow model is that it virtually ignores the diffusion processes by which information made available by an advertiser spread through the market. The fundamental concept of the diffusion-model approach to the economics of advertising, which has been developed in papers by Stigler and Ozga, is that not all the individuals comprising the market will become aware of a particular piece of information the instant it is announced, but instead there will be some period of time during which individuals learn of the information by coming in contact with an advertising medium or by word of mouth.[10] Models incorporating such diffusion processes in the analysis of advertising policy have a number of appealing features. First, the idea that it takes time for information to spread through a market has more appeal on empirical grounds than the assumption that any level

---

[8]Nerlove and Arrow, *op. cit.*, footnote 3, p. 130 (parenthetical comments added). It is interesting to note that empirical work tends to confirm the hypothesis that there are disceconomies of scale in advertising. See Lester Telser, "Advertising and Cigarettes," *Journal of Political Economy*, 70 (1962), pp. 471–499, and J. L. Simon, "Are There Economies of Scale in Advertising?" *Journal of Advertising Research*, 5, No. 2 (1965), pp. 15–19.

[9]For this policy to be optimal, it is assumed that when the optimal level changes, it either increases or that its proportional rate of decrease is less than the rate of depreciation. The reason for this, as the authors note, is that when the optimal level of goodwill is expected to decrease at a more rapid rate (proportionally) than δ at, say, t^*, it is likely that the optimal policy will be to keep A below its instantaneous optimum level for some period before t^*.

[10]G. Stigler, "The Economics of Information," *Journal of Political Economy* (1961), pp. 213–225.

S. Ozga, "Imperfect Markets through Lack of Knowledge," *Quarterly Journal of Economics* (1960), pp. 29–52.

of goodwill can be achieved instantly given a large enough advertising expenditure. Second, the very concept of goodwill is somewhat fuzzy and seems to have been adopted by Nerlove and Arrow for lack of a more satisfactory name for the cumulative effect of advertising expenditures. In contrast, the introduction of a diffusion process permits a more natural and obvious definition of this cumulative effect of advertising: the number of individuals who are aware of the given piece of information at each point in time.[11] Third, the explicit introduction of a diffusion process provides a means of examining the effects that an alternative information-diffusion process will have on the optimal advertising policy. This may be quite useful in comparing the advertising policies of firms which face different mechanisms of information spread and allows for some interesting comparative dynamic analyses.

To be more concrete, we now turn to a discussion of two particular models of information spread.

1
THE STIGLER AND
OZGA MODELS OF
INFORMATION SPREAD

The first model to be considered will be a continuous version of a discrete model discussed by Stigler.[12] Let

$K(t)$ = number of individuals who know of the firm at time t $[K(0) = K_0]$

N = total number of individuals in the market $N \geq K(t)$

b = forgetfulness coefficient, that is, the instantaneous proportional rate at which individuals forget the message

$u(t)$ = contact coefficient or the instantaneous proportional rate at which individuals become aware of the firm

As has been mentioned, we will treat $K(t)$ as being active customers of the firm. The total number of individuals in the market, N, will be regarded as fixed throughout the period of analysis for reasons which shall be made clear below. The interpretation of b should become clearer in what follows, but some important characteristics of this coefficient may be noted at this point. First, it is assumed that b represents the rate of loss of customers arising from all causes: forgetting, switching to another brand, changing tastes, etc. Second it is assumed

---

[11]There remains the problem of giving a precise definition to the concept of knowing the piece of information. For purposes of this paper we will take this to mean that the individual is an active customer of the firm. The fact that there are probably decreasing returns to scale in acquiring active customers will be recognized by introducing a nonlinear function for advertising expenditures.

[12]Stigler, *op cit.*

that b remains constant throughout the period of analysis. This is a pretty questionable assumption, because changes in the advertising policy of other firms and changes in prices are quite likely to change b. The assumption is useful, however, to facilitate the analysis, and we can consider at a later stage what effects loosening this assumption may have on the results. It should be noted that this assumption is equivalent to the assumption of constant δ in the Nerlove–Arrow model. Third, although it is true that in a discrete-time model b would be bounded between zero and one, in the continuous-time model to be introduced here, the only constraint on this parameter is that it be nonnegative, because it is an instantaneous rate. The coefficient $u(t)$ is treated as a function of time, because this is the parameter of the diffusion model that will be determined by the firm's (dynamic) advertising policy. As in the case of the coefficient b, the only constraint on $u(t)$ is that it be nonnegative, because it is an instantaneous rate.

The relationships among these variables and parameters may be written as follows:

$$K(t + dt) = K(t)(1 - b\,dt) + u(t)\,dt(N - K(t)). \qquad (6)$$

Equation (6) can be described as follows: The number of individuals who know of the advertising message at time $t + dt$ (where dt represents a small time interval) is equal to the number who knew at time t less those who "forget" the message the interval dt plus those that are newly informed in the interval dt. The coefficient b and $u(t)$, being rates per unit time, must be multiplied by dt to maintain the correct dimensionality in the above expression. Note also that $u(t)\,dt$ is multiplied by $N - K(t)$, because it is only this number of people that can be *newly* informed of the message. It is assumed that any individual who already knows the information will not be affected by repeated exposure to the message.[13] Dividing both sides of (6) by dt and rewriting,

$$\frac{K(t + dt) - K(t)}{dt} = u(t)N - (b + u(t))K(t). \qquad (6a)$$

The limit of (6a) as dt approaches zero yields the differential equation

$$\dot{K}(t) = u(t)N - (b + u(t))K(t). \qquad (6b)$$

Consider for a moment the special case where $u(t)$ is taken as a constant. In this case, the general solution to (6b) is

$$K(t) = \frac{uN}{b + u} + \left(K_0 - \frac{uN}{b + u}\right)e^{-(b+u)t}, \qquad (6c)$$

---

[13]It would be possible to develop a model in which n exposures to the message are needed before a person becomes "informed." Such refinements, although of obvious interest, will not be dealt with here.

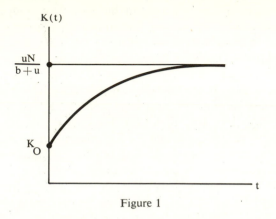

Figure 1

where $K_0 = K(0)$. As is clear from (6c), the path of K *for fixed u* is an exponential growth path [or decay if $uN/(b + u) < K_0$] with its equilibrium at $uN/(b + u)$. An example of such a path is given in Figure 1, where it can be seen that the equilibrium K will be less than N as long as $b > 0$. It should be emphasized that, in general, the optimal path will not be characterized by a constant u, so that Figure 1 is in no sense typical of the path which maximizes the integral introduced in the introduction.

The second model of information spread differs from the first in some important ways. The key difference is that information spreads by word of mouth rather than an impersonal advertising medium, so that in the absence of forgetting, the likelihood of a given individual becoming informed of the message increases over time.[14] The model to be considered here has been analyzed by Ozga in a related context.[15] Let $K(t)$, N, and b be the same as above and let $c(t)$ be the contact coefficient. The parameter $c(t)$ represents the number of persons contacted per unit time by each individual. It is assumed that when two persons come into contact, each tells the other whatever information he has about the advertised product. It is also assumed that by increasing advertising expenditures $c(t)$ can be increased.[16]

As in the previous model, forgetting occurs at the proportional rate, b, so that if $K(t)$ people know of the message at time t, only

$$K(t)(1 - b \, dt)$$

[14]This is because, as time goes on, an increasing number of individuals know of and are communicating the message to others. In contrast, the likelihood of a given individual learning the message remains constant over time for the first model with $b = 0$ and fixed $u > 0$, because this likelihood is not affected by the number of persons who know of the message.

[15]Ozga, *loc. cit.* Those interested in more sophisticated and presumably more realistic diffusion models should see N. T. J. Bailey, *The Mathematical Theory of Epidemics* (Hafner, New York, 1957).

[16]See Ozga's paper for a more detailed discussion of these assumptions.

of these people will remember it after the interval dt. The word-of-mouth advertising during the interval dt will offset this loss from forgetting, however. In particular, the $K(t)(1 - b\,dt)$ people who remember the message will contact and inform a total of

$$K(t)(1 - b\,dt)c(t)\,dt$$

individuals during dt of which the proportion

$$1 - \frac{K(t)(1 - b\,dt)}{N}$$

will not know of the message at the time of contact. Combining these results we have

$$K(t + dt) = K(t)(1 - b\,dt)$$
$$+ K(t)(1 - b\,dt)c(t)\,dt\left[1 - \frac{K(t)(1 - b\,dt)}{N}\right]. \qquad (7)$$

Dividing both sides of (7) by dt and rewriting,

$$\frac{K(t + dt) - K(t)}{dt}$$
$$= -bK(t) + K(t)(1 - b\,dt)c(t)\left[1 - \frac{K(t)(1 - b\,dt)}{N}\right]. \qquad (7a)$$

The limit of (7a) as dt approaches zero yields the differential equation

$$\dot{K}(t) = -bK(t) + c(t)K(t)\left[1 - \frac{K(t)}{N}\right]. \qquad (7b)$$

For *fixed c* this differential equation has the solution

$$K(t) = \frac{(c - b)N}{c + \{[(N/K_0) - 1]c - (N/K_0)b\}e^{(b-c)t}}. \qquad (7c)$$

An example of such a solution for $K_0 < N$ and $c > b$ is shown in Figure 2, where it can be seen that the equilibrium K, for given c, is $N[1 - (b/c)]$. An obvious difference between Figures 1 and 2 is that the path in Figure 1 is concave everywhere, whereas the path in Figure 2 is convex in the early periods. It is worth repeating that the path illustrated in Figure 2 assumes that c remains constant over time, and this will not, in general, be the optimal policy, as the following analysis indicates.

Before going on to dynamics, it is worth taking a brief look at some of the comparative statics of these two models. Once it is observed that for given finite values of b, c, u, and N only some fraction of the N potential customers will know about the firm in equilibrium, it is nat-

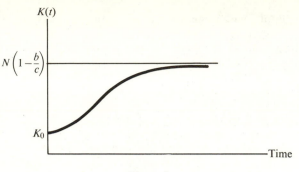

Figure 2

ural to ask if a firm can be a monopolist with respect to those customers who know only of that firm and no others.[17] Assuming a two-
firm industry for concreteness, the answer to this question depends on
knowing the number of buyers in each of the following groups: (a) those
who know of the first firm but not the second, (b) those who know of
the second but not the first, (c) those who know of both, and (d) those
who know of neither. The firms may be able to act as monopolists with
respect to groups (a) and (b). Put another way, the first firm can consistently charge a higher price than the second and not lose all its customers if group (a) is not empty. This much is obvious. What is surprising is that Stigler and Ozga disagree about the number of buyers
in each of these groups. In particular, Stigler claims that in equilibrium
there will be some buyers in each of the four groups, whereas Ozga
argues that groups (a) and (b) will be empty in the stationary state.
What may be even more surprising is that each is correct with respect
to his own particular model. To resolve the apparent conflict, it is
convenient to sketch the arguments presented by each author.

Stigler observes that the equilibrium proportion of persons knowing of either firm, given that u and b are the same for each firm, is
$\lambda = u/(b + u)$.[18] Thus, using the binomial distribution, one obtains

Number in group 1	$\lambda(1 - \lambda)N$
Number in group 2	$\lambda(1 - \lambda)N$
Number in group 3	$\lambda^2 N$
Number in group 4	$(1 - \lambda)^2 N$
Total	N

It is clear that there will be some persons in each of the four groups if
$1 > \lambda > 0$ and $N > 0$.

---

[17]In Stigler's version $[u/(b + u)] N$ buyers will know of the firm in equilibrium and in
Ozga's version $N(1 - b/c)$ will know of the firm in equilibrium. The fraction for the
Stigler version differs from that given in his article (*op. cit.*, eq. 4 on p. 221) because we
use continuous rather than discrete time in this paper.

[18]The assumption that c and b are the same for each firm is essential to Ozga's argument
and, for purposes of comparison, the analogous assumption is made here.

Ozga arrives at his result by the following reasoning:

Suppose that the products of the two firms (two brands of chocolate, for instance) are on the market. The knowledge of the existence of these products is then the result of information being passed on through social contact. Three pieces of information are in fact being passed on: (1) there is chocolate in the market, (2) there is chocolate of firm A, and (3) there is chocolate of firm B. (The first is passed on implicitly when either the second or third is passed on; the possibility of its being passed on independently of either the second or the third is here neglected.) The process of the diffusion of these three pieces of information takes place within the same group of buyers, with the same contact coefficient, and subject to the same rates of growth and removal. It must, therefore, lead, in the limit, to exactly the same number of buyers in possession of each of them. There cannot be more buyers who know of the existence of chocolate in general than there are buyers who know that there is chocolate A and than there are those who know there is chocolate B. All of them must be, therefore, the same buyers, those who know of both A and B, and implicitly the existence of chocolate in general. If it were not so, then it would be possible to increase the number of people informed beyond the limit imposed by the contact coefficient and the rates of growth and removal simply by making the information more detailed; i.e., by adding to the general information that there is chocolate on the market the details that there is chocolate A and chocolate B.[19]

Ozga's argument can be expressed notationally as follows. Let N_{i0} be the number of people who know only of firm i ($i = A, B$), let N_{AB} be the number who know of both, let N_i be the total number that know of firm i ($i = A, B$), and, finally, let N_C be the total number who know there is chocolate on the market. Thus

$$N_A = N_{A0} + N_{AB},$$
$$N_B = N_{B0} + N_{AB},$$
$$N_C = N_{A0} + N_{B0} + N_{AB}.$$

Now, as Ozga argues, for a given set of parameters c, b, N (the same for each firm) the equilibrium number of people knowing each piece of information will be the same, so that $N_A = N_B = N_C$. Hence from $N_A = N_C$ it follows that $N_{B0} = 0$, and from $N_B = N_C$ it follows that $N_{A0} = 0$, as asserted.

What leads to this difference? The answer, it seems to me, is implicit in Stigler's use of the binomial distribution to determine the number of persons who will be in each class. For this distribution to be used, it must be assumed that the probability that a person learns of one firm is independent of his knowledge of the other firm and remains constant over time. Both assumptions are consistent with Stig-

---

[19] Ozga, *op. cit.*, p. 41.

ler's specification as long as advertisements of the two firms are not presented to the consumer in a way that he cannot learn of one without learning of the other. Given this specification a person can enter the market at *any* time t and know of only one of the firms at time $t + 1$ with probability $\lambda(1 - \lambda)$.[20] In contrast, the probability of learning about either firm in the Ozga model increases over time as more and more persons become informed. Thus, in the Ozga model, the probability that a person can enter the market and meet someone who knows of only one firm approaches zero as t approaches infinity. As time goes on, the "word-of-mouth" mechanism in the Ozga model ultimately leads to complete dependence in the sense that there is no way to learn of A without learning of B. In the Stigler model, on the other hand, the number of people who currently know of a firm has no effect on the probability of an uninformed person learning about that firm, so that complete independence is maintained at all times.

It is quite clear that neither model is entirely acceptable by itself. Certainly there are many ways of learning about one seller in an industry without learning of all the others in that industry, so that Ozga's model is somewhat unrealistic.

Similarly, Stigler's implicit assumption that the probability of learning of a seller is independent of the consumer's knowledge of other sellers and the additional assumption that this probability is independent of the number of persons who know of the seller are both of dubious realism. It appears desirable, therefore, to develop a more general model which recognizes both word-of-mouth and inanimate media as mechanisms of information spread. However, our main interest is in examining the sensitivity of optimal advertising policy to the underlying processes of information spread, so we choose to analyze each of these models by itself. It is important to note, however, that in doing so we are focusing attention on situations that may be atypical and unusual in some important respects.

2
THE OPTIMAL POLICY FOR THE NERLOVE–ARROW MODEL WITH NONLINEAR COSTS FOR ADDING TO GOODWILL

In this section, we extend the Nerlove–Arrow model by relaxing the assumption that the costs of adding to goodwill are linear. Instead, we introduce the twice continuously differentiable cost function $w(a)$,

---

[20]We switch here to discrete-time representation for purposes of exposition.

where for $a \geq 0$,

$$w(a) > 0, \tag{8a}$$
$$w'(a) > 0, \tag{8b}$$
$$w''(a) > 0. \tag{8c}$$

As equations (8) indicate, the cost of adding to goodwill is positive and the marginal cost of adding to goodwill is positive and increasing. It is also assumed that $\pi(A)$ is twice continuously differentiable and that for $A \geq 0$

$$\pi'(A) > 0,$$
$$\pi''(A) \leq 0.$$

The problem may be formally stated as

$$\max_{0 \leq a(t)} \int_0^\infty e^{-rt}[\pi(A) - w(a)] \, dt \tag{9}$$

subject to

$$\dot{A} = a - \delta A,$$
$$A(0) = A_0.$$

Observe first that the concavity of $\pi(A)$ and the convexity of $w(a)$ imply that the integral in (9) has a finite upper bound over all feasible paths. Moreover, the concavity of the integrand in (9) and the linearity of the constraints means that if an optimum path exists, it is unique.[21] Thus, since the problem has the structure of an optimal control problem with a variable right end point, it is necessary to show that there exists a path which satisfies the conditions of Pontryagin's maximum principle with $A(0) = A_0$ and a finite stationary point (a^*, A^*).[22] The Hamiltonian expression for (8) is

$$\mathcal{H}(A, a, \psi) = e^{-rt}[\pi(A) - w(a) + \psi(t)(a - \delta A)],$$

and the maximum principle establishes that the optimum path will maximize this expression for all t. Thus a necessary condition is

$$\frac{\partial \mathcal{H}}{\partial a} = e^{-rt}[-w'(a) + \psi(t)] = 0.$$

Moreover, the partial derivative $-\partial \mathcal{H}/\partial A$ will equal $de^{-rt}\psi(t)/dt = -re^{-rt}\psi + \dot{\psi}e^{-rt}$. Thus, according to the maximum principle, the

---

[21]This can be shown following a line of proof similar to that used by Uzawa on pages 4 and 5 of "Optimal Growth in a Two-Sector Model of Capital Accumulation," *Review of Economic Studies*, 31 (1964).

[22]L. S. Pontryagin et al., *The Mathematical Theory of Optimal Processes* (John Wiley & Sons, Inc., New York, 1962).

optimal path must satisfy[23]

$$\dot{\psi} = (r + \delta)\psi - \pi'(A), \tag{10a}$$

$$\psi = w'(a), \tag{10b}$$

$$\dot{A} = a - \delta A. \tag{10c}$$

Differentiating (10b) with respect to time and using the resulting expression and (10b) to eliminate $\dot{\psi}$ and ψ from (10a) we obtain the following system of nonlinear differential equations

$$\dot{a} = \frac{1}{w''(a)} [(r + \delta)w'(a) - \pi'(A)],$$

$$\dot{A} = a - \delta A. \tag{11}$$

Since the system (11) is autonomous, its behavior can be conveniently analyzed in the (a, A) phase space.[24] The singular curve for $\dot{A} = 0$ is given by $a = \delta A$. Moreover, since

$$\left.\frac{da}{dA}\right|_{\dot{a}=0} = \frac{\pi''}{(r + \delta)w''} \le 0,$$

the singular curve for $\dot{a} = 0$ has a negative slope. At points above the $\dot{A} = 0$ curve, $\dot{A} > 0$ and at points below this curve, $\dot{A} < 0$. Furthermore, since

$$\frac{\partial \dot{a}}{\partial A} = -\frac{\pi''(A)}{w''(a)} \ge 0,$$

it follows that at points to the right of the $\dot{a} = 0$ curve, $\dot{a}$ is positive, while for points to the left of the $\dot{a} = 0$ curve, $\dot{a}$ is negative. From an important theorem on the behavior of the trajectories of a system such as (11), we know that if the equilibrium state (i.e., that point at which both $\dot{a} = 0$ and $\dot{A} = 0$) is a saddle, then there exists exactly two trajectories of the system of differential equations which lead to this

---

[23]In addition, the optimal path should satisfy the transversality condition

$$\lim_{t \to \infty} \psi e^{-rt} = \lim_{t \to \infty} w'(a)e^{-rt} = 0$$

and the Weierstrauss–Erdmann corner conditions. The fact that a must remain finite to prevent the integral (9) from becoming infinitely negative guarantees that the transversality condition will be met. The assumptions on the continuity of the derivatives of $w(a)$ and $\pi(A)$ rules out corners and we may ignore the Weierstrauss–Erdmann conditions. In the latter respect, it should be made explicit that our primary concern is with cases for which A_0 is less than the long-run optimal level of goodwill. If A_0 was above this level, the optimal path may require that $a(t) = 0$ during some time intervals and the corner conditions would be relevant. Moreover, if A_0 was above the stationary level of A, there may be a problem of irreversibilities in moving from interior to boundary solutions.

[24]It would not be possible to analyze the system in this way if we had introduced exogenous, time-dependent variables into the demand function. Similarly, it is for this reason that δ (and b on the following models) is assumed to be independent of time.

equilibrium as $t \to \infty$.[25] Linearizing the system (11) around its stationary point (a^*, A^*) we get[26]

$$\begin{bmatrix} \dot{A} \\ \dot{a} \end{bmatrix} = \begin{bmatrix} \alpha_{11} & \alpha_{12} \\ \alpha_{21} & \alpha_{22} \end{bmatrix} \begin{bmatrix} A \\ a \end{bmatrix}. \tag{12}$$

The point (a^*, A^*) will be a saddle if the eigenvalues of the matrix $\|\alpha_{ij}\|$ in (12) are real and opposite. These eigenvalues are given by

$$\lambda = \frac{r \pm \sqrt{r^2 + 4\left(\delta(r + \delta) - \dfrac{\pi''(A)}{w''(a)}\right)}}{2},$$

which are real and opposite in sign, because

$$\delta(r + \delta) - \frac{\pi''(A)}{w''(a)} > 0.$$

These results are illustrated in the phase diagram in Figure 3, where the optimum path is given by the heavy arrows approaching (a^*, A^*).

It is clear from the above analysis and Figure 3 that the unique path to (a^*, A^*) is the optimal path, because all other paths ultimately lead either to infinitely large (A, a) or to a zero level of goodwill, and

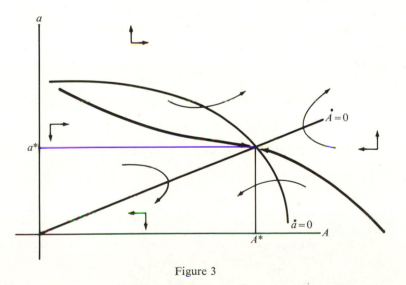

Figure 3

[25]L. S. Pontryagin, *Ordinary Differential Equations* (Addison-Wesley Publishing Company, Inc., Reading, Mass., 1962), p. 246.

[26]The α_{ij} represent the relevant partial derivatives of the right-hand sides of the system (11) evaluated at the point (a^*, A^*), which makes $\dot{a}$ and $\dot{A}$ zero simultaneously. It is denoted generically for reference in the analysis of the following systems.

these solutions have been shown to be nonoptimal.[27] As can be seen from the phase diagram, the optimal policy for $A_0 < A^*$ is to advertise most heavily in the initial periods and continually decrease the level of advertising expenditures as A increases toward the equilibrium level A^*.

An interesting special case arises when it is assumed that $\pi(A) = \gamma A$, where γ is a positive constant. This situation may arise when the firm is a competitor with constant returns to scale in production.[28] In this situation, the $\dot{a} = 0$ curve becomes a straight line at $a^* = \delta A^*$. The eigenvalues for the system (12), given the assumption that $\pi(A) = \gamma A$, are

$$\lambda = \frac{r \pm \sqrt{r^2 + 4(\delta + r)\delta}}{2},$$

and these are real and opposite for r, δ greater than zero. As is clear from the phase diagram in Figure 4, the unique path approaching the saddle point (a^*, A^*) is collinear with the $\dot{a} = 0$ line, because all other paths must diverge. Thus, when operating profits are linear in A, the optimal policy is to maintain advertising expenditures at the constant

---

[27]To rule out the optimality of a solution having a zero level of goodwill in the stationary state, we assume that the parameters of the model are such that an "ϵ policy" with $\epsilon > 0$ gives the firm a larger present value than a policy which maintains $(a, A) = (0, 0)$ for all t. By an ϵ policy is meant a policy of maintaining $a = \epsilon$ for all t. If $a = \epsilon$ for all t, then

$$A(t) = \frac{\epsilon}{\delta}(1 - e^{-\delta t}) + A_0 e^{-\delta t}.$$

Differentiating the integral

$$\int_0^\infty e^{-rt} [\pi(A) - w(\epsilon)] \, dt$$

with respect to ϵ, therefore, we obtain

$$\int_0^\infty e^{-rt} \left\{ \pi'(A) \left[\frac{1 - e^{\delta t}}{\delta} \right] - w'(\epsilon) \right\} dt, \tag{a}$$

which represents the change in present value from a small increment in ϵ. If the firm is in a position of zero goodwill (i.e., $A_0 = 0$) and (a) is evaluated at $\epsilon = 0$, we obtain, for the change in present value given an ϵ policy with some small but nonzero ϵ, the expression

$$\frac{\pi'(0)}{r(r + \delta)} - \frac{w'(0)}{r}. \tag{b}$$

If (b) is greater than zero, the firm will not find it optimal to maintain a zero level of goodwill. Thus from (b) we have that a sufficient condition for ruling out the optimality of a solution having a zero stationary level of goodwill is

$$\pi'(0) > (r + \delta)w'(0). \tag{c}$$

For purposes of this paper, condition (c) is assumed to hold.

[28]Advertising is not inimical to the idea of competition as long as we recognize that the concept of a firm embodies the costs of informing the market of its existence. The requirement that the knowledge possessed by the market is "perfect" does not preclude the possibility that information is an economic good. Those interested in a carefully developed argument making a similar point should see Lester Telser, "Advertising and Competition," *Journal of Political Economy*, 72 (1964), pp. 537–562.

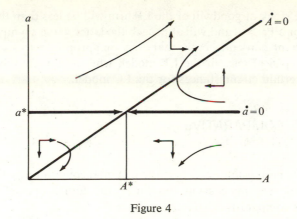

Figure 4

level $a^* = \delta A^*$.[29] The values a^* and A^* are determined from the system

$$w'(a^*) = \frac{\gamma}{r + \delta},$$

$$A^* = \delta a^*. \tag{13}$$

It is clear from (13) that increases in r or δ will decrease the amount of advertising expenditures, and an increase in the marginal profit of goodwill, γ, will increase advertising expenditures. An upward shift in the marginal advertising cost function, $w'(a)$, will decrease a^*.

It is interesting to observe that the optimal policy in the case of constant marginal profitability of goodwill, as developed here, looks superficially identical to the optimal policy determined by Nerlove and Arrow for the case of linear costs when in fact these policies differ significantly. If we were to fix A^* at a given level for a linear profit (LP) firm and for a linear cost (LC) firm we would observe that $a^*(t)$ would be the same for both firms for $t > 0$ if δ is the same for each. At $t = 0$, however, the LP firm would have $a^*(0) = \delta A^*$, whereas the LC firm would have $a^*(0) = \infty$, when A_0 is less than A^*. As a result, the LC firm will have

$$\dot{A}(t) = 0, \qquad t > 0$$

and the LP firm will have

$$\dot{A}(t) = \delta(A^* - A(t)), \qquad t \geq 0,$$

---

[29]A corresponding result has been established in models of investment in physical capital for a firm with costs of adjusting capital stock. See J. P. Gould, "Adjustment Cost, in the Theory of Investment of the Firm," *Review of Economic Studies*, 35 (1968), pp. 47–55; and Arthur Treadway, *Optimal Investment Dynamics and Distributed Lag Models*, unpublished, Ph.D. dissertation, University of Chicago, 1966.

so that the stock of goodwill of the LP firm will be less than that of the LC firm for all $t > 0$ and will approach the latter value asymptotically. An important consequence is that it is inappropriate to use current sales in empirical tests of the LP model, whereas this may be appropriate in certain circumstances for the LC model.

3
SOME COMPARATIVE DYNAMICS

Once it has been established that the instantaneous jump policy is not optimal if advertising costs are nonlinear, the door is opened for some interesting comparative dynamic analyses.[30]

We begin by considering what effect a downward shift in the marginal profit of goodwill function will have on the optimal path of advertising. This may be accomplished by comparing the optimal paths associated with the two marginal profit functions $\pi_1'(A)$ and $\pi_2'(A)$, where, for all A,

$$\pi_2'(A) > \pi_1'(A).$$

It can be seen from the system of equations (11) that the $\dot{a} = 0$ curve associated with π_1' will be below the one associated with π_2' in the (a, A) phase space and that there is no change in the $\dot{A} = 0$ curve, so that $A_1^* < A_2^*$.

We now show that it is impossible for the optimal path associated with π_1' to intersect the optimal path associated with π_2'.[31] Since the slopes of the optimal paths are negative except at the stationary point, no intersection can occur for $A_1^* < A < A_2^*$, as should be clear from Figure 5. If the optimal paths ever intersect to the left of A_1^*, the first such intersection to the left of A_1^* must have $da/dA|_{\pi_1'} < da/dA|_{\pi_2'}$. From the system (11) we obtain

$$\left.\frac{da}{dA}\right|_{\pi_i'} = \left.\frac{\dot{a}}{\dot{A}}\right|_{\pi_i'} = \frac{(r + \delta)w'(a) - \pi_i'(A)}{w''(a)[a - \delta A]} .$$

At a point of intersection the values of a, A, r, and δ will be the same, so that the inequality

$$\left.\frac{da}{dA}\right|_{\pi_1'} < \left.\frac{da}{dA}\right|_{\pi_2'}$$

---

[30]It is worth noting that the instantaneous jump policy arises in part because of the assumption of continuity. As Telser and Graves have shown in a related context, a discrete problem will *not* have instantaneous adjustment even when the continuous version of the problem does. See L. G. Telser and R. L. Graves, "Continuous and Discrete Time Approaches to a Maximization Problem," *Review of Economic Studies*, 35 (1968), pp. 307–325.

[31]The line of analysis employed here has been used by Treadway to show the effect of change in the interest rate on the investment function in a "cost-of-adjustment" model of the firm. See Treadway, *op. cit.*, Chap. V.

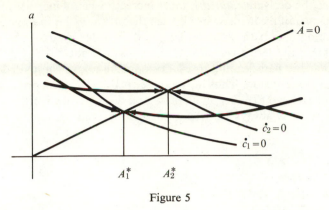

Figure 5

holds only if

$$\pi_1'(A) > \pi_2'(A),$$

which is a contradiction.[32] Thus it has been shown that when the marginal profit of goodwill is decreased for all A, the optimal path of advertising expenditure is shifted downward and the stationary level of A will be decreased.

Similar analyses can be used to show that if r is increased or if $w'(a)$ shifts up by a constant, the optimal path of advertising is shifted downward. When δ increases, the $\dot{c} = 0$ curve shifts downward and the $\dot{A} = 0$ curve shifts upward. This must necessarily reduce A^*, but the stationary value of a can either increase or decrease, as indicated in Figure 6.

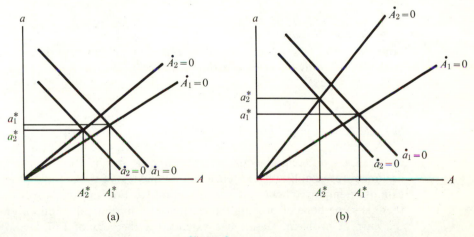

(a)   (b)

Figure 6

[32]Note that a similar contradiction can be established for interactions to the right of A_2^*.

Since the derivative, da/dA, must increase when δ increases we can conclude that if the increase in δ is such that $a_1^* > a_2^*$ [as in Figure 6(b)], then the optimal path of advertising is shifted downward. If $a_2^* > a_1^*$, the fact that the derivative, da/dA, increases does not rule out the possibility that the path leading to a_1^* does not lie above the path leading to a_2^* in some region. Thus an increase in the rate of depreciation of goodwill can lead to either an increase or a decrease in advertising, even though it must always lead to a smaller optimal stationary level of goodwill.

4

THE OPTIMAL POLICY FOR
THE FIRST DIFFUSION
MODEL

Proceeding in a manner analogous to that used in the Nerlove–Arrow model, one obtains an operating profit function $\pi(K)$, where K is the number of persons in the market who know of the firm's advertising message. It is assumed that $\pi'(K) > 0$ and $\pi''(K) \leq 0$ for $K \geq 0$.

The contact coefficient, u, is assumed to be related to advertising expenditures by the cost function $w(u)$, where $w'(u) > 0$ and $w''(u) > 0$. It is also assumed that $\pi'(0) > [(b + r)/N]w'(0)$.[33] The formal problem, using the diffusion process given by (6b), thus becomes

$$\max_{u(t) \geq 0} \int_0^\infty e^{-rt}[\pi(K) - w(u)]\, dt \tag{14}$$

subject to

$$\dot{K} = u(t)N - (b + u(t))K(t),$$
$$K(0) = K_0.$$

Note that $\pi(N) > \pi(K)$ for $K_0 \leq K < N$ and that K can be maintained at the level N only for $u = \infty$ as long as $b > 0$. Thus, since

$$\lim_{u \to \infty} w(u) = \infty,$$

(14) has a finite upper bound over all feasible paths.

A serious problem remains, however. The lack of concavity of the constraining differential equation in u and K means that Uzawa's argument for establishing existence and uniqueness of the optimal path cannot be employed here as it was in Section III. Fortunately, however, there is some hope of proving the existence of an optimal solution for the current problem. Cesari has extended a theorem of Fillipov to

---

[33]This assumption rules out the possibility that the optimum stationary K is zero and is derived by "ϵ-policy" technique (described footnote 27).

establish existence of optimal controls in Pontryagin problems for which the Hamiltonian is concave in the control variable but not necessarily in the state variable.[34] Since the constraining differential equation is linear in the control, and since the integrand of (14) is concave in K and u, there is a possibility of applying the Cesari result. Indeed, for a finite horizon problem where K and u lie in a compact set, the Cesari results would apply directly. The catch is that the problem we are dealing with is an infinite horizon problem and also the range of u is unbounded from above. The latter difficulty can be handled in a reasonably straightforward manner because the finite upper bound on $\pi(K) - w(u)$ means that it would never be optimal for the firm to maintain u above some finite level $\bar{u}$. Hence the problem is not significantly altered if we add the constraint $u(t) \leq \bar{u}$, where $\bar{u}$ is some large finite number. It appears that the remaining difficulty, the assumption of an infinite horizon, can also be handled as Drandakis and Hu have shown in a related context by the use of Helly's theorem.[35] It thus appears that the existence of an optimal control can be established for the present problem, although no formal proof of this assertion is provided here. We now turn to an examination of the necessary conditions for the present problem.

The Hamiltonian for (14) is

$$\mathcal{H} = e^{-rt}\{\pi(K) - w(u) + \psi[uN - (b + u)K]\},$$

from which follow the necessary conditions

$$\dot{\psi} = (b + u + r)\psi - \pi'(K), \tag{15a}$$

$$\psi = \frac{w'(u)}{N - K}, \tag{15b}$$

$$\dot{K} = u(N - K) - bK. \tag{15c}$$

These conditions yield the following system of differential equations:

$$\dot{u} = \frac{1}{w''}\left\{\left(b + r + \frac{bK}{N - K}\right)w' - (N - K)\pi'(K)\right\}, \tag{16a}$$

$$\dot{K} = Nu - (b + u)K. \tag{16b}$$

From (16b) we see that the singular curve $\dot{K} = 0$ in the (K, u) phase

---

[34]L. Cesari, "Existence Theorems for Optimal Solutions in Lagrange and Pontryagin Problems," *Journal of SIAM Control*, Series A (1965), pp. 475–498.

[35]E. M. Drandakis and S. C. Hu, "On the Existence of Optimal Policies with Induced Technical Progress" (unpublished manuscript, presented at the December 1968 meeting of the Econometric Society). I should make clear that I owe a great debt of gratitude to these authors and their paper for bringing the Cesari and Fillipov results to my attention and for showing how these results provide a way of dealing with the existence of solutions to infinite horizon problems which do not have concavity in the constraints.

space is given by

$$K = \frac{uN}{b + u},$$ (17)

where

$$\frac{dK}{du}\bigg|_{\dot{K}=0} = \frac{bN}{(b + u)^2} > 0,$$

$$\frac{d^2K}{du^2}\bigg|_{\dot{K}=0} = \frac{-2bN}{(b + u)^3} < 0.$$

Similarly from (16a), the $\dot{u} = 0$ curve is determined by those (K, u) for which

$$\left(b + r + \frac{bK}{N - K}\right) w'(u) - [N - K]\pi'(K) = 0.$$ (18)

The total differential of (18) yields

$$\frac{dK}{du}\bigg|_{\dot{u}=0} = \frac{\left(b + r + \dfrac{bK}{N - K}\right) w''(u)}{(N - K)\pi'' - \pi' - \dfrac{Nb}{(N - K)^2} w'(u)} < 0$$

for $K \leq N$. It is clear from (17) that $\dot{K} > 0$ for points (K, u) below the $\dot{K} = 0$ singular curve and that $\dot{K} < 0$ for points above this curve. Moreover, since

$$\frac{\partial \dot{u}}{\partial K} = \frac{1}{w''}\left[\frac{Nb}{(N - K)^2} - (N - K)\pi'' + \pi'\right] > 0$$

for $K < N$, it follows that $\dot{u} > 0$ for points above the $\dot{u} = 0$ curve and $\dot{u} < 0$ for points below this curve.

It is now necessary to show that the point of intersection of $\dot{K} = 0$ and $\dot{u} = 0$ is a saddle. The system (16) is linearized around the stationary point (K^*, u^*) in a manner analogous to that used in (12) with the vectors $[A, a]$ and $[\dot{A}, \dot{a}]$ replaced by the vectors $[u, K]$ and $[\dot{u}, \dot{K}]$. The components of $\|\alpha_{ij}\|$ are now given by

$$\alpha_{11} = \frac{\partial F}{\partial u}\bigg|_{\substack{u=u^* \\ K=K^*}} = r + b + u^*,$$

$$\alpha_{12} = \frac{\partial F}{\partial K}\bigg|_{\substack{u=u^* \\ K=K^*}} = \frac{w'(u^*)}{w''(u^*)}\left[\frac{(b + u^*)^2}{bN}\right] - \frac{(N - K^*)\pi''(K^*) - \pi'(K^*)}{w''(u^*)},$$

$$\alpha_{21} = \frac{\partial G}{\partial u}\bigg|_{\substack{u=u^* \\ K=K^*}} = N - K^* = \frac{bN}{b + u^*},$$

$$\alpha_{22} = \frac{\partial G}{\partial K}\bigg|_{\substack{u=u^* \\ K=K^*}} = -(b + u^*),$$

where $F(u, K)$ and $G(u, K)$ denote the right-hand sides of (16a) and (16b), respectively. The eigenvalues of $\|\alpha_{ij}\|$ are

$$\lambda = \frac{(\alpha_{11} + \alpha_{22}) \pm \sqrt{(\alpha_{11} + \alpha_{22})^2 - 4(\alpha_{11}\alpha_{22} - \alpha_{12}\alpha_{21})}}{2}. \quad (19)$$

These eigenvalues will be real and opposite if $(\alpha_{11}\alpha_{22} - \alpha_{12}\alpha_{21}) < 0$, and this is in fact the case because $\alpha_{11} > 0$, $\alpha_{22} < 0$, $\alpha_{12} > 0$, and $\alpha_{21} > 0$. Thus the point (u^*, K^*) is a saddle and there exists a unique path approaching it in the (K, u) phase space. These results are depicted in the phase diagram shown in Figure 7.

The general qualitative properties of the optimal path are similar to those found for the Nerlove–Arrow model with nonlinear costs of adding to goodwill. In particular, for $K_0 < K^*$ the optimum policy is to advertise most heavily at the start of the campaign and continually decrease advertising expenditures as K approaches K^*. In contrast to the Nerlove–Arrow model, this general pattern of advertising expenditures is maintained even when it is assumed that $\pi'(k)$ is constant. It is also interesting to note that the $\dot{u} = 0$ singular curve intersects the K axis at $K = N$ and, since the optimal $u^*(t)$ path lies to the right of this singular curve, the optimal policy always has $u^*(0) > 0$ even if $K_0 > K^*$. Thus it can be seen that the nature of the diffusion process has some important effects on the optimal advertising policy. This is even more obvious for the model analyzed in Section V.

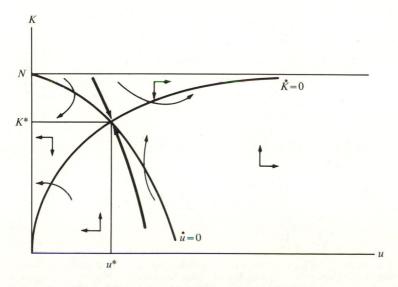

Figure 7

5
THE OPTIMAL ADVERTISING POLICY FOR THE SECOND DIFFUSION

If information spread is assumed to occur according to the model (7b), where the firm affects the parameter $c(t)$ through its advertising policy, then, reasoning along the lines used in the last two sections, the formal problem becomes

$$\max_{0 \le c(t)} \int_0^\infty e^{-rt}[\pi(K) - w(c)] \, dt \qquad (20)$$

subject to

$$\dot{K}(t) = -bK(t) + c(t)K(t)\left[1 - \frac{K(t)}{N}\right].$$

The constraining differential equation is linear in the control, c, so the kinds of existence arguments alluded to in Section IV should also apply in the present case.[36]

The Hamiltonian expression for (20) is

$$\mathcal{H} = e^{-rt}\left\{\pi(K) - w(c) + \psi(t)\left[(c - b)K(t) - \frac{c}{N}K(t)^2\right]\right\},$$

from which we obtain

$$\dot{\psi} = \psi\left[r - c + b + 2\frac{c}{N}K\right] - \pi'(K), \qquad (21a)$$

$$\psi = \frac{w'(t)}{K - (K^2/N)}, \qquad (21b)$$

$$\dot{K} = (c - b)K - \frac{c}{N}K^2. \qquad (21c)$$

Eliminating ψ and $\dot{\psi}$ from (21a) and (21b), we obtain after some manipulation

$$\dot{c} = \frac{1}{w''}\left\{w'\left[r + \frac{bK}{N - K}\right] - \left[K - \frac{K^2}{N}\right]\pi'\right\}, \qquad (22a)$$

$$\dot{K} = (c - b)K - \frac{c}{N}K^2. \qquad (22b)$$

---

[36]It is clear that for both this model and the model of Section IV, additional work on both existence and sufficiency proofs is in order. Since this would entail a substantial increase in the amount of mathematical analysis in what is already an overly long paper, I have decided to leave these considerations for a later work. It should be emphasized that such further analysis may lead to modifications in the results of this paper.

There are *two* singular curves for $\dot{K} = 0$; the line $K = 0$ and

$$K = N\left(1 - \frac{b}{c}\right) \tag{23}$$

for $K \neq 0$. From (23) it follows that

$$\left.\frac{dK}{dc}\right|_{\substack{\dot{K}=0 \\ K \neq 0}} = N\left(\frac{b}{c^2}\right) > 0,$$

$$\left.\frac{d^2K}{dc^2}\right|_{\substack{\dot{K}=0 \\ K \neq 0}} = -N\left(\frac{2b}{c^3}\right) < 0.$$

These two singular curves divide the (K, c) phase space into four relevant subspaces.[37] For $0 < K < N$,

$$\frac{\partial \dot{K}}{\partial c} = K\left(1 - \frac{K}{N}\right) > 0,$$

and this expression is negative for $K < 0$. These results are illustrated in Figure 8.

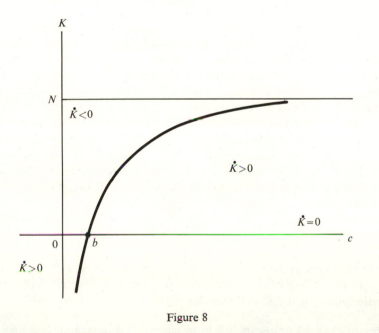

Figure 8

[37]We ignore the behavior of $\dot{K}$ for points above the $K = N$ line.

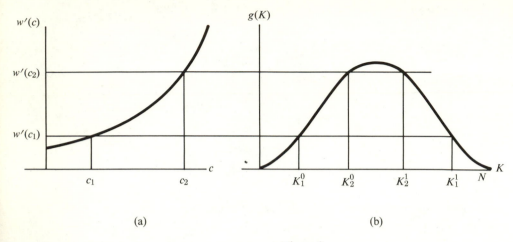

Figure 9

Turning to the $\dot{c} = 0$ singular curve, (22a) will be zero for points (K, c) satisfying

$$w'(c) = \frac{K\left(1 - \dfrac{K}{N}\right)\pi'(K)}{r + \dfrac{bK}{N - K}} = h(K). \qquad (24)$$

Inspection of the right-hand side of (24) [which is denoted $h(K)$] indicates that the shape of $h(K)$ is typified by graph (b) of Figure 9. Graph (a) of Figure 9 illustrates a typical $w'(c)$ curve. As may be seen from Figure 9, when c is small, there will be two values of K associated with each such c. For example, at $c = c_1$, $\dot{c}$ is zero for $K = K_1^0$ and $K = K_1^1$. Similarly, the values K_2^0, K_2^1 are associated with c_2 on the $\dot{c} = 0$ curve. As c gets larger, the associated values of K get closer together, and for large enough c there is no solution at all. Since $w'(0) > 0$ and $h(0) = h(N) = 0$, it follows that at $c = 0$ the $\dot{c} = 0$ singular curve intersects the K axis at two points between 0 and N. It follows from

$$\left.\frac{\partial \dot{c}}{\partial c}\right|_{\dot{c}=0} = r + \frac{bK}{N - K} > 0 \qquad (K < N)$$

that for points to the right of the $\dot{c} = 0$ singular curve, $\dot{c} > 0$, and for points to the left of this curve, $\dot{c} < 0$. Combining these results with those found for the $\dot{K} = 0$ singular curve we obtain Figure 10.[38]

[38]It should be noted that Figure 10 is by no means the only conceivable configuration. For example, the $\dot{c} = 0$ and $\dot{K} = 0$ may not intersect at all or they may intersect only at a single point of tangency.

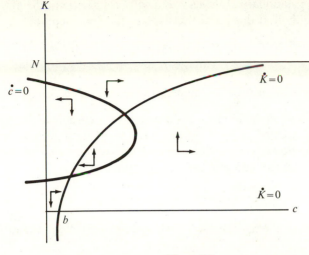

Figure 10

There are two stationary points in this phase diagram and it is necessary to examine the behavior of the system at each. We linearize the system as in (12), replacing $[\dot{A}, \dot{a}]$ and $[A, a]$ by $[\dot{K}, \dot{c}]$ and $[K, c]$, respectively, and recognizing $\|\alpha_{ij}\|$ as the relevant matrix of partial derivatives evaluated at the stationary point. Specifically,

$$\alpha_{11} = \left.\frac{\partial \dot{K}}{\partial K}\right|_{\substack{K=K^* \\ c=c^*}} = b - c^*,$$

$$\alpha_{12} = \left.\frac{\partial \dot{K}}{\partial c}\right|_{\substack{K=K^* \\ c=c^*}} = K^* \left(1 - \frac{K^*}{N}\right),$$

$$\alpha_{21} = \left.\frac{\partial \dot{c}}{\partial K}\right|_{\substack{K=K^* \\ c=c^*}} = \frac{1}{w''} \left\{ \left(r + \frac{b}{(N-K^*)^2}\right) w' - \left(1 - \frac{2K^*}{N}\right)\pi' \right. $$
$$\left. - \left(K^* - \frac{K^{*2}}{N}\right)\pi'' \right\},$$

$$\alpha_{22} = \left.\frac{\partial \dot{c}}{\partial c}\right|_{\substack{K=K^* \\ c=c^*}} = r + c^* - b.$$

The stationary points are such that $c^* > b$ and $K^* = N(1 - b/c^*) < N$, so that $\alpha_{11} < 0$, $\alpha_{12} > 0$, $\alpha_{22} > 0$ and the sign of α_{21} is ambiguous, since it depends on the size of K^* relative to N. To facilitate the analysis, it is convenient to introduce the following:

Lemma. The stationary point (K^*, c^*) will be a saddle in the above system if and only if at this point the slope of the $\dot{c} = 0$ curve

$$\left(\frac{dc}{dK}\bigg|_{\dot{c}=0}\right)$$

is less than the slope of the $\dot{K} = 0$ curve $(dc/dK|_{\dot{K}=0})$.

Proof: The lemma is simply a geometric interpretation of the fact that the eigenvalues of $\|\alpha_{ij}\|$ at a stationary point must be real and opposite if that point is a saddle. From (19) it can be seen that the eigenvalues will be real and opposite if and only if

$$-\alpha_{11}\alpha_{22} + \alpha_{12}\alpha_{21} > 0. \tag{25}$$

Given the signs of the α_{ij}'s in the above system, (25) is equivalent to the condition

$$\frac{\alpha_{21}}{\alpha_{22}} > \frac{\alpha_{11}}{\alpha_{12}}. \tag{26}$$

At (K^*, c^*), the slope

$$\frac{dc}{dK}\bigg|_{\dot{c}=0} = -\frac{\alpha_{21}}{\alpha_{22}}$$

and the slope

$$\frac{dc}{dK}\bigg|_{\dot{K}=0} = -\frac{\alpha_{11}}{\alpha_{12}}.$$

Combining these expressions and (26) we see that (K^*, c^*) is a saddle point if and only if

$$\frac{dc}{dK}\bigg|_{\dot{c}=0} = -\frac{\alpha_{21}}{\alpha_{22}} < -\frac{\alpha_{11}}{\alpha_{22}} = \frac{dc}{dK}\bigg|_{\dot{K}=0}.$$

A stationary point that is not a saddle will be an unstable node if the eigenvalues of $\|\alpha_{ij}\|$ are real and positive, and it will be an unstable focus if these eigenvalues are complex with positive real parts. Since in the above system $\alpha_{11} + \alpha_{22} = r > 0$, we obtain, from (19) and the lemma, the following:

Corollary. If, in the system (22), the slope of $\dot{c} = 0$ is greater than the slope of the $\dot{K} = 0$ curve at a stationary point, then that stationary point is unstable.

Returning to Figure 10, we see that at the stationary point with the larger K^*, the $\dot{c} = 0$ curve has negative slope and the $\dot{K} = 0$ curve has positive slope, so that, according to the lemma, this is a saddle point. At the stationary point with the smaller K^*, the $\dot{c} = 0$ curve

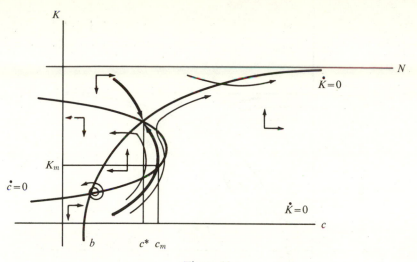

Figure 11

cuts the $\dot{K} = 0$ curve from above, so that $dc/dK|_{\dot{c}=0} > dc/dK|_{\dot{K}=0}$ and we know from the corollary that this is an unstable stationary point.

It is interesting to observe that the diffusion process used in this model is such that if K_0 is zero, there is no way of achieving any positive level of K no matter how much the firm spends on advertising. This means that for certain values of K_0 the path to the saddle point is not optimal, because for small emough K_0 it is presumably optimal to keep c at zero indefinitely. For the remainder of this paper, however, it is assumed that K_0 is large enough to put the firm on the unique path which leads to the saddle point. The optimum path in Figure 11 differs significantly from that found in the previous two models. In the earlier models, the optimum path of advertising expenditures always requires the heaviest outlays in the early periods with continuous reductions in expenditures as K (or A) approaches its equilibrium level. In contrast, the optimum path for the present model may begin with a low level of expenditure, build up to a maximum of c_m, which is greater than the equilibrium level c^*, and then cut back toward c^* as K approaches K^*. Thus, while K increases all along the optimum path, c first increases and then decreases over time.[39] Of course, it is not always true that this pattern will be followed in the present model. If, for example, K_0 is larger than K_m (where K_m is the ordinate of the point where the optimum path intersects the $\dot{c} = 0$ singular curve), then advertising expenditures will be continuously decreasing all along the

[39]It is interesting to note that for $K_0 > K^*$ the optimum path for c is monotonically increasing and does not reverse as it may when $K_0 < K^*$.

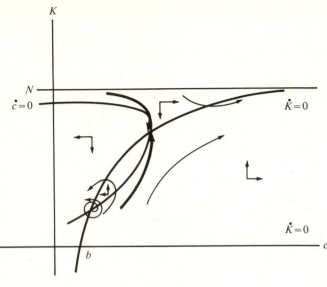

Figure 12

optimum path. On the other hand, consider Figure 12, where the slope of the $\dot{c} = 0$ curve is positive at both stationary points. At the stationary point with the larger K^*, the $\dot{c} = 0$ curve cuts the $\dot{K} = 0$ curve from below so that $dc/dK|_{\dot{c}=0} < dc/dK|_{\dot{K}=0}$, and according to the lemma this is a saddle point. The other stationary point is unstable, since the $\dot{c} = 0$ curve cuts the $\dot{K} = 0$ curve from above. Thus the heavy line indicates the optimal path and, as can be seen, for $K_0 < K^*$, advertising expenditures start at a low level and *increase* along the entire path as K approaches K^*.[40]

<h1 style="text-align:center">6
SUMMARY AND
CONCLUSIONS</h1>

This paper has extended the Nerlove–Arrow model of the dynamic optimal advertising policy for the firm by relaxing their assumption of a linear advertising cost function and also by recognizing that there exist alternative hypotheses about the way in which information spreads through a market. As Nerlove and Arrow noted in their paper, the introduction of a nonlinear advertising cost function invalidates the optimality of the instantaneous "jump" policy which they established for the linear case. This nonlinear cost function also affects the optimal policy for periods following the initial expenditure (although this

[40]For $K_0 > K^*$, c starts low, increases, and then decreases as K approaches K^*.

point is not entirely clear in the Nerlove–Arrow paper) and, as a consequence, a number of the Nerlove–Arrow results are only "quasi-dynamic" in some respects.

The introduction of different processes of information spread leads to an extremely varied set of patterns for the optimal path as outlined in Table 1.

As can be seen from the table, the process of information spread has significant effects on the optimal advertising policy. It is interesting to note that, although it is clearly useful to exploit the "capital-stock" aspects of advertising, the analogy should not be pushed too far. It is somewhat counterintuitive, in the context of an investment model, to think of making the smallest increments to capital stock when the gap between desired and actual capital stock is the greatest and then decrease the rate of investment as the gap narrows. Nonetheless, this pattern may occur with the contagion model of information spread, as shown in the last sections of this paper.

There remain a great many unanswered questions, and it is worthwhile to mention at least some of these at this point. First, for reasons of analytical convenience, it has been assumed that exogenous parameters remain stationary in the above analysis. This is clearly unrealistic. It is very likely that the entrance of competing brands or changes in competitors' price and advertising policies will affect the forgetfulness coefficient b. Furthermore, there certainly will be shifts in the demand function over time. While the precise effect of such changes cannot be developed in detail here, it is clear that the firm will take into account the future time path of these exogenous variables in making current

Table 1

Shape of Optimal Path of Advertising Expenditures for $A_0 < A^*(K_0 < K^*)$ and $A^*(K^*)$ Stationary	Model[a]
Instantaneous jump to optimum	Nerlove–Arrow with linear advertising cost function
Constant	Nerlove–Arrow with nonlinear advertising cost function and profit linear in goodwill
Monotonically decreasing	Nerlove–Arrow, diffusion, and contagion (if K_0 is sufficiently large) with nonlinear advertising cost function
Increasing, then decreasing	Contagion with nonlinear advertising costs and sufficiently low initial K_0
Monotonically increasing	Contagion with nonlinear advertising costs (for certain values of K^*)

[a]For purposes of distinction, the Stigler model is called a "diffusion" model and the Ozga model is called a "contagion" model in this table. These titles, although somewhat arbitrary, seem to capture the flavor of the different diffusion processes.

decisions. Thus, if it is expected that demand will shift downward at some future time, it is likely that the firm will advertise less in the current period than it would if demand were expected to remain constant or increase in the future.

Finally, it should be emphasized that the models used in the above analysis probably represent extremes. A more plausible assumption is that information spreads through a more general process. It is useful, nonetheless, to gain insight into this combined process by examining the extreme cases in isolation.

On the Theory of
Price Dynamics*

DONALD F. GORDON and
ALLAN HYNES

The present paper was motivated by the authors' interest in the logical foundations of disequilibrium price dynamics, including behavior relations such as the Phillips curve and its elaborations. Our fundamental interest is in the possibility of deriving the behavioral relationships expressed in the equations used in disequilibrium price dynamics from the maximizing postulate which has long been the basis for comparative statics. In Section 1 we examine briefly some aspects of the existing theory of such price adjustments in both competitive and monopolistic markets. We conclude that disequilibrium price dynamics are impossible to derive from the maximizing assumption unless some form of imperfect information is introduced into the model, and we elaborate a necessary condition for such a state of imperfect information. In Section 2 stochastic demand functions are introduced and are extended beyond their common usage in inventory theory toward a more general theory of unemployed resources. A major conclusion here is that as long as the economic unit is assumed to know the probability distribution of his demand, we are dealing with comparative statics, and that to speak of disequilibrium price movements between

*This study was financed by a grant from the National Science Foundation. An earlier version was presented at the meetings of the Western Economic Association in August 1965. We are indebted to numerous colleagues at the University of Washington and at the University of Rochester for helpful discussions at numerous points.

positions of comparative statics, we must assume a state of uncertainty as opposed to risk to use the distinction put forth by F. H. Knight. In such a state the price movements represent the results of learning. In Section 3 we deal with disequilibrium price dynamics themselves. The major conclusion here is that the instability of the Phillips curve is but a special case of the general principle that any stable equation describing disequilibrium dynamic price behavior is inconsistent with maximizing postulates. Finally, Section 4 indicates certain implications of our findings for currently contested issues in the theory of inflation.

1
THE CURRENT THEORY
OF PRICE ADJUSTMENTS

A. The Competitive Model   From well before the time of Adam Smith, the literature of economic theory has contained arguments to the effect that in competitive markets prices will rise when there is excess demand and fall when there is excess supply. In 1941, apparently for the first time, this "law of supply and demand" was given a formal interpretation by Samuelson[1] when he wrote for an isolated market,

$$\frac{dp}{dt} = F(D - S), F(0) = 0, \text{ and } F' > 0, \tag{1a}$$

$$D = D(p, a), \qquad S = S(p), \tag{2a}$$

where p is the market price, D and S are the quantities demanded and supplied per unit time, and a is a shift parameter. For multiple interconnected markets the equivalent equations are

$$\frac{dp_i}{dt} = F_i(D_i - S_i), F_i(0) = 0, \text{ and } F_i' > 0 \quad (i = 1, 2, \ldots, n), \tag{1b}$$

$$D_i = D_i(p_1, p_2, \ldots, p_i, \ldots, p_n, a_i),$$
$$S_i = S_i(p_1, p_2, \ldots, p_i, \ldots, p_n). \tag{2b}$$

The seemingly innocuous clarification contained in these equations has formed a basis for research in the pure theory of price dynamics and for empirical investigations of labor markets in disequilibrium. The latter research has led some economists to suggest the possibility of a trade-off between alternative rates of inflation and levels of employment.

   Theoretical work, following the leads of Professor Samuelson's own research, has been primarily directed at determining the formal

---

[1]Samuelson's early contributions are summarized in P. A. Samuelson, *The Foundations of Economic Analysis* (Harvard University Press, Cambridge, Mass., 1947), pp. 257–349.

requirements for dynamic stability in multiple markets. These studies have been concerned with deriving the necessary and sufficient conditions for dynamic relations of the form shown in (1a) or (1b) to yield time paths of prices that approach equilibrium values from arbitrary disequilibrium points.[2]

Professor Phillips and others have attempted to estimate a form of (1a) for labor markets,[3] and this negative functional relationship has been used in support of the belief that with more or less free labor markets a trade-off is available to policy-makers between the rate of increase of money wages and the level of unemployment. Despite empirical findings that at best must be regarded as highly inconclusive, the "Phillips curve" has become embedded in the conventional economic wisdom to the extent that it now appears in standard elementary texts.

Although the use of (1a) and (1b) as a basis for theoretical and policy analysis has been extensive, important conceptual weaknesses have been recognized in the hypothesized dynamic process.[4] First, (1a) and (1b) are essentially arbitrary with respect to motivation. The properties of static demand and supply functions are derived on the basis of the proposition that households and firms maximize the familiar objective functions, while dynamic properties, on the other hand, are never deduced as the maximizing response of economic units to changing data.[5] Second, the economic actors are not defined. When all prices are taken by traders as given (as in the competitive model), the question naturally arises: Who or what is the economic unit whose behavior is described by (1a) and (1b)? It has been conjectured that in well-organized markets, "we may imagine an auctioneer who, as the incarnation of the competitive force in the market, raises the prices of the commodities at a rate proportional to the dif-

[2]The work in this area is summarized in T. Negishi, "The Stability of a Competitive Economy," *Econometrica*, 30 (October 1962), pp. 635–669.

[3]Earlier work in this area is critically surveyed in G. Perry, *Unemployment, Money Wage Rates, and Inflation* (M.I.T. Press, Cambridge, Mass., 1966). Of course, some economists might argue—against the viewpoint taken in this paper—that the Phillips curve does not represent labor markets in *disequilibrium*. The point is discussed at length in Section 3.

[4]For example, see K. Arrow, "Toward a Theory of Price Adjustment," *The Allocation of Economic Resources*, M. Abramovitz et al., eds. (Stanford University Press, Stanford, Calif., 1959), pp. 41–51; and T. Koopmans, *Three Essays on the State of Economic Science* (McGraw-Hill, Inc., New York, 1957). The Marshallian dynamic system, where dx/dt is a function of the difference between demand price and supply price, will not be discussed in this paper.

[5]Another aspect of the problem concerns the issues raised by the correspondence principle as stated by Samuelson and developed in the literature under the general topical heading of qualitative economics. The principle states that economists should examine the requirements for dynamic stability as an independent source of restrictions on the static functions of economic systems. This methodology is anomalous, and may not yield powerful operational theorems, precisely because the adjustment mechanisms are not linked to the analysis of utility or profit-maximizing behavior of the relevant economic units in the disequilibrium positions.

ference between demand and supply."[6] In point of fact, the auctioneer is a *deus ex machina* introduced into the analysis to salvage the equations despite their contradiction with the logical structure of competitive markets.[7]

Finally, (1a) and (1b) are subject to criticism on an altogether different level. Since they are introduced to summarize price behavior in a true disequilibrium situation, they do not describe movements that arise because of the presence of adjustment costs; adjustments arising from the latter would represent a moving equilibrium. But to hypothesize the stability of *any* functions such as these makes little sense in a private market inhabited by maximizing traders. Stability of (1a) implies that given an initial price and level of excess demand, the course of future prices is predictable. But if this were true, profit opportunities would exist and private traders exploiting these opportunities would act in a manner to destroy the stability of the hypothetical differential equation. The logic of this argument is identical to that which suggests that stock market prices may be represented by a random walk.[8]

When the analysis is extended to multiple markets, the problem is more complicated. Equation (1b) implies a predictable course of any one price for a given set of all prices, and it may be more difficult for persons to detect the form of the true relationship. Nevertheless, any systematic relationship may be expected to be discovered if it recurs persistently, and again incentives would exist to buy and sell in a manner that would nullify the original function.[9]

B. The Monopoly Model   Because the competitive model is so completely unsatisfactory as a framework within which to analyze

---

[6]Negishi, *loc. cit.*

[7]Of course, it should not be surprising that the traditional dynamics attributed to competitive markets prove inconsistent with an important axiom of that model. When demand does not equal supply, it is logically inadmissible that each and every trader can buy or sell unlimited quantities at the given prices; therefore, the competitive model in its logically complete form cannot apply.

A number of other incongruities appear in the current literature on price dynamics, particularly in discussions of macroeconomic theory and policy. In many analyses of positions of less than full employment it is assumed that the supply of labor is perfectly elastic until full employment is reached. Second, it is maintained that sellers' inflation occurs when firms or unions raise prices or wages before full employment is attained. These propositions contradict (1a) or (1b) as well as each other and of course are not derived from the usual axiom of maximizing behavior. Later we make more positive criticisms of (1a) and (1b).

[8]See P. Cootner, ed., *The Random Character of Stock Market Prices* (M.I.T. Press, Cambridge, Mass., 1964).

[9]In anticipation of results to be arrived at later from a different line of reasoning, it is interesting to note that the above analysis may be extended to the examination of the Phillips curve or any more elaborate equation attempting to predict the economy's price and output response to a change in aggregate demand. If aggregate demand does fluctuate, and if a stable function describes the economy's price and output response, profit opportunities will appear and their exploitation will eliminate them, thereby destroying the postulated stability of the function under consideration.

price dynamics, it is natural to utilize the model of monopoly for the study of disequilibrium behavior. Here, at least, we have no trouble identifying the economic agent who changes prices. Thus for the rest of this paper we will drop the competitive assumption of price-taking, as we surely must if we are to discuss price-changing. However, important sources of ambiguity remain. Oscar Lange has postulated a price-adjustment relation for monopolists who face a nonstochastic demand schedule.[10] His statement is equivalent to

$$\frac{dp}{dt} = G(R' - C'), \ G' < 0, \text{ and } G(0) = 0, \tag{3}$$

where R' and C' are marginal revenue and marginal cost, respectively. The immediate question is: What is the economic situation characterized by (3)? After all, why should the monopolist ever be at a non-maximizing position? Two possibilities appear relevant: The monopolist may be assumed to know the entire demand schedule, but, given a shift of the schedule, instantaneous adjustment will not occur if costs of changing price increase with the rate of price change; alternatively, he may be assumed to know only a point, and (3) describes a process by which he searches the schedule.

If the former model is adopted, a formal analysis showing his maximizing behavior over time can support an adjustment relation of the form stated in (3). We feel hard pressed, however, to cite examples of economic costs that would give rise to this model; thus it seems rather sterile as a source of important propositions about price dynamics. Why should the process of making price changes per unit time be more costly for large changes than for small? (Note that we are not discussing costs of production.)

This leaves the process of acquiring information as the most tenable explanation of dynamic behavior relationships, and this is the position taken in the remainder of this paper. However, before entering upon an analysis of the effects of incomplete information, we wish to examine an ambiguity frequently implied in the literature and to point out a condition that must hold if lack of information is to be an important economic consideration.

C. A Condition for the Existence of Nonequilibrium Prices

Conventional analysis of demand, cost, and supply functions defines the commodity transacted as a flow; there are, though, two possible interpretations. The variable can be defined as time-continuous—that is, as an instantaneous rate of change in a stock with the derivative being continuous with respect to time. Alternatively, the variable can

---

[10]O. Lange, *Price Flexibility and Full Employment* (The Principia Press, Bloomington, Ill., 1944), p. 107.

be defined as discrete quantities transacted at discrete time intervals, which can be transformed to a flow by averaging over time. This is the elementary logical distinction between a derivative and an average difference. Of little importance for purposes of examining many theoretical problems in comparative statics, the distinction becomes crucial in understanding disequilibrium behavior.

A substantial fraction of existing theoretical literature seems to assume that *transactions* are continuous, which requires that the commodity is perfectly divisible. But if this interpretation is adopted, it would appear that the search of an unknown demand schedule would be (virtually) costless and instantaneous. Because transacting is continuous, the seller possesses a critical type of information. The rate of output to be taken by demanders at a quoted price is known instantaneously, and any shift in demand is immediately registered as a change in sales. The seller could then run his price over any range in an arbitrarily short period of time and trace out his new demand curve. The market would in the limit always be in equilibrium, and the rate of price change would go to infinity.

Consequently, we will henceforth apply the analysis to markets in which transactions occur at discrete points in time. It may appear that this view of purchases and sales is being adopted on rather formal grounds—based on the desire to derive finite rates of change in price from maximizing behavior. This is true. Although for many purposes of comparative statics these aspects of reality are not crucial and have properly been ignored, it is apparent that for analysis of price dynamics the proposed view is not only critically important but fully realistic.

Consider, first, physical commodities. A very large proportion of such commodities possess indivisibilities which are costly or, in the limit, technically impossible to overcome. Examples are clothing, durable consumer or capital goods, or—to go to the extreme—matches. There are, of course, material goods which may be considered physically infinitely divisible—gases or liquids—but even these are traded in finite increments because of economies of scale in transactions. Thus one does not trade 5 cents' worth of common stock or so many thimblefuls of gasoline; more exactly, one does not purchase such commodities in a continuous stream or flow. Transacting in the real world is the exchange of finite quantities at discrete points in time.

The services of physical wealth are naturally infinitely divisible because time has this property. But transactions in these services are not continuous; rather, they occur at intermittent points and for finite blocks of time (i.e., for the present value of a stream of services). The costs of continuous transacting are prohibitive, so that one rents office space, hotel rooms, or apartments for discrete periods.

The above observations are generally applicable to labor markets and other factor markets as well as to product markets. For markets characterized by the presence of legal contracts, such as union markets, the applicability appears obvious. For those labor markets where no legal contracts exist, we are accustomed to think of the services as purchased and sold in a time-continuous fashion, because either the employer or the employee may terminate the relation at any instant. In actual fact, however, it is clear that when a bargain is struck, both parties consider it an implicit agreement to exchange services for a finite, though undetermined, duration. Costs of search for both employee and employer and the cost of formal and informal job training prevent either from wishing to recontract continuously.[11]

For our purposes the important aspect of markets where purchases and sales are in discrete units is that in an important sense the seller is always between transactions and cannot observe at any instant in time his current demand. Strictly speaking, the only observable prices and quantities are those at which past contracts were closed. This is true even where the increments sold are fairly trivial, such as successive packages of cigarettes. Under these circumstances only future demand exists, and the usual sharp distinction between present and future is replaced by the less exact difference between immediate and "further" future. It is natural in these circumstances to introduce stochastic demand functions[12]—an analytical tool that has been extensively applied in inventory theory—and to this we now turn.

2
STOCHASTIC DEMAND SCHEDULES AND PRICE ADJUSTMENTS

A. The Standard Inventory Model We have thus far argued that disequilibrium price dynamics must entail some form of imperfect information. In this section we will first point out that if such lack of information is introduced with a known but stochastic demand schedule, the results contradict the zero excess supply postulate of (1a) and (1b). Second, we will argue that ordinary stochastic models, where the seller knows the probability distribution of his demand, are insufficient to produce "true" disequilibria such as occur in business cycles; the latter must be produced by uncertainty in the Knightian sense, where the parameters of the relevant distributions are not known. Third, we

---

[11]Economists have become accustomed to think of transactions in two categories—stocks and flows—and for many purposes such a distinction is crucial. It is therefore difficult to keep in mind that in fact all transactions are exchanges of assets.

[12]Stochastic models introduce a form of uncertainty into the analysis, and there may thus be additional reasons why persons would not be willing to transact continuously. The notion of risk aversion also raises the possibility that utility, rather than wealth-maximizing models, should be the framework of the analysis. In this paper wealth-maximizing models are used—thus implicitly assuming linear utility functions and/or perfect capital markets.

will show in simplified examples how the "optimal unemployment" of inventory theory can be extended to other markets, including the labor market.

The logical implications of stochastic demand models for the theory of price adjustment are conveniently summarized by the simple monopoly model. The seller is assumed to have imperfect information in that he does not know what quantity will be sold at a particular price, but it is assumed that he knows the parameters of the probability distribution of demand. Thus the demand function may be specified as

$$x = f(p, V, u), \tag{4}$$

where x is the quantity demanded per unit time, p is the price per unit of quantity, $V = (v_1, \ldots, v_m)$ is a vector of information or prediction variables, and u is a random variable with zero mean and constant variance. In the general case (when a firm's horizon extends beyond one period) positive returns will be attached to end-period inventories and positive costs will be associated with shortages. It is a well-known result[13] that maximization of expected income subject to a demand function of the form in (4) and a normal cost function $c(x)$ will yield a solution dictating that the firm maintain an optimum level of inventories, or "unemployed" resources. This result naturally contradicts the equilibrium axiom of traditional dynamics, which states that $F(0) = 0$.

Observed prices in these models will not be stable but will fluctuate from period to period, continually maintaining equilibrium stocks of commodities, given the observation on demand in the prior period. If a random observation were relatively high, inventory would subsequently be relatively low; with an increasing marginal cost function, price would therefore be higher in the subsequent period. The change in price is therefore a positive function of $(D - S)$, where D is the *observed* demand rather than the expected quantity demanded. These movements are not, though, analogous to movements from a non-equilibrium position toward an equilibrium position; rather they are continuously maintaining equilibrium, given an unchanging set of known parameters defining the demand and cost functions. Moreover, if the parameters were changing in a way that the seller has learned to predict—say, because of a steady continuous inflation—prices will be changing so as to maintain equilibrium levels of unemployed resources. Thus if (4) fully specified the forces positioning the demand schedule—including the time path of monetary and fiscal policy subject only to a random component—long runs of abnormal levels of unemployed resources would not be observed. For example, assume sellers did

---

[13]For example, see E. S. Mills, *Price, Output, and Inventory Policy* (John Wiley Sons, Inc., New York, 1962), Chap. IV.

know the distribution of their demand and that aggregate demand were serially correlated in a known manner. Past values of aggregate demand will be included in the predictive variables, and prices will adjust to allow for the known correlation. For any given demand function, expected unemployment $(D - S)$ would in each period be the optimal or equilibrium level. Successive periods of deficient demand would represent a "highly unlikely" run. The probability of runs such as occur during a prolonged depression would be virtually zero; they would be replaced by larger fluctuations in prices.

The above discussion naturally implies that disequilibrium is most meaningfully defined as a situation where the seller is not certain about the true values of the parameters describing the position of his demand function; and disequilibrium price changes may then be defined as those changes that arise as the seller discovers the "true" values of these parameters. It is presumably unnecessary to argue in detail that such disequilibrium positions do exist. The distribution of u in (4) may in principle be partitioned into separate components for firm, industry, and aggregate demand. Economic units would have to know the parameters of the distribution functions of each of these components for disequilibrium situations to be the exception rather than the rule.

A theory of price dynamics is therefore in reality a theory of learning. The mysterious motivational character of disequilibrium price dynamics embodied in (1a) and (1b) can therefore be interpreted as maximizing behavior but with a lag due to the process of learning. A formal decision process for this learning is not possible in a world where the underlying stochastic process is not stable. It is true that the response sellers make to new data can, *ex post*, be described as the rational response to subjective prior distributions. However, since there is not sufficient information to accumulate relative frequencies, these subjective estimates will depend, in part at least, on "judgment," will differ among rational persons confronted with the same measurable data, and will also alter from period to period in an unpredictable manner on the basis of information external to the individual's own sampling experience. Such differences and volatility are presumably the operational distinction between risk and uncertainty in the Knightian sense. Later we will investigate the question of whether such learning can produce a stable function relating price adjustments to $(D - S)$, or other variables current or past, which the seller may utilize in estimating demand.

B. Other Sources of Optimal Unemployment Before investigating disequilibrium behavior in more detail we would like to show briefly that the notion of optimal unemployment in inventory theory can be extended to a more general theory of unemployed resources.

Most economists easily accept the notion that in product markets optimal behavior in the face of uncertainty implies the maintenance of buffer stocks of "unemployed" inventories which are distinguished from speculative holdings in that they will be created and maintained even if future demand functions are expected to remain unchanged. In the prior analysis the existence of buffer inventories was clearly dependent on the lack of information embodied in the stochastic demand schedule. Few would suggest that in product markets such assets, kept unemployed for private gain, cause social losses. However, for other kinds of transactions where sellers face stochastic demand curves a different view seems to prevail. This is particularly obvious in the attitude toward labor wherein unemployment is clearly thought to be a social waste, burdensome to the laborer.[14]

But the logic of the argument is similar for many markets. A labor union, for example, with effective control over the wage, may be thought of as facing a demand function such as (4). It presumably attempts to maximize some preference function. In a state of equilibrium, i.e., where the union knows the true probability distribution of demand, this will, in general, not lead it to set a wage such that expected unemployment approaches zero. Again, in the real world of disequilibria, it will have a learning and forecasting problem very similar to the single seller.

Other aspects of optimal unemployment may be seen by considering the sale of a single asset. This polar case illuminates important characteristics of a wide variety of transactions important in the analysis of inflexible prices and unemployment. Obvious cases are the sale of a house, an apartment, or a commercial building. There are, though, less obvious situations; the owner of an apartment wishing to rent it for a finite length of time is selling the present value of a stream of services—i.e., an asset. Similarly, the nonunionized unit of labor seeking to sell his service stream for a finite, though undefined, period is also selling an asset.

In analyzing the sale of a single asset the relevant stochastic variable is not the quantity per unit time, but rather the length of time required to make a transaction. A hypothetical seller does not face a demand function as defined by (4) but rather works with a function giving the probability of selling the asset in a unit time period as a function of price. It is intuitively plausible that assets will vary greatly in the relative range of prices over which the probability of selling goes from zero to one. This range is dependent on the heterogeneity of the asset and the resulting differences in the cost of information needed to make a transaction. Heterogeneous assets are those whose quality is defined

---

[14]A notable exception is expressed in A. Alchian and W. Allen, *University Economics* (Wadsworth Publishing Co., Belmont, Calif., 1968), Chap. XXV. In this work the authors arrive at results similar, in important respects, to those presented in this section.

by a large number of components; these many attributes are expensive to describe and can usually be appraised only by direct inspection. These costs are well known to anyone who has purchased a house. The cost of search is, of course, itself an economic variable, determined primarily by the value of time to the searcher; although the number of potential buyers may be large, only a small fraction of them can evaluate and price any particular house in the unit time period.

Consider the problem of selling a house as contrasted to that of selling a relatively homogeneous asset such as a block of common stock of a particular company. We may suppose that for any buyer there is some price at which he would buy the house, but because of dissimilarities of taste the distribution of these prices may have a wide range. If the seller can sample only a small number of buyers in a time period, no matter how many total buyers would buy at any particular price, he would have to lower the price drastically to raise the probability of selling in the period close to unity. On the other hand, because of the homogeneity of different shares of the common stock, a very large portion of the potential buyers can acquire the relevant information quickly; and because the seller is in touch with a large portion of the market via brokers and the exchange, a relatively small drop in price will raise the probability close to one.

A function that might apply to a seller of a house is illustrated in Figure 1, where Π, the probability of selling the asset in the unit time interval, is a function of the asking price S[15]; i.e., $\Pi = h(S)$, where $0 \leq \Pi \leq 1$ for some $S' \leq S \leq S''$. Hence the period T in which the asset will be sold is a random variable where the probability that $T = t$ is $\Pi(1 - \Pi)^{t-1}$. Assuming the seller knows the true state of the market, and that this state will continue into the future, he can be assumed to maximize expected present value and will thus choose a

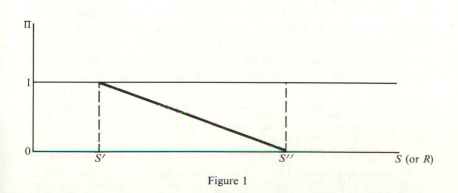

Figure 1

---

[15]The function is assumed linear for the sake of simplicity only. While the function in the figure might represent the demand for a residential dwelling, that for a block of widely traded common stock would be almost vertical.

380 DONALD F. GORDON AND ALLAN HYNES

price that maximizes

$$S\Pi \sum_{j=0}^{\infty} \left(\frac{1-\Pi}{1+r}\right)^j, \qquad (5)$$

where r represents the cost of not selling the house per period of time, expressed as a percentage of the selling price.[16] Thus if the house is otherwise going to be empty and if it does not depreciate, r is simply the interest rate on his nonrealized funds. More generally r would be increased by depreciation and decreased by income from other (inferior) uses of the house (e.g., imputed or actual rent). Summing this geometric series and setting the derivative with respect to price equal to zero, we obtain

$$S^* = -\frac{h(S^*)[h(S^*)+r]}{rh'(S*)}, \qquad (6)$$

where S^* is the maximizing price. Of course the optimum sales price implies an optimum Π^*, which in turn implies an optimum expected period $(1-\Pi^*)/\Pi^*$ in which the asset will on the average be on the market without finding a buyer.[17]

Although the above is probably the simplest characterization of the structure of the problem, it still affords important insights. The maximizing price is solely a function of the parameters that determine $h(S)$; unless these parameters shift, the asking price will remain unchanged no matter how long the asset has remained unsold. If the parameters change, and assuming the owner knows the change, his asking price will immediately be moved to the new equilibrium price.

An interesting and important variant of the problem is that of renting, rather than selling, a unique asset. For simplicity, assume again that the seller maximizes expected wealth and that now there is no rate of discount. The probability of renting per time period, Π, is a function, $g(R)$, of R, the rent asked, a function which the seller again expects to remain stable. The time to rental, T, will be distributed geometrically, with the expected value of T being $(1-\Pi)/\Pi$. If other costs are ignored, the assumptions about the discount rate imply that the expected value of the asset will be maximized when the expected flow of revenue

---

[16]In the example it is assumed that transactions take place at the beginning of the period. Also, it should be noted that the analysis implicitly assumes that the population from which potential buyers are sampled must undergo change; otherwise the function approaches the vertical as t goes to infinity.

[17]The "liquidity" of different assets could be ranked by the length of the period $(1-\Pi^*)/\Pi^*$.

The notion of an optimal expected time of selling, on the one hand, and the optimum search time for a buyer, on the other, throws doubt on the usefulness of models in monetary theory in which the demand for money is instantaneously, or almost instantaneously, equated to the supply. An increased demand for money may be immediately realized if it entails selling highly marketable securities but not if it entails selling a house. Similarly, a decreased demand for money and an increased demand for houses might involve a long optimum search time for buyers.

is maximized. Thus R, the rental price, will be chosen to maximize

$$\frac{RL\Pi}{\Pi(L-1)+1},\tag{7}$$

where L is the term of the lease; although this latter variable is assumed given, a more complete analysis would treat it as an endogenous variable.[18] Differentiating (7) with respect to R gives

$$R^* = -\frac{g(R^*)\{g(R^*)[L-1]+1\}}{g'(R^*)},\tag{8}$$

where R^* is the maximizing price. Finally, we may solve for the optimum expected vacancy rate in terms of the parameters of $g(R)$ and L; at R^* this expected vacancy rate will be

$$\frac{1-g(R^*)}{g(R^*)(L-1)+1}.\tag{9}$$

Again, the formal relation between the stochastic element of the problem and what may be termed frictional unemployment is illustrated. If the owner knows or maintains his estimate of $g(R)$, he will for maximizing rather than for institutional reasons maintain a price that creates this vacancy rate. "Unemployed" resources will be observed, but this simply reflects the costs of operating in a stochastic world.

This analysis of optimal rental decisions is, in its formal aspects, directly applicable to certain characteristics of the behavior of non-unionized labor markets. A unit of labor searching for a job faces the same conceptual decision as does the owner of an apartment; the laborer wishes to lease a block of his services for a finite length of time. Given his knowledge of market conditions as reflected in $g(R)$—which may include other variables—he will seek employment until he is hired at his asking price. He will not alter this wage, no matter how long he has remained unemployed, as long as $g(R)$ remains unchanged. This result is, of course, analogous to that obtained for more familiar forms of stochastic demand schedules; sellers are always in equilibrium for known values of the parameters which position their stochastic decision functions. Disequilibrium price changes emerge in response to the accumulation of knowledge concerning the values of parameters whose magnitudes are unknown.

We have assumed in the above discussion and for the most part will continue to assume that sellers make all price quotations—but

[18]If Π is the probability of renting in one month, then $(1-\Pi)/\Pi$ is the expected time in which it will be rented (when renting starts at the beginning of the month). $L+[(1-\Pi)/\Pi]$ will then be the expected time between successful rentals and $L/\{L+[(1-\Pi)/\Pi]\}$ will be the expected proportion of time that it is rented. Multiplication by R yields (7).

of course do not determine prices. For some markets—labor markets being an important example—this assumption is obviously not realistic. To introduce buyers' wage quotations, a more complete analysis would be required: This would incorporate the interrelation between the demand for products and the demand for labor as a factor of production. The firm that operates in a stochastic world will naturally have a stochastic demand function for labor (and for other inputs) derived from the stochastic product demand schedule. It is obvious that cost considerations which are identical in nature to those previously discussed will dictate against the firm transacting continuously for a flow of labor services. (Of particular importance in this respect are those aspects of on-the-job training which impart specificity to the existing labor force of the firm.) As a consequence of these factors the firm will find it profitable to hold an equilibrium inventory of labor. In the formulation of an optimal maintenance policy, account must be taken of the fact that the quit rate will have a stochastic component,[19] while in the market for new labor the firm will face a supply function that relates the probabilities of obtaining various quantities of labor in the unit time interval to the wage offered. Given the expected term of employment there will be an equilibrium (i.e., profit maximizing) wage that the firm will announce, and this quote will not be altered as long as the parameters defining the relevant probability distributions remain unchanged; a lower wage will not in the long run maintain the labor force at its equilibrium level, while a higher wage imposes unnecessary costs. Given an unknown increase in aggregate demand, for example, the firm will observe runs of quit rates that are higher than have come to be regarded as normal and will also have difficulty obtaining the desired flow of labor at the old equilibrium wage offer. However, with respect to the use of this information, no issues appear special to the problem that have not been discussed above. The disequilibrium adjustments of the wage offer by the firm, as with product-price adjustments and adjustments in wages asked by workers, occur as the firm acquires information about the values of the unknown parameters. It is to this latter issue that we now turn.

3
DISEQUILIBRIUM PRICE RESPONSES

A. Price Adjustments in a Disequilibrium Setting Section 2 has emphasized the crucial distinction between equilibrium and dis-

---

[19]The decision on the part of a worker to quit involves the balancing of the costs and returns of searching the market while employed versus those when he is not working. A full discussion of these issues that is in important ways complementary to our work is presented by Armen Alchian in his paper in this volume.

equilibrium price adjustments. This section will pick up the thread of the argument at this point. The analysis will focus specifically on the question of whether learning in a world characterized by true "Knightian" uncertainty (as defined above) will produce price be-havior of the type postulated by the fundamental equations (1a) or (1b) or by their difference-equation analogs. To clarify the discussion, (4) may be generalized and rewritten as

$$x^e = f^e(V, p, u_1, u_2, u_3, \alpha^e), \qquad (10)$$

where x^e is the estimate of demand; u_1, u_2, and u_3 are the random components of firm, industry, and aggregate demand, respectively; and α^e is an estimate of a shift variable. Although introduced in the context of the standard monopoly model, this relation may also be applied to the interpretation of rental markets; here the seller may be thought of as possessing a number of apartments which he is renting, and x^e may then be reinterpreted as the fraction of the units which will be filled in a particular period.[20]

For analytical simplicity and to establish the argument in a context most applicable for examining its implications for the theory of in-flationary trade-offs, assume the economy is one where the monetary authorities have for a long period maintained on average a stable level of money prices. In addition, it is assumed for the moment that the only unpredictable shifts in demand result from changes in monetary policy; u_1 and u_2 are being temporarily suppressed. In this hypothetical econ-omy, consider, in isolation, a once-and-for-all increase in the nominal quantity of money that would necessitate a rise in the level of money prices of 10 percent in the current period if equilibrium were to be reestablished "instantaneously."[21]

During the inflationary deviation, excess demands will appear in the form of declines in vacancy rates, inventories, and levels of un-employment in labor markets. Consider a "representative" seller in this environment whose demand function is described by (10) and whose behavior is summarized in Figure 2. Suppose he has set a price consistent with an "optimum" vacancy rate or level of inventories (denoted by U^* in Figure 2), given his estimate of α^e based on evidence from the long period during which there has been no trend in prices.

---

[20]The renter of a single asset—the "laborer"—does not observe a vacancy rate but rather observes different intervals between rentals. Of course, it is unrealistic to assume that this is his only source of information. In addition to his own experience, he will also gather information from other traders in the market.

[21]Strictly speaking, if the economy were expanding, a constant price level would require an equilibrium rate of monetary expansion, and a once-and-for-all deviation in the rate of monetary expansion would require a once-and-for-all adjustment in prices.

We have chosen this simple textbook example for illustrative purposes. Our analysis would be equally applicable if the change in aggregate demand arose from a change in fiscal policy.

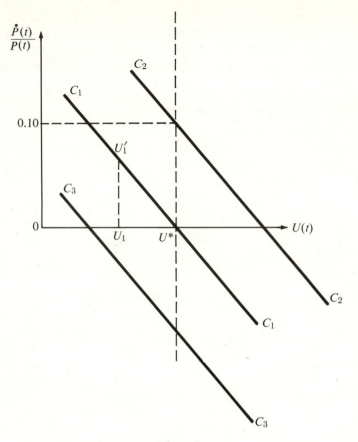

Figure 2

Because of the shift in demand resulting from the change in the quantity of money, an inventory level U_1, less than U^*, is observed. Sellers aware of the presence of uncertainty will, of course, not give full weight to the current reduction in the level of unemployed resources when they form their new estimate of α^e; past values will still enter into the calculation. Thus the price rise $U_1 U_1'$ will be less than sufficient to restore equilibrium in the current period. Actually, the observed price rise can be conceptually partitioned into two components: (a) that part which results from the seller's change in his estimate of α^e caused by the addition of the current observation to his data; and (b) that part arising from his use of new information, if any, contained in the variables in V. [If (1a) and (1b) are now reinterpreted as forecasting equations, they are arbitrarily misspecified as a consequence of the omission of the variables in (2), and their explanatory power will be diminished. The success of the inclusion of "institutional" variables in Phillips curve regressions may be due to the fact that they have informational content and thus aid in forecasting.][22]

Perhaps the most natural way to conceptualize the behavior involved is in terms of the terminology of Bayesian analysis. The seller possesses a subjective prior distribution of α^e which is modified by the most recent information. (Presumably, for any one seller, the longer the past history of stable prices, the smaller is the weight attached to the current deviation and thus the smaller will be the price adjustment.) The problem of detecting the shift in aggregate demand is further complicated by the reintroduction of the potential effects of u_1 and u_2— the subjective random components for firm and industry effects. These serve to make the subjective variance larger, thereby inducing the seller to assign a smaller weight to the current observation relative to past experience.[23]

For some time after the reestablishment of the long-run equilibrium policy consistent with stable prices, the above reasoning implies that the actual level of money prices will be too low. During this second phase prices will be observed to increase more rapidly than had previously been thought consistent with the long-run monetary policy. (In fact, there seems no a priori reason why prices may not increase more rapidly than during the prior period of an inflationary expansion in the quantity of money.) Once price-setters have become cognizant of an abnormal increase in aggregate demand, they must also learn that it is only a transitory deviation from the equilibrium policy. The addition of recent inflationary experience to the total experience will lead to a revision of what is thought to be the normal policy, and this revision will in the short run cause prices to continue to increase above the equilibrium level consistent with the long-run monetary policy. The latter phase—of rising prices that produce temporary "excess supplies"—is required to ultimately convey the information that monetary expansion has been restored to the long-run equilibrium level. The specific path to equilibrium—and thus the observed relation between the rate of change of prices and measures of excess demand— will depend on the learning path. Given a world of true uncertainty as defined earlier, this path will be dependent on the particular his-

---

[22]Examples of studies that report the success of such variables, but give very different interpretation, are O. Eckstein and T. A. Wilson, "Determination of Money Wages in American Industry," *Quarterly Journal of Economics*, 76 (August 1962), pp. 379–423; and O. Eckstein, "Wage Determination Revisited," *Review of Economic Studies*, 35 (April 1968), pp. 133–144. In particular, it is very plausible that the addition of rates of change of unemployment improves the explanation of wage changes. In the course of business cycles this would tend to produce anticlockwise loops into the usual Phillips curve.

[23]The implicit reasoning underlying this proposition is analogous to the result in the theory of sequential analysis which states that the number of observations required to reach a decision at a given probability level is an increasing function of the variance.

torical environment within which each adjustment takes place. Nevertheless, if the long-run monetary policy has been consistent with stable money prices, we would expect a scatter of observations, for a representative seller, around $U*$ in Figure 2—where $U*$ is the equilibrium level of unemployed resources. Successive observations to the right of $U*$ would represent positions of involuntary unemployment due to the inherent uncertainty of sellers, while successive observations to the left would represent situations of involuntary overemployment. Both positions are essentially due to the fact that government authorities, by changing their behavior in an unpredictable manner, can temporarily fool the economy.

While many reasons indicate that a simple relationship between $\dot{p}(t)/p(t)$ and $U(t)$ would not be very stable, adjustments arising from deviations of the kind outlined above, in a regime of trendless monetary policy, may be expected to fluctuate around the line C_1C_1 in Figure 2. The monetary authorities would, of course, be mistaken to regard this Phillips curve as tracing out available equilibrium trade-offs. Suppose that, observing this historical relationship, the authorities shift to a new equilibrium policy (unannounced or, if announced, not fully believed) consistent with a trend rate of inflation of 10 percent, with the goal of achieving a lower equilibrium level of unemployment. For some time in the transitory state the authorities will be able to look back and observe an increase in measured output as a consequence of their new policy. Yet if, as we have hypothesized, individuals eventually learn of any stable environment and react to it, they will in time incorporate into their predictive variables a stable general 10 percent rate of inflation, thereby raising their money prices at an annual rate of 10 percent, reestablishing equilibrium relative prices, and again maintaining $U*$ through time. The Phillips curve will shift to C_2C_2; and trade-offs resulting from transitory deviations in the rate of monetary expansion will be scattered about this line. Similarly, a long-run deflationary policy would result in a Phillips curve C_3C_3. Short-run trade-offs, though they may be unstable, will occur because of learning lags in an uncertain world; however, for a given permanent rate of monetary expansion no equilibrium trade-off between inflation and the level of unemployment is available. The long-run Phillips curve is a vertical line through $U*$.[24] Given that economic units maximize objective functions that are homogeneous of degree zero in all money variables, this analysis is consistent with any degree of competition or monopoly; it is not necessary to attribute rising Phillips curves to increases in monopoly power in product or factor markets.

---

[24]After completing an earlier draft of this paper, we discovered two works that reach the same conclusion about the possibility of long-run trade-offs. See E. S. Phelps, "Phillips' Curves, Expectations of Inflation and Optimal Unemployment over Time," *Economica,*

B. On the Possibility of a General Price Dynamics   The preceding argument states that the monetary authorities cannot choose between alternative equilibrium rates of inflation and equilibrium levels of unemployed resources because decision units will eventually discover—or, more accurately, will form unbiased estimates of—the equilibrium rate of change of prices. Casual inspection of the argument may appear to indicate that monetary authorities could on average maintain a U less than U^* by continually increasing the rate of monetary expansion, thus making sellers' estimates of the "true" or equilibrium rate of inflation continually biased. However, if we invoke the assumption that economic units will eventually learn of any stable situation, they will become aware of such a stable policy consistently effecting the acceleration of the money supply (and thus of prices) and will incorporate this information into their estimating functions, thus preventing such policy from inducing consistently biased estimates and maintaining levels of U less than U^*.

This reasoning may usefully be illustrated by considering a learning model widely employed by economists. Suppose sellers were to use the adaptive expectations model with respect to α^e:

$$\alpha_t^e = \alpha_{t-1}^e + \lambda(\alpha_t - \alpha_{t-1}^e), \tag{11}$$

where λ is the fixed coefficient of expectations. It is well known that the solution to this difference equation is

$$\alpha_t^e = \lambda \sum_{i=0}^{i=\infty} (1 - \lambda)^i \alpha_{t-i}. \tag{12}$$

If individuals were to follow this model rigidly, they could be perpetually deceived by the monetary authority; after forecasting the behavior

34 (August 1967), pp. 254–281; and M. Friedman, "The Role of Monetary Policy," *American Economic Review*, 63 (March 1968), pp. 1–17.

Certain differences appear between our argument and that of Professor Friedman concerning the emergence of transitory states. Friedman pictures the temporary Phillips curve as arising from the fact that an unexpected inflation will lead workers to think that an increase in money wages represents an increase in real wages—they do not anticipate increased prices that will nullify the rise in money wages. With some elasticity of supply this will lead to an increase in employment. This is possible but it is not necessary for Phillips curve phenomena when stochastic demand curves are introduced. An apartment-house owner has a completely inelastic supply in the short run; an increase in aggregate demand will reduce his vacancy rate. For a representative unemployed laborer, an increase in demand will reduce the expected unemployment period. Measured output will increase in both situations. However, the apparent increase in "measured" real output will not necessarily be an increase if properly construed; there will be some misallocation of apartments or laborers.

Also, it should be recognized that asymmetry in expectations between buyers and sellers in a market is not a necessary condition for inflation to have real effects. An employer may believe that an increased demand for his product is random, and his employee may believe the same for the resulting increase in demand for his labor, yet real output will rise.

pattern of the economy, the authority could simply create demand for the ensuing period which would differ from the expected amount by any desired percentage. By means of such a strategy they could induce price-setters to raise prices by a smaller amount than would have been optimal for them had they known the true state of demand rather than estimated it from (12). Of course, even with this model, the monetary authorities would have to accept a continually rising rate of inflation in order to maintain a level of unemployment less than U^*—they could not enjoy a simple Phillips curve trade-off. However, we reject the idea that economic units would continue to follow (12) when it became clear to them (given the government policy) that each time they did so they were making a mistake; we reiterate that decision units would recognize the consistent acceleration policy and incorporate this information when making decisions. Like the Phillips curve, (12) would cease to be valid if the government attempted to use it as a device to maintain a level of unemployment to the left or right of U^*.[25]

These considerations form the basis for a critique of the modification of the simple adaptive expectation model that has recently been proposed by Allais.[26] He suggests that the coefficient of adjustment (the λ in our notation), rather than being considered a constant, should itself be specified as a function of past rates of change of the variable to be predicted. This formalizes the plausible view that individuals will be more sensitive to current data (λ will be larger) when recent rates of change are larger. However, this model is subject to the same fundamental criticism as applied to the more naive model: The monetary authorities only have to alter the rate of acceleration of prices in order to fool persons and induce biased expectations; the fiscal-monetary authority could calculate on the basis of any pattern of past data what the economy expects for the future, and then make the expectation fall short of the "true" value by any desired amount. But again the axiom prevails that persons eventually learn. If the authorities follow a consistent policy when increasing the acceleration of prices, the rational individual will adjust his price formation to incorporate this knowledge and render the policy ineffective as a means of

[25]The argument may be stated in a slightly different form. Equation (12) has been shown to be an optimal, unbiased forecast for certain stationary stochastic processes. See J. Muth, "Optimal Properties of Exponentially Weighted Forecasts," *Journal of the American Statistical Association*, 56 (June 1960), pp. 299–306; and J. Muth, "Rational Expectations and the Theory of Price Movements," *Econometrica*, 29 (July 1961), pp. 315–335. Because the monetary-fiscal authority is the generator of the relevant time series, it may appear to them that by shifting the governing parameters in a manner unknown to private traders they may render (12) a biased forecast and thus move the economy in the desired manner. However, rational traders are not going to act in a consistently biased fashion; they will learn of the underlying change, modify their forecasting equation, and thereby nullify the attempted monetary action.

[26]M. Allais, "A Restatement of the Quantity Theory of Money," *American Economic Review*, 61 (December 1966), pp. 1123–1157.

inducing trade-offs.[27] This argument leads to the formal generalization that there is no stable difference equation of the form

$$H[\Delta^n \ln p(t), \ldots, \Delta \ln p(t), \ln p(t), t; Y] = 0,$$

where Y is a vector of current and past variables, including measures of the level of excess supply, which govern learning and expectations, on which the monetary authorities can choose an arbitrary equilibrium value of U. The government cannot learn about how persons learn and take advantage of this knowledge to alter equilibrium employment; to conclude otherwise is to conclude they do not learn.

Although the foregoing analysis has focused specifically on the possibility of the existence of trade-offs between rates of inflation and levels of employment, the general conclusions have immediate implications for a wider range of issues of current interest in the theory of monetary policy. Recent developments, placing great emphasis on the dynamic aspects of monetary policy, have stressed the need to acquire evidence on the structure of lags in various channels through which monetary policy operates. The findings presented here indicate that any results of research into lag structures may be of little use to the monetary authority. Adjustments of price and quantity in response to a monetary action lag (in large part) because it takes time for individuals to learn the new equilibrium values of the variables that enter their decision functions; a particular form of this lag observed in a given historical experience cannot be expected to remain stable in the face of attempts on the part of the monetary authorities to exploit this knowledge. Any persistent attempt on the part of the authorities to move the economy along the observed learning function will result in consistently incorrect forecasts by individuals—who will eventually learn of the goals and effects of the monetary action, include this information in their decision functions, and thereby invalidate the previously observed learning path as a norm of market behavior.[28,29]

A decade and a half ago Friedman, surveying the state of economic theory, wrote:

[27]Friedman, *op. cit.*, p. 10, appears to concede too much when he writes, "A rising rate of inflation may reduce unemployment, a high rate will not." On the contrary, a rising rate should *increase* unemployment if it rises at a slower rate than has generally been true for a past period. He further suggests that we have "systematic evidence" on the length of time it takes the economy to adjust money interest rates to inflation, but that we do not have this information for employment. Such evidence on interest rates should prove as transitory as the Phillips curve if the government were to attempt to exploit it.

[28]A similar conclusion was anticipated in footnote 9. There the argument abstracted from interrelationships between the monetary authorities and private traders and did not require the dynamic relationship to specifically reflect learning and the formation of expectations. The reasoning was simply that any stable equation describing price behavior in disequilibrium would be discovered by private traders, and they, through their exploitation of the profit opportunities thus present, would act in a manner that would destroy the stability. In the context of that argument one may raise the question whether private

The weakest and least satisfactory part of current economic theory seems to me to be in the field of monetary dynamics, which is concerned with the process of adaptation of the economy as a whole to changes in conditions and so with short-period fluctuations in aggregate activity. In this field we do not even have a theory that can appropriately be called "the" existing theory of monetary dynamics.[30]

The argument of this paper suggests that there are very good reasons why this has been the case, and should continue to be the case.

4
SELLERS' INFLATION AND THE THEORY OF PRICE DYNAMICS

A. Cost-Push Illusion and Boom-Bust Reality   In the years following World War II, professional economists as well as interested laymen evinced renewed interest in the age-old proposition that inflation can arise as the result of economic units "autonomously" increasing money wages and prices in attempts to increase their shares of national income. This phenomenon, it is held, is characteristic of economies that contain imperfectly competitive markets. More recently it has been suggested that cost-push inflation takes the form of an autonomous shift in the Phillips curve.

We assume it is accepted that as a proposition in comparative statics the idea of sellers' inflation surely makes no sense. Change on

---

individuals—without the resources of government grants, computers, and professional economists—could find such a function if it did exist. If they ccould not, this fact might justify the grants. But the successful economist would have to keep the results to himself and his employing institution. Once the finding was announced, the action of private traders would create a situation where the relationship no longer held. Of course, the announcement could take into account the effect of the announcement. Since the effect of the announcement would be to move prices immediately into equilibrium, the announcement would be that future prices or an unbiased estimate of future prices will be current prices plus a normal rate of return on all costs. This is precisely the random walk hypothesis for stock prices generalized to all prices.

Note that the learning involved in the argument in the text here is simpler, and to that extent the argument is stronger, than the earlier discussion. There private traders had to discover a dynamic function from data gathered from many points on the function. Here, if the government persists in inducing the economy into overemployment situations, private traders will merely have to notice *ex post* that they have always been wrong in *one* direction, in order to change the hypothesized behavioral relation.

[29]Of course, it could be argued that the government should not attempt to fool the economy by reducing employment below the optimum indicated by U^* in Figure 2, even if it could permanently do so. In a world of perfect information Pareto optimality requires that a good be sold to the highest bidder. In a world of stochastic demand curves the analogous proposition would be to sell the services of labor or assets at the highest expected income, and this would entail creating unemployment of U^*.

[30]Milton Friedman, *The Methodology of Positive Economics* (University of Chicago Press, Chicago, 1953) p. 42. Of course, our reasoning is also highly consistent with Friedman's well-known finding, that there is a long and variable lag in the effects of monetary policy, particularly the word "variable." See "The Lag in the Effect of Monetary Policy," *Journal of Political Economy* (October 1961), pp. 447–466.

the part of any economic unit, whether operating in a perfectly or imperfectly competitive market, that maximizes a stable decision function which is homogeneous of degree zero in all money variables must be viewed as merely responsive if it is maximizing before as well as after a change occurs. However, when the movement of prices from one equilibrium to another is analyzed as a problem of forecasting future demand in a world of uncertainty, the adjustment will generate evidence that could mislead the eclectic observer to perceive the causal mechanism of inflation as one of cost push.

The issues are clearly illustrated by reconsidering the example presented in Section 2 to illustrate the theory of disequilibrium price adjustments: The monetary authorities, having long maintained a stable price level, now pursue a deviation in policy that requires a once-and-for-all adjustment in prices of 10 percent. One conclusion of Section 2 was that in a world of uncertainty, price setters will not give full weight to the current increase in demand, and thus prices will rise in the current period less than required to immediately restore equilibrium. Thus, after the reestablishment of the normal policy, prices will continue to be too low, a state of excess demand will still exist, and prices will continue to rise in the face of a policy that the monetary authorities have come to regard as consistent with stable prices. Once price-setters do detect a true increase in demand, they must learn that it was a one-time deviation. The addition of an inflationary period to their total experience will cause them to revise upward their estimate of the normal rate of inflation, and in adjusting to these new expectations they will raise prices through the new equilibrium level. The information that the equilibrium rate of inflation has not altered will be conveyed by the emergence of excess supplies in association with rising prices.

The possibilities for misinterpretation of the evidence are obvious. Upon examining the period in which the transitory increase in the quantity of money took place, and the ensuing periods, an observer may well be tempted to label the initial period as one of demand-pull inflation and the succeeding periods (in which it must be determined that the equilibrium has remained unchanged) will appear as sellers' inflation. In these latter phases prices will seem to increase autonomously. The tightening of monetary policy implicit in the return to the normal policy will appear to be ineffective against price increases that are, in fact, simply delayed responses to the past increase in aggregate demand.

Popular economic thinking has long believed in the reality of a boom-bust sequence. "What goes up must come down." The preceding sketch suggests that this notion, contrary to cost-push, has a reasonable foundation. During the period in which actual prices are below the equilibrium level in our stylized example, the economy will be characterized by overfull employment, whereas when prices rise above the new equilibrium level as the result of temporary formation of inflationary expectations, involuntary unemployment will emerge. The correction of expectations requires the bust in the boom-bust ordering.[31]

B. Administered Prices and Relative Price Adjustments The literature on sellers' inflation, because of its emphasis on the causal role in the inflationary process of "autonomous" increases in factor and product prices, has contrasted prices set by the "automatic" and "natural" forces of the market with prices "administered" by firms and unions possessing "market power"—the latter phrase presumably embodying some implicit assumption of a degree of monopoly. More specifically, the empirical content of this distinction is that economic units are identified as "administering" prices when they have exhibited long lags in adjusting prices in response to changes in aggregate demand and thus generate such evidence as rising prices in the presence of unemployed resources. Our analysis suggests that such behavior, rather than being associated with some static measure of monopoly power involving the slope properties of demand and cost functions, is more fruitfully linked to the degree of uncertainty and the resulting problems of learning that face the decision-maker.

Consider, as an example, two sellers with stochastic demand schedules as given by (10) with identically distributed error terms for aggregate demand, but distinguished by the fact that one seller has larger variances for his intrafirm and intraindustry stochastic components. If they are initially in equilibrium with estimates of α^e equal to the true value of α, then for any given shift in the true α as the result of changes in aggregate demand, holding other parameters constant, the individual with the larger variances will take longer to detect the shift and thus will be slower in adjusting his price. For a shift of a given magnitude, successive periods of "disequilibrium" will be more likely for the seller with the larger stochastic components.[32] Thus a firm (or labor union) could potentially be faced with demand and cost functions that would imply a very small degree of monopoly power in the textbook sense and yet be slow to adjust to a fundamental disequilibrium because of large variances in demand that have come to be regarded as normal.

A similar line of reasoning applies to asset demand curves of the type illustrated in Figure 1. The steeper the demand curve, the lower will be the optimum price,[33] the higher the optimum probability, the

[31]It should be noted that this implied cyclical behavior is to be distinguished from that generated by systems with arbitrarily postulated distributed lags. The reasoning of this paper is that the boom-bust sequence is necessary to convey information and to correct fallacious expectations.

[32]The logic of this argument is the same as that discussed in footnote 23.

[33]This follows because rotating the curve toward the vertical lowers the cost, in terms of price foregone, of a given rise in the probability of selling.

shorter the expected time to sale, and the smaller the variance in the time to sale. The latter two factors will cause such a seller to discern more promptly a shift in demand. It is also true that a given shift in the true equilibrium price will change the true probability by more, the steeper is the demand function. For all these reasons the seller with the greater degree of information, as reflected in the steeper function, will be more rapid in adjusting his price.

C. Some Historical Interpretations: Exercises in Casual Empiricism On the basis of this analysis it is possible to reinterpret at least qualitatively certain forms of historical wage-employment phenomena that have been presented to shed doubt on demand-pull hypotheses and as being consistent with cost-push mechanisms of inflation. Three examples are: (a) "Even in the early 1900's, before the advent of large industrial unions, average hourly earnings tended to increase faster than productivity when the unemployment rate was below 6 percent"[34]; (b) "at comparable rates of unemployment average hourly earnings in manufacturing tended to rise more rapidly in the post war years than in the period prior to 1930"[35]; and (c) the cost-push observations of the second half of the 1950s (rising prices and excess supplies) and the long boom with relatively stable prices of the early 1960s.

The first may be explained by the inflationary developments of the period. Prices rose at the annual rate of 2.5 percent from 1896 to 1914, and it is reasonable to presume that rises in money wages incorporated inflationary anticipations. The second fact can be related to the differential rates of inflation between the two periods and the corresponding differences in expectations. Finally, the third sequence can be interpreted as arising from the tight fiscal monetary policy of the late 1950s following the inflation of the early 1950s. The former caused a downward revision in expectations that in turn permitted expansion to occur in the early 1960s with relatively low rates of inflation.

---

[34]W. G. Bowen, "Wage Behavior and the Cost-Inflation Problem," in *Labor and the National Economy*, W. G. Bowen, ed. (W. W. Norton & Co., Inc., New York, 1965), p. 84.
[35]Bowen, *ibid.*, p. 85.

Market Clearing for
Heterogeneous Capital Goods*

DONALD A. NICHOLS

This paper develops, within the context of a simple model, a few propositions that characterize markets for heterogeneous capital goods. Primary attention is devoted to the determination of an equilibrium rate of unemployment in that model. The word inventories is more common than unemployment when markets other than those for labor are being discussed, but the nature of the model is such that it is particularly applicable to labor markets. The unemployment that results is, in fact, an optimal level of inventories in the sense that it is preferred to all other levels of unemployment by the sellers of the heterogeneous asset. It is a level of unemployment that fulfills the expectations of the market participants. The term frictional unemployment has been loosely used in the past to describe unemployment of this sort. This paper, then, explains why there should exist a level of frictional unemployment in a market for heterogeneous assets.

The stimulus for the study was the desire to find an explanation for the casual observation that unemployment is most apparent in markets for commodities that are not homogeneous: labor, housing, fixed capital goods, etc. The model developed below is of a market for a heterogeneous asset—assets that are similar but not identical.

*The authur gratefully acknowledges the financial support of the Federal Deposit Insurance Corporation and the Research Committee of the Graduate School of the University of Wisconsin.

It is shown that such assets can be expected to experience higher unemployment rates than assets that are homogeneous. Under very restrictive assumptions, it is shown how such markets exhibit economies of scale—that as the size of the market increases, buyers can buy at lower prices, sellers sell at higher prices, and the level of unemployment can fall.

To isolate the impact of heterogeneity from that of other factors which contribute to the existence of an equilibrium level of unemployment, the model below was constructed in such a way that unemployment is zero at equilibrium unless the commodity is heterogeneous.

The simultaneous existence of unsold commodities and unsatisfied demand can occur only if the commodities are heterogeneous. Heterogeneity in this model can be thought of as the economic reason that frictional unemployment exists. Unemployment of the kind observed in labor markets (where the unemployment rate never equals zero) exists below only if the asset in question is heterogeneous.

The reason why heterogeneity is the critical factor in this analysis is that it permits the simultaneous existence of many different prices. Buyers and sellers can find it optimal to wait for better offers under certain conditions. This would not be true in markets for homogeneous assets if there were no search costs. There are no search costs as such imposed in this model, but there are waiting costs. That is, after examining all the commodities for sale, a buyer may choose to wait for additional commodities to come on the market. The costs are connected with waiting, not examining.

As an aside, we might note that search costs only become relevant for heterogeneous assets. If assets are homogeneous, then buyers need only know prices to know which commodity to buy. With heterogeneous assets, however, a detailed inspection may be necessary to learn of the many characteristics of a commodity. To realize the importance of heterogeneity, one need only compare the process of buying a house with that of buying common stocks of an equivalent value. Thus the previous literature concerning search costs pertains primarily to heterogeneous assets.[1]

This paper is not concerned with the response of unemployment rates to changes in the demand for the commodity. It is, therefore, complementary to other recent works on the labor market which are concerned solely with dynamics but which ignore those factors which determine the equilibrium level of unemployment.[2] The model does, however, give insight into a way in which heterogeneity may affect

---

[1]See J. Stigler, "The Economics of Information," *Journal of Political Economy*, 61 (June 1961), pp. 213–225, and J. MacQueen, "Optimal Policies for a Class of Search and Evaluation Problems," *Management Science*, 10, No. 4 (July 1964).

[2]See, for example, R. E. Lucas, Jr., and L. A. Rapping, "Real Wages, Employment, and Inflation," this volume.

the formation of expectations. A brief concluding discussion indicates how a variant of this model might include expectations and yield a price-adjustment equation of the Phillips variety. The derivation of the unemployment rate from its equilibrium value in such a model would be likely to depend significantly on one's expectations about future prices. In this context, one would characterize as erroneous price expectations the "money illusion" that has been attributed to Keynes' labor-market participants.

My procedure is to develop a simple optimizing model of buying and selling assets. As the purpose of the model is to explore the conditions under which markets clear, no attention is paid to the decision to enter the market. As price rises, less buyers and more sellers enter, of course. But the decision-making that occurs after they are in the market is independent of the decision to enter. Once in, they must remain until they have bought or sold. This simplifying assumption is not thought to affect the character of the results in any substantial manner.

To study inventory models, one must deal with durable goods. Inventories exist because the owner expects that he will receive more by selling the commodity in the future than in the present. The good must be durable for that possibility to exist; thus the word "capital" appears in the title of the paper.

1
THE MODEL

The model we will construct here can be briefly summarized as follows: Individuals who have entered a market observe present and expected future prices. They decide to buy (or sell) in that period which will minimize (maximize) the expected present value of the purchase (sale). A decision by a potential seller to not sell in the current period is a decision to place the commodity in inventory or can be viewed as a decision to be unemployed. The third possibility, that of renting the asset, is not allowed here.[3]

The decision to sell or wait revolves around two simple functions: the level of prices and interest costs—both expressed as functions of time. A typical decision involves a seller observing that future prices are higher than present prices and then calculating whether it is worth holding the asset and paying interest between now and the future in order to be able to sell at the higher price.

The following simplifying assumptions are made in order that the model be able to deal with situations where unique commodities are

---

[3]The effect of a rental can be obtained by purchase and resale once borrowing is allowed. We do not restrict borrowing in this model.

sold. Each seller has one unit of the commodity to sell; each buyer wishes to buy one unit. Once a seller or buyer enters the market, he remains there until his transaction is completed. Price elasticity of demand and supply is attained by varying the number of entrants to the market per time period as a function of price.

Mathematically, these assumptions are expressed in (1) through (4), where

$S(t)$ = the number of sellers in the market at time t

$D(t)$ = the number of buyers in the market at time t

$s(t) = dS(t)/dt$ = the change in the number of sellers at time t

$d(t) = dD(t)/dt$ = the change in the number of buyers at time t

$s^*(t)$ = number of sellers who enter the market exogenously at time t

$d^*(t)$ = number of buyers who enter the market exogenously at time t

$q(t)$ = number of transactions completed at time t

$P(t)$ = the average price of the transactions completed at time t

$$s(t) = s^*(t) + \alpha P(t) - q(t), \qquad \alpha > 0, \tag{1}$$

$$d(t) = d^*(t) - \beta P(t) - q(t), \qquad \beta > 0, \tag{2}$$

$$S(t) = \int_{-\infty}^{t} s(v)\, dv, \tag{3}$$

$$D(t) = \int_{-\infty}^{t} d(v)\, dv. \tag{4}$$

Equations (1) through (4) determine the number of buyers and sellers as a function of the history of prices and transactions. They do not tell us the nature of the maximizing behavior that buyers and sellers undergo once they are in the market. By varying this behavior and the assumptions about the exogenous forces on the market, we can derive alternative results about the time paths of price, inventories (S), and unsatisfied demand (D).

The stock of inventories (S) is proportional to the amount of unemployment because of a crucial assumption—that once a seller enters the market, he can only consume a fraction of the services of the asset he wishes to sell. This assumption is justified by the following simple observation: If the value of services to a seller equals their value in the market, he should not be a seller. If an unemployed person values his leisure at the market wage rate, he will not search for work—he is not unemployed. Thus we assume that a man becomes a seller when he values the services of an asset below their market value. To simplify the analysis, we say that the value to him is a constant proportion $(1 - k)$ of the market value of the service.

We also assume that a, the flow of services yielded by the asset, is constant over time. Thus kS is a measure of the stock of unemployed resources (measured in men or houses), and kaS is a measure of the flow (measured in man-hours or house-days.) With a market price (p_a) for a, kap_aS becomes the value of the wasted resources.

Symmetrically, buyers are buyers because they place a value on the asset which exceeds its market value. Thus buyers undergo a waiting cost which can be thought of as utility foregone because of not owning the asset. This, too, is assumed to be a constant fraction (g) of the value of asset. Thus gaD is a measure of the services lost by buyers who are in the market but have not yet bought, and P_agaD is a measure of the value of those services.

Buyers and sellers are assumed to optimize given some information about future prices. Sellers maximize the present value of the sale price plus the value of the returns obtained from the asset before the sale. Assume that the discount rate (r) is constant. Then to the seller, the value of the asset at t if it is to be sold in time T is expressed by (5). If future prices are uncertain, think of $P(T)$ as the expected price in time T.

$$PV(t) = P(T)e^{-r(T-t)} + \int_t^T (1 - k)\, p_a(v)ae^{-r(v-t)}\, dv. \qquad (5)$$

The seller maximizes (5) with respect to T to find the optimal time in which to sell:

$$\frac{dPV(t)}{dT} = P'(T)e^{-r(T-t)} - rP(T)e^{-r(T-t)}$$

$$+ (1 - k)p_a(T)ae^{-r(T-t)} = 0. \qquad (6)$$

Therefore,

$$r = \frac{P'(T)}{P(T)} + \frac{(1 - k)ap_a(T)}{P(T)}.$$

The result is that the optimal time to sell is when the rate of interest equals the capital gain plus the value of the physical rate of return to the seller. Second-order conditions tell us that this is a maximum if r exceeds its value in (6) when $t > T$. We can also see from (6) a set of future prices for the asset which make the seller indifferent between holding it and selling it.

Figure 1 indicates three alternative paths of prices that would leave the seller indifferent, owing to alternative assumptions about k. If $k = 1$ (the asset's services have no value for the seller), then the

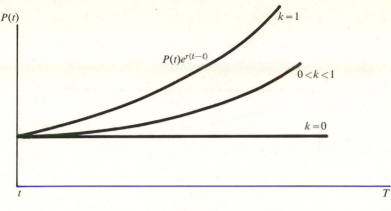

Figure 1

price must appreciate at exactly the rate of interest to make him indifferent. If $k = 0$, then no price appreciation is necessary to make him willing to hold the asset, as the value of the services are the same to him as to the rest of the market. If $0 < k < 1$, some path in between leaves him indifferent. Define $\lambda(T)$ as that rate of price appreciation which makes him indifferent between buying and selling:

$$\lambda(T) = r - \frac{(1 - k)ap_a(T)}{P(T)}. \tag{7}$$

Note that if there are no transaction costs, the sale should not be viewed as a once-and-for-all event. In fact, the seller should be viewed as owning the house whenever price appreciation is expected to exceed $\lambda(T)$ and selling it when prices begin to rise by less than $\lambda(T)$. Thus T will not be unique. The previous analysis should then be applied to the initial decision to sell, as we are interested in the length of time that an asset remains unsold.

The buyer minimizes an equation identical to (5) except that the $(1 - k)$ is replaced by $(1 + g)$. The buyer wishes to buy at as cheap a price as possible, but he also feels a loss when not owning the asset, owing to the fact that he values its services more highly than does the market. Minimizing the buyer's function with respect to T yields (8), which is a minimum if r is less than that value for $t > T$:

$$r = \frac{P'(T)}{P(T)} + \frac{(1 + g)ap_a(T)}{P(T)}. \tag{8}$$

Equation (8) also yields a set of future prices that make the buyer indifferent between buying now and buying in the future. Figure 2 shows that if $g = 0$, a constant expected price will make the buyer indifferent between buying or not buying the asset. If $g > 0$, the buyer

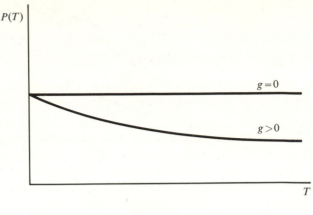

Figure 2

values the services more highly than does the rest of the market and
he will be indifferent about buying it only if its price is expected to fall.

Define ρ as the rate of price decline which makes buyers indifferent
between buying and waiting:

$$\rho(T) = r - \frac{(1 + g)ap_a(T)}{P(T)}.\qquad(9)$$

Once prices fall by less than $\rho(T)$, buyers buy; but they will sell
when prices are expected to fall by more than $\rho(T)$.

To close the model, we need only discuss the assumptions that
determine the future prices. Once these are known, buyers and sellers
will behave as indicated above. We now look at how different sets
of assumptions lead to different results concerning the level of unemployment and price behavior.

2
MARKET CLEARING FOR
HOMOGENEOUS GOODS

In this section we simply list a few obvious results that can be derived
from the model above if the markets in questions are those for homogeneous commodities. This is done to be able to compare these with
the results we obtain in Section III for heterogeneous commodities.

It is clear from the discussion above that unless prices are expected
to appreciate, sellers will sell immediately. Thus no unemployment or
inventories will exist unless the seller feels that future prices will exceed
current prices. Symmetrically, buyers will not wait to buy unless they
feel that prices are going to fall. Thus if everyone forms expectations
in the same manner, it is impossible to have both unsatisfied demand
and unsatisfied supply (inventories). Also, if an equilibrium is attained

wherein prices are expected to remain constant, there can be neither unsatisfied demand nor unsatisfied supply.

Given equations (1) and (2), a long-run equilibrium is attained for constant s^* and d^* when price attains the value shown in (10):

$$P = \frac{d^* - s^*}{\alpha + \beta}. \qquad (10)$$

If, initially, excess supply exists, then a lower price will exist which increases at rate $\lambda(T)$ until P is attained. The initial lower price must be exactly low enough so that all the excess supply will be absorbed by the time the price attains its equilibrium value. It must increase at rate $\lambda(T)$ if sellers are to be content to hold some of the asset as inventory.

If s^* and d^* are variable but perfectly forecast, there is still a price path that will keep buyers and sellers content with their decisions to act or wait. Specifically, if prices increase at a rate less than λ, then there can be no excess supply. If a large future increase in demand is foreseen, prices can increase at rate λ to build up a stock of inventories to help satisfy that demand. The higher price encourages more sellers to enter the market as well as discouraging buyers.

Typical time paths of P, $D - S$ and d^* are plotted in Figure 3 to show how the first two of these variables will respond to forecast increases in d^* that lasts for one period.

If the change in d^* is unforeseen, discrete moves in the price level become possible. Price will increase with an increase in d^* to such a level that all the unsatisfied demand will be satisfied by the time the equilibrium price is reattained. P must fall at rate ρ after its initial discrete upward move.

This discussion has been based on the assumption that everyone knows the long-run values of d^*, s^*, and therefore P^*. If, alternatively,

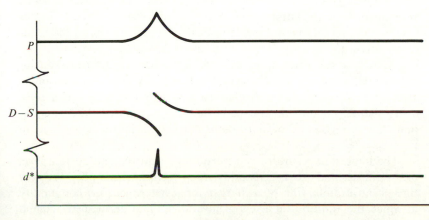

Figure 3

we assume that they are not known, then we must include some function to determine the expected level of d^*. A commonly used function makes expected d^* a weighted average of present and past values of d^*, with the weights declining geometrically with increases in distance from the present. Let δ be the weight given the current period's d^*, $(1 - \delta)\delta$ the weight for last period's d^*, $(1 - \delta)^2\delta$ for the d^* of two periods ago, etc. Then, for $\delta = 1$ (expected d^* equals current d^*), we have that the expected long-run price must be given by (11) if it is to be able to clear the market:

$$P(t) = \frac{d^*(t) - s^*(t)}{\alpha + \beta}. \tag{11}$$

If, alternatively, $\delta = 0$ and we begin with a given expected value for d^*, all changes will be viewed as temporary. For an increase in d^*, price will increase by just enough so that the stock, D, can be expected to be worked off as P adjusts to its long-run expected equilibrium value. This adjustment will occur by having P fall at rate $\rho(t)$, of course. If, in fact, a change does occur in d^*, so that it remains constant at a level above its expected value, the excess demand will not be eliminated by the price increase just described. In fact, every period there will be more excess demand, leading to increases in D and therefore $P(t)$, but the increases in P will be large enough to eventually satisfy D only if d^* reverts to its expected level. If d^* remains at its higher level, an equilibrium is approached wherein P is high enough so that there are no more increases in D. That is, P is at the level that sets s equal to d. The existing stock of D will remain, however.

This example could be thought of as a long-run money illusion. Buyers expect lower prices in the future and are content to wait for them at some cost. Lower prices never materialize, however.

The two cases just discussed are polar cases, one with instantaneous adjustment of expectations, one with no adjustment. In the former case, prices are volatile but markets clear instantaneously. In the latter case, prices adjust very slowly and markets need not ever clear. In between these extremes lie cases in which prices adjust less than instantaneously but in which markets eventually clear. These intermediate positions yield a price-adjustment equation which can have many shapes, none of them exactly that of the original Phillips equation. One possible set of time paths for the variables is graphed in Figure 4.

The important result for our purposes is that the equilibrium level of inventories and excess demand is always zero in this model. We now turn to an examination of a market for a heterogeneous commodity in which the equilibrium levels of inventories and unsatisfied demand are positive.

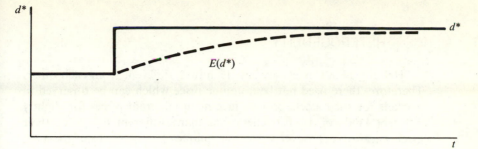

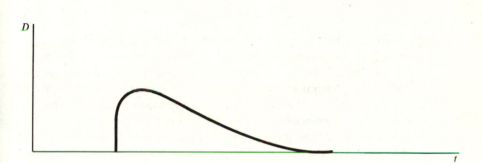

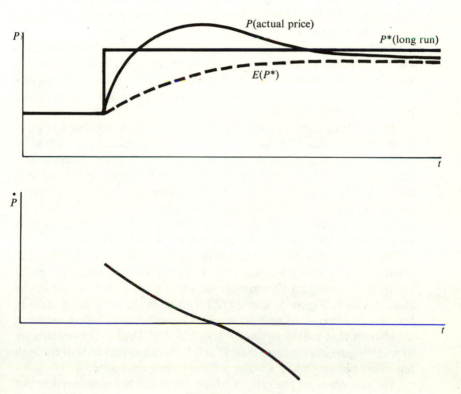

Figure 4

3
HETEROGENEITY

Heterogeneous assets are, by definition, different from each other. Therefore, there need not be a unique price which can be observed in markets for such assets. Buyers face many different prices for slightly different kinds of assets. Sellers face many different offers for their asset, because each buyer values the unique characteristics of the asset differently. We now look at how buyers and sellers behave in such markets.

A. Selling a Heterogeneous Asset A seller will face many different offers for his asset. We will initially approach his decision-making problem as if he is certain about the distribution from which the offers are generated but uncertain as to the order in which they will be received. The offers are random samples from a known distribution. Given his knowledge of the distribution of possible offers, he can answer the following question: If I charge price P', how long must I wait until I find someone who is willing to pay that price? The answers to that question for all possible prices yield an expression in waiting time as a function of the price charged. The higher the price he charges, the longer the seller can expect to wait before he finds a buyer who will pay the price.

To keep the problem simple, we assume that the seller's actions are not affected by the existence of uncertainty. He acts as if he can sell the asset for sure at a certain price on a certain day and not one day sooner. Thus the inverse function will tell the seller an expected price for each future time period.

His actions, then, are just like those studied in Section I. He refrains from selling if prices are expected to appreciate in excess of $\lambda(t)$. He decides to sell in the first period in which prices increase at a rate less than or equal to $\lambda(t)$. But the expected price appreciation is now a result of the fact that different buyers will offer him different amounts for the asset he is selling. There need be no generally expected increase in prices for him to observe that his expected selling price is an increasing function of time. This can be shown as follows.

We assume that the seller knows the density function from which the price offers are drawn. For any price P' that he might choose, the probability of receiving an offer greater than that price is represented by the shaded area in Figure 5, where $f(P)$ represents the probability density function. The expected number of offers he will receive before receiving an offer in that region is simply $1/p(P > P')$. Thus if the probability of receiving an offer greater than P' is 0.1, he can expect to wait through ten offers before finding a buyer willing to pay that price.

He also observes the rate at which offers are being received, n per

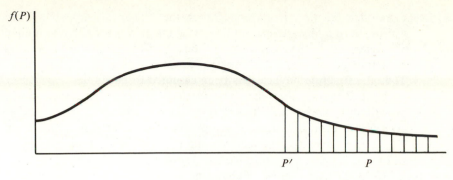

Figure 5

unit of time. This tells him how long he must wait before receiving the tenth offer. Thus expected waiting time (T) is given in (12) as a function of the price he demands:

$$E(T) = \frac{1}{np(P > P')} . \tag{12}$$

The seller maximizes the expected present value of the sale, which is given in (13):[4]

$$PV(\text{sale}) = P'e^{-rT(P')} + \int_0^{T(P')} (1 - k)ap_ae^{-rt}\, dt. \tag{13}$$

Equation (13) expresses the present value of the sale as the present value of the price plus the value of the services received from the asset before it is sold. As above, these are taken to be a constant proportion $(1 - k)$ of their market value. Maximizing (13) with respect to P' gives (14):

$$rP' = (1 - k)ap_a + \frac{1}{dT/dP'} ,$$

$$P' = \frac{(1 - k)ap_a}{r} + \frac{1}{r\, dT/dP'} . \tag{14}$$

This tells him that he must plan to sell in that period in which the interest cost of holding the asset is just offset by the value of the services of the asset plus the expected price appreciation.[5] This is the same condition we had for selling a homogeneous asset except that now the price appreciation occurs without an increase in the mean of the

[4]A similar problem has been studied previously in S. Karlin, "Stochastic Models and Optimal Policy for Selling an Asset," *Studies in Applied Probability and Management Science* (Stanford University Press, Stanford, Calif., 1962), pp. 149–158.
[5]This is a maximum if $d^2T/dP'^2 > 0$.

price-offer function he faces. Rather the higher price results from waiting until a buyer comes along whose tastes value highly the unique characteristics of the asset for sale. Thus there are returns from waiting even though the seller does not expect prices in general to increase. The offer function he faces has been assumed to be stable.

Note that once the seller has selected the price to charge, he will be willing to accept an offer of that amount whenever it is made — even if that means immediate acceptance of an offer. The equilibrium T is only an expected number of time periods. The actual number he waits may be much greater or much less than T.

If there exists a stock of unsatisfied demand, it is possible that an offer in the acceptable range already exists and that no waiting is required. If this is the case, the offer is accepted. If not, the stock of unsatisfied demand does not affect the price he charges, as they do not affect the amount of time he expects to wait before receiving an acceptable offer.

B. Buying a Heterogeneous Asset   The buyer's problem differs from the seller's in that buyers must explicitly take account of the heterogeneity that exists. Sellers, on the other hand, must sell what they own regardless of its characteristics. Buyers have to decide not only what price to offer but which asset to buy.

Assume that the assets differ by some subjective characteristic k. There can be differences of opinion over the quantity of k that each asset contains. Alternatively, k could be thought of as an objective value that depends on thousands of characteristics, each of which has some value to a buyer but which cannot be bought individually.[6] Buyers observe the assets for sale. Their observations consist of a set of points that denote the price and the quantity of k associated with each asset. For all those assets of a given quantity of k (say $k*$) the buyer can form a function with waiting time just the way the seller did. Minimizing this function gives him a price at which he can expect to buy an asset of quality $k*$ and the number of periods he can expect to wait until one comes along. Point b in Figure 6 stands for such a point. It is the price at which $k*$ can be bought which involves the lowest present value of outlay of cash plus waiting time.

Points such as b exist for every possible value of k. Linking these points gives the buyer a frontier in P, k space which shows him the present value of the outlay he must expect to make if he is to acquire any asset of characteristic k. This is shown in Figure 7.

The buyer has preferences which can be expressed over k and P. Such preferences should tell him which point on the frontier in Figure

---

[6]A house, for example, may have a location which has a view, is close to shopping, distant from traffic, near noisy neighbors, or subject to mudslides. Each buyer could value the location differently because the market would not permit him to sell the characteristics separately.

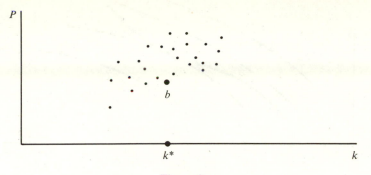

Figure 6

7 will yield him the greatest satisfaction. These preferences are represented by indifference curves in Figure 8. Assuming the appropriate convexity, etc., a tangency will exist which indicates the kind of asset he will attempt to buy and the price he will offer for it.

He can, of course, make offers for assets with different quantities of k, but he does not expect that they will be accepted before the offer at the tangency will. The other offers he makes, of course, must also be on indifference curve I_1. It is his expectation that these other offers will be accepted much later than the offer he makes for that k indicated in Figure 8. If there is no cost involved in making an offer, he will make these other offers as well, because they may, in fact, be accepted first.

C. Buyers and Sellers   Here we look at the implications of having buyers and sellers act as indicated above. The most striking difference between the behavior in heterogeneous markets and the behavior in homogeneous markets is that, in the former case, both buyers and sellers can wait for better prices in the future and both can be satisfied!

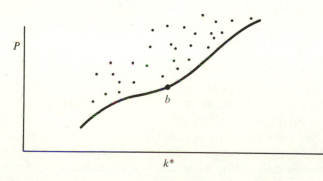

Figure 7

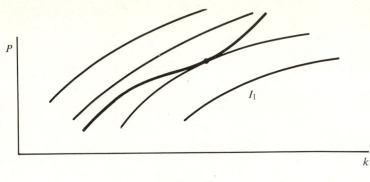

Figure 8

That is, it may be rational for both buyers and sellers to wait. Buyers will find lower prices in the future while sellers will find higher ones. In fact, the only thing to keep sellers from waiting forever to sell is the interest cost of holding the asset.

Thus we observe the simultaneous existence of unsold assets and unsatisfied demand. This was not possible in the markets for homogeneous assets. One sufficient condition for frictional unemployment or for frictional levels of inventories that rarely go to zero is that the commodity in question be heterogeneous.

These results are qualitative. Quantitative results will be derived only for the means of the distributions. The decisions we have analyzed are those of individual sellers and buyers. Given their particular tastes and the assets they own, they will face specific distributions and have specific waiting costs. Thus variables to characterize whole markets can only be averages. Price and waiting time will be different for different people. But market statistics such as "the wage rate" or "the duration of unemployment" can be constructed as simple means of the observations, and it is these means that interest us now.

The average expected waiting time for sellers can be denoted T_s. As, in equilibrium, $\bar{s}$ new sellers enter the market each time period, in equilibrium the number of waiting sellers is $\bar{s}T_s$. These constitute the unemployed or the inventory of the asset. These sellers are waiting for buyers whose tastes match their assets.

The equilibrium number of waiting buyers is similarly $\bar{d}T_d$, where $\bar{d}(=\bar{s})$ is the equilibrium number of new buyers entering the market and T_d is the average waiting time of buyers. There is no a priori reason to believe that T_d equals T_s; their relative magnitude is determined by the numbers of offers received and the distributions from which the offers are drawn. It is possible, for example, that sellers advertise publicly, thereby making offers to all buyers while buyers are very selective in their offers. Thus sellers may receive less offers than buyers and may wait longer for a sale than buyers do.

Given $\bar{s} = \bar{d}$, equilibrium unemployment is clearly determined by T_s. And it is obvious from (22) that the determinants of T_s are the number of offers one receives and the distribution from which they are drawn. If an increase in the size of the market increases the number of offers one receives from a given distribution, then T_s will fall if P' is held constant.[7] The simultaneous determination of T and P' may, of course, warrant an increase in P' to such an extent that T increases. That is, if one receives offers at an increased rate, he will not have to wait as long for an acceptable offer. Alternatively, he may raise the price he asks and hold T constant, or he may do some combination of these two actions. In fact, there are distributions for which one may increase price to such an extent that waiting time actually increases. The derivation of results for any specific market will therefore require an empirical study of the distribution of offers. No further generalizations can be made.

D. A Future Extension The assumptions with which we have been working in this section must be modified before this model can be used to derive results about the nature of a Phillips curve. In Section II we examined how an assumption concerning the formation of expectations can yield an expression for the adjustment in prices. In this section we have made assumptions that are equivalent to certainty about the prevailing market price, that is, that the distributions of price offers do not vary. Their means remain constant. We did not examine how a market for heterogeneous goods would adjust to a change in demand.

One obvious way to extend this analysis to include changes in demand would be to formulate it as a Bayesian decision problem. The buyers and sellers would have prior distributions concerning the price offers. These priors would be modified by the offers that one received. Thus after receiving many low offers, one might lower his asking price. In this way changes in demand or supply would be slowly perceived by the market participants. The slowness in adjusting priors would result in temporary changes in the unemployment rate above or below its long-run equilibrium level. That is, if demand expanded, sellers would observe more offers per time period and could therefore raise prices. Buyers would then perceive that the commodities had become more expensive and they would have to raise their price offers if they expect success with the same amount of waiting as before. Sellers would then perceive offers which were, on average, above the means of their prior distributions. Thus the priors would be raised and, with them, the sellers' asking price. Before the priors are raised, however, the higher

---

[7] If there are no costs to making offers, then offers received will be at a rate proportional to s.

offers that sellers receive would result in an increase in the number of offers accepted—therefore a reduction in inventories. Thus a relationship between price adjustment and unemployment could be derived from such a model. This is not done here.

4
CONCLUSIONS

Summarizing the results of Section III, we have that unemployment may exist side by side with unsatisfied demand in markets that have no search costs if the markets are for heterogeneous commodities; that such markets exhibit economies of scale in the sense that buyers' outlays' (including waiting time) for the commodities are lower in large markets and sellers receipts are higher than they are in small markets; and that the form of the distribution of offers determine how these gains are distributed between price changes and waiting-time changes. An additional result not mentioned above but that follows directly from the indeterminacy of the previous result with respect to waiting time is that we cannot, in general, say that markets which are more heterogeneous than others have higher unemployment rates. By more heterogeneous, we mean that they have a larger variance of price offers. This last result contradicts one's intuition. It may, of course, be true that for most distributions, increasing the variance will result in an increase in the level of unemployment.

I have argued that if assets are heterogeneous, it will be rational for market participants to expect the future to bring them better opportunities than the present. Buyers will be able to buy at lower prices—sellers sell at higher prices. Waiting costs prevent them from waiting forever before conducting a transaction. Thus owners of assets determine the optimal amount of time which their asset will be unemployed. Markets for heterogeneous assets will have a frictional level of unemployment.

Heterogeneity is therefore the characteristic of assets which makes them illiquid. Tobin has defined illiquidity as the length of time one must prepare to sell an asset before expecting to receive a certain percentage of its full value.[8] Here we have not discussed what the value of the asset is independent of waiting costs. Heterogeneous assets are illiquid, however, as the receipts to be expected from selling them increase with the time one waits for buyers.

A long-run equilibrium level of unemployment does not require the existence of "money illusion." Erroneous price expectations may, however, be necessary if levels of unemployment other than the equilibrium level are to be observed.

[8]James Tobin, *unpublished manuscript.*

User Cost, Output, and Unexpected Price Changes*

PAUL TAUBMAN and
MAURICE WILKINSON

The purpose of this paper is to analyze the production and factor-utilization decisions of the competitive firm experiencing product and factor price changes which were unexpected but that are expected to regress gradually to their previous levels. The unique feature of our model is that the flow of services from a given stock of capital is not fixed but is subject to the control of the firm. The static version of this model has been analyzed by us in an earlier paper.[1] Both the cases of irreplaceable and replaceable assets will be considered.

The outline for this paper is as follows: Section I contains a brief discussion of the model of asset utilization and the user cost of non-reproducible assets. The necessary conditions for the maximization of the net worth of a competitive firm are next derived by means of the calculus of variations. These conditions are utilized to examine production and factor-utilization decisions given a set of price expectations. The paper concludes by considering the case of reproducible assets.

*The authors wish to thank Edmund S. Phelps and Donald Katzner for substantially improving earlier versions of this work.

[1] P. Taubman and M. Wilkinson, "User Cost, Capital Utilization, and Investment Theory," *International Economic Review* (forthcoming).

1
NONREPRODUCIBLE ASSETS

In this section we will consider the case for nonreproducible assets. This category covers two different types of capital. First, there may be natural resources. Second, there are those assets which are reproducible in the long run, which is determined by the interval necessary to plan and produce these items. In this section we assume that by the time the firm could obtain this capital, the temporary and unexpected price change will be within (an epsilon of) expiring.

To aid in the production process, a piece of capital must yield services. The rate of utilization and services generally is not fixed by engineering rules but is subject to the choice of the firm. Variations in the rate of utilization can be achieved by altering the length of time that capital is operated within a calendar day or altering the intensity of use or speed of operation of capital per unit of time. Such alterations of utilization are not free but are subject to a "user cost."[2]

This user cost is measured, in physical terms, by loss of future capital services and output while the monetary cost is computed in the prices of the future. This loss of future capital services can occur for several reasons. First, for natural resources, such as a body of ore, the "capital" is depleted automatically as it renders its services. For machines more use will be at the expense of preventive maintenance and future breakdowns. Drills and farming machines are worn out by use, while metal fatigue, etc., depend on cumulated use and intensity of use. Some of the user cost-induced reduction in capital services can be offset by repairs and maintenance, but such repairs should be classified as investment and are only relevant for the reproducible-asset section. It might be noted now, however, that in certain cases the firm will benefit in a temporary inflation if it can use the capital now and replace it later at a lower price.

If the asset is not reproducible, the firm must choose between using the asset now and preserving it to be used later on. This choice will, in part, depend upon the firm's expectations regarding prices.

In our earlier paper we considered the implications of user cost and capital utilization for capital and investment theory when the firm expected no future price changes. This model consists of the following variables:

H = index of capital utilization
S = physical amount of depreciation per unit of capital per unit of time

---

[2]If there were no cost attached to varying capital utilization the firm should always employ the maximum utilization rate and the problem reduces to the case in which there are no variations in the rate of capital utilization.

K = capital stock, in number of units
P_k = current replacement price of capital, i.e., market price
L = man-hours per unit of time
w = wage rate
m = money interest rate
Q = output
P = price of output

which can be combined in the equations

$$S = S(H), \tag{1}$$

$$Q = F(H, K, L). \tag{2}$$

Equation (1) is an engineering relationship, twice differentiable at all points. In some instances it is possible that $\partial S/\partial H < 0$ for some H (e.g., a canal will silt up faster if not used at all); however, our analysis will be restricted to the case where $\partial S/\partial H > 0$ while $\partial^2 S/\partial H^2 \lessgtr 0$. The production function (2) is twice differentiable where we assume that F_1, F_2, and $F_3 > 0$, while F_{11}, F_{22}, and F_{33} are all < 0. Capital services are a function of H and K but not necessarily simply the product of H and K. If the production function, $Q = G(HK, N)$, is assumed, none of our conclusions will be altered in any major way.

Thus far we have talked about a temporary but unexpected inflation without defining it. We define such an inflation in the following way:

$$P_t^e = \overline{P} + (P_0 - \overline{P})e^{-gt}, \qquad 0 < g \tag{3}$$

where P_t^e is the expected price of output at time t while $\overline{P}$ is the expected long-run or steady-state price level. Suppose that for a long time, until $t = 0$, each P_t actually equaled $\overline{P}$ but for some reason P_0 unexpectedly exceeds $\overline{P}$. Then future prices will be expected to return to $\overline{P}$. Moreover, representing the time derivative of P^e by $\dot{P}^e$, the percentage change in expected prices will be

$$\frac{\dot{P}_t^e}{P_t^e} = -g\left(\frac{P_t^e - \overline{P}}{P_t^e}\right) \tag{4}$$

Thus in each period g percent of the current disequilibrium will be eliminated.

We will assume that the expected wage rate and, when capital is reproducible, its expected selling price are always proportional to P_t^e. Thus

$$w_t^e = \alpha P_t^e, \tag{5}$$

$$P_{kt}^e = \beta P_t^e. \tag{6}$$

Finally, we will assume that the firm does not expect the nominal rate of interest to fall as much as the product and factor prices:

$$m = i + \delta \left(\frac{\dot{P}^e}{P^e}\right)_t, \qquad 0 \le \delta < 1. \tag{7}$$

where i is the expected long-run or steady-state interest rate and m is the expected nominal rate of interest.[3]
    If V is the net worth of the firm, we wish to maximize,

$$V = \int_0^\infty e^{-mt}[P_t^e F(H_t, K_t, L_t) - \dot{w}_t^e L_t]\, dt, \tag{8}$$

subject to the constraints

$$\int_0^\infty (\dot{K}_t + S_t K_t)e^{-mt}\, dt = 0, \tag{9}$$

and, of course, (1), which will be incorporated in (9) from here on.
    The Euler–Lagrange equations from the calculus of variations yield the following necessary conditions for (8), to be maximized subject to (9)[4]

$$P_t^e F_H + \lambda S_t' K_t = 0, \tag{10}$$

$$P_t^e F_K + \lambda(S_t + m_t) - \dot{\lambda} = 0, \tag{11}$$

$$P_t^e F_L - w_t^e = 0, \tag{12}$$

$$\dot{K}_t + S_t K_t = 0, \tag{13}$$

where λ is the Lagrangian multiplier and is negative, while $\dot{\lambda}$ is $d\lambda/dt$. From (10) we obtain the implicit rental price of capital utilization:

$$S_t' K_t \lambda = -P_t^e F_H. \tag{14}$$

Thus λ is the ratio of the value of the marginal product of capital utilization (valued at the expected output price) to the physical depreciation of the capital stock. The shadow price of capital, η, is obtained from (11) as

$$\eta = \lambda(S_t + m_t) - \dot{\lambda}. \tag{15}$$

While λ enters into the shadow price of H and K, the integration by

[3]This assumption is made by Lucas and Rapping, who also discuss the empirical evidence upon which interest rate expectations are at least partly based. R. E. Lucas, Jr., and L. A. Rapping, "Real Wages, Employment, and the Price Level," this volume, pp. 257–305.
[4]To obtain (11) it is necessary to eliminate the derivative with respect to time of the variational in K. This is accomplished by integrating by parts and evaluating the resulting terms at $t = 0$ and $t = \infty$.

parts yields the terms in m and $\dot{\lambda}$. As will be shown shortly, it is the behavior of $\partial m/\partial P_0$ that determines our answer. When integration by parts is not required because there is no user cost and no control over K, m will not influence our result.

To determine the effects of the unexpected but temporary price inflation on the firm, differentiate (10) through (12) with respect to P_0, simplify with the aid of the price expectation (4) through (7), make use of (14) to determine $\dot{\lambda}$, and arrange in matrix form:

$$DV + W = P, \tag{16}$$

where

$$D = \begin{bmatrix} P^e F_{KK} & P^e F_{KH} + \lambda S' & P^e F_{KL} & S + m \\ P^e F_{HK} + \lambda S' & P^e F_{HH} + \lambda KS'' & P^e F_{LH} & S'K \\ P^e F_{KL} & P^e F_{HL} & P^e F_{LL} & 0 \\ S & S'K & 0 & 0 \end{bmatrix},$$

$$V = \begin{bmatrix} \partial K/\partial P_0 \\ \partial H/\partial P_0 \\ \partial L/\partial P_0 \\ \partial \lambda/\partial P_0 \end{bmatrix};$$

and W, a matrix of time derivatives that would be utilized in the analysis of the adjustment path of the firm if expectations about prices were not changed, is obtained as follows:

$$W = \begin{bmatrix} \dfrac{P_t^e \partial [d(F_H/K_t S_t')/dt]}{\partial P_0} \\ 0 \\ 0 \\ \dfrac{\partial \dot{K}}{\partial P_0} \end{bmatrix}.$$

The price vector, P, is

$$P = \begin{bmatrix} + \dfrac{e^{-gt}}{P_t^e}[\lambda(S_t + m_t) - g\dfrac{\bar{P}}{(P_t^e)}\lambda + g\delta\dfrac{\bar{P}}{(P_t^e)}\lambda] \\ + \dfrac{e^{-gt}}{P_t^e}(\lambda S_t' K_t) \\ 0 \\ 0 \end{bmatrix}. \tag{17}$$

Consider first $\partial\lambda/\partial P$. Note that the first element in each item of the price vector is proportional to the fourth column of D and expansion by these elements must yield a sum proportional to $|D|$. Thus, with $|D|$ indicating the determinant of D and $|D_{ij}|$ the $i^{th}j^{th}$ cofactor,

$\partial \lambda / \partial P_0$ is

$$\frac{\partial \lambda}{\partial P_0} = \frac{e^{-gt}}{P_t^e}\left[1 + \frac{g\overline{P}}{P_t^e}(1-\delta)\frac{|D_{14}|}{|D|}\right]\lambda. \tag{18}$$

If we multiply through by P_0/λ and evaluate at $t = 0$, we find that the elasticity of λ with respect to P_0 is

$$\frac{\partial \lambda}{\partial P_0}\frac{P_0}{\lambda} = \left[1 + g\frac{\overline{P}}{P_t^e}(1-\delta)\frac{|D_{14}|}{|D|}\right]. \tag{19}$$

Thus, if the money interest rate adjusts fully to expected percentage price changes, i.e., if $\delta = 1$, then λ as well as P_K^e and w^e remains proportional to P^e. In this situation, as will be shown shortly, H, K, L, and Q are unaffected by the unanticipated inflation. If, however, $0 < \delta < 1$, then λ will rise less than proportionately than P_0 provided $|D_{14}|/|D| < 0$. $|D|$, of course, is the determinant of the second-order conditions of our calculus-of-variations problem and, for a maximum, must be less than zero. While $|D_{14}|$ is an off-diagonal minor, it can be shown that it must be positive.[5] Thus λ must rise proportionately less than P.

As noted previously, the first element in the price vector is proportional to the elements in the fourth column of D. By the usual rules of expansion of determinants, the use of the elements in another column yields a sum of zero. Therefore, these terms can be ignored in finding $\partial H/\partial P_0$, $\partial K/\partial P_0$, and $\partial L/\partial P_0$. We can write

$$\frac{\partial Q}{\partial P_0} = \frac{\partial H}{\partial P_0}F_H + \frac{\partial K}{\partial P_0}F_K + \frac{\partial L}{\partial P_0}F_L. \tag{20}$$

Let

$$A = -g\frac{e^{-gt}}{(P_t^e)^2}\overline{P}\lambda(1-\delta) > 0. \tag{21}$$

Then we have

$$\frac{\partial H}{\partial P_0} = -\frac{A|D_{12}|}{|D|}, \tag{22}$$

$$\frac{\partial K}{\partial P_0} = \frac{A|D_{11}|}{|D|}, \tag{23}$$

$$\frac{\partial L}{\partial P_0} = \frac{A|D_{13}|}{|D|}. \tag{24}$$

Then

$$\frac{\partial Q}{\partial P_0} = \frac{A}{|D|}(-F_H|D_{12}| + F_K|D_{11}| + F_L|D_{13}|) \tag{25}$$

[5] $|D| < 0$ but $|D| = -S|D_{14}| + KS'|D_{24}|$. Now $|D_{14}|$ must be > 0 whenever $|D_{24}| \geq 0$. However, expanding $|D_{14}|$ and $|D_{24}|$, it can be shown that even if $|D_{24}| < 0$, $|D_{14}| > 0$.

or

$$\frac{\partial Q}{\partial P_0} = \frac{A}{|D|} |G|,$$

where

$$G = \begin{bmatrix} F_K & F_H & F_L & 0 \\ P^e F_{HK} + \lambda S' & P^e F_{HH} + \lambda K S'' & P^e F_{LH} & S'K \\ P^e F_{LK} & P^e F_{LH} & P^e F_{LL} & 0 \\ S & K_t S'_t & 0 & 0 \end{bmatrix}. \tag{26}$$

The conditions for the equilibrium of a competitive firm require that $|G| < 0$ and $|D| < 0$ while $A \geq 0$ if $\delta \leq 1$. Thus, $\partial Q/\partial P_0 > 0$ if $\delta < 1$.[6]

In short, if in response to a price rise that is expected to be temporary, monetary policy is expected to allow the long-run equilibrium rate of interest to remain constant while the nominal rate of interest falls, then output will increase if the firm has the above price expectations.

Thus, with nonreproducible capital, it can be shown that an expected inflation of the type defined in (3) through (7) will raise λ less than proportionately if the nominal interest rate does not fully include an adjustment for $\dot{P}^e/P^e$. In this case, the rental price of H and K will decline in real terms and output will expand. Perhaps the easiest way of understanding this result is the following: When prices rise but are expected to fall, it becomes possible to "borrow" output from the future and sell it at the higher price. The funds so obtained can be placed in a bond. If the interest rate adjusts fully to expected price changes, there is no benefit—as opposed to the situation without inflation—by obtaining more revenue sooner. When interest rates do not adjust fully, it is possible for the firm to increase its net worth by switching its portfolio.

Before considering the case of reproducible assets, the following points should be emphasized. For a $\delta < 0$, the nonproportional price effect only occurs because it is necessary to compute $d(e^{-mt}\lambda) \, dt$ when integrating by parts in (11). In turn, this integration is only required because K is *controllable* through variations in H. If a nonreproducible asset does not have the possibility of variable utilization associated with a user cost, then only (12) is relevant for the firm. In (12) w^e/P^e is always constant; hence $\partial Q/\partial P_0$ would be zero. Thus it is the introduction into the problem of capital and its utilization cost that yields $\partial Q/\partial P_0 > 0$ for a temporary inflation where the nominal interest rate is expected to fall less than output and factor prices.

[6] G can be rearranged into a principal minor of the production function bordered by its marginal products.

2
REPLACEABLE CAPITAL
STOCK CASE

Consider the more typical case where the capital stock of the firm is replaceable. We will analyze the simplest case in which $\partial P_K / \partial I = 0$. The firm now wishes to maximize its net worth,

$$R = \int_0^\infty \{e^{-mt}[P_t^e F(H, L, K) - w_t^e L_t - P_{Kt}^e I_t]\} \, dt \qquad (27)$$

subject to (1) and to the following constraint:

$$\int_0^\infty \{e^{-mt}[\dot{K}_t + S_t K_t - I_t]\} \, dt = 0. \qquad (28)$$

The necessary first-order conditions are

$$P_t^e F_H + \lambda^* S_t' K_t = 0, \qquad (29)$$

$$P_t^e F_K + \lambda^*(S_t + m_t) - \lambda^* = 0, \qquad (30)$$

$$P_t^e F_L - w_t^e = 0, \qquad (31)$$

$$-P_{K_t}^e - \lambda^* = 0, \qquad (32)$$

$$\dot{K}_t + S_t K_t - I_t = 0. \qquad (33)$$

From (32) we see that λ^* is now the expected market price of capital. Substitute (32) for λ^*, divide by P^e, differentiate (29) through (33) with respect to P_0 using (3) through (7), and arrange in matrix form:

$$\begin{bmatrix} F_{KK} & F_{KH} - S_t' & F_{KL} & S_t \\ F_{HK} - S_t' & F_{HH} - \beta K_t S_t'' & F_{HL} & S_t' K_t \\ F_{LK} & F_{LH} & F_{LL} & 0 \\ S_t & K_t S_t' & 0 & 0 \end{bmatrix} \begin{bmatrix} \partial K / \partial P_0 \\ \partial H / \partial P_0 \\ \partial L / \partial P_0 \\ \partial \lambda / \partial P_0 \end{bmatrix}$$

$$+ W = \begin{bmatrix} \beta \dfrac{\partial m}{\partial P_0} - \beta g \dfrac{\partial P_t^e}{\partial P_0} \cdot \dfrac{\bar{P}}{(P_t^e)^2} \\ 0 \\ 0 \\ 0 \end{bmatrix} \qquad (34)$$

or

$$Ck + W = r. \qquad (34a)$$

The first term in the price vector can be simplified to

$$B = \left[\beta \left(g \cdot \dfrac{\bar{P} e^{-gt}}{(P_t^e)^2} \right) (1 - \delta) \right]. \qquad (35)$$

Thus

$$\frac{\partial Q}{\partial P_0} = \frac{B}{|C|} \left(-F_H |C_{12}| + F_K |C_{11}| + F_L |C_{13}| \right), \tag{36}$$

and following the argument in Section I, when $\delta < 1$, and $\beta > 0$, $\partial Q / \partial P_0 > 0$.

Thus if investment in replaceable assets is allowed and if P_k is not affected by I or $\dot{K}$, the price expectations described above result in the same qualitative result for $\partial Q / \partial P_0$ as was derived for the case of non-reproducible assets. In addition, it can be shown that for $t = 0$ the quantitative result for $\partial Q / \partial P_0$ is the same provided that the absolute value of the shadow price of the nonreproducible asset, (12), equals the selling price of capital.

To see this, compare the nonzero price effects given in (35) and (21). The former was derived by dividing through by P_t^e; however, the same operation was not performed to obtain (21). Correcting for this, the ratio of the two expressions reduces to

$$\frac{B}{A} = \frac{P_k^e}{-\lambda}. \tag{37}$$

For the long-run equilibrium of a perfectly competitive market B/A should be unity. The quantitative impact or our inflation is thus the same if new investment and/or variations in capital utilization are allowed. It should also be realized that if the rate of capital utilization cannot be altered, $\partial Q / \partial P_0$ would still be nonzero if $\delta < 1$, because firms would find it profitable to rearrange their portfolios.

3
SUMMARY AND
CONCLUDING REMARKS

The following conclusions can be drawn from the above analysis:

a. Once the neoclassical theory of the firm is expanded to include capital utilization, unforeseen price movements combined with adaptive expectations can produce a change in output even if wage rates are not expected to change relative to output price and capital cannot be purchased. This result follows from the assumption that the nominal interest rate is not expected to change proportionately to output and factor prices.

b. If investment in capital is allowed, the same results follow, given the same set of price (including interest rate) expectations.

c. In addition, if the market price of capital is expected to vary with either gross or net investment (in the sense of Eisner–Strotz and Lucas), the possibility of varying the rate of capital utilization would lead to an even greater change in output than if this were not possible.

d. The above model of output and factor utilization under unforeseen price movements and adaptive expectations complements the Lucas and Rapping[7] analysis of labor supply under the same conditions. If the two models are combined, a general equilibrium analysis might be possible.

e. Finally, it would seem that our model would have some relevance to the problem of standby equipment. While excess capacity may be of the most modern vintage, standby equipment is usually of an older vintage. A formal vintage capital model with capital utilization is beyond the scope of this paper; however, it would seem possible to measure the number of idle machines by variations in H. Thus our analysis would indicate that the temporary inflations considered in this paper would cause standby equipment to be brought into operation.

[7]Lucas and Rapping, *op. cit.*

Index